Colin A. Ireland
**The Gaelic Background of Old English Poetry before Bede**

# Publications of the Richard Rawlinson Center

**Editorial Board and Special Advisors**
Lindy Brady, University College Dublin, Ireland
Kees Dekker, Rijksuniversiteit Groningen, the Netherlands
Nicole Guenther Discenza, University of South Florida, USA
Helen Foxhall Forbes, Durham University, England
Timothy Graham, University of New Mexico, USA (**Series Editor**)
Susan Kim, Illinois State University, USA
Rosalind Love, Robinson College, Cambridge University, England

Colin A. Ireland
# The Gaelic Background of Old English Poetry before Bede

—

DE GRUYTER

This publication has been aided by subventions from
The College of Global Studies
at Arcadia University, Glenside, Pennsylvania
and from
The Mícheál Ó Cléirigh Institute
for the Study of Irish History and Civilization
at University College Dublin

ISBN 978-1-5015-2214-7
e-ISBN (PDF) 978-1-5015-1387-9
e-ISBN (EPUB) 978-1-5015-1393-0

**Library of Congress Control Number: 2021943321**

**Bibliographic information published by the Deutsche Nationalbibliothek**
The Deutsche Nationalbibliothek lists this publication in the Deutsche Nationalbibliografie; detailed bibliographic data are available on the Internet at http://dnb.dnb.de.

© 2023 Walter de Gruyter GmbH, Berlin/Boston
This volume is text- and page-identical with the hardback published in 2022.
Cover image: Durrow High Cross, © National Monuments Service of the Department of Heritage, Ireland
Typesetting: Integra Software Services Pvt. Ltd.
Printing and binding: CPI books GmbH, Leck

www.degruyter.com

I ndilchuimhne ar Honóra
Mo sholas treorach
Spreagadh m'intinne
Mo ghrá geal
Ar feadh níos mó ná
Ceithre bhliain agus triocha

# Acknowledgements

I owe much to good mentors. At UCLA Patrick Ford agreed to help me create an independent, inter-disciplinary PhD in Celtic Studies and Early English. He instructed me in Early Gaelic and Middle Welsh and laid a firm foundation in the literatures of those languages. Daniel Calder (d. 1994) agreed to serve as co-chairman of my PhD committee and deepened my appreciation of Old English literature. When I arrived in Dublin James Carney (d. 1989) was enthusiastic about my cross-cultural interests and unstintingly generous with his vast knowledge. I am grateful to all three for their guidance and wisdom.

When I retired from International Education and was able to devote myself to full time research, I was again fortunate in my colleagues and friends. As this project took shape, I found their in-depth discussions, their sharing of recondite knowledge, and constructive feedback, invaluable. More could be named, but those who merit special mention are: Mary Clayton, Anthony Harvey, David Howlett, Daniel Mc Carthy, Juliet Mullins, Dáibhí Ó Cróinín, and Immo Warntjes. The reader should not conflate their well-intended contributions with any of my erroneous conclusions. Robert Bjork and Howard Clarke encouraged the project and advised me on the publication process. Sarah Gearty efficiently produced maps and a chart. Laura Napran created an informative index for the reader. The editorial staff of the series and the press were always helpful.

I want to express my appreciation for my former employers, The College of Global Studies at Arcadia University, Glenside, Pennsylvania, for their willingness to support the research of an *emeritus* and, likewise, my colleagues in University College Dublin at the School of English, Drama and Film, and at the Mícheál Ó Cléirigh Institute for the Study of Irish History and Civilization. Thank you all for your support.

My wife Honóra, who did not live to see its publication, never wavered in her enthusiasm and encouragement for this project. *Beidh mé fíorbhuíoch di go brách*. This work is dedicated to her memory.

# Preface

Readers of this book live in a world where speakers of English have been at the forefront of cultural, political, social, and scientific affairs. There has been a tendency, therefore, for scholarship from this English-speaking world to impose a template onto the early medieval world that parallels and reflects modern circumstances. Because of the pre-eminence of modern English as a world language a large amount of scholarship has been produced about literature in Old English and the Anglo-Saxon peoples who created it. By way of illustration, contrast the number of universities worldwide with English departments containing active medievalists against the few universities that have Celtic Studies departments. The diminished status of the Gaelic (Irish and Scottish) and Brittonic (Welsh) languages in the modern world has allowed their influence in, and contributions to, the medieval insular world to be either overlooked or undervalued.

As Christianity spread across Western Europe it brought literacy in Latin from the Mediterranean world to peoples who had not yet developed written literatures in their own native languages. After the arrival of Latin literacy, the first written vernacular literatures in Western Europe were developed in Ireland and Britain, and texts in the Gaelic, Brittonic, and Germanic languages and dialects were preserved. The long-established Gaelic and Brittonic languages produced rich and varied literatures, of both secular and ecclesiastical import, that transmitted much indigenous lore and tradition while reflecting their early conversions to Christianity. Old English also produced a vernacular literature, preserved in the blended dialects of Germanic immigrants to Britain, but one narrowly confined to ecclesiastical subjects or topics derived from written sources of the Mediterranean world. Old English texts about native lore or local concerns are made significant by their paucity.

Although last to arrive in the archipelago, Old English has become the most widely known and studied of the early medieval insular vernacular literatures. However, it is the least informative about indigenous lore and local cultural traditions. For researchers interested in the archipelago's indigenous traditions, the written resources are much richer and more plentiful in the Gaelic and Brittonic vernaculars. More importantly, the cultural traditions transmitted through Old English did not evolve independently, but rather in association with their well-established Gaelic and Brittonic Christian neighbors.

A feature of modern Old English and Anglo-Latin criticism can be called the "appeal to Rome." Anglo-Saxon culture stressed its relations with Rome beginning with the Augustinian mission sent to Canterbury by Pope Gregory (d. 604). The "appeal to Rome" was reinforced through those early mission activities,

Roman sojourns of clerics like Wilfrid and Benedict Biscop, the writings of Aldhelm and Bede, the tenth-century Benedictine Reform, and the writings, especially the homilies, of Ælfric and Wulfstan. The notion of Anglo-Saxon "orthodoxy" is based on the contents of the writings of a few named, historical authors. It must downplay the breadth of subject matter that exists elsewhere in the Old English corpus, whether secular (e.g., *Beowulf, Widsith, Deor*) or ecclesiastical (e.g., anonymous homilies). The "appeal to Rome" has allowed critics to dismiss the older Gaelic and Brittonic traditions as "heterodox" or "schismatic." This is unwarranted, particularly in the case of the seventh-century Gaelic Christian literary tradition, in both Latin and Old Gaelic.

Many modern Old English and Anglo-Latin scholars apparently saw their academic discipline as beginning with Bede's *Historia ecclesiastica gentis Anglorum*, proceeded through an examination of a select few named Anglo-Saxon authors, in either Latin or Old English, and shaped their discipline into the *Historia ecclesiae Romae apud gentem Anglorum*. Modern academics of Old English have made a virtue of a vernacular literature that, with notable exceptions, is remarkably incurious about its own indigenous cultural traditions and which can be rigidly derivative in its adherence to a purported Roman "orthodoxy" with identifiable sources.

But the Church itself has never, throughout its long history, promulgated a consistent view of its own "orthodoxy." Such a modern critical view is anachronistic and leaves unexplained numerous anonymous Old English texts, both ecclesiastical and secular, that do not respond to the "appeal to Rome." More crucially it has encouraged critics to ignore possibilities of influence from contiguous insular cultures of the Gaels and Britons. This study proposes a necessary corrective to that narrow doctrinal approach to insular vernacular literatures.

# Contents

Acknowledgements —— VII

Preface —— IX

List of Figures —— XIII

Introduction —— 1

**Chapter One**
Early Vernacular Poetic Practice —— 7

**Chapter Two**
Early Historical Poets before Bede —— 49
    Appendix 2.a: Historical Poets after Bede to ca. 1100 —— 87

**Chapter Three**
Professional Poets and Vernacular Narratives —— 105

**Chapter Four**
The Church and the Spread of Bilingual Learning —— 163
    Appendix 4.a: Aldhelm in a Gaelic World —— 220
    Appendix 4.b: Bede in a Gaelic World —— 229

**Chapter Five**
The Ethnic Mix of Anglo-Saxon Empire —— 245

**Chapter Six**
The Long Century of Anglo-Saxon Conversion —— 299

**Chapter Seven**
Cædmon's World at Whitby —— 353

Afterword —— 371

Bibliography —— 375

Index —— 425

# List of Figures

**Figure 1.a** Map Showing Major Locations of *Táin Bó Cúailnge* —— 18
**Figure 1.b** Map of Scandinavia Showing Locations Mentioned in *Beowulf* —— 24
**Figure 2.a** Cædmon's *Hymn* in the "Moore Bede" Manuscript —— 66
**Figure 2.b** Schaffhausen Manuscript Containing *Vita Sancti Columbae* —— 77
**Figure 2.c** Map of the Four Major Old English Dialects —— 84
**Figure 2.d** Extracts from the Prologue of *Félire Óengusso* "Martyrology of Oengus" —— 93
**Figure 2.e** Extracts from "Slán seiss, a Brigit," a Poem by Orthanach úa Cóellámae —— 95
**Figure 2.f** Three Contemporary Literary Kings —— 99
**Figure 3.a** Conferring a Grade (*grád*) on a Poet (*fili*) —— 109
**Figure 3.b** Divine and Human Sources of Inspiration —— 151
**Figure 4.a** Pope Gregory the Great in the Works of Seventh-Century Gaels —— 172
**Figure 4.b** Map of the Locations of Seventh-Century *Sapientes* —— 180
**Figure 4.c** *Maith dán ecnae*, Attributed to Flann Fína mac Ossu (Aldfrith *sapiens* son of Oswiu) —— 195
**Figure 4.d** Gaelic Names in Bede —— 231
**Figure 5.a** Three Gaelic-Speaking Northumbrian Kings —— 258
**Figure 5.b** Chart of Oswiu's Liaisons and Offspring —— 263
**Figure 5.c** Map of Aldfrith's Network of Influence —— 290
**Figure 6.a** Differing Paschal Cycles —— 305
**Figure 6.b** Map of Rath Melsigi's Networks in Ireland, Britain, and the Continent —— 336
**Figure 6.c** Map of locations in the Barrow Valley —— 348
**Figure 7.a** The Gaelic Ethos of Whitby —— 354

# Introduction

The recording of the earliest Old English poetry has a multi-faceted background and at least one of those facets is Gaelic. Understanding the background of insular vernacular literatures should include perspectives on shared poetic practice; the named personnel involved; the subject matters of their crafts; their relationship with ecclesiastical culture; and the multi-ethnic, intra-cultural blend of their working environments. Old English is the most widely known and most thoroughly studied of the medieval vernacular literatures of Western Europe. But it is neither the earliest nor most extensive, and it did not evolve in isolation.

The chronological heart of this study is the crucial century from 635 (foundation of Lindisfarne) to 735 (death of Bede). Anglo-Latin writers of the late seventh and early eighth centuries commonly refer to Gaels living and working among the Anglo-Saxons in Britain, as well as to Anglo-Saxons who lived and studied in Ireland among the Gaels. Bede's *Historia ecclesiastica gentis Anglorum*, in fact, is an important source for the activities and accomplishments of several seventh-century Gaels. Despite ample evidence for cross-cultural contacts provided by Aldhelm, Bede, Stephen of Ripon, Felix of Crowland, and others, few modern scholars of Old English and Anglo-Latin literatures have investigated what Gaelic learned culture had to offer the Anglo-Saxons who partook of, and benefited from, those contacts. The present study aims to expose in seven chapters that neglected facet of "Gaelic background."

## Chapter One: Early Vernacular Poetic Practice

The first chapter demonstrates that rich vernacular poetic traditions co-existed on the island of Britain in the early medieval period. It opens by examining poems and stories that preserve the names of mythico-legendary poets of the Brittonic, Gaelic, and Anglo-Saxon traditions.

The second part of this first chapter examines vernacular poetic practices as described in three Old English poems – *Beowulf*, *Widsith*, *Deor* – and compares those passages to similar examples from Gaelic tradition. The examples demonstrate that both traditions stressed poets performing at court, their reliance on indigenous lore and stories, and their functions of praising patrons. The reliance on courtly patrons and the poets' freedom to travel widely suggest a recognition of special status or professional ranking for poets.

## Chapter Two: Early Historical Poets before Bede

This chapter surveys named historical Anglo-Saxon writers who likely composed in the vernacular, concluding with Bede (d. 735), in the context of their more numerous Gaelic contemporaries. Three persons from this period may have composed Old English poetry: Cædmon certainly, Bede quite possibly, Aldhelm perhaps, based on circumstantial evidence. Six persons had Old Gaelic poems attributed to them. Secular encomiastic diction converted for ecclesiastical purposes is recorded for both traditions. All nine named authors had, or developed, ecclesiastical affiliations.

The appendix to Chapter Two, "Poets from Bede to ca. 1100," surveys historical vernacular authors from after Bede until the end of the Anglo-Saxon period (ca. 1100). Three contemporary kings from the period ca. 900 were involved in the production of poetry. Six persons surveyed have Old English texts attributed to them. Twenty-five historical Gaelic poets are cited. The appendix concludes with Gilla in Choimded (fl. 1100) who wrote a sixty-three quatrain retrospective poem on iconic poets and jurists of Gaelic tradition.

## Chapter Three: Professional Poets and Vernacular Narratives

This chapter describes the Gaelic literary tradition, first in terms of the personnel who produced it, and then of the contents of the texts they produced. The professional status of poets (*filid*) is recorded in four eighth-century vernacular lawtracts. Gaelic poets undertook formal training to attain the highest levels of their profession. Top ranking poets enjoyed the same privileges as the chief secular and ecclesiastical authorities in Gaelic society. The contents of the now lost manuscript *Cín Dromma Snechtai* provide a sense of the lore (*senchas*) and tales (*scéla*) controlled by the *filid*. The named texts, which survive in other manuscripts, date linguistically to the late seventh and early eighth centuries, roughly the period covered by this study.

A ninth-century etiological legend discusses the poets' recovery of the epic *Táin Bó Cúailnge* after it had been exchanged for Isidore's *Etymologiae*. The events, portrayed as taking place in the seventh century, acknowledge the debt of indigenous traditions to Latinate learning. A review of tales from the tenth-century tale lists, which survive in modern editions, illustrates the functioning of the poetic profession. Some tales emphasize the Irish Sea cultural region and encompass both Ireland and Britain.

Several Old Gaelic texts on "poetics" survive. They are unique among the vernaculars of Western Europe for this early period of the Middle Ages. The nature of poetic inspiration, as well as prophecy, divination, and dream visions expressed through poetry, are discussed.

## Chapter Four: The Church and the Spread of Bilingual Learning

Both Anglo-Saxons and Gaels shared a rich Latinate heritage, but the Gaels quickly developed a bilingual learned culture. The achievements of the Gregorian mission to Canterbury and the Iona mission to Northumbria are set in context. The Gaels absorbed late Antique and patristic texts from the Continent as reflected by their reception of Gregory the Great's writings. Texts by Columbanus (d. 615), *peregrinus* from Bangor to the Continent, demonstrate the depth of Latinate learning developed by the late sixth century. By the late seventh century Bangor was associated with vernacular literature as well.

Bede highlighted the third quarter of the seventh century as a time when multitudes of Anglo-Saxons took advantage of free education offered by the Gaels. This period coincides with the floruits of several *sapientes*, Gaelic scholars who represent the learning available to Anglo-Saxon students. Six named *sapientes* have surviving works attributed to them. Three wrote in Latin, three wrote in Gaelic, emphasizing the bilingual nature of Gaelic intellectual life, both ecclesiastical and secular.

A survey of seventh-century Hiberno-Latin hagiography shows the degree to which the Gaels were indebted to fourth- and fifth-century late Antique continental sources. Eighth-century Anglo-Latin hagiography reveals a familiarity with these Gaelic models. The two appendices place the careers of Aldhelm and Bede within the larger world of contemporary Gaelic ecclesiastical culture.

## Chapter Five: The Ethnic Mix of Anglo-Saxon Empire

Anglo-Saxon kings from the sixth through the eighth century had to interact with their multi-ethnic neighbors. Bede described three Northumbrian kings as having ruled empires (Edwin, Oswald, Oswiu). Anglo-Saxon kings often either allied with or fought against Britons, Picts, and Gaels; but also cooperated with missionary projects conducted by Gaels. In the critical century from 635 to 735 Northumbria was ruled for fifty-five years by Gaelic-educated, fluent Gaelic-speaking kings (Oswald, 634–642; Oswiu, 642–670; Aldfrith, 685–704).

King Oswiu had three marital liaisons: the first with a Brittonic woman, the second with a Gael, the third with an Anglo-Saxon. Each liaison produced a son who became a king: Ealhfrith (ca. 655–664), Aldfrith, Ecgfrith (670–685). Ealhfrith helped instigate the "synod" of Whitby (664). Ecgfrith's reign saw the foundation of Bede's monastery at Wearmouth-Jarrow (673x681). His half-brother Aldfrith *sapiens* nurtured the incipient intellectual climate in Northumbria.

## Chapter Six: The Long Century of Anglo-Saxon Conversion

The conversion of the Anglo-Saxons, and their subsequent ecclesiastical training, relied to varying degrees on neighboring Britons and Gaels. For example, King Edwin (617–633) was converted by Paulinus of the Gregorian mission who is equated with Rhun mab Urien in some Brittonic sources. Fursa and his companions were established among the East Angles in the 630s and 640s. King Oswald (634–642) introduced the successful Iona mission into Northumbria. Later, major contentions arose because Iona, and many Britons and Picts, followed older Easter traditions no longer considered orthodox. However, Bede declared that many churches in Ireland already followed Roman orthodoxy for decades before the "synod" of Whitby (664) where the issue was resolved for Northumbria.

After the "synod" Bishop Colmán left Lindisfarne, along with thirty Anglo-Saxon monks, returned to Iona, and by ca. 673 had established "Mayo of the Saxons" with the aid and approval of a local chieftain. It successfully attracted Anglo-Saxons well into the ninth century. Rath Melsigi in the Barrow valley was another establishment frequented by Anglo-Saxons. Bede praised the achievements of its named trainees who returned to labor among their kin in Britain or who went to the Continent as missionaries to Germanic pagans. At no time from the foundation of Lindisfarne through Bede's lifetime did Gaelic contacts in Britain among the Anglo-Saxons cease, north or south.

## Chapter Seven: Cædmon's World at Whitby

This chapter about Cædmon highlights a specific example of how "Gaelic background" can manifest in Old English literary history. The Gaelic ethos of Whitby can be shown from its inception under Abbess Hild (657–680) and through her successor Abbess Ælfflæd (680–714). Cædmon's name is Brittonic, and circumstances at the time in Whitby's locale imply that he was a bilingual Briton. Bede's account of Cædmon is the most thorough description of how an Old English poet composed. It records events that took place within the timeframe of the two abbesses. The composition methods Bede described for Cædmon are not unique or unusual. They are all found in Gaelic poetic culture, as discussed, primarily, in chapter three. Cædmon's gift of "divine grace" (*gratia divina*) is explained in Old Gaelic texts on poetics. They note that poetic inspiration can have either a human or a divine source, and that "divine grace" (*rath déoda*) can produce inspired poems.

# Chapter One
# Early Vernacular Poetic Practice

Modern English holds a distinguished and prominent status as a world language, spoken as a mother tongue, and a commercial, political, and learned language, on every continent of the globe. Nevertheless, the early history of the English language and its literature cannot be separated from the other vernacular literary cultures that existed beside it on the island of Britain. The first part of this chapter seeks to give a sense of Britain's early vernacular literatures through works ascribed to or associated with named mythico-legendary poets from each of three traditions. The second section examines descriptions of poets at their work from three Old English poems – *Beowulf*, *Widsith*, and *Deor* – and compares them with analogous passages from Old Gaelic texts. In both cultures, poets were prominent in the royal courts; they were expected to control a large corpus of native stories and lore; they performed encomia for their patrons, but also practiced satire as the counterpart of praise; their freedom to travel widely implies their special social rôle; and their reliance on the patronage of nobles and chieftains suggests a professional status.

Beyond the literatures in Greek and Latin of the Mediterranean world, the first recorded literatures of Western Europe were written on the fringes of that world on the islands of Ireland and Britain. With their conversion to Christianity certain of the islands' inhabitants, having become literate in Latin, began to record information, besides short inscriptions, in their own indigenous languages (poems, narratives, etc.). So it is that the oldest vernacular literatures in Western Europe are found in the insular world of the western archipelago. Poetic texts and narratives from the early Middle Ages have survived from the Brittonic, Gaelic, and Old English vernaculars.

The island of Britain had a much greater ethnic diversity than did Ireland whose linguistic and cultural uniformity did not exist in contemporary Britain. The Venerable Bede (d. 735), in his Church history of the Anglo-Saxons, *Historia ecclesiastica*, noted that there were five languages in use in Britain in his time: Old English, in the various dialects of the Anglo-Saxons; Brittonic, in the various ancestral Celtic languages related to modern Welsh; Gaelic, spoken by the peoples of Ireland and much of northern Britain; Pictish, the language of peoples found mainly in what is now Scotland; and Latin, which for all the peoples of the archipelago was the language of the Church.[1] Bede acknowledged the ability of

---

**1** For a survey of the late Antique background to Britain and Ireland, see Yorke, "Britain and Ireland." For a survey of insular vernacular literatures in this early period, see Ní Mhaonaigh,

each language to express important and worthy thoughts and concepts, implicitly placing the four vernacular languages on a par with Latin which served all insular ethnic groups as a *lingua franca*. He stated that just as the divine law in the Bible is divided into the first five books, that is the *Pentateuch*, all insular languages are "devoted to seeking out and setting forth one and the same kind of wisdom, namely the knowledge of sublime truth and of true sublimity (*HE* i 1)."[2] Of the five languages noted only Pictish has not left a corpus of literature beyond a few inscriptions, the evidence of place and personal names, and a few scattered words.

Latin provided the literature and learning that speakers of all four vernacular languages in Britain shared, and through the Latin of the Church they all partook of common Biblical, patristic, and other late antique sources. The Bible and the writings of early Church fathers helped open the wider Mediterranean world of post-Classical, late Antique learning to the inhabitants of Britain and Ireland. The Anglo-Saxons, Gaels, and Britons each enhanced and elaborated a store of native lore with Latinate learning to create rich, new amalgams in their vernacular literatures. A rich bilingual intellectual culture was developed by all three peoples, and some of the named historical poets to be discussed in chapter two composed in both Latin and their vernaculars.

Named vernacular poets whose historicity cannot be verified survive in the three traditions. Some are mythic and have no plausible historicity. They may have evolved as iconic or symbolic characters. Some are legendary, meaning they may or may not have a historical basis, but their historicity cannot be, or has not been, verified. In the second section of this chapter, descriptions of Old English and Gaelic poets are compared. The social structure of these early medieval societies overlapped in many features and so it is assumed that descriptions of poets and their functions in one tradition can be productively compared to those in another.

The timeframes of Old English and Old Gaelic literatures must be noted. The period of Old English extended from ca. 600, the time of the papal mission to Canterbury in Kent, to ca. 1100, roughly a generation after the Norman conquest of Anglo-Saxon Britain. A commonly used period for Old Gaelic extends from ca. 600 to ca. 900, by which latter date the diachronic changes to the language had been great enough that from ca. 900 to ca. 1200 the language is

---

"Bede's 'five languages and four nations'." For the importance of insular vernaculars, see Hall, "Interlinguistic Communications." For Britain's language mix from a Brittonic viewpoint, see Charles-Edwards, *Wales and the Britons*, 89–115.

2 "unam eandemque summae ueritatis et uerae sublimitatis scientiam scrutatur et confitetur": Colgrave and Mynors, *Ecclesiastical History*, 16–17. Colgrave and Mynors will be the standard edition used for this work and will be referred to as *HE* (*Historia ecclesiastica*) throughout the body of the text.

considered Middle Gaelic.[3] Note that the Old and Middle Gaelic periods overlap with, and encompass, the Old English period. The period from ca. 600 to ca. 1100 can be bookended in the Gaelic tradition by citing the poetic fragments preserved from the professional poet Colmán mac Lénéni (d. ca. 606), while the date of ca. 1100 can be summarized for the Gaelic tradition by a long poem on named poets and jurists, "Aimirgein Glúngel Tuir Tend," by Gilla in Choimded Úa Cormaic dated between ca. 1050–ca. 1150.[4]

This study concentrates on, but is not limited to, the period from the foundation of Lindisfarne (635) to the death of the Venerable Bede (735). That century falls well within the limits of the Old English and Old Gaelic linguistic periods. Most texts referred to will fall within the Old Gaelic period (600–900) which, for the Old English vernacular, extends to and encompasses the life and translated works associated with the court of King Alfred the Great of Wessex (d. 899).[5]

The typical word for "poet" in Old English was *scop* (pl. *scopas*) with another commonly used term being *glēoman* (pl. *glēomen*) which can imply a "musician" or someone more like a later medieval "minstrel." In Old Gaelic the word for a fully qualified "poet" was *fili* (pl. *filid*), but another common term was *éices* with both words implying a "learned person." The abstract nouns from these two Gaelic terms, *filidecht* and *éicse* respectively, refer to both the poetic art and the indigenous lore that forms its basis.

There is a rich vocabulary for poets of various ranks and duties in the Gaelic world. For example, *bard* describes a poet of lower status and less formal training than either the *fili* or *éices*.[6] On the other hand, *bard(d)* was the word used most regularly for poet among the Britons.[7] Early Gaelic law-tracts of the eighth century confirm the professional status and functions of poets and other "people of the arts" (*áes dána*). The *áes dána* were people who achieved social status through specifically acquired knowledge or skills and included the various grades of poets and entertainers, lawyers, physicians, wrights, smiths, and others who produced manufactured goods.[8] Their status is outlined in eighth-century Gaelic law-tracts, a phenomenon that does not occur among the Anglo-Saxons.

---

[3] These approximate dates for linguistic periods of early Gaelic will vary from authority to authority. There are no convenient historical events to frame the early Gaelic time periods as exist for Old English, rather there is a shifting consensus among linguists based on diachronic linguistic changes.
[4] Smith, "Aimirgein Glúngel Tuir Tend"; Ó Corráin, *Clavis*, iii, 1583–84 §1190.
[5] For a convenient overview of his life and times, see Keynes and Lapidge, *Alfred the Great*.
[6] Breatnach, *Uraicecht na Ríar*, 87–88, 99–100.
[7] The term bard came to be used by many early critics writing about the imagined traditions of poetry among the Anglo-Saxons: Thornbury, *Becoming a Poet*, 12–14.
[8] For an overview, see Kelly, *Guide*, 43–65.

The high social ranking of Early Gaelic poets stands in marked contrast to historical, named Anglo-Saxon poets for whom no evidence of professional status survives.[9] The named historical Anglo-Saxon poets are known by other social functions they fulfilled, such as priest, abbot, king, not by their rôles as poets. Gaelic poets, as members of a recognized, respected professional organization, have their high social rank acknowledged and defined in Gaelic law-tracts. These will be discussed in chapter three. No equivalence exists in Anglo-Saxon society. The professional status of poets accounts for their high profile social rank in Gaelic cultural histories.[10]

## Poets of Myth and Legend

Rich vernacular traditions of Ireland and Britain have preserved stories and poems about their poets into modern times. The named legendary poets, who may have some degree of historicity, tend to have existed around the sixth and seventh centuries.

Named Brittonic poets, that is, those who spoke the non-Gaelic Celtic languages of Britain, appear in the ninth-century *Historia Brittonum* (History of the Britons).[11] This work places early Britain in world history and traces the origins of the Brittonic peoples in the context of neighboring Picts, Gaels, and Anglo-Saxons. Two of the five late sixth- to early seventh-century poets named in *Historia Brittonum* have poems attributed to them that are preserved in manuscripts of the thirteenth century or later. There are difficult issues with regard to linguistic confirmation of the early dates of these poems that are referenced in footnotes. Nevertheless, as the immediate neighbors of the Anglo-Saxons for many centuries, the portrayal of Brittonic traditions is important for comparison and contrast.

The surviving records for named Gaelic poets are the most extensive of all. This is probably due to the social prestige and professional rank accorded poets in Gaelic law-tracts. Some named poets are mythical with no prospect of any historicity. Some are legendary, implying that they may have derived from historical persons or events no longer firmly identifiable. Others are plausibly historical, typically of the seventh century, but their historicity has not yet been

---

**9** "there is no solid evidence that a professional class of poets existed in Anglo-Saxon England": Thornbury, *Becoming a Poet*, 34.
**10** See arguments in Ireland, "Vernacular Poets."
**11** In the past this work was attributed to a certain "Nennius" who cannot be shown to have existed: Sharpe, *Handlist*, 382 §1072.

confirmed by modern scholarship. Far more historical poets can be verified for the Gaelic tradition than for any other insular peoples.

Three Old English poems describing poets at work will form the basis for cross-cultural comparison in this chapter. The poems *Widsith* and *Deor* derive their editorial names from characters in whose voices the poems are related.[12] Both poems name characters from Germanic history, legend, and myth. The epic *Beowulf* also pictures poets at work.[13] These three poems, and the poets described in them, provide the basis for comparison with Gaelic traditions in the second half of this chapter.

**Mythico-legendary Brittonic Poets**

The ninth-century *Historia Brittonum* named five poets who were pre-eminent among the Britons in the late sixth century, during the time of the Northumbrian King Ida and his sons. According to the *Anglo-Saxon Chronicles* Ida assumed kingship in 547 and reigned for twelve years.[14] Ida established Bamburgh as a royal seat and began the process of unifying two formerly Brittonic regions, Deira (Deur) and Bernicia (Berneich), into a single kingdom. The five Brittonic poets are named thus:

> Tunc Talhaearn Tad Awen in poemate claruit; et Neirin [Aneirin], et Taliesin, et Blwchfardd, et Cian, qui vocatur Gwenith Gwawd, simul uno tempore in poemate Brittanico claruerunt.

> (Then Talhaearn Tad Awen [Talhaearn Father of the Poetic Muse] was famed in poetry; and Aneirin and Taliesin and Blwchfardd and Cian, who was known as "Wheat of Song," were all famed in Brittonic verse at that time.)[15]

These five named poets are portrayed as having been active when Northumbria was first being united as an Anglo-Saxon kingdom. It would have been an era of warbands and "bards" who praised the chieftains and described the deeds of their warriors.[16] Note that the first named poet, Talhaearn, is called the "father

---

12 Krapp and Dobbie, *Exeter Book*, 149–53 (*Widsith*), 178–79 (*Deor*).
13 Fulk, Bjork, Niles, *Klaeber's Beowulf*.
14 Swanton, *Anglo-Saxon Chronicles*, 16–17 s.a. 547 (from chronicles A and E).
15 I have regularized spelling to more modern forms of the personal names. For an edition, see Morris, *Nennius*, 37 §62 (English), 78 (Latin). For background to these poems, see Koch, "Why Was Welsh Literature First Written Down?"
16 For a concise defense for the study of these early Brittonic poets, known in Modern Welsh as *cynfeirdd*, see Koch, "Waiting for Gododdin."

(*tad*) of the poetic muse (*awen*)."[17] It is a commonplace among the Britons and Gaels that their best poets claimed to possess and control "poetic inspiration." *Awen* described the notion of poetic inspiration among the Britons, just as *aí* referred to it among the Gaels.[18]

The name Blwchfardd may have been intended as metaphorical. It is a compound for which the first element *blwch* means "box, chest," and the second *bardd* is a poet.[19] This name, or epithet, suggests the concept of a *wordhord* (word-hoard), a compound found in *Beowulf* and other Old English poems.[20] The poet Cian is known as "Wheat of Song" (*Gwenith Gwawd*) implying that his poetry supplied sustenance of superior quality. The poets named as Aneirin and Taliesin both proliferate in subsequent legend and have surviving texts attributed to them. However, linguistic dating counsels caution with regard to confident equation of text to poet.[21]

The *Gododdin* survives in a thirteenth-century manuscript known as the "Book of Aneirin" (*Llyfr Aneirin*; Cardiff, Central Library, MS 2.81).[22] The poem is a collection of heroic eulogies which celebrate, or commemorate, the participants at the battle of Catraeth, the presumed Catterick on the River Swale at the northern end of the Vale of York. The battle, or battles, took place in the late sixth or early seventh centuries.[23] Two scribes have preserved the collected poems which can be divided into three recensions, each with differences in linguistic features and subject matter. All recensions place the origins of the Brittonic forces in the north of Britain, that is, around Edinburgh and across to Strathclyde, and mention Picts as fellow participants. They are, in other words, *Gwyr y Gogledd* (Men of the North), a term for which greater subtlety is needed

---

[17] "poetic gift, genius or inspiration, the muse"; *Geiriadur*, 240.
[18] "poetic inspiration, learning, metrical composition"; eDIL: http://www.dil.ie, s.v. 2 *aí* or dil.ie/715.
[19] The modern spelling of the second element as –*fardd* reflects the lenition required in the second element of a compound.
[20] See Fulk, Bjork, Niles, *Klaeber's Beowulf*, 11, line 259; and the first line of *Widsith*: Hill, *Minor Heroic Poems*, 31, line 1.
[21] Nerys Ann Jones surveyed the poets (*gogynfeirdd*) of the later Middle Ages for references to named poets, and heroes, from texts assigned to this earliest poetry from the North: Jones "Hengerdd." Oliver Padel argued that the poetry attributed to these two named poets is likely to be of the ninth or tenth centuries: Padel, "Aneirin and Taliesin."
[22] CODECS: https://www.vanhamel.nl/codecs/Cardiff,_Central_Library,_MS_2.81; for a survey of poems attributed to Aneirin, see Charles-Edwards, *Wales and the Britons*, 364–78.
[23] For arguments that *Y Gododdin* should be read as depicting varied border skirmishes and not a single battle at Catraeth, which is likely a conventional name for a battle, see Dunshea, "The Meaning of Catraeth."

to distinguish competing polities. The most recent recension allows that the battle may have been a victory, but the two earlier recensions portray the endeavor as a disastrous defeat for the "Men of the North."[24] In each recension the enemy is either Deira or both Deira and Bernicia combined.[25] In the manuscript, at the beginning of the *Gododdin*, but as part of what is considered the most recent, more innovative recension, is the line *Hwn yw e gododin. Aneirin ae cant* (This is the *Gododdin*, Aneirin sang it).[26]

Whether or not any faith is placed in such an ascription, this collection of poems reflects a heroic age ethos and demonstrates a major rôle filled by early poets with regard to panegyric, encomium, and eulogy. The poems typically name individual participants and describe their social status and background, deeds in battle, and, often, how they faced death. The men are frequently described as having paid with their lives for the wine and mead provided by their lords, a reminder of descriptions of the Anglo-Saxon *comitatus* at court or in the mead hall. In the two later recensions the Britons and their Pictish allies are portrayed as Christians at a time when the Northumbrians were still pagan or, at most, within the first generation of conversion.[27] The encomiastic diction and vocabulary of Cædmon's *Hymn* can be viewed in this context of heroic warriors and bards.

In another thirteenth-century manuscript, called the "Book of Taliesin" (*Llyfr Taliesin*; Aberystwyth, NLW, Peniarth MS 2),[28] are preserved poems that praise leaders whose influence spread over north Wales, the midlands of Britain, and southwestern Scotland. As in most of the *Gododdin* poems, the heroes are portrayed as Christians, and the day of the week in which the action takes place is often named. Urien Rheged and his son Owain are praised in poems that describe their victories against enemies, be they Picts or Anglo-Saxons. A formulaic ending appended to many of these poems reflects the ethos of a culture where a poet might attach himself to an important chieftain as patron.

> Ac yny vallwyf y hen
> ym dygyn agheu aghen.
> Ny bydif ym dirwen
> na molwyf vryen.[29]

---

24 For discussion, see Koch, *Gododdin of Aneirin*, xiii–xxxiv.
25 Koch, *Celtic Heroic Age*, 318–19.
26 Williams, *Canu Aneirin*, 1.
27 See Yorke, "Anglo-Saxon Kingdoms," 76–77.
28 CODECS: https://www.vanhamel.nl/codecs/Aberystwyth, National Library of Wales, Peniarth MS 2; for an overview of Taliesin, see Charles-Edwards, *Wales and the Britons*, 378–80.
29 For slight variations, see Williams, *Poems of Taliesin*, 3, 4, 5, 6, 7, 9, 11.

(And until I grow old
in the dire compulsion of death's allotment,
I shall not be happy,
unless I praise Urien.)[30]

Many poems surviving in the Brittonic records portray an encomiastic tradition that praised warriors and their chieftains, much as has been assumed for the earliest Anglo-Saxons.[31] They paint a militaristic war-like society where success in combat was a valued virtue and lasting fame the greatest reward.

## Mythico-Legendary Gaelic Poets

As in the Brittonic traditions, much survives among the Gaels that reveals a reliance on secular eulogy and encomium of noted ancestors and living chieftains. The recorded cultural history of the Gaels is more extensive than for either the Britons or Anglo-Saxons. Several mythico-legendary named poets are cited as experts and authorities in an eighth-century "pseudo-historical prologue"[32] to the seventh-century collection of law-texts known as the *Senchas Már* (Great Tradition), as will be seen below.[33] The law-tracts of the *Senchas Már* already look back centuries to earlier traditions and name important, precedent-setting poets. The poem by Gilla in Choimded (ca. 1100) reviews hundreds of years of Gaelic cultural history from the arrival of the Gaels in Ireland before the Christian era to the fifth-century conversion attributed to St. Patrick and forward to a time contemporary with the end of the Old English era.[34] The following discussion of

---

**30** From the translation of John Koch, with modernized spelling of Urien: Koch, *Celtic Heroic Age*, 357, 359, 361, 362, 364. For arguments against the authenticity of this coda, see Padel, "Anierin and Taliesin," 136–37.

**31** See arguments in Koch, "Why Was Welsh Literature First Written Down?" Marged Haycock has noted that for later Welsh poets these early poetic traditions comprise "a virtual realm of 'beyond and before', and like the old common Germanic homeland, a shareable, adaptable and expandable resource" much as *Beowulf* and *Widsith* potentially served for Anglo-Saxons: Haycock, "Early Welsh Poets," 19.

**32** McCone, "Dubthach Maccu Lugair"; Carey, "Dubthach's Judgment"; Carey, "Pseudo-Historical Prologue."

**33** For the full context of early law and individual manuscripts, see Ó Corráin, *Clavis*, ii, 863–72 §668, 905–7 §679, 909–11 §682, 915–16 §687, 918–19 §691, 921 §695; Kelly, *Guide*, 48 (*filid*), 242–46 (texts included within). For dating, contents, and general discussion, see Breatnach, *Senchas Már*. Many law tracts are attributed to named characters: Chapman-Stacey, "Law and Literature," 68–75.

**34** Smith, "Aimirgein Glúngel Tuir Tend"; Ó Corráin, *Clavis*, iii, 1583–84 §1190.

mythico-legendary Gaelic poets does not attempt to follow any chronological order.

The Leinster dynastic poems, composed perhaps at the end of the sixth or early seventh centuries, portray illustrious ancestors and suggest the importance of a secular tradition of encomium.[35] These poems are integrated into the Leinster genealogies.[36] References to Biblical characters and items of Latinate vocabulary show the Christian background of the audience being addressed in one of the longer poems.[37] The same dynastic poem refers to Góedel Glas, the eponymous ancestor of the Gaels (Goidels) according to the origin legends developed in *Lebor Gabála Érenn* (The Book of Invasions of Ireland) in the Middle Gaelic period,[38] but who is also encountered in the early eighth-century vernacular grammar *Auraicept na nÉces*.[39] Some of the rhyming Leinster dynastic poems are attributed to Laidcenn mac Bairchedo, a poet of the Dál nAraidi, a people located in present-day Co. Antrim.[40] Among these dynastic poems are fragmentary verses called the rhymeless Leinster poems which show the same characteristics of glorifying illustrious ancestors,[41] many of whom are portrayed in later tenth-century prosimetric narratives.[42]

A certain Luccreth maccu Chíara has poems attributed to him which are complex and linguistically early, but not later than the seventh century.[43] The poem *Conailla Medb míchuru* (Medb enjoined illegal contracts) has long been recognized as one of the texts that foreshadows events and characters of the

---

35 For translations of some of these poems, see Koch, *Celtic Heroic Age*, 53–59 §§67–72.
36 See O'Brien, *Corpus genealogiarum Hiberniae*, 1–9.
37 These are found in the poem beginning *Núada Necht* which is attributed to the poet Find Rossa Ruaid: O'Brien, *Corpus genealogiarum Hiberniae*, 1. Some of the Biblical characters include Noah and Methuselah (§48), Enoch (§49), and Adam (§50): Koch, *Celtic Heroic Age*, 57.
38 Koch, *Celtic Heroic Age*, §68 ¶42. For discussion of the evolution and introduction of the origin legend to seventh-century Ireland, see Howlett, "Irish Foundation Legend." For the *Lebor Gabála*, see Ó Corráin, *Clavis*, iii, 1531–39 §1141.
39 Ahlqvist, *Early Irish Linguist*; Ó Corráin, *Clavis*, ii, 1130–34 §850.
40 Poems attributed to Laidcenn mac Bairchedo include one beginning "*Énna, Labraid luad cáich*": O'Brien, *Corpus genealogiarum Hiberniae*, 4–7; and another beginning "*Nidu dīr dermait*": O'Brien, *Corpus genealogiarum Hiberniae*, 8–9; for a translation of the latter, see Koch, *Celtic Heroic Age*, 53–54 §67. For discussion of the socio-political background, see Charles-Edwards, *Early Christian Ireland*, 454–58.
41 Carney, "Accentual Poems," 65–73. See also Corthals, "Observations on the Versification"; Corthals, "Rhymeless 'Leinster Poems'"; Ó Corráin, *Clavis*, ii, 1122–23 §845.
42 The prose narrative *Orgain Denna Ríg* will be discussed in chapter three. See an edition in Greene, *Fingal Rónáin*, 16–26; Ó Corráin, *Clavis*, iii, 1423–24 §1086.
43 Carney, "Accentual Poems"; Charles-Edwards, *Early Christian Ireland*, 537–40; Carney, "Language and Literature," 482, 485.

*Táin Bó Cúailnge* before that prosimetric narrative was preserved in writing.[44] It also purportedly explains the descent of various Munster groups from northern ancestors such as Fergus mac Roíg, an important protagonist of the *Táin*. A poem in the genealogies on the Eoganachta of Munster is also attributed to Luccreth.[45]

As with Laidcenn mac Bairchedo and Luccreth maccu Chíara, there are other named poets who are in the pantheon of cultural icons. Some, however, have little or no historical confirmation. Amairgen Glúngel (Amairgen White-knee) is the quasi-mythical poet of the Milesian invasion of Ireland.[46] According to *Lebor Gabála Érenn*, the "sons of Míl" (Milesians) were the original Gaels and Amairgen was their chief poet and judge.[47] In his rôle as judge Amairgen gave the first legal judgement in Ireland, which implies that poets once fulfilled the functions of judges. Amairgen's first judgement is cited in the eighth-century "pseudo-historical prologue" to the *Senchas Már*.[48] Amairgen is also cited as an inspired poet and authority in an early eighth-century text on poetics and the nature of poetic inspiration, the anonymous "Caldron of Poesy."[49] Amairgen as judge is cited in Gilla in Choimded's poem.[50]

Ferchertne *fili* (Ferchertne the poet) debated with Néide mac Adnai for the position of chief poet at the court of Conchobar mac Nessa in Emain Macha (Navan Fort, Co. Armagh). The legendary setting is the time of the *Táin Bó Cúailnge* (The Cattle Raid of Cooley), around the time of Christ.[51] Their debate is preserved in an Old Gaelic text known as *Immacallam in Dá Thuarad* (Colloquy of the Two Sages).[52] Ferchertne won the debate, but their language was so obscure and unintelligible to their audience at court that it was decided that judicial functions could not be left to the domain of poets alone. In the "pseudo-historical

---

44 For an edition, see Henry, "*Conailla Medb Míchuru*." For discussion of its relationship to the *Táin*, see Olmstead, "Earliest Narrative Version."
45 O'Brien, *Corpus genealogiarum Hiberniae*, 199–202 (148b30–149a11); Charles-Edwards, *Early Christian Ireland*, 537–40.
46 Rees and Rees, *Celtic Heritage*, 96–100; O'Rahilly, *Early Irish History and Mythology*, 196–99.
47 Carey, *Origin-Legend*. For prophetic and mantic poetry attributed to Amairgen, see Macalister, *Lebor Gabála Érenn*, 110–17. For background, see Scowcroft, "Leabhar Gabhála Part I"; Scowcroft, "Leabhar Gabhála Part II"; Ó Corráin, *Clavis*, iii, 1531–39 §1141.
48 McCone, "Dubthach Maccu Lugair," 9; Carey, "Pseudo-Historical Prologue," 19 §10.
49 Henry, "Caldron of Poesy," 123; Breatnach, "Caldron of Poesy," 62–63; and Ó Corráin, *Clavis*, ii, 1129–30 §849.
50 Smith, "Aimirgein Glúngel Tuir Tend," 124–38 §§1, 14, 16, 40, 45, 63.
51 For general background, see Ó hUiginn, "Development of *Táin Bó Cúailnge*."
52 Stokes, "Colloquy of the Two Sages"; see also Thurneysen, *Die irische Helden- und Königsage*, 518–23; Ó Corráin, *Clavis*, iii, 1396–98 §1070.

prologue" this debate is cited as the reason that poets lost their rôle as judges.[53] Gilla in Choimded repeated aspects of the legend and named both Ferchertne and Néide.[54]

In the ninth-century recension of the *Táin Bó Cúailnge*, a composite text, a female poet evoked the scenario for the narrative's plot in a poem that results from her poetic inspiration.[55] As the combined armies of Ireland are about to set out for their raid against Ulster, they encounter a grown maiden. Queen Medb asks her to identify herself and she replies that she is Fedelm *banfili* (poetess) from Connacht. She is also referred to as *banfáith* (prophetess) in the narrative, with justification. When she is asked where she has come from she replies that she has just returned from Britain (*Albu*) having learned *filidecht* (poetic art). Medb then asked if she possessed *imbas for·osna* (great knowledge which illumines), a divinatory skill claimed by adept poets. When Fedelm answered in the affirmative, Medb asked her to "look" and see how the expedition would turn out. Three times Fedelm predicted disaster for the expeditionary force with Medb insisting each time that their defeat was impossible.[56] Fedelm then uttered a prophetic poem telling of the victorious feats of the Ulster hero Cú Chulainn which begins: *Atchíu fer find firfes cles* (I see a fair man who will perform feats).[57] Fedelm is an iconic example of the *fili* with prophetic powers and divinatory skills.

Morann mac Moín is credited with *Audacht Morainn* (The Testament of Morann), the oldest vernacular *speculum principum* in Europe, dated to ca. 700.[58] The concern with just rule and proper kingship is reflected in many Gaelic texts from this period. John Carey argued that *Audacht Morainn*, among other texts, can be dated to the time of Fínsnechta Fledach (675–95) and that they are derived from the lost manuscript *Cín Dromma Snechtai*, which will be discussed in chapter three.[59] Fínsnechta held the high-kingship of Tara at the time that King Ecgfrith

---

53 McCone, "Dubthach Maccu Lugair," 9–19; Carey, "Pseudo-Historical Prologue," 19 §10.
54 See Smith, "Aimirgein Glúngel Tuir Tend," 192–237 §§30, 46, 59 (Ferchertne); §§30, 46, 55 (Néide mac Adnai).
55 For the *Táin*, see Ó Corráin, *Clavis*, iii, 1445–68 §1103. This episode can be found in O'Rahilly, *Táin: Recension I*, 2–3, lines 29–98 (Gaelic); 126–28 (English). For dating and background, see Ó hUiginn, "Development of *Táin Bó Cúailnge*."
56 This episode is discussed for its visual aesthetics in Ireland, "Visionary Poets," 129–30.
57 O'Rahilly, *Táin: Recension I*, 2–3, lines 29–67 (Gaelic); 126–27 (English). The same incident is related in the Middle Gaelic Book of Leinster recension: O'Rahilly, *Táin Book of Leinster*, 5–7, lines 183–234 (Gaelic); 143–44 (English).
58 Kelly, *Audacht Morainn*, xxxii (dating); Ó Corráin, *Clavis*, ii, 1188–90 §908.
59 CODECS: https://www.vanhamel.nl/codecs/Cín_Dromma_Snechtai; Carey, "*Cín Dromma Snechtai* Texts," 86–89; Ó Corráin, *Clavis*, ii, 1053–54 §815.

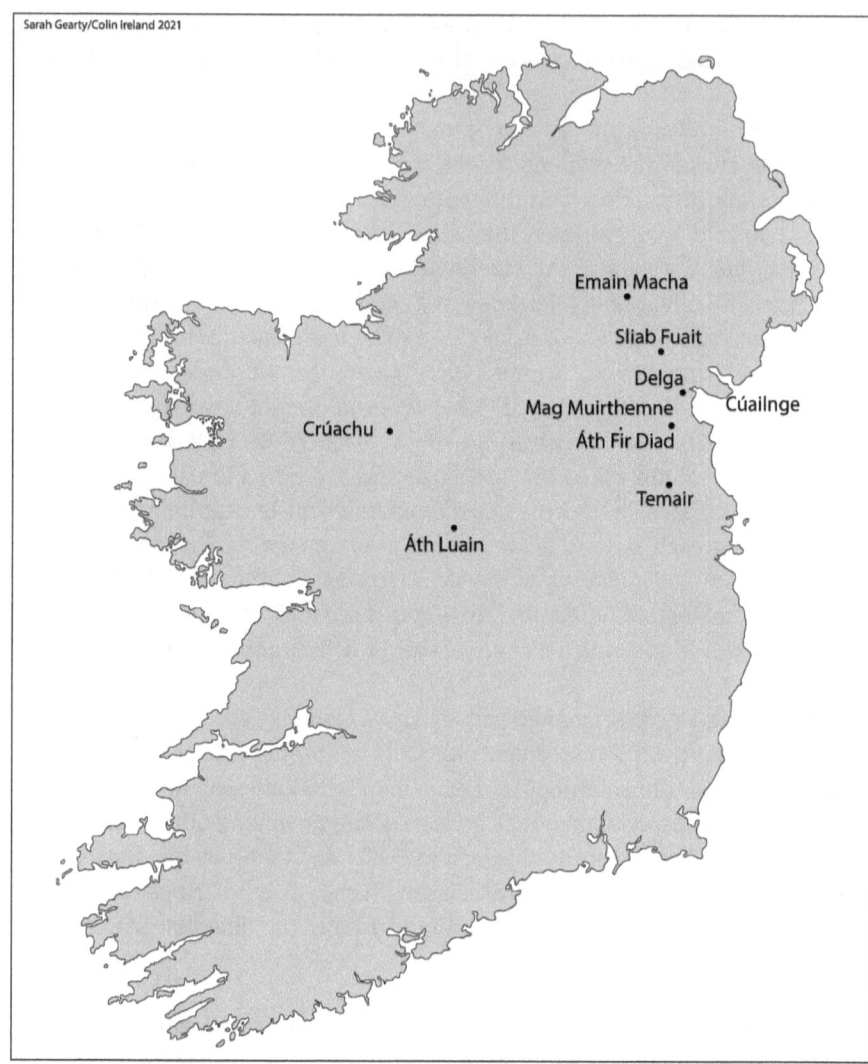

**Figure 1.a:** Cúailnge = Cooley, Co. Louth; Crúachu = Rathcroghan, Co. Roscommon; Emain Macha = Navan Fort, Co. Armagh; Temair = Hill of Tara, Co. Meath; Sliab Fuait = The Fews Mountains, Co. Armagh; Delga = Dundalk, Co. Louth; Mag Muirthemne = Plain south of Dundalk; Áth Fir Diad = Ardee, Co. Louth; Áth Luain = Athlone, Co. Westmeath.

All significant peoples and events mentioned in the *Táin Bó Cúailnge* are found in identifiable locations in Ireland. The sequence of events and their locations can be traced on a modern map. *Dindṡenchas* (place lore) is an important literary genre among the Gaels.

sent his *dux* Berht on a raid into Brega in 684 (*HE* iv 26 [24]).⁶⁰ The prophetic poem on the kingship of Tara, *Baile Chuinn*, derives from the same manuscript and timeframe with the last firmly identifiable king in the list being Fínsnechta.⁶¹ These two vernacular texts, a political prophecy and a *speculum principum*, emphasize the importance of proper kingship among the Gaels.

In style and content *Audacht Morainn* is related to law-texts known as *Bretha Nemed* (Judgements of Privileged Persons) and is referred to as the *Nemed* school.⁶² Morann descended from one of the *aithechthúatha* (vassal tribes) and Morann's ancestor, Cairpre Cattchenn, led a successful revolt against the sons of Míl.⁶³ Another legend tells of Morann's collars which distinguished between truth and falsehood, good judgement and bad judgement by expanding or contracting accordingly.⁶⁴ *Audacht Morainn* is cited in the "pseudo-historical prologue" as an example of a text which resulted from the dissolution of the poets' monopoly in jurisprudence.⁶⁵ Gilla in Choimded included Morann in his poem.⁶⁶

Aithirne Áilgesach (Aithirne the Importunate) is a poet noted for his greediness which he satisfies by threatening satire against those who fail to comply with his excessive requests. Aithirne's self-serving behavior reveals the negative aspects of poetic privilege in Gaelic society and is thoroughly portrayed in the late Old Gaelic narrative text *Talland Étair*, often translated as the "Siege of Howth."⁶⁷ He regularly uses his privilege to make demeaning demands, such as sexual favors from the wives of those who provided him hospitality, as he went on circuit throughout Ireland. The loss of reputation through satire feared by the higher social ranks displays the obverse function of praise poets who would normally create fame for those same patrons through encomia and panegyric.⁶⁸

---

60 Colgrave and Mynors, *Ecclesiastical History*, 426–29; for Fínsnechta Fledach, see Byrne, *Irish Kings*, 104, 146, 254; Pelteret, "Attack on Brega."
61 Carey, "*Cín Dromma Snechtai* Texts," 86–89. For an edition, see Murphy, "Dates of Two Sources," 145–51; Bhreathnach and Murray, "*Baile Chuinn Chétchathaig*"; Ó Corráin, *Clavis*, iii, 1525–26 §1135.
62 Kelly, *Audacht Morainn*, xviii–xix; Kelly, *Guide*, 235–36 (*Audacht Morainn*), 246 (*Nemed* school). For *Bretha Nemed* texts, see Breatnach, *Companion*, 184–88 §5.15 (*Bretha Nemed Dédenach*); 188–91 §5.16 (*Bretha Nemed Toísech*).
63 Mac Neill, *Celtic Ireland*, 64–69; O'Rahilly, *Early Irish History and Mythology*, 159–60.
64 Stokes, "Irish Ordeals," 206–9.
65 McCone, "Dubthach Maccu Lugair," 10; Carey, "Pseudo-Historical Prologue," 19 §11.
66 Smith, "Aimirgein Glúngel Tuir Tend," 126–37 §§10, 26, 36, 51, 54.
67 Ó Dónaill, *Talland Étair*; Ó Corráin, *Clavis*, iii, 1475–76 §1109.
68 See the wide-ranging introduction in McLaughlin, *Early Irish Satire*, 1–40; Breatnach, "Satire, Praise."

Dallán Forgaill is remembered as chief poet of Ireland who eulogized the historical St. Columba upon his death in a poem known as *Amrae Coluim Chille*.[69] Columba died in 593 and is, of course, firmly historical, Dallán Forgaill is not.[70] According to legend Dallán praised Columba in verse because of the saint's support of the poets at the *Mórdál Dromma Ceta* (Convention of Druimm Cet).[71] While the poem may contain a genuinely old core, it is now argued that the surviving poem is a composite of probably the ninth century.[72] In chapter two we will see how Bécán mac Luigdech also praised Colum Cille, although the poets' styles differ, in poems assigned to the seventh century with greater confidence.

According to the Middle Gaelic commentaries Dallán composed *do chennaib*, literally "from heads."[73] The poetic skill known as *díchetal di chennaib* (chanting from heads) is taken to represent extempore composition.[74] Along with *imbas for·osna*, a skill displayed by the poetess Fedelm, it is one of the three skills required of a fully qualified poet by the late Old Gaelic period.[75] From the Old English tradition the most graphic description of extempore composition is the *scop* who praised Beowulf after his deadly combat with Grendel.[76]

*Amrae Coluim Chille* is addressed to an ecclesiastical authority rather than a secular leader. The poem emphasizes Columba's patristic, Latinate learning and presents him as a warrior who struggles against temptations and strives for his heavenly home in a manner similar to that seen in Old English poems such as *Andreas* or the *Dream of the Rood*, in the character of Christ himself in the latter poem. The *Amrae* uses obscure, archaicizing language with frequent alliteration, and uses stanzaic structure and rhyme borrowed from Latin hymns.[77] This vernacular poem acknowledges Latinate literacy and learning when Columba is

---

[69] For an edition and translations, see Bisagni, *Amrae Coluimb Chille*; Stokes, "Amra Choluimb Chille," 30–55, 132–83, 248–87, 400–437; Henry, *Saoithiúlacht*, 191–212; Clancy and Márkus, *Iona*, 104–15; Ó Corráin, *Clavis*, ii, 1117–20 §843.

[70] For the date of Columba's death, see Mc Carthy, "Chronology of St Columba's Life." For Dallán, see Herbert, "Preface to *Amra*"; Charles-Edwards, *Early Christian Ireland*, 192, 306 (Dallán); 180, 192–93, 289–90 (*Amrae Coluim Chille*).

[71] Stokes, "Amra Choluimb Chille," 35–37; Herbert, *Iona, Kells, and Derry*, 244–47 (Gaelic), 265–69 (English); Mac Airt and Mac Niocaill, *Annals of Ulster*, 86–87 s.a. 575. For a broad discussion of the poet and background to the poem, see Ní Dhonnchadha, "Irish Vernacular Literary Tradition," 566–73.

[72] See general conclusions in Bisagni, *Amrae Coluimb Chille*, 250–57.

[73] Stokes, "Amra Choluimb Chille," 132–35.

[74] Meyer, "Sanas Cormaic," 64 §756; Carey, "Three Things," 44–47.

[75] Carey, "Three Things."

[76] Fulk, Bjork, Niles, *Klaeber's Beowulf*, 31, lines 867b–74a.

[77] Murphy, *Early Irish Metrics*, 17–18; but see fuller discussion in Bisagni, *Amrae Coluim Chille*, 158–98.

praised for reading the Psalms,[78] for following the books of Solomon, for making known law-books and the books that Cassian loved,[79] for reading the sages and Scripture,[80] for obeying Basil's (of Caesarea) judgements,[81] and for studying Greek grammar.[82] The legend that has accrued around the poem shows a professional, secular poet praising an ecclesiastic in the manner of a secular lord, but highlighting qualities valued by the Church rather than martial skills valued in secular chieftains of warbands.

Senchán Torpéist is cited in Gilla in Choimded's poem as the "apex of speech" (*rind ráid*).[83] He is associated with the historical king Guaire Aidni of Connacht in some narratives. Guaire Aidni died ca. 663[84] and is important in both historical and literary contexts.[85] We may, therefore, place Senchán's *floruit* in the middle of the seventh century.[86] He traveled throughout Ireland with his large retinue which created a burden for those who hosted him. He is the main protagonist in an important etiological legend called *De Failsigiud Tána Bó Cúailnge* (the finding (recovery) of the *Táin*).[87] In the narrative Senchán must send out named pupils to help recover the *Táin* epic because it had been exchanged for Isidore of Seville's encyclopedic *Etymologiae*. Fergus mac Roíg, a major character in the *Táin*, figures in this legend as the character who related the *Táin* to the student poets. This etiological legend will be discussed in greater detail in chapter three.

Dubthach maccu Lugair is a legendary *fili* who is portrayed as an early, and influential, convert of St. Patrick in the late seventh-century *Vita Patricii*

---

78 Bisagni, *Amrae Coluimb Chille*, 270–71; Stokes, "Amra Choluimb Chille," 252–53; Clancy and Márkus, *Iona*, 106–7.
79 Bisagni, *Amrae Coluimb Chille*, 270–71; Stokes, "Amra Choluimb Chille," 254–55; Clancy and Márkus, *Iona*, 106–9.
80 Bisagni, *Amrae Coluimb Chille*, 270–73; Stokes, "Amra Choluimb Chille," 256–57; Clancy and Márkus, *Iona*, 108–9.
81 Bisagni, *Amrae Coluimb Chille*, 270–71; Stokes, "Amra Choluimb Chille," 180–81; Clancy and Márkus, *Iona*, 106–7.
82 Bisagni, *Amrae Coluimb Chille*, 276–77; Stokes, "Amra Choluimb Chille," 404–5; Clancy and Márkus, *Iona*, 112–13.
83 Smith, "Aimirgein Glúngel Tuir Tend," 133, 137 §57.
84 Mac Airt and Mac Niocaill, *Annals of Ulster*, 134–35; Stokes, "Annals of Tigernach," 197–98 [Felinfach i 157–58]; Mc Carthy, D., http://www.irish-annals.cs.tcd.ie/, s.a. 663.
85 For historical contexts, see Byrne, *Irish Kings*, 239–46. For literary contexts, Ó Coileáin, "Structure of a Literary Cycle"; Ó Coileáin, "*Tromdám Guaire*"; Ó Coileáin, "Problems of Story and History."
86 Thurneysen, "Colmān mac Lēnēni"; Carney, "Accentual Poems," 68, 73 and note; Johnston, "Senchán Torpéist"; Carney, "Language and Literature," 468, 469, 474–75.
87 Ó Corráin, *Clavis*, iii, 1361–62 §1039; Murray, "Finding of the *Táin*."

by Muirchú maccu Machtheni.[88] The context is the fifth-century conversion by St. Patrick of the pagan royal court at Tara under King Lóegaire mac Néill. Dubthach plays a central rôle in the eighth-century "pseudo-historical prologue" to the *Senchas Már*, as noted above.[89] In the "prologue" Dubthach must pass judgement in a legal case that is pivotal in the conversion of Lóegaire's court. His judgement is delivered, after submitting himself to God's will, as a complex poem.[90] The successful outcome of his legal judgement, in a symbolic elaboration of the legend, resulted in the formation of a named nine-man commission comprised of three secular rulers, three churchmen, and three learned men in native lore. Among the learned men was the *fili* Dubthach himself. The commission's brief was to syncretize indigenous tradition with Church teachings and ensure that those native practices that were maintained did not contravene Christian conscience. This legend is crucial to understanding cooperation between the order of professional poets and ecclesiastical authority that resulted in, among other things, the bilingual intellectual culture so evident by the late seventh century. The "prologue" is also given expression in another *Senchas Már* text of the seventh century, *Córus Bésgnai* (The Regulation of Proper Behaviour).[91] Dubthach appears in later texts, such as vernacular saints' lives and prose narratives. Poems about Leinster dynastic families and their ancestral heroes are also ascribed to Dubthach.[92] The late poems about Leinster families attributed retrospectively to Dubthach come from the twelfth century and are contemporary with the end of the Anglo-Saxon period.

Dubthach and the nine-man commission are cited in Gilla in Choimded's poem where Dubthach and another poet, Fergus *fili*, are praised for augmenting the *Senchas Már*.[93] Subsequently in Gilla in Choimded's poem, the members of the nine-man commission are named and acknowledged for their contributions.[94]

---

[88] Bieler, *Patrician Texts*, 92–93 (*Vita Patricii*); Howlett, *Muirchú Moccu Macthéni's*, 80–83; Ó Corráin, *Clavis*, i, 261–66 §217. See discussion of Dubthach in Ireland, "Vernacular Poets," 49–52, 55–58.

[89] The "pseudo-historical prologue" expressed a sense of *natio* for the island of Ireland through the power of Uí Néill kings: Wadden, "Pseudo-Historical Origins."

[90] McCone, "Dubthach Maccu Lugair"; Carey, "Dubthach's Judgment"; Carey, "Pseudo-Historical Prologue"; Ireland, "Vernacular Poets," 55.

[91] Breatnach, *Córus Bésgnai*, 32–35 §§31, 35, 37. See further Ó Corráin, Breatnach, Breen, "Laws of the Irish," 385–86, 399; McCone, "Dubthach Maccu Lugair," 10, 20–26; Carey, "Dubthach's Judgment," 2–3, 8.

[92] Ireland, "Vernacular Poets," 58 and notes; Ó Corráin, *Clavis*, iii, 1606–8 §§1208–20.

[93] Smith, "Aimirgein Glúngel Tuir Tend," 129, 136 §33.

[94] Smith, "Aimirgein Glúngel Tuir Tend," 130, 136–37 §§37–40.

Dubthach's purported rôle in establishing the *Senchas Már* is a reminder of the place of the *filid* in Early Gaelic social order and law.

## Mythico-legendary Anglo-Saxon Poets

The Old English poems, *Beowulf*, *Widsith*, and *Deor*, depict poets practicing their art and allow us to reconstruct some early Germanic poetic practices. Note that none of the three Old English poems named here can be placed on the island of Britain in an explicitly Anglo-Saxon context,[95] whereas early Brittonic and Gaelic poetic traditions are firmly insular in their geographical descriptions. For the Old English poems it is the fact of language itself that allows us to assume that their Anglo-Saxon audiences understood the references to mythico-legendary and historical characters and events, and to the poetic practices described in them.

Each of the three Old English poems survives as a single copy. The copy of *Beowulf* has a complicated manuscript history and is found in the composite London, British Library, Cotton Vitellius A.xv.[96] Both *Widsith* and *Deor* are found in the Exeter Book (*Codex Exoniensis*; Exeter Cathedral Library, MS 3501) which can be dated to the late tenth century and gives a *terminus ante quem* for when these two poems were composed.[97]

*Beowulf* is an epic poem that takes its name from its main protagonist and may be contemporary with the Old Gaelic *Táin Bó Cúailnge* in their surviving written forms.[98] Despite the relative closeness in age of the two texts as preserved,

---

[95] Frank, "Anglo-Saxon Oral Poet," 28. While *Beowulf* is clearly set in Sweden and Denmark, it is not at all specific as to place and generally seems disinterested: Orchard, *Companion to Beowulf*, 172–73. For more thoughts on this aspect of the poem, see Niles, "How Real Are the Geats?" 67–71. The anonymous Old English poems *Battle of Maldon*, *Battle of Brunanburh*, and *Durham*, on the other hand, all use personal and place names that situate the poems on the island of Britain.

[96] Gneuss and Lapidge, *Anglo-Saxon Manuscripts*, 322–23 §399; Fulk, Bjork, Niles, *Klaeber's Beowulf*, xxv–xxxv. For an illustration of the manuscript, see Breay and Story, *Anglo-Saxon Kingdoms*, 230–31.

[97] Gneuss and Lapidge, *Anglo-Saxon Manuscripts*, 201–3 §257; Krapp and Dobbie, *Exeter Book*, 149–53 (Widsith), 178–79 (Deor); Butler, "Glastonbury."

[98] Linguistic dating of *Beowulf* can be assigned most probably to the first half of the eighth century: Fulk, Bjork, Niles, *Klaeber's Beowulf*, clxxix; but see the wide array of supporting evidence in the collection of essays edited by Neidorf, *Dating of Beowulf*. Linguistic dating for the first written text of the *Táin Bó Cuailnge* is assigned to the eighth or ninth centuries in the form as we have it. But earlier textual evidence for its existence will be cited throughout. See, for example, Corthals, "*Aided Chonchobuir*"; Meid, *Táin Bó Fraích*.

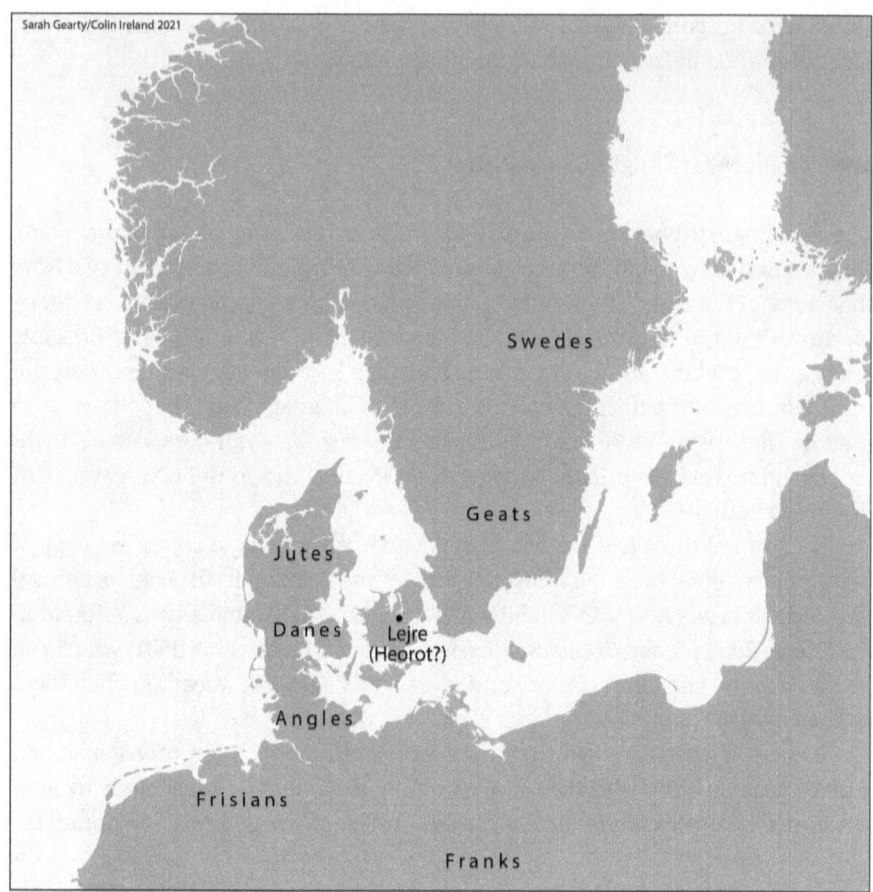

**Figure 1.b:** *Beowulf* is preserved in a mixture of Old English dialects. The Anglo-Saxons of Britain are the poem's intended audience. However, all peoples and events central to the main narrative are found on the Continent in what is now Denmark and Sweden, with digressive references to people and events in Frisia.

they depict different ages in their narratives. Based on references to historical events in *Beowulf* it would appear to represent a sixth-century timeframe.[99] *Táin Bó Cúailnge* is intended to represent events in Gaelic society from around the time of Christ.[100] Another difference is that the persons and events of *Beowulf* are not

---

**99** Fulk, Bjork, Niles, *Klaeber's Beowulf*, li; Biggs, "Frisian Raids."
**100** Kelleher, "*Táin* and the Annals." This article was challenged by Dumville, "Ulster Heroes." However, shortcomings in Dumville's arguments were pointed out by Mc Carthy, *Irish*

associated with parts of Britain occupied by Anglo-Saxon peoples but rather with Denmark and Sweden,[101] whereas all events in *Táin Bó Cúailnge* take place in Ireland and the action of the narrative can be traced on the modern Irish landscape.[102] One broad similarity in the two narratives is that they each depict the serial single combats of their respective heroic protagonists, Beowulf and Cú Chulainn.

The poems *Widsith* and *Deor* are named after *personae* in the poems whose voices recite the poems themselves. The names are rare, though both occur in the prosopography of the Anglo-Saxons, but each only once in surviving records.[103] The name Widsith is a compound composed of the adjective *wīd* (broad, spacious) and the noun *sīð* (journey; venture; occasion).[104] It is a personal name that anticipates the contents of the poem. Widsith is a "wide-traveler" in both space and time. *Deor* is an adjective meaning "bold, brave" in Old English,[105] but its use as a personal name may originate in Brittonic.[106]

*Widsith* cites Germanic heroes, tribes, and events that cover a vast geographical and chronological expanse, as well as citing peoples and events known from the Bible and from classical and antique sources.[107] *Widsith* may be among the oldest of surviving Old English poems.[108] It appears to name a second poet, Scilling, who was apparently comrade and colleague of Widsith.[109] *Widsith* and the knowledge portrayed in the poem hint at origin legends of Germanic peoples and can be compared to catalog texts produced in Britain, *Historia Brittonum*, and in Ireland, *Lebor Gabála Érenn*.[110] Widsith may be compared with the Gaelic characters Fintan

---

*Annals*, 100–101. See a text of the early eighth century that places King Conchobar in the time of Christ: Corthals, "*Aided Chonchobuir.*"
101 Bjork and Obermeier, "Date, Provenance," 18–28 (Date and Provenance); Niles, "How Real Are the Geats?"; Woolf, "Sutton Hoo and Sweden."
102 See the maps that accompany the translation of the *Táin* by the poet Thomas Kinsella: Kinsella, *The Tain*.
103 Prosopography of Anglo-Saxon England (PASE): http://www.pase.ac.uk/index.html.
104 Hill, *Minor Heroic Poems*, 128.
105 Hill, *Minor Heroic Poems*, 99.
106 Breeze, "Celtic Etymology."
107 Niles, "Anthropology of the Past."
108 Neidorf, "Dating of *Widsið.*"
109 It is possible that Scilling refers to the poet's harp, since Scilling implies a sound: Hill, *Minor Heroic Poems*, 121.
110 Widsith has already been compared to the Brittonic *Cad Goddeu* and *Taliesin's Travels* and to the Gaelic *Amargein's Song*: Calder, Bjork, Ford, Melia, *Sources and Analogues*, 101–5. For *Historia Brittonum*, see Sharpe, *Handlist*, 382 §1072; for *Lebor Gabála*, see Ó Corráin, *Clavis*, iii, 1531–39 §1141.

mac Bóchra[111] and Tuán mac Cairill,[112] both of whose longevity allowed them to recount the past of the various peoples of Ireland.

The poem *Deor* relates several episodes from Germanic lore: mythical, legendary, and historical. For example, from myth Weland and Beadohild are named and a historical Theodoric also, but which person of that latter name is not clear. Whether to mythical or historical persons, the oblique references in *Deor* imply that the audiences were expected to be able to identify the circumstances referred to. The theme of the poem highlights the poet Deor's loss of patronage to a competing poet named Heorrenda.[113]

Widsith and Deor appear to represent conventional names for poets rather than any legendary poets such as Taliesin and Aneirin among the Britons, or quasi-mythical personages such as Amairgen or Fedelm among the Gaels. The remainder of this chapter sets out to compare and contrast the Anglo-Saxon and Gaelic poetic traditions in greater detail.

## Descriptions of Poets at Work

A number of texts from the early Middle Ages depict the courts of kings and chieftains as having storytellers or poets and music, in the form of harps or other instruments, available for edification or entertainment of those gathered. The three Old English poems noted above – *Beowulf*, *Widsith*, and *Deor* – provide pictures of early poets at work. By comparing the poets depicted in these poems with similar depictions of poets from Early Gaelic society we can recreate something of early medieval insular practice or, at least, how early insular cultures imagined their ancestors in a distant, heroic past to have performed storytelling or poetry, sometimes accompanied by music.

### Poets at Court

In an early scene from *Beowulf* (lines 89b–90a) men are gathered at a mead feast of the Danish king Hrothgar, enjoying comradeship in the hall named *Heorot* (literally, hart, stag). The scene of pleasure in the mead hall includes the

---

[111] Best, "Manor of Tara."
[112] Carey, "*Scél Tuáin meic Cairill*."
[113] Hill, *Minor Heroic Poems*, 111.

presence of a poet (*scop*) and harp music. The expressions of human joy in the hall dismay and perturb the otherworldly monster Grendel who will soon make his destructive presence felt as the narrative unfolds:

> þær wæs hearpan swēġ,
> swutol sang scopes (lines 89b–90a).[114]

(There was harp music, (and) the clear song of a *scop*.)

The evidence from insular cultures indicates that poetry and music were complementary arts and performed in tandem, yet it appears that the personnel who performed the two functions were often, if not typically, separate. Unfortunately, the example just cited does not make it clear if the harp music and song are produced by the same person or two different people. In Gaelic society the high-ranking poet may have had someone else declaim his composition in performance at court often accompanied by a third person playing a stringed instrument.[115] Harp players were granted a social status on a higher level than other skilled professionals in the law-tracts and were frequently present at court functions. Among Gaels, the *fili* (poet) was *sóernemed* (noble *nemed*; a noble dignitary), the *cruit* (harpist) was *dóernemed* (base *nemed*; a dependent professional). But both poet and harpist were *nemed* (privileged), whereas in Anglo-Saxon tradition no official status was defined for either position and some descriptions suggest they are the same person. Some Anglo-Saxon evidence suggests a similar separation of the functions of poetry and music, although there is ambiguity in the few cases that can be cited.[116]

The immediately following lines in *Beowulf* (90b–98) are frequently referred to as the "Song of Creation" and describe how God created the world and humankind within it. Creation as a theme recurs in many contexts in insular literature, both in Latin and in the vernaculars. In this context, the discussion of God's creation sets up the introduction of Grendel, a malevolent aspect of the created world. Creation as a poetic theme will be reviewed in chapter seven.

An early eighth-century Gaelic law-tract on the status of the lay grades, *Críth Gablach* (Branched Purchase), offers an idealized picture of the historical king's house and retinue which should contain both a poet (*éices*) and a harper

---

**114** Fulk, Bjork, Niles, *Klaeber's Beowulf*, 6.
**115** Buckley, "Music in Ireland," 748.
**116** Jeff Opland made the most thorough study of the situation and tended to the view that the *scop* did not accompany himself on the harp, but that the gleeman (*gleōman*) might do so: Opland, *Anglo-Saxon Oral Poetry*, 192–99, 219–22, 257–60. For a contrary view, see North, "Singing Welsh Bishop."

(*cruit*), just as portrayed in Hrothgar's hall in *Beowulf*.¹¹⁷ The immediately following passage in *Críth Gablach* includes the *cuislennach* (piper), *cornaire* (horn player), and *clessamnach* (juggler) among the retinue, indicating that entertainment was an important aspect of the chieftain's court in the insular world.¹¹⁸

A narrative of the early tenth century, *Orgain Denna Ríg* (The Destruction of Dind Ríg), tells about the internecine dynastic struggles of Leinster imagined as having occurred about 300 B.C.¹¹⁹ In a scene at the court of King Cobthach Cóel in Tara, the poet Ferchertne *fili* and his harper Craiphtine are present among the nobles and *áes admolta* (people of praising).¹²⁰ Their interactions with the king and his court imply that their presence and function of providing *encomia* was not only normal but expected.

The complementarity of music and poetry is stressed in a series of poems from an Old Gaelic law-text on "the privileges and responsibilities of poets," *Bretha Nemed Dédenach* (The Later Judgements of Privileged (or Professional) Persons).¹²¹ The poems are referred to as the *Áiliu* poems and Johan Corthals states of the series, "this text must primarily have been meant to be recited to the accompaniment of musical instruments and dance and partly in processional movement towards the festive hall."¹²² The initial two lines of the first poem provide a sense of what he means:

> Áiliu seinm sernar n-imbus,
> indel crott, cuislennaig córai.
>
> (I pray for music, by which great learning is displayed,
> Arrangement of harps, harmoniousness of the flutist.)¹²³

The importance of harpers and harp music is emphasized in the Old Gaelic tale *Cath Maige Tuired* (The [Second] Battle of Mag Tuired) which is set in an indeterminate period in Ireland's prehistory and deals with the war between the

---

117 "éccis íar su[i]dib; cru[i]tti íar su[i]di[b]": Binchy, *Críth Gablach*, 23, line 589. It should be noted that in this passage the words for poet (*éices*) and harper (*cruit*) are both nominative plurals. Joan Radner discussed some early Gaelic tales that treat the origins of poetry and harp music and their relationships with each other: Radner, "'Men Will Die'."
118 In the text each of these terms are nominative plurals: Binchy, *Críth Gablach*, 23, line 590. Current archaeological evidence suggests significant differences in the size of structures used for courtly gatherings in the Anglo-Saxon and Gaelic worlds: Woolf, "Court Poet in Early Ireland."
119 Carney, "Language and Literature," 480–81.
120 Greene, *Fingal Rónáin*, 19, lines 344, 347.
121 Gwynn, "Privileges and Responsibilities"; Breatnach, *Companion*, 184–88.
122 Corthals, "*Áiliu* Poems," 74.
123 Corthals, "*Áiliu* Poems," 75 (Gaelic), 78 (English). The *cuislennach* may have been a piper rather than a flutist.

Tuatha Dé Danann and the Fomoiri, two supernatural races. Many "firsts" in Gaelic cultural history are recorded in the text. The harper of the Dagda (the Good God) was named Uaithne and he was able to play three types of music that all subsequent harpers should master in order to validate their rank. The three types of music were *súantraí* (sleep music) which caused its audience to sleep soundly, *gentraí* (joyful music) which made its audience laugh and be merry, and *goltraí* (sorrowful music) which caused its audience to weep and lament.[124] These types of music, either as a triad or singly, are referred to in numerous tales and contexts. For example, in *Orgain Denna Ríg* mentioned above, the harper Craiphtine plays *súantraí* to induce deep sleep in his audience on two occasions. The first time was so that the narrative's hero, Labraid Loingsech, could complete a tryst with his lover Moriath; the second time was to place the defenders of the fortress Dind Ríg in a stupor so that Labraid and his allies could recapture it from his rivals.[125]

The following excerpt from *Beowulf* describes the entertainment in the mead hall after the monster Grendel has been killed by the hero Beowulf. Gifts are dispensed to Beowulf's men and his achievement celebrated:

> Þær wæs sang ond swēġ    samod ætgædere
> fore Healfdenes    hildewīsan,
> gomenwudu grēted,    ġid oft wrecen,
> ðonne Healgamen,    Hrōþgāres scop
> æfter medobenċe    mænan scolde
> Finnes eafer*an* (lines 1063–68a).[126]
>
> (there was song and music together
> before the battle leader of the Half-Danes,
> the entertainment wood (harp) was plucked, lore recited often,
> when Healgamen, Hrothgar's *scop*,
> along the mead-bench would tell of
> Finn's offspring.)

The phrase "battle leader of the Half-Danes" is assumed to refer to King Hrothgar and Healgamen is taken as the personal name of his *scop*, thus adding to our list of named poets in the Old English corpus. *Healgamen* has in the past

---

124 Gray, *Cath Maige Tuired*, 70–71 §§163–64. The three types of harp music are also listed in the Triads of Ireland: Meyer, *Triads of Ireland*, 16–17 §122. I have modernized the spellings of the types which in older texts would be: *súantraige, gentraige, goltraige*.
125 Greene, *Fingal Rónáin*, 20, lines 367–74; 21, lines 396–407; for an outline and discussion of the tale, see Dillon, *Early Irish Literature*, 74–77.
126 Fulk, Bjork, Niles, *Klaeber's Beowulf*, 37. The last word in the passage has been emended from manuscript *eaferum* (dative plural) to a form equivalent to the accusative singular: Fulk, Bjork, Niles, *Klaeber's Beowulf*, 180.

been treated by editors literally as "hall joy, hall entertainment" which works well in the context when translating the passage. But the most recent editors have opted to take the term as an epithet used as a personal name of the poet similar to that for Widsith.[127] The reference to "Finn's offspring" reflects the recitation of Germanic lore by the *scop*, a topic that will be expanded on presently.

There is precedence in the Gaelic tradition for poets performing or chanting poems more or less as songs. For example, in the late seventh-century *Vita sancti Columbae* by Adomnán, abbot of Iona (d. 704), an anecdote intended to highlight Columba's prophetic abilities mentions a Gaelic poet (*scoticus poeta*) named Crónán. While on a journey with Columba, sometime in the second half of the sixth century, the group of monks met up with the poet. Some of the monks asked Columba, "why did you not according to the custom ask for a song of his own composition, sung to a tune?"[128] The monks were disappointed not to have been entertained by the poet as was the custom (*ex more*). Columba, relying on his prophetic abilities, had opted not to make the request because he could foresee the unfortunate poet's impending violent death.

Early vernacular narratives also emphasize the expectation of music and entertainment at court. For example, in *Táin Bó Fraích* (The Cattle Raid of Fróech) (ca. 700),[129] when Fróech travels with his retinue to visit the court of King Ailill and Queen Medb at Crúachu in Connacht he brings his harpers and other entertainers with him. There are at least two reasons for the splendor of Fróech's retinue. The first has to do with his personal background because his mother is Bé Find, a "faerie" (*síd*) woman and the faerie world is typically described as being resplendent. But Fróech has also arrived to woo Finnabair, daughter of his hosts Ailill and Medb, so he has every desire to impress.

There is an elaborate description of Fróech's three harpers and their highly ornamented harps which seem to have decorative moving parts that were activated when the harps were played.[130] Twelve men died of weeping and sorrow at the playing. The narrative then provides a version of the tale of the Dagda's harper Uaithne noted above from *Cath Maige Tuired* and the three types of harp

---

127 For Healgamen treated as proper name designating Hrothgar's poet, see Fulk, Bjork, Niles, *Klaeber's Beowulf*, 180–81. The name does not appear in Anglo-Saxon Prosopography.
128 "Cur, aiunt, a nobis regrediente Cronano poeta aliquod ex more suae artis canticum non postulasti modolabiliter decantari?": Anderson and Anderson, *Life of Columba*, 76–77, i 42. The dating range for the *Vita Columbae* is from ca. 688 to ca. 704 when Adomnán died.
129 The editor dated this text on linguistic data to ca. 700 but not later than 750: Meid, *Táin Bó Fraích*, xxv. James Carney had argued for a wider range of dates, 680–775, based on contents and philological data: Carney, *Literature and History*, 26–27.
130 For discussion of this scene in a larger context, see Whitfield, "Lyres Decorated with Snakes."

music: *súantraí, gentraí, goltraí*.¹³¹ The power of music is reiterated later in the narrative when Fróech, having been injured, was brought into Ailill's and Medb's court for his cure in a special bath and his horn players (*cornairi*) precede him. Their playing was so effective that it caused thirty of Ailill's noblest men to die of longing (*sírdecht*).¹³² The exaggeration is deliberate to stress Fróech's connection to the otherworldly *áes síde* (faerie people). These hyperbolic descriptions of music and entertainment at court could only work if the audience were already familiar with more quotidian examples from real life.

In the *Táin Bó Cúailnge* Queen Medb, from jealousy and worry, complains of the efficiency of the Galeóin troops compared to others in her composite army formed from the various regions of Ireland as they prepare for their raid against Ulster. Medb notes that the Galeóin are always at least one step ahead of the others in the muster and complains that by the time the others have sheltered for the night and prepared their food, the Galeóin have done all that and are relaxing as their harpers play for them.¹³³ Medb is concerned that the Galeóin, in their superior efficiency, will take credit for any success the expedition achieves. But the example shows that Old Gaelic storytellers pictured a military muster of their epic ancestors from around the time of Christ traveling with harpers for entertainment, just as Fróech also traveled with a retinue that included harpers and other musicians.

## Lore and Stories

The passage above from *Beowulf* that named Healgamen, Hrothgar's *scop*, introduced a section of the narrative referred to as the Finn episode (lines 1063–159a). It tells of a conflict between (Half-)Danes, who are related to the family line of characters in *Beowulf*, and Frisians whose king was the eponymous Finn. The presence of this so-called "digression," and others in the narrative of *Beowulf*, suggest that Anglo-Saxon poets, like Healgamen, were expected to know Germanic lore and recite it as stories or narrative poems for their audiences.¹³⁴ The Finn episode is particularly important because the chance survival of another

---

131 Meid, *Romance of Froech*, 43 §10 (Gaelic), 67 §10 (English). See also Meid, *Táin Bó Fraích*, 4–5, lines 100–112, §10; see translation Gantz, *Irish Myths and Sagas*, 117–18.
132 Meid, *Romance of Froech*, 46 §20 (Gaelic), 70–71 §20 (English). See also Meid, *Táin Bó Fraích*, 9, lines 229–231, §20; Gantz, *Irish Myths and Sagas*, 121.
133 "ro bátár a cruti ocaó n-airfitiud": O'Rahilly, *Táin: Recension I*, 5, line 153 (Gaelic); 129 (English).
134 For digressions and episodes, see Fulk, Bjork, Niles, *Klaeber's Beowulf*, lxxxiv–lxxxvi.

short text of forty-eight lines, called the Finnsburh Fragment,[135] or the Fight at Finnsburg, argues in favor of the former existence of such a related corpus of tales from Germanic lore.[136] The Finnsburh Fragment, which exists separately from *Beowulf*, emphasizes the heroic ethos in a fight between feuding Danes and Frisians while the Finn Episode, existing within the poem *Beowulf*, stresses the personal loss, particularly of the woman (peace-weaver) Hildeburh, wife of the Frisian king Finn, but daughter of Hoc and sister of Hnæf, both opposing Danes involved in the feud.

Long lists of Early Gaelic tales and lore have been preserved by the tenth century and titles from those same lists survive from the manuscript tradition as tales which have been edited and studied by modern scholars. As we shall see, there is evidence that these tales were known and recited by qualified *filid* for elite audiences. In the idealized schematization of the Gaels there were three hundred and fifty such named tales.[137] The introduction to the tale list in the Book of Leinster makes clear its purpose: "What follows here below concerns the qualifications of poets (*filid*) in regard to stories and *coimgne*[138] to be narrated to kings and chieftains."[139] The preface specifically states that *filid* narrated tales to audiences that included kings and chieftains. "Digressions" such as the Finn episode in *Beowulf* suggest that Anglo-Saxon poets, like the *scop* Healgamen, must have performed the same or similar functions.

After Beowulf and his retinue depart Denmark and return to their people, the Geats in Sweden, Beowulf relates to the Geatish king Hyġelāc his adventures and combats with Grendel and Grendel's mother. The passage below (lines 2105–14) is part of Beowulf's description to King Hyġelāc of the celebrations at the court of King Hrothgar in Heorot. It is possible to interpret this passage below, or portions of it, as describing Hrothgar's recitation of lore or personal lament while being accompanied, or accompanying himself, on the harp. Such an interpretation is supported by taking the phrases *gomela Scilding* (aged Scylding) and *rūmheort cyning* (large-hearted king) to refer to Hrothgar. Not all agree about this interpretation,

---

[135] Hill, *Minor Heroic Poems*, 27–29 (discussion), 42–43 (edition), 52–56 (textual notes).
[136] For editions and discussions, see Fulk, Bjork, Niles, *Klaeber's Beowulf*, 273–90; Hill, *Minor Heroic Poems*, 27–29, 42–43, 52–56.
[137] Mac Cana, *Learned Tales*; Toner, "Earliest Irish Tale Lists"; Breatnach, *Uraicecht na Ríar*, 102–3 §2. For the notion of an "anthology" of Ulster death-tales, see Clancy, "Die Like a Man?" 82–84.
[138] This term will be discussed in chapter three.
[139] "Do nemthigud filed i scélaib ⁊ i comgnimaib inso sís da nasnís do rígaib ⁊ flathib": Mac Cana, *Learned Tales*, 41.

however, and the complexities of Old English poetic syntax help maintain ambiguity in interpretation.[140]

> Þær wæs ġidd ond glēo;   gomela Scilding,
> felafricgende    feorran rehte;
> hwīlum hildedēor    hearpan wynne,
> gome(n)wudu grētte,    hwīlum ġyd āwræc
> sōð ond sārliċ,    hwīlum sylliċ spell
> rehte æfter rihte    rūmheort cyning;
> hwīlum eft ongan    eldo ġebunden,
> gomel gūðwiga    ġioguðe cwīðan,
> hildestrenġo;    hreðer (in)ne wēoll
> þonne hē wintrum frōd    worn ġemunde (lines 2105-14).[141]

> (There was lore and music; an aged Scylding,
> well informed told of olden times;
> sometimes a brave warrior touched the entertainment wood [harp],
> pleasure of the harp, at times recited lore
> true and sorrowful, sometimes the large-hearted king
> truthfully narrated a wonderful story;
> at other times bound by old age,
> the old warrior began to lament [lost] youth
> and battle-strength; his heart surged within
> when, wise in winters, he remembered so much.)

There are precedents in both Anglo-Saxon and Gaelic societies for kings to be renowned as poets. It is acknowledged that King Alfred (d. 899) instigated a major translation project during his reign and may have participated in the translations himself.[142] In Gaelic tradition there are closely contemporaneous *rígbaird* (kingly bards) such as Flannacán mac Cellaig (d. 896) and Cormac mac Cuilennáin (d. 908; Figure 2.f).[143] The fact that these Gaelic kings are designated by the term *bard* shows that either they had not participated in the formal training of the *filid* or, if they had, they had not advanced to the higher ranks.[144] All three kings are discussed in the appendix to chapter two.

Bede, in his *Historia ecclesiastica*, offers an example that indirectly links playing the harp (*cithara*) with the production of poetry in his account of Cædmon (*HE* iv 24). The context is different from the example in *Beowulf* above

---

140 See the notes to these lines: Fulk, Bjork, Niles, *Klaeber's Beowulf*, 233-34; Opland, *Anglo-Saxon Oral Poetry*, 199-201.
141 Fulk, Bjork, Niles, *Klaeber's Beowulf*, 71-72.
142 But see Godden, "Did King Alfred Write Anything?"
143 Breatnach, *Uraicecht na Ríar*, 50-51; Breatnach, "Satire, Praise."
144 For distinctions between *bard* and *fili*, see Breatnach, *Uraicecht na Ríar*, 87-88, 99-100; for other named *rígbaird*, see Breatnach, *Uraicecht na Ríar*, 50-51.

because Cædmon is at a social gathering at a monastery and is of low social status while King Hrothgar is at his royal court in Heorot. Cædmon used to attend feasts (*convivia*) where, as entertainment (*laetitia*), participants would sing (*cantare*) and play the harp. Cædmon would never take his turn on the harp and sing but, instead, preferred to leave the gathering when he saw the harp approaching for his turn (*HE* iv 24).[145] Bede does not indicate if participants at these feasts, where Cædmon was present, were singing known, established songs or if they were extemporizing when the harp came their way. Similarly, in the case from *Beowulf*, we cannot know if it was Hrothgar who was playing the harp and extemporizing as "the old warrior began to lament [lost] youth and battle strength." But there is an Old Gaelic text on poetry that provides contexts for both scenarios to be about extemporizing poems or songs. "The Caldron of Poesy" discusses the potential of individuals to produce poetry and acknowledges that even those without any training or inherent skill can produce poetry when either sorrow (*brón*) or joy (*fáilte*) inspires an individual.[146] Both cases discussed here provide the potential for oral, extemporaneous composition. Cædmon, as we will see, was transformed into an acknowledged talented poet.[147] Hrothgar was not likely considered a poet by people at his court. If he was indeed performing, his performance was personal.[148]

Another passage from *Beowulf* provides a more graphic description of a poet at work and one that suggests an extemporizing performance. The lines describe the celebration at Heorot after Beowulf has defeated Grendel:

> Hwīlum cyninges þeġn,
> guma ġilphlæden,    ġidda ġemyndiġ,
> sē ðe eal fela    ealdġeseġena
> worn ġemunde,    word ōþer fand
> sōðe ġebunden;    secg eft ongan
> sīð Bēowulfes    snyttrum styrian
> ond on spēd wrecan    spel ġerāde,
> wordum wrixlan; (lines 867b–74a)[149]

(at times a thegn of the king,
a man ready with praise, mindful of lore,
one who remembered a great many

---

[145] Colgrave and Mynors, *Ecclesiastical History*, 414–17.
[146] Breatnach, "Caldron of Poesy," 66–67 §8; Henry, "Caldron of Poesy," 124–25.
[147] Ireland, "Vernacular Poets," 45–48.
[148] Associating Hrothgar with traditional lore and music enhances his portrait "as warlord . . ., commander and builder . . ., magnanimous host . . ., spokesperson for timeless wisdom . . ., patron of music and song": Fulk, Bjork, Niles, *Klaeber's Beowulf*, 234.
[149] Fulk, Bjork, Niles, *Klaeber's Beowulf*, 31.

of the old traditions, found other words
truthfully joined together; the man in turn began
wisely to narrate Beowulf's adventure
and to relate skillfully an apt story
by varying the words;)

This passage has been taken to represent a clear expression of extemporaneous oral improvisation in Old English. Nevertheless, there is not universal agreement with this view.[150] Among scholars of the Gaelic tradition there is similar disquiet about portrayals, or their lack, of extemporaneous orally improvised poetry or lore. In a famous Gaelic triad, referred to as "three things required of a poet," the third element, rendered typically as *díchetal di chennaib* (chanting from heads [?]), is assumed to refer to extemporaneous oral composition.[151] If the interpretation is accurate it places improvisation or extemporaneous composition quite high among the requirements for qualified Gaelic poets. A famous example of its supposed use is found in the Middle Gaelic prose preface to *Amrae Coluim Chille*, a complex poem in praise of St. Columba. As the story goes, the poet Dallán Forgaill went to Columba to recite the preface of the poem he had composed to honor the saint, but Columba forbade the poet to proceed stating that praise should be reserved only for those who had died.[152] So it was that upon Columba's death Dallán finished his praise poem *di chennaib* (extemporaneously).[153]

In the section (lines 874b–914) that follows immediately from the passage cited above, Beowulf is implicitly compared to another hero named Sigemund in a "digression" that describes how Sigemund slew a dragon and which presages Beowulf's own accomplishments at doing the same.[154] The description of the talented *cyninges þegn* (king's thegn) above encourages us to see him as the person who related the Sigemund episode and supports the notion that talented individuals, in both traditions, acted as repositories of lore and created, at times extemporaneously, appropriate tales and poems by relying on a font of tradition for narrative models and poetic diction.

---

150  Fulk, Bjork, Niles, *Klaeber's Beowulf*, 165–66; Opland, *Anglo-Saxon Oral Poetry*, 202–4.
151  Meyer, *Triads of Ireland*, 16–17 §123; Carey, "Three Things," 44–47, 54–56.
152  Note how this retrospective portrait of Columba's attitude parallels the Germanic heroic ethos as stated nearby at line 885 in *Beowulf*. The line reads, *æfter dēaðdæge dōm* (renown after death): Fulk, Bjork, Niles, *Klaeber's Beowulf*, 168, see discussions at lxxiii, cxxix.
153  Stokes, "*Amra Choluimb Chille*," 132–34. John Carey discussed other examples from the literature of the phrase *di chennaib* in the apparent meaning of "extempore": Carey, "Three Things," 45 and 45n22. For a discussion of the sophistication of the preface itself, see Herbert, "Preface to *Amra*."
154  Fulk, Bjork, Niles, *Klaeber's Beowulf*, 165–68; Opland, *Anglo-Saxon Oral Poetry*, 105–10.

If that same "king's thegn" was ġidda ġemyndiġ (mindful [or knowledgeable] of lore), it can be assumed that he carried in his memory a repository of tales from the Germanic past. We have seen above that the Gaelic poets were supposed to carry a large corpus of tales in their minds for presentation to noble audiences. In a prose narrative from the early eighth century about the hero Mongán, we are told that while Mongán was exercising his kingship at court in Ráth Mór in Mag Line (Moylinny, Co. Antrim), he was visited by the poet (*fili*) Forgoll. The poet used to tell a story to Mongán every night "from Halloween to May Day" (*ó Samuin co Beltaine*).[155] Mongán acted as patron and provided "treasures and food" (*séuit ocus biad*) for the poet and his other guests.[156] This early eighth-century anecdote explicitly states that a *fili* told a tale each night of the winter months at a king's court and was well rewarded for this service.

**Praise and Patronage**

From this point on we will examine three passages, two from *Widsith* and one from *Deor*, which provide pictures of Anglo-Saxon poets as functionaries at court. They portray poets seeking patronage from lords and help confirm the place of encomium and eulogy in the interplay between poet and patron. The wide-ranging topics of *Widsith*, with lists of mythic and historical characters and events, place the poet centrally in the interplay of patron and poet, which implies that the targeted audience was the nobility.[157] Encomium and panegyric are at the heart of this interplay between poet and audience.[158] Neither Old English poem, however, clarifies the relationship between poet and harpist, as seen in the following lines from *Widsith*:

> Ðonne wit Scilling    sciran reorde
> for uncrum sigedryhtne    song ahofan,
> hlude be hearpan    hleoþor swinsade (lines 103–5).[159]

> (When Scilling and I, with clear voice,
> raised a song before our victorious lord,
> the sound resonated loudly to the harp.)

---

155 White, *Compert Mongáin*, 73 §1 (Gaelic), 79 (English).
156 White, *Compert Mongáin*, 73 §1 (Gaelic), 79 (English).
157 Niles, "Anthropology of the Past," 196–97.
158 Maring, "Bright Voice of Praise."
159 Hill, *Minor Heroic Poems*, 35; see also Krapp and Dobbie, *Exeter Book*, 152.

The passage apparently names a second person Scilling and the use of dual pronouns seems to confirm that. Yet there are at least three possible interpretations of the situation. Scilling may be a second poet and the two poets, Widsith and Scilling, perform together as a team, or Scilling may be the name of Widsith's harpist. Scilling is recorded as a personal name in Anglo-Saxon prosopography. It has also been suggested that Scilling may be the name of Widsith's harp.[160] There is a verb with the forms *scillan* or *scellan* that means "to make a noise, resound" and Anglo-Saxon poetry has other examples of inanimate objects that have been personified.[161] Ambiguity as to the performance of music during the poets' delivery of praise to a noble patron exists in the Gaelic tradition as well.

Seventh-century Gaelic hagiography, specifically Muirchú maccu Machtheni's *Vita sancti Patricii*, provides an example of poets appearing together at court, although there is no indication that they perform together. In fact, the two poets, Dubthach maccu Lugair and Fiacc Finn Sléibte, are master poet and pupil respectively. The scenario is the fifth-century court of King Lóegaire mac Néill at Tara as Patrick and his retinue work to convert the pagans.[162] We have already seen an example of a named poet, Ferchertne, and his harper, Craiphtine, together at court in the Old Gaelic narrative *Orgain Denna Ríg*, which complements the argument that Scilling may be the name of Widsith's harpist. This same tale paints a court scene where, apparently, multiple "poets" (*áes admolta*; people of praising)[163] are present and performing before an audience of high-status people, also portrayed as being in Tara, an important royal and ritual site. The text of *Orgain Denna Ríg* describes the court scene as follows: "the 'people of praising' were in the center praising the king and the queen and the princes and the lesser nobles."[164] This scene takes place as all present "are consuming the feast" provided by King Cobthach.[165]

The *sigedryhten* (victorious lord) praised by Widsith and Scilling should be seen in the context of neighboring peoples of the Anglo-Saxons on the island of Britain who also had a tradition of eulogizing lords and heroes. As noted, the Brittonic poet Taliesin purportedly praised the leaders Urien Rheged and his

---

160 Hill, *Minor Heroic Poems*, 121.
161 A phenomenon most frequently seen in the riddles, but also in the poem "Dream of the Rood": Krapp, *Vercelli Book*, 61–65, 130–32.
162 Ireland, "Vernacular Poets," 49–58.
163 The term implies that these people who "praise" are of varying social rank, such as *baird*, and not limited to *filid* who are of a higher rank: Breatnach, *Uraicecht na Ríar*, 87–88, 99–100.
164 "bātar int aes admolta for in lár oc admolad in rīg ⁊ na rīgna ⁊ na flathi ⁊ na n-ōcthigern": Greene, *Fingal Rónáin*, 19, lines 340–41.
165 "ic tomailt na fesse": Greene, *Fingal Rónáin*, 19, line 340.

son Owain in their battles against the Anglo-Saxons in the late sixth century. The collected verses in the *Gododdin* praised warbands that engaged Anglo-Saxon forces, supposedly at Catraeth, thought to be Catterick in North Yorkshire (*HE* ii 14).[166]

Gaelic poems and poetic fragments, perhaps of the seventh century if not earlier, preserved in the genealogies of the peoples of Leinster praise illustrious ancestors and their martial prowess.[167] One of the fragments relates directly to persons and events narrated in *Orgain Denna Ríg* (The Destruction of Dind Ríg). The fragment reads as follows:

> Dind Rīg | ruad Tuaim   Tenbad,
> trīcha(it) nairech | fo brōn   bebsait.
> Brūisius, brēosuis | bār niad lonn   Labraid,
> lāth Elgca | hūa Luircc   Lōegaire.
> Lugaid lōeg | lonn sanb   Sētna
> sochla Cōel | Cobthach māl   muiredach.
> Mandrais armu | [athair] athar   Ollomon
> ort Mōen | macco āin   Augaine.

(Dind Ríg (was) red Túaim Tenbad. Thirty nobles (?) died sorrowfully. He crushed (and) burnt them, the bold wise champion Labraid, the warrior of Elg [Ireland], the grandson of Loegaire Lorc: the calf (= the beloved) Lugaid, the bold, . . . Sétnae, the renowned Coel, Cobthach the chief (and) lord. He destroyed (their) weapons, the father of the father of (Óengus) Ollam. Móen of the family of glorious Augaine slew (them).[168]

The Dind Ríg of the fragment is named in the title of the prose narrative. As noted, the events are represented as having taken place around 300 B.C.[169] All of the personal names in the fragment refer to ancestors of the Leinstermen, while only hinting at the events that are described more fully in the Old Gaelic narrative. The presumed location of Dind Ríg is only a few kilometers from the

---

**166** The place is associated by Bede with King Edwin's reign and the success of Bishop Paulinus at baptizing large numbers of people: Colgrave and Mynors, *Ecclesiastical History*, 188–89.
**167** These poems can be found in their genealogical contexts in O'Brien, *Corpus genealogiarum Hiberniae*, 1–9, 18, 19, 20, 21, 22, 23, 25, 70, 71, 72–73. Their importance has been discussed by Meyer, "Über die Älteste irische Dichtung"; and by Carney, "Dating of Early Irish Verse"; Carney, "Archaic Irish Verse." Their place in the genealogical tradition has been highlighted by Ó Corráin, "Irish Origin Legends," 56–63, 89–90nn12–18; Ó Corráin, "Church and Secular Society," 265, 269–71. For editions and translations of some of these poems see Corthals, "Observations on the Versification"; Corthals, "Rhymeless 'Leinster Poems'"; Koch, *Celtic Heroic Age*, 51–59.
**168** Edition and translation from Corthals, "Observations on the Versification," 117.
**169** A different version of the poem is found in the Old Gaelic *Organ Denna Ríg* where it is attributed to Ferchertne *fili* of the tale: Greene, *Fingal Rónáin*, 23, lines 453–69.

site of Rath Melsigi, mentioned frequently by Bede as the location of an important school that trained Anglo-Saxon clerics and missionaries in the seventh and eighth centuries (*HE* iii 13, 27, iv 3, v 9–11).

It is ironic that a poetic genre as important as praise poetry is not more abundantly represented in the Old Gaelic period, especially since it is so common in the post-Norman period. Many fragments and quatrains survive in later texts such as the metrical tracts or in genealogies and prose narratives.[170] Proinsias Mac Cana, through a review of these poetic fragments, was able to suggest names of historic poets such as Colmán mac Lénéni (d. 606), Rechtgal úa Siadail (fl. 780–790), and Dallán mac Móre (fl. 900–920), to whom were attributed praise poems.[171]

These identifications of poets can be partially substantiated by reference to historical kings named in fragments and quatrains attributed to them. So, for example, fragments by Colmán may refer to Domnall, king of Tara (ca. 565); Fergus Tuile, a contemporary king of Uí Liatháin in the region of Cloyne where Colmán founded a monastery; and Áed Sláine (ca. 604), a king of Tara from whom are descended the Síl nÁedo Sláine. Persons likely praised by Rechtgal include Donnchad Midi mac Domnaill, king of Ireland (770–797); Muirgius mac Tommaltaig, a king of Connacht (792–815); and Rígnach, wife of the king of Loch Léin in Kerry, whose fragment is cited as an example of *ró molta* (excess of praise). Dallán may have praised Cerball mac Muirecáin, king of Leinster (ca. 900–920); he also eulogized Cormac mac Cuilennáin, king/bishop of Cashel (d. 908), a recognized poet and scholar himself. The kings Cerball and Cormac had fought on opposing sides at the battle of Belach Mugna (908) where Cormac was killed.[172]

Liam Breatnach used references from the law-tracts to confirm the *filid* as disseminators of encomium and panegyric by first identifying passages in the laws about the denigration of reputation of potential noble patrons through poetic satire. The recognition of the power of satire, and the need to regulate through law its justified and unjustified use by the *filid*, implies that the obverse also obtained and that the *filid* had the responsibility of dispensing praise to noble patrons in proper circumstances. The *Bretha Nemed Dédenach* explains that the *filid* should use praise to ennoble high-ranking people, and that they should expect appropriate remuneration for their poetic skills from those who have been praised: "You are only to ennoble, only to make known a king or a

---

170 Many of these fragments and quatrains have been gathered by Meyer, "Bruchstücke."
171 Mac Cana, "Praise Poetry," 18–20.
172 Mac Cana, "Praise Poetry," 18–20.

noble, for it is from them that is due great wealth as a result of which prosperity increases."¹⁷³

A Gaelic panegyric preserved, in what was traditionally called the *Codex sancti Pauli* (St. Paul im Lavanttal, Stiftsbibliothek, MS 86a/1),¹⁷⁴ on the continent is the most complete vernacular poem of its type from the Old Gaelic period.¹⁷⁵ It has been dated to the early ninth century but may be older. It praises a prince named Áed mac Diarmata who cannot be certainly identified. Tomás Ó Cathasaigh has made the most thorough study yet of the poem.¹⁷⁶ Many stereotypical features expected of panegyric are found here such as describing the person praised as a tree trunk, or house post, or pillar that is able to support many households.¹⁷⁷ These features imply his quality as protector and his generosity. Áed's genealogy is traced, naming father and grandfather, as well as establishing his family's locale by naming identifiable places in the province of Leinster.¹⁷⁸ Ó Cathasaigh points out that, as in the Old English examples, the poem is ambiguous as to whether or not the praise poem is recited to music.¹⁷⁹ All is presented as taking place at an ale-feast (Old English *gebeorscipe*; Latin *convivium*), and liquor serves as a symbol of sovereignty.¹⁸⁰ A poem in the Old Gaelic narrative *Scéla Cano meic Gartnáin* refers to the "ale of sovereignty" of various regions of the Gaelic world, as well as among the Picts and Anglo-Saxons.¹⁸¹

*Dúnad* (conclusion; closure) is a common feature of Early Gaelic verse in which the poem is concluded with a word or phrase used to begin the poem. So, for example, our poem's first word is the personal name *Áed* in nominative singular and the concluding word is the same name in genitive singular, *Áeda*.¹⁸² In another ninth-century Gaelic manuscript on the continent, Codex Ambrosianus C.301 (Milan, Biblioteca Ambrosiana MS C 301)¹⁸³ containing a commentary on the Psalms, the glossator observed that Psalm 8 concluded with the same

---

173 "Ní sóerae, ní sloinde acht ríg nó airig, ar is doib dligid mórmainbthe dia moaiget moín": Breatnach, "Satire, Praise," 67–68.
174 CODECS: https://www.vanhamel.nl/codecs/Áed_oll_fri_andud_n-áne.
175 Stokes and Strachan, *Thesaurus*, ii, 295.
176 Ó Cathasaigh, "Making of a Prince."
177 Ó Cathasaigh, "Making of a Prince," 145 §§2, 7, 149.
178 Ó Cathasaigh, "Making of a Prince," 146–47.
179 Ó Cathasaigh, "Making of a Prince," 152–53.
180 Ó Cathasaigh, "Making of a Prince," 147–48, 152–54. The political prophecy *Baile Chuinn Cétchathaig* is a *locus classicus* for the depiction of liquor as a symbol of sovereignty: Bhreathnach, "Political Context"; Bhreathnach and Murray, "*Baile Chuinn Chétchathaig*."
181 Ó Cathasaigh, "Making of a Prince," 153–54; Binchy, *Scéla Cano*, 16–19.
182 Stokes and Strachan, *Thesaurus*, ii, 295; Ó Cathasaigh, "Making of a Prince," 144–45.
183 CODECS: https://www.vanhamel.nl/codecs/Milan,_Biblioteca_Ambrosiana,_MS_C_301_inf.

words with which it began. He then noted: "Amal as hō molad ocus adamrugud in Choimded in-tinscana in salmsa, is [s]amlaid for-centar dano, amal dundgniat ind filid linni cid in sin" (As this psalm begins with praise and admiration of the Lord, it is thus moreover that it is concluded, even as the poets do with us).[184] The glossator recognized the psalmist's technique of ending the psalm with the same phrase with which it began as an example of *dúnad*.

The glossator would have recognized the psalmist's praise of the Lord as a natural feature of poetry. The Gaels had already extended panegyric from secular leaders to clerical ones, so that various forms of praise and encomium were not restricted to secular contexts. As noted previously, *Amrae Coluim Chille*, attributed to Dallán Forgaill, eulogized a church leader upon his death but shifted many of the typical tropes from secular to ecclesiastical contexts.[185] Two substantial seventh-century poems by Bécán mac Luigdech in praise of St. Columba survive and will be discussed in chapter two.

Among the oldest Gaelic poetry that can be attributed to a named, historical poet are fragments by Colmán mac Lénéni (d. 606). Colmán began his professional life as a praise poet but eventually joined the church and founded a monastery at Cloyne (*Cluain Uama*, Co. Cork).[186] Among the surviving poetic fragments attributed to him, which include both secular and religious subjects, are lines in praise of Áed Sláine (d. 604), an overking of the Uí Néill who founded the dynastic family known as Síl nÁedo Sláine whose territory covered Brega (*Mag Breg*) wherein lies the site of Tara. The fragment reads:

> Ní séim anim i n-anmib áne
> Ár for Áed Sláine
>
> (It is not a minor blemish among blemishes of splendor;
> Slaughter (death) upon Áed Sláine.)[187]

We can already see an important aspect of Gaelic literary culture in the form of paronomasia. There is an implied pun on the word *ainim* (blemish, defect) used in the poem, and *ainm* (name) and, by extension in the context of praise poetry,

---

184 Stokes and Strachan, *Thesaurus*, i, 51.10; text and translation as in Murphy, *Early Irish Metrics*, 43–44; discussion in Ó Cathasaigh, "Making of a Prince," 146.
185 The poem as preserved is not contemporary with the saint's death: Bisagni, *Amrae Coluimb Chille*.
186 Thurneysen, "Colmān mac Lēnēni"; Carney, "Accentual Poems," 63–65; and MacCotter, *Colmán of Cloyne*.
187 Ireland, "Cædmon and Colmán," 180. For another version of the poem, see MacCotter, *Colmán of Cloyne*, 130.

"reputation." The loss of so great a "name" as Áed Sláine was not an insignificant "blemish" on the polity of the midlands of Ireland.

This seemingly "minor" poetic fragment may feel remote from Anglo-Saxon affairs, but there are possible connections. King Aldfrith's maternal grandfather, according to the genealogies, was Colmán Rímid (d. 604) who shared the high-kingship of Tara with Áed Sláine as recorded in certain annal entries.[188] Just the year before Aldfrith assumed the Northumbrian throne, his half-brother Ecgfrith sent an army into Ireland at Brega (684) and destroyed many churches (*HE* iv 26). This attack took place during the reign of Fínsnechta Fledach (675–695) who was a member of Síl nÁedo Sláine.[189] Áed Sláine is the eponymous ancestor of this dynastic family of the southern Uí Néill. Bede regretted this attack, carried out for Ecgfrith by an ealdorman named Berht, and stated that the action had "devastated a harmless race that had always been most friendly to the English" (*HE* iv 26).[190] These incidental facts suggest how closely the Gaels and Anglo-Saxons could be tied at this early period.

## Freedom to Travel

The next passage, also from *Widsith*, confirms the importance of praise for the nobility and their rôle as patrons of the poets and musicians at their courts. The passage also emphasizes the importance of the poets' freedom to travel across borders,[191] a point that is not so obvious for Anglo-Saxon poets, but is made explicit in the tradition for poets among the Gaels and Britons and confirms their higher status and privilege compared to other ranks in society.

> Swa scriþende   gesceapum hweorfað
> gleomen gumena   geond grunda fela,
> þearfe secgað,   þoncword sprecaþ,
> simle suð oþþe norð   sumne gemetað
> gydda gleawne,   geofum unhneawne,
> se þe fore duguþe wile   dom aræran,
> eorlscipe æfnan,   oþ þæt eal scæceð,

---

[188] Mac Airt and Mac Niocaill, *Annals of Ulster*, 100–101; Stokes, "Annals of Tigernach," 164–65 [Felinfach i 124–25]; Byrne, *Irish Kings*, 104, 281, 283; Ireland, "Aldfrith and the Irish Genealogies," 68.
[189] Pelteret, "Attack on Brega."
[190] Colgrave and Mynors, *Ecclesiastical History*, 426–27.
[191] Mac Cana, "Early Irish Ideology," 74; Bromwich, *Trioedd Ynys Prydein*, lxviii–lxix.

leoht ond lif somod;   lof se gewyrceð,
hafað under heofonum   heahfæstne dom (lines 135–43).[192]

(So with wandering as their destiny
the poets (*gleomen*) of men roam throughout many lands,
they tell of their need, and speak their thanks,
ever south or north they meet someone
discerning of lore, not grudging with gifts,
one who desires to raise his reputation among his retinue,
to perform valorous acts, until all passes away,
light and life together; the one who gains praise
has lasting fame under heaven.)

The first thing to be noted here in this passage is that the word translated as "poet" is not *scop*, but rather *gleoman*. It has been argued that this latter term is better treated as something like "entertainer, musician," whereas the *scop* is more specifically a "poet."[193] It is not clear how much this distinction matters in Anglo-Saxon society, but in Gaelic society the professional status of the top-ranking poets, who have undergone rigorous formal training, is distinguished from the lower, less prestigious grades of poets and entertainers.

In the poem, as his name implies, Widsith wanders widely through both space and time. The passage implies that it is the fate of *gleomen* to roam. Gaelic poets are portrayed as having the freedom to travel, but it implies a privilege awarded their high social status. Fedelm, in the *Táin Bó Cúailnge*, has just returned from Britain[194] having studied and learned poetry (*filidecht*) there. Poets who travel with large retinues and demand hospitality from the lords they visit, under threat of satire, are portrayed in Gaelic narrative.[195] In the tale *Talland Étair* the *fili* Aithirne traveled with his retinue on a circuit of the royal houses of Ireland and his demands for hospitality were acceded to wherever he went because his hosts feared the punitive power of his satire.[196] Poets could be portrayed in other negative ways as well. For example, in *Tromdám Guaire* (Guaire's Burdensome Troop), the chief poet Senchán Torpéist traveled around Ireland with his overly large retinue straining the hospitality of those he visited.[197]

---

192  Hill, *Minor Heroic Poems*, 36; see also Krapp and Dobbie, *Exeter Book*, 153.
193  Opland, *Anglo-Saxon Oral Poetry*, 187–88, 190–91, 221–22 (*gleoman*), 213–16 (*scop*).
194  For an inconclusive discussion of whether Albu refers only to northern Britain, the entire island, or somewhere else, see Dumville, "Ireland and Britain."
195  Retinue sizes depending on the rank of the poet are outlined in Breatnach, *Uraicecht na Ríar*.
196  Ó Dónaill, *Talland Étair*. For discussions of satire, see McLaughlin, *Early Irish Satire*.
197  Dillon, *Cycles of the Kings*, 90–98; Breatnach, "Satire, Praise."

The *Additamenta*, a text (ca. 700) from the Patrick dossier in the Book of Armagh (Dublin, Trinity College, MS 52),[198] tells of how the poet Fiacc Finn Sléibte was chosen to become Patrick's first bishop in Leinster in the fifth century. When Patrick asked the *poeta optimus* (*ollam filed*; chief poet) Dubthach maccu Lugair to name a likely candidate for bishop after describing the qualities he sought, Dubthach suggested from his household (*muinter*) the young poet Fiacc "who has gone from me into the lands of Connacht."[199] The ninth- or early tenth-century macaronic *Bethu Phátraic*, or *Tripartite Life of Patrick*, explains that Fiacc was "hi tír Connacht co mbairtni donaib rígaib" (in Connacht with *bairdne* for the kings).[200] *Bairdne* is the abstract noun for the "art of the bard," in other words, Fiacc had left his native Leinster and was on a poetic circuit selling encomium to the chieftains and lords of Connacht.

In the *Táin Bó Cúailnge* the Ulster heroes, such as Conall Cernach, have among their responsibilities the guarding of territorial borders "to protect anyone who came that way with poetry" (fri snádud neich dothíssad co n-airchetul).[201] The term translated as "protect" (*snádud*) is a legal term which covers the responsibility to provide protection or safe conduct through a given territory.[202] It is a term, and concept, that we will see repeated in some of the early poems to be discussed in the next chapter. The term translated as "poetry" is *airchetal*. It implies firstly "metrical composition, poem," or the "ability to compose poetry."[203] It is the verbal noun of *ar-cain* (sings, chants, recites) which can be applied to poetry, charms, magical formulae, legal pronouncements, or maxims.[204] The use of the term *airchetal*, with its broad semantic range, suggests that "poets" or "entertainers" well below the rank of *fili* were welcomed and provided with safe passage. The use of *gleoman* in the passage from *Widsith* above implies that the Anglo-Saxon chieftains and nobles also made an array of "poets" and "entertainers" welcome at their courts as they traveled about.

---

[198] CODECS: https://www.vanhamel.nl/codecs/Dublin,_Trinity_College,_MS_52.
[199] "duchooid huaim-se hi tíre Connacht": Bieler, *Patrician Texts*, 176–77, §13 (3). For Fiacc Finn, see Ireland, "Vernacular Poets," 51–55.
[200] Mulchrone, *Bethu Phátraic*, 115, lines 2224–25. Ó Cathasaigh, "Early Irish *bairdne*."
[201] O'Rahilly, *Táin: Recension I*, 21, line 668–69 (Gaelic), 144 (English); see also the fuller, later version in O'Rahilly, *Táin Book of Leinster*, 27, lines 998–1003 (Gaelic); 165 (English).
[202] eDIL, http://www.dil.ie, s.v. *snádud* or dil.ie/38113; Binchy, *Críth Gablach*, 106–7.
[203] eDIL, http://www.dil.ie, s.v. *airchetal* or dil.ie/1707.
[204] eDIL, http://www.dil.ie, s.v. *ar-cain* or dil.ie/3993.

## Professional Status

The *gleomen gumena* (poets of men) are those who wandered throughout the land in search of someone who was generous with gifts and who was discerning of poetry and lore. These characteristics are found in the Gaelic tradition as well and indicate that insular societies recognized a professional class of poets, and entertainers, who relied on the patronage of "one who desires to raise his reputation among his retinue" (se þe fore duguþe wile dom aræran) and who was willing "to perform valorous acts" (eorlscipe æfnan) as a means of winning "lasting fame" (heahfæstne dom). A reciprocally beneficial relationship developed between those lords and nobles, whatever their ethnic origins, who sought to spread their reputations and gain fame, and those poets who broadcast that fame for them into the wider world.

Both Anglo-Saxon and Gaelic literatures portray individuals of such disposition. Beowulf is described, in the last word of the poem, as being *lofgeornost* (most eager for praise).[205] His three extraordinary combats show that he was willing "to perform valorous acts" (eorlscipe æfnan). Likewise, in the *Táin Bó Cúailnge*, when Cú Chulainn, as a young boy, hears the druid Cathbad declare that on that particular day the omens were good that anyone who took up arms would gain fame forever.[206] The young Cú Chulainn immediately set about requesting arms and equipment from King Conchobar. The wise and mature king demanded to know who had predicted good prospects for the boy. When he realized that Cú Chulainn had simply overheard the druid but had not been advised by him, he was exasperated because he knew it meant an early death for the boy. The young Cú Chulainn replied, "Provided I be famous, I am content to be only one day on earth."[207] These examples show that both traditions were aware of their ancestors' expectations that heroes should desire lasting fame and both societies had professionals who traveled from court to court to spread that fame.

The last passage of Old English to be discussed is from the poem *Deor*. This passage seems to be the only instance in Old English literature in which a

---

205 Fulk, Bjork, Niles, *Klaeber's Beowulf*, 109, line 3282b. See discussion, including dissenting views that see this term as negative, at least in a Christian context: Fulk, Bjork, Niles, *Klaeber's Beowulf*, 271–72.
206 "Asbert Cathbud ócláech no gébad gaisced and forbíad a ainm Hérind co bráth ar gním gascid ₇ no mértaís a airscéla co bráth": O'Rahilly, *Táin: Recension I*, 19, lines 613–15 (Gaelic); 142 (English).
207 "Acht ropa airderc-sa, maith lim cenco beind acht óenlá for domun": O'Rahilly, *Táin: Recension I*, 20, lines 640–41 (Gaelic); 143 (English); Davies, "Warrior Time," 273–74.

character refers to himself as a *scop*.[208] There is some ambiguity in the passage where the *scop* appears to name himself as Deor.[209] The Heodeningas represent a tribal group descended from someone named Heoden. A poet named Heorrenda, who competed for the lord's patronage, is also named.[210]

>
> Þæt ic bi me sylfum     secgan wille,
> þæt ic hwile wæs     Heodeninga scop,
> dryhtne dyre;    me wæs Deor noma.
> Ahte ic fela wintra     folgað tilne,
> holdne hlaford,    oþ þæt Heorrenda nu,
> leodcræftig monn,     londryht geþah
> þæt me eorla hleo    ær gesealde (lines 35–41).[211]

(I want to tell about myself,
that I was once *scop* of the Heodenings,
dear to my lord; I was called Deor.[212]
For many years I had a good position,
and a gracious lord, until now when Heorrenda,
a man skilled in song, received the estate
that the protector of earls before had presented to me.)

The passage suggests that poets could expect to fulfill a formal service with a lord who acted as the poet's patron. The relationship portrayed in these lines appears to confirm that Germanic poets could achieve something resembling professional status. It shows that poets competed for a lord's patronage and the privileges and benefits (*londryht*) that accrued from that patronage could be won or lost.[213]

---

**208** Thornbury, *Becoming a Poet*, 16.

**209** Hill, *Minor Heroic Poems*, 99.

**210** For surviving Scandinavian legends dealing with characters with these names, see Hill, *Minor Heroic Poems*, 108 s.n. Hagena (2).

**211** Hill, *Minor Heroic Poems*, 38; Krapp and Dobbie, *Exeter Book*, 179.

**212** This line has traditionally been taken to be the poet telling us his name since Deor is attested as a proper name. But it seems odd that he should name himself in the past tense. It also seems unusual to use a dative personal pronoun rather than a possessive pronoun. If the poet is really naming himself we might expect something like *\*Deor is min noma*. It seems possible that the poet is referring to his unnamed lord. *Deor* as an adjective means "bold, brave, fierce." For a poet, whose principal function is praise, it seems likely that he might say of his former patron "His name was fierce to me" (*Me wæs deor (sin) noma*). This "fierceness" seems apt in light of the misfortune later suffered by the poet at the hands of his former patron. The poet is perhaps playing on *dyre* and *deor*. Such word play is common among the Gaels and Britons. If *Deor* is, in fact, a proper name then it apparently has Celtic origins: Breeze, "Celtic Etymology."

**213** The suggestion that *Deor* may be a "blame poem" derives from the fact that a poet can threaten a patron with satire, a common feature of the Gaelic tradition. See inconclusive arguments citing Scandinavian and Gaelic analogues in Biggs, "Blame Poem."

The contention between Deor and Heorrenda can be compared with the competition for the position of *ollam filed* (chief poet) between the established Ferchertne *fili*[214] and the young Néide mac Adnai in *Immacallam in dá Thuarad*.[215] This Gaelic text as preserved is perhaps of the tenth century, according to its editor. But references to the tale in other contexts prove that the story itself is centuries older. The surviving version is set at Emain Macha (Navan Fort, Co. Armagh) in the time of Conchobar mac Nessa. The poets competed with each other for a post that was left vacant when the "chief poet" Adnae, father of Néide, died and Ferchertne *fili* of Ulster was appointed to fill Adnae's post. This happened while Néide was away in Britain studying poetry (*éicse*), a parallel situation to what we saw for Fedelm in *Táin Bó Cúailnge*. Néide was so advanced in his studies that his heightened sensibilities allowed him to ascertain the death of his father, and Ferchertne's appointment to his father's post, by observing waves without a human intermediary.[216] Néide's teacher, recognizing his advanced talents, encouraged him to return to Ireland to compete for his father's post.

The poetic confrontation between Ferchertne and Néide resulted in such convoluted dialogue that none present, except for the two poets themselves, were able to understand.[217] While the competition ended with the senior poet keeping the post, it resulted in mutual respect and admiration between Ferchertne and Néide. The "dark speech" of the two contestants had wider implications for Gaelic society. Their abstruse, contentious dialogue made King Conchobar separate the functions of poets and judges ever after. This result is related in the "pseudo-historical prologue" to the *Senchas Már*.[218] In Gilla in Choimded's legal poem the dispute is mentioned twice.[219]

The poets and their audiences had other ways to contend with each other. In one of the tales about Mongán mentioned above, the poet Forgoll stayed at the court of Mongán and related tales to him nightly through the winter, but Mongán was not afraid to query the poet about the ancient lore and challenge

---

**214** Not to be confused with the Ferchertne *fili* of the tale *Orgain Denna Ríg* which is a Leinster tale.
**215** Stokes, "Colloquy of the Two Sages"; Ó Corráin, *Clavis*, iii, 1396–98 §1070.
**216** "ar bá baile fallsigthe éicsi dogrés lasna filedu for brú usci" (for the poets deemed that on the brink of water it was always a place of revelation of science): Stokes, "Colloquy of the Two Sages," 8–9 §II. For examples of metaphors of water and inspiration in Late Antiquity, see Thornbury, "Aldhelm's Rejection," 77–78.
**217** Discussed by Nagy, *Conversing with Angels*, 203–4. For competition among poets see Carey, "Obscure Styles."
**218** McCone, "Dubthach Maccu Lugair," 19 where the editor suggests it may be as early as the eighth century; Carey, "Pseudo-Historical Prologue," 9.
**219** Smith, "Aimirgein Glúngel Tuir Tend," 129 §30, 131 §46 (Gaelic), 136, 137 (English).

him when the poet answered wrongly, despite the threat of satire from the poet.[220] Another tale about Mongán, from the early Old Gaelic period, tells how Eochu *rígéices* (royal poet) was bested at knowledge of local sites (*dindṡenchas*) by clerical students and youths who were associates of Mongán. This besting of Eochu took place while the poet was on a royal circuit of the land of Mongán's father, Fiachnae. Eochu realized that Mongán was the instigator of the youths' ability to provide superior knowledge, involving quoting authenticating verses, about the local sites. Eochu proved the danger of offending high-ranking poets by cursing Mongán so as to deprive him of noble offspring.[221]

In the *Prull* episode from *Sanas Cormaic* (Cormac's Glossary),[222] the chief poet Senchán Torpéist was challenged to finish a verse by a female poet who had been stranded on the Isle of Man. The chief poet, unable to answer the challenge, was bested by an ugly youth who accompanied Senchán's retinue against their wishes. The ugly, but knowledgeable, youth was later transformed into a handsome youth and revealed to be *spiritus poematis*.[223]

---

[220] White, *Compert Mongáin*, 73 §2 (Gaelic), 79 (English).
[221] Knott, "Why Mongán was Deprived."
[222] Ó Corráin, *Clavis*, ii, 1171–74 §887.
[223] Ford, *Celtic Poets*, 35–42; Ní Dhonnchadha, "*Prull* Narrative."

# Chapter Two
# Early Historical Poets before Bede

Most of the early vernacular texts produced by the Anglo-Saxons and Gaels are anonymous. Nevertheless, many texts are attributed, in both vernaculars, to named historical persons.[1] The present chapter examines some of those historical authors from both traditions. In both societies a working relationship with the Church was a prerequisite for having surviving texts attributed to a historical author.

Throughout Anglo-Saxon literary history only a handful of named poets have been recorded in the tradition.[2] Why so few historical poets are known is not clear. Commentators on Old English poetic culture have tended to assume the existence of a professional class of poets, but there is no convincing historical evidence to support this view.[3] However, in the previous chapter the poems *Widsith* and *Deor* provided evidence that some kind of professional status existed among *scopas* and *gleomen* who relied on patronage from secular lords.

The anonymity of the Anglo-Saxon poetic tradition suggests that *scopas* did not rank high socially. The tradition has preserved scant information about poets apart from the three Old English poems discussed in chapter one. Poets are not mentioned in hagiography, homilies, law-tracts, chronicles, or other such texts. There is no surviving evidence for a system of formal training, as supported by the emphasis placed by scholars a few decades ago on oral-formulaic composition and "learning by listening."[4]

By contrast, named poets from the Gaelic tradition are more numerous. The preservation of works by named historical poets appears to result from the fact

---

[1] There is an extensive literature about "poets" in early medieval societies but it is not my intention to define and explain so vast a concept in disparate societies. See, for example, Chadwick and Chadwick, *Growth of Literature*, 592–634 (The Author). For a broad study of the poet in Anglo-Saxon society, see Opland, *Anglo-Saxon Oral Poetry*; Bredehoft, *Authors, Audiences*. Several chapters were devoted to various named poets and their poetic topics by Henry, *Saoithiúlacht*. A wide-ranging study of poets in medieval societies has concentrated on their functions as bearers of wisdom and tradition: Bloomfield and Dunn, *Role of the Poet*. For the difficulties in defining the medieval poet, see Bloomfield and Dunn, *Role of the Poet*, 1–5. Bloomfield emphasized the didactic character of much early literature and noted that "Early poets were teachers, diviners, prophets, and preservers of tradition": Bloomfield and Dunn, *Role of the Poet*, 4.
[2] Thornbury, *Becoming a Poet*, 243–47 (Appendix 1); Bredehoft, *Authors, Audiences*, 3–7.
[3] Thornbury, *Becoming a Poet*, 34.
[4] Magoun, "Bede's Story of Cædmon," 56; Fry, "Formulaic Poet," 233. Fry based his arguments on Albert Lord's *Singer of Tales*, 21–26. For a synopsis, see O'Donnell, *Cædmon's Hymn*, 3–4, 23–24, 67–68.

that Gaelic poets were well-placed in the social order and had a formal educational and apprenticeship system.[5] The high status of Gaelic poets recorded in the law-tracts outlines their social privileges and cultural responsibilities as described in the eighth-century *Uraicecht na Ríar* (Primer of the Stipulations).[6] The social status and professional training of Gaelic poets will be discussed in chapter three.

The lack of secondary commentary from the Anglo-Saxons about their poets may owe much to the vagaries of manuscript preservation. But there is a marked contrast to the Early Gaelic literary corpus where secondary commentary from within the culture itself is, by comparison, prolific. The literary self-awareness of Gaelic culture is striking when several anecdotes, narratives, and etiological legends survive whose protagonists are poets. There is frequent intertextual cross-referencing in a variety of contexts.[7] Many Gaelic poets are named from the earliest period.[8] Despite numerous anonymous texts, several are plausibly ascribed to historically identifiable persons.[9] In both traditions, named vernacular authors are frequently clerics, or associated with the Church and Latinate learning in other ways.

The poets to be discussed flourished in the period prior to the death of Bede. Possible Old English poets include Cædmon (fl. 670), Aldhelm (d. 709), and Bede himself (d. 735). The Gaelic authors to be discussed include Colmán mac Lénéni (d. 606), a professional poet who founded a monastery. Bécán mac Luigdech (fl. 670) must also have trained as a professional poet. His two substantial poems praise St. Columba and convert secular encomiastic *topoi* for ecclesiastical themes. The three *sapientes* Cenn Fáelad mac Ailello (d. 679), Banbán (d. 686), Aldfrith son of Oswiu (d. 704), and the abbot Adomnán of Iona (d. 704) are included here but will be discussed more fully in chapter four. This chapter outlines their output, looks for connections between the traditions, and notes the survival of distinct dialects in Old English and the lack of dialect in Early Gaelic written records.

---

5 This point is discussed in Ireland, "Vernacular Poets."
6 Breatnach, *Uraicecht na Ríar*.
7 See discussion in Ireland, "Vernacular Poets."
8 Various scholars have attempted to catalogue the named historical and legendary Gaelic poets: O'Reilly, *Four Hundred Irish Writers*; Meyer, *Primer of Irish Metrics*. Early texts which list named Gaelic poets have been edited from manuscript: Stokes, "List of Ancient Irish Authors"; Carney, "*De Scriptoribus Hibernicis*"; Smith, "Aimirgein Glúngel Tuir Tend." A survey of Gaelic literature has acknowledged both historical and legendary poets from the Early Gaelic period: Welch, *Companion to Irish Literature*.
9 For an attempt to date early Gaelic verse texts and name poets to whom these texts are attributed, see Carney, "Dating of Early Irish Verse," 182–89.

As a complement to this chapter Appendix 2.a treats named authors who wrote in the vernacular after Bede's death (735) until the end of the Anglo-Saxon period (ca. 1100).

## Colmán mac Lénéni (d. ca. 606)

Colmán mac Lénéni[10] trained and practiced as a secular professional poet before turning to a life in religion. He was a contemporary of such churchmen as St. Columba (d. 593),[11] founder of Iona, and the *peregrinus* to the continent Columbanus (d. 615), who departed from Bangor, Co. Down. Their three names show that already by the mid sixth century names based on Latin *Columba* (Gaelic *Col(u)m*; dove) had become common.[12] Several fragments of verse attributed to Colmán were identified by Rudolf Thurneysen from a variety of sources such as Middle Gaelic metrical tracts or *Sanas Cormaic* (Cormac's Glossary), a compendium of rare words and cultural references.[13] Only eight fragments of poems survive, comprising less than forty lines, but both encomiastic and religious topics are included.[14]

Colmán used his poetic skills to compose religious verse and he used his social status to establish a monastery at Cloyne (*Cluain Úama*, Co. Cork).[15] He apparently descended from the Cattraige, a family resident in the area near Emly (*Imlech Ibair*, Co. Tipperary).[16] Colmán was recognized as an *athláech* (ex-layman) by the early eighth century. In the early generations of conversion this

---

[10] Colmán apparently died early in the first decade of the seventh century. This date is taken from Mac Airt, *Annals of Inisfallen*, 82–83. Charles-Edwards dated this to 604 by comparing dates for other events from the Annals of Ulster, Tigernach, and the Chronicum Scottorum: Charles-Edwards, *Chronicle of Ireland*, 124.

[11] Mc Carthy, http://www.irish-annals.cs.tcd.ie/, s.a. 593; Mac Airt and Mac Niocaill, *Annals of Ulster*, 97–97 s.a. 595; Stokes, "Annals of Tigernach," 160 [Felinfach i, 120]. For a full discussion, see Mc Carthy, "Chronology of St Columba's Life."

[12] See the numerous saints named Col(u)m or Colmán (*Colm* + diminutive *–án*): Ó Riain, *Dictionary*, 183–215. Even in secular genealogies names based on Columba are frequent: O'Brien, *Corpus genealogiarum Hiberniae*, 551–53.

[13] Thurneysen, "Colmān mac Lēnēni." For more up-to-date treatment, see Ó Corráin, *Clavis*, ii, 1120–22 §844.

[14] These are translated by Donnchadh Ó Corráin in Appendix C of MacCotter, *Colmán of Cloyne*, 129–32.

[15] In "The Triads," an Old Gaelic wisdom-text, the monastery at Cloyne is equated with the "jurisprudence of Ireland" (féinechas Hérenn): Meyer, *Triads of Ireland*, 2–3 §12.

[16] MacCotter, *Colmán of Cloyne*, 49. See also Ó Corráin, "Creating the Past," 198–99.

title honored those who gave up a secular career and opted for life in religion.[17] Colmán's recognition by the Church is registered in *Félire Óengusso* (Martyrology of Oengus), a text of ca. 830, at November 24.[18] Turning from secular to religious life is appreciated, and highlighted, by Bede in such figures as Cuthbert,[19] Tilmon (*HE* v 10), and Eostorwine.[20] A similar status was implied for Cædmon, as discussed in chapter seven.

Some fragments attest to Colmán's training as a secular praise poet. One such from early in his career has stanzaic structure, wordplay, end-rhyme, and linking alliteration, in which the last word of a line alliterates with the first word of the following line.[21] The poet, through a series of favorable comparisons, praises a patron named Domnall for the gift of a sword. The poem follows:

| | |
|---|---|
| Luin oc elaib | (Blackbirds to swans, |
| ungi oc dīrnaib | Ounces to heavy weights, |
| delba[22] ban n-athech | Forms of common women |
| oc rōdaib rīgnaib | To splendid queens, |
| rīg oc Domnall | Kings to Domnall, |
| dord oc aidbse | A drone to choral music, |
| adand oc caindill | A rushlight to a candle: |
| calg oc mo chailgse[23] | Swords to my sword.)[24] |

Gerard Murphy had argued that stanzaic structure and end rhyme had been borrowed from late Antique Latin hymns and blended with indigenous features such as linking alliteration.[25] Each of the fragments by Colmán mac Lénéni cited here show these metrical features. The fragment above was preserved in order to cite arcane vocabulary: *aidbse* (singing, chanting) in the Middle Gaelic

---

**17** Hull, "Conall Corc," 900; Ní Dhonnchadha, "Irish Vernacular Literary Tradition," 556–57.
**18** Stokes, *Félire Óengusso*, 236–37.
**19** Colgrave, *Lives of Saint Cuthbert*, 172–73, c. 6 (*Vita prosa*).
**20** Grocock and Wood, *Abbots of Wearmouth*, 40–41 §8 (*Historia abbatum*).
**21** Murphy, *Early Irish Metrics*, 18; Mac Cana, "Praise Poetry," 18–19.
**22** The translation, called "A Spendid Sword," is by Lehmann, *Early Irish Verse*, 62–63, 110 §57. Two words, *delb* (pl. *delba*; form, figure, shape) and *drech* (pl. *drecha*; face, countenance), have been suggested as substitutions for manuscript *crotha* (sg. *cruth*; form, shape, appearance) in order to restore alliteration: Thurneysen, "Colmān mac Lēnēni."
**23** MacCotter, *Colmán of Cloyne*, 129.
**24** Lehmann, *Early Irish Verse*, 62, 110 §57 (translating *delba* (forms, figures) instead of *drecha* (faces), both alliterating substitutes for manuscript *crotha* (forms, shapes)).
**25** Murphy, *Early Irish Metrics*, 18. His views have been supported by Corthals, "Late Antique Background."

prose preface to *Amrae Choluim Cille*,[26] and *adand* (*adann*; rushlight) in *Sanas Cormaic*.[27]

James Carney had proposed a chronology for Colmán mac Lénéni that encompassed the secular and religious aspects of his career (ca. 530 to ca. 606).[28] Carney suggested that the Domnall praised in the poem above was Domnall (Ilchelgach)[29] mac Muirchertaigh (ca. 565/6)[30] who shared the high-kingship of Tara with his brother Forggus. The brothers were of Cenél nEogain, the sept to which King Aldfrith *sapiens* belonged, and were victors at the Battle of Cúl Dreimne, the battle which was the purported cause of St. Columba's exile to Iona.[31] In another encomium Colmán mac Lénéni praised Áed Sláine (d. 604), the eponymous ancestor of Síl nÁedo Sláine, as cited in chapter one.[32]

Another poetic fragment praises a certain Fergus Tuile, king of Uí Liatháin, the territory where Cloyne is located. The fragment suggests that Colmán, though now a cleric, praised the person in whose territory Cloyne was situated and who was his likely patron:[33]

| | |
|---|---|
| Ó ba mac cléib | (Since he was a child in the cradle |
| caindlech ser | the bright star |
| sirt cach n-ainm | the name of Man-Strength (Fer-gus) |
| ainm gossa fer | surpassed every name)[34] |

The wordplay on the personal name Fergus (*fer* "man" and -*gus* "strength"; here in the genitive singular *gossa*) is a core aspect of the verse.[35] This Fergus Tuile would have ruled Uí Liatháin in the time of Colmán and probably not long

---

[26] This word was used in the *Amrae Choluim Cille* and had to be explained in the glosses: Stokes, "*Amra Choluimb Chille*," 180–83 §49; Thurneysen, "Colmān mac Lēnēni," 198.
[27] Meyer, "*Sanas Cormaic*," 7 §69; Thurneysen, "Colmān mac Lēnēni," 199.
[28] Carney, "Accentual Poems," 63–65.
[29] Domnall's epithet, *Ilchelgach*, means "of many swords." See his genealogy at Byrne, *Irish Kings*, 283.
[30] Muirchertach is also called Mac Ercae: Byrne, *Irish Kings*, 102. For his *obit*, see Mac Airt and Mac Niocaill, *Annals of Ulster*, 84–85; Mc Carthy, http://www.irish-annals.cs.tcd.ie/, s.a. 565.
[31] Byrne, *Irish Kings*, 95–96, 102–2; Herbert, *Iona, Kells, and Derry*, 27–28.
[32] Mac Cana, "Praise Poetry," 18–19.
[33] MacCotter, *Colmán of Cloyne*, 129–30 (Appendix C). There is a genealogical tradition that credits Coirpre mac Crimthainn of the Éoganacht of Munster (d. ca. 580) with bequeathing Cloyne: Ó Corráin, "Creating the Past," 198–99.
[34] MacCotter, *Colmán of Cloyne*, 129–30.
[35] The last two lines of the stanza state that Fergus "the name of strength of men [*ainm gossa fer*] surpassed every name."

after a certain Cormac of the Uí Liatháin, a seafarer and *miles Christi*, founded a monastery as part of Columba's *familia* operating from Iona. Cormac the seafarer establishes a link between Uí Liatháin and Iona that suggests that Colmán mac Lénéni could have been known in Northumbria through Iona's mission.[36]

So far the fragments discussed have been examples of encomium. But as a poet turned cleric, Colmán also composed on religious topics. The following is an example:

| Ropo thānaise | (It was the second twilight watch |
| Triuin crapscuil | (i.e., the second twilight third, i.e., the dawn watch) |
| Ceirdd promthaidi | the manner of testing |
| Petair apstail. | Of the apostle Peter.)[37] |

This fragment refers to the apostle Peter's denial of Christ three times before cockcrow (Matthew 26:34, 26:75; Mark 14:30, 14:72; Luke 22:34, 22:61) as found in the Synoptic Gospels and noted by Donnchadh Ó Corráin.[38] An important aspect of the insular Paschal controversy was the differing accounts between the Synoptic Gospels, just listed, and the Gospel of John. Those Gaels who followed the *latercus*, that is, Iona and Lindisfarne, relied on the account of the passion and crucifixion in the Gospel of John, the apostle favored by Christ.[39] Theological divisions based in Scripture separated the parties at the "synod" of Whitby.[40]

A four-line fragment by Colmán refers to sleep that resulted in a poem, a phenomenon analogous to the account of Cædmon as told by Bede (*HE* iv 24).[41] Colmán's fragment precedes Cædmon's performance by as much as eighty years. The fragment presents difficulties in translation because it lacks a larger context, it contains legal terminology, and has a *hapax legomenon*.

Nī fordiuchtror for duain indlis
iar cotlud chaīn bindris.

---

[36] Anderson and Anderson, *Life of Columba*, 166–71, ii 42 (94b–97b); 206–7, iii 17 (118a). See, Ireland, "Cædmon and Colmán," 174, 178–79.
[37] Donnchadh Ó Corráin, who translated these fragments, changed manuscript *apstail* (apostle) to the earlier form *axail*: MacCotter, *Colmán of Cloyne*, 131.
[38] MacCotter, *Colmán of Cloyne*, 131.
[39] Walsh and Ó Cróinín, *Cummian's Letter*, 69n89.
[40] Pelteret, "Apostolic Authority."
[41] Discussed previously in Ireland, "Precursor of Cædmon"; MacCotter, *Colmán of Cloyne*, 130–31.

Briathar chorgais cen nach ndīchmaircc,
deog nepnairc⁴² rath rīgmaicc.

(I do not awaken to an unworthy poem
After beautiful and sweet-dreamed sleep.
(It is) a Lenten promise without anything unpermitted,
(It is) a present drink of Christ's grace.)

The poet's sleep results in a poem to which he is pleased to awaken. It fulfils the requirements of his religious beliefs and satisfies his desire to praise the "royal son" (*rígmac*). The Christian message is unmistakable with reference to *Corgus* (Lent; genitive singular *corgais*). The kenning referring to Christ is an early example of secular diction turned to religious use. It is paralleled in Cædmon's and other Old English poems by terms for an earthly lord applied to God.

The Middle Gaelic interlinear glosses to this fragment found in Dublin, Trinity College, MS 1316 (H.2.15a)⁴³ reveal the congruity in Gaelic Christian culture between the inspired *fili* and religious subject matter. In the following I print the text of the poem in italics in [square brackets] and translate the glosses below.

[*Nī fordiuchtror for duain indlis iar cotlud*].
.i. ni for duain is indlis dam duiscim iar codludh, inge is for scel mbinn, moladh righ .uii. nimhe.

(It is not to a poem which is worthless to me that I awaken after sleep, but it is to pleasant tidings, the praise of the king of the seven heavens.)

The beginning of the gloss is essentially a paraphrase of the original text. The legal term *dúan indlis* means "a poem not entitled to recompense."⁴⁴ Colmán's poem is just the opposite and is "worthy" or "entitled," and implies his professional status. Notice that the pleasant tidings are "praise of the king" of the seven heavens.

[*chaīn bindris*]
.i. is taithnemach binn in scel tarfas dam .i. nem 7 talam 7 ifirn.

(The tidings revealed to me are resplendent and pleasant, i.e., heaven and earth and hell.)

---

42 This *hapax legomenon* has not been explained. I follow Thurneysen's suggestion and translate *frecndairc* (present (in time), actual). Thurneysen's own translation is "gegenwärtiger Trunk aus den (künftigen) Gnadengaben Christi": Thurneysen, "Colmán mac Lēnēni," 203. Ó Corráin, in his translation, treated the word as *écndairc* in the sense "prayer for the dead, requiem"; MacCotter, *Colmán of Cloyne*, 130–31.
43 CODECS: https://www.vanhamel.nl/codecs/Dublin,_Trinity_College,_MS_1316.
44 Watkins, "Etymology of Irish *Dúan*," 275.

The tidings have been revealed through "inspired" sleep. In Cædmon's inspired sleep he was commanded to sing of the creation. Though Colmán's poem does not refer to creation, or the world, it appears in the gloss, apparently, because Early Gaelic Christianity was preoccupied by the concept as, for example, in the Hiberno-Latin *Altus Prosator*.

> [*briathar chorgais*]
> .i. briathar is coir a chorgus
>
> (A promise which is appropriate to Lent)

As noted above, Lent is an unambiguous Christian reference.

> [*cen nach ndīchmaircc*]
> .i. briathar cen dichmairc, .i. cen go aei
>
> (A promise without something unpermitted, i.e., without a falsehood in law)

This gloss stresses the correctness, literally the legality, of the Lenten promise. Cædmon's song had to undergo inspection and approval by "more learned men" (*viri doctiores*).

> [*deog nepnairc rath rīgmaicc*].
> .i. in deog dobeir mo rímac damh, is a nécnairc nímhe dosbeir, 7 is machtnadh són in éicse dobeir dia moladh fein.
>
> (The drink my Christ (royal son) gives to me, it is from the *nécnairc* (?) of heaven that he gives it, and it is a matter of wonder, the poetic revelation (*éicse*) that he gives for his own praise.)

St. Columbanus, a close contemporary of Colmán mac Lénéni, wrote a sermon on Christ as the "fountain of life" and the abundant drink granted from it.[45] In the gloss the "drink" (*deog*) given by Christ is related to the "poetic revelation" (*éicse*) granted by the Lord to the poet for the Lord's own praise.

Cultural and literary historical awareness by Gaelic poetic families were recorded centuries after the fact, as suggested by Gilla in Choimded's retrospective poem on poets and legal authorities. That sense of self-awareness and inheritance of the poetic classes is clearly demonstrated by a later poet named Gofraidh Fionn Ó Dálaigh (d. 1387). Gofraidh Fionn claimed Colmán mac Lénéni as the patron of the Uí Dhálaigh (O'Daly) poetic family because their eponymous ancestor, Dálach, had been the *daltae* (fosterling, pupil) of Colmán mac Lénéni.[46] Gofraidh

---

**45** Walker, *Sancti Columbani Opera*, 114–21 (*Instructio xiii*).
**46** Bergin, *Irish Bardic Poetry*, 70–72 (Gaelic), 242–44 (English).

Fionn's praise of, and family claim to, Colmán involved a retrospective look of nearly eight hundred years going back to the late sixth century. Gofraidh Fionn's *floruit* is contemporary with the florescence of Middle English poetry in figures such as Geoffrey Chaucer, William Langland, and the *Gawain*-poet. Yet Gofraidh Fionn has the sustained historical perspective to acknowledge Colmán as the originator of his own family line as poets.

## Bécán mac Luigdech (fl. 670)

Two substantial encomiastic poems in praise of St. Columba of Iona survive from the second half of the seventh century. As preserved, they each contain twenty-five stanzas and are both attributed to Bécán mac Luigdech (fl. 670).[47] They describe St. Columba as a pilgrim saint who left his home in Ireland and sacrificed himself for God.[48] The poems apply the diction of secular encomia to an ecclesiastical figure and each poem appears to have had the protective power of a *lorica*.[49]

Praise songs with protective power are confirmed in *Vita Columbae* where certain lay people, who were guilty of bloodshed, nevertheless were protected from their enemies by vernacular songs (scoticae linguae . . . carmina) in praise of Columba. The people had been surrounded in their house by enemies, but those who sang in praise of Columba escaped the flames, spears, and swords unharmed, while those who neglected to sing perished. Adomnán assured his readers of the numerous witnesses to these and similar events throughout Ireland and Britain (in Scottia et Britannia) as proof of their veracity.[50]

Bécán was a member of Cenél nÉogain of the Northern Uí Néill[51] and appears to have been connected with the monasteries of Tech Conaill[52] near Bray,

---

[47] The form of his name cannot be identified for certain. His name may be Béc(c)án, as the late manuscript containing one of the poems suggests, with a long first vowel. His father's name, in the genitive, may have been Lugdach, from Lugad, rather than with the slender consonant cluster of Luigdech. The variant forms of both names can be found in surviving records.
[48] Kelly, "Poem in Praise"; Kelly, "Tiughraind Bhécáin." For another translation, see Clancy and Márkus, *Iona*, 129–63; Ó Corráin, *Clavis*, ii, 1147–49 §§858–59.
[49] Hughes, "Irish Influence"; Herren, *Hisperica Famina: II*, 23–31.
[50] Anderson and Anderson, *Life of Columba*, 16–17, i 1 (9b–10a).
[51] Kelly, "Poem in Praise," 3; Kelly, "Tiughraind Bhécáin," 66, 73–75; Ó Riain, *Corpus Genealogiarum Sanctorum Hiberniae*, 7 §32. For the Cenél nÉogain, see Byrne, *Irish Kings*, 70–105.
[52] Ó Riain, *Corpus Genealogiarum Sanctorum Hiberniae*, 7 §32; Ó Riain, *Dictionary*, 92 (Beagán of Churchtown).

Co. Wicklow and Cluain Aird Mo-Bécóc[53] near Aherlow, Co. Tipperary. Given the peripatetic nature of early monastic education both foundations may have legitimate claim to him. If he was a trained poet, as he appears to have been, there is no reason why he should not produce encomium for someone outside of his kin group. The Annals of Ulster record the death of Do-Bécóc of Cluain Aird in 690.[54] Because Bécán praised St. Columba there is a tendency to associate him with Iona. It is possible that a certain Beccán *solitarius*, a recipient of Cummian's Paschal letter (632) addressed to Abbot Ségéne of Iona, may also be the poet.[55] But Beccán *solitarius* was more likely Beccán of Rùm, an island monastery north of Iona.[56] Beccán of Rùm died in 677.[57] Whatever about the specific identity and location of our poet, his *floruit* was in the second half of the seventh century, in agreement with the linguistic analysis of the poems.[58] Bécán's poems reveal his place in a well-established tradition and not at its inception.

Of the two poems, the one beginning "*Fo réir Choluimb*" has seven syllable lines with four-line stanzas,[59] and the other beginning "*To·fed andes*," described in its manuscript as *Tiughraind Bhécáin* (last stanzas of Bécán), has twelve syllable lines with two-line stanzas.[60] They each have end rhyme with the pattern in "*Fo réir Choluimb*" being ac and bd. The poems also have linking alliteration with the last word of each line alliterating with the first word of the following line, and the last word of each stanza alliterating with the first word of the following stanza. Both poems have caesurae in the lines with alliteration across the caesurae. Syllabic verse with regular rhyme likely derived from Late Antique Latin

---

53 The scholia in *Félire Óengusso* associate him with both locations: Stokes, *Félire Óengusso*, 136–37; but the entry in the martyrology itself, at May 26, associates him with Cluain Aird: Stokes, *Félire Óengusso*, 126.
54 Mac Airt and Mac Niocaill, *Annals of Ulster*, 152–53; Stokes, "Annals of Tigernach," 211. Both Mo-Bécóc and Do-Bécóc, each of Cluain Aird, are hypocoristic forms of the diminutive Béc(c)án.
55 Walsh and Ó Cróinín, *Cummian's Letter*, 8–9, 11.
56 Ó Riain, *Dictionary*, 93 (Beagán of Rum).
57 Mac Airt and Mac Niocaill, *Annals of Ulster*, 144–45; Stokes, "Annals of Tigernach," 204 [Felinfach i, 164].
58 Kelly, "Tiughraind Bhécáin," 66–69.
59 The only complete version of this poem is found in the seventeenth-century manuscript Dublin, National Library of Ireland, MS G 50: Kelly, "Poem in Praise," 1; CODECS: https://www.vanhamel.nl/codecs/Dublin,_National_Library_of_Ireland,_MS_G_50.
60 This poem is known only from the sixteenth-century manuscript Oxford, Bodleian Library, MS Laud Misc. 615: Kelly, "Tiughraind Bhécáin," 66; CODECS: https://www.vanhamel.nl/codecs/Oxford,_Bodleian_Library,_MS_Laud_Misc._615. All citations of the two poems are from the editions and translations of Fergus Kelly.

poetry and hymns.⁶¹ The form and style of these poems by Bécán support such a contention.

The poems preserve features that are assumed to have been part of the secular encomiastic tradition. They praise Columba, highlighting his illustrious family background, his rôle as protector – and whose protection (*snádud*) the poet actively seeks⁶² – his strength, not so much as a warrior but as one willing to make self-sacrifices. Both poems stress Columba's seafaring as a deliberate separation from his kin and sacrifice for the sake of others.

"*Fo réir Choluimb*" describes the saint as "Columb Cille, candle of Níall" (Columb Cille, caindel Néill; 14c) emphasizing his descent from Níall Noígíallach (Níall of the Nine Hostages), eponymous ancestor of the extended Uí Néill septs. Using similar language "*To·fed andes*" makes clear the geographical reach of Columba's influence and declares the saint to be:

> Caindel Connacht | caindel Alban | amrae fíadat (4a)
>
> (Candle of Connachta, candle of Britain, wonderful lord.)

"*Fo réir Choluimb*" emphasizes his greatness in the statements that "his name shone like the sun" (tindis a ainm amal gréin; 4c) and that his name was "the name which is nobler than [other] people's" (a n-ainm as úaisliu doínib; 5d). He was not only great and high-ranking, but because of him "safe is every one in peril to whom he is a fort" (slán cach eslán asa dún; 6b).

This latter line serves to remind that the poems have characteristics of protective *loricae*, which were also produced in Latin as seen in the *lorica* by Laidcenn mac Baíth *sapiens* (d. 661),⁶³ which was recorded in later Anglo-Saxon prayer books.⁶⁴ "*Fo réir Choluimb*" declares "may the fair one in the seven heavens protect me" (find for nimib snáidsium secht; 1b)⁶⁵ and the concern with the

---

61 McCone, *Pagan Past*, 39, plus other citations in text and notes. For the inheritance of Late Antique Latin hymns in early vernacular texts beyond the styles discussed here, see Corthals, "Late Antique Background."
62 *Snádud* (protection) was first noted in chapter one as protection offered to poets and entertainers who crossed territorial boundaries. For the legal concept, see Binchy, *Críth Gablach*, 106–7.
63 Herren, "So-called *Lorica Gildae*"; Herren, *Hisperica Famina: II*, 42–45, 76–89.
64 Hughes, "Irish Influence." See discussion in chapter four.
65 This short line has two significant features. Firstly, the verb, *snáidid* (protects; provides safe conduct; eDIL: http://www.dil.ie, s.v. *snáidid*; dil.ie/38121), is used of warriors acting as escorts for visiting poets (*filid*). Secondly, the early Gaels emphasized the significance of the number seven in both ecclesiastical and secular matters. For the use of seven by Aldhelm in order to impress King Aldfrith, see Ireland, "Where Was King Aldfrith Educated?" 37–39.

final judgement is evident in the line "may he carry me past the king who inhabits the fire" (berthum sech ríg trebas tein; 23c). This last line is reminiscent of the threat of punishing fires in the visions of Fursa (*HE* iii 19) and Dryhthelm (*HE* v 12) as related by Bede.

Both poems are full of heroic images turned to religious purpose as, for example, in the shared expression "he broke desires" (brisis tola; "*Fo réir Choluimb*," 12c; "*To·fed andes*," 3a). In "*Fo réir Choluimb*," using a striking seafaring image of exile and sacrifice, we are told "he crucified . . . his body on the green waves" (crochais . . . a chorp for tonna glass; 2cd). It is reminiscent of images of the nobility of a willing self-sacrifice in the Old English *Dream of the Rood* when Christ, described as a "young hero" (geong hæleð), ascends the cross:

> Ongyrede hine þā geong hæleð, (Þæt wæs god ælmihtig),
> strang ond stīðmōd; Gestāh hē on gealgan hēanne,
> mōdig on manigra gesyhðe, Þā hē wolde mancyn lȳsan (lines 39–41).[66]
>
> (The young hero undressed himself, (that was God almighty),
> strong and resolute. He mounted the high gallows,
> courageous in sight of many, when he would redeem mankind.)

Images of secular lords as a stout oak or a source of security are combined with notions from monastic life in the description of St. Columba from "*To·fed andes*";

> Ba dair nduillech | ba dín anmae | ba hall nglinne,
> ba grían manach | ba már coímdiu | Columb Cille (14ab)
>
> (He was a leafy oak, he was a protection of the soul, he was a rock of security,
> he was the sun of monks, he was a great lord, Columb Cille.)

"*Fo réir Choluimb*" continues this inversion of heroic images for monastic and ecclesiastical purposes. For example, the image of the generous lord, as found in all insular heroic literatures, is overturned in the following line: "he has freed his monks from riches" (ro·sóer a manchu moínib; 5b). Contrast line 1102a in *Beowulf*, in the Finn episode, where the slain lord Hnæf is lamented and described as *bēaggyfa* (ring-giver). And the inversions of cultural images continue: "He was uniquely victorious over lust" (Ba óen-búadach boí for tuil; 8a); "he was the spear-cast, falsehood was destroyed" (ba hé roüt, goítae gáu; 10d); "He fought with the flesh familiar battles" (Fích fri colainn catha íuil; 13a). Even the notion of the band of men acting together is changed from a secular warband to a religious setting:

---

66 Swanton, *Dream of the Rood*, 95.

Dánae arbar asa chrúas,
clér co n-imlúad aingel cert (15ab)

(Brave is the host whose toughness is his,
a band with the movement of true angels.)

Both poems by Bécán contain seafaring images and stress the notion of voluntary exile undertaken by the saint. Since the 1950s Old English scholars have argued that the poem *Seafarer* can be read as the meditations of one who becomes a *peregrinus*, whether that is understood literally or allegorically.[67] That notion can be seen in the evolving outlook of the first-person speaker in the following lines:

                    For Þon cnyssað nu
heortan geÞohtas    Þæt ic hean streamas,
sealtyÞa gelac,        sylf cunnige – (33a–35)

(and so the thoughts
trouble my heart now that I myself am to venture
on the deep [or towering] seas – )[68]

                    Þæt ic feor heonan
elÞeodigra            eard gesece – (37a–38)[69]

(that I far hence
should seek the land of foreigners – )

The poem provides a motivating mindset for this seemingly drastic decision in the following lines:

                  for Þon me hatran sind
Dryhtnes dreamas   Þonne Þis deade lif
læne on londe (64a–66a).

(for the joys of the Lord are warmer
[more living or inspiring] to me than this dead, transitory life on land.)[70]

Similar notions and seafaring images about Columba in the poems by Bécán suggest the degree of shared experience of early Christian "exiles" who left their homelands. For example, from "*To·fed andes*" we have the lines:

---

**67** Dorothy Whitelock argued for a literal interpretation of the *Seafarer* as a *peregrinus*: Whitelock, "Interpretation"; whereas G. V. Smithers argued for an allegorical interpretation: Smithers, "Meaning." Both interpretations can be applied to Anglo-Saxons who studied in Ireland in order to become missionaries to their Germanic brethren on the continent: Ireland, "*Seafarer*."
**68** Gordon, *Seafarer*, 37–38 and notes (text and translation).
**69** Gordon, *Seafarer*, 38.
**70** Gordon, *Seafarer*, 42 and notes (text and translation).

> Cechaing tonnaig | tresaig magain | mongaig rónaig (5a)
>
> (He traversed the wavey tumultuous place, foaming, full of seals.)

Further seafaring images are applied to Columba in the poem "*Fo réir Choluimb*";

> cechaing noïb nemed mbled . . .
> fairrge al druim dánae fer (12b and d)
>
> (he traversed in ships the whale's sanctuary, . . .
> a brave man over the ridge of the sea.)

The Gaelic phrase *nemed mbled* (whale's sanctuary) chimes well with Old English *hronrād* (whale road) as a kenning in *Beowulf* for the ocean, or from the Old English *Seafarer*, terms like *hwæles ēþel* (whale's homeland) or *hwælweg* (path of the whale).[71] The next example reminds us that Columba did not travel alone, but was accompanied by a dozen monks in his pilgrimage into exile:[72]

> Lessach, línmar, sláin co céill,
> curchaib tar sál sephtus cló; (14ab).
>
> (Successful, numerous, in safety,
> a wind swept them over the sea in boats.)

In both poems there are several encomiastic references to Columba's emphasis on scholarship and learning as opposed to the heroic ideals of a warlord or secular leader. A good example is found in these lines from "*To·fed andes*";

> Techtaiss liubru | lécciss la slán | selba aithri,
> ar ṡeirc léigind | lécciss coicthiu | lécciss caithri. (18ab)
>
> (He kept books, he abandoned without claim (?) the possessions of [his] paternal kin,
> for love of learning, he abandoned battles, he abandoned fortresses.)

The following lines from the same poem indicate the geographic spread of his and his establishment's influence. Note that the word *ecnae* (wisdom) is frequently used as the equivalent of Latin *sapientia*. *Sapiens* began to be used in the seventh century as a title or epithet to designate important scholars who worked in both Latin and the vernacular.

> Birt búaid n-eccnai | hi cúairt Éirenn | combo hardu,
> amrae n-anmae | ailtir Lethae | líntair Albu. (6ab)

---

[71] For the example from *Beowulf*, see Fulk, Bjork, Niles, *Klaeber's Beowulf*, 3, line 10a. For the example from the *Seafarer*, see Gordon, *Seafarer*, 41, line 60a; 42, line 63a.
[72] An appendix, added later to the Life, names the twelve companions with details of some of their backgrounds: Anderson and Anderson, *Life of Columba*, 238–39.

(He brought the virtue of wisdom throughout Ireland, so that it was more elevated, wonderful name, Armorica is nourished, Britain is filled.)

The following line from "*Fo réir Choluimb*" resonates well with the preceding stanza from the other poem about the value of his learning to the wider world: "the wisdom of his mouth is the glory of Britain" (tendál Alban ecnae a béoil; 19a). A stanza from this same poem combines motifs discussed so far. Columba's battles were of a spiritual kind and learning was one of his weapons, while he willingly accepted a self-imposed foreign exile across the sea.

> Fích fri colainn catha íuil,
> légais la sin suíthe n-óg,
> úagais, brígais benna síuil,
> sruith tar fairrgi, flaith a lóg. (13a–d)

> (He fought with the flesh familiar battles,
> in addition to that, he read pure wisdom,
> he sewed, he displayed sail-tops,
> a sage over the sea, Heaven his reward.)

Both poems reveal composition by a well-trained, professional Gaelic poet who, like Colmán mac Lénéni before him, had turned his poetic talents to use by the Church. Most particularly in "*To·fed andes*" certain vocabulary items support this notion of formal training and professional status. The poet described Columba as:

> dín mo anmae | dún mo uäd | hauë Conail (12b)

> (protection of my soul, fort of my poetic art, descendant of Conal.)

The poet described the saint as the fort (*dún*) of his *aí* (poetic inspiration, learning; metrical composition),[73] which appears in the genitive singular form *uäd*. The Gaelic *aí* is equivalent to the Brittonic *awen* (poetic inspiration) encountered in chapter one. This vocabulary tends to be restricted to the sphere of the highly trained, professional poet. This one line has the encomiastic quality of reminding us of Columba's descent from Conall son of Níall Noígíallach. The line displays the qualities of the *lorica* in describing Columba as the protection (*dín*) of the poet's soul and fortress (*dún*) of his poetic inspiration. The same poem also contains the phrases "[It is] Columb of whom we sing . . . according to the demands of poetic knowledge" (Columb canmae . . . ríaraib imbaiss; 21ab). *Imbas* (great knowledge; poetic talent, inspiration), in the poem as the genitive singular *imbais(s)*, is a word that appears in the phrase *imbas for·osna* (encompassing knowledge which illuminates) and is claimed by the *filid* as a specialized inspirational skill that they

---

73 eDIL: http://www.dil.ie, s.v. 2 *aí* or dil.ie/715.

controlled and cultivated.[74] It was the special divinatory skill that Medb asked Fedelm if she possessed as the armies set forth on the *Táin Bó Cuailgne*, noted in chapter one. These vocabulary items concerning poets will be discussed more fully in chapter three. But their use by the monastic poet Bécán implies that he had undertaken formal training as a professional poet before composing these poems in praise of St. Columba.

## Cædmon (fl. 670)

Cædmon is the earliest named Old English poet from whom any poetry survives. Although he is a close contemporary of Bécán mac Luigdech, the backgrounds of the two are quite different. While Bécán is associated with monastic establishments it is clear that his poetic training was extensive, perhaps involving a period of secular professional service before actively joining the Church, not unlike what we observed for the career of Colmán mac Lénéni. Cædmon's work is known only through the account given by Bede in the *Historia ecclesiastica* and its later Old English translations (*HE* iv 24).[75] Bede, however, gave only a Latin translation of the "hymn."[76]

Cædmon differs from every other poet discussed in this chapter by being a low status layman who was already mature in years when his poetic talent manifested itself. According to Bede, Cædmon was illiterate, had no prior training as a poet, and never demonstrated any poetic skill or desire to perform in public. It could be argued that Bede's portrayal of Cædmon was intended to contradict his audience's expectations of the function and practice of a typical Anglo-Saxon poet. Yet Cædmon's nine-line hymn in praise of God as Creator has a style and encomiastic diction which, many have argued, are reflected throughout the corpus of Old English poetry.

Modern criticism of the Old English poetic corpus has consistently used Cædmon as its starting point for an analysis of the tradition.[77] Cædmon composed at Whitby probably during the period when Hild was abbess, that is, between 657

---

74 Kelly, *Guide*, 44–45; Carey, "Three Things."
75 Colgrave and Mynors, *Ecclesiastical History*, 414–21; Wallace-Hadrill, *Historical Commentary*, 165–67. See also Ireland, "Vernacular Poets," 43–48.
76 For a study of the sophistication of Bede's Latin version and its comparison to surviving vernacular versions, see Howlett, *British Books*, 262–74.
77 Frantzen, *Desire for Origins*, 130–67. For other examples of how Cædmon's *Hymn* helps unlock the poetic tradition, see O'Brien O'Keeffe, *Visible Song*, 23–46; Bredehoft, *Authors, Audiences*, 14–17.

and 680 or slightly later.[78] The numerous manuscript copies of Bede's *Historia ecclesiastica* which contains the account of Cædmon and his *Hymn*, in both Latin and Old English, have bolstered its cultural importance.

The manuscript tradition of Cædmon's *Hymn* reveals very little about the cultural milieu in which Cædmon worked. Twenty-one Old English witnesses of the hymn from medieval sources have been identified, all in manuscripts of the *Historia ecclesiastica*, but three have subsequently been either destroyed or severely damaged.[79] No copy of the hymn is found in other contexts, such as in chronicles, hagiography, sermons, law tracts, or other narratives, as often happens in Gaelic tradition where famous poets might be quoted to illustrate a point or authenticate a claim.[80] Bede provided only a Latin version of the hymn, but vernacular versions were recorded close to the time of Bede's writing or shortly after his death.[81] No instances of the hymn independent of the *Historia* survive. Bede's *Historia* is our only context for a discussion of the Cædmon story and the *Hymn* itself.[82]

Old English literature reflects the survival of dialects and the copies of Cædmon's *Hymn* are no exception. Gaelic literature, on the other hand, reveals a geographic linguistic homogeneity. The earliest vernacular copies of Cædmon's *Hymn* are in the Northumbrian dialect. The poem survives in various versions, with a major distinction at line 5b between a recension that reads "for the sons of the earth" (*eordu barnum/eorðan bearnum*), or "for the sons of men" (*aelda barnum/ylda bearnum*). Such differences are to be expected in any text preserved in multiple copies.

The following version of the hymn is the reconstructed "hypothetical written ancestor to all surviving recensions of the poem" made by Daniel O'Donnell.[83] The reconstruction is based on the "Moore Bede" dated ca. 734x737 (Figure 2.a).[84]

---

[78] For arguments supporting a later dating of ca. 684, see Cronan, "Cædmon's *Hymn*." Others have argued that Cædmon's death, but not necessarily his composition, is covered by this later dating: O'Donnell, *Cædmon's Hymn*, 10n6.

[79] O'Donnell, *Cædmon's Hymn*, 78–97.

[80] See, for example, a list of annalistic verse in Mc Carthy, *Irish Annals*, 364–67 (Appendix Two); for the law-tracts, see Breatnach, *Companion*, 355–67; for examples in narrative, see Ní Mhaonaigh, "Poetic Authority."

[81] Dobbie, *Manuscripts*, 12; O'Donnell, *Cædmon's Hymn*, 89–90 ("Moore Bede" dated ca. 734x737; Cambridge, University Library, Kk.5.16), 92–93 ("St. Petersburg Bede" or "Leningrad Bede" dated ca. 731/2x746; St. Petersburg, National Library of Russia, lat.Q.v.I.18).

[82] For a contrast with the Gaelic poetic cultural history, see Ireland, "Vernacular Poets."

[83] O'Donnell, *Cædmon's Hymn*, 205.

[84] For illustrations from the manuscript, see Breay and Story, *Anglo-Saxon Kingdoms*, 35, 78–79.

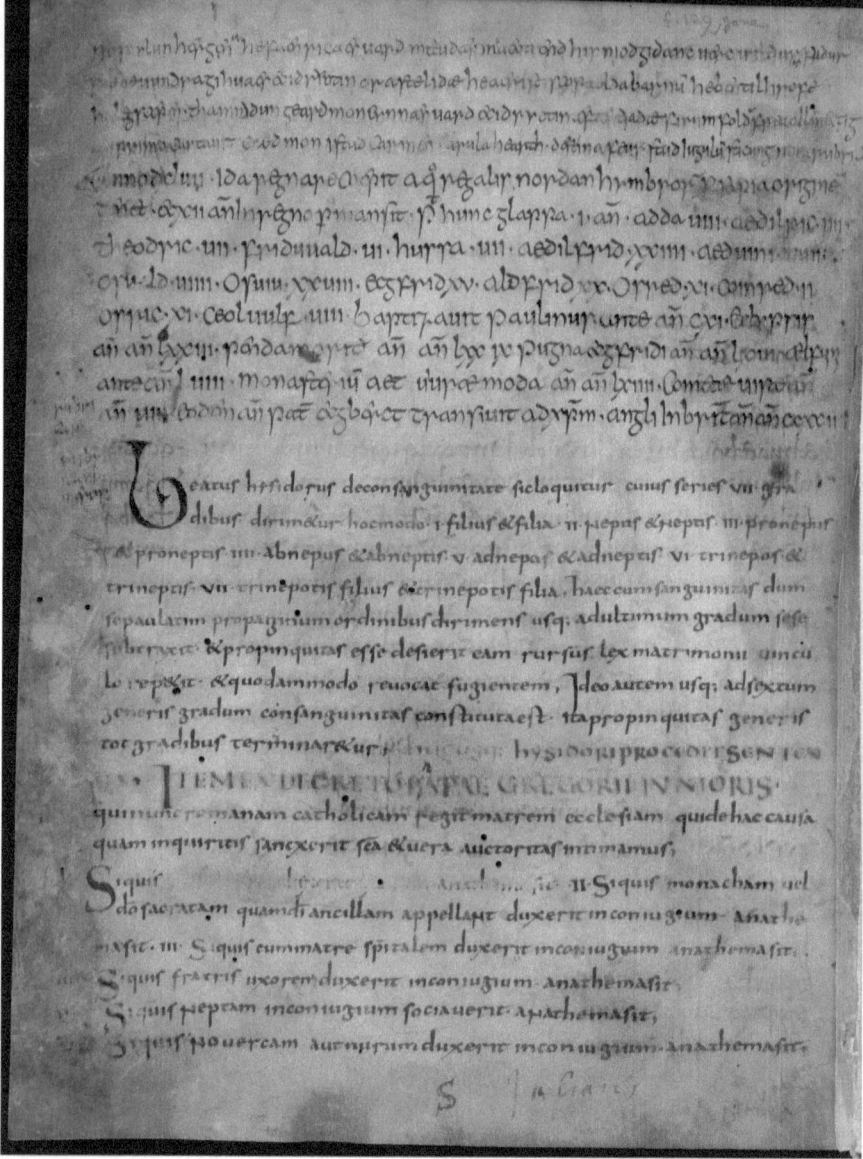

**Figure 2.a:** Folio 128v of Cambridge, University Library, MS Kk.5.16, known as the "Moore Bede," contains one of the earliest vernacular copies of Cædmon's *Hymn*. The dialect is Northumbrian and the manuscript is dated to 734x737. The poem appears in the first three cramped lines at the top of the folio. Reproduced by kind permission of the Syndics of Cambridge University Library.

| | |
|---|---|
| Nu scylun hergan | hefaenricaes uard, |
| metudæs maecti, | end his modgidanc, |
| uerc uuldurfadur – | sue he uundra gihuaes, |
| eci dryctin, | or astelidæ! |
| He aerist scop | eordu barnum |
| heben til hrofe, | haleg sceppend; |
| tha middungeard, | moncynnæs uard, |
| eci dryctin, | æfter tiadæ |
| firum foldu, | frea allmectig.[85] |

(Now we should praise the Guardian of the Heavenly Kingdom, the might of the Creator and His purpose, the work of the Glorious Father – as He, Eternal Lord, created the beginnings of every wondrous thing! He first made for the sons of earth heaven as a roof, the Holy Shaper; then the Guardian of Mankind afterwards adorned the world for men on earth, the Eternal Lord, Almighty Ruler.)

The older Northumbrian version above can be compared to the more recent poem in West Saxon dialect, the dialect in which the greatest amount of Old English literature is preserved. Below is a critical edition, also by Daniel O'Donnell, of the probable recension for the West Saxon archetype:

| | |
|---|---|
| Nu sculon herigean | heofonrices ƿeard,[86] |
| meotodes meahte, | ond his modgeþanc, |
| ƿeorc ƿuldorfæder – | sƿa he ƿundra gehƿæs, |
| ece drihten, | or onstealde! |
| He ærest sceop | eorðan bearnum |
| heofon to hrofe, | halig scyppend; |
| þa middangeard, | moncynnes ƿeard, |
| ece drihten, | æfter teode |
| firum foldan, | frea ælmihtig.[87] |

The one translation above accurately reflects the two dialect versions. There is a long history of seeking analogues and sources for Cædmon's *Hymn*.[88] P. L. Henry had proposed the following quatrain as a ninth-century Gaelic analogue, similar in tone and theme:

---

85 O'Donnell, *Cædmon's Hymn*, 205.
86 Note that the Old English letter ƿ (wynn; wen), derived from the runic alphabet, represents the sound /w/. In the earliest written records in Northumbrian dialect this sound is often represented by the digraph (uu) or simply (u). Note that here it is found in the later West Saxon dialect and not in the earlier Northumbrian.
87 O'Donnell, *Cædmon's Hymn*, 208. For other illustrations of dialect variations, see Smith, *Three Northumbrian Poems*, 39, 41. For an earlier discussion of both dialect versions, see Dobbie, *Anglo-Saxon Minor Poems*, xciv–c, 105–6, 198–99.
88 Most thoroughly traced in O'Donnell, *Cædmon's Hymn*, 29–59. For a recent study that sees Bede's account in an Indo-European context: Beechy, "Consumption, Purgation."

Adram in Coimdid
    cusnaib aicdib amraib,
nem gelmár co n-ainglib,
    ler tonnbán for talmain.

(Let us adore the Lord, maker of wondrous works, great bright Heaven with its angels, the white-waved sea on earth.)[89]

While it is clear that a ninth-century poem could not have influenced a seventh-century poetic act, the parallels include similar openings, themes, and structure in their short forms.[90] The theme of God as creator and emphasis on his creation was frequent in the contemporary insular world. For example, at the beginning of the seventh century in a sermon on the faith (*De fide*), Columbanus argued that in order to know God one must "understand the creation, if you wish to know the Creator" (Intellege, si vis scire Creatorem, creaturam).[91] The seventh-century grammarian Virgilius Maro Grammaticus referred frequently, in what might be described as digressions, to cosmology and the creation.[92] The seventh-century abecedarian poem from Iona, *Altus Prosator* (High Creator), was known to Aldhelm and by its very name is a poem about the Creator and His creation.[93] The *Hisperica Famina* shows that a scholar's world was concerned with the Creator's creation.[94] Exegesis on Genesis was known in the Gaelic world at the time.[95] The theme of "creation" was common in both the vernaculars and Latin of the Gaels and Anglo-Saxons.

---

**89** Murphy, *Early Irish Lyrics*, 4, 174. The poem is preserved in *Mittelirische Verslehren*, ii, §54, as an example of *breccbairdne* in which the final words of lines b and d rhyme, and all lines consonate on the final word. See also Henry, *English and Celtic Lyric*, 212.

**90** Although discussing analogues to the *Hymn*, O'Donnell dismisses this Gaelic example by saying that "What resemblances there are are almost certainly the product of their treatment of a common theme rather than direct textual influence"; O'Donnell, *Cædmon's Hymn*, 47. But his statement shows that he was thinking, as so many Anglo-Latin and Old English scholars do, in terms of a direct source for the *Hymn* rather than for a close analogue. P. L. Henry, in contrast, made compelling arguments for why the two short poems should be compared: Henry, *English and Celtic Lyric*, 213.

**91** Walker, *Sancti Columbani Opera*, 64–65 (*Instructio I*); Ó Corráin, *Clavis*, i, 416–19 §328; Sharpe, *Handlist*, 90–91 §201.

**92** Law, *Wisdom, Authority and Grammar*, 38–40; Ó Corráin, *Clavis*, ii, 717–23 §564; Sharp, *Handlist*, 704 §1882.

**93** Clancy and Márkus, *Iona*; Stevenson, "Altus Prosator"; Ó Corráin, *Clavis*, i, 374–76 §267.

**94** Herren, *Hisperica Famina: I*; Ó Corráin, *Clavis*, ii, 733–36 §570.

**95** Ó Cróinín, "Commentary on Genesis"; Ó Corráin, *Clavis*, i, 94–107 §§38–61.

The eulogistic tone of Cædmon's *Hymn* has long been recognized. In nine lines, eight phrases are used which mean "Lord."[96] The short poem can be seen as a litany listing alternative names for God based on terms for an earthly lord. Its vocabulary appears to derive from secular praise tradition applied to a religious theme. As a monastic tenant, Cædmon would have been exposed to such vocabulary shifts in the Bible. Jeff Opland noted, "it is possible that the most elevated form of early Germanic poetry was eulogy, and that the poets who propagated this tradition were intimately connected with the kingship."[97] Kemp Malone stated, "The *Hymn* as a whole follows the pattern traditional for the eulogy of a prince in the poetry native to the English."[98] J. B. Bessinger re-wrote Cædmon's "hymn" into an encomium appropriate to *Beowulf*. His alterations, without changing alliteration or meter, show how easily a secular praise poem could be created from it.

Below is Bessinger's reconstruction in "Beowulfian" style. Instead of heaven, Heorot the hall of King Hrothgar of the Scyldings is named. References to the protector and ruler of the Scyldings imply an encomium for King Hrothgar. The *Beowulf*-poet had referred to the creation of Heorot by Hrothgar at lines 67b–70 and 74–82a.[99] Bessinger's version is in the West Saxon dialect and follows the recension "for the sons of men" (*ielda/ylda bearnum*) at line 5b. The words and phrases altered from Cædmon's *Hymn* are italicized:

Nu sculon herian    *heall-ærnes* weard,
*mann-dryhtnes* meahta    and his mod-geÞanc,
weorc *weorod-Þeodnes*,    swa he wundra gehwæs,
*eorla* dryhten,    or astealde.
He ærest scop    ielda bearnum
*Heorot* to hrofe,    *helm scieldinga*;
Þa *mæran heall*    *magu-dryhte* weard,
*eorla* dryhten    æfter teode –
firum *fold-bold*    frea *scieldinga*.[100]

(Now we should praise the guardian of the hall[-building], the might of the prince of men and his purpose, the work of the band-chieftain, as he, prince of heroes, brought about the beginnings of every wondrous thing. He first made for the sons of men Heorot as a roof, protection of the Scyldings; then the guardian of the band of retainers afterwards adorned the wondrous hall, prince of heroes, the building for men, ruler of the Scyldings.)

---

**96** For a discussion of secular epithets applied to religious themes, see Strauss, "Compounding."
**97** Opland, *Anglo-Saxon Oral Poetry*, 29.
**98** Malone, "Cædmon and English Poetry," 194.
**99** Fulk, Bjork, Niles, *Klaeber's Beowulf*, 5–6. See discussion in Neville, *Representations*, 62–69.
**100** Bessinger, "Homage to Cædmon," 91.

Thus we see Bessinger replace "heavenly kingdom" (*hefaenrice/heofonrice*) with *heall-ærnes* (hall-building; 1b); the Creator (*metud/meotod*) becomes *manndryhten* (prince of men; 2a); Glorious Father (*uuldurfadur/puldorfæder*) is changed to *weorod-þeoden* (band-chieftain; 3a); the Eternal Lord twice becomes "prince of heroes" substituting *eci/ece* (*dryctin/drihten*; eternal (lord)) for *eorl* (hero; *eorla* = genitive plural; 4a, 8a); heaven (*heben/heofon*) is transformed into *Heorot* (6a), the great hall in *Beowulf*; the Holy Shaper (*haleg sceppend/ halig scyppend*) is replaced by "protection of the Scyldings" (*helm scieldinga*; 6b), solidifying the Beowulfian references; the wider "world" (*middungeard/middangeard*) is reduced to *mæran heall* (wondrous hall; 7a); "mankind's" (*moncynnæs/moncynnes*) guardian becomes a guardian for a "band of retainers" (*magu-dryht*; 7b); the earth's surface (*foldu/foldan*) is changed into a "building" (*fold-bold*; 9a); and finally, the Almighty Ruler (*frea allmectig/ælmihtig*) is reduced to another Beowulfian reference in "ruler of the Scyldings" (*frea scieldinga*; 9b).

Part of Bessinger's purpose in "rewriting" Cædmon's *Hymn* was to demonstrate how, in poetry reliant on formulae, many semantic alternatives exist with appropriate alliteration and stress patterns. By converting the hymn into a Beowulfian encomium Bessinger showed how Cædmon could have used the building blocks of Old English encomia to create a song of praise for the Creator. In Bécán mac Luigdech's poems we saw the use of encomiastic language to praise ecclesiastical rather than secular leaders. Cædmon applied the same technique which was repeated in subsequent Old English poems. Both traditions found this precedent in the Bible.[101]

The Anglo-Saxons were in regular contact with neighbors who had their own tradition of encomiastic, panegyric verse such as poems attributed to Taliesin and Aneirin that dealt with conflicts between the Britons and Anglo-Saxons. Similarly, Gaelic poets praised illustrious ancestors and their deeds. Early in the Gaelic tradition Colmán mac Lénéni and Bécán mac Luigdech praised both secular and ecclesiastical leaders.

## Cenn Fáelad *sapiens* (d. 679)

The most famous of the *sapientes* is Cenn Fáelad mac Ailello, a member of Cenél nÉogain, the same northern Uí Néill branch to which Bécán mac Luigdech and King Aldfrith *sapiens* belonged.[102] Cenn Fáelad and Aldfrith appear together

---

[101] This argument was made several decades ago: Howlett, "Theology."
[102] History and legend are mixed in the story of Cenn Fáelad: see, McCone, *Pagan Past*, 23–24, 41–42, 75; Nagy, *Conversing with Angels*, 4; Ireland, "Learning of a *Sapiens*," 68–71; Ireland, "Case of Cenn Fáelad."

in the same genealogy.[103] An important Middle Gaelic etiological legend grew up around Cenn Fáelad that involved the syncretism of Latinate and native forms of learning. He is associated with the ecclesiastical establishment at Derryloran (*Daire Lúráin*, Co. Tyrone) in Uí Thuirtri territory. All texts associated with Cenn Fáelad are in Old Gaelic. None, however, have yet been dated firmly on linguistic criteria to the seventh century.

Modern scholars first noticed Cenn Fáelad because several quatrains in annal entries of the sixth and seventh centuries are attributed to him.[104] The quatrains had been added by later scribes as authenticating witnesses to information in annals about battles of the Northern Uí Néill, often against Leinster neighbors.[105] These isolated quatrains suggest that Cenn Fáelad composed poems about Uí Néill families similar to those preserved in the Leinster genealogies.

A poem in an early eighth-century prose narrative is attributed to Cenn Fáelad. *Brislech Mór Maige Muirthemni* (the Great Rout of Muirthemne Plain) contains an episode described as the "Death of Cú Chulainn."[106] The twenty-four-line poem is about Cú Chulainn's death and the numbers that he slew.[107] The editor, Bettina Kimpton, noted that the poem has linguistic features that point to a late seventh- or early eighth-century date.[108] It may be the earliest surviving text attributed to Cenn Fáelad. The poem has features of *dindśenchas* (place lore), noting locations of significant events and the place of Cú Chulainn's death at Airbe Rofir.[109] It is introduced with the following words: "Conid dé as·bert Cenn Fáelad mac Ailella i nAidedaib Ulad" (So it is of that Cenn Fáelad mac Ailella said in the Death-tales of the Ulstermen).[110] The use of a dative plural (*aidedaib*) implies that Cenn Fáelad had contributed to more than one "death tale" (*aided*).[111] This line implies that his contribution to the preservation of early vernacular narratives may have been greater than other evidence suggests. Cenn Fáelad will be discussed further in chapter four.

---

103 O'Brien, *Corpus genealogiarum Hiberniae*, 135 (140 a 37–40); Ireland, "Irish Genealogies," 68–69, 72–73n50.
104 See, for example, the survey of annalistic verse in Mc Carthy, *Irish Annals*, 364–67.
105 Mac Néill, "Pioneer of Nations."
106 Kimpton, *Death of Cú Chulainn*; Ó Corráin, *Clavis*, iii, 1269–71 §960.
107 Kimpton, *Death of Cú Chulainn*, 24–25, 43–44 §24.
108 Kimpton, *Death of Cú Chulainn*, 61.
109 Kimpton, *Death of Cú Chulainn*, 24, 43 §24; 26, 44 §27.
110 Kimpton, *Death of Cú Chulainn*, 24, 43 §24. The introduction implies that Cenn Fáelad had input into other "death tales."
111 For arguments that such an "anthology" once existed, see Clancy, "Die Like a Man?" 82–84.

## Banbán *sapiens* (d. 686)

Banbán is another seventh-century *sapiens* who composed in the vernacular. He is associated in the Annals of Tigernach and the Fragmentary Annals with Kildare (*Cill Dara*) and has been described as *fer léigind* or *scriba* there.[112] In other sources he is associated with Old Leighlin (*Lethglenn*, Co. Carlow)[113] not far from Rath Melsigi where Anglo-Saxons trained. Banbán is named in the seventh-century commentaries on the Catholic Epistles where he is associated with Manchéne of Min Droichit (d. 652) and Laidcenn *sapiens* (d. 661).[114] The vernacular law-tract *Cáin Fhuithirbe*, which survives only in fragments, is attributed in part to Banbán.[115] The text's ecclesiastical background is clear from its contents. It is associated with Munster in style and content, including its name.[116] It has been dated ca. 680.[117]

Banbán is credited with writing *Cáin Fhuithirbe* as part of a team.[118] Although fragmentary, reconstructed text relies on linking and internal alliteration for ornamentation, and some is written as syllabic verse. Liam Breatnach demonstrated its ecclesiastical associations which stress the relationship between secular rulers and the Church, implying cooperation between their hierarchies. Such preoccupations suggest the genre of *speculum principum* and the vernacular *Audacht Morainn*[119] and the Latin *De duodecim abusivis*.[120] Banbán will be discussed further in chapter four.

---

[112] Ireland, "Learning of a *Sapiens*," 71. For *fer léigind*, see Stokes, "Annals of Tigernach," 209 [Felinfach i, 169]). For *scriba*, see Radner, *Fragmentary Annals*, 36–37.
[113] Stokes, *Félire Óengusso*, 248 (scholium for November 26); Ireland, "Learning of a *sapiens*," 72; Ó Riain, *Dictionary*, 85.
[114] Ó Corráin, *Clavis*, i, 125–26 §94; Grosjean, "Quelques Exégètes," 78–80; Breatnach, "*Cáin Fhuithirbe*," 47; Richter, *Ireland and Neighbhours*, 192; Ó Corráin, "Church and Secular Society," 301.
[115] Breatnach, "*Cáin Fhuithirbe*," 46–47; Ó Corráin, *Clavis*, ii, 911–14 §§683–84.
[116] Fuithirbe has been located in the Muckross Demesne near Loch Léin in Co. Kerry: Ó Coileáin, "Mag Fuithirbe Revisited," 24–26.
[117] It was first dated to between 678 and 683 by Binchy, "*Uraicecht Becc*," 53. In his edition of some of the fragments Liam Breatnach stated of Binchy's dating of the text, "there can be no objection to this conclusion"; Breatnach, "*Cáin Fhuithirbe*," 46; Breatnach, *Companion*, 216–18.
[118] "Díblíne is said to have instituted *Cáin Fhuithirbe*, Banbán to have written it, and Amairgen to have arranged it"; Breatnach, "*Cáin Fhuithirbe*," 46.
[119] Kelly, *Audacht Morainn*; Ó Corráin, *Clavis*, ii, 1188–90 §908.
[120] The most obvious relationship here is with the section on the *rex iniquus*: Clayton, *Two Ælfric Texts*; Ó Corráin, *Clavis*, ii, 745–48 §576.

## Aldhelm (d. 709)

Aldhelm is the first Anglo-Saxon man of letters and a noted poet in Latin.[121] He served as abbot of Malmesbury (ca. 675–705) and bishop of Sherborne (705–709). Towards the end of his *Epistola ad Acircium*, an erudite letter to King Aldfrith *sapiens*, he boasted of himself that "no one born of the offspring of our race and nourished in the cradles of a Germanic people has toiled so mightily in a pursuit of this sort before our humble self."[122] Aldhelm is acknowledged as an Anglo-Latin poet for his *Enigmata*,[123] for his *Carmen de Virginitate*,[124] and for his *Carmen rhythmicum*,[125] among other works. Bede recognized Aldhelm's learning and described him as a *vir undecumque doctissimus* (*HE* v 18), a phrase he also used of Aldfrith *sapiens* (*HE* v 12). In Aldhelm's "letter" to Aldfrith, which included detailed discussion of poetry and metrics, Aldhelm displayed knowledge of Roman and late Antique poets and grammarians.[126] He also knew the work of Virgilius Maro Grammaticus and the *Altus Prosator*, an abecedarian poem from Iona.[127] According to William of Malmesbury, his teacher had been the Gael Máeldub who gave his name to Malmesbury (*Maildubi urbs*), where Aldhelm served as abbot (*HE* v 18).[128] Aldhelm displayed the learning he acquired from both the Gaels and the Continent.

If Aldhelm composed in the vernacular, none of his poems survive. Some modern critics include Aldhelm among Old English poets based on a story told in the twelfth-century *Gesta pontificum* by William of Malmesbury where it is said he composed vernacular poems and performed on the harp to attract people into church.[129] Faricius, who wrote a late tenth-century *life* of Aldhelm, also implied

---

121 Sharpe, *Handlist*, 46 §89.
122 Lapidge and Herren, *Aldhelm*, 45; Lapidge and Rosier, *Aldhelm*, 19.
123 Pitman, *Riddles of Aldhelm*; Lapidge and Rosier, *Aldhelm*, 61–69 (introduction), 70–94 (translation). For an illustration of a manuscript, see Breay and Story, *Anglo-Saxon Kingdoms*, 104–5.
124 Lapidge and Rosier, *Aldhelm*, 97–101 (introduction), 102–67 (translation).
125 Lapidge and Rosier, *Aldhelm*, 171–76 (introduction), 177–79 (translation); Barker, *Aldhelm and Sherborne*: the end of this volume includes separate translations of the poem by Michael Lapidge, David Howlett, and Katherine Barker.
126 Lapidge and Herren, *Aldhelm*, 31–32.
127 Orchard, *Poetic Art of Aldhelm*, 54–60; Stevenson, "Altus Prosator." For an edition, translation, and attribution of the poem to Virgilius, see Howlett, "'Altus Prosator'."
128 Winterbottom, *William of Malmesbury*, i, 502–5, c. 5 §189.
129 Winterbottom, *William of Malmesbury*, i, 506–7, c. 5 §190; Frank, "Anglo-Saxon Oral Poet"; Niles, "Anglo-Saxon Oral Poet." For a discussion of Aldhelm as a possible vernacular poet see Opland, *Anglo-Saxon Oral Poetry*, 120–29; Lapidge, "Aldhelm's Latin Poetry"; Thornbury, *Becoming a Poet*, 135–59.

that Aldhelm successfully used his "eloquence" to attract people to attend mass, but said nothing specific about producing poetry in the vernacular.[130]

Aldhelm is referred to as a "noble *scop*" (*æþele sceop*) in a single tenth-century manuscript in a macaronic poem inserted before the salutation of his *Prosa de virginitate*.[131] His reliance on formulae in Latin poetry suggests his familiarity with Old English poetry. Michael Lapidge suggested that his rather wooden quantitative Latin poems rely too much on formulae.[132] David Howlett suggested that the Leiden Riddle may represent a Northumbrian translation of an *enigma* by Aldhelm done at Aldfrith's court.[133]

Ute Schwab examined the possibility that Aldhelm preceded Cædmon as a vernacular poet.[134] William of Malmesbury made very little of Bede's Cædmon, referring to him without naming him, but he made a great deal more of Aldhelm as a vernacular poet, declaring that Aldhelm was a favorite of King Alfred's as related in his *Handboc* which no longer survives.[135] William's championing of Aldhelm over Cædmon may be no more than his Wessex bias. Many modern critics include Aldhelm among the named Old English poets although no vernacular works by him survive. The differences between the two are vast. Cædmon was an illiterate layman, advanced in years when his inspired poetic skills were revealed. Aldhlem was a well educated ecclesiastic who, apparently, eschewed any notion of relying on inspiration, divine or otherwise.[136] Appendix 4.a views Aldhelm in the larger Gaelic world.

## Aldfrith *sapiens* (d. 704)

King Aldfrith *sapiens* descended through his mother from the Cenél nÉogain, the same Uí Néill sept to which Cenn Fáelad *sapiens* and Bécán mac Luigdech belonged. As king of Northumbria he drew together the intellectual worlds of the

---

130 O'Donnell, *Cædmon's Hymn*, 13–14 §1.22, 39–41 §§2.17–19, 43–44 §2.22.
131 The manuscript is Cambridge, Corpus Christi College, MS 326: Thornbury, *Becoming a Poet*, 24; Howlett, *British Books*, 285; Dempsey, "High Ecclesiasticism," 49.
132 Lapidge, "Aldhelm's Latin Poetry," see notes in article. Despite Lapidge's suggestion that Aldhelm's quantitative poetry is unimaginative, Thornbury suggests that Aldhelm hoped that Aldfrith would learn to compose quantitative verse from him: Thornbury, *Becoming a Poet*, 153.
133 Howlett, *British Books*, 288; Dobbie, *Anglo-Saxon Minor Poems*, cviii–cx, 109, 199–201; Smith, *Three Northumbrian Poems*, 17–19, 44, 46.
134 Schwab, *Caedmon*; Schwab, "Miracles of Cædmon."
135 Lapidge, "Aldhelm's Latin Poetry," 228–29. Frank, "Anglo-Saxon Oral Poet."
136 Thornbury, "Aldhelm's Rejection."

Gaels and Anglo-Saxons, including Southumbrians, through his personal relationships with his contemporaries, Adomnán of Iona and Aldhelm of Malmesbury.

After Aldfrith ascended the throne Aldhelm sent him the compilation known as the *Epistola ad Acircium*.[137] From the personal nature of the exordium and epilogue it is clear that Aldhelm and Aldfrith had studied together in their youths. Unfortunately, no location can be firmly established, although it was among the Gaels, probably in Ireland. It is plausible that they studied at Bangor together.[138] Aldfrith's connections to Bangor are discussed in chapter four.

Adomnán of Iona referred to Aldfrith as *Aldfridus amicus*. On a visit ca. 687, Adomnán presented him with a copy of *De locis sanctis* and Aldfrith ensured its distribution throughout his kingdom. Bede was one beneficiary and created an epitome of the work ca. 703, which may have been dedicated to Aldfrith, as discussed in Appendix 4.b. Two chapters of Bede's *Historia ecclesiastica* recapitulate material derived from *De locis sanctis* (*HE* v 16–17).[139]

A large collection of maxims, known as *Bríathra Flainn Fhína maic Ossu*, are ascribed to Flann Fína mac Ossu, that is, Aldfrith son of Oswiu.[140] The texts are linguistically Old Gaelic, but as preserved cannot be dated firmly to the seventh century. Within the collection is a poem which contrasts the benefits of *ecnae*, a Gaelic word that frequently translates *sapientia*, with the deficiencies of *láechdacht* (the lay life) (Figure 4.c). Aldfrith *sapiens* and these wisdom texts will be discussed in chapter four. King Aldfrith will be discussed in chapter five.

## Adomnán (d. 704)

Adomnán was abbot of Iona from 679 to 704. Like Iona's founder, Columba, he was of the Cenél Conaill branch of the northern Uí Néill. Adomnán is known for three major works, two written in Latin and one in Gaelic. Shorter works in both languages are also attributed to him. Adomnán's best known work among the Gaels is *Vita sancti Columbae*, the life of St. Colum Cille, Iona's founder.[141] His

---

[137] For an introduction, see Lapidge and Herren, *Aldhelm*, 31–33 (discussion), 34–47 (translation).
[138] Ireland, "Where Was King Aldfrith Educated?" 37–40.
[139] For the possible dedication, see Hunter Blair, *World of Bede*, 185–86. For a translation of Bede's epitome, see Foley and Holder, *Bede*, 1–25. The two chapters in the *Historia* are derived from Bede's epitome: Brown and Biggs, *Bede*, ii, 13.
[140] Ireland, *Bríathra Flainn Fhína maic Ossu*; Ó Corráin, *Clavis*, ii, 1190–92 §909.
[141] Anderson and Anderson, *Life of Columba*; Ó Corráin, *Clavis*, i, 280–90 §230; Sharpe, *Handlist*, 25 §49.

most widely renowned work was *De locis sanctis*.[142] After Adomnán presented a copy to Aldfrith *sapiens* the latter ensured its distribution throughout Northumbria (*HE* v 15).[143] Bede created an epitome and cited parts in *Historia ecclesiastica* (*HE* v 16–17).[144]

A short Latin poem preserved in an Anglo-Saxon prayer book originally from Winchester is very likely by Adomnán (London, British Library, Cotton Galba A.xiv).[145] *Adiutor laborantium* has the quality of a petition and the style of a litany which lists titles or epithets for God, a stylistic feature noted previously in Cædmon's vernacular *Hymn*.

Adomnán also wrote the vernacular law-tract *Cáin Adomnáin* (known as *Lex Innocentium* in Latin), intended to protect non-combatants[146] and promulgated in 697 at a synod at Birr (*Birra*) in Ireland's midlands.[147] The guarantor list for this law-tract reveals Adomnán's adept abilities as diplomat and statesman. It includes both ecclesiastical and secular authorities across Ireland and Britain throughout Gaelic regions, several Picts, and even an Anglo-Saxon present in Ireland.[148]

Among the lesser-known vernacular poetic texts ascribed to Adomnán is *Colum Cille co Día domm eráil* (May Colum Cille commend me to God).[149] This poem is found in the manuscripts with the *Amrae Coluim Chille*. It has qualities of *loricae* and emphasizes the notion of *snádud* (protection). It is sometimes referred to as a *cathbarr* (battle helmet), but also as a hymn or prayer. It is an alliterating, unrhymed poem.

James Carney felt that the ascription to Adomnán of the vernacular poem beginning *A maccucáin, sruith in tíag* (Young boy, venerable is the satchel)

---

142 Meehan, *De Locis Sanctis*; Ó Corráin, *Clavis*, ii, 727–32 §§568–69.
143 Meehan, *De Locis Sanctis*, 3–6; Colgrave and Mynors, *Ecclesiastical History*, 508–9.
144 For a translation of the epitome, see Foley and Holder, *Bede*, 1–25. For the chapters Bede included in his *History*, see Colgrave and Mynors, *Ecclesiastical History*, 508–13; Brown and Biggs, *Bede*, ii, 13.
145 Clancy and Márkus, *Iona*, 69–80, 235n3; Gneuss and Lapidge, *Anglo-Saxon Manuscripts*, 256 §333. For a discussion of the poem and its authorship, see Márkus, "*Adiutor laborantium*."
146 Meyer, *Cáin Adamnáin*; Ní Dhonnchadha, "Birr and the Law of the Innocents"; Ní Dhonnchadha, "Law of Adomnán"; Ó Corráin, *Clavis*, ii, 802–3 §622.
147 Mac Airt and Mac Niocaill, *Annals of Ulster*, 156–57; Stokes, "Annals of Tigernach," 215 [Felinfach i 175].
148 Ní Dhonnchadha, "Guarantor List." Ichtbricht epscop (bishop Wihtberht) is listed at no. 29, but this person was identified by Ní Dhonnchadha with Ecgberht of Rath Melsigi: Ní Dhonnchadha, "Guarantor List," 180, 193–94. Dáibhí Ó Cróinín corrected that identification to Wihtberht: Ó Cróinín, "Rath Melsigi, Willibrord," 25–26.
149 See Clancy and Márkus, *Iona*, 164–76; Ó Corráin, *Clavis*, i, 342–48 §251 (at 346).

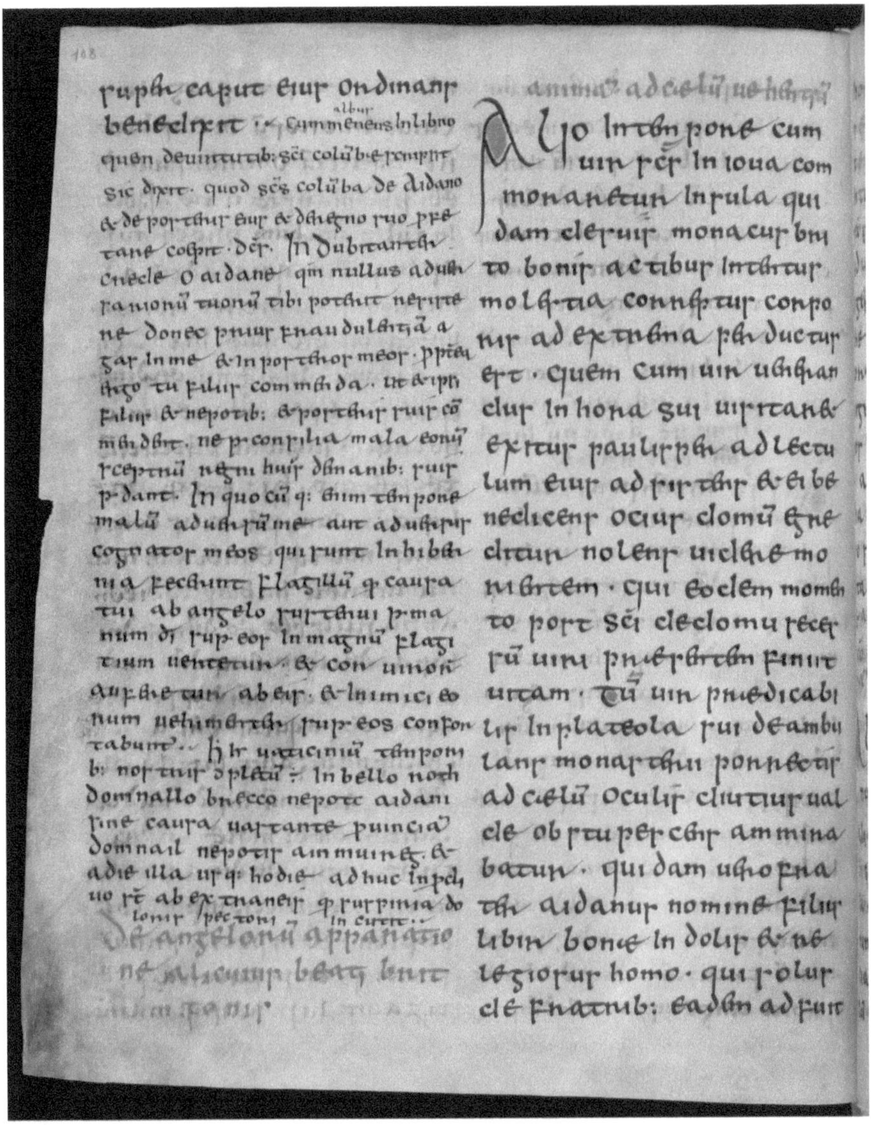

**Figure 2.b:** The left-hand column pictured here from the Schauffhausen manuscript, Generalia I, page 108, contains what survives of *De virtutibus sancti Columbae* by Cummeneus Albus (657–669), abbot of Iona. It has been incorporated into Adomnán's *Vita Columbae* (688x704). The scribe was Dorbbéne (d. 713). Schaffhausen, Stadtbibliothek, Gen. 1: Adamnanus de Iona, Vita Columbae. (http://e-codices.ch/en/list/one/sbs/0001).

should be accepted.[150] Although surviving manuscript versions proved difficult to reconstruct, he concluded "on linguistic grounds there is no reason to reject the authorship of Adomnán."[151] It contains nineteen quatrains with the rhyming pattern bd. Carney argued that the poem was intended as a metaphorical expression of the "relics" and other contents of a young scholar's book satchel.[152] It included the Four Gospels, the Acts of the Apostles, important saints like the desert fathers Paul and Anthony, Sulpicius Severus's *Life* of St. Martin, and an array of Early Gaelic saints. The most recent saint named was Mo-Chutu (a hypocoristic form for Carthach) of Lismore, Co. Waterford and Rathan, Co. Offaly (d. 637).[153]

The *lorica* qualities of the poem can be seen in verbs derived from *snádud* (protection) in its first and eighteenth stanzas, reproduced below respectively:

A maccucáin, sruith in tíag
    nod·gaibi fort muin;
méite nom·snádad i tíag
    for tír ocus muir.

(Young boy, venerable (*sruith*) is the satchel you take upon your back; it were a likely thing that that it would protect me when I travel on land or sea.)[154]

Noíb do·ruirmius – rígdae a ndám –
    rom· snádat sech drong
com chorp ocus com anmain
    óm chiunn com da bonn.

(The saints I have enumerated – kingly their company – may they protect me against a host (= an evil host), my body and soul from my head to my two feet.)[155]

The second half of the first stanza creates the picture of someone who expects to have to "travel on land and sea" as part of his duties as Adomnán himself

---

**150** Carney, "*A maccucáin*"; for a diplomatic edition, see Ó Riain, *Corpus Genealogiarum Sanctorum Hiberniae*, 163–65 §714; Ó Corráin, *Clavis*, ii, 1151 §862.
**151** Carney, "*A maccucáin*," 30.
**152** Clancy and Márkus left this poem out of their book on Iona's poetry because they felt that the cult of relics would not have developed that early: Clancy and Márkus, *Iona*, 166. However, Cummian's letter of ca. 632 mentions testifying before relics: Walsh and Ó Cróinín, *Cummian's Letter*, 94–95, lines 283–88. Bishop Colmán, after the "synod" of Whitby, arrived in Inishboffin from Iona in 668 "with relics of the saints" to establish a monastery there: Mac Airt and Mac Niocaill, *Annals of Ulster*, 138–39. See further discussion in Wycherley, *Cult of Relics*.
**153** Mac Airt and Mac Niocaill, *Annals of Ulster*, 120–21; Stokes, "Annals of Tigernach," 184 [Felinfach, i 144]; Ó Riain, *Dictionary*, 470–73.
**154** Carney, "*A maccucáin*," 32 §1.
**155** Carney, "*A maccucáin*," 36 §18.

had done. The second quatrain above is clear in its qualities as a *lorica* which stresses both spiritual and physical protection.[156] It is easy to imagine the contents of the satchel as containing a small pocket Bible or, more specifically, the Gospels, from the following verse:

> Fil and soiscélae in maicc máir
>   Maire maínig múaid;
> is findithir gelbáin ngréin
>   lebrán Eöin úaig.
>
> (There is the gospel of the great Son, treasure-endowed and famous, of Mary;
> Fair as the gleaming white sun is the booklet of virgin John.)[157]

The traditions of Iona during Adomnán's time followed the *latercus* in the Easter practice which meant that they privileged the Gospel of John over the Synoptic Gospels.[158] This can be seen in the arguments placed in the mouths of those at the "synod" of Whitby in both Stephen of Ripon's and Bede's versions.[159] But, whether they followed the *latercus* or were orthodox in Easter practices, the Gaels tended to revere the apostle John as *Eoin bruinne* (John of the breast) and considered him the most beloved apostle of Jesus.[160]

However, Bede claimed that Adomnán, after a visit to Aldfrith's Northumbria ca. 687, having been "earnestly advised by many who were better instructed than himself," decided to alter his observance of Easter and followed orthodox practices.[161] Adomnán apparently became an advocate for orthodox Paschal traditions and, according to Bede, endeavored to convince many to alter their practices, but he was never able to convince his own monastery of Iona.[162]

If we accept Bede's version of Adomnán's efforts to convert Gaels who followed the *latercus*, then the last quatrain has special significance for the diplomatic

---

156 We see these same features in the *lorica* of Laidcenn *sapiens* (d. 661): Herren, *Hisperica Famina: II*, 76–89; Howlett, "Five Experiments," 8–18.
157 Carney, "*A maccucáin*," 32 §2.
158 Pelteret, "Apostolic Authority."
159 Colgrave, *Life of Bishop Wilfrid*, 20–23, c. 10; Colgrave and Mynors, *Ecclesiastical History*, 294–309, bk. iii, c. 25. For a full development of these ideas, see Pelteret, "Apostolic Authority."
160 Walsh and Ó Cróinín, *Cummian's Letter*, 69n89; Monge Allen, "Metamorphosis of *Eoin Bruinne*."
161 "sed et a pluribus, qui erant eruditiores, esset sollerter admonitus": Colgrave and Mynors, *Ecclesiastical History*, 506–7, bk. v, c. 15. For discussion of Adomnán in Northumbria, see Ireland, "Lutting of Lindisfarne."
162 Immo Warntjes has argued that Adomnán converted from the *latercus* to the Dionysiac method at this time which put him at odds with both his own monastery of Iona and with the Gaels of Ireland who followed the Victorian reckoning: Warntjes, "Victorius vs Dionysius."

mission Adomnán had set himself. Keep in mind that the *Cáin Adomnáin* of 697 confirms his negotiating abilities and diplomatic skills. The following quatrain suggests that Adomnán did not wish to alienate those who disagreed with him regarding that "strange and wonderful tale" of the crucifixion and resurrection related at Easter:

> Ciped cruth nond·ráidet Scuitt
> a scél n-amra n-aitt,
> sruith a n-aithne ad·noär duitt,
> 'Ba idan, a maicc.'
>
> (Whatever be the manner in which the Scotti [Gaels] relate that strange and wonderful tale, wise is the injunction that is given to you: Be worthy (*idan*), my son.)[163]

Adomnán endeavored throughout his career to be a peacemaker and negotiator of conflicting traditions.[164] Adomnán represents the monastically trained Gaelic intellectual of the seventh century who was as comfortable producing works in Latin as in the vernacular, or in prose as well as in verse. His contributions will be discussed further in chapter four.

## Bede (d. 735)

Bede himself is named among the likely Old English poets. He is most famous for the *Historia ecclesiastica*.[165] At the end of the *Historia* he listed extensively his works composed in Latin (*HE* v 24). In his letter to Bishop Ecgberht, Bede related that he had translated the Apostles' Creed and the Lord's Prayer into Old English for many ignorant priests.[166] He felt this was necessary for the benefit of lay people so that they might chant them. The *Epistola Cuthberti de obitu Bedae* stated that Bede was translating certain texts into the vernacular including the Gospel of John, up to a specific point, and a section of Isidore's "On the Wonders of Nature," with which he had disagreements.[167] While no vernacular

---

163 Carney, "*A maccucáin*," 36 §19.
164 See the arguments in Stancliffe, "'Charity with Peace'."
165 Bede recorded a long list of works which he himself wrote: *HE* v 24. The critical literature on Bede is extensive: Sharpe, *Handlist*, 70–76 §152. See further Hunter Blair, *World of Bede*; Bonner, *Famulus Christi*; Brown, *Bede the Venerable*; Brown and Biggs, *Bede*. For Bede's interest in understanding the Bible, see Biggs, "Two Scribal Additions." For Bede as poet, see Lapidge, *Bede the Poet*.
166 Grocock and Wood, *Abbots of Wearmouth*, 130–33 §5 (*Epistola Bede ad Ecgbertvm Episcopvm*).
167 Colgrave and Mynors, *Ecclesiastical History*, 582–83 (*Epistola de obitu Bedae*).

texts survive that can be confidently assigned to Bede, it is certain that he translated Latin texts into the vernacular. However, it cannot be firmly established whether or not he composed vernacular texts.

A five-line poem called Bede's "Death Song" is included in the Northumbrian dialect in some copies of the *Epistola Cuthberti*, written shortly after his death.[168] It is the one surviving vernacular verse attributed to Bede. Cuthbert stated simply that it is a poem he knew and recited "in our own language, for he was familiar with English poetry, speaking of the soul's dread departure from the body."[169] This poem, because of its brevity, diction, and subject matter, provides little information about Old English poetic tradition or Bede's rôle, if any, in developing it. Unlike Bede's account of Cædmon, Cuthbert's letter quotes the poem in Old English, not in Latin. This short poem has been preserved, like Cædmon's *Hymn*, in both Northumbrian and West Saxon dialects and shared a similar manuscript history.[170] Below is the Northumbrian version followed by a copy of the West Saxon version. The translation comes from the edition by Colgrave and Mynors:

Fore thaem neidfaerae      naenig uuiurthit
thoncsnotturra,            than him tharf sie
to ymbhycggannae           aer his hiniongae
huaet his gastae           godaes aeththa yflaes
aefter deothdaege          doemid uueorthae.[171]

(Facing that enforced journey, no man can be
More prudent than he has good call to be,
If he consider, before his going hence,
What for his spirit of good hap or of evil
After his day of death shall be determined.)[172]

---

**168** Colgrave and Mynors, *Ecclesiastical History*, 582–83. For further discussion of the context in which the poem appears, see Bolton, "*Epistola Cuthberti*"; Twomey, "*Bede's Death Song*"; Bredehoft, *Authors, Audiences*, 20–23.
**169** "in nostra quoque lingua, ut erat doctus in nostris carminibus, dicens de terribili exitu animarum e corpore": Colgrave and Mynors, *Ecclesiastical History*, 580–81n4. George Hardin Brown stated that "there is no compelling evidence that he composed the five-line poem": Brown, *Bede the Venerable*, 77. But later he came to accept it as composed by Bede: Brown and Biggs, *Bede*, i, 217–18; Michael Lapidge concurred: Lapidge, *Bede's Latin Poetry*, 39, 553–55.
**170** Dobbie, *Anglo-Saxon Minor Poems*, c–cvii, 107–8; Dobbie, *Manuscripts*; Smith, *Three Northumbrian Poems*, 4–7, 15–17, 23–26, 42–43.
**171** Dobbie, *Anglo-Saxon Minor Poems*, 107.
**172** Translation in Colgrave and Mynors, *Ecclesiastical History*, 583.

Below is the later West Saxon version of Bede's "Death Song" for which the translation above is appropriate:

| For þam nedfere | næni wyrþeþ |
|---|---|
| þances snotera, | þonne him þearf sy |
| to gehicgenne | ær his heonengange |
| hwæt his gaste | godes oþþe yfeles |
| æfter deaþe heonon | demed weorþe.[173] |

A specific source for such a succinct poem is unlikely to be identified. There are several analogous Latin texts by Gaelic scholars that deal with the transitory nature of the world and the inevitability of impending death. One example is the longish poem by Columbanus, *De mundi transitu*. It is a much more substantial work and does not attempt to limit itself to aphoristic crispness. Columbanus wrote the poem in the late sixth century before he departed for the continent.[174] A short passage that comes from a Gaelic writer that Bede knew, Virgilius Maro Grammaticus, is more succinct and yet conveys that same consciousness of inevitable death. Vivien Law, in discussing Virgilius's rhetorical style and contents, quoted from fragments: "Wisdom reveals itself only to those who despise greed. Contempt of greed is not to be found without mindfulness of roving death."[175] There is much in these philosophical fragments that would have appealed to Bede.

A ninth-century Gaelic quatrain from the margins of Codex Boernerianus (Dresden, Saxon State Library, MS A 145b) of the circle of Sedulius on the continent, echoes the tone and message in the poem "that Bede knew." While it is close to the Old English poem in content, it can only be an analogue given its later date:

Mór báis, mór baile
    mór coll céille, mór mire
olais airchenn teicht do écaib
    beith fo étoil maic Muire.[176]

---

[173] Dobbie, *Anglo-Saxon Minor Poems*, 108; see a variant at Smith, *Three Northumbrian Poems*, 43. For a discussion of both dialect versions, see Dobbie, *Anglo-Saxon Minor Poems*, c–cvii, 107–8, 199.

[174] For an edition of the poem, see Walker, *Sancti Columbani Opera*, 182–85. For discussions, see Schaller, "Siebensilberstrophen 'de mundi transitu'"; Schaller, "'De mundi transitu'."

[175] "Sapientia non nisi contemptoribus cupiditatis apparet. Cupiditatis autem contemptus sine uagi leti recordatione non accipitur": Law, "*Epitomae* of Virgilius," 121.

[176] Stokes and Strachan, *Thesaurus*, ii, 296.

(Much folly, much frenzy,
Much loss of sense, much madness (it is),
Since going to death is certain,
To be under the displeasure of Mary's son.)[177]

There is much in the career of Bede that acknowledges his debt to Gaelic intellectual culture, as reviewed in Appendix 4.b. The Gaels reciprocated by referring to Bede to as *sapiens* in the annals.[178] That title places him among the respected *sapientes* of the Gaelic world.[179] A few centuries later a portion of his *Historia ecclesiastica* was translated into Middle Gaelic.[180]

## The Significance of Dialect

Both Cædmon's *Hymn* and the so-called "Death Song" of Bede are preserved in Northumbrian and West Saxon dialects. Four major dialects have long been recognized in Old English texts: Northumbrian, Mercian, Kentish, and West Saxon.[181] In longer poems, such as *Beowulf*, a blend of dialect forms is evident throughout and aids philologists in linguistic dating of the poem.[182] Some feel that the blend of dialects represented a *koinē*, a common poetic dialect that blended forms from each region, and that each *scop* and *gleoman* could avail of this poetic dialect when composing or performing.[183]

If there was a poetic *koinē*, it implies the existence of training or schooling, for which no evidence survives.[184] *Widsith* and *Deor* suggest the existence of professional status dependent upon patronage from secular chieftains. The emphasis on oral-formulaic composition and "learning by listening" provides

---

**177** See Flower, *Irish Tradition*, 39–40 for translation of the poem and description of its background as coming from the "circle of Sedulius."
**178** Mac Airt and Mac Niocaill, *Annals of Ulster*, 188–89 s.a. 735; Stokes, "Annals of Tigernach," 239 [Felinfach i 199]; Mac Airt, *Annals of Inisfallen*, 106–7 s.a. 735.
**179** For an overview of *sapientes*, see Johnston, *Literacy and Identity*, 102–12; Ireland, "Learning of a *Sapiens*."
**180** Ní Chatháin, "Bede's Ecclesiastical History."
**181** These dialects are noted in any standard grammar of the Old English language: Moore and Knott, *Elements of Old English*, 1; Mitchell and Robinson, *Guide to Old English*, 11, 118–19; Baker, *Old English*, 9–10.
**182** Fulk, Bjork, Niles, *Klaeber's Beowulf*, cxxix–clix, especially cliv–clix §§28–30. For perspectives on the importance of linguistic issues, see Fulk, "*Beowulf* and Language History."
**183** Fulk, Bjork, Niles, *Klaeber's Beowulf*, cliv–clv §28.
**184** Thornbury, *Becoming a Poet*, 34–36.

**Figure 2.c:** There are four major dialects of Old English: Kentish, West Saxon, Mercian, Northumbrian. The two northern dialects are sometimes classed under the rubric Anglian. Early Gaelic does not preserve identifiable dialects in surviving written forms, although diachronic changes are traceable in the language from the earliest written records through the seventeenth century. The formal training of the poets, scholars, and jurists is the most likely reason for this linguistic uniformity that survived until the dismantling of the Gaelic order.

the best scenario for an informal, yet apparently effective, system of training among poets of Old English.[185]

Kenneth Sisam argued in the 1950s that the dialect-leveling evident in the Old English poetic corpus suggested a poetic *koinē*. As he stated:

> More attention should be given to the probability that there was a body of verse, anonymous and independent of local interest, which was the common stock for the entertainment or instruction of the English people . . . . A poet might prefer to take his models from the common stock rather than from the less-known work of his own district. In this way poems could be produced that do not belong to any local dialect.[186]

In contrast to Old English, Old Gaelic written records do not reveal regional dialect distinctions even though diachronic language change can be traced through the centuries.[187] Modern Gaelic has clear regional dialects whose basis must have existed in the past. But centuries of written evidence do not reveal identifiable regional dialects. The formal training and freedom to travel of the Gaelic poets, jurists, and ecclesiastical scholars appear to be the best explanation for this uniformity.

Attempts to identify dialectal variation in the early language have concentrated on regional preferences for animal names or the distribution of placename forms.[188] While slight differences have been detected, they do not lead to the identification of regional dialects. Early records distinguish levels of register and distinctions in varieties of language so that, for example, *gnáthbérla* (everyday language) is distinguished from *bérla na filed* (language of the poets), *bérla Féne* (jurists' language), *iarmbérla* (cryptic language). The term *bérla etarscartha* (divided language) suggests that the pseudo-etymological parsing found in Isidore's *Etymologiae* also applied to the vernacular.[189] Although the later metathesized form *bérla* (language) has been used here, the original form *bélrae* reveals its etymology as what is produced with the *bél* (mouth).[190]

---

[185] Magoun, "Bede's Story of Cædmon"; Fry, "Formulaic Poet." Fry based his arguments on Albert Lord's *Singer of Tales*, 21–26. For a synopsis, see O'Donnell, *Cædmon's Hymn*, 3–4, 23–24, 67–68.

[186] Sisam, *Old English Literature*, 138. For a book length study, see Opland, *Anglo-Saxon Oral Poetry*.

[187] Thurneysen, *Grammar of Old Irish*, 12 §16; McCone, "An tSean-Ghaeilge," 63 §1.7; Russell, "'What was best of every language'," 439–43.

[188] For animal names, see Kelly, "Dialekte im Altirischen?"; Russell, "'What was best of every language'," 442. For placenames, see Murray, "Dialect in Medieval Irish?".

[189] For these terms, see Calder, *Auraicept na n-Éces*, 100–105; Russell, "'What was best of every language'," 448–49.

[190] eDIL: http://www.dil.ie, s.v. *bélrae* or dil.ie/5638.

Evidence for formal training and apprenticeship for the *filid* is described in *Uraicecht na Ríar*. A *fili* must progress through the poetic grades over a course of seven years.[191] The poets' freedom to travel throughout the Gaelic-speaking world aided in dialect leveling. As noted in chapter one, the poetess Fedelm and the young challenger Néide had both studied poetic arts (*filidecht, éicse*) in Britain. The poets Aithirne and Senchán Torpéist made circuits of Ireland. Brittonic poets also enjoyed the privilege of travel.[192]

Despite the well recorded diachronic evolution of Early Gaelic,[193] the lack of distinct dialects in the written record, until after the dismantling of the Gaelic order in the seventeenth century, can be explained by the formal training of the *filid*. This written uniformity reveals a unitary sense of *natio* at a socio-cultural level among the Gaels that was not mirrored in the political sphere.[194] The named historical poets discussed above would have contributed to that sense of Gaelic cultural unity, aided by their association with the Church.

---

**191** Breatnach, *Uraicecht na Ríar*, 81–89.
**192** In the Mabinogi tale *Math fab Mathonwy* the characters Gwydion and Gilfaethwy travel from the north to the south of Wales *yn rith beird* (in the guise of bards) in order to gain entry to the court of Pryderi. For a translation, see Ford, *Mabinogi*, 92.
**193** McCone, "An tSean-Ghaeilge"; Breatnach, "An Mheán-Ghaeilge."
**194** See the arguments in Mac Cana, "Early Irish Ideology"; Mac Cana, "Literary Language." A similar situation among the Britons is noted in: Bromwich, *Trioedd Ynys Prydein*, lxviii–lxix. But for a more cautious approach to the dialect-free records of early Gaeldom in the context of learned communities, see Johnston, *Literacy and Identity*, 22.

## Appendix 2.a: Historical Poets after Bede to ca. 1100

This appendix surveys named historical poets and authors from both Old English and Gaelic traditions as one way of contrasting the two traditions. The period covered is from the death of Bede (735) until the end of the Anglo-Saxon period (ca. 1100). Six named authors wrote in Old English, twenty-five Gaelic poets are listed. The survey of Gaels does not pretend to be complete. Some historical Old English writers are not remembered as poets but rather as writers of prose.[195] All Gaels listed are known for producing verse. Most authors are noted only briefly, but several who worked before the end of Alfred's career (ca. 900) are examined in greater detail: Blathmac mac Con Brettan, Colcu úa Duinechda, Cynewulf, Óengus mac Óengobann (Figure 2.d), Orthanach úa Cóellámae (Figure 2.e), Máel Muru Othna, Flannacán mac Cellaigh, Alfred the Great, and Cormac mac Cuilennáin. The last three named, all contemporaries with *obit*s ca. 900, were kings who produced poetry or encouraged its production (Figure 2.f).

The authors are listed in approximate chronological order, since some dates are uncertain, concluding with the retrospective poem *Aimirgein Glúngel Tuir Tend* (White-kneed Aimirgein, a firm pillar) by Gilla in Choimded Úa Cormaic (ca. 1100). A contemporary Old English analogue to Gilla in Choimded's poem is the anonymous *encomium urbis Durham*, a poem of twenty-one lines, which harkens back to the "age of saints" at Lindisfarne and names historical persons, both Anglo-Saxon and Gael, all of whom are named in Bede's *Historia ecclesiastica*.

Ruman mac Colmáin (d. 747) was a contemporary of Bede. He is cited in the Annals of Ulster as *poeta optimus*, equivalent of the vernacular *ollam filed* (chief poet).[196] He was a member of a royal family and descended from an ecclesiastical one.[197]

Blathmac mac Con Brettan (fl. 750–770) produced two major poems that survive in a seventeenth-century manuscript.[198] He was a member of the Fir Rois (Men of Ross) of Airgíalla, in the counties of Monaghan and Louth.[199] Carney

---

[195] The easy distinction between verse and prose in Old English has been effectively challenged by Bredehoft, *Authors, Audiences*.
[196] Mac Airt and Mac Niocaill, *Annals of Ulster*, 202–3; Stokes, "Annals of Tigernach," 249 [Felinfach i 209].
[197] Johnston, *Literacy and Identity*, 138 and notes.
[198] This manuscript (Dublin, National Library of Ireland, MS G 50) also contains the only complete copy of "*Fo réir Choluimb*" discussed in chapter two: Carney, *Poems of Blathmac*, ix; Ó Corráin, *Clavis*, ii, 1149–50 §860.
[199] Byrne, *Irish Kings*, 72–74, 82–83, 114–18, 124–28; Bhreathnach, "Airgíalla Charter Poem," 95–99.

argued that Blathmac was likely a member of the *Céili Dé* movement.[200] There appear to have been two poems, the first contains one hundred and forty-nine quatrains.[201] Intricate metrical features, combined with scriptural and apocryphal subjects, reveal a formally trained poet with a monastic vocation.[202]

The poem contains encomiastic vocabulary applied to Mary and Jesus. The qualities praised seem to be reversed from those for a secular lord. Such encomiastic diction applied for ecclesiastical purposes is known from Old English poetry. Blathmac described the crucifixion of Christ as a case of *fingal* (kin-slaying). Mary's own people crucified her son.[203] Such killings, whether purposeful or accidental, were viewed as tragic in societies that relied on vengeance and the collection of honor-price to compensate for such losses.[204] Kin-slaying left survivors without recourse to an outside source from which revenge or compensation can be taken.

In *Beowulf* a digression relates how a certain Hæðcyn, brother of the Geatish king Hygelac, accidently killed their eldest brother Herebeald when an arrow went astray.[205] The distraught father, Hreðel, who could only lament his son's tragic death since the lost son could not be avenged on his own brother, ultimately "chose God's light" (*Godes lēoht ġecēas*), distributed his possessions and land, and left this life.[206]

---

**200** Carney, *Poems of Blathmac*, xv; Lambkin, "Blathmac and the Céili Dé"; Follet, *Céli Dé in Ireland*, 168–70.
**201** The second poem, or continuation of the first, contains one hundred and nine quatrains in Carney's edition. For an attempt to gather the remaining fragmentary quatrains of the second poem, see Ní Shéaghdha, "Poems of Blathmac."
**202** Among the apocrypha known to Blathmac is the story of Longinus present at the crucifixion who, when Jesus's side is pierced with his spear, allows the flowing blood to baptize Adam whose head was buried at the foot of the cross: Carney, *Poems of Blathmac*, 20–21 §§55–58, 123 notes for lines 227–28. See also Herbert and McNamara, *Biblical Apocrypha*, 16 §§51–53; McNamara, *Apocrypha*, 23 §5 (poem on Adam's head of tenth or eleventh century), 81 §69 (Longinus).
**203** For legal implications of *fingal*, see Kelly, *Guide*, 127–28. An Old Gaelic tale, *Fingal Rónáin* (The Kin-slaying of Rónán) tells of the tragic killing of Máel Fhothartaigh due to the jealousy of his father King Rónán: Greene, *Fingal Rónáin*, 1–12. For a discussion and synopsis, see Dillon, *Cycles of the Kings*, 42–48.
**204** In *Beowulf* the character Ūnferð is treated with suspicion because he was apparently guilty of kin-slaying: Fulk, Bjork, Niles, *Klaeber's Beowulf*, 22, lines 587–88a; 41, lines 1165b–68b; civ, 149–51 (discussion of Ūnferð). For a discussion of accidental killing and kin-slaying in a Germanic context, see Fulk, Bjork, Niles, *Klaeber's Beowulf*, xlvii–xlviii; Orchard, *Companion to Beowulf*, 246. The early Gaels had to deal with similar situations, especially within intra-familial struggles for kingship: Byrne, *Irish Kings*, 36, 96; Ó Cróinín, *Early Medieval Ireland*, 76.
**205** Fulk, Bjork, Niles, *Klaeber's Beowulf*, 83–84, lines 2435–43.
**206** Fulk, Bjork, Niles, *Klaeber's Beowulf*, 84–85, lines 2462b–71, quote line 2469b; Donahue, "*Beowulf* and Christian Tradition," 102–3. The tragic case of King Hreðel and his sons is compared to a father who must see his son hang (apparently as a punishment) for which he cannot

Another topos in Blathmac's poem was inspired by an unidentified apocryphon. At the crucifixion, in sympathy with the cross of wood, the trees of the world all bleed.[207] Carney noted that this motif occurred in the Old English *Christ III*.[208] Such parallels in motifs and language suggest a confluence in the thought worlds of the two societies that reflect a common source in apocrypha.

Blathmac's father Cú Brettan mac Congusa (d. 740) was king of Fir Rois.[209] Three quatrains describing the Battle of Allen (*Cath Almaine*) in 722[210] are attributed to him in the Annals of Tigernach[211] and the Chronicum Scotorum.[212] Some historical kings, *rígbaird*, who wrote poetry are noted in the law-tract *Bretha Nemed Dédenach*.[213]

Rechtgal úa Siadail (fl. 790), mentioned in chapter one, worked sometime toward the end of the same century.[214] Among the kings he is likely to have praised are Donnchad Midi mac Domnaill (770–797) and Muirgius mac Tommaltaig (792–815).

Colcu úa Duinechda (d. 796)[215] of Clonmacnoise is the likely author of *Scúap Chrábaid* (Broom of Devotion),[216] which displays features of the "enumerative" and "litanic" styles that appear in Old English homiletic literature.[217] He may have been a *scriba*, bishop, and anchorite. Colcu appears in the ninth-century monastic memoir "The Monastery of Tallaght," which associates him with the *Céili*

---

claim recompense or compensation: Fulk, Bjork, Niles, *Klaeber's Beowulf*, 84, lines 2444–62a. See a discussion in the context of other Germanic traditions: Orchard, *Companion to Beowulf*, 116–19.

**207** Carney, *Poems of Blathmac*, 22–23 §64, 124.
**208** Carney assumed that this example from Christ III should be attributed to Cynewulf, but current scholarship would only attribute Christ II to Cynewulf: Carney, *Poems of Blathmac*, 22–23 §64, 124; Carney, "Language and Literature," 497. For the Old English, see Krapp and Dobbie, *Exeter Book*, 35, lines 1174–76a; Biggs, *Apocrypha*, 14–15; McCormack, "Those Bloody Trees."
**209** Mac Airt and Mac Niocaill, *Annals of Ulster*, 194–95.
**210** Mac Airt and Mac Niocaill, *Annals of Ulster*, 176–77; Ó Riain, *Cath Almaine*, 66.
**211** Stokes, "Annals of Tigernach," 229–30 [Felinfach i 189].
**212** Hennessy, *Chronicum Scotorum*, 122–23. See also Mc Carthy, *Irish Annals*, 366.
**213** Breatnach, *Uraicecht na Ríar*, 50–51; Gwynn, "Privileges and Responsibilities," 42, lines 19–23.
**214** Ó hAodha, "Rechtgal úa Siadail."
**215** Mac Airt and Mac Niocaill, *Annals of Ulster*, 250–51.
**216** Meyer, "Scúap Chrábaid"; Plummer, *Irish Litanies*, 30–45; Ó Corráin, *Clavis*, ii, 1159–60 §874. For a discussion of the differences in these two editions, see O'Sullivan, "*Scúap Chrábaid*."
**217** Wright, "Irish 'Enumerative Style'"; Wright, *Irish Tradition*, 49–105 (enumerative), 243–48, 262–64 (litanic). Tomás O'Sullivan noted the fluidity of litanic texts intended for liturgical purposes in the different surviving versions: O'Sullivan, "*Scúap Chrábaid*."

Dé movement.[218] Alcuin of York apparently addressed a letter to him.[219] Alcuin named in that letter another Gael, Joseph, who was abbot at Clonmacnoise (d. 794).[220] The name Joseph is not common among the Gaels but several are associated with Clonmacnoise.[221] Alcuin's letter mentioned problems between Charlemagne and Offa of Mercia. The Annals of Ulster at 796 cite Offa's death.[222] Colcu, Joseph, and Offa appearing together in Alcuin's letter imply regular communications from the Continent, through York and Mercia, to Clonmacnoise.

Cynewulf (eighth–tenth centuries [?]) is the most prolific of the historical Old English poets.[223] *Fates of the Apostles* and *Elene* appear in the Vercelli Book (Vercelli, Biblioteca Capitolare di Vercelli, MS CXVII).[224] *Christ II*, also known as "the Ascension," lines 440–866 of the *Christ* group, and *Juliana* are found in the Exeter Book (Exeter, Exeter Cathedral Library, MS 3501).[225] Cynewulf included his name in runes near the ends of the four poems just named.[226] A fifth poem about the Mercian saint Guthlac may be included among Cynewulf's poems.[227]

Cynewulf has not been firmly dated nor accurately identified. He was, apparently, a trained cleric and literate in Latin. His dialect is Anglian, probably Mercian rather than Northumbrian. Estimates for his dates vary widely, the later dating based on the age of the manuscripts that contain his poems. Most of Cynewulf's *œuvre* can be sourced in the Latinate traditions of the Church and late Antiquity.

---

**218** Gwynn and Purton, "Monastery of Tallaght," 148 §56, 153 §65, 159 §77, 161 §81. For possible relationship with *Céili Dé* movement, see Follet, *Céli Dé in Ireland*, 163–65.
**219** Meyer, "Scúap Chrábaid," 92–93. For a translation of Alcuin's letter, see Whitelock, *English Historical Documents*, 840–42 §192; Allott, *Alcuin of York*, 42–43 §31. Some have assumed that Alcuin addressed a Gaelic scholar resident at York: Kenney, *Sources*, 534 §340n; Ryan, *Clonmacnois*, 41 §31. See the remarks of Byrne, "Church and Politics," 664 and n12.
**220** Mac Airt and Mac Niocaill, *Annals of Ulster*, 248–49.
**221** For example, Mac Airt and Mac Niocaill, *Annals of Ulster*, 354–55 s.a. 904. There is a Joseph at Clonmacnoise in the family background of the scribe Máel Muire: Best and Bergin, *Lebor na Huidre*, xii.
**222** "Offa rex bonus Anglorum moritur": Mac Airt and Mac Niocaill, *Annals of Ulster*, 250–51. This entry stands out because Offa is called a "good" king of the "Angles." Typically the Gaels referred to Anglo-Saxons as "Saxons," from wherever they came in Britain.
**223** For overviews of Cynewulf, see Calder, *Cynewulf*; Anderson, *Cynewulf*; Bjork, *Cynewulf Reader*.
**224** Krapp, *Vercelli Book*, 51–54, 123–26 (*Fates*); 66–102, 132–52 (*Elene*).
**225** Krapp and Dobbie, *Exeter Book*, 15–27, 250–55 (*Christ II*); 113–33, 280–88 (*Juliana*).
**226** Frese, "Cynewulf's Runic Signatures." For arguments that the runic passages should be treated separately from the body of the poems, see Bredehoft, "Date of *Beowulf*," 104–7. For an illustration in the Exeter Book, see Breay and Story, *Anglo-Saxon Kingdoms*, 34.
**227** Bjork, *Poems of Cynewulf*, 33–75 (translation), 239, 246–47 (notes).

Juliana refused to relinquish her Christian faith and marry a pagan.[228] Cynewulf's version is likely based on anonymous *acta*.[229] *Juliana* is listed in *Félire Óengusso* at February 16.[230] In *Christ II* Cynewulf drew widely for his Latinate sources.[231]

*Fates of the Apostles* describes their martyrdoms. No specific Latinate source has been identified, but Gaelic influences have been suggested.[232] Verses from Blathmac portray the martyrdoms of several apostles in a manner reminiscent of Cynewulf.[233] Cynewulf, like the Gaels, emphasized the apostle John (*Iōhannes*) as the most beloved of Jesus.[234]

*Elene*, involving the "finding of the true cross," has multiple sources including *acta* of St. Cyriacus.[235] Adomnán's *De locis sanctis* may be the earliest documented exposure of the Anglo-Saxons to the story. Bede made an epitome of Adomnán's text.[236] Adomnán discussed the basilica constructed by Emperor Constantine near Calvary to commemorate the finding of the cross (*HE* v 16).[237] He also told of the *rotunda mirae magnitudinis lapidea eclesia* (the very celebrated round stone church) in Constantinople where the reliquary was kept.[238]

Cynewulf used the triad "thought, word, deed" in *Elene*. By the middle of the seventh century the Gaels had made it a feature of their exegesis.[239] Cynewulf worked the triad into the epilogue, after the section where he had identified himself with runes.[240]

---

228 Greenfield and Calder, *New Critical History*, 167–71. Muirchú's *Vita Patricii* relates a similar tale about Monesan: Bieler, *Patrician Texts*, 98–101.
229 Calder and Allen, *Sources and Analogues*, 121–32.
230 Stokes, *Félire Óengusso*, 61, 74–75.
231 Greenfield and Calder, *New Critical History*, 188–93; Calder and Allen, *Sources and Analogues*, 78–83. For doctrinal orthodoxy of Cynewulf's work: Garde, *Old English Poetry*, 131–58.
232 Brooks, *Andreas*, xxx–xxxi; Calder and Allen, *Sources and Analogues*, 35–39.
233 Carney, *Poems of Blathmac*, 84–87 §§247–55.
234 Brooks, *Andreas*, 56, lines 26–27a; Krapp, *Vercelli Book*, 52; Walsh and Ó Cróinín, *Cummian's Letter*, 69n89. For the development of *Eoin bruinne* in Gaelic tradition, see Monge Allen, "Metamorphosis of *Eoin Bruinne*."
235 Calder and Allen, *Sources and Analogues*, 59–69; Greenfield and Calder, *New Critical History*, 171–76. For doctrinal orthodoxy of *Elene*: Garde, *Old English Poetry*, 159–88.
236 For a translation, see Foley and Holder, *Biblical Miscellany*, 5–25.
237 Meehan, *De Locis Sanctis*, 48–51, bk. 1, c. 6.
238 Meehan, *De Locis Sanctis*, 108–111, bk. 3, c. 3, quote at 108. For Bede's epitome, see Foley and Holder, *Biblical Miscellany*, 24 (Constantinople).
239 Sims-Williams, "Thought, Word and Deed." See Appendix 4.b for Bede's use of this Gaelic triad.
240 Krapp, *Vercelli Book*, 101, lines 1281b–86a; Wright, *Irish Tradition*, 79, 226.

Robert Bjork analyzed the rhetorical sophistication of Cynewulf's *Elene* and *Juliana*.[241] The dialogic characteristics of Gaelic literature are suggested by *immacallam* (dialogue, conversation) in titles such as *Immacallam in dá Thuarad*, discussed in chapters one and three.[242] A comparison of Cynewulf's two strong female characters with Emer from the Ulster Cycle tales would reward the effort.[243]

Óengus mac Óengobann maic Óebleáin (fl. 830) created the versified *Félire Óengusso* (The Martyrology of Óengus; 828x833).[244] Óengus was associated with Máel Ruain of Tallaght of the *Céili Dé* movement.[245] The martyrology comprises three hundred and sixty-six quatrains to cover the full year, including leap years, in addition to a substantial prologue and epilogue. Middle Gaelic prose prefaces attribute great reward to anyone who praised the saints through poetry.[246]

The prologue contrasts ancient regal sites now deserted (Tara, Rathcroghan, Knockaulinn, Navan Fort) against the vibrant ecclesiastical foundations (Armagh, Clonmacnoise, Kildare, Glendalough) of Óengus's day (Figure 2.d). The word for "cemetery" (*rúam*) in two quatrains is literally "Rome," a term that came to mean a thriving monastic settlement and, by extension, the cemetery where all the faithful are buried.[247] Nothing preserved in Old English literature so explicitly contrasts the legendary or ancient historical Germanic past with the vital, thriving Christian present.

*Félire Óengusso* named saints from the wider Christian world of the Mediterranean and Near East. Insular saints are also named including Anglo-Saxons.[248] King Oswald, listed at August 5, may have developed a cult among the Gaels

---

241 Bjork, *Verse Saints' Lives*, 45–61 (*Juliana*), 62–89 (*Elene*).
242 See further Carey, "Lough Foyle Colloquy Texts." The story involving Bran had been discussed earlier by Carney, "Bran Material."
243 For the character of Emer, see Findon, *Woman's Words*. For dialogic approach to Gaelic narrative, see Nagy, *Conversing with Angels*.
244 Stokes, *Félire Óengusso*; Ó Corráin, *Clavis*, i, 353–55 §254; ii, 1180 §899. See further, Ó Riain, "Martyrology of Óengus." It has always been accepted as an Old Gaelic text, but dating arguments have varied from early to late in the ninth century. Pádraig Ó Riain first asserted the dates listed above: Ó Riain, "Tallaght Martyrologies." However, David Dumville questioned the dating criteria and asserted its composition to be late ninth century: Dumville, "*Félire Óengusso*." Liam Breatnach supported the earlier dating (797x808) established by Rudolf Thurneysen: Breatnach, "Poets and Poetry," 74–75 §4.4. Pádraig Ó Riain has re-asserted the dates from 828x833 for the Tallaght martyrologies: Ó Riain, *Feastdays*, 97–98, 118.
245 Carney, "Language and Literature," 497–98; Follet, *Céli Dé in Ireland*, 117–21.
246 Stokes, *Félire Óengusso*, 8–9 (Leabhar Breac), 10–11 (Ms Laud 610).
247 eDIL: http://www.dil.ie, s.v. 1 *rúam*; dil.ie/35630.
248 Pádraig Ó Riain argued that, since Gaelic martyrologies do not appear until the ninth century, they may owe their evolution to Anglo-Saxon influence which helps account for the Anglo-Saxons in the present martyrology: Ó Riain, *Anglo-Saxon Ireland*.

> 165. Tara's mighty ramparts perished
>   at the death of her princes:
>   With a multitude of venerable champions
>   the Height of Machae (Armagh) abides.
> 169. Right valiant Lóegaire's pride
>   has been quenched – great the anguish:
>   Patrick's name, splendid, famous,
>   is on the increase.
> 173. The Faith has grown,
>   it will abide till Doomsday:
>   Guilty pagans who are carried off,
>   their *ráth*s are not dwelt in.
> 177. Rathcroghan (*Ráth Crúachann*) has vanished
>   with Ailill offspring of victory:
>   Fair the sovereignty over princes that is here
>   in the monastery of Clonmacnoise.
> 189. Knockaulinn's (*Ailenn*) proud ramparts have perished
>   with its warlike host:
>   Great is victorious Brigit,
>   fair is her multitudinous cemetery (i.e., Kildare).
> 193. Emain's (Navan Fort's) ramparts have vanished,
>   save that stones remain:
>   The cemetery of the west of the world
>   is multitudinous Glendalough.
>
> In the three hundred and forty lines of the prologue to his "Martyrology" Óengus mac Óengobann (fl. 830) championed the triumphant Christian churches (e.g., Armagh, Clonmacmoise, Kildare, Glendalough) that thrived while the old pre-Christian royal sites (e.g., Tara, Rathcroghan, Ailenn, Emain [Macha]) have lapsed into ruin. Nevertheless, Óengus showed a firm knowledge of the Gaels' native past (*senchas*), their heroes, and significant sites. Óengus was a contemporary of Orthanach úa Cóellámae.
>
> (Translation based on edition by Stokes, *Félire Óengusso*, 24–25.)

**Figure 2.d:** Extracts from the Prologue of *Félire Óengusso* (Martyrology of Oengus).

before it developed among the Anglo-Saxons, as discussed in chapter five.[249] Wihtberht studied at Rath Melsigi and undertook a mission to Frisia, as discussed in chapter six. He is named in the guarantor list of *Cáin Adomnáin*

---

[249] Stokes, *Félire Óengusso*, 174. For the concept of "high-kingship" among Anglo-Saxon rulers, see Higham, *Ecgfrith*, 20–24. Bede referred to Oswald's *imperium*, and Adomnán described Oswald as "emperor of all Britain ordained by God" (totius Brittanniae imperator a deo ordinatus): Anderson and Anderson, *Life of Columba*, 16, i 1.

(697).²⁵⁰ He appears, as a "seafarer," at December 8 in *Félire Óengusso*.²⁵¹ King Aldfrith *sapiens* is cited under his Gaelic name Flann (Fína) at December 15.²⁵² He is called the "enduring heir of Bangor," discussed in chapters four and five, as is appropriate for a *sapiens*.

Orthanach úa Cóellámae (d. 839) was bishop of Kildare from ca. 834 to his death. An epithet attached to his name, *Cuirrigh* (of the Curragh), the open plain near Kildare, attests to his origins there. A number of poems attributed to him praise the ancestors of the Leinstermen and implies concerns with contemporary politics.²⁵³ Some have considered that another Orthanach was the poet.²⁵⁴

One poem attributed to Orthanach begins *Slán seiss, a Brigit* (sit safely, Brigit) (Figure 2.e).²⁵⁵ In twenty-six stanzas it praises the triumph of St. Brigit and the spread of Christianity throughout Leinster. The poem names the ancient regal sites Knockaulin (*Cnoc Ailinne* [*Ailenn*]) and Dind Ríg, as well as the Liffey plain and the Curragh of Kildare. The poet states that despite the magnificence of the regal sites and the greatness of the rulers who once controlled them, Brigit is now supreme (Figure 2.e). The penultimate stanza states of Brigit: "thy fame has outshone the fame of the king – thou art over them all" (rogab do chlú for a chlú in ríg, is tū fordatá).²⁵⁶

The degree of shared tradition can be demonstrated by a comparison with the tenth-century narrative *Orgain Denna Ríg* (The Destruction of Dind Ríg), a place named in Orthanach's poem, and discussed in chapter three.²⁵⁷ Characters such as Ailill Áine, Lóegaire Lorc, Cobthach Cóel, and Labraid (Loingseach), are found in *Orgain Denna Ríg* and in Orthanach's ninth-century poem, as well as in dynastic poems from the genealogies, some attributed to the seventh-century

---

**250** Ní Dhonnchadha, "Guarantor List," 180, 193–94 §29. Ní Dhonnchadha equated Ichtbricht with Ecgberht of Rath Melsigi. Dáibhí Ó Cróinín corrected the reference to Wihtberht: Ó Cróinín, "Rath Melsigi, Willibrord," 25–26.
**251** Stokes, *Félire Óengusso*, 250; Ireland, "Seafarer," 9.
**252** Stokes, *Félire Óengusso*, 251; Ireland, "Where Was King Aldfrith Educated?" 63–69.
**253** Among the poems attributed to Orthanach are: Meyer, "Masu de chlaind Echdach aird"; Ó Corráin, *Clavis*, iii, 1595 §1202; and O Daly, "A chóicid choín Chairpri Crúaid"; Ó Corráin, *Clavis*, iii, 1594–95 §1203.
**254** James Carney favored another Orthanach, abbot of Kilbrew (Cell Foibrig) near Slane, who died in 814. Both were churchmen. See Francis J. Byrne's discussion of the political background: Byrne, "Church and Politics," 671–72. Carney discussed the poems in the context of kingship and the Leinster ancestors: Carney, "Language and Literature," 480–83.
**255** Meyer, *Hail Brigit*; Ó Corráin, *Clavis*, iii, 1593–94 §1201.
**256** Meyer, *Hail Brigit*, 18–19 §25.
**257** Greene, *Fingal Rónáin*, 16–26; Ó Corráin, *Clavis*, iii, 1423–24 §1086. For a synopsis of the tale, see Dillon, *Cycles of the Kings*, 4–10.

Quatrain 1)
Sit safely, triumphant Brigit
upon the edge of Liffey to the sea's strand,
you are the female sovereign with hosts of troops
who presides over the children of Catháir Már.

Quatrain 2)
God's counsel to the whole of Ireland would be a greater telling in each era.
Though bright Liffey is yours today
It has been the land of others in their turn.

Quatrain 4)
Lóegaire was king as far as the sea,
Ailill Áne, a mighty bargain,
the Curragh with its splendor lives on,
no king who was upon it remains.

Quatrain 5)
Abundant Labraid Loingsech lives no more
having crushed the thirty nobles
in Dind Ríg – it was a well-known dwelling –
since he brought doom to Cobthach Cóel.

Quatrain 13)
Bresal Brecc was king over Elg (Ireland),
Fiachra Fobrecc himself with fierceness,
Fergus of the Sea, Finn son of Roth,
they loved to be in lofty Knockaulinn (Ailenn).

Quatrain 26)
You possess eternal rule with the King
apart from the land that holds your grave.
Grandchild of Bresal son of Dian,
sit safely, triumphant Brigit.

This poem of twenty-six quatrains is attributed to Orthanach úa Cóellámae (d. ca. 839), bishop of Kildare, the Leinster seat of St. Brigit. The poem begins and ends with praise for St. Brigit (notice the *dúnad* (closure), similar opening and closing lines). However, the majority of quatrains are taken up with legendary and historic heroes and their royal sites throughout Leinster, such as Dind Ríg and Ailenn. Orthanach was a contemporary of Óengus mac Óengobann.

(Translation based on edition by Meyer, *Hail Brigit*, 12–13, 14–15, 18–19.)

**Figure 2.e:** Extracts from "Slán seiss, a Brigit," a Poem by Orthanach úa Cóellámae.

Laidcenn mac Bairchedo, mentioned in chapter one. The prose tale cites poems by Flann mac Lonáin (d. 896) and Orthanach himself, whose two stanzas are extracted from one of his longer poems beginning *A chóicid choín Chairpri chrúaid* (fair province of stern Cairpre).[258] Orthanach was a churchman, but he used his poetic talents to serve both secular and ecclesiastical agendas.

Daniél úa Líathaiti (d. 863) was abbot of Lismore and Cork.[259] He is noted for a poem refuting the advances of a woman, among other works.[260] Aspects of the poem can be compared to the anonymous enigmatic dialogue between Líadain and Cuirithir, about a love affair that is not consummated because of commitments to the Church.[261] The poems are roughly contemporary.

Máel Muru Othna (d. 887) may have been a cleric.[262] His name and epithet mean "devotee of Muru of Fahan." St. Muru founded (ca. 600) the monastery at Fahan (*Othain*) in the Cenél nEogain territory of Inishowen. Máel Muru Othna is called *fili eolach* (learned poet) in the Chronicum Scotorum and *rígfili* (kingly poet) in the Annals of Ulster.[263]

Four surviving poems have been attributed to him. Two of them, *Flann for Érinn* (Flann over Ireland)[264] and *Tríath ós tríathaib Tuathal Techtmar* (Chieftain over chieftains Tuathal Techtmar),[265] appear to have been written under the patronage of Flann Sinna, a king of Clann Cholmáin of the southern Uí Néill.[266] A third poem, *Áth Lïac Find, cid dia tá* (the ford of Fionn's stone, whence [its name]), is a poem about place-lore.[267] It relates the combats of Fionn mac Cumhaill (Umhaill) at a ford somewhere on the River Shannon.[268]

Máel Muru's most influential poem, *Can a mbunadus na nGoídel* (Whence the source of the Gaels), purportedly relates the Biblical and pseudo-classical origins of the Gaels, their arrival in Ireland, and their interactions with otherworldly

---

[258] Greene, *Fingal Rónáin*, 23, lines 445–52; O Daly, "A chóicid choín Chairpri Crúaid"; Ó Corráin, *Clavis*, iii, 1594–95 §1203.
[259] Mac Airt, *Annals of Inisfallen*, 132–33.
[260] Murphy, *Early Irish Metrics*, 6–9 §7 and notes 175–77.
[261] Meyer, *Liadain and Curithir*; Murphy, *Early Irish Metrics*, 82–85 §35 and notes 208–11.
[262] Johnston, *Literacy and Identity*, 128–29, 144. See also Carney, "Dating Early Irish Verse," 178, 187; Welch, *Oxford Companion*, 350.
[263] Hennessy, *Chronicum Scotorum*, 142–43; Mac Airt and Mac Niocaill, *Annals of Ulster*, 342–43 s.a. 887; Carey, "Mael Muru Othna," 430–33.
[264] Ó Corráin, *Clavis*, iii, 1552–53 §1149.
[265] Ó Corráin, *Clavis*, iii, 1497 §1123.
[266] Carey, "Mael Muru Othna"; Byrne, "Ireland and Her Neighbours," 865, 867.
[267] Gwynn, *Metrical Dindshenchas*, iv, 36–39.
[268] For an early eighth-century tale in which the protagonist and a poet disagree over the details of a place-lore story, see White, *Compert Mongáin*, 73–74, 79–81.

races already resident.[269] It forms the basis for much of *Lebor Gabála Érenn*.[270] Máel Muru is the earliest of the numerous poets associated with the *Lebor Gabála* project that relied on learned texts such as the *Historiae adversum paganos* of Orosius (d. ca. 418), the *Chronicle* of Eusebius (d. ca. 339), and the *Etymologiae* of Isidore (d. 636).[271] The work by Orosius formed part of the translation project initiated by King Alfred. The reliance on Isidore implies that the *Lebor Gabála* project had been incubating among learned Gaelic scholars since the seventh century.[272]

Flann mac Lonáin (d. 896) was killed by the Déisi of Munster.[273] He was described as "Virgil of the Scots, chief poet of the Gaels" in the seventeenth-century Annals of the Four Masters.[274] Poems attributed to him survive in *duanairí* (poetry anthologies) of the sixteenth century and later.[275]

Flannacán mac Cellaigh (d. 896) was a king of Brega.[276] A poem attributed to him confirms the prior existence of tales from the tenth-century lists, discussed in chapter three.[277] Flannacán was killed by Norsemen, a reminder that King Alfred had to deal with their depredations.[278]

Flannacán is named in *Bretha Nemed Dédenach* along with other identifiable kings as a *rígbard*, that is, he was both king and *bard*. Liam Breatnach translated the following passage, but I have included additional information in square brackets: "[T]he *rígbard*, i.e. he has kingship and bardic art, as was Tnúthgal son of Cellach [CGH 324a19],[279] the king of Múscraige Mittine, or Bran Finn son of Máel Ochtraig [AU 671], over the Déisi, or Flannacán son of Cellach [AU 896], over the men of Brega, or Écnechán son of Dálach [AU 906], over Cenél Conaill."[280] The geographical spread across Ireland, from south to north,

---

269 Ritari, "'Whence is the Origin of the Gaels'," 160–65; Ó Corráin, *Clavis*, iii, 1530–31 §1140.
270 Scowcroft, "*Leabhar Gabhála* Part II," 8, 9, 11, 17, 41, 51–52; Carey, *Origin-Legend*, 15–18; Bhreathnach, *Ireland in the Medieval World*, 5–7.
271 For a survey of the larger tradition, see Ó Corráin, *Clavis*, iii, 1531–39 §1141.
272 Howlett, "Irish Foundation Legend."
273 Mac Airt and Mac Niocaill, *Annals of Ulster*, 350–51 s.a. 896.
274 O'Donovan, *Four Masters*, i, 549 s.a. 891.
275 Dobbs, "Flann mac Lonáin"; Findon, "Dangerous Siren"; Ó Corráin, *Clavis*, ii, 1238–39 §948, 1142–43 §953.
276 Mac Airt and Mac Niocaill, *Annals of Ulster*, 350–51.
277 Thurneysen, *Die irische Helden- und Königsage*, 19.
278 For some of the political background to his reign, see Mulchrone, "Flannacán mac Cellaigh," 80–82; Bhreathnach, *Ireland in the Medieval World*, 46–47.
279 O'Brien, *Corpus genealogiarum Hiberniae*, 371, line 324a19.
280 Breatnach, *Uraicecht na Ríar*, 50–51; Gwynn, "Privileges and Responsibilities," 42, lines 19–23. Only Tnúthgal could not be dated in the Annals of Ulster (AU), but he is found in the genealogies: O'Brien, *Corpus genealogiarum Hiberniae*, 371.

and the chronological span, from the seventh to the tenth centuries, show the phenomenon of *rígbard* to have been widespread.

In a poem of twenty-eight quatrains several tales are referred to, recognizable by the characters and events noted.[281] The second stanza refers to the Battle of Mag Tuired (*Cath Maige Tuired*), cited in chapters one and three.[282] Flannacán's poem lists the deaths of heroes by the day of the week on which they died, a characteristic found in the *Gododdin*, and poems attributed to Taliesin.[283] For example, the legendary Ulster hero Cú Chulainn died on a Wednesday. This traditional death day is confirmed in the early eighth-century tale *Brislech Mór Maige Muirthemni*.[284] The word for Wednesday (*cétaíne*; first fast) is a Christian one, as is the concept of organizing time into weeks of seven named days.[285]

Flannacán's poem lists four deaths of Ulster cycle heroes on a Monday: 1) King Conchobar (§6),[286] discussed in chapters one and three, 2) the sons of Uisliu (§8),[287] 3) the seer Dubthach Dóel (§9), discussed in chapter three,[288] and 4) Conall Cernach (§10), noted in chapters one and three.[289] The semi-historical Conall Gulbain, eponymous ancestor of Cenél Conaill of the northern Uí Néill, died on a Friday (§22). Muirchertach mac Ercai (d. 534)[290] died on a Thursday (§17). Mongán mac Fiachnai (d. 625)[291] died on a Wednesday (§14). Mongán's

---

281 Mulchrone, "Flannacán mac Cellaigh"; Ó Corráin, *Clavis*, iii, 1553 §1150.

282 Mulchrone, "Flannacán mac Cellaigh," 83 §2. The name here is given as *Mag Tuire*. For an edition of the text, see Gray, *Cath Maige Tuired*.

283 For translations from the most archaic section of *Gododdin* and from a poem dealing with Rheged, see Koch, *Celtic Heroic Age*, 323 (*Gododdin*), 361 (*Gweith Argoet Llwyfein*).

284 Kimpton, *Death of Cú Chulainn*, 30, lines 602–3, 47 §33.

285 Ó Cróinín, "Days of the Week."

286 Meyer, *Death-tales*, 2–21. See also the early elaboration of the tale which synchronizes his death with the crucifixion: Corthals, "*Aided Chonchobuir*."

287 This is the tragic story of the beautiful Deirdre. See Hull, *Longes mac n-Uislenn*; for a synopsis of the tale, see Dillon, *Early Irish Literature*, 13–16.

288 For an episode involving Dubthach Dóel as seer, see O'Rahilly, *Táin: Recension I*, 107, lines 3527–36 (Gaelic); 219–20 (English).

289 Conall Cernach appears in numerous tales involving Ulster heroes. In chapter one he was noted as guarding the borders in order to provide safe passage for visiting poets: O'Rahilly, *Táin: Recension I*, 21, line 664–86 (Gaelic); 143–44 (English).

290 Mac Airt and Mac Niocaill, *Annals of Ulster*, 70–71; Stokes, "Annals of Tigernach," 132–34 [Felinfach i 92–94]. A twelfth-century tale of magic and mystery relates the death of Muirchertach mac Ercai: Nic Dhonnchadha, *Aided Muirchertaig meic Erca*; see discussion at Ní Bhrolcháin, *Early Irish Literature*, 131.

291 Mac Airt and Mac Niocaill, *Annals of Ulster*, 112–13; Stokes, "Annals of Tigernach," 178 [Felinfach i 138].

father Fiachnae helped Áedán mac Gabráin against the Anglo-Saxons (*HE* i 34),²⁹² discussed in chapter three.

Alfred the Great (d. 899), king of Wessex (871–899), instituted an ambitious translation project of Latin works into Old English. We know about Alfred and his court because the Briton Asser wrote *De Vita et Rebus Gestis Alfredi*.²⁹³ Alfred searched beyond his kingdom to fill his court with competent scholars. There were at least four Mercians: Plegmund, who became archbishop of Canterbury; Wærferth, eventually bishop of Worcester; and two priests, Werwulf and Æthelstan.²⁹⁴ From further afield came Grimbald from Francia, and John from Saxony.²⁹⁵

> Flannacán mac Cellaigh (d. 896) composed a poem that confirms information from the tenth-century Tale Lists:
> Twenty-eight quatrains on the death of heroes (mythico-legendary and historical) and the day of the week on which they died
> Alfred (d. 899) instituted a translation project that included:
> Pope Gregory's *Dialogues*
> Pope Gregory's *Pastoral Care*
> Boethius's *Consolation of Philosophy*
> Augustine's *Soliloquies*
> Fifty Psalms from the Psalter
> Orosius's *Histories against the Pagans*
> Bede's *Historia ecclesiastica*
> Cormac mac Cuilennáin (d. 908) may have composed two surviving poems and has the compilation of an important glossary attributed to him:
> *Uga Cormaic meic Cuilennáin* (Cormac's Choice), a poem about spiritual pilgrimage
> *Amrae Senáin*, a poem in praise of Senán of Scattery Island in the Shannon Estuary
> *Sanas Cormaic* (Cormac's Glossary), a collection of recondite vocabulary and *senchas* (ancient lore).

**Figure 2.f.** Three Contemporary Literary Kings.

Alfred's open court welcomed (891) three Gaels who had set themselves adrift for the love of God: Dub Sláine, Mac Bethad, Máel Inmain.²⁹⁶ The same Chronicle

---

292 White, *Compert Mongáin*, 71–72, 78–79 (*Compert Mongáin*).
293 Keynes and Lapidge, *Alfred the Great*. See also Discenza and Szarmach, *Companion to Alfred the Great*. For an illustration of a manuscript containing Asser's work, see Breay and Story, *Anglo-Saxon Kingdoms*, 179.
294 It has been argued that Æthelstan composed *Andreas* relying on *Beowulf* and the works of Cynewulf: North and Bintley, *Andreas*.
295 Greenfield and Calder, *New Critical History*, 42.
296 Swanton, *Anglo-Saxon Chronicles*, 82–83.

entry noted the death of Suibne "the best teacher among the Scots," that is, Suibne mac Maíle Umai (d. 891) of Clonmacnoise, *ancorita et scriba optimus*.[297]

Alfred's agenda was extensive, and the texts chosen reveal something of the king's character. The first text was Pope Gregory's *Dialogues* which Wærferth of Mercia undertook.[298] The second was Gregory's *Cura Pastoralis*.[299] Another was *De consolatione Philosophiae* by Boethius.[300] Some texts were free adaptations, or interpretations, such as Augustine's *Soliloquies* which drew on a wide array of additional sources.[301] The first fifty psalms were also translated.[302] The Old English *Martyrology* may have been an outgrowth of this project.[303]

Alfred's laws represent an eclectic gathering. Their preface drew on the Hiberno-Latin *Liber ex lege Moysi*.[304] Three historical texts attracted the attention of Alfred's project: Orosius's *Historiae adversum Paganos*,[305] Bede's *Historia ecclesiastica*,[306] and the creation of the *Anglo-Saxon Chronicles*.[307] When viewed in the context of encroaching Norse power and the expansion of the Danelaw, Alfred's translation project, whatever his personal contribution,[308] is all the more impressive.

Cormac mac Cuilennáin (d. 908) was a scholar and cleric who undertook the kingship of Cashel around 901 and became known as a king/bishop. A number of persons in Gaelic society combined ecclesiastical office and secular kingship.[309]

---

**297** Mac Airt and Mac Niocaill, *Annals of Ulster*, 346–47.
**298** Greenfield and Calder, *New Critical History*, 42–43; Godden, "Wærferth and King Alfred."
**299** Greenfield and Calder, *New Critical History*, 43–46; Breay and Story, *Anglo-Saxon Kingdoms*, 182–83.
**300** Greenfield and Calder, *New Critical History*, 46–51. Alfred may have composed the *Metres of Boethius*: Thornbury, *Becoming a Poet*, 200, 224, 244; Breay and Story, *Anglo-Saxon Kingdoms*, 252–53.
**301** Greenfield and Calder, *New Critical History*, 51–54.
**302** Greenfield and Calder, *New Critical History*, 54–55; O'Neill [Ó Néill], *First Fifty Psalms*; Breay and Story, *Anglo-Saxon Kingdoms*, 240–41.
**303** Greenfield and Calder, *New Critical History*, 61–62; Rauer, *Old English Martyrology*, 11–14.
**304** Carella, "Laws of Alfred"; Ó Corráin, *Clavis*, ii, 799–800 §620.
**305** Greenfield and Calder, *New Critical History*, 55–57. The Orosius is, in many ways, a paraphrase. Accounts of voyages to the Baltic by Ohthere and Wulfstan were inserted. Both had visited Alfred's court. Orosius was central to the *Lebor Gabála* project.
**306** Greenfield and Calder, *New Critical History*, 57–59; Breay and Story, *Anglo-Saxon Kingdoms*, 186–87.
**307** Greenfield and Calder, *New Critical History*, 59–61; Breay and Story, *Anglo-Saxon Kingdoms*, 176–78, 192–93, 360–61, 386–87.
**308** Godden, "Did King Alfred Write Anything?"
**309** For examples, see Hughes, "Irish Church," 642–43. See further Ó Riain, *Dictionary*, 225–26 (Cormac mac Cuilennáin), 312 (Fedlimid mac Crimthainn), 330–31 (Fínsnechta mac Colcan), 346–49 (Flannán mac Tordelbaig).

He may have been over sixty years old when he became king. He appears to have been motivated by a desire to curtail the expansion of the Uí Néill.[310] Nonetheless, he was killed in battle in 908 at Belach Mugna by his Uí Néill rival Flann Sinna mac Máele Sechnaill of Clann Cholmáin.[311]

His reputation as a poet and scholar grew after his death. How much was deserved in his lifetime is uncertain. A twenty-nine-quatrain poem *Uga Corbmaic meic Cuilendain* (Cormac mac Cuilennáin's choice),[312] opens with images of a pilgrim voyage, foregoing the comforts of family and possessions (§§1–11). But it soon becomes clear that "the pilgrim does not propose to chart a course himself."[313] The image shifts from physical voyage to a metaphorical journey through life and relates "how a variety of Biblical figures were pardoned by God and taken to everlasting bliss."[314] *Uga Corbmaic* implies that God's grace can provide relief and forgiveness whatever our circumstances or personal shortcomings.[315]

The Old Gaelic *Amrae Senáin* was likely by Cormac.[316] It praises Senán, the patron of *Inis Chathaig* (Scattery Island) in the Shannon Estuary. This poem displays the qualities of a *lorica* and asks Senán to protect the poet from blindness. The poem's recondite vocabulary suits the attribution to Cormac.

The most influential text attributed to Cormac is the erudite, arcane glossary *Sanas Cormaic* (Cormac's Glossary).[317] It organizes words into roughly alphabetical order. Explanations may rely on Gaelic, Latin, Greek or Hebrew.[318] The obscure word *adann* (rushlight), found in a fragment by Colmán mac Lénéni cited in chapter two, is explained in *Sanas Cormaic*.[319] One entry contains a short narrative on "poetics," discussed in chapter three, that evolves out of an

---

**310** Byrne, *Irish Kings*, 203, 214. For this genealogy, see O'Brien, *Corpus genealogiarum Hiberniae*; 217, 150b28.
**311** Mac Airt and Mac Niocaill, *Annals of Ulster*, 356–57.
**312** Henry, *English and Celtic Lyric*, 54–63; see discussion in Ní Mhaonaigh, "Cormac mac Cuilennáin," 116–22; Ó Corráin, *Clavis*, ii, 1154 §867. Other poems attributed to Cormac include one on pilgrimage starting *Mithidh damhsa tairired* (Time for me to proceed on a journey): Henry, *English and Celtic Lyric*, 64–66. A Middle Gaelic poem about Cormac's "Testament" was edited by Poppe, "Cormac's Metrical Testament."
**313** Henry, *English and Celtic Lyric*, 54.
**314** Henry, *Early English and Celtic Lyric*, 54.
**315** Compare the mood in the refrain in *Deor*: *þæs oferēode, þisses swā mæġ*, which Pope translated freely "That (misfortune just alluded to) has passed over, so may this (whatever is troubling us now)"; Pope, *Seven Old English Poems*, 93.
**316** Breatnach, "*Amra Senáin*"; Ó Corráin, *Clavis*, ii, 1153–54 §866.
**317** The standard edition is still Meyer, "*Sanas Cormaic*"; Ó Corráin, *Clavis*, ii, 1171–74 §887.
**318** For discussions of *Sanas Cormaic* and related texts and glossaries, see Russell, "Sounds of a Silence"; Russell, "*Dúil Dromma Cetta*."
**319** Meyer, "*Sanas Cormaic*," 7–8 §69.

explanation of the adverb *prull*.[320] Some have doubted Cormac's authorship of the glossary, but it is plausible that he was involved as editor or compiler.[321] Cormac, like Alfred, may have initiated the *Sanas Cormaic* project, perhaps composing entries himself, while the final compilation was undertaken by scholars continuing the project beyond his lifetime.

Dallán mac Móre (fl. 900) was the court poet of Cerball mac Muirecáin, king of Leinster, and contemporary of Cormac mac Cuilennáin.[322]

Uallach ingen (daughter) Muinecháin (d. 934), a rare example of official recognition of a female poet, is entered in the Annals of Inisfallen.[323]

Owun (tenth century), a scribe with a Brittonic-looking name, signed himself in a colophon in the MacRegol Gospels (Oxford, Bodleian Library, MS Auct. D.2.19) which he was glossing in Old English.[324]

Cináed úa hArtacáin (d. 975), a widely cited poet, composed praise poems, place-lore (*dindsenchas*), and an important poem on Gaelic heroes.[325]

Flann mac Maíle M'Áedóc (d. 979), *airchinnech* (monastic superior) of Killeshin (*Glenn Uissen*), Co. Laois, composed about the heroes of the Leinstermen.[326]

Urard mac Coisse (ca. 990), credited with the narrative tale *Airec menman* (Mental stratagem) which contains tale lists discussed in chapter three, was a noted poet.[327]

Eochaid úa Flainn (d. 1004) contributed to the evolution of the *Lebor Gabála* project.[328] Eochaid descended from an aristocratic line and was related to important ecclesiastics and scholars at Armagh.

Ælfric (d. ca. 1012), abbot of Eynsham, was noted as "the greatest prose writer of the Anglo-Saxon period."[329] He was a prolific homilist and composer of saints' lives.[330] His pedagogical works included the first vernacular grammar

---

320 Meyer, "*Sanas Cormaic*," 90–94 §1059; Ní Dhonnchadha, "*Prull* Narrative."
321 Russell, "Sounds of a Silence," 10–15.
322 For poems attributed to Dallán, see Ó Corráin, *Clavis*, iii, 1595–98 §§1204–9.
323 Mac Airt, *Annals of Inisfallen*, 150–51; Johnston, *Literacy and Identity*, 140.
324 Thornbury, *Becoming a Poet*, 67, 247; Breay and Story, *Anglo-Saxon Kingdoms*, 210–11.
325 Ó Corráin, *Clavis*, iii, 1553–56 §§1151–55.
326 Ó Corráin, *Clavis*, iii, 1608 §1221.
327 Mac Cana, *Learned Tales*, 33–38; O'Leary, "Poet(s) Mac Coisi"; Ó Corráin, *Clavis*, iii, 1295–96 §982.
328 Smith, *Politics and Land*; Ó Corráin, *Clavis*, iii, 1539–41 §1142.
329 Greenfield and Calder, *New Critical History*, 75. For a more nuanced view, see Bredehoft, *Authors, Audiences*, 146–70 (What Has Ælfric to Do with *Maldon*?).
330 Clemoes, *Aelfric's Catholic Homilies*; Godden, *Aelfric's Catholic Homilies*; Clayton and Mullins, *Old English Lives of Saints*. See further Breay and Story, *Anglo-Saxon Kingdoms*, 250–51.

of the Latin language, a glossary, and a colloquy for the classroom.[331] He also engaged in Biblical translation.[332] He relied on the Hiberno-Latin *De duodecim abusivis* for some of his exegetical writing.[333]

Airbertach mac Coisse Dobráin (d. 1016) produced poems on world geography and the creation of the world in the psalter text *Saltair na Rann*.[334] Airbertach was *fer légind* at Ros Ailithir, now Roscarberry, Co. Cork.[335]

Mac Liag (d. 1016) was court poet to Brian Boru (*Bóroime*; d. 1014), a Munster king who successfully challenged the Uí Néill domination of the high-kingship of Ireland. Mac Liag has many poems attributed to him.[336]

Byrhtferth (d. ca. 1020) of Ramsey wrote *Enchiridion*, a mixture of Latin and Old English intended to teach his students computus.[337]

Wulfstan (d. ca. 1023) completed his career as archbishop of York. He too was noted for homilies and sermons. The most famous, *Sermo Lupi ad Anglos*, criticized the Anglo-Saxons for their shortcomings.[338] He relied often on the writings of Ælfric, and like him referenced *De duodecim abusivis* in his political theory, such as *Institutes of Polity*.[339]

Cúán úa Locháin (d. 1024) wrote prolifically on place lore (*dindśenchas*) and the prerogatives of kings.[340]

Flann Mainistrech (d. 1056) of Monasterboice (*Mainister Buite*, Co. Louth) wrote widely on world history, the kings of Tara, and the mythical race of the Tuatha Dé Danann, who will be noted in chapter three in the discussion of *Cath Maige Tuired*. All of these topics contributed to the development of the *Lebor Gabála* tradition.[341]

---

[331] For an illustration of his grammar, see Breay and Story, *Anglo-Saxon Kingdoms*, 248–49.
[332] Greenfield and Calder, *New Critical History*, 75–88; Breay and Story, *Anglo-Saxon Kingdoms*, 244–45.
[333] Clayton, *Two Ælfric Texts*.
[334] Kenney, *Sources*, 681–83 §§545–47; Ó Corráin, *Clavis*, i, 97–98 §§45–46, 105–6 §59; ii, 1156–57 §§870–71.
[335] For the rôle of *fer légind*, see Johnston, *Literacy and Identity*, 107–9, 124–26.
[336] Ó Corráin, *Clavis*, iii, 1625–26 §1238, 1627 §1241, 1628–31 §§1243–46.
[337] Baker and Lapidge, *Byrhtferth's Enchiridion*; Stephenson, *Politics of Language*, 39–67; Breay and Story, *Anglo-Saxon Kingdoms*, 272–73.
[338] Breay and Story, *Anglo-Saxon Kingdoms*, 356–57; Bredehoft, *Authors, Audiences*, 26–38, 174–80 for other works by Wulfstan.
[339] Greenfield and Calder, *New Critical History*, 88–95. He also engaged in writing laws, see Breay and Story, *Anglo-Saxon Kingdoms*, 366–67.
[340] Downey, "Cúán Ó Lothcháin"; Ó Corráin, *Clavis*, iii, 1556–64 §§1156–66.
[341] Mac Airt, "Poems on World Kingship"; Smith, "Poem of the Kings of Mide"; Ó Corráin, *Clavis*, iii, 1568–75 §§1172–79a.

Gilla Cóemáin (d. 1072) wrote many poems on historical topics, including lists of kings and culture heroes.[342] It is not certain that all his work was intended to contribute to the *Lebor Gabála* project, but much of his poetry found its way into various recensions.

Máel Ísu úa Brolcháin (d. 1086) wrote devotional and didactic poems and was a respected religious poet of his time.[343]

Dublittir úa Úathgaile (fl. 1090), *fer légind* of Killeshin, composed *Sex Aetates Mundi*, dealing with the six ages of the world and the periodization of history, intended as a textbook in the monastic schools.[344]

Gilla in Choimded Úa Cormaic (fl. 1100) composed the substantial poem of sixty-three quatrains beginning "Aimirgein Glúngel tuir tend" which is a retrospective look at famous poets and jurists of the Gaelic tradition, both mythico-legendary and historical.[345] It is a poem that pays homage to a lengthy Gaelic literary history, reflecting a cultural awareness that was not duplicated in Anglo-Saxon writings.

---

**342** Smith, *Three Historical Poems*; Smith, "*Tigernmas mac Follaig aird*"; Ó Corráin, *Clavis*, iii, 1575–81 §§1180–86.
**343** Kenney, *Sources*, 727–28 §585; Murphy, *Early Irish Metrics*, 52–59 §§22–25 and notes 194–99; Ó Corráin, *Clavis*, ii, 1165 §882.
**344** Ó Cróinín, *Sex Aetates Mundi*; Ó Corráin, *Clavis*, i, 152–55 §§119–20.
**345** Smith, "Aimirgein Glúngel Tuir Tend"; Ó Corráin, *Clavis*, iii, 1583–84 §1190.

# Chapter Three
# Professional Poets and Vernacular Narratives

The present chapter concentrates on the Gaelic literary tradition and its practitioners to help place it within the broader "background" of insular vernacular literatures. It begins with the professional status of Gaelic poets, their social rank and privilege, their program of schooling, and their place in the law-tracts among entertainers and craftsmen. The poets' prestige came, partially at least, from the fact that "the patrons of the poets were normally either kings and nobles, or the Church."[1] In both traditions the early historical poets were associated with the Church.

A sense of the lore controlled by the *filid* is demonstrated by the tales once contained in the now lost manuscript *Cín Dromma Snechta*. Its tales constitute a corpus of seventh- and eighth-century texts that include allegorical sea voyages, a political prophecy, the earliest vernacular *speculum principum*, conception tales, stories about an historical culture hero, and a vatic poem that presages events of the epic *Táin Bó Cúailnge*, among others. These vernacular texts are roughly contemporary with the chronological heart (635–735) of this study.[2]

A ninth-century etiological legend, whose events are set in the seventh century, relates how the *Táin* had to be recovered because the epic had been exchanged for Isidore's *Etymologiae*. It is an explicit expression of the interchange between indigenous vernacular traditions and Latinate learning from the Continent. The legend cites fore-tales (*remscéla*), which are known to modern scholarship, that provide background to the *Táin*. Their existence parallels the "digression" in *Beowulf*, related to the Finn episode, as noted in chapter one.

A vast corpus of narrative tales survives. Two tenth-century tale lists provide just under two hundred tale titles. This study examines surviving tales which have been treated in modern editions. The discussion provides a sense of the array of contents for these tales; their intertextual cross-referencing; the rôle of poets, musicians, and entertainers; and the appearance of individual characters in multiple tales. In the Old English corpus Weland the smith appears in *Deor*, in *Beowulf*, in the Alfredian translation of Boethius's *Consolatio Philosophiae*, and pictorially on the Franks Casket.[3]

---

1 Breatnach, *Uraicecht na Ríar*, 89, but see more fully 89–94.
2 For broad introductory surveys of Gaelic literature that extend beyond the contents of the *Cín*, see Ó Cathasaigh, "Literature of Medieval Ireland"; Ní Mhaonaigh, "*Légend hÉrenn*."
3 Frank, "Germanic Legend," 92.

Some tales emphasize the Irish Sea as a cultural region with characters and events moving between Ireland and Britain. Gaelic tales tend to be accurately locatable within these islands, whereas for legendary characters and events in Old English literature "none of the stories takes place in the British Isles."[4] The *Widsith* poet claims to have spent time among Scots and Picts but does not impute to them any legendary material.[5]

Finally, texts on poetics survive. In a society where poets enjoyed such prestige it is only logical that texts describing their art, and justifying their claims as "inspired" individuals, should form part of their corpus. Poems created through sleep or trance, or resulting from dreams, are discussed.

## Gaelic Poets in the Law-Tracts

A professional class of poets existed among the Gaels who participated in a system of formal training and apprenticeship that included hereditary privileges for poets who descended from poets. Gaelic poets enjoyed higher social status than their Anglo-Saxon counterparts. Hierarchies of poets, with named divisions based on analogy to the seven grades of the church, are recorded in vernacular law-tracts. The amount of training, skills and qualifications, honor-price, and privileges – such as size of retinues and freedom to travel – are designated for each poetic rank. These hierarchies extended to all divisions of society and the professions.

Early Gaelic society was "hierarchical and inegalitarian"[6] and the law-tracts lay "great stress on distinctions of rank and profession."[7] The chief distinctions were between those who were *nemed* (privileged), and those who were non-*nemed*. The original meaning of *nemed* was "consecrated place; sanctuary" and when applied to persons implied "sacredness; privileged or dignified status." In a legal context *nemed* referred to "persons possessing legal status or privilege."[8] Within the *nemed* social ranks and professions was the further distinction of those who were *sóernemed* (noble *nemed*; a noble dignitary) and those who were *dóernemed* (base *nemed*; a dependent professional).[9] The only profession with *sóernemed* status was the poet (*fili*).[10] All other professions were *dóernemed* or

---

4 Frank, "Germanic Legend," 89.
5 Krapp and Dobbie, *Exeter Book*, 152, line 79; Hill, *Minor Heroic Poems*, 34, line 79.
6 Kelly, *Guide*, 7.
7 Kelly, *Guide*, 16.
8 eDIL: http://www.dil.ie, s.v. *neimed* or dil.ie/33032.
9 Kelly, *Guide*, 9–10.
10 Kelly, *Guide*, 43.

non-*nemed*. Some *dóernemed* professions included lawyers (*brithem* and *aigne*), the physician (*liaig*), the woodworker (*sáer*), the blacksmith (*gobae*), the silversmith (*cerd*), and coppersmith (*umaige*). Entertainers also figure as professionals, but only the harper (*cruit*) achieved *dóernemed* status. All other entertainers were non-*nemed* and considered *fodána* (subordinate professions) such as the piper (*cuislennach*), the horn player (*cornaire*), the juggler (*clesamnach*), and the jester (*fuirsire*).[11]

This brief survey of professional ranks confirms the prominence assigned to poets and harpers among the Gaels, and *Widsith* implies something similar in the Old English tradition. While among the Anglo-Saxons there is no conclusive evidence that the two rôles were filled by the same person, among the Gaels the two were kept separate, at least at the professional levels. The poets' *sóernemed* status was equal to the highest secular or ecclesiastical ranks. The harper was *dóernemed*, a status that nevertheless placed him well above other entertainers in the social hierarchy.

The introduction to the seventh-century law-tract collection *Senchas Már* (The Great Tradition) lists five social positions that are awarded the highest *díre* (honor price, compensation), a term roughly equivalent to Old English *wergild*.[12] Those five are a king (*rí*), a bishop (*epscop*), a "pillar of the law of Scripture" (*áige rechto litre*), in other words an ecclesiastical scholar, a master poet (*suí filed*), and a hospitaller (*briugu*).[13] Later law-tracts kept four of these top categories, but removed the *briugu*, so that kings, bishops, ecclesiastical scholars, and master poets all retained *sóernemed* status, but the *briugu* retained equal *díre* (honor price) with the other top ranks.[14]

Four eighth-century law-tracts adumbrate the status of poets in the larger society.[15] The earliest of the four, *Bretha Nemed* (Judgments of Privileged Persons), dated to the second quarter of the eighth century,[16] was composed sometime after

---

11 Kelly, *Guide*, 51–65. For a discussion of distinctions in woodwind instruments, see Bisagni, "Flutes, Pipes."
12 For the *Senchas Már*, see Ó Corráin, *Clavis*, ii, 863–72 §668, 905–7 §679, 909–11 §682, 915–16 §687, 918–19 §691, 921 §695; iii, 1583–84 §1190.
13 Breatnach, *Senchas Már*, 4–5 §4.
14 For discussion of the *briugu*, see Kelly, *Guide*, 36–38.
15 The social status of poets is outlined in Kelly, *Guide*, 43–49. The knowledge purportedly controlled by the *filid* included meters, narrative tales, genealogies, law, prophecy. For some studies that attempt to convey that breadth, see Murphy, "Bards and Filidh"; Mac Airt, "*Filidecht* and *Coimgne*"; Ó Cathasaigh, "Aspects of Memory and Identity."
16 Breatnach, "Canon Law and Secular Law," 442–44 for dating. This law-tract was composed by three kinsmen, one of whom, Máel Tuile úa Búireucháin, was a poet. There are two related tracts called *Bretha Nemed*, one designated *toísech* (early), and one *dédenach* (late). See further, Kelly,

the *Collectio canonum Hibernensis* ca. 725.[17] *Bretha Nemed* distinguished four divisions of those with "noble privilege" (*sóernemed*). They were the ecclesiastical scholar (*ecnae*), churchman (*eclais*), lord (*flaith*), poet (*fili*).[18] While using different vocabulary, the *Bretha Nemed* agrees with the earlier *Senchas Már* in placing these four categories at the highest social levels. In both law-tracts top-ranking poets were equal to the highest ranks of secular (*flaith*) and ecclesiastical authorities (*ecnae* and *eclais*). Two law-tracts, *Uraicecht Becc* (Small Primer)[19] and *Míadšlechtae* (Sections on Rank),[20] were composed after the middle of the eighth century. Both refer to poets who are ranked within the top echelons of the social hierarchy.

The most recent of the four, *Uraicecht na Ríar* (Primer of the Stipulations),[21] is devoted entirely to poets, their grades, their qualifications, their training, and the size of their retinues. While each law-tract differs with regard to details, they all agree in the esteem accorded poets as a learned class within the Gaelic social hierarchy.

*Uraicecht na Ríar* divides the hierarchy of poets into seven named grades based on the seven grades of the Church. Other eighth-century law-tracts, *Bretha Nemed*, *Uraicecht Becc*, *Córus Bésgnai*,[22] *Míadšlechta*, and *Críth Gablach*,[23] also use seven grades based on the ecclesiastical model.[24] Aldhelm's treatise on the number seven, included in his *Epistola ad Acircium* sent to Aldfrith *sapiens*, may have been intended to impress the new king with his understanding of why the number seven mattered so to the Church.[25]

---

*Guide*, 268–69, §14 (*toísech*), §15 (*dédenach*); Breatnach, *Uraicecht na Ríar*, 20–57; Breatnach, *Companion*, 184–91, §5.15 (*dédenach*), §5.16 (*toísech*); Ó Corráin, *Clavis*, ii, 907–9 §680, 915 §686, 1174 §894, 1197 §914 (*dédenach*); ii, 907–9 §680, 909–11 §682, 919 §692 (*toísech*).

17 For dating limits of the *collectio*, see Russell, "'What was Best of Every Language'," 445; Charles-Edwards, *Early Christian Ireland*, 265. See the edition and translation by Flechner, *Hibernensis*; Ó Corráin, *Clavis*, ii, 769–70 §585; Sharpe, *Handlist*, 93 §207, 599 §1599.

18 Breatnach, "*Bretha Nemed Toísech*," 8–9 §1.

19 MacNeill, "Ancient Irish Law," 272–81; Kelly, *Guide*, 267; Breatnach, *Uraicecht na Ríar*, 3–19; Breatnach, *Companion*, 315–18; Ó Corráin, *Clavis*, ii, 863–72 §668, 900–901 §670, 902 §673, 909 §681, 916 §688.

20 MacNeill, "Ancient Irish Law," 311–13; Kelly, *Guide*, 267; Breatnach, *Uraicecht na Ríar*, 19; Breatnach, *Companion*, 264–65; Ó Corráin, *Clavis*, ii, 911–14 §§683–84.

21 Breatnach, *Uraicecht na Ríar*, 77 (for dating to "the second half of the eighth century"); Kelly, *Guide*, 268 §13; Breatnach, *Companion*, 320–21; Ó Corráin, *Clavis*, ii, 901–2 §673, 905–7 §679, 915 §686, 922–24 §698.

22 Breatnach, *Córus Bésgnai*; Ó Corráin, *Clavis*, ii, 905–7 §679.

23 Binchy, *Críth Gablach*; Ó Corráin, *Clavis*, ii, 863–72 §668, 911–13 §683.

24 Breatnach, *Uraicecht na Ríar*, 81–89.

25 Ireland, "Where Was King Aldfrith Educated?" 38–39 and nn46–48.

*Uraicecht na Ríar* names the seven poetic grades from highest to lowest: *ollam, ánṡruth, clí, cano, dos, macfuirmid, fochloc*.[26] Ironically, this same section also names three sub-grades (*fográda*) of poets: *taman, drisiuc, oblaire*.[27] All ten named divisions of poets are found in the literature and prove that such distinctions existed in society. However, the ten named divisions suggest that Gaelic social structures based on the model of the Church was a recent fiction devised by the juridical classes. The Gaelic jurists were schematizing an already hierarchical Gaelic society based on the prestige model of the Church.

> §6. How is a grade conferred on a poet? Not difficult; he shows his compositions (*dréchta*) to an *ollam* (highest grade of poet) – and he (the *ollam*) has seven grades of knowledge – and the king receives him in his full grade in which the *ollam* declares him to be on the basis of his compositions, and his guiltlessness, and his purity, that is, purity of learning, and purity of mouth, and purity of hand and marital union.
>
> This extract from *Uraicecht na Ríar*, a law-tract of the second half of the eighth century, treats the grades and qualifications of poets. Note how "purity of marital union" implies the acceptance by the poets of Church authority in such personal matters and emphasizes the cooperation between the professional poets and the Church. The verb translated as "shows" (*do·aisféna*) can also be translated as "sets forth, declares, recites" and need not imply a written "composition."
>
> (Translation based on edition by Breatnach, *Uraicecht na Ríar*, 104–5 §6).

**Figure 3.a:** Conferring a Grade (*grád*) on a Poet (*fili*).

The chief poet (*ollam filed*) must have three hundred and fifty *dréchta* (compositions), and he must be knowledgeable in each *coimgne*, translated here as "historical science," as well as in the "jurisprudence of Irish law" (*brithemnacht fénechais*).[28] Through his poetic craft (*éicse*) and integrity (*idnae*) he "illuminates nobility" (*for úaisli –osnai*), a reference to duties of encomium for the upper classes.[29] Offending or violating an *ollam* carried heavy penalties. Achieving that rank required not only rigorous training and proven competence, but an *ollam* must be the son of an *ollam* and the grandson of one as well.[30]

---

26 Breatnach, *Uraicecht na Ríar*, 102–3 §1.
27 Breatnach, *Uraicecht na Ríar*, 102–3 §1.
28 Breatnach, *Uraicecht na Ríar*, 102–3 §2.
29 Breatnach, *Uraicecht na Ríar*, 102–3 §3.
30 This is referred to as the "three generation requirement": Breatnach, *Uraicecht na Ríar*, 102–3 §3.

The trained *fili* possessed an array of specialized skills. In addition to a general knowledge of *senchas* (e.g., traditional tales, genealogies, native law) the *fili* should control the performance of *imbas for·osna* (great knowledge which illumines), the vatic skill purportedly displayed by the poetess Fedelm, noted in chapter one.[31] The poet must also perform *díchetal di chennaib* (chanting from heads), representing extempore composition, like the poet in *Beowulf* who knew the old stories (*ġidda ġemyndiġ*; line 868b) and varied the words (*wordum wrixlan*; line 874a).[32]

It is not certain what is intended by *drécht*, but it is often equated with a "tale." It will become clearer as to why when the tale lists are discussed. The tract explains that the *ollam* has fifty *dréchta* for each of the seven grades.[33] This number demonstrates the learned achievement attained through training. The number of *dréchta* required of each grade does not progress by increments of fifty, however.[34] In fact, the next grade below *ollam*, the *ánṡruth*, is required to possess one hundred and seventy-five *dréchta*, half the amount for the *ollam*.[35] But each grade of poet must progress through a course of study (*frithgnam*). If a *drécht* equates to a tale, then we should recall the poet Forgoll telling a tale (*scél*) each night of winter.[36]

Many legal points are illustrated by the jurists in narrative sequences in the law-tracts. Conversely, in narratives such as the *Táin*, many episodes can only be understood by reference to the laws.[37] Examples of the first type were published by Myles Dillon and "are all written in prose so as to provide a fuller background to certain incidents alluded to in the canonical text of the two *Bretha Nemed* tracts."[38] The collection of legal anecdotes thus becomes a reference book for jurists in story form such that "nowhere else is the referential function of narratives

---

[31] For a fuller discussion of the special skills required of a *fili*, see Carey, "Three Things"; For the broad skills of a *fili* and their implications for Gaelic cultural unity, see Ó Cathasaigh, "Aspects of Identity and Memory."

[32] Fulk, Bjork, Niles, *Klaeber's Beowulf*, cxxi–cxxii, 31, lines 867b–74a, notes at 165–66; Thornbury, *Becoming a Poet*, 17–19.

[33] Breatnach, *Uraicecht na Ríar*, 102–3 §2.

[34] The requirements are outlined in a chart: Breatnach, *Uraicecht na Ríar*, 176 (Table 1). According to *Uraicecht na Ríar*, the *fochloc* must have thirty *dréchta*, the *macfuirmid* forty, the *dos* fifty, the *cano* sixty, the *clí* eighty-seven, the *ánṡruth* one hundred and seventy-five. The fully qualified *ollam* must have twice the number of *dréchta* as the grade below him.

[35] Breatnach, *Uraicecht na Ríar*, 108–9 §12.

[36] White, *Compert Mongáin*, 73 (Gaelic), 79 (English) §1 of text 2: *Scél as-a:mberar combad hé Find mac Cumaill Mongán*.

[37] See, for example, Breatnach, "Law and Literature," 233–35; Qiu, "Ulster Cycle in the Law Tracts"; Ó Cathasaigh, *Táin Bó Cúailnge and Early Irish Law*.

[38] Qiu, "Narratives in Early Irish Law," 119; Breatnach, "Law and Literature," 224–31. For the editions and translations, see Dillon, "Stories from Law-Tracts."

more explicit" for explaining the law-tracts.[39] Many tales from the Ulster Cycle deal with legal matters.[40] One important example, discussed in chapter one, related how King Conchobar abrogated the function of judge for the *filid* because of the obfuscating language of two poets debating at court.[41] Nevertheless, in other Ulster Cycle tales poets function as judges, negotiators, and litigants in legal debates.[42] The legal rôle of poets never disappeared and they continued to function as learned men.[43] As stated in *Uraicecht na Ríar*, a top-ranking poet (*ollam*) was expected to be conversant in the "jurisprudence of Irish law" (*brithemnacht fénechais*).[44]

The importance of the term *coimgne* (earlier *coimcne*) is obvious from the requirement that an *ollam* be knowledgeable in it. However, its full meaning remains uncertain.[45] It has sometimes been translated as "synchronism" but there is already a specific term (*comaimserad*) to cover that meaning.[46] *Coimgne* has also been translated more widely as "historical science."[47] It is reasonable that chronology be included in its definition, but the emphasis on matters chronological appears to derive from the earlier translation as "synchronism." Seán Mac Airt noted that, based on its proposed etymology from *com-* (together, mutually, equally)[48] and *ecnae* (wisdom, knowledge, enlightenment), but more specifically "acquired knowledge,"[49] its meaning "would seem to be something like 'joint knowledge' (σύγγνωσις), 'all-embracing knowledge'."[50] Taking Mac Airt's suggestion further, *coimgne* appears to represent a synthesizing or harmonizing of various branches of knowledge. *Coimgne* would thus designate a process; an eclectic blending of different branches of *ecnae* (knowledge), from both indigenous and Latinate traditions, in order to achieve innovative and complementary results.

---

**39** Qiu, "Narratives in Early Irish Law," 120.
**40** For an example of how legal points form the pivot of an episode in the *macgnímrada*, see Ireland, "From Protected to Protector."
**41** This is the tale *Immacallam in dá Thuarad*. See further Breatnach, "Law and Literature," 217–21.
**42** Qiu, "Ulster Cycle in the Law Tracts," 15–18. For more detailed discussion, see Hollo, "Depiction of Senchae mac Ailella."
**43** Breatnach, "Law and Literature," 231–33.
**44** Breatnach, *Uraicecht na Ríar*, 102–3 §2.
**45** See discussions of its possible meanings: Mac Airt, "*Filidecht* and *Coimgne*"; Mac Cana, *Learned Tales*, 123–27; Ó Cathasaigh, "Aspects of Identity and Memory," 203–5, 214.
**46** eDIL: http://www.dil.ie, s.v. *comaimserad* or dil.ie/10611.
**47** Breatnach, *Uraicecht na Ríar*, 102–3 §1; Ó Cathasaigh, "Aspects of Identity and Memory," 202–4.
**48** eDIL: http://www.dil.ie, s.v. 1 *com-* or dil.ie/10554.
**49** eDIL: http://www.dil.ie, s.v. 1 *ecna(e)* or dil.ie/19605.
**50** Mac Airt, "*Filidecht* and *Coimgne*," 143.

The seventh-century introduction to the *Senchas Már* describes *senchas* (tradition) as the "joint recollection of two elders, transmission from one ear to another, chanting of poets."[51] That is an accurate description of indigenous oral culture. However, it is to be augmented by "the law of Scripture" (*recht litre*),[52] the literate, Latinate culture of Christianity and the Bible. Indigenous and Latinate cultural traditions, both oral and literate, are combined and reconciled in a syncretic process. Later in the introduction, the necessity of honoring verbal contracts (*coir*; sg. *cor*) is exemplified by Adam's bad bargain of losing the world in exchange for a single apple.[53] The native requirement of honoring both advantageous and disadvantageous (oral) contracts is illustrated syncretistically by an *exemplum* from the Bible.

The eighth-century "pseudo-historical prologue" to the *Senchas Már* illustrates an early test case on the Christian law of forgiveness. The case is played out in an allegory telling how a group of nine high-status men were convened to reconcile the Church's teachings with the laws and customs of the pre-Christian Gaels. The nine-man group consisted of three named kings, three named bishops, and three named learned men, two of whom were poets: Dubthach maccu Lugair and Fergus *fili*.[54] Their deliberations concluded that those indigenous customs and practices that did not contravene Scripture and Church teachings, and which did not conflict with the consciences of Christians, could be kept. The result of their efforts was the entire legal corpus of the *Senchas Már*.[55]

Thus we have in the "pseudo-historical prologue" to the *Senchas Már*, allegorically, secular rulers, ecclesiastical authorities, and indigenous scholars and poets working together to "syncretize" native Gaelic traditions with Latinate, ecclesiastical practices. They reconciled native practice and law so as to complement the new Christian dispensation but allow as much native custom as practicable to continue.[56] It has been proposed that this "syncretic" approach among the Gaels helps explain the Christian coloring so noticeable in *Beowulf*.[57]

---

[51] "Comchuimne dá šen, tindnacul clúaise di araili, díchetal filed": Breatnach, *Senchas Már*, 4–5 §1.
[52] "Tórmach ó recht litre": Breatnach, *Senchas Már*, 4–5 §1.
[53] Breatnach, *Senchas Már*, 6–7 §10. *Di Astud Chor* (On the Securing of Contracts), a separate legal tract, uses this same *exemplum*: McLeod, *Early Irish Contract Law*, 36, 128–29 §4, 140–41 §15, 164–65 §33.
[54] McCone, "Dubthach Maccu Lugair," 8–10, §§6–8; Carey, "Pseudo-Historical Prologue," 18–19, §§7–11. For a discussion in the context of vernacular poets, see Ireland, "Vernacular Poets," 55–56.
[55] McCone, "Dubthach Maccu Lugair," 9; Carey, "Pseudo-Historical Prologue," 18–19 §7. For a list of the forty-seven titled texts that make up the *Senchas Már*, see Breatnach, *Senchas Már*, 1–2.
[56] For a sensitive survey of this process, see Carey, "Learning, Imagination and Belief." For a wider discussion of religious speculation and philosophical inquiry related to this syncretic process, see Carey, *Single Ray of the Sun*.
[57] Hill, "*Beowulf* and Conversion History," 200–201.

The clearest allegorical expression of *coimgne* as a harmonizing of disciplines is found in the Middle Gaelic legend that evolved around the historical Cenn Fáelad *sapiens* (d. 679). According to the later legend he learned *légend* (Latinate, ecclesiastical learning), *fénechas* (native law), and *filidecht* (poetry and native lore) because three schools dedicated to each of those subjects stood at Tuaim Drecain (Tomregan, Co. Cavan) where he was recovering from a head wound suffered at the Battle of Mag Roth (639; Moira, Co. Down). Cenn Fáelad was able to blend, or synthesize, the three major disciplines in poetic form.[58] The legendary Cenn Fáelad came to represent those synthesizing endeavors. The historical person will be discussed further in chapter four.

This evidence reveals the cooperation between the Church and the poetic classes. The career of Colmán mac Lénéni (d. 606), discussed in chapter two, is a case in point. Muirchú's seventh-century *Vita Patricii* portrays the poets Dubthach maccu Lugair and Fiacc Finn Sléibte at the pagan court of Lóegaire mac Néill cooperating with the saint.[59] Dubthach played a central rôle in the syncretic "pseudo-historical prologue." Cenn Fáelad *sapiens* blended in verse the indigenous and Latinate learning that he acquired at the three schools according to later legend.

Among the Anglo-Saxons critics have noted the harmonizing of Christian and heroic values in *Beowulf*.[60] *Widsith*, as preserved, juxtaposes legendary and historical characters from Germanic tradition alongside peoples from world history such as Israelites, Egyptians, and Indians.[61] The iconography of the Frank's Casket portrays scenes from Germanic myth, from the Bible, and from Rome's own etiological legend.[62] As among the Gaels, historical Anglo-Saxon poets were either clerics or wrote on topics of importance to the Church. The *filid* utilized their prestige status to influence the harmonization and blending of indigenous traditions and Latinate practices approved by the Church.

## Cín Dromma Snechtai

Rudolf Thurneysen first reconstructed the original contents of a lost manuscript known as *Cín Dromma Snechtai* (The Book of Druimm Snechtai) based on

---

58  Ireland, "Case of Cenn Fáelad."
59  Bieler, *Patrician Texts*, 92–93, §I 19 (18); Ireland, "Vernacular Poets."
60  Fulk, Bjork, Niles, *Klaeber's Beowulf*, lxvii–lxxix; Hill, "*Beowulf* and Conversion History."
61  Hill, *Minor Heroic Poems*, 34, lines 79–84 and glossary.
62  Webster, "Franks Casket."

references to its contents in later manuscripts.[63] The *Cín* itself no longer survives.[64] The manuscript was named for a minor ecclesiastical foundation at Druimm Snechtai (literally "ridge of snow"; Drumsnat, Co. Monaghan), a daughter house of Bangor, Co. Down. Druimm Snechtai was founded by Mo-Lua (d. ca. 612), the hypocoristic name of Lugaid maccu Óchae, who had been fostered and trained by St. Comgall, founder of Bangor, in the mid sixth century.[65] Mo-Lua also founded Clonfertmulloe (*Cluain Ferta Mo-Lua*; Kyle, Co. Laois), a monastery which received Cummian's letter on the Paschal controversy (ca. 632), to be discussed in chapter four.[66] Clonfertmulloe was the establishment of Laidcenn *sapiens* (d. 661), and he will be discussed in chapter four. The monastery Mo-Lua founded at Drumsnat, and Bangor where he trained, are both associated with the evolution of vernacular literature.

The *Cín* is usually assigned to the early eighth century, although it has been argued that it may be tenth century.[67] Other commentators note that there is a tenth-century node in the transmission of texts from the *Cín*, but there is general agreement that those same texts have an Old Gaelic core dated linguistically to the eighth century, with some being assigned to the seventh.[68] Whether or not the *Cín* was an eighth- or a tenth-century manuscript, the texts associated with it constitute a significant corpus of early Old Gaelic literature from the seventh and eighth centuries.

Some of the *Cín* texts are derived from the Ulster Cycle and predate the earliest, ninth-century recension of the *Táin Bó Cúailnge*.[69] *Compert Chonchobuir* (The Conception of Conchobar)[70] and *Compert Con Chulainn* (The Conception

---

63 Ó Corráin, *Clavis*, ii, 1053–54 §815; Thurneysen, "Zu irische Handschriften," 23–30; Thurneysen, *Die irische Helden- und Königsage*, 15–18; Ó Concheanainn, "Connacht Medieval Literary Heritage."
64 The word *cín* comes from Latin *quinio* and means "booklet; book": eDIL: http://www.dil.ie, s.v. *cín*, dil.ie/9105; Thurneysen, *Grammar of Old Irish*, 571 §920; Souter, *Glossary of Later Latin*, 339 s.v. "group of five."
65 Ní Dhonnchadha, "Irish Vernacular Literary Tradition," 574–75.
66 Walsh and Ó Cróinín, *Cummian's Letter*, 91n262.
67 Thurneysen, "Zu irische Handschriften," 26; for arguments of a tenth-century origin, see Appendix 1 of Mac Mathúna, *Immram Brain*, 421–69.
68 McCone, *Echtrae Chonnlai*, 67–70; White, *Compert Mongáin*, 35–37. For arguments of possible seventh-century origins, see Carey, "*Cín Dromma Snechtai* Texts."
69 The earliest surviving recension is a composite from four manuscripts. For an edition and translation, see O'Rahilly, *Táin: Recension I*; Ó Corráin, *Clavis*, iii, 1445–68 §1103.
70 For an edition and translation, see Hull, "Conception of Conchobor." For a more recent translation, see Koch, *Celtic Heroic Age*, 59–63 §73; Ó Corráin, *Clavis*, iii, 1347–49 §1026.

of Cú Chulainn)[71] are both early eighth-century texts and give important background details for two major characters in the *Táin*. *Verba Scáthaige* (The Words of Scáthach) is probably a seventh-century text.[72] Scáthach is the female martial arts instructor in Britain (*Albu*) who honed the fighting skills of Cú Chulainn. The poem is uttered by Scáthach through *imbas for·osna* (great knowledge which illumines). The poem prophesies Cú Chulainn's participation in the *Táin* and his combat successes against great odds. It names the protagonists Ailill and Medb and cites the denouement of the *Táin* in the combat between the two bulls Finnbennach and Donn Cúailnge. These three texts provide evidence for the existence of the epic *Táin* before the earliest surviving recension was preserved in writing.

The *Cín* contained narratives that combined elements of indigenous lore and Latinate learning, a phenomenon discussed above. This blending aspect of the early literature can be seen in *Echtrae Chonnlai* (The Faring Forth of Connlae)[73] and *Immram Brain* (The Voyage of Bran).[74] Both texts involve high-status men at their courts who encounter mysterious "otherworldly" women who describe wondrous lands across the sea, inhabited only by women, where there is neither sorrow nor death. Commentators agree that the texts should be read allegorically, but there is little consensus as to the details of interpretation.[75]

The Connlae of *Echtrae Chonnlai* is the son of Conn Cétchathach (Conn of the Hundred Battles) an ancestor figure to both the Connachtmen and the Uí Néill. The mysterious woman has been taken as a symbol for the Church, supported by Biblical precedent, but that would not exclude interpreting her as an indigenous "goddess" of sovereignty.[76] The text acknowledges "otherworldly" beings, and plays on the double meaning of *síd* as "peace" and as the "faerie folk."[77] There is contention

---

**71** For an edition, see van Hamel, *Compert Con Culainn*, 1–8. For a translation of this earliest version, see Gantz, *Irish Myths and Sagas*, 130–33; Ó Corráin, *Clavis*, iii, 1344–47 §1025.
**72** For an edition and translation, see Henry, "*Verba Scáthaige*"; Ó Corráin, *Clavis*, iii, 1501–2 §1127.
**73** McCone, *Echtrae Chonnlai*; Ó Corráin, *Clavis*, iii, 1364–66 §1042.
**74** van Hamel, *Immrama*, 1–19; Meyer, *Voyage of Bran*; Mac Mathúna, *Immram Brain*; Ó Corráin, *Clavis*, iii, 1398–400 §1072.
**75** For a cogent discussion of allegory in these works, see Carney, *Literature and History*, 280–95; Carney, "Bran Material," 183–93; Hollo, "Allegoresis." For broader views see Scowcroft, "Abstract Narrative"; and Carey, "Rhetoric."
**76** McCone, *Pagan Past*, 157–58.
**77** Carney, "Deeper Level," 165; Carey, *Single Ray of the Sun*, 27–29. For discussion of the semantic range of *síd*, see Ó Cathasaigh, "Semantics of 'Síd'."

in *Echtrae Chonnlai* between the mysterious woman and Conn's druid Corann, with the woman denigrating druidism and, apparently, foretelling the coming of Christ. *Immram Brain* presents similar situations, with an "otherworldly" woman describing a land of women far over the sea who exist without original sin and death. She also foretells a "great birth" of one who will rule over many, and this man's mother will not have known a mate.[78] She appears to refer to the birth of Christ.

Isidore of Seville, in his *Etymologiae*, attributed accuracy to the vaticinations of the sibyls of the Classical world with regard to God and Christ, so that there was an established precedent of pagan prophecies about the coming Christian dispensation.[79] One can see in the female characters of *Echtrae Chonnlai* and *Immram Brain* a reference to a personified *Sapientia* appropriate to either a pre-Christian or Christian milieu.[80] Both Gaelic texts describe places where plenty never diminishes but is replenished. One is reminded of the Gaelic metaphor of the *ubera sapientiae* where "Wisdom" offers her breasts to many sons, but however many partake, her breasts remain full.[81] Aldhelm used this metaphor to describe his pupil Heahfrith as having spent six years in Ireland "sucking the teat of wisdom."[82]

The female figure *Philosophia* consoled the imprisoned Boethius (d. 524) and helped him search for the Good in an unjust world where wealth and security are transitory. *De consolatione Philosophiae*, without specific reference to Christian doctrine, became a central text of the Christian Middle Ages. The "otherworldly" women of *Echtrae Chonnlai* and *Immram Brain* offer a land where there is no sin and no death, but at the price of leaving behind the known, transitory world. As Connlae contemplates departing with the "otherworldly" woman, he summarizes the dilemma: "It is not easy for me and besides I love my people."[83] The seventh-century macaronic *Cambrai Homily* noted that "white martyrdom" (*bán martre*) meant that a person would separate himself from all that he loved for the sake of God.[84] There are Old and New Testament precedents that would have been widely

---

[78] Meyer, *Voyage of Bran*, 14–15 §26; Mac Mathúna, *Immram Brain*, 37 (Gaelic), 50 (English) §26. See also McCone, *Pagan Past*, 79–82.
[79] "Quarum omnium carmina efferuntur, in quibus de Deo et de Christo et gentibus multa scripsisse manifestissime conprobantur": Oroz Reta and Marcos Casquero, *Etimologías*, 1:710–13, viii 8.7.
[80] Hollo, "Allegoresis," 122–27.
[81] Richter, *Ireland and Her Neighbours*, 159–60; Bayless and Lapidge, *Collectanea Pseudo-Bedae*, 122–23 §1, 199n1; Orchard, "*Hisperica Famina* as Literature," 30–32.
[82] Lapidge and Herren, *Aldhelm*, 161 (translating *uber sofiae sugens*).
[83] "Ní réid dam, sech caraim mu doíni": McCone, *Echtrae Chonnlai*, 123 §13, 184 (translation).
[84] Stokes and Strachan, *Thesaurus*, ii, 247. See further Ó Néill, "*Cambrai Homily*"; Stancliffe, "Red, White and Blue Martyrdom"; Ó Corráin, *Clavis*, ii, 1125 §847.

known to the monastic audiences of these early texts. The patriarch Abraham was encouraged to leave his country, his relations, his homeland, and go to a land which he would be shown (Genesis 12:1). In the New Testament the apostles are told that anyone who left homes, or brothers, or sisters, or father, or mother, or wife, or children, or lands for the Lord's sake would receive back a hundredfold and gain eternal life (Matthew 19:29). Such parallels would not be missed by the monastic audience of *Echtrae Chonnlai* and *Immram Brain*.

In *Immram Brain* Bran accepts the "otherworldly" woman's invitation to undertake a voyage across the sea. He sets sail accompanied by three times nine men. After two days and nights at sea Bran encounters the sea-god Manannán mac Lir. In addition to making another prediction of the advent of Christ, in an intertextual reference whose full details are told in *Compert Mongáin* (The Conception of Mongán), Manannán declares that he is on his way to Ireland to father a son, Mongán mac Fíachnai of the Dál nAraidi in Northern Ireland. Details from this tale relate to battles in northern Britain at the time of Áedán mac Gabráin and Æthelfrith reported by Bede (*HE* i 34). The references to Mongán and the Dál nAraidi reflect Bangor affiliations in this early literature.

Manannán states that, while Bran sees only a vast sea from his boat, for Manannán himself the sea is an expansive flowered plain over which he travels in a two-wheeled chariot. For Manannán the sea is a beautiful plain of sport and delights, a perspective that Bran and his men cannot share. A striking image created by Columbanus in a letter to Pope Boniface (608–615) portrays Christ as a charioteer, relying on his two steeds (Peter and Paul) to bear his message from Rome westwards to Ireland over the surging seas: "the Most Highest [sic] Pilot of that carriage [*currus*] Who is Christ, the true Father, the Charioteer of Israel, over the channels' surge, over the dolphins' backs, over the swelling flood, reached even unto us [i.e. the Gaels]."[85] The passage is a strong statement from Columbanus of the relationship between Rome and the early Gaels and the debt owed to Rome by the latter. The author of *Immram Brain* may have been indebted to Columbanus for the striking image of Christ as charioteer riding across the surging sea.[86]

---

85 "supremus ipse auriga currus illius, qui est Christus, Pater verus, agitator Israel, trans euriporium rheuma, trans delfinum dorsa, trans turgescentem dodrantem ad nos usque pervenit": Walker, *Sancti Columbani Opera*, 48–49, §11, lines 27–30.
86 First mentioned by Oskamp, *Voyage of Máel Dúin*, 80–81; discussed by others, including McCone, *Echtrae Chonnlai*, 111–13.

Four tales contained in the *Cín* are about Mongán mac Fiachnai, a historical person whose death is noted in the annals at ca. 625.[87] He apparently predeceased his father Fiachnae mac Báetáin by one year.[88] They were from Dál nAraidi, the same sept to which belonged St. Comgall, founder of Bangor. In the four tales Mongán plays the rôle of a "culture hero." Although portrayed as a prince or chieftain, he does not excel in physical prowess or martial endeavors, rather "his tools and weapons are of an intellectual sort."[89] He is seen to best poets at their professional skills and knowledge.

We noted above that *Immram Brain* drew a direct connection to Mongán when Manannán mac Lir told Bran that "after long ages" (*íar n-aimseraib cíanaib*) he would go to Ireland and father a son Mongán mac Fiachnai.[90] The details of Mongán's "supernatural" birth are related in *Compert Mongán* where we learn that Manannán will sleep with Mongán's mother in a deal to protect Fiachnae, his human father, while Fiachnae is across the sea in Britain helping his friend Áedán mac Gabráin fight against the Anglo-Saxons. The timeframe fits Bede's account (*HE* i 34) of the combat between Æthelfrith and Áedán mac Gabráin which culminated in the battle of Degsastan (603; *HE* v 24).[91]

Many of the *Cín* texts have a northern emphasis and relate to Ulster Cycle events dealing with Cú Chulainn and other heroes. *Immram Brain* is connected with Mongán mac Fiachnai through Manannán mac Lir's declaration that he would be Mongán's "otherworldly" father. *Immram Brain* also signifies its northern bias through Bran's father, Febal, who gave his name to Lough Foyle on the eastern side of the Inishowen peninsula. The four Mongán tales have as their main protagonist a member of the Dál nAraidi located in Co. Antrim. The monastery of Bangor was founded by a member of that sept. Several commentators have proposed Bangor as the driving force for the production of early vernacular texts represented in the *Cín Dromma Snechtai*.[92]

---

[87] See synchronisms by Mc Carthy, D., http://www.irish-annals.cs.tcd.ie/, s.a. 627; Mac Airt and Mac Niocaill, *Annals of Ulster*, 112–13 s.a. 625; Stokes, "Annals of Tigernach," 178 [Felinfach, i 138]. For editions of the four texts, see White, *Compert Mongáin*; Ó Corráin, *Clavis*, iii, 1419–21 §1084.

[88] Mc Carthy, D., http://www.irish-annals.cs.tcd.ie/, s.a. 628; Mac Airt and Mac Niocaill, *Annals of Ulster*, 114–15 s.a. 626; Stokes, "Annals of Tigernach," 179 [Felinfach, i 139].

[89] Stifter, "Ulster Connections," 29.

[90] Meyer, *Voyage of Bran*, 16–17 §32; Mac Mathúna, *Immram Brain*, 38 (Gaelic), 51 (English) §32.

[91] What is historical here can be examined against the career of Columbanus of Bangor: Ó Cróinín, "Political Background," 60–64. For concerns that Bede confused his sources, see Duncan, "Bede, Iona, and the Picts," 16–18.

[92] For example, Mac Cana, "Mongán mac Fiachna," 103–6; Ó hUiginn, "Development of *Táin Bó Cúailnge*," 62; Byrne, "Church and Politics," 678–79; White, *Compert Mongáin*, 67–70,

*Táin Bó Fraích* (Driving the Cattle of Fróech) is an early vernacular text (ca. 700) that has no associations with *Cín Dromma Snechtai* but which points to Bangor as its source.[93] The text's narrative action anticipates the events of *Táin Bó Cúailnge* and explains how Fróech joined Ailill's and Medb's expedition against Ulster. Fróech is descended from the *síd* (faerie folk) through his mother, reflecting native traditions. Yet, in a unique turn for such an early text, Fróech must venture onto the continent to the Lombards of northern Italy which suggests the tale's relationship to Bangor through the Columbanian monastery of Bobbio. The tale concludes with an etymological anecdote that explains how the strand at Bangor (*Bennchor*) received its name.[94] This tale will be discussed more fully later in this chapter.

Bangor's importance in disseminating Latinate learning, but often with a secular purpose, can be seen in the *Hisperica Famina* which, it has been argued, derives from Bangor.[95] The *lex diei* (rule of the day) in the A-text describes a student's life as well as his surroundings.[96] This section of the *Hisperica Famina* appears to be a contemporary account of Bede's Anglo-Saxon students, among others, taking advantage of free education offered by the Gaels (*HE* iii 27). The importance of Bangor to Northumbrian cultural developments is reflected in the likelihood that King Aldfrith *sapiens* owed his own education to Bangor.[97] It has been reasonably suggested that Agilberht, participant at the "synod" of Whitby (664), had been schooled at Bangor, most likely in the 640s or early 650s.[98]

John Carey proposed that four texts from *Cín Dromma Snechtai*, all of which he considered to be late seventh century, should constitute a "Midland group":[99] *Echtrae Chonnlai* (The Faring Forth of Connlae), *Togail Bruidne uí Derga* (The Destruction of Uí Derga's Hostel),[100] *Baile Chuinn Chétchathaig* (The Frenzy of Conn

---

emphasizes the relationship with Dál nAraidi rather than pointing specifically to Bangor; Stifter, "Ulster Connections," 28–30 35–37.

93 Meid, *Táin Bó Fraích*; Meid, *Romance of Froech*; Ó Corráin, *Clavis*, iii, 1471–73 §1106. For a study of intertextual references and relationship to landscape, see McCarthy and Curley, "Exploring the Nature of the *Fráoch Saga*."
94 This episode is discussed in Ireland, "Whitby *Life* of Gregory," 152–53.
95 Stevenson, "Bangor and the *Hisperica Famina*"; Ó Corráin, *Clavis*, ii, 733–36 §571.
96 Herren, *Hisperica Famina: I*, 74–91. See further Ireland, "Study Abroad Destination."
97 Ireland, "Where Was King Aldfrith Educated?" 63–69.
98 Hammer, "'Holy Entrepreneur'," 62.
99 Carey, "*Cín Dromma Snechtai* Texts," 86–89.
100 The exact form of this text is not known. A text of mixed date, with possible seventh-century sections survives and is edited by Knott, *Togail Bruidne Da Derga*; Ó Corráin, *Clavis*, iii, 1488–93 §1120. For some of the complexities see Ó Cathasaigh, "*Cín Dromma Snechta* Version."

of the Hundred Battles),[101] and *Audacht Morainn* (The Testament of Morann).[102] All four texts have themes that deal, directly or indirectly, with kingship.

*Echtrae Chonnlai* has already been discussed above. It was included in the Midland group because the setting is the royal site of Uisnech in Co. Westmeath, the geographical center of Ireland. Connlae is portrayed as having opted for an "alternative" life, having been coaxed into departing by the "otherworldly" woman, leaving his brother Art to carry on a secular "worldly" life to become an important ancestor of the Uí Néill.

Kingship is the central theme of *Togail Bruidne Da Derga*, assuming it descends directly from *Togail Bruidne uí Derga*. It highlights the king of Tara's duties and responsibilities. *Togail Bruidne Da Derga* contains descriptions of *tarbfeis* (bull feast; bull sleep), a purported divinatory ritual used for predicting a future king. It will be discussed more thoroughly later in this chapter. Bertram Colgrave had noted how St. Cuthbert's use of his prophetic abilities to divulge Aldfrith's succession of his half-brother Ecgfrith has affinities with the Gaelic tradition.[103]

The opening sequence of *Togail Bruidne Da Derga*,[104] in an example of intertextuality, provides background details for another *Cín* text, *Tochmarc Étaíne* (The Wooing of Étaín).[105] *Tochmarc Étaíne* tells of the pursuit of a beautiful faerie (*síd*) woman through various incarnations by her lover Midir, another denizen of the faerie world. Neither *Togail Bruidne Da Derga* nor *Tochmarc Étaíne*, in their surviving forms, can be assumed to represent the texts that were once in *Cín Dromma Snechtai*.

Political prophecy about the kingship of Tara is highlighted in *Baile Chuinn Chétchathaig* (The Frenzy of Conn of the Hundred Battles).[106] The text is presented as a prophetic utterance by Conn Cétchathach, an ancestor of the Connachtmen and Uí Néill, in which he names those who will imbibe the liquor of sovereignty, that is, will attain the kingship of Tara.[107] The text reflects Uí Néill

---

101 Murphy, "Dates of Two Sources," 145–51; Bhreathnach and Murray, "*Baile Chuinn Chétchathaig*"; Bhreathnach, "Political Context"; Ó Corráin, *Clavis*, iii, 1525–26 §1135.
102 For edition and translation, see Kelly, *Audacht Morainn*; Ó Corráin, *Clavis*, ii, 1188–90 §908.
103 Colgrave, *Lives of Saint Cuthbert*, 329 notes (*Vita anonyma*, bk. 3, c. 6; Bede's *Vita prosa*, c. 24).
104 Knott, *Togail Bruidne Da Derga*, 1–3.
105 Bergin and Best, "*Tochmarc Étaíne*." For a brief outline, see Dillon, *Early Irish Literature*, 54–58; Ó Corráin, *Clavis*, iii, 1482–84 §1114.
106 Murphy, "Dates of Two Sources," 145–51; Bhreathnach and Murray, "*Baile Chuinn Chétchathaig*"; Bhreathnach, "Political Context."
107 See a list of the kings named in the context of other king lists: Byrne, *Irish Kings*, 276–77.

propaganda for their dominance of the Tara kingship. In the 1950s Gerard Murphy had pointed out that the last firmly identifiable king named was Fínsnechta Fledach (675–695) of Síl nÁedo Sláine in Brega. However, since he is identified by a play on his name, *snechta fína* (snow of wine), Murphy argued that the original poem was composed just before he took the kingship. The Anglo-Saxons entered the scene when, in the middle of Fínsnechta's reign, King Ecgfrith sent his *dux* Berht into Brega in 684 in a smash and grab raid which Bede deplored (*HE* iv 26 [24]).[108] Within a year Ecgrith had been defeated and killed by the Picts and his half-brother Aldfrith *sapiens* acquired the rule of Northumbria (*HE* iv 26). The *Cín* text *Baile Chuinn* has important textual descendants that expand its core political prophecies and which will be discussed presently.

The fourth *Cín* text of the Midland group is *Audacht Morainn* (The Testament of Morann), Europe's oldest vernacular *speculum principum*. The text is presented as advice from the illustrious judge Morann to the king Feradach Find Fechtnach, an ancestor of Conn Cétchathach. It emphasizes the important trope that through "justice of the ruler" (*fír flathemon*) peace, wealth, and natural abundance are ensured.[109] Another interesting feature is a classification of kings as 1) *fírflaith* (true ruler), 2) *cíallflaith* (wily ruler), 3) *flaith congbále co slógaib* (ruler of occupation with hosts), 4) *tarbflaith* (bull ruler).[110] Several vernacular and Latin *specula* were created by the Gaelic intelligentsia in subsequent centuries.

Of the *Cín Dromma Snechtai* texts, the Midland group appears to be the oldest, probably late seventh century. Most texts reveal their northern bias, specifically the northeast of Ireland in the province of Ulster. The monastic establishment that has the greatest likelihood of encouraging the production of this early vernacular literature, as noted by the manuscript named for one of its daughter houses, is Bangor in Co. Down.

## The Finding of the *Táin Bó Cúailnge*

The narrative *De Faillsigiud Tána Bó Cúailnge* (Finding [or "Recovery"] of the *Táin*) is an etiological legend that contains a list of fore-tales (*remscéla*) to the epic *Táin*.[111] The chief poet Senchán Torpéist, mentioned in the first chapter, is the main protagonist. The legend proclaims the "recovery" of the *Táin* by

---

108 Pelteret, "Attack on Brega."
109 Kelly, *Audacht Morainn*, 6–7 §§13–21.
110 Kelly, *Audacht Morainn*, 18–19 §§59–62.
111 Murray, "Finding of the *Táin*"; Ó Corráin, *Clavis*, iii, 1361–62 §1039.

Senchán's pupils and implies that Latinate learning had been emphasized to the neglect of native lore since the younger poets confess to Senchán that they know "only fragments" (*ach bloga nammá*) of the *Táin*.[112] The tale acknowledges the debt of Gaelic *intelligentsia* to Latinate learning while expressing the desire to maintain indigenous lore and native tales. This Book of Leinster (Dublin, Trinity College, MS (1339) H.2.18) version is linguistically of the ninth century, though the tale is set in the seventh.[113]

Senchán sent out his *daltai* (students) to recover the *Táin* in return for his blessings. The *Táin* had been exchanged for Isidore's *Etymologiae* by a scholar (*suí*) who had traveled eastward onto the continent. Two students, Émíne úa Nínine and Muirgen mac Sencháin, traveled eastward to recover the *Táin* until they came upon the standing stone at Énloch, the burial place of Fergus mac Róig.[114] Fergus was a major protagonist of the *Táin* epic where, as an exiled Ulsterman fighting on the side of Queen Medb and King Ailill of Connacht, he served as their eyewitness informant about Cú Chulainn and the Ulstermen generally.

Muirgen addressed the standing stone in verse as if he were addressing Fergus himself.[115] The revenant Fergus, described graphically, came in a mist and recited the entire *Táin* from start to finish to the young poets over the course of three days and nights.[116] The syncretic character of the legend is highlighted when the indigenous tale, lost in exchange for Isidore's *Etymologiae*, is recovered by the apprentice poets who received the tale orally from a central participant of the *Táin*, as if they were recording an eyewitness report.[117]

This legend acknowledges variant versions which have been outlined and discussed by James Carney.[118] They vary in detail but agree in making Senchán Torpéist the chief protagonist. Senchán must either recover the *Táin* himself or enlist his apprentices to help. In all versions Fergus mac Róig is the intercessor who relates the *Táin* to the poets.

---

112 Murray, "Finding of the *Táin*," 21.
113 Best and O'Brien, *Book of Leinster*, v, 1119, lines 32879–909; Murray, "Finding of the *Táin*," 17–23, edition based on the Book of Leinster and four other manuscripts.
114 The location is apparently in Mag Aí in Connacht: Hogan, *Onomasticon*, 398.
115 Murray, "Finding of the *Táin*," 22–23. For a reconstruction, translation, and interpretation of the poem, see Carey, "Address to Fergus's Stone"; Corthals, "Why Did Fergus Rise."
116 For a discussion of this episode in contrast to Old English poetic style, see Ireland, "Visionary Poets," 128–29.
117 See the lucid discussion in Davies, "Cultural Memory," 83–95.
118 Carney, *Literature and History*, 165–88; Thurneysen, *Die irische Helden- und Königsage*, 251–67; Nagy, *Conversing with Angels*, 307–17.

Separate intertextual references from Fergus's death-tale (*aided*) note that Fergus brought the *Táin* to the poets.[119] However, not all versions of the legend include the motif of the *Táin* having been exchanged for Isidore's *Etymologiae*. This legend evolved over time with the growth of Gaelic literature and has become the denouement of the early Classical Gaelic story *Tromdám Guaire* (The Burdensome Troop of Guaire).[120] Seán Ó Coileáin dated this tale to the late thirteenth or early fourteenth century.[121] Carney outlined the tale in detail in his study.[122] The legend continued to evolve over the centuries and became even more elaborate in the later narrative *Imtheacht na Tromdháimhe* (The Expedition of the Burdensome Troop).[123]

Intertextual evidence from other Old Gaelic sources shows how widespread the legend had already become. The ninth-century wisdom-text "The Triads of Ireland" (*Trecheng Breth Féne*) comprises lore preserved, typically, in groups of three. One triad lists the three wonders concerning the *Táin Bó Cúailnge* as follows:

> Trí hamrai la Táin Bó Cúailnge: .i. in cuilmen dara héisi i nÉrinn; in marb dia haisnéis don bíu .i. Fergus mac Róig dia hinnisin do Ninníne Éicius i n-aimsir Corbmaic maic Fáeláin; intí dia n-aisnéther, coimge bliadna dó.[124]

> (Three wonders concerning the *Táin Bó Cúailnge*: (1) that the *Cuilmen* [i.e., Isidore's *Etymologiae*] came to Ireland in its stead; (2) the dead relating it to the living, i.e., Fergus mac Róig reciting it to Ninníne Éices [Ninine the poet] in the time of Cormac mac Fáeláin; (3) one year's protection to him to whom it is recited.)

When this entry from the "Triads" is compared with the "Finding of the *Táin*" the first two elements agree in outline though not in detail. In the first element, the *Cuilmen* (Isidore's *Etymologiae*)[125] being exchanged for the *Táin*, we see the debt of the Early Gaelic *intelligentsia* to the Latinate world of the continent. By referring to the *Etymologiae* as the *cuilmen* (from Latin *culmen*; the top, summit) the Gaels implied its pre-eminence. Many of Isidore's (d. 636) works, not just the *Etymologiae*, begin appearing in the texts of Gaelic scholars by the middle

---

119 Meyer, *Death-tales*, 32–33 (*Aided Fergusa maic Róich*).
120 Joynt, *Tromdámh Guaire*; Ó Corráin, *Clavis*, iii, 1495–97 §1122.
121 Ó Coileáin, "*Tromdám Guaire*," 66.
122 Carney, *Literature and History*, 170–79.
123 Connellan, "Imtheacht na Tromdhaimhe."
124 Meyer, *Triads of Ireland*, 8–9 §62, for dating, see x; Ó Corráin, *Clavis*, ii, 1195–96 §912. Ó Coileáin suggested that this triad is not as old as the collection as a whole since it appears in only one of four manuscripts: "*Tromdám Guaire*," 49.
125 eDIL: http://www.dil.ie, s.v. *cuilmen*; dil.ie/13530; Ó Máille, "Authorship of the Culmen."

of the seventh century. The *Etymologiae*, among other Isidorean texts, are cited by Laidcenn *sapiens*,[126] by Virgilius Maro Grammaticus,[127] in commentaries of the Catholic Epistles,[128] in the *Hisperica Famina*,[129] in *De duodecim abusivis*,[130] and in *De locis sanctis* by Adomnán.[131] The influence of Late Antiquity and Visigothic Spain generally can be traced in the intellectual world of the Gaels before the end of the seventh century.[132]

The second element, having Fergus mac Róig recite the *Táin* to a poet (*éices*),[133] varies in details involving personnel and historical points. For example, the triad states that Nitríne himself received the *Táin* from Fergus, whereas the legend as cited above states that Muirgen, son of Senchán, received it and that Émíne, grandson of Nitríne, was Muirgen's companion. Senchán Torpéist is associated with the Connacht king Guaire Aidni who died ca. 663.[134] Nitríne Éices is difficult to confirm historically, but he is associated with figures of the seventh century.[135] Cormac mac Fáeláin, however, is not firmly identified. The Annals of Tigernach list the death of a certain Cormac mac Fáeláin uí Shilne in an entry that equates with the Annals of Ulster 756.[136] The context suggests that he was a cleric. Apparently, Cormac's father, Fáelán úa Silne (*obit* 711), was a guarantor of *Cáin Adomnáin* (697).[137] Versions that emphasize Senchán Torpéist and Nitríne Éices place the events in the seventh century, but Cormac mac Fáeláin is, if accurately identified, an eighth-century cleric.

The third element of the triad invites discussion about the nature of vernacular literatures in the early Middle Ages. It implies that the *Táin* epic has the qualities of a charm or protective *lorica*, and that simply by hearing it recited (*intí dia n-aisnéther*) one earns a year's protection (*coimge bliadna*). The

---

126 Hillgarth, "Ireland and Spain," 8; Herren, "So-called *Lorica Gildae*," 47–49; Richter, *Ireland and Her Neighbours*, 189.
127 Hillgarth, "Ireland and Spain," 8; Herren, "Life of Virgilius," 45–46. It is important to contrast the ideas of Virgilius with those of Isidore: Law, *Wisdom, Authority and Grammar*, 98–101.
128 Hillgarth, "Ireland and Spain," 8; Breen, "Hiberno-Latin Texts," 207–10; Richter, *Ireland and Her Neighbours*, 193.
129 Hillgarth, "Ireland and Spain," 8; Herren, *Hisperica Famina: I*, 20–22.
130 Hillgarth, "Ireland and Spain," 8; Kenney, *Sources*, 182 §109.
131 O'Loughlin, "Monasteries and Manuscripts," 56.
132 Hillgarth, "Ireland and Spain"; Howlett, "Irish Foundation Legend."
133 Mac Mathúna, "Functions and Knowledge of the Irish Poet," 235–36.
134 Mc Carthy, http://www.irish-annals.cs.tcd.ie/, s.a. 663; Mac Airt and Mac Niocaill, *Annals of Ulster*, 134–35; Stokes, "Annals of Tigernach," 197–98 [Felinfach i 157–58].
135 Dobbs, "Nínine Écess"; Ó Fiaich, "Cérbh é Ninine Éigeas?"
136 Stokes, "Annals of Tigernach," 256 [Felinfach i 216].
137 Ní Dhonnchadha, "Guarantor List," 196 §40, who suggests that he may be associated with Imblech Ibair (Emly, Co. Tipperary).

colophon that concludes the early twelfth-century Book of Leinster recension of the *Táin* has a very different spirit. This Middle Gaelic version differs greatly in style and length from the ninth-century Recension One version cited in this study. The colophon in the Book of Leinster *Táin* states in Gaelic: "A blessing (*bendacht*) on every one who shall faithfully memorize (*mebraigfes go hindraic*) the Táin as it is written here and shall not add any other form to it."[138] Here, however, the active rôle of memorization is required, passive reception, as stated in the Triad, is not enough to derive benefit. But the Latin colophon appended to the Gaelic, by the same hand that copied the epic, disparages the tale as "deceptions of demons" (*praestrigia demonum*), and concludes that much in the narrative was intended for the "amusement of foolish men" (ad delectationem stultorum).[139] Rather than a legitimate *historia*,[140] the writer of the Latin colophon considered the epic to be a misleading *fabula*.[141]

One aim of *De faillsigiud Tána Bó Cúailnge* is to list twelve fore-tales (*remscéla*) of the *Táin*. The legend thus becomes an early surviving list of narrative tales. Although the anecdote states that there are twelve tales, only ten can be fore-tales, as the compiler noted that the last two tales named represent episodes within the narrative of the *Táin* itself.[142] Such "internal" tales are not unlike the "digressions" of *Beowulf* that indicate the existence of stories beyond the main narrative.[143] In chapter one we noted the story of Sigemund's fight with a dragon which presages Beowulf's own dragon fight.[144] The digression about Fremu and Offa (lines 1931b–62) suggests a "moral" tale contrasting the qualities of queens.[145] Another interpolation about a certain Ingeld, sometimes called the Heaðo-Beard episode, revolves around the theme of revenge.[146] Roberta Frank noted that the *Beowulf* poem draws on about twenty legends.[147]

---

138 O'Rahilly, *Táin Book of Leinster*, 136, lines 4919–20 (Gaelic), 272 (English).
139 O'Rahilly, *Táin Book of Leinster*, 136, lines 4921–25 (Latin), 272 (English).
140 It is clear that for many the *Táin* was considered *historia*: Poppe, "Medieval Irish Literary Theory," 36–37; Toner, "Historiography or Fiction?"
141 For discussion, see Ó Néill, "Colophon to the 'Táin Bó Cúailnge'." A disparaging attitude toward the vernacular languages and literature can sometimes be seen in ecclesiastical writers who wrote in Latin such as Muirchú, Adomnán, Aldhelm, Bede, and Alcuin. For the varying levels at which we must read early narratives, see Davies, "Protocols of Reading."
142 Backhaus, "List of *Remscéla*," 20 and n7.
143 Fulk, Bjork, Niles, *Klaeber's Beowulf*, lxxxiv–lxxxvi, xcv–xcvii (Non-linear Narrative).
144 See the textual notes in Fulk, Bjork, Niles, *Klaeber's Beowulf*, 166–69.
145 See the textual notes in Fulk, Bjork, Niles, *Klaeber's Beowulf*, 222–27.
146 See the textual notes in Fulk, Bjork, Niles, *Klaeber's Beowulf*, 229–33.
147 Frank, "Germanic Legend," 98. See also Scowcroft, "Irish Analogues to *Beowulf*."

It has been argued that these fore-tales were organized based on "the main characters of the tales, the chronological structure of the list, and the plots of the tales."[148] Another modern classification of the fore-tales argues that there are "Background *remscéla*; Causal *remscéla*; *Remremscéla* (i.e., fore-fore-tales); and Referential *remscéla*" depending on how their events relate to the *Táin* epic.[149] The relationship between a fore-tale and events in the *Táin* may be loose, such as a prophetic anticipation of events that will transpire. Although events, and characters, in a particular fore-tale may have no concrete relationship to the *Táin*, by supplying background explanation of future episodes they represent a concrete intertextuality. As such, the example of the *Táin*'s *remscéla* helps explain vague references to past events in digressions and interpolations in *Beowulf* that seem to apply to current episodes as the narrative unfolds.

It would seem that the aim of the redactor of the *Táin Bó Cúailnge* "was to construct a history of the cattle-raid of Cooley following normal medieval historiographical practices."[150] Important characters and events in Old Gaelic narratives were accepted as historical by medieval *literati*, even where they noted contradictions in the narrative flow and offered differing versions of various episodes.[151] For example, entries in the Annals of Tigernach assume precise dating for events related in some Ulster tales, and make Cú Chulainn and Conchobar contemporaries of Christ.[152] An authenticating example is found in the death-tale of King Conchobar (*Aided Chonchobuir*) where his death is caused by his learning of the contemporaneous crucifixion of Christ.[153] Some manuscripts of the death-tale contain an early eighth-century poem in heightened style (*retoiric*) in which Conchobar regrets that he did not personally meet Christ whom he would have protected from crucifixion with his martial prowess.[154] The editor of the *retoiric* stated that "The poem describes Conchobar's conversion from being a pagan king, who would resort instinctively to the force of the sword, to being a Christian believer."[155] This is an important case of the Gaels attributing the acceptance of Christianity to illustrious ancestors before the arrival of the faith

---

148 Backhaus, "List of *Remscéla*," 26.
149 Chadwin, "*Remscéla*," 70.
150 Toner, "Historiography or Fiction?" 6.
151 Toner, "Historiography or Fiction?" 11–13.
152 Poppe, "Medieval Irish Literary Theory," 41–42; Kelleher, "*Táin* and the Annals"; McCone, *Pagan Past*, 74, 197–98; Mc Carthy, *Irish Annals*, 278–79.
153 Meyer, *Death-tales*, 2–21. For the notion of an "anthology" of Ulster death-tales, see Clancy, "Die Like a Man?" 82–84.
154 The term *retoiric* is derived from Latin *rhetorice* and refers to unrhymed chants or rhapsodies. For a fuller discussion see Mac Cana, "Term *Retoiric*"; Breatnach, "Zur Frage der *Roscada*."
155 Corthals, "*Aided Chonchobuir*," 51.

through Church missions. The Christian coloring noted in *Beowulf* arose in a similar cultural milieu to that which created Conchobar's *retoiric*.[156]

## Tales from the Tenth-Century Tale Lists

The legend about the "recovery" of the *Táin* concluded with a list of tales involving intertextual episodes appropriate to the *Táin Bó Cúailnge*. But in five manuscripts there are lists of tales that comprise a vast corpus of learned tales many of which survive. The lists divide into two groups called simply List A and List B, this latter found as part of a narrative called *Airec menman Uraird maic Coise* (The Stratagem of Urard mac Coise).[157] Both lists derive from the tenth century, although many surviving texts are demonstrably older.[158] For example, some *Cín Dromma Snechtai* texts, discussed above, are included in the tale lists. The tale *Airec menman* is a long allegory in which a wronged poet, Urard mac Coise, takes his complaint for redress to the king of Tara, Domnall mac Muirchertaig (d. 980). When the king asks for his "tidings" (*scéla*) the poet deliberately takes the word in its meaning "stories, tales" and tells the king that he has them in abundance. Urard uses the deliberate misunderstanding to enumerate his long list of tales making sure to conclude with a tale he has made up in order to recount the incident of how he had been wronged. The king, naturally, requested that Urard recount the last named tale.[159]

Many of the tales named by Urard (List B) overlap with the first list (List A).[160] These lists divide the tales by categories that reflect the contents of the action, typically classed by the first word of the title, so that, for example, there are *tána* (sg. *táin*; drivings off (of cattle)), *togla* (sg. *togail*; destructions), *catha* (sg. *cath*; battles),

---

156 "[T]he poet is a Christian whose intellectual horizons have been expanded to include not only biblical learning but the wider world of Christian-Latin culture in general": Robinson, "*Beowulf*," 142. See also Hill, "*Beowulf* and Conversion History."
157 Ó Corráin, *Clavis*, iii, 1295–96 §982. The two manuscripts that contain List A are: Dublin, Trinity College MS H.2.18 (Book of Leinster); Dublin, Trinity College, MS H.3.17. The three manuscripts that contain List B from the narrative *Airec Menman* are: Dublin, Royal Irish Academy, MS 23 N 10; Oxford, Bodleian Library, MS Rawlinson B.512; and London, British Library, MS Harley 5280.
158 Mac Cana, *Learned Tales*, 33–40; Toner, "Earliest Irish Tale Lists."
159 Mac Cana, *Learned Tales*, 34–35; the tale is synopsized in Dillon, *Cycles of the Kings*, 115–17. See a literary historical discussion in Poppe, "Medieval Irish Literary Theory," 43–47, 53.
160 There are two shorter lists found in a tract on the *filid* (Edinburgh, Advocates' Library, MS VII) and in the introduction to the *Senchas Már* (London, British Library, Harleian MS 432): Mac Cana, *Learned Tales*, 64–65; Toner, "Earliest Irish Tale Lists," 90.

*immrama* (sg. *immram*; sea voyages), *oitte* (sg. *aided*; violent deaths), *echtrai* (sg. *echtra*; adventures), *serca* (sg. *serc*; loves), *tochmarca* (sg. *tochmarc*; wooings). The modern scholarly classification favors grouping tales by their characters who interact regularly, so that we have the Mythological cycle, the Ulster (Heroic) cycle, the Fenian (Finn) cycle, the King (Historical) cycle.[161] Note that these lists and classifications, in contrast with Old English literature, do not include the rich vernacular hagiographical texts.

*Airec menman* and the Old English *Widsith* have common features. They both reflect the need for *fili* and *scop* to seek patronage from local rulers. In the case of *Airec menman* Urard seeks to have a wrong redressed by the king, and does so successfully by disguising his circumstances as a traditional *scél* (tale). Widsith makes no appeal to a specific chieftain, but the "emphasis on kings' liberality in rewarding scops' endeavors has suggested to some that *Widsith* was a 'begging' poem, a real scop's plea for patronage."[162] Both poets demonstrate their control of arcane traditional lore and, by implication, their rôles as storytellers (*senchaid*). Urard recited a list of tales, many known to modern scholarship, and which he claimed to know. Widsith, in essence, does the same by naming legendary and historical characters and peoples from the Germanic world in what has been called a "catalogue" poem.

The two differ in that Urard mac Coise is a historical figure, although biographical uncertainty remains because of confusion with other poets named mac Coise.[163] Widsith is a fictitious, idealized, all-knowing poet. By contrast, Urard mac Coise appears in the annals with an *obit* of 990, contemporary with King Domnall (d. 980).[164] Two debate poems against other poets are attributed to Urard,[165] reminiscent of competition between Deor and Heorrenda. The Gaelic debate poem *Immacallam in dá Thuarad* was cited in chapter one and will be addressed further below.

The tale list in the twelfth-century Book of Leinster purports to contain three hundred and fifty titles consisting of two hundred and fifty primary tales and one hundred sub-tales. In fact, each of the five tale lists comprises somewhat less than two hundred titles apiece. The Book of Leinster list begins with the prescription that the ability to recite the stories to kings and

---

161 For a broad discussion, see Poppe, *Of Cycles and Other Critical Matters*. For discussion of the problematical nature of the first named cycle, see Carey, *Mythological Cycle*.
162 Greenfield and Calder, *New Critical History*, 147.
163 O'Leary, "Poet(s) Mac Coisi," 69.
164 Mac Airt and Mac Niocaill, *Annals of Ulster*, 422–23 (Urard), 414–15 (Domall); O'Leary, "Poet(s) Mac Coisi," 70.
165 O'Leary, "Poet(s) Mac Coisi," 70.

nobility (*da n-asnís do rígaib 7 flathib*) conferred privileged status (*nemed*) on the *poets* (*filid*).[166] As noted above, the *filid* were the only professionals to have *sóernemed* status.

The emphasis on three hundred and fifty tales is likely a fiction devised to enhance the prestige of the *filid*. It seems to draw on the dictum in *Uraicecht na Ríar* that the *ollam filed* (chief poet) must be competent in three hundred and fifty *dréchta*. He must also be knowledgeable in *coimgne* (synthesis) and in Gaelic jurisprudence.[167] The discrepancies between the three hundred and fifty *dréchta* and less than two hundred tale titles suggest that *dréchta* involve more than *scéla* (tales). *Dréchta* most likely include other forms of compositions, both prose and verse.

The recitation of tales by Forgoll each night of winter to Mongán and his court portray the *fili* as a storyteller (*senchaid*).[168] In *Cath Maige Tuired* (The (Second) Battle of Mag Tuired) the multi-talented (*samildánach*) hero Lug sought entrance to the court at Tara by declaring that he was both poet (*fili*) and reciter of lore (*senchaid*). The doorkeeper, however, replied that the court already had someone, Én mac Ethamain, qualified in both skills.[169] In *Beowulf* these two functions appear in individual performers.

Gregory Toner has demonstrated how the tale lists reflect important aspects of poetic culture. He noted that List A was closest to a now lost original, and that both Lists A and B derive from an original that he designated as X.[170] He also noted that the titles of List A constitute "an extended alliterative list" which was the deliberate work of the compiler.[171] He observed that alliteration is so prevalent in List A that it must reflect an earlier core list, derived from X, which he called O.[172] His study shows that O "contained around 140 of the titles now found in List A" and that this alliterative list was compiled in the tenth century, in agreement with Mac Cana's findings.[173] Such an elegant and complex alliterative list was suited as a mnemonic for memorization. Its underlying structure suggests that it was the product of *filid*.

---

166 The introduction of the tales and the list are found in Best and O'Brien, *Book of Leinster*, iv, 835–37. For discussion see, Mac Cana, *Learned Tales*, 33–65.
167 Breatnach, *Uraicecht na Ríar*, 102–3, §2.
168 "In·féded in fili scél cacha haidche do Mongán": White, *Compert Mongáin*, 73 (Gaelic), 79 (English) §1.
169 Gray, *Cath Maige Tuired*, 40–41 §62.
170 Toner, "Earliest Irish Tale Lists," 91–92.
171 Toner, "Earliest Irish Tale Lists," 101.
172 Toner, "Earliest Irish Tale Lists," 105.
173 Toner, "Earliest Irish Tale Lists," 114; Mac Cana, *Learned Tales*, 36.

A substantial number of tales from the two lists survive and are known to modern scholarship. The following discussion concentrates on tales whose names are found in all five manuscript versions of the tale list as discussed by Mac Cana. Most of these tales have an Old Gaelic linguistic core that reveals subsequent revision and expansion in the Middle Gaelic period. The *Táin Bó Cúailnge* is the most famous of these tales. It is part of a vast, interrelated network of tales as noted in the etiological legend about the "recovery" of the *Táin*. The evolution of Gaelic literary style can be seen by comparing the Old Gaelic Recension One[174] of the *Táin* with the Middle Gaelic version in the Book of Leinster.[175] The latter is written in a florid, at times prolix, style. Yet the narrative flow and individual episodes are easily recognized from the earlier version.

The two narratives *Beowulf* and *Táin Bó Cúailnge* have much in common including arguments that their written forms may have origins from as early as the eighth century.[176] References throughout the literature point to the previous existence of the *Táin* narrative, its characters, and episodes, before the earliest written recension.[177] Two such texts from the *Cín Dromma Snechtai*, *Compert Con Culainn*[178] and *Verba Scáthaige*,[179] are from the late seventh or early eighth century. The poem attributed to Cenn Fáelad *sapiens* (d. 679) in the "death tale" of Cú Chulainn is dated linguistically to the late seventh or early eighth century, as noted in chapter two.[180] *Táin Bó Fraích*, a text of ca. 700, is predicated on Fróech's participation in Ailill and Medb's military expedition to Cúailnge. The early eighth-century *retoiric* (stylized poem)[181] in *Aided Chonchobuir* (Death Tale of Conchobar), laments the king's inability to have protected Christ at his crucifixion.

Both *Beowulf* and *Táin Bó Cúailnge* highlight the prowess of the hero through spectacular combats. Beowulf engaged in three fights that saved communities from destruction by defeating first, the monster Grendel, then Grendel's mother and, finally, by slaying a dragon. In this last combat Beowulf lost his own life. In the *Táin*, Cú Chulainn, by imposing a heroic honor code, delayed the invasion of the province of Ulster by the united armies of Ailill and Medb through a series of

---

174 O'Rahilly, *Táin: Recension I*; Ó Corráin, *Clavis*, iii, 1445–68 §1103.
175 O'Rahilly, *Táin Book of Leinster*.
176 Fulk, Bjork, Niles, *Klaeber's Beowulf*, clxxix.
177 Chadwin, "Remscéla."
178 van Hamel, *Compert Con Culainn*.
179 Henry, "Verba Scáthaige."
180 Kimpton, *Death of Cú Chulainn*, 24–24 (Gaelic), 43–44 §24 (English), 61 notes. For the notion of an "anthology" of Ulster death-tales, see Clancy, "Die Like a Man?" 82–84.
181 Corthals, "Aided Chonchobuir."

single combats with champions from the opposing armies, some of whom, tragically, are personally close to him such as his own foster-brother Fer Diad.[182]

There are differences in the narratives, of course. While Beowulf died at the end of the epic in his combat with the dragon, Cú Chulainn survived the invasion of Ulster that he delayed. His death is told in separate tales, the earliest of which is the eighth-century *Brislech Mór Maige Muirthemni* (The Great Rout of Muirthemne Plain).[183] Another major difference in the narratives reflects the divergent histories of the two peoples. The language of *Beowulf* is Old English, of mixed dialect, but the intended audience were Anglo-Saxons living in Britain. All narrative action, however, transpires between the modern lands of Denmark and Sweden (Figure 1.b).[184] This feature of the epic emphasizes the Anglo-Saxons' own recognition of their immigration onto the island of Britain from the continent, related by Bede as having begun as precisely as 449 A.D., based on the *annus Domini* dating of co-emperors Marcian and Valentinian (*HE* i 15).[185] From identifiable characters and events, all continental, the period depicted in *Beowulf* points to the first half of the sixth century or slightly earlier.[186]

The narrative action of the *Táin*, by contrast, all happens in identifiable locations in the northern half of Ireland (Figure 1.a). In fact, the onomastic references are explicit enough to allow the flow of events to be traced on a modern map.[187] Many present-day place names are derived from events depicted in the *Táin*. This reflects the tradition of *dindšenchas* (place lore) common throughout Gaelic cultural history. Although no firm historical facts emerge from the narrative, events are definitively placed at the time of Christ in the annals and in narratives associated with the *Táin* as, for example, in the *retoiric* about Conchobar.[188]

General knowledge of the tales among learned scholars is revealed in a marginal note in the early twelfth-century *Lebor na hUidre* (Dublin, Royal Irish Academy, MS 23 E 25) version of the *Táin*. In the tale Cú Chulainn reckons the size of the invading army by examining their confused and jumbled tracks. The note, in triadic fashion, states that this is one of the three cleverest, yet most

---

182 For *comrac Fir Diad 7 Con Culaind*, see O'Rahilly, *Táin: Recension* I, 78–95, lines 2567–3153 (Gaelic); 195–208 (English).
183 Kimpton, *Death of Cú Chulainn*. Ó Corráin, *Clavis*, iii, 1269–71 §960.
184 Fulk, Bjork, Niles, *Klaeber's Beowulf*, lii–lxvii; Frank, "Germanic Legend."
185 See Howe, *Migration and Mythmaking*, 143–80 (*Beowulf* and the Ancestral Homeland).
186 Fulk, Bjork, Niles, *Klaeber's Beowulf*, li. Biggs, "Frisian Raids."
187 See Kinsella, *The Tain* for helpful maps.
188 Corthals, "*Aided Chonchobuir*"; Kelleher, "*Táin* and the Annals." The Annals of Tigernach note the death of Virgil in the same year as the cattle-raid: Clarke, "Furies and the Morrígan," 103.

difficult, reckonings ever made in Ireland.[189] The other two reckonings were, firstly, when Lug calculated the dead of the Fomoiri after the battle of Mag Tuired in *Cath Maige Tuired*[190] and, secondly, when Ingcél reconnoitered the size and characteristics of the assembly at the hostel in *Togail Bruidne Da Derga* after a single glance through his one eye.[191] This marginal note is attributed to Máel Muire, one of the scribes.[192] Máel Muire descended from an ecclesiastical learned family with bishops and abbots in his lineage. He has been described as a fine scribe who "is a scholarly editor of texts, a writer and a teacher."[193] The three tales cited in the note are known to current scholarship and are available in modern editions.

The tales in the following discussion all occur in both lists from all five manuscripts. They are well known to modern scholarship and exist in accessible editions and translations. They are sometimes of mixed date, but all have an Old Gaelic linguistic core that places them before ca. 900. The rôle of kingship is frequently highlighted and, consequently, the pre-eminence of Tara (*Temair*), whether portrayed as historical or mythical. The *áes dána* (people of the arts) feature regularly with poets and musicians playing prominent parts. Vision and prophecy are frequent aspects of their learned skills. The texts show an awareness of the larger world referring to peoples throughout Ireland and Britain including Picts, Britons, and Saxons. They are also aware of the continent and specific peoples there.

*Cath Maige Tuired* (The (Second) Battle of Mag Tuired)[194] has a ninth-century linguistic core with signs of reworking in the eleventh or twelfth centuries. An aside in the tale shows the synchronizing tendencies of Gaelic *intelligentsia* when it notes that the battle took place at the same time as the destruction of Troy.[195] It depicts a battle between mythical races, the Fomoiri and the Tuatha Dé Danann,

---

189 "Is sí seo in tres árim is glicu 7 is dolgiu dorigned i nÉrind .i. árim Con Culaind for feraib Hérend ár Tána, 7 árim Loga for slúag Fomórach, ar Cath Maigi Tured 7 árim Ingciúil for slog Bruidni Da Dergae": Best and Bergin, Lebor na Huidre, 151; O'Rahilly, *Táin: Recension I*, 11 (Gaelic), 134 (English). This note is in the hand of Máel Muire, one of the chief scribes.
190 Gray, *Cath Maige Tuired*, 66–67 §§146–48.
191 Knott, *Togail Bruidne Da Derga*, 19 §71 begins the sequence; Borsje and Kelly, "'The Evil Eye'"; Borsje, "Approaching Danger"; O'Connor, *Destruction of Da Derga's Hostel*, 159–92 §6 (The Perfect Spy); O'Connor, "Compilation as Creative Artistry."
192 Best and Bergin, *Lebor na Huidre*, xv, 151.
193 Ó Corráin, "Máel Muire, the Scribe," 25–26. Ó Corráin refers to this marginal note in the same context as above: "Máel Muire, the Scribe," 26–27.
194 Gray, *Cath Maige Tuired*; Ó Corráin, *Clavis*, iii, 1335–38 §1019; Ó Cathasaigh, "*Cath Maige Tuired*."
195 Gray, *Cath Maige Tuired*, 40–41 §69.

which is caused when Bres, the king of the two peoples and descended from both, acts unjustly toward the Tuatha Dé. In that sense, this text is about the responsibilities of good kingship. Bres's downfall is precipitated by the poet Cairpre of the Tuatha Dé who satirizes Bres for his lack of hospitality, a fatal flaw in a king. The episode highlights the power of satire, the obverse of praise, among Gaelic poets.[196]

Major protagonists in the ensuing battle are Balor "of the evil eye"[197] who fights for the Fomoiri, and Lug *samildánach*[198] who assumes the kingship of the Tuatha Dé at Tara and leads them to victory. Lug's epithet implies he was equally gifted in many arts and highlights the value of the *áes dána* (people of the arts). When Lug first arrived at Tara's court it was ruled by Núada *Airgetlám* (silverhand) who had replaced the deposed Bres. Núada had lost a hand in the first battle of Mag Tuired and had it substituted by an artificial silver one. As such he was considered blemished by some of his subjects.

Initially Lug was not permitted to enter Núada's court unless he offered some special skill or knowledge. Lug presented himself as skilled in each of the following: *sáer* (wright), *gobae* (smith), *trénfer* (champion), *cruitire* (harper), *nía* (warrior), *corrguinech* (magician), *liaig* (physician), *deogbaire* (cupbearer), *cerd* (artisan), *fili* (poet), *senchaid* (reciter of lore; historian).[199] The rôles of *fili* and *senchaid* were combined as though one person should fulfil both duties.

The doorkeeper told Lug that someone with each of the skills was already at the court and he named the person who possessed each skill. Lug then demanded to know if anyone at court possessed all of those skills equally. Eventually Lug was admitted to court and among the demonstrations of his skills was to play on the harp the three kinds of music, *súantraí*, *goltraí*, and *gentraí*,[200] noted in chapter one.

*Togail Bruidne Da Derga* (The Destruction of Da Derga's Hostel), known from the *Cín Dromma Snechtai* as *Togail Bruidne uí Derga*, is another text that has the responsibilities of kingship at its core.[201] It is not clear what differences in content, if any, the differing titles represent. The tale as preserved has an early eighth-century linguistic core with signs of reworking in the eleventh

---

**196** Breatnach, "Satire, Praise"; McLaughlin, *Early Irish Satire*.
**197** Borsje and Kelly, "'The Evil Eye'."
**198** Lacey, *Lug's Forgotten Donegal Kingdom*.
**199** The rôles of *fili* and *senchaid* are presented together much as in *Beowulf* where the duties of poet and reciter of lore are bound into a single person: Gray, *Cath Maige Tuired*, 40–41 §62.
**200** Gray, *Cath Maige Tuired*, 42–43 §73.
**201** Knott, *Togail Bruidne Da Derga*; Ó Corráin, *Clavis*, iii, 1488–93 §1120; O'Connor, *Destruction of Da Derga's Hostel*, 250–86 §9 (Conaire, Saul and Sacred Kingship).

century. The beginning serves as a fore-tale for the well-known *Tochmarc Étaíne* (The Wooing of Étaín),[202] a text also found in the *Cín Dromma Snechtai*. The thrust of the narrative is that King Conaire failed to reprimand his foster-brothers when they participated in *díberg* (brigandage). He therefore exposed his own kingdom to attack from brigands from Britain under the leadership of the one-eyed Ingcél in league with Conaire's foster-brothers. Conaire's reign began auspiciously enough. In fact, his rule was foreseen through a ritual called *tarbfeis* (bull feast; bull sleep) which predicts or prophesies a forthcoming king. *Tarbfeis* will be discussed presently.

Another text in the tale lists is *Fís Chuinn Chétchathaig .i. Baile in Scáil* (The Vision of Conn of the Hundred Battles, that is, the Vision [Frenzy] of the Phantom),[203] a text which prophesies the kings of Tara and helps confirm the notion of a Gaelic *natio*. The B List has this double name under one heading, but under the headword *baile* the three B List manuscripts also include *Baile in Scáil* so this tale is, in essence, listed twice in the B List.[204] The Gaelic word *fís* (vision) derives directly from Latin *visio* and has retained the original Latin meaning. In both tale lists *fís* is the headword for a small group of four tales. *Baile in Scáil* may have a ninth-century core with additions and changes up to the first half of the eleventh century.[205] It is a political prophecy uttered by the *scál* (phantom) emphasizing the Uí Néill high-kings in the presence of Conn Cétchathach, an important Uí Néill ancestor figure. *Baile in Scáil* is related to the much earlier *Baile Chuinn*,[206] a text from *Cín Dromma Snechtai*, in which Conn himself enumerated kings who would follow him in the kingship. The last identifiable king in *Baile Chuinn* is Fínṡnechta Fledach (675–695),[207] who ruled Mag Breg when Anglo-Saxon forces invaded the region in 684 (*HE* iv 26 [24]).

*Fís Fursa* (The Vision of Fursa) is one of four tales listed under the headword *fís* (vision). This is significant since Fursa's vision of the punishments and rewards of the afterlife is an ecclesiastical topic. Bede's chapter devoted to Fursa's vision, which he took from a *libellus* (little book), is its most widely known account (*HE* iii 19). Fursa most likely came from Co. Louth,[208] and had his vision

---

202 Bergin and Best, "*Tochmarc Étaíne*."
203 Murray, *Baile in Scáil*; Ó Corráin, *Clavis*, iii, 1526–27 §1136.
204 Mac Cana, *Learned Tales*, 56, 58.
205 Murray, *Baile in Scáil*, 4.
206 Murray, "Manuscript Tradition."
207 Murphy, "Dates of Two Sources"; Carey, "*Cín Dromma Snechtai* Texts." See more recently Bhreathnach, "Political Context"; Bhreathnach and Murray, "*Baile Chuinn Chétchathaig*."
208 Ó Riain, *Dictionary*, 357–59. This is also the region where Cuanu and the *Táin* likely originated: Kelleher, "*Táin* and the Annals"; Ó hUiginn, "Development of *Táin Bó Cúailnge*," 57–62.

ca. 629.[209] Fursa, along with named companions, settled among the East Angles at Cnobheresburg (Burgh Castle) and cooperated with two local kings before proceeding onto the Continent (*HE* iii 19).[210] Their time in East Anglia overlapped with the bishopric of Felix and with Abbess Hild's stay there, discussed in chapter six.

*Fís Fursa* (Vision of Fursa) is important for appearing in the tenth-century tale lists because it is a religious text and yet involves historical characters whose activities can be traced from Ireland, through Britain and onto the Continent. However, *Fís Fursa* may be a late addition to the tale lists, as its appearance breaks the alliterative pattern of the list.[211] Fursa's cross-cultural importance is recorded in the Martyrology of Óengus[212] and the Old English Martyrology[213] at January 16, and in Ælfric's homilies.[214]

*Táin Bó Fraích* (Driving the Cattle of Fróech) is from the early eighth century, if not earlier.[215] The tale is notable for blending indigenous lore and episodes on the Continent. Fróech's mother's people are *a sídib* (from the faerie mounds), implying that his origins were "otherworldly." His connection with the *síd* is demonstrated in elaborately descriptive passages that portray the elegance and splendor of the *síd* world and its denizens.[216] In his retinue are three harpers descended from Uaithne, harper of the Dagdae. In the tale their names are equivalent to the three types of music, sleep inducing music (*suantraí*), laughter inducing music (*gentraí*), and laments (*goltraí*), recorded in *Cath Maige Tuired*.[217] Fróech's hornplayers also had the ability to mesmerize their audience with their music.[218]

The tale is divided into two unequal halves. The first involves Fróech's wooing of Finnabair, daughter of Ailill and Medb of Connacht at Crúachu.[219] Finnabair is

---

209 See synchronisms Mc Carthy, www.irish-annals.cs.tcd.ie; Mac Airt and Mac Niocaill, *Annals of Ulster*, 114–15 s.a. 627; Stokes, "Annals of Tigernach," 180 [Felinfach i 140].
210 Colgrave and Mynors, *Ecclesiastical History*, 270–71.
211 Toner, "Earliest Irish Tale Lists," 111–12.
212 Stokes, *Félire Óengusso*, 36, 44–47 (scholia).
213 Rauer, *Old English Martyrology*, 48–49 §21, 237 (commentary).
214 Warner, *Early English Homilies*, 109–115. See further, Clemoes, *Aelfric's Catholic Homilies*; Godden, *Aelfric's Catholic Homilies*.
215 The editor argued from linguistic evidence that the text "can hardly be later than 750, indeed it may be as early as 700"; Meid, *Táin Bó Fraích*, xxv; Ó Corráin, *Clavis*, iii, 1471–73 §1106. James Carney argued that the dating limits were likely from 680 to 775: *Literature and History*, 27.
216 See discussion in Ireland, "Visionary Poets," 130–31.
217 Meid, *Romance of Froech*, §10, 43 (Gaelic), 67 (English).
218 Meid, *Romance of Froech*, §20, 46 (Gaelic), 70 (English).
219 Archaeological evidence, in the form of ogham inscriptions, suggests the depth of traditions about a character named Fróech in this region: Waddell, "Cave of Crúachain," 81, 84, 85–86.

already in love with Fróech before seeing him because his *airscél* (reputation) has preceded him. A deal is reached whereby Fróech will accompany Ailill and Medb's expedition on the *Táin Bó Cúailnge* as part of Finnabair's bride price. This early tale may be thought of as a fore-tale of the *Táin*, despite not being referred to as such anywhere in the literature.

Intertextual cross-referencing between Fróech's tale and Recension One of the *Táin Bó Cúailnge* is striking. The section in Recension One called *Aided Fraích* (The Violent Death of Fróech) depicts the single combat between Fróech and Cú Chulainn in the waters of a ford. In *Táin Bó Fraích* Fróech was portrayed as an effective fighter in water and defeated a water monster though wounded in the process. When Fróech encountered Cú Chulainn in Recension One he deliberately challenged Cú Chulainn to fight in the water of a ford. Cú Chulainn, as expected, defeated and killed Fróech, at whose death elaborately dressed faerie women lamented him and took his body with them back to the *síd*. In typical *dindsenchas* fashion it bore the name *Síd Fraích* (Faerie Mound of Fróech) ever after.[220] In *Táin Bó Fraích*, when Fróech was wounded in the fight with the water monster, even more elaborately dressed faerie women lamented Fróech's condition and transported him to the *síd* where he was healed overnight and returned next day to the court of Ailill and Medb, whole and unblemished. Since *Táin Bó Fraích* is earlier than surviving versions of *Táin Bó Cúailnge*, it serves as another witness among several to the prior existence of the epic *Táin* before it was first preserved in written form.

The second half of the tale involves Fróech traveling onto the continent accompanied by Conall Cernach,[221] a hero from the Ulster cycle. Fróech and Conall must cross the Alps to the land of the Lombards (*Langbaird*)[222] in order to recover cattle stolen from Fróech. They were special faerie cattle that he had received from his mother's family. This tale is unusual for having a major episode transpire on the Continent, while at the same time having characteristics firmly within insular indigenous traditions. The tale concludes with an etymological anecdote that describes how Bangor got its name.[223] Columbanus's monastery at Bobbio explains how the monks at Bangor were familiar with the Continent and the Lombards.

---

[220] O'Rahilly, *Táin: Recension I*, 26–27, lines 834–57 (Gaelic); 148–49 (English).
[221] Conall Cernach is portrayed in genealogies as ancestor of various groups including the Dál nAraidi, the Uí Echach, and the Lóiges. See further Meid, *Romance of Froech*, 249–50.
[222] Familiarity with the Lombards among scholars in Bangor is suggested by the continued presence of Irish at Bobbio: Richter, *Bobbio*, 13–23 (background), 67–68 (Comgall), 89–96 (Cummian).
[223] Ireland, "Whitby *Life* of Gregory," 152–53.

Seventh-century records confirm the rise of the Uí Néill in the polity of the northern half of Ireland and the inexorable decline of the Laigin, especially in Ireland's midlands. The Laigin are the people who gave their name to the province of Leinster.[224] A substantial literature addresses the traditions of the Laigin. Oxford, Bodleian Library, MS Rawlinson B 502 preserves the largest collection of this traditional material, for example, a large corpus of verse, *Laídšenchas Laigen* (Versified Traditional Lore of Leinster),[225] as well as many narrative texts in the *Scélšenchas Laigen* (Narrative Traditional Lore of Leinster). Some of this material is also found abundantly in other manuscript sources. In the genealogies of the same manuscript, but not limited to it, are a number of poems dealing with the ancestors of the Laigin.[226] These poems from the Leinster genealogies were mentioned in chapter one in the context of *encomia* and praise of ancestors.

*Orgain Denna Ríg* (The Destruction of Dind Ríg) is the first text in the *Scélšenchas Laigen* and contains the origin legend of the Laigin. The story is set in the third century before the Christian era. As preserved the tale is probably of the tenth century.[227] The tale relates how Labraid Loingseach[228] recovers his patrimony from Cobthach Cóel a relative who had killed Labraid's grandfather and father in order to secure the kingship for himself.[229] The tale assumes the pre-eminence of Tara as a royal site whose territory at the time is under the control of the Laigin. Cobthach Cóel held the *feis Temrach* (feast of Tara) at which the king, queen, princes, and lesser nobles were being praised by the eulogists (*áes admolta*). Among the "eulogists" were Ferchertne *fili*[230] and the harper Craiphtine, both of whom were loyal to Labraid.

Craiphtine twice during the course of the narrative played "sleep-inducing music" (*suantraí*) to put hosts to sleep to the advantage of Labraid. Two poems are quoted, reputedly by Ferchertne, that relate to the events of the tale.

---

**224** Byrne, *Irish Kings*, 130–64; Smyth, *Celtic Leinster*.
**225** Bhreathnach, "Kingship of Leinster."
**226** For example, see O'Brien, *Corpus genealogiarum Hiberniae*, 1–9, 18–23. Corthals, "Observations on the Versification"; Corthals, "Rhymeless 'Leinster Poems'."
**227** Greene, *Fingal Rónáin*, 16. For *Orgain Denna Ríg*, see Ó Corráin, *Clavis*, iii, 1423–24 §1086.
**228** Later traditions about Labraid are varied and complex. For versions preserved in the preface to *Amrae Coluim Chille*, see Dillon, *Cycles of the Kings*, 7–10; Clarke, "Medieval Irish Bookshelf"; Carey, "From David to Labraid."
**229** Another version about "Móen" includes the "horse's ears"; see Clarke, "Medieval Irish Bookshelf."
**230** There is another Ferchertne *fili* in the Ulster cycle of tales at the court of Conchobar, also famous from the text *Immacallam in dá Thuarad* which portrays the competition for position of court poet between the established poet Ferchertne and the younger Néide mac Adnai, whose father Adnae had recently died leaving the post of court poet open.

Versions of these two poems are found in the genealogies of the Laigin.²³¹ Two historical poets are quoted as part of the tale. In both cases the quotations serve as external confirmation of details in the narrative by citing well-known poets on the topic in question. A quatrain attributed to Flann mac Lonáin (d. 896)²³² retells in verse events already related in prose. Two unattributed quatrains in the text come from a poem that begins *A chóicid choín Chairpri crúaid*, attributed elsewhere to Orthanach úa Cóellámae (d. ca. 839),²³³ a bishop of Kildare discussed in Appendix 2.a (Figure 2.e). This poem is included among the *Laídšenchas Laigen*.²³⁴

There are two destructions of Dind Ríg in the tale. The first allows Labraid to reassert control over the territory around Dind Ríg.²³⁵ The second destruction allows Labraid to take vengeance on Cobthach Cóel by killing him and thirty other kings in a specially made iron house in which they are burned alive after being invited to a feast there. Charles Wright identified this episode with the iron house from *Orgain Denna Ríg* as being the closest analogue of the "iron house" motif in the Old English Vercelli Homily IX.²³⁶ The traditional site for Dind Ríg is on the River Barrow, near Leighlinbridge, only a few miles from Rath Melsigi, the site Bede identified as an important training center for Anglo-Saxon students (Figure 6.c). The monk Ecgberht spent several decades there. The proximity of Rath Melsigi and the presumed site of Dind Ríg suggest that the unusual motif of the "iron house" found in a tenth-century Gaelic narrative might resurface in an Old English homily of the same century.

## Tales from the "Irish Sea Culture-Province"

Surviving titles, and tales, in the tale lists demonstrate interactions between the peoples of Ireland and Britain and show that the Irish Sea served as a highway

---

**231** O'Brien, *Corpus genealogiarum Hiberniae*, 18; Corthals, "Observations on the Versification," 117 §1, 118 §2. For discussions of the poems in this tale, see Ó Cathasaigh, "Observations on *Orgain Denna Ríg*," 10–13.
**232** He was killed by the Déisi of Munster: Mac Airt and Mac Niocaill, *Annals of Ulster*, 350–51. Flann mac Lonáin appears in Appendix 2.a.
**233** Byrne, "Church and Politics," 671–72; Mac Cana, *Learned Tales*, 102 and n92. See discussion in Appendix 2.a.
**234** Bhreathnach, "Kingship of Leinster," 301, 302.
**235** See the discussion of the term *rechtas*, in Ó Cathasaigh, "Observations on *Orgain Denna Ríg*," 7–10.
**236** Wright, *Irish Tradition*, 194–204. For a wider discussion, see Sims-Williams, *The Iron House*.

rather than a barrier. Proinseas Mac Cana used a term derived from archaeologists who speak of the "Irish Sea culture-province" comprising all the peoples and lands that border the Irish Sea, including the Gaels, Britons, Picts, and Anglo-Saxons.[237]

From an early period, tales were created and preserved that are based on historical persons who may, at times, interact with supernatural characters. Two tales from the *Cín Dromma Snechtai*, *Immram Brain* and *Compert Mongáin*, deal with Manannán mac Lir, a manifestation of an indigenous sea god,[238] and the historical Mongán mac Fiachnai (d. 625) who, according to stanzas in the annals, was killed by a Briton.[239] Both tales from the *Cín* are dated to the early eighth century, if not earlier, and tell of the supernatural conception of Mongán. His father, Fiachnae Lurgan mac Báetáin (d. 626),[240] is described in *Compert Mongáin* as being friendly with Áedán mac Gabráin (d. ca. 604)[241] in the north of Britain.

Fiachnae went to help Áedán in battle against his Anglo-Saxon enemies. The intervention by Manannán mac Lir in *Compert Mongáin* was to save the life of Fiachnae from a great warrior sent by the Anglo-Saxons.[242] The story has Áedán and Fiachnae emerge successful in the battle. According to Bede, the Bernician king Æthelfrith (d. 616) defeated Áedán mac Gabráin at the battle of Degsastan (ca. 600; 603 in Bede, *HE* i 34, v 24).[243] Gaelic annals recorded Áedán's defeat a few years earlier than Bede's date for Degsastan. Bede declared that no Gaelic king in Britain dared engage in combat against the Anglo-Saxons after that (*HE* i 34).[244] Bede's history confirms that subsequent Anglo-Saxon kings continued to pursue aggression against the Gaels, Britons, and Picts.

---

237 Mac Cana, "Mongán mac Fiachna," 105.
238 Even in the Old English Martyrology the ocean can manifest as Garsecg: Rauer, *Old English Martyrology*, 166–67 §162 (under Bartholomew, August 25), 284 (commentary).
239 Mac Airt and Mac Niocaill, *Annals of Ulster*, 112–13; Stokes, "Annals of Tigernach," 178 [Felinfach i, 138]; Hennessy, *Chronicum Scotorum*, 78–79.
240 Mac Airt and Mac Niocaill, *Annals of Ulster*, 114–15; Stokes, "Annals of Tigernach," 179 [Felinfach i, 139]; Hennessy, *Chronicum Scotorum*, 80–81.
241 Mc Carthy, http://www.irish-annals.cs.tcd.ie/, s.a. 604; Mac Airt and Mac Niocaill, *Annals of Ulster*, 104–5; Stokes, "Annals of Tigernach," 167 [Felinfach i, 127]; Hennessy, *Chronicum Scotorum*, 70–71.
242 White, *Compert Mongáin*, 71–72 (Gaelic), 78–79 (English).
243 Mc Carthy, http://www.irish-annals.cs.tcd.ie/, s.a. 599; Mac Airt and Mac Niocaill, *Annals of Ulster*, 98–99, s.a. 600; Stokes, "Annals of Tigernach," 163 [Felinfach i, 123]; Hennessy, *Chronicum Scotorum*, 70–71. For arguments about Bede's confusion of sources, see Duncan, "Bede, Iona, and the Picts," 16–18.
244 "Neque ex eo tempore quisquam regnum Scottorum in Brittania aduersus gentem Anglorum usque ad hanc diem in proelium uenire audebat": Colgrave and Mynors, *Ecclesiastical History*, 116.

The remaining tales to be discussed exist only as titles, no actual narratives survive. One such title from List A only, *Echtrae Mongáin maic Fiachnai* (The Adventure of Mongán son of Fiachnae), names Mongán again. We have no indication of the tale's contents. It may be an alternative name for a surviving tale about Mongán contained in *Cín Dromma Snechtai*, but it is equally likely that it related another noteworthy adventure.

Another List A title, *Echtrae Áedáin maic Gabráin* (The Adventure of Áedán son of Gabrán) suggests that a historical tale, or cycle of tales, about this king of Dál Ríata once existed. It would be more surprising if there had not been tales extant about Áedán (d. ca. 604) since he is mentioned prominently in Adomnán's *Vita sancti Columbae*, in Bede's *Historia ecclesiastica*, and his battles, both victories and defeats, are cited in Gaelic annals, along with mentions of his sons and grandsons.[245] For example, Áedán appears in the vernacular Life of St. Berach (*Betha Beraigh*) when Áedán asked his druids to ascertain the source of miracles performed by Berach.[246] A twelfth-century poem recounts that Áedán and Brandub mac Echach, king of Leinster (d. ca. 605) were brothers.[247]

A title from both lists, *Slúagad Fiachnai maic Báetáin co Dún nGuaire i Saxanaib* (The Military Expedition of Fiachnae son of Báetán to Dún Guaire (Bamburgh) among the Saxons), appears to contradict Bede's statement that Áedán mac Gabráin was the last Gaelic king to engage the Anglo-Saxons in combat. Although no such tale survives, the title names Mongán's father, Fiachnae mac Báetáin, and implies that he led a campaign against the Anglo-Saxons at Bamburgh (Dún Guaire).[248] Support seems to come from an annal entry ca. 623, "expugnatio Rátha Guali la Fiachnae mac Báetáin" (the storming of Ráth Guala by Fiachnae son of Báetán).[249] This interpretation takes the name *Guala* as a corruption of *Guaire* and *ráth* as a substitute for *dún* both describing a "fortified enclosure." This otherwise unexplained annal entry suggests that an event not recorded in Anglo-Saxon records was developed into a narrative tale.[250] Such

---

245 Summarized in Plummer, *Venerabilis Baedae opera*, ii, 64–65.
246 Plummer, *Bethada Náem nÉrenn*, i, 34–5; ii, 33–34 §§54–59.
247 O'Brien, "Birth of Áedán mac Gabráin."
248 The Gaelic and Brittonic names for Bamburgh are related: Morris, *Nennius*, 37–38, 78–79 §§61, 63 (Historia Brittonum); Byrne, *Irish Kings*, 112.
249 Mc Carthy, http://www.irish-annals.cs.tcd.ie/, s.a. 624; Mac Airt and Mac Niocaill, *Annals of Ulster*, 112–13, s.a. 623; Stokes, "Annals of Tigernach," 176 [Felinfach i, 136]; Hennessy, *Chronicum Scotorum*, 76–77. Both the Annals of Ulster and Tigernach have quatrains inserted at the entry for the battle, but they provide no clarification. See discussions in Byrne, *Irish Kings*, 112; Ó Cróinín, *Early Medieval Ireland*, 74.
250 Byrne, *Irish Kings*, 112; Charles-Edwards, *Chronicle of Ireland*, 132–33n8; Ó Cróinín, *Early Medieval Ireland*, 74.

an event, if it occurred, would have been during Edwin's reign (617–633). However, Bede made much of the peacefulness of his *imperium* (*HE* ii 16), as discussed in chapter five.

The title *Echtrae Maíl Umai maic Báetáin* (The Adventure of Máel Umai son of Báetán), found in List A, puts the conflict of Æthelfrith with the Gaels into more secure historical context. Máel Umai, of the Cenél nÉogain, appears in the same genealogy with Aldfrith (Flann Fína) and Cenn Fáelad, two important *sapientes*.[251] In the genealogy Máel Umai is styled *rígféinnid* (royal champion). He participated at Degsastan and, according to the Annals of Tigernach, had slain Eanfrith, described as Æthelfrith's brother.[252] However, Bede reported that Æthelfrith's brother Theobald had been slain (*HE* i 34; *A. S. Chron.* E 603). Eanfrith, Æthelfrith's son, may have been confused with Theobald by the annalist.[253] Máel Umai was the brother of Colmán Rímid, Aldfrith's maternal grandfather.[254] Colmán Rímid shared the high-kingship with Áed Sláine (d. 604).[255] Bishop Fínán (651–ca. 661) of Lindisfarne may also have been a son of Colmán Rímid.[256]

Bede's description of Æthelfrith at the battle of Degsastan has an epic quality. The fighting resulted in heavy losses on both sides. Bede stated that Áedán's army was cut to pieces and he fled with his survivors. But Theobald, Æthelfrith's brother, was slain along with all of his army (*HE* i 34). Bede's statement that no Gaelic king waged war against the Anglo-Saxons after the battle may not be accurate. Bede described Æthelfrith as very brave and "most eager for glory" (fortissimus et gloriae cupidissimus: *HE* i 34), words reminiscent of Beowulf as *lofgeornost* (most eager for praise).[257] No ruler had subjected more land to his control, either by exterminating or conquering the natives, than Æthelfrith had (*HE* i 34). It is little wonder that the Gaels celebrated Máel Umai *rígféinnid* (royal champion).

Another title from both lists, *Slúagad Néill maic Echach co Muir nIcht* (The Expedition of Níall son of Echu to the English Channel), would have been about Níall Noígíallach (Níall of the Nine Hostages), the eponymous ancestor of the Uí Néill. Níall's epithet reflects traditions of hostage taking throughout Ireland, as

---

251 Ireland, "Irish Genealogies," 69.
252 "Cath Saxonum la hAedan, ubi cedidit Eanfraith frater Etalfraich la Maeluma mac Baedan, in quo uictus erat": Stokes, "Annals of Tigernach," 163 [Felinfach i, 123].
253 Plummer, *Venerabilis Baedae opera*, ii, 66.
254 O'Brien, *Corpus genealogiarum Hiberniae*, 135; Ireland, "Irish Genealogies," 69. The genealogies as preserved cannot always be taken at face value.
255 Byrne, *Irish Kings*, 104, 275; Ó Cróinín, "Ireland, 400–800," 210.
256 Ireland, "Irish Genealogies," 74; Ó Cróinín, "Ireland, 400–800," 210.
257 Fulk, Bjork, Niles, *Klaeber's Beowulf*, 109, line 3182b and nn271–72.

well as from Picts, Britons, Anglo-Saxons, and Franks on the continent, as a way of securing his rule.[258] Muir nIcht refers to the English Channel. Such traditions are a reminder that the purview of the early Gaels extended beyond the archipelago and onto the Continent.

The last title, also from both lists, is *Tochomlud Dáil Ríata i nAlbain* (The Advance of Dál Ríata into Britain). It must have portrayed the sea voyages, conquests, and alliances required to create Dál Ríata which extended from Ireland into northern Britain. Iona, from which Northumbria was evangelized, is in Dál Ríata. Áedán mac Gabráin was one of its most famous kings.[259] Despite Æthelfrith's aggression against Dál Ríata, it is where his sons sought refuge after his death and throughout the reign of his rival Edwin (617–633). The exile during Edwin's reign ensured that two major Northumbrian kings, Oswald (634–642) and Oswiu (642–670), were educated and baptized among the Gaels.

Kings Oswald (*HE* iii 3) and Oswiu (*HE* iii 25) were fluent Gaelic speakers, as was Oswiu's son Aldfrith *sapiens* (685–704). They would have been familiar with local lore, such as the strife between Æthelfrith and Áedán mac Gabráin, or Dál Ríata's expansion. In the context of an "Irish Sea culture-province," Northumbria was ruled for fifty-five years by three Gaelic-speaking kings (Figure 5.a). The tale titles discussed above leave an impression of the *senchas* these three kings would have known.

## Gaelic Texts on "Poetics"

A unique aspect of insular cultural history is the existence of Old Gaelic texts on "poetics." The Gaels developed treatises to describe how poetry was created and as explanations for the social prestige enjoyed by poets. Aldhelm apparently attempted to create an Anglo-Latin poetics in his *Epistola ad Acircium*, specifically with his *De metris* and *De pedum regulis*.[260] It has also been suggested that Aldhelm hoped Aldfrith *sapiens* would learn to compose quantitative Latin verse from this letter.[261] Whatever Aldhelm had expected to achieve with regard to

---

[258] See discussions in O'Rahilly, *Early Irish History and Mythology*, 218–22; Byrne, *Irish Kings*, 76–78.
[259] Byrne, *Irish Kings*, 107–114. See discussion of later traditions: Wadden, "Dál Riata."
[260] Discussed and translated by Neil Wright in Lapidge and Rosier, *Aldhelm*, 183–219. For a discussion of "poetic inspiration" in the Latin poetry of Late Antiquity, with an acknowledgement of vernacular parallels, see Ziolkowski, "Classical Influences."
[261] Thornbury, *Becoming a Poet*, 153–54.

Anglo-Latin poetics, no vernacular counterparts survive from the Old English corpus.[262]

The ninth-century "Triads of Ireland" describe characteristics of an array of persons, places, and activities.[263] The three skills that each *fili* must possess in order to sustain "privileged" (*nemed*) status are:

> Tréde neimthigedar filid: immas forosna, teinm læda, dichetal di chennaib.[264]
>
> (The three things that confer privilege on a poet: *imbas for·osnai, teinm láeda, díchetal di chennaib.*)

Two of these specialized skills have been discussed in chapter one. The first, *imbas for·osnai* (great knowledge which illuminates), was possessed by Fedelm *banfili* (poetess) who prophesied the outcome of Medb's and Ailill's expedition against Ulster in the opening sequences of the *Táin*. The third item, *díchetal di chennaib* (chanting from heads), represented extemporaneous oral composition, as attributed to Dallán Forgaill and an unnamed poet in *Beowulf*. Both of these poetic skills, or similar ones, are cited in the introduction of the seventh-century *Senchas Már*. It describes a master poet (*suí filed*) "who chants extempore, whom inspiration illuminates" (di·chain di chennaib, for·osnai imbas).[265] The *Senchas Már* was compiled ca. 660–680 at Armagh, probably as an aspect of the growing cult of St. Patrick.[266]

An earlier form of the triad was likely derived from the law-tracts and included *imbas for·osnai* and *díchetal di chennaib*. But the third item was, apparently, *anamain* which refers to poetic meters.[267] The original triad probably included *imbas* as great knowledge or "inspiration," without reference to divination or mantic abilities, *díchetal di chennaib* as improvisation or extemporaneous composition, and *anamain* as knowledge of meters or technical expertise generally.[268]

The triad shows that by the late Old Gaelic period these items had become stereotyped as skills required of poets. They are repeated in a variety of texts that suggest an evolving fiction to boost the prestige of poets. For example, they

---

262 Although no texts on poetics written in Old English have survived, modern scholars have recreated a poetics for the literature. See, for example, Tyler, *Old English Poetics*.
263 Meyer, *Triads of Ireland*; Ó Corráin, *Clavis*, ii, 1195–96 §912.
264 Meyer, *Triads of Ireland*, 16–17 §123.
265 Breatnach, *Senchas Már*, 4–5 §4.
266 Breatnach, *Senchas Már*, 38–42.
267 Breatnach, *Uraicecht na Ríar*, 36, 59, 177, 183.
268 Carey, "Three Things," 47. For examples from *Bretha Nemed* see Breatnach, *Uraicecht na Ríar*, 36–37; and for other examples of *anamain*, see Breatnach, *Uraicecht na Ríar*, 59, 177, 183.

are required of qualified poets in *Airec Menman*, the tenth-century tale that included tale-lists.[269] Elsewhere, the items are named in the preface to a ninth-century poem attributed to the legendary hero Fionn mac Cumhaill:

> Ro fogluim-sim in trēide nemt[h]igius filid .i. teínm lāega ocus imus for-osna ocus dīc[h]edul di c[h]ennaib. Is ann sin do-róine Finn in lāig-si oc fromad a éicsi.[270]
>
> (He learned the three things which confer privilege (*nemed*) on a *fili*, that is, *teinm láeda* and *imbas for·osnai* and *díchetal di chennaib*. It is then that Fionn made this lay to prove his *éicse* (poetic revelation, divination).)

*Teinm láeda* is a skill associated with Fionn mac Cumhaill acquired when, in his youth, he burned his fingers while cooking the "salmon of knowledge." From then on, whenever he put his finger or thumb in his mouth (or chewed with his "tooth of knowledge") he could access hidden knowledge which he expressed in verse. T. F. O'Rahilly argued that *teinm* is a verbal noun of *tennim* (I cut open, I cleave) and that *láeda* is genitive singular of *láed* (pith, marrow). He would translate *teinm láeda* as "the chewing of the pith."[271] Other descriptions of Gaelic divinatory practices emphasize chewing, but not swallowing, and are reminiscent of metaphors of "rumination" as meditation or deep thinking as applied by Bede to Cædmon (*HE* iv 24 [22]).[272]

A full description of *imbas for·osnai* is preserved in "Cormac's Glossary," attributed to Cormac mac Cuilennáin (d. 908; see Appendix 2.a). It is contemporary with the "Triads." There are good reasons not to accept its accuracy as a description of a rite or technique practiced by *filid*. For example, *imbas for·osnai* and *teinm láeda* are both condemned in "Cormac's Glossary" as rejecting the faith because they require sacrifices to demons. It is tempting to see this condemnation as the influence of Cormac himself in his rôle as bishop. Nevertheless, both practices are cited in a variety of texts throughout the tradition. The following is the entry from *Sanas Cormaic*:

> Imbass forosnae .i. dofūarascaib sec[h]ip rēt bas maith lasin filid 7 bes adlaic dó d'foillsiugad. Is amlaid didiu dognīther ōn .i. concnā in file mīr do c[h]arna dirg muice nō c[h]on nō c[h]ait ocus dobir īarom for lic īar cūl na comlad 7 dichain dīchetal fair 7 adopair do dēib īdal 7 cotagair dó 7 nī fagaib īarnabāroch, 7 dochain īarom for a dī bois 7 congair dēo īdal cuige arnā tarmascthar a c[h]odlud 7 dobeir a dī bois ima dī lecain 7 contuli 7 bīthir og a foraire ar nachn-imparræ 7 nach toirmescae neach, agas doadbanar dō īarom annī

---

269 Mac Cana, *Learned Tales*, 35, 37–38.
270 Murphy, "Finn's Poem," 89.
271 O'Rahilly, *Early Irish History and Mythology*, 337–38.
272 For rumination metaphors, see West, "Rumination"; Wieland, "Caedmon, the Clean Animal."

aradmbí co cend nómaide nō a dōu nō a trī, fut ngair conmessad ocind audpairt. Et ideo imbas dicitur .i. bas disīu 7 bass anall im a agaid nō im a c[h]end. Atrorbe Pātraic anīsin, 7 an teinm laoda 7 fotroirgell a brīathar nā bad nimhe nā talman nach aon dogēnai, ar is dīultad bathis. Dīc[h]etal doc[h]ennaib immorro fodrācbad sōn i cōrus c[h]erdæ, ar is soas fodera sōn: nī ēcen audbairt do demnaib oca, acht aisnēis do c[h]ennaib a chnāmae fochēdōir.[273]

(*Imbas for·onsai*, i.e., it discovers whatever thing the *fili* would like and that he desires to have revealed. This is how it is done. The *fili* chews a piece of red meat, either of pig or dog or cat, and then places it upon the flagstone behind the door and intones a spell over it and makes an offering to idol gods and summons them to him. And he does not discover it the next day, [but] chants upon his two palms [of the hand] and summons idol gods to him in order that his sleep is not disturbed. And he places his two palms about his two cheeks and sleeps, and there is someone watching over him in order that he not turn over and that no one may disturb him. And that which is in store for him for up to a *nómad* [period of time][274] or two or three is revealed to him in a short time in order that he may assess it during the sacrifice. And for this reason it is called *imbas*, because each palm [*bas*] is placed about [*im*] either side of his face or his head. Patrick forbade that, as well as *teinm láeda*, and testified by his word that anyone who performed it would not be of heaven or earth because it is a rejection of the faith. *Díchetal di chennaib* however, was left as proper to the arts, for it is knowledge which produces it. A sacrifice to demons is not necessary [for its performance], rather [it is] an extemporaneous recitation from the tips of his bones.)[275]

This account smacks of antiquarianism, as though the redactor were trying to recreate imagined practices of pre-Christian ancestors. The reference to Patrick's condemnation of *imbas for·osnai* and *teinm láeda* recalls the "pseudo-historical prologue" to the *Senchas Már* and the nine-member committee who syncretized native practice with Christian doctrine and conscience. The description is reminiscent of a ritual called *tarbfeis* (bull sleep or bull feast), to be discussed presently.[276] The purpose of *tarbfeis* was to predict a future king. The description of *imbas for·osnai* in *Sanas Cormaic* took place while lying in a structure. Chewing meat without swallowing suggests rumination. The information sought by the *fili* was revealed through sleep. These features are all reproduced in Bede's description of Cædmon (*HE* iv 24).

The modern linguistic etymology of *imbas* is taken to consist of an intensive prefix, *imb*, and *fios* (knowledge), and translated as "great knowledge" or

---

273 Meyer, "*Sanas Cormaic*," 64. Slight variations in the description are preserved in other manuscripts. For more on *Sanas Cormaic*, see Ó Corráin, *Clavis*, ii, 1171–74 §887.
274 Breatnach, "Meaning of *Nómad*."
275 For an early discussion, see Chadwick, "Imbas Forosnai." For other translations, see Bergin, *Irish Bardic Poetry*, 10; Ford, *Celtic Poets*, 46–47.
276 The descriptions are found in two tales: *Togail Bruidne Da Derga* and *Serglige Con Culainn*.

"encompassing knowledge."[277] The description from *Sanas Cormaic* above, based on "expository" etymology, as found in Isidore's *Etymologiae*, treats *imbas* as the preposition *im* (about, around) and the noun *bas* (palm of the hand). It implies that the poet's hands are covering his face, as though to shade his eyes, blocking out the light and creating a darkened ambience for composing.

No lengthy descriptions, however suspect in detail, survive for the other two members of the triad, *teinm láeda* and *díchetal di chennaib*. As noted, *teinm láeda* is associated with Fionn mac Cumhaill which he performed by putting his finger or thumb into his mouth, allowing him to access hidden knowledge.[278] *Díchetal di chennaib* (extempore incantation) has no clear descriptions, but references to it support that interpretation.[279] The fullest reference is found in later commentary to *Amrae Coluim Chille*. Dallán Forgaill intended to praise St. Columba (Colum Cille). But Columba did not allow Dallán to compose beyond the preface (*remfocul*) because only the deceased should be praised in such a manner. So Dallán waited until he learned of Columba's death and then composed the *Amrae* "extemporaneously" (*di chennaib*). The commentary even provides alternative locations for where Dallán was when he learned of Columba's death.[280]

*Immacallam in dá Thuarad* (The Colloquy of the Two Sages), noted for its arcane and deliberately obscure vocabulary, reveals much about Early Gaelic poetics.[281] It is cited in the "pseudo-historical prologue" to the *Senchas Már*,[282] and in *Sanas Cormaic* which expounds on rare vocabulary items found in it. As preserved in its tenth-century form it seems to refer to Norse invaders. It has been transformed through time, yet its core themes, the obscurity of the poetic contest and the derogation of judicial duties away from poets, can be identified in earlier texts. An outline of the narrative reveals many stereotypical characteristics of the Gaelic professional poets' world, discussed in chapter one and below.

When Néide mac Adnai arrived at Emain Macha to challenge Ferchertne *fili* the latter was away from court teaching his apprentices (*éicsíni*). Néide sat in Ferchertne's chair and draped the special poet's robe around himself. Because of his youth Néide took a handful of grass and cast a spell on it so that it would look like a beard. When Ferchertne received word of the interloper, he returned to the court and the two began their cryptic dialogue, a challenge to prove to

---

277 Thurneysen, "*Imbas for·osndai*."
278 Carey, "Three Things," 41–42.
279 See, for example, Carey, "Three Things," 45–46, 53–54.
280 Stokes, "*Amra Choluimb Chille*," 131–35. See further discussion in Herbert, "Preface to Amra."
281 Stokes, "Colloquy of the Two Sages"; Ó Corráin, *Clavis*, iii, 1396–98 §1070.
282 Carey, "Pseudo-Historical Prologue," 13, 19 §10.

each other, and to all present, that each possessed the recondite knowledge of a skilled poet and deserved to fill the post of *ollam filed* (chief poet).

Ultimately the senior poet Ferchertne bested the young Néide, but they concluded with deep respect for each other. None of the audience at court understood the poets' obscure language, with the result that legal judgements were removed from poets by King Conchobar and consigned to jurists only.[283] Gilla in Choimded devoted five stanzas to the contentious dialogue, King Conchobar's decision, and the poets' "dark speech" (*dublabrae*).[284] Despite Conchobar's decision, *Uraicecht na Ríar* stipulates that the *ollam filed* must be knowledgeable in "jurisprudence of Irish law" (brithemnacht fénechais).[285] The *Immacallam* suggests a context for the competition between the poets Deor and Heorrenda for the patronage of the lord (*dryhten*) of the Heodeningas.[286]

One of the longer glossarial entries in "Cormac's Glossary" relates a short narrative built around the adverb *prull* (greatly, excessively).[287] It has generated discussion among modern scholars about how to interpret it.[288] Senchán Torpéist, the legendary poet of the "Finding of the *Táin*," undertook a poetic circuit that included a visit to the Isle of Man. As his retinue was about to set off they were joined by a hideous youth whose appearance was repellent to all, but who was allowed to accompany them because he insisted that his presence would be of greater benefit to Senchán than any of his retinue. The youth's hideous appearance is elaborately described in the account.

When the retinue arrived on the Isle of Man they encountered a haggard woman gathering seaweed. Despite her ragged clothing, they noticed the noble appearance of her hands and feet. She was, in fact, the *leccerd* (*lethcherd*), a kind of poet, daughter of úa Dulsaine from Múscraige of Lia Toll in Munster.[289] She had gone on a poetic circuit of the Gaelic-speaking world, Ireland, Britain, and the Isle of Man, but all of her retinue had died. Her brother, also a poet, had searched for her throughout Ireland without success. When she saw Senchán and his retinue arrive she enquired as to who they were. One of the retinue

---

[283] McCone, "Dubthach Maccu Lugair," 9–10; Carey, "Pseudo-Historical Prologue," 19 §10.
[284] Smith, "Aimirgein Glúngel Tuir Tend," 131–32 (Gaelic), 137 (English), §§46–50; *dublabrae* at §47.
[285] Breatnach, *Uraicecht na Ríar*, 102–3 §2.
[286] For a discussion of the *Immacallam* in a wider European context, see Wright, "From Monks' Jokes to Sages' Wisdom."
[287] Meyer, "*Sanas Cormaic*," 90–94 §1059.
[288] Dooley, "Early Irish Literature," 68–71; Ford, "Blind, the Dumb, and the Ugly"; Ní Dhonnchadha, "*Prull* Narrative."
[289] For examples of *lethcherd*, see Breatnach, *Uraicecht na Ríar*, 34–35, 39–41.

responded that she must be from another country if she did not know Senchán, the poet (*éices*) of the whole island of Ireland.

She then asked Senchán if he would hear what she had to say. After his positive response she quoted half a quatrain to him and asked that he complete it. But Senchán and all his retinue seemed stunned into silence. With that the hideous youth interceded and told the woman that it was not appropriate for her to address Senchán. She should, rather, address him (the hideous youth). So she asked the youth to complete the quatrain, which he did correctly. The woman then asked Senchán to complete a second verse that contained the word *prull*. Again, the hideous youth reminded her that Senchán would not speak with her and so she asked the youth to complete the second verse, which he again did. The conclusion of the verse identified the haggard woman as the lost poet (*cerd*), daughter of úa Dulsaine.

Senchán then asked the woman if she was, indeed, the lost poet. When she confirmed her identity, she was bathed and dressed in fine garments and returned to Ireland with Senchán, as befit her status. Upon the retinue's return to Ireland it was noticed that the hideous youth, having proven his poetic skills, had been transformed into a handsome youth and was elegantly dressed. The youth then went around Senchán and his retinue right hand-wise (*dessel*) and has never been seen since.[290] The narrative concludes, in Latin, that the youth was, without doubt, the "spirit of poetry" (*spiritus poematis*).

While many details in this narrative are open to differing interpretations, it contains several stereotypical features that apply to Gaelic poets. Poets enjoyed the privilege of travel throughout the Gaelic-speaking world; high-ranking poets had large retinues; poets challenged each other and competed to test their knowledge and abilities; there were different ranks and types of poets; their status was reflected in their clothing; and women participated in the profession.

We have noted the presence of Fedelm "poetess" (*banfili*) and "prophetess" (*banfáith*) in the *Táin Bó Cúailnge*. Another "poetess" (*banéices*) from the vernacular prosimetric tradition was named Liadain. Her frustrated love affair with the poet (*éices*) Cuirithir was due to commitments to the Church but left some touching, emotive verse.[291] Their "spiritual advisor" (*anmcharae*) was Cuimmíne Fota *sapiens*, who will be discussed in chapter four. Ambiguities in the circumstances of their relationship have intrigued modern scholars in a manner reminiscent of the narrative voices in the Old English poems "Wulf and Eadwacer" and "The

---

**290** The implication is that moving right hand-wise or sunwise (*dessel*) is lucky or auspicious.
**291** Meyer, *Liadain and Curithir*; Ó Corráin, *Clavis*, iii, 1349–50 §1027. See further, Larson, "Veiled Poet."

Wife's Lament."[292] Historical confirmation of women professional poets is found in the Annals of Inisfallen which note the death (934) of Uallach, daughter of Muinechán, poetess (*banfili*) of Ireland, as noted in Appendix 2.a.[293]

The eighth-century text with the modern editorial title "Caldron of Poesy" demonstrates how poetic inspiration had many sources. It could be acquired through training and knowledge, as an inherent part of learned culture.[294] But strong emotions could also impel those without training to produce poems. This text originated near the time that Bede wrote his account of Cædmon. It names three metaphorical caldrons that lie within a person and affect the potential to produce poetry under differing circumstances. The caldron may assume three possible positions. It may stand upright, implying fullness; it may be inclined on its side, that is, half full; or it may be upside down, implying emptiness. These varying positions are metaphors for the potential poetic ability residing in each individual. The Gaels recognized that the vicissitudes of life could shift, figuratively, the position of a caldron within a person. They also recognized that study and learning, that is, the training and apprenticeships of professional poets, enhanced their contents and helped alter the positions of these metaphorical caldrons.

Each caldron (*coire*) is given a name. The *Coire Goiriath* applied to the beginning stages or foundations of acquiring poetry. The mythico-legendary poet Amairgen proclaimed it, having received it from God, as establishing knowledge of language, speech, grammar, meter, writing.[295] The *Coire Sofis* referred to knowledge of all arts and sciences which are useful as background for the efficient production of poetry and the maintenance of poetic art.[296] These two caldrons signify that applied study and wide learning from an early age, and throughout one's life, enhanced the likelihood of achieving "inspiration."

The greatest part of the text is taken up with explanations of the *Coire Érmai* and how "inspiration" is manifested, from the person who displays no predisposition for poetry to the one who is brimming with it.[297] One section on

---

[292] Krapp and Dobbie, *Exeter Book*, liv–lvii §15, 179–80 (Wulf and Eadwacer), lvii–lx §16, 210–11 (The Wife's Lament).
[293] "Quies Huallaige ingene Muinecháin, banfile Herend": Mac Airt, *Annals of Inisfallen*, 150–51; discussed in Johnston, *Literacy and Identity*, 140. See further Clancy, "Women Poets."
[294] This important text has been edited twice, unbeknownst to the different editors, and published close in time to each other. In this discussion I rely primarily on Breatnach, "Caldron of Poesy." The other edition is useful for comparisons: Henry, "Caldron of Poesy." See further Ó Corráin, *Clavis*, ii, 1129–30 §849.
[295] Breatnach, "Caldron of Poesy," 48 (introduction), 62–63 §1 (text), 74–75 (etymology of *goiriath*).
[296] Breatnach, "Caldron of Poesy," 49 (introduction), 62–63 §2 (text), 79 (etymology).
[297] Breatnach, "Caldron of Poesy," 49 (introduction), 64–73 §§6, 8–15 (text), 82–83 (etymology).

*Érmae* is attributed to Néide mac Adnai, the young poet who challenged Ferchertne the *ollam filed* in *Immacallam in dá Thuarad*.[298] The section stresses the centrality of *imbas* (great knowledge; inspiration) which must be developed and nurtured for each person to be successful. The "Caldron of Poesy" is linguistically earlier than the surviving version of *Immacallam in dá Thuarad*, so the mention of Néide mac Adnai proves that he existed as an iconic figure from before the redaction of the text by which he is now best known.

The text inquires whether the source of a person's poetic ability is of the body or the soul. For those who answer the soul, it is because the body does nothing without the soul. For those who say the body, it is because some inherit their skills from a parent or grandparent. This latter statement emphasizes the hereditary aspects of rank and privilege among the poets.[299] It is noted that some people never display poetic ability "since God does not equally provide for all."[300]

The *Coire Érmai* deals with varying aspects of "inspiration." The eighth section states that the caldron is upside down in every second person, that is, in those who are ignorant and display little knowledge or poetic skill. The caldron is on its side for those who practice lower levels of the poetic arts. But the caldron is upright in the person who achieves the level of *ánsruth* in general knowledge and poetic art. In the hierarchical Gaelic system the *ánsruth* has attained the highest level of skill and knowledge in a specific profession or craft, but may be held back from occupying the top station, either because it is already occupied or because the *ánsruth* does not have the necessary hereditary background.[301] Part of *Bríathra Flainn Fhína*, attributed to King Aldfrith *sapiens*, stated that *ecnae* (learning; *sapientia*) could turn one into an *ánsruth* (Figure 4.c).[302] Study can shift the position of the metaphorical caldron within a person. For those who do not apply themselves to learning, either sorrow or joy can sometimes lift the caldron into an upright position, that is, inspire a "poetic" outpouring.

Section nine states that the four causes of sorrow that release inspiration are: 1) longing, 2) grief, 3) jealousy and 4) exile for God (*ailithre ar Día*). The fourth item makes clear that this text evolved under the influence of the Church and ecclesiastical personnel. The first two causes, longing and grief, are reminiscent of King Hrothgar, or the *gomela Scilding* (aged Scylding) of *Beowulf*, when he lamented his

---

**298** Breatnach, "Caldron of Poesy," 68–71 §13 (text).
**299** For context and discussion of the "three generation requirement" to achieve and maintain social status, see Breatnach, *Uraicecht na Ríar*, 93–98.
**300** "dath nád inonn airlethar Día do cach dóen": Breatnach, "Caldron of Poesy," 62–63 §1.
**301** Breatnach, *Uraicecht na Ríar*, 94.
**302** Ireland, *Bríathra Flainn Fhína maic Ossu*, 90–91 §7.

lost youth and vigor.[303] The tenth section defines the two forms of joy as "divine joy" (*fáilte déoda*) and "human joy" (*fáilte dóenda*). The four divisions of "human joy" are: 1) sexual longing, 2) safety and security from care and want, 3) joy in success at studying poetry, and 4) joy at the acquisition of *imbas*. Note how the last two items are about progressing within the educational hierarchy of the professional poets.

---

From the "Caldron of Poesy" (early eighth century):

§10. There are, then, two divisions of joy through which it is converted into the Caldron of Knowledge (*Coire Sofis*), that is, divine joy and human joy.

§11. As for human joy (*fáilte dóendae*), it has four divisions: 1) the force of sexual longing, 2) the joy of safety and freedom from care, 3) joy at the prerogatives of poetry after studying it well, and 4) joy at the arrival of *imbas* (encompassing knowledge; inspiration).

§12. Divine joy (*fáilte déodae*), moreover, is the coming of divine grace (*rath déodae*) to the Caldron of *Érmae*, so that it converts it into the upright position, and as a result there are people who are both divine and secular prophets (*fáidi déodai ⁊ dóendai*) and commentators both on matters of grace (*rath*) and of (secular) learning (*frithgnam*), and they then utter godly utterances and perform miracles, and their words are maxims and judgements, and they are an example for all speech.

(Translation based on the edition by Breatnach, "Caldron of Poesy," 66–69.)

From *Vita Guthlaci* (ca. 730–ca. 740):

A certain *librarius* named Wigfrith, part of the retinue of Bishop Headda on a visit to St. Guthlac, hearing of the saint's prophecies, told his companions that he would be able to discern the nature of the saint's abilities because he had lived among the Gaels (*inter Scottorum populos*) and had seen there "false hermits and pretenders of various religions, whom he found able to predict the future and to perform other miracles." He said that there were others "who were followers of the true religion and abounded in many signs and miracles."

(Citations from Colgrave, *Life of Saint Guthlac*, 142–43, c. 46.)

---

**Figure 3.b:** Divine and Human Sources of Inspiration.

Divine joy, described in section twelve, is caused by the arrival of "divine grace" (*rath déoda*) which, following the metaphor, turns the *Coire Érmai* upright in a person. This would seem to be how the "miracle" of Cædmon's "gift of song"

---

**303** Fulk, Bjork, Niles, *Klaeber's Beowulf*, 71–72, lines 2105–14.

came about.[304] He was, after all, that "certain brother who was specially marked out by the grace of God" (frater quidam diuina gratia specialiter insignis; *HE* iv 24 [22]).[305] Bede had no hesitation in discussing miracles, but he never described Cædmon's poetry as a miracle.[306] The fact that so many modern scholars describe Cædmon's "gift of song" as a miracle suggests that they have not examined parallels and analogues from contiguous insular poetic traditions.[307]

Divine grace was not restricted to the religious, as both divine and secular prophets (fáidi déoda, dóenda) may make godly pronouncements, perform miracles, and comment on matters so that their words are remembered as important judgements or become wise sayings.[308] The recognition of both divine and secular prophets in an early eighth-century Gaelic text reflects the observations in *Vita Guthlaci* of Wigfrith who had lived among the Gaels and had seen "false hermits and pretenders of various religions, whom he found able to predict the future and to perform other miracles" (pseudo-anachoritas diversarum religionum simulatores vidisse, quos praedicere futura et virtutes alias facere: Vita Guthlaci c. 46).[309] Recognition by the Gaels of both divine and secular prophets, confirmed by a contemporary Anglo-Saxon source, shows that the Gaels distinguished between the secular and ecclesiastical spheres of life without relinquishing their Christian world view.

Core concepts of the "Caldron of Poesy" are derived from Christian perspectives on human life, beginning with the duality of body and soul and the benefits of divine grace. This dual division is expounded by Isidore in the *Etymologiae*.[310] The image of three caldrons is metaphorical.[311] Johan Corthals has shown that these metaphors have parallels in the Late Antique Mediterranean world. He cited, by way of example, a text by Apuleius, transmitted under the name *Florida*, which used bowls metaphorically to designate, by their contents, stages

---

**304** The description of Cædmon's production of poetry as a miracle is surprisingly common in the critical literature. See, for example, Wrenn, "Poetry of Cædmon," 288; Magoun, "Bede's Story of Cædmon," 58; Ward, "Miracles and History," 73–74; Mitchell and Robinson, *Guide to Old English*, 204; O'Donnell, *Cædmon's Hymn*, 4–12, 25–28; Thornbury, "Aldhelm's Rejection," 86–87.
**305** Colgrave and Mynors, *Ecclesiastical History*, 414–15.
**306** For miracles in Bede, see Colgrave and Mynors, *Ecclesiastical History*, xxxiv–xxxvi; Colgrave, "Bede's Miracle Stories"; McCready, *Miracles*.
**307** For surveys of the miracle story of Cædmon, see O'Donnell, *Cædmon's Hymn*, 4–12, 25–28.
**308** Breatnach, "Caldron of Poesy," 68–69 §12.
**309** Colgrave, *Life of Saint Guthlac*, 142–43.
**310** Oroz Reta and Marcos Casquero, *Etimologías*, 12–15 (XI.1.6–16). But note the discussion of arguments from Virgilius Maro Grammaticus about whether humankind is dual or tripartite in nature: Law, *Wisdom, Authority and Grammar*, 60–66.
**311** Breatnach, "Caldron of Poesy," 47; Corthals, "'Caldron of Poesy'," 80.

of education such as: 1) elementary lessons, 2) a grammarian's teachings, and 3) a rhetorician's eloquence.[312] As Corthals stated, "the pursuit of *sapientia* or intellectual perfection, which . . . is the real subject of our text, runs as a common denominator throughout the whole of intellectual life in ancient Greek, Roman, and christian cultures."[313] The "Caldron of Poesy" can be interpreted as describing one's elevation from ignorance to "inspired" intelligence through education and training, specifically in this case, the Gaelic poets' striving after *imbas* (great knowledge). The concluding lines summarize succinctly the goals of an education in poetic knowledge: "berid co hecnae, echtraid fri borbu" (it brings one to wisdom (*sapientia*), it separates one from the ignorant) (cf. Figure 4.c).[314]

The "Caldron of Poesy," and its parallels and analogues from the Mediterranean world, make Aldhelm's "rejection of the Muses" seem artificial and overstated. As Emily Thornbury has noted, the *locus classicus* for this rejection comes from a later reworking of Aldhelm's *Carmen de uirginitate*.[315] Was Aldhelm simply showing off his knowledge of classical myth and geography, much as he had done in his letter to Wihtfrith? One logical conclusion to draw from Aldhelm's letter to Wihtfrith is that Gaeldom was brimming with knowledge of classical pagan mythology.[316] But our brief survey of narratives and poetry from the Early Gaelic period prove that indigenous traditions were abundantly preserved.

The "Caldron of Poesy" shows that the *filid*, as a privileged cohort ranked as *sóernemed*, were interested in training their members to the highest professional standards. Those same professional standards, derived from native traditions and practice, had to blend coherently with the teachings of the Church, as expounded most cogently in the "pseudo-historical prologue" to the *Senchas Már*.

## The Rôle of Vision and Divination

The stereotype of the poets' reliance on inspiration became institutionalized in the narrative tradition. The appearance of *teinm láeda* or *imbas for·osnai* in

---

312 Corthals, "'Caldron of Poesy'," 80–81.
313 Corthals, "'Caldron of Poesy'," 84. The metaphor of a caldron, or cup, was often expanded to include a womb, and the creative process could be described as a pregnancy, even in male poets: Mulligan, "Pregnant Poets."
314 This is my translation. It is translated slightly differently in the two editions: "it brings one to wisdom, it separates one from fools": Breatnach, "Caldron of Poesy," 73; "It brings (him) to (the grade of) a scholar, He departs from the unlearned": Henry, "Caldron of Poesy," 127.
315 Thornbury, "Aldhelm's Rejection," 89–90.
316 See evidence for knowledge of Classical myths and legends known to Gaels and to Bede: Holford-Strevens, *The Disputatio Chori*.

early narratives should not be taken as representing historical practice. Their presence in the literature more accurately reflects the aura of knowledge and accomplishment that surrounded the *filid* and which they themselves promoted to enhance their own prestige. For example, *teinm láeda* was associated with Fionn mac Cumhaill, but not with historical poets. The following discussion includes two examples of *imbas for·osnai* from prosimetric narratives, but in neither case is any ritual described that remotely resembles the depiction from *Sanas Cormaic*.

The description from Recension One of *Táin Bó Cúailnge* of the female poet Fedelm is the first example. It was discussed briefly in chapter one. The heroic setting is around the time of Christ. King Ailill and Queen Medb have mustered the armies of Ireland and are about to set out from Connacht on their campaign against Ulster. Medb is in her chariot at the head of the army when they encounter Fedelm who has just returned from Britain having learned *filidecht*. Note the detailed physical description of Fedelm. The reader is made to "see" Fedelm before she demonstrates her own prophetic power and recites her poem describing what she herself "foresees":

> In tan didiu dosoí in t-ara forsin carpat 7 lotair do thecht ass co n-accatár in n-ingin macdacht remib. Folt buidi furri. Bratt brecc impe, delg n-óir and. Léine c[h]ulpatach co nderggintŝlaid impe. Dá assa co foraib óir impu. Agad fochóel forlethan. Dí broí duba dorchaidi. Abrait duib dáin co mbentaís foscod i mmedón a dá grúaide. Indar latt ropo di partaing imdéntai a beóil. Indar lat ba fross do némannaib boí inna bélaib .i. a fíaclai. Teóra trillsi fuirri .i. dí thriliss immo cend súas, trilis tara haiss síar co mbenad a dá colptha inna díaid. Claideb corthaire do findruine inna láim, esnaid óir and. Trí meic imlisse cechtar a dá súla. Gaisced lasin n-íngin 7 dá ech duba foa carput.
> "Cía do chomainm-siu?" ol Medb frisin n-ingin.
> "Fedelm banfili do Chonnachtaib mo ainm-sea," or ind ingen.
> "Can dothéig?" or Medb.
> "A hAlbain iar foglaim filidechta," or ind ingen.
> "In fil imbass forosna lat?" or Medb.
> "Fil écin," or ind ingen.
> "Décai dámsa didiu co bbia mo fechtas."
> Dosnéce ind íngen íarum. Is and asbert Medb:
> "A Feidelm banfáith, co acci in slúag?"
> Frisgart Fedelm co n-epert:
> "Atchíu forderg, atchíu rúad."[317]

(Then when the charioteer turned the chariot and made to go forth they saw a grown maiden before them. She had yellow hair, and a vari-colored cloak about her with a gold brooch on it. She wore about her a hooded tunic with red embroidery. Her two shoes had gold clasps on them. Her face was narrow below and broad above with two black, austere eyebrows. Her fine black eyelashes cast shadows to the middle of her two cheeks. You

---

317 O'Rahilly, *Táin: Recension I*, 2, lines 29–50.

would have thought that her lips were adorned with Parthian red. You would have thought that her teeth were a shower of pearls in her mouth. She wore her hair in three plaits, two plaits up about her head, the third hung behind her so that its end struck her two calves. In her hand was a weaver's beam of white bronze inlaid with gold. There were three pupils in each of her two eyes. The maiden was armed and two black horses pulled her chariot.
"What is your name?" said Medb to the maiden.
"Fedelm poetess [*banfili*] of the Connachtmen is my name," said the maiden.
"Where have you come from?" said Medb.
"From Britain, having learned *filidecht*," said the maiden.
"Do you have *imbas for·osnai*?" asked Medb.
"I have, indeed," replied the maiden.
"Look for me then. How will my expedition turn out?"
The maiden looked into herself. Then Medb said:
"Oh Fedelm prophetess [*banfáith*], how do you see the army?"
Fedelm answered and said:
"I see it all bloody, I see it red.")[318]

The description of Fedelm is strongly visual with emphasis on color, shape, and shadow. Her formal study of *filidecht* in Britain has equipped her to control *imbas for·osnai*. Her divinatory response to Medb was repeated three times. Each time Medb protested and insisted that the Ulstermen were incapable of effective countermeasures against her amassed armies. Fedelm then recited a forty-six-line mantic poem foretelling the feats of the Ulster hero Cú Chulainn, as yet unknown to Queen Medb, King Aillil, and their armies. The poem begins:

> Atchíu fer find firfes cles
> co lín créchta fora chnes
>
> (I see a fair man who will fulfill great feats
> with many wounds on his flesh)

Note the poem's rich alliteration and end rhyme. It prophesies the confrontation of Medb's armies against Cú Chulainn and the destruction he will wreak, even before her armies encounter the aroused Ulstermen. The prophetic force of this poem is strengthened by the fact that Cú Chulainn is unknown outside of Ulster and has not yet been tested in combat. Fedelm must also "foresee" him drastically change his appearance in his battle distortions (*ríastrad*).[319]

---

[318] This is my translation, but should be compared with O'Rahilly, *Táin: Recension I*, 126. This example is discussed elsewhere in the context of Old English poetic formulae. See Ireland, "Visionary Poets," 129–30.

[319] eDIL: http://www.dil.ie, s.v. *ríastrad* or dil.ie/35242. The physical distortions of Cú Chulainn's battle rage encourage comparison with the Old Norse *berserkr*.

Another example of *imbas for·osnai* is now contained in *Tochmarc Emire* (The Wooing of Emer), a prosimetric tale of mixed date, from the early eighth to eleventh centuries.[320] Cú Chulainn wooed Emer and the two pledged their love to each other. But Emer's father tricked Cú Chulainn into traveling to Britain to train in advanced combat in the hopes that he would not return. Nevertheless, Cú Chulainn trained successfully with Scáthach, his female instructor, and increased his already prodigious skills. When Cú Chulainn had mastered the full array of elaborately named martial feats taught by Scáthach he prepared to depart for home. Scáthach used her *imbas for·osnai* to foretell Cú Chulainn's future:

> 7 asbert íarom Scáthach fris íar sin aní aridmbái dia forciund 7 ro cachain dó tria imbas forosnai. Conid and asbert na bríathra so dó.[321]
>
> (And then Scáthach told him that which was before him and sang to him through her *imbas for·osnai*, so that she said these words to him.)

The cryptic poem in the rhythmical, alliterative style she uttered is the *Verba Scáthaige*, from the *Cín Dromma Snechtai*, discussed earlier in this chapter.[322] It describes Cú Chulainn's future battles in graphic detail. *Verba Scáthaige* provides details that anticipate episodes from the later Recension One of the *Táin* such as the final combat between the rival bulls.[323]

Another divinatory ritual in the narrative literature is *tarbḟeis*. It was performed to determine the identity of a future king. As discussed previously in this chapter, several texts from *Cín Dromma Snechtai* have kingship at their core, such as the political prophecy *Baile Chuinn Chétchathaig* or the speculum principum *Audacht Morainn*.

The brief description of *tarbḟeis* overlaps with the entry in *Sanas Cormaic* for *imbas for·osnai*. It suggests that mantic or divinatory practices had been conflated in the imagination of the redactors. The following account comes from *Serglige Con Culainn* (The Sickbed of Cú Chulainn), another prosimetric narrative of mixed Old and Middle Gaelic sections.[324]

---

[320] van Hamel, *Compert Con Culainn*, 16–68. For translation, see Kinsella, *The Tain*, 25–39. See further Ó Corráin, *Clavis*, iii, 1480–82 §1113.

[321] van Hamel, *Compert Con Culainn*, 57 §78.

[322] Henry, "*Verba Scáthaige*."

[323] The final combat of the two bulls concludes the tale in Recension I: O'Rahilly, *Táin: Recension I*, 124, lines 4133–55 (Gaelic); 237 (English).

[324] Dillon, *Serglige Con Culainn*, xiii–xiv (dating). See further Ó Corráin, *Clavis*, iii, 1439–42 §1099.

> Dogníther íarom tarbḟes léo and sin co fíastais esti cía dia tibértais rígi.
>
> Is amlaid dogníthe in tarbḟes sin .i. tarb find do marbad 7 óenḟer do chathim a ṡátha día eóil 7 dá enbruthi, 7 chotlud dó fón sáith sin, 7 ór fírindi do chantain do chethri drúdib fair, 7 atchíthe dó i n-aislingi innas ind ḟir no rígḟaide and asa deilb 7 asa thúarascbáil 7 innas ind oprid dogníth. Díuchtrais in fer asa chotlud, 7 adfíadar a res dona rígaib.[325]
>
> (A *tarbḟeis* was performed by them there so that they could find out from it to whom they should give the kingship.
>
> This is how that *tarbḟeis* was done, that is, a white bull was killed and one individual consumed his fill of its meat and of its broth, and he slept having eaten his fill, and an incantation of truth was sung over him by four druids, and in a vision he would see as to form and description the kind of man who would be made king, and also the kind of works he would perform. The man awoke from his sleep and told his dream to the kings.)

The four druids and their "incantation of truth" (*ór fírindi*) serve to ensure the reliability of the vision. In a similar manner Cædmon had to describe his dream "in the presence of a number of the more learned men" (multis doctioribus uiris praesentibus) in order to ensure its acceptability to the Church (*HE* iv 24).

Another depiction of *tarbḟeis* comes from the narrative *Togail Bruidne Da Derga* (The Destruction of Da Derga's Hostel), which is likely a later version of *Togail Bruidne uí Derga* from the *Cín Dromma Snechtai*.[326] It highlights the duties and responsibilities of proper kingship.

> Marb in rí íarum .i. Eterscéle. Con-grenar tairbḟeis la firu Hérenn .i. no marbad tarb leó 7 no ithead oenfear a ṡáith de 7 no ibead a enbruithi 7 no chanta ór fírindi fair ina ligiu. Fer at-chichead ina chotlad is é bad rí, 7 at-baildis a beóil in tan ad-beiread gaí.[327]
>
> (Then the king, that is Eterscéle, died. A *tarbḟeis* was convened among the men of Ireland. A bull was killed by them and one individual ate his fill of it and drank its broth and an incantation of truth was sung over him where he lay. The man that he would see in his sleep is the one who would be king, and he [the diviner] would die if he told a lie.)

The two accounts of *tarbḟeis* agree in their essential details. Although no druids are mentioned in the second account, an "incantation of truth" was sung over the diviner. No enforcing authorities were described, but the penalty for the diviner of uttering a falsehood was death.

Prophecies concerning kings, predicting either their future or their demise, have confirmation from both Gaelic and Anglo-Saxon contemporary texts. *Baile*

---

[325] Dillon, *Serglige Con Culainn*, 8–9, lines 244–51.
[326] For a discussion of its transmission, see Ó Cathasaigh, "*Cín Dromma Snechta* Version."
[327] Knott, *Togail Bruidne Da Derga*, 4, §11, lines 122–26.

*Chuinn* is an early prophecy of future Uí Néill kings of Tara.³²⁸ Bertram Colgrave had noted that when St. Cuthbert foretold the kingship of Aldfrith *sapiens* for Abbess Ælfflæd in the anonymous *Vita Cuthberti* (c. 6), he was following others such as Bishop Aidan who prophesied the death of King Oswine (*HE* iii 14) and Bishop Cedd doing the same for King Sigeberht (*HE* iii 22).³²⁹ *Vita Columbae* has St. Columba foresee the violent deaths of two kings.³³⁰ He also foresaw the successful reigns of Echaid Buide mac Áedáin and Óengus mac Bronbachaill.³³¹ Of significance in the Anglo-Saxon world, Columba ordained Áedán mac Gabráin and prophesied his success and that of his descendants. For this episode, Adomnán would have relied on *De virtutibus sancti Columbae* by an earlier abbot, Cuimmíne Find (Albus; 657–669).³³² In this context, Cædmon's inspired *Hymn*, full of terms for lords and lordship, was not so much foretelling a new king, but rather a new dispensation.

The name *tarbḟeis* itself helps explain the ritual. The first element, *tarb*, means "bull." The second element, *feis*, can mean "spending the night, sleeping" or "feast, festival."³³³ Both meanings are manifest in the descriptions. The descriptive overlap of the two accounts of *tarbḟeis* suggests either that one is derived from the other, or that they reflect a vaguely remembered practice of the "secular prophets" (*fáidi dóendai*) who, through grace and learning, were able to "utter godly utterances and perform miracles, and their words are maxims and judgements" as described in the "Caldron of Poesy."³³⁴

Practices reminiscent of *tarbḟeis* are described in later insular accounts. For example, the thirteenth-century Welsh satiric tale *Breudwyt Ronabwy* (The Dream of Rhonabwy) has the main character sleep on the yellow skin of a heifer. He was granted a vivid dream of the days of King Arthur, described in detail, and only awoke after three days.³³⁵ Geoffrey Keating (Seathrún Céitinn) described, in the early seventeenth-century *Foras Feasa ar Éirinn*, a "History of Ireland" (ca. 1634), a form of conjuration used by druids of old. They would place the hide of a freshly sacrificed ox, flesh-side up, on rowan hurdles to get information from

---

328 Byrne, *Irish Kings*, 276–77 and notes. Murphy, "Dates of Two Sources," 145–51; Bhreathnach and Murray, "*Baile Chuinn Chétchathaig*."
329 Colgrave, *Lives of Saint Cuthbert*, 329n.
330 Anderson and Anderson, *Life of Columba*, 36–37, i 12.
331 Anderson and Anderson, *Life of Columba*, 32–33, i 9 (Echaid); 36–37, i 13 (Óengus).
332 Anderson and Anderson, *Life of Columba*, 188–91, iii 5; Sharpe, *Handlist*, 93 §209.
333 eDIL: http://www.dil.ie, s.v. *feis(s)*, *fess* or dil.ie/21506.
334 "conid íarum labrait inna labarthu raith 7 do-gniat inna firtu, condat fásaige 7 bretha a mbríathar": Breatnach, "Caldron of Poesy," 68–69 §12.
335 Richards, *Breudwyt Ronabwy*, 2–3. For translation, see Jones and Jones, *Mabinogion*, 138–39.

"demons," as conjurers did in Keating's own day.³³⁶ Accounts of the Hebrides published in the early eighteenth century describe a man being wrapped in a cow's hide and left overnight to conjure hidden information.³³⁷

Anglo-Saxon confirmation of such practices is found in the eighth-century *Vita Guthlaci*. The *librarius* Wigfrith had lived among the Gaels and had seen "false hermits and pretenders" who were able to "predict the future and to perform other miracles."³³⁸ This argument from *Vita Guthlaci* does not confirm that the Gaels practiced divinatory rituals as described above for *imbas for·osna* and *tarbfeis*, but it does show that segments of Anglo-Saxon society believed that they did. Bede's account of Cædmon must be seen in the context of prophetic and inspired utterances as described in texts of the Gaels and Britons and accepted by Anglo-Saxons.

## Poems from Dreams or Visions

Gaelic poets portrayed themselves as relying on both divine and human inspiration to produce poems. The following section illustrates examples of dreams or visions resulting in verse or heightened, stylized speech. What follows describes what Ingcél saw in Conaire Mór's chamber when he reconnoitered the assembly at the hostel in *Togail Bruidne Da Derga*. This excerpt is from the manuscript *Lebor na hUidre*. The "tender youth" (*móethóclach*) is Conaire Mór himself.

> Ro boí iarom in móethóclach ina chotlud ₇ a chossa i n-ucht indala fir ₇ a chend i n-ucht araile. Doríusaig iarom assa chotlud ₇ atraracht ₇ ro chachain in laid se.³³⁹
>
> (The tender youth was asleep with his feet in the lap of one man and his head in the lap of another. He awoke then out of his sleep and arose and sang this lay.)³⁴⁰

There follows cryptic verse which hints at the imminent attack and eventual destruction of the hostel and then the line:

---

**336** Keating, *History of Ireland*, ii, 350.
**337** Martin, *Western Isles of Scotland*, 111–12; O'Rahilly, *Early Irish History and Mythology*, 324 and notes.
**338** Colgrave, *Life of Saint Guthlac*, 142–43 c. 46.
**339** Best and Bergin, *Lebor na Huidre*, 227, lines 7429–31. See also Knott, *Togail Bruidne Da Derga*, 31, lines 1045–48.
**340** This position is very reminiscent of that of the Welsh ruler in the fourth branch of the *Mabinogi*, Math fab Mathonwy, who could not live without his feet being in the lap of a maiden, unless war prevented it: Williams, *Pedeir Keinc*, 67; for a translation, see Ford, *Mabinogi*, 91.

> Cotlais afridise ⁊ díuchtrais ass ⁊ canais in retoric se.[341]

> (He slept again and awoke from it and sang this *retoiric*.)

Another cryptic poem follows, but one which is more specific about the impending attack on the hostel and its disastrous results. Sleep, or a trance-like state, is often an integral prelude to the production of poetic and prophetic utterances. In the following example from Recension One of the *Táin* the editor chose to translate the verbal noun *cotlud* (act of sleeping, sleep) as "trance."

> Ba isin n-aidchi sin adchondairc Dubthach Dóel Ulad in aislingi a mbádar ind tslóig for Gáirich ⁊ Irgáirich. Is and asbert triana chotlud.[342]

> (That was the night when Dubthach Dóel Ulad saw a vision in which the army stood at Gáirech and Irgáirech, and in his trance he spoke.)[343]

There follows what is called the *aislinge* (vision) of Dubthach in which "a wonderful morning for a battle" is described. During that morning armies would be thrown into confusion, kings overthrown, men's necks broken, and sand red with blood, as the Ulstermen, led by Conchobar, would defeat the armies of Ireland. Dubthach's vision then concludes:

> Dofochtradar tria chotlud la sin.

> (Thereupon he awoke from his trance.)[344]

Neither Conaire Mór nor Dubthach are described as poets. But their utterances are in the heightened style typically reserved for such speeches. The earliest example of a Gaelic poet whose "inspired" sleep results in a poem is Colmán mac Lénéni (d. ca. 606), discussed in chapters one and two. Two lines of a fragment discussed in chapter two are worth repeating here:

---

**341** Best and Bergin, *Lebor na Huidre*, 228, lines 7438. In the edition by Knott the equivalent line reads *co clos ní a rithise* (something was heard again): Knott, *Togail Bruidne Da Derga*, 31, lines 1045–48.
**342** O'Rahilly, *Táin: Recension I*, 107, lines 3527–29.
**343** O'Rahilly, *Táin: Recension I*, 219.
**344** O'Rahilly, *Táin: Recension I*, 107, line 3536 (Gaelic); 220 (English). Different prepositions were used in the two accounts. In the *Togail* Conaire awakened *assa chotlud* (out of his sleep), whereas in the *Táin* Dubthach uttered his "vision" *triana chotlud* (through his sleep/trance). It is not possible to discern whether or not the use of the prepositions *a* (out of) or *tre* (through) are intended to convey a difference in the manner of production or the nature of their utterances.

Ní fordiuchtror for duain indlis
iar cotlud chaín bindris.³⁴⁵

(I do not awaken to an unworthy poem
after beautiful, harmonious sleep.)

These lines by a contemporary of St. Columba reveal a poet producing a poem through sleep. Calvert Watkins argued that the phrase *dúan indles* is a technical legal term that means a "poem not entitled to recompense."³⁴⁶ Therefore, the poem to which Colmán awakens is due compensation, an important outcome for a professional poet.³⁴⁷ The poet, trained to tap his inspiration, awakens with the poem in mind. The poem may be the cause of his awakening, much as one might awaken from a dream. But the poem is also the product of the poet's sleep and is worthy of reward.

Religious poems of the tenth or eleventh centuries express the desire to receive visions through sleep. The two examples below are anonymous. The first two stanzas of the first poem are:

Rop tú mo baile,
    a Choimdiu cride:
ní ní nech aile
    acht Rí secht nime.

Rop tú mo scrútain
    i lló 's i n-aidche;
rop tú ad-chëar
    im chotlud caidche.³⁴⁸

(May you be my vision
Oh Lord of my heart,
No one else is anything
except for the king of the seven heavens.

---

**345** MacCotter, *Colmán of Cloyne*, 130. This fragment has been discussed in the context of Cædmon: Ireland, "Precursor of Cædmon."
**346** Watkins, "Etymology of Irish *Dúan*," 275.
**347** *Fordiuchtror* is a *hapax legomenon*, but must derive from the verb *do·fiuch(t)ra* (awakes). It is first person singular, present indicative (deponent ending). This form is apparently made up of *do·fiuch(t)ra* (awakes) with the additional pre-verb *for·* from the preposition *for* (on, upon; over, above). In this *hapax* the prefix seems to have a similar semantic sense to the *for-* which, when compounded with *canaid* (sings, recites), yields *for·cain* (teaches, instructs; prophesies, predicts). The apparent doubling of the pre-verb *for-* by the following preposition *for* results in difficulties in translation, although the sense seems clear enough.
**348** Murphy, *Early Irish Lyrics*, 42.

> May you be my meditation
> by day and by night;
> may you be that which I see
> in my sleep forever.)

This poem survives as a hymn in a translation by Eleanor Knott called "Be Thou My Vision" found in modern hymnals. The first two stanzas of the second poem are:

> Tórramat do nóebaingil,
>     a Chríst meic Dé bí,
> ar cotlud, ar cumsanad,
>     ar lepaid co llí.
>
> Físsi fíra foillsiget
>     'nar cotaltaib dún
> a Ardflaith inna n-uile,
>     a Ruire na rún.[349]
>
> (Oh Christ, son of the living God,
> may your holy angels care for
> our sleep, our rest,
> our beds with brightness.
>
> May they reveal true visions
> to us in our sleep,
> Oh high Lord of all,
> Oh great king of the mysteries.)

Such lines as "may you be that which I see in my sleep forever," and "may they reveal true visions to us in our sleep" in Middle Gaelic poems of religious purpose reveal how the notions of poetry and dream visions were intertwined in Gaelic poetic culture. Cynewulf may provide the closest example in Old English poetic culture when, in a rhymed section of *Elene*, he expressed the anxiety of his nightly meditations.[350]

---

[349] Murphy, *Early Irish Lyrics*, 44, 46.
[350] Calder, *Cynewulf*, 134–35.

# Chapter Four
# The Church and the Spread of Bilingual Learning

By the eighth century the Gaels had created etiological legends to explain the cooperation between the Church and poetic orders which they described as beginning with St. Patrick. That cooperation resulted in a bilingual intellectual culture. Colmán mac Lénéni, poet and monastery founder, and contemporary of Pope Gregory the Great, is an early manifestation of that cooperation.

This chapter charts how the Gregorian mission to Canterbury and Iona's mission to Northumbria introduced Christianity with its Latinate learning to the Anglo-Saxons. Texts produced by Columbanus and his contemporaries delineate the depth of Bangor's learning by the late sixth and early seventh centuries. Cummian's Paschal letter (632) reveals a vast knowledge of computistics. His intellectual world is set against the historical context of peoples and events in both Britain and Ireland. The reception of works by Gregory the Great and Isidore reflect Gaelic openness to Continental influences. Works by *sapientes* outline the bilingual education available to Anglo-Saxon students who came to Ireland. Seventh-century Hiberno-Latin hagiography reveals its debt to late Antique sources while reflecting the indigenous cultural milieu that created it. The Anglo-Saxons used those Gaelic innovations as models as revealed in their own eighth-century hagiographies.

The Latinate learning that came with the conversion to Christianity began in Britain before the third century under the Roman Empire's influence.[1] Christianity spread throughout southern and central Britain and was firmly established in the indigenous Brittonic populations by the time the Anglo-Saxons began their expansion across Britain (*HE* i 7).[2] The greatest ecclesiastical writer among the Britons from this period is the sixth-century Gildas whose writings were popular among learned Anglo-Saxons and Gaels of the seventh and eighth centuries.[3] The conversion of the Gaels was well underway by the fifth century and the writings of Patrick mark the beginnings of recorded literate, Latinate

---

[1] For brief surveys of education and learning in Britain and Ireland, see Ryan, "Latin Learning and Christian Art," 178–84 (Education and Learning); Riché, *Education and Culture*, 307–36.
[2] Bede is aware of the Christian Britons and relates the story of St. Alban, the first British martyr: Colgrave and Mynors, *Ecclesiastical History*, 28–35.
[3] Charles-Edwards, *Wales and the Britons*, 202–19; Winterbottom, *Gildas*; Lapidge and Dumville, *Gildas*.

culture in Ireland.[4] Much of the early conversion of Ireland took place under the aegis of Christian Britons as can be traced in the vocabulary of the Gaelic Church.[5]

Both the Gaels and the Anglo-Saxons had to learn Latin as a second language in order to develop and evolve their bilingual intellectual cultures.[6] The surviving literatures in Latin and in both vernaculars demonstrate the high levels of linguistic ability attained.[7] The Gaels studied late antique grammarians such as Donatus and Priscian. The consciousness of parts of speech acquired through their study of Latin as second-language learners resulted in changes in how the written word was presented. The Gaels made the change from using *scriptio continua* and began to separate individual words when writing Latin and developed forms of punctuation suitable to their needs.[8] This approach to the written word was soon applied to the vernacular. The Anglo-Saxons learned these habits from their Gaelic teachers.[9] The use of Cambro-Latin and Hiberno-Latin texts at the school of Canterbury would have helped advance these developments.[10] The Anglo-Saxons almost certainly learned about writing their own vernacular, and adopted their choices of alphabet characters, from their Gaelic teachers at the schools in Ireland described by Bede (*HE* iii 27).[11] For example, the use of the digraph *th* among early

---

**4** For the gradual transformation during conversion, see Johnston, *When Worlds Collide?* For works on Patrick generally, see Howlett, *Book of Letters*; Dumville et al., *Saint Patrick*; O'Loughlin, *Discovering Saint Patrick*. For a survey of intellectual life, see Stevenson, "Beginnings of Literacy." For books known to the Gaels throughout the Old Gaelic period (to ca. 900), see Sharpe, "Books from Ireland."

**5** Charles-Edwards, *Wales and the Britons*, 181–87; Mc Manus, "Chronology of the Latin Loan-Words."

**6** For arguments that Latin was spoken well enough to be used as a *lingua franca*, see Harvey, "Juvencus Glosses." For examples of Old Gaelic being used in Latin computistical texts of the late seventh and early eighth centuries, see Bisagni and Warntjes, "Latin and Old Irish"; Bisagni and Warntjes, "Old Irish Material."

**7** Ó Corráin, *Clavis*, i, 23–25 §3. The levels of Latin fluency attained by Gaelic scholars are demonstrated by Bisagni, "Study of Code-Switching." Frequently included in this facility with Latin, was an understanding of Greek: Moran, "Language Interaction."

**8** Ó Corráin, *Clavis*, i, 35 §7; Parkes, *Scribes, Scripts and Readers*, 1–18 (The Contribution of Insular Scribes in the Seventh and Eighth Centuries to the "Grammar of Legibility"); Ó Cróinín, "First Century of Anglo-Irish Relations," 6–8.

**9** Parkes, *Scribes, Scripts and Readers*, 13–16; and see Parkes, *Pause and Effect*, 20–29 (Changing Attitudes to the Written Word: Components in a "Grammar of Legibility"); Howlett, "Insular Latin Poetry," 82–85; Stansbury, *Iona Scribes*.

**10** These reading and writing habits were encouraged, if not developed, at the school of Canterbury with Theodore and Hadrian: Howlett, "Insular Latin Poetry," 82–93.

**11** The transformations that the Gaels themselves were undergoing in the representation of their own language are sometimes reflected in choices made by the Anglo-Saxons: O'Neill, "Origins of the Old English Alphabet."

Northumbrians, rather than the "thorn" (þ) or "eth" (ð) more typical of their southern kinsmen, was likely derived from the practice of their Gaelic teachers.[12] Gaelic scribes working at Anglo-Saxon establishments, such as Ultán mentioned in Æthelwulf's *De abbatibus*, are given greater prominence in this early period than any Anglo-Saxon scribes, although the concentration is often on illuminated manuscripts.[13]

## The Gregorian Mission to Canterbury

The mission to the Anglo-Saxons sent by Pope Gregory the Great was established at Canterbury in 597. The veneration of Pope Gregory was firmly established by the eighth century among the Anglo-Saxons who credited Gregory with first bringing the faith to them.[14] Among the early personnel at Canterbury mentioned by Bede are Augustine, Mellitus, Laurentius, Justus, and Paulinus. However, the Anglo-Saxon tradition has little to say about the missionaries themselves. For example, no hagiography about the founding missionaries, such as Augustine, was produced during the Anglo-Saxon period although Paulinus plays a large part in the early eighth-century *Vita Gregorii*.[15] Patrizia Lendinara suggests that Augustine and his fellow missionaries are largely ignored by the Anglo-Saxons due, perhaps, to the veneration for Gregory.[16]

However, mention of Gregory among the Anglo-Saxons is not clearly marked until the late seventh century. Aldhelm is the first to refer to him and his works explicitly, and the calendar of Willibrord (Wilbrord) marks the second instance.[17] However, these two early cases must be seen against the Gaelic background in both Aldhlem's and Willibrord's ecclesiastical educations. The argument that the school of Theodore promoted the cult of St. Gregory[18] must be examined against the relative paucity of references to Gregory and his works in the Biblical commen-

---

12 Harvey, "Reading the Genetic Code," 162–63.
13 Campbell, *Æthelwulf*, 18–23, lines 206–69 §viii; Nees, "Ultán the scribe"; Brown, "Columba to Cormac." For more background, see Howlett, "*De abbatibus*."
14 Patrizia Lendinara states that the "early recognition gained by the pope in England is unparalleled in any other country in Europe": Lendinara, "Forgotten Missionaries," 381. See further Meyvaert, *Bede and Gregory*; Ortenberg, "Anglo-Saxon Church and the Papacy"; Thacker, "Memorializing Gregory."
15 Lendinara, "Forgotten Missionaries."
16 Lendinara, "Forgotten Missionaries."
17 Thacker, "Memorializing Gregory," 76 (Aldhelm), 78 (Willibrord).
18 Thacker, "Memorializing Gregory," 60, 75–77, 83.

taries preserved from the Canterbury school.[19] By the eighth century references to Gregory the Great are as plentiful in the *Collectio canonum Hibernensis* as in any Anglo-Saxon sources.[20]

An appreciation of Gregory and his works can be traced among Gaelic churchmen throughout the seventh century, starting in Gregory's own papacy. Gregory's emphasis on the monastic life, as opposed to the clerical life, met with approval from the Gaels. The Gaelic appreciation of Gregory can be traced beyond the Whitby *Vita Gregorii* as noted in discussions to follow.[21]

The rôle of Gregorian missionaries at Canterbury is outlined in Bede's *Historia ecclesiastica*. He noted the relative lack of success of the Canterbury missionaries when compared with those operating in Northumbria from Iona and Lindisfarne. Bede wrote the *Historia ecclesiastica* encouraged by Abbot Albinus who, along with the priest Nothhelm, assisted from Canterbury (*HE* preface). Information gathered at Canterbury came from written records (*monimentis litterarum*) or old traditions (*seniorum traditione*). Albinus passed along through Nothhelm to Bede "whatever seemed worth remembering" (de his quae memoria digna uidebantur). Bede received this information "either in writing or by word of mouth" from Nothhelm (siue litteris mandata siue ipsius Nothelmi uiua uoce referenda, transmisit). Bede noted that afterwards, implying once all written and oral local sources had been exhausted, Nothhelm retrieved additional information from Rome through permission of Pope Gregory II (715–731) and, on the advice of Albinus, brought selected information to Bede upon his return from Rome.

Although Bede stated that he gathered written records from Canterbury, there is no surviving evidence of a *schola* that produced writings or preserved records there until the arrival of Theodore and Hadrian ca. 670. Pope Vitalian's letter to King Oswiu (*HE* iii 29), which detailed the decision to send Theodore and Hadrian, included holy relics of Pope Gregory. Despite the credit given to Theodore and his school for promoting Gregory's cult, written evidence is disappointingly thin.[22] A perusal of modern studies on the Biblical commentaries or the "Laterculus Malalianus" produced at the Canterbury School reveals little evidence for direct reading of Pope Gregory's extensive writings.[23] The productivity of the Canterbury School is suggested by the fact that the earliest synods

---

**19** Bischoff and Lapidge, *Biblical Commentaries*.
**20** For edition and translation, see Flechner, *Hibernensis*. For a discussion of citations, see Davies, "'Mouth of Gold'."
**21** See, for example, Herbert, "Gregory the Great."
**22** Thacker, "Memorializing Gregory."
**23** Bischoff and Lapidge, *Biblical Commentaries*; Stevenson, "*Laterculus Malalianus*."

and councils among the Anglo-Saxons, with the exception of the "synod" of Whitby, were not enacted until after the arrival of Theodore and Hadrian.[24]

## Iona, its Mission, and its Learning

The first missionary saint of the Gaels had a far-reaching influence on Britain. Iona was established by Columba ca. 562 and within a few generations exerted profound influence in Northumbria in the middle of the seventh century.[25] Columba evangelized the northern Picts in the sixth century and can be compared to Ninian (Nynias) earlier among the southern Picts (*HE* iii 4). Ninian operated from Whithorn (*Candida Casa*), built of stone, which for Bede implied the influence of Rome and the continent.[26] Bede stated that Ninian had been trained in Rome and was orthodox in practice (*HE* iii 4). This area along the north Solway Firth may have constituted the Brittonic region of Rheged. It is possible, as suggested by Molly Miller, that Rheged was already orthodox when it entered Northumbria's sphere of influence in the seventh century.[27]

The traditional *obit* for Columba (597) makes his death coincide with the Gregorian mission to Canterbury. But his death date is, in fact, more likely four years previous ca. 593.[28] The explanation for the later date is hagiographical necessity. Adomnán wanted Columba to have died on a Sunday. The *Vita Columbae* has a chapter that elaborately extends his death by four extra years.[29] One of the witnesses to Columba's distress at learning that he must remain in this world is an Anglo-Saxon in the Iona community named Pilu.[30] Gaelic annalistic records point to a date earlier than 597, the date in Adomnán's hagiography. Bede

---

**24** Cubitt, *Anglo-Saxon Church Councils*, 19 (Table 1.1 Northumbrian Synods), 22–23 (Table 1.2 Canterbury Provincial Synods).
**25** Mc Carthy, http://www.irish-annals.cs.tcd.ie/, s.a. 562; Mac Air and Mac Niocaill, *Annals of Ulster*, 82–83 s.a. 563. Bede gives the date as 565 (*HE* iii 4, v 24): Colgrave and Mynors, *Ecclesiastical History*, 220–21, 562–63.
**26** Hawkes, "*Iuxta morem Romanorum*."
**27** Molly Miller had suggested, based on the equation of Rhun mab Urien with Paulinus in *Historia Brittonum* and on Bede's statement that Ninian had trained in Rome and was orthodox in practice, that Rhun and Rhiainfellt, a wife of King Oswiu, may have been orthodox: Miller, "Dates of Deira," 47n3.
**28** Mc Carthy, "Chronology of St Columba's Life."
**29** Anderson and Anderson, *Life of Columba*, 214–35, iii 22–23.
**30** Anderson and Anderson, *Life of Columba*, 214–15, iii 22.

never stated that Columba died in 597, but other dates and time spans he did cite add up to that date and suggest his familiarity with *Vita Columbae* (*HE* iii 4).[31]

Iona participated in the achievements in Latinate and vernacular learning among the Gaels of Ireland. The oldest Gaelic manuscript, the Cathach (Dublin, Royal Irish Academy, MS 12 R 33), a Gallican version of the Psalms in Jerome's Vulgate, dates from the end of the sixth century.[32] By tradition Columba copied it and, given the stories of him as scribe, tradition may be accurate.[33] Iona's influence extended beyond Northumbria as seen in the *Altus Prosator* known to Aldhelm in Malmesbury.[34] Bécán mac Luigdech's poems eulogizing Columba, discussed in chapter two, are from the period that produced *Altus Prosator*.

The majority of texts associated with Iona were penned by its seventh abbot, Adomnán.[35] They include prose and verse texts in both Latin and the vernacular. *De locis sanctis* was the best known of Adomnán's works among the Anglo-Saxons (*HE* v 15).[36] King Aldfrith *sapiens* helped disseminate it in Northumbria. Bede created an epitome of it and based two chapters in *Historia ecclesiastica* on it (*HE* v 16–17).[37] The vernacular law-tract *Cáin Adomnán*, known as *Lex innocentium* in Latin, was promulgated in 697 at Birr, Co. Offaly.[38] It was intended to protect noncombatants, women, children, and clergy from the violence of warfare.[39] The law is important for its innovative contents and the diplomatic initiative required to promulgate it, with ecclesiastical and secular authorities in Ireland and northern Britain, both Gaelic and Pictish, who endorsed it.[40] The poem *Adiutor laborantium*, with characteristics of a *lorica*, lists epithets for God reminiscent of Cædmon's short *Hymn*.[41] *Adiutor laborantium* survives in an Anglo-Saxon prayer book.[42]

---

[31] Bede had Columba found Iona in 565 and die 32 years later, i.e., 597: Mc Carthy, "Chronology of St Columba's Life," 4–6.
[32] Ó Corráin, *Clavis*, i, 45–46 §12; https://www.ria.ie/cathach-psalter-st-columba.
[33] Herity and Breen, *Cathach*, 1–7 (legend and background); O'Neill, *Irish Hand*, 12–13.
[34] Stevenson, "Altus Prosator"; Orchard, *Poetic Art of Aldhelm*, 54–60.
[35] Sharpe, *Handlist*, 25 §49; for a historical overview, see Lacey, *Adomnán*, 7–119.
[36] Ó Corráin, *Clavis*, ii, 727–30 §568; Meehan, *De Locis Sanctis*. See further O'Loughlin, "Adomnán's *De locis sanctis*"; O'Loughlin, "*De locis sanctis* as a Liturgical Text"; Aist, "Adomnán, Arculf"; Hoyland and Waidler, "Adomnán's *De Locis Sanctis*."
[37] For a translation of Bede's epitome, see Foley and Holder, *Biblical Miscellany*, 1–25.
[38] Ó Corráin, *Clavis*, ii, 802–3 §622.
[39] Meyer, *Cáin Adamnáin*; and articles in O'Loughlin, *Adomnán at Birr*. For the law's innovative approach to *jus in bello* before the modern era, see Fraser, "Adomnán and the Morality of War," 96; Houlihan, *Adomnán's Lex Innocentium*, 47–48, 188–90.
[40] Ní Dhonnchadha, "Guarantor List."
[41] Clancy and Márkus, *Iona*; Márkus, "*Adiutor laborantium*."
[42] Lapidge and Sharpe, *Bibliography of Celtic-Latin Literature*, 344 §1302; Gneuss, *Handlist*, 64 §333; Gneuss and Lapidge, *Anglo-Saxon Manuscripts*, 256 §333.

Vernacular poems attributed to Adomnán, *Colum Cille co Día domm eráil*[43] and *A maccucáin, sruith in tíag*,[44] were discussed in chapter two.

Bede appreciated Adomnán's learning and implicitly compared him to others he respected. In his epitome of *De locis sanctis* Bede described Admonán as "most learned in the scriptures" (eruditissimus in scripturis) and used a similar phrase (*doctissimus in scripturis*) to describe both King Aldfrith *sapiens* (*HE* v 15) and Ecgberht of Rath Melsigi (*HE* iii 4).

## The Learning of Bangor at Home and Abroad

A few years before Gregory initiated the mission to Canterbury, a Gaelic *peregrinus* to the continent, Columbanus, began his own successful *peregrinatio* in 590. Columbanus was from Leinster where he began his boyhood training. He studied with Sinilis (Sinlán/Sillán; Mo-Sinu maccu Min), probably on Lough Erne in Co. Fermanagh, before attending the monastery at Bangor on Belfast Lough in Dál Fiatach territory.[45] He spent many years at Bangor, founded ca. 557 by Abbot Comgall of the Dál nAraidi,[46] before he left for the Continent. There he established foundations at Annegray, Luxeuil, and Fontaine in Burgundy, and lastly at Bobbio in northern Italy with the patronage of the Lombard king Agilulf.[47]

Bangor gained a reputation for its learning. The *Hisperica Famina* likely originated at Bangor.[48] Michael Herren argued that it was compiled in the period 651–664, highlighted by Bede for Anglo-Saxons studying among the Gaels (*HE* iii 27).[49] The Antiphonary of Bangor (680–691), a collection of hymns and

---

43 Clancy and Márkus, *Iona*.
44 Carney, "*A maccucáin*."
45 Bullough, "Career of Columbanus," 4; Charles-Edwards, *Early Christian Ireland*, 178–80; Breen, "Columbanus' Monastic Life"; Woolf, "Columbanus's Ulster Education."
46 Mac Airt and Mac Niocaill, *Annals of Ulster*, 78–79 s.a. 555, 80–81 s.a. 559; Mc Carthy, www.irish-annals.cs.tcd.ie, s.a. 557.
47 Bullough, "Career of Columbanus"; Richter, *Bobbio*, 26–27. For an understanding of Columbanus's *modus operandi* and strategies in selecting sites, see O'Hara, "Columbanus ad Locum."
48 Herren, *Hisperica Famina: I*; Ó Corráin, *Clavis*, ii, 733–36 §570; Lapidge and Sharpe, *Bibliography of Celtic-Latin*, 93–96 §§325–30. For likely origins in Bangor, Co. Down, see Stevenson, "Bangor and the *Hisperica Famina*."
49 Herren, *Hisperica Famina: I*, 32–39; Ireland, "Study Abroad Destination," 68–71.

poems, is also a product of this monastery.[50] Abbot Comgall took a great interest in Faustus of Riez, whose influence appears in works produced by Columbanus.[51] Among the earliest texts to be associated with Bangor are a "computus" attributed to Mo-Sinu (maccu Min), the hypocoristic name for Sillán (maccu Min), Columbanus's teacher at Lough Erne.[52] Mo-Sinu's pupil Mo-Chuaróc maccu Sémuine put the "computus" into verse sometime in the late sixth century.[53] That text is now known as *Nonae Aprilis*.[54]

Columbanus's training received at Bangor is revealed in his writings, some produced while still a young man in Ireland, but most after 590 on the continent.[55] Two rhythmical poems, or hymns, may have been written before he came to Bangor. The hymn, *Precamur patrem* (we pray to the Father), preserved in the Antiphonary, is accepted as a late sixth-century poem by Columbanus.[56] It is full of striking images, rich in rhyme, rhythm, and alliteration.[57] Another poem, or hymn, appropriate to the life of a *peregrinus*, about the transitory nature of the world, begins *Mundus iste transibit* (this world shall pass).[58]

Columbanus produced monastic rules for his followers on the continent, one for the individual monk, *Regula monachorum*, and another to aid in the conduct of the communal life, *Regula coenobialis*.[59] Jane Stevenson observed that "Columbanus's *regulae* are, in effect, the earliest evidence for monastic practice in the Irish church."[60] Growing evidence suggests that Columbanus's

---

50 Warren, *Antiphonary of Bangor*; Curran, *Antiphonary of Bangor*; Ó Corráin, *Clavis*, i, 386 §281, 455–58 §341.
51 Charles-Edwards, *Wales and the Britons*, 199–202; Stancliffe, "Thirteen Sermons," 197; Ó Corráin, *Clavis* i, 419–22 §329.
52 Lapidge and Sharpe, *Bibliography of Celtic-Latin*, 77–78 §288; Ó Cróinín, "Mo-Sinnu moccu Min." For an edition and translation of this text, see Howlett, "Music and the Stars," 113–15.
53 Ó Cróinín, "Mo-Sinnu moccu Min," 285–89.
54 For an edition of this text, see Howlett, "Music and the Stars," 115–19.
55 For editions of texts, see Walker, *Sancti Columbani*. For studies of his works, see Lapidge, *Columbanus*.
56 Lapidge, "Columbanus and the 'Antiphonary'"; Lapidge, "'*Precamur patrem*'."
57 For an edition with translation and discussion, see Howlett, "Earliest Irish Writers," 1–10; Howlett, *Celtic Latin Tradition*, 169–77.
58 Walker, *Sancti Columbani Opera*, lv–lvi, 182–85; Schaller, "Siebensilberstrophen 'de mundi transitu' "; Schaller, "'*De mundi transitu*'." For an edition with translation and discussion, see Howlett, *Celtic Latin Tradition*, 156–69.
59 Walker, *Sancti Columbani Opera*, 122–43 (*Regula monachorum*), 142–69 (*Regula coenabialis*); Ó Corráin, *Clavis*, i, 422–28 §330 (*Regula monachorum*), §331 (*Regula coenabialis*); Stevenson, "Monastic Rules of Columbanus."
60 Stevenson, "Monastic Rules of Columbanus," 207.

works helped formulate the Benedictine Rule.[61] Columbanus was concerned that his monks have the correct mental attitude to control their words and deeds.[62] The concern for proper attitudes and personal control is also seen in his penitential.[63] It described spiritual advisors as "doctors of souls" and the penance they prescribed was medicine to heal the soul's wounds. This medical metaphor appears in the anonymous *Vita Gregorii* from Whitby a century later.[64] Columbanus used the metaphor of being wounded by Christ's love, and stated that Christ was the physician who healed the wounds of the soul.[65] The emphasis on divine "medicine" in treating spiritual "wounds" helps explain the prevalence of *loricae* and other prophylactic compositions.[66]

A corpus of thirteen sermons (*instructiones*) is accepted as being by Columbanus. They were written to benefit his monks at Bobbio and, therefore, come from the end of his career. They are rich in references to Church fathers, and others, and reveal the breadth of his training and education.[67] Five of Columbanus's letters survive.[68] He wrote his earliest surviving letter to Pope Gregory.[69] Columbanus's letter, "written probably in 600, is an appeal to Pope Gregory the Great (ob. 604) to resolve Columbanus's dispute with the Gallic clergy, primarily over the notorious issue of Easter celebration."[70] Although Columbanus challenged the pope, as bishop of Rome, regarding differences over Easter, he addressed Gregory as "the fairest Ornament of the Roman Church," complimented him on his *Regula Pastoralis* and requested a copy of his recent "Homilies on Ezekiel."[71] At the time of this first letter Columbanus was still in Gaul and had not yet left for Italy.

---

61 See Ó Cróinín, "Benedict and Columbanus"; Dunn, "Columbanus, Charisma."
62 Stevenson, "Monastic Rules of Columbanus," 206.
63 Walker, *Sancti Columbani Opera*, 168–81; Bieler, *Irish Penitentials*, 96–107; Ó Corráin, *Clavis*, i, 428–30 §332; Charles-Edwards, "Penitential of Columbanus."
64 Walker, *Sancti Columbani Opera*, 172–73; Bieler, *Irish Penitentials*, 98–99; Ireland, "Whitby *Life* of Gregory," 165–67.
65 Walker, *Sancti Columbani Opera*, 120–21 (Instructio xiii).
66 Davies, "Place of Healing," 50–52.
67 Walker, *Sancti Columbani Opera*, 60–121; Ó Corráin, *Clavis*, i, 419–22 §328; Stancliffe, "Thirteen Sermons."
68 Walker, *Sancti Columbani Opera*, 2–57; Ó Corráin, *Clavis*, i, 416–19 §328; Lapidge and Sharpe, *Bibliography of Celtic-Latin*, 165–68 §§639–42; Wright, "Columbanus's *Epistulae*."
69 Walker, *Sancti Columbani Opera*, 2–13; Howlett, *Celtic Latin Tradition*, 82–91. See the remarks of a skeptical reviewer about the quality of Columbanus's prose: Grocock, "Review," 384.
70 Wright, "Columbanus's *Epistulae*," 29.
71 Walker, *Sancti Columbani Opera*, 10–11; Ireland, "Whitby *Life* of Gregory," 146.

> **Columbanus (d. 615)**
> In a letter to Pope Gregory, he praised *Regula pastoralis* and requested a copy of "Homilies on Ezekiel" (ca. 603).
>
> **Cummian (d. 662[?])**
> In his letter *De controversia Paschali* (632) Cummian referred to Pope Gregory as "Golden Mouth" and stated that Gregory "is deservedly to be preferred to all" Church fathers.
>
> **Laidcenn *sapiens* mac Baíth Bannaig (d. 661)**
> He wrote an epitome of Pope Gregory's *Moralia in Iob* called *Egloga de moralibus in Iob*. His Life of St. Mo-Lua displays great interest in Gregory.
>
> **Ailerán *sapiens* (d. 665)**
> He used Gregory as a source in his *Interpretatio mystica progenitorum Domini Iesu Christi*.
>
> **Anonymous *Liber de ordine creaturarum* (pre-680)**
> Gregory was used as a source in this anonymous text known to Bede.
>
> **Adomnán, abbot of Iona (d. 704)**
> Both *Vita sancti Columbae* (688–704) and *De locis sanctis* (pre-687) used Gregory's *Dialogues* as a source. *De locis sanctis* was made known throughout Northumbria by Aldfrith *sapiens*.
>
> **Cambrai Homily (ca. 700)**
> This macaronic homily of mixed Old Gaelic and Latin text cited Gregory's *Homilia in Evangelia*.

**Figure 4.a:** Pope Gregory the Great in the Works of Seventh-Century Gaels.

His second and third letters also address the vexing Easter issue. In his fifth letter, to Pope Boniface IV (608–615), Columbanus described the Gaels as disciples of saints Peter and Paul and expressed his concerns about Arianism among the Lombards who opposed Rome's authority which, in this case, he supported.[72] While differing with the pope on Easter observance, Columbanus portrayed himself and the Gaels as following universal practice, claiming a unity in diversity in the face of larger threats to Rome.[73] Columbanus died in 615 at Bobbio.

The land of the Lombards was described in *Táin Bó Fraích* (ca. 700) as "a grim, terrible country, with fierce warriors."[74] This vernacular tale is based on traditional Gaelic *topoi*, but a major episode transpires on the Continent among the Lombards, as discussed in chapter three. Near the tale's end etymological

---

[72] Walker, *Sancti Columbani Opera*, 38–39 (Epistola v); Bracken, "Authority and Duty."
[73] Bracken, "Rome and the Isles," 78–80, 85, 95.
[74] Meid, *Táin Bó Fraích*, 14, lines 345–46; Meid, *Romance of Froech*, 49, line 321; 73 (translation).

wordplay associates the tale's action with Bangor (*Bennchor*).⁷⁵ These plot details reflect the Bangor monks' knowledge of the Lombards through Columbanus's foundation at Bobbio.

## Computus and Cummian's World post-632

In 632 a certain Cummian (*Cummianus*) sent a letter on the Easter controversy to Abbot Ségéne of Iona and Beccán *solitarius*, probably of Rùm in the Hebrides, "along with their sages" (cum suis sapientibus).⁷⁶ Cummian wrote to persuade Iona and its sympathizers, including many Picts and Britons, to eschew the *latercus*, with its 84-year Paschal cycle, and accept orthodox practices as observed in Rome. Although Cummian was arguing for unity of observance, Rome itself had not yet firmly established just what universal practice was to mean.⁷⁷

Cummian cited a decision reached at Mag Léne (ca. 630) in support of "orthodox" practice. He named five ecclesiastical establishments that were represented. Since they were identified only by their founders' names there is uncertainty as to which five were intended. The five founders and their likely churches are: 1) Ailbe of Emly (*Imblech Ibair*), 2) Ciarán of Clonmacnoise (*Cluain maccu Nóis*), 3) Brénann of Clonfert (*Cluain Ferta Brénainn*) or Brénann of Birr (*Birra*), 4) Nessan of Mungret (*Mungairit*), 5) Lugaid of Clonfertmulloe (*Cluain Ferta Mo-Lua*).⁷⁸ All of the foundations listed are either in the Irish midlands or further south. This list has encouraged modern scholars to think of Bede's orthodox "southern provinces" of Ireland in an artificial geographical sense, as if a line were drawn east to west from Dublin to Galway.⁷⁹

Cummian's letter showed a consciousness of the wider Christian world when he noted that in previous years delegates who supported the *latercus* had gone to Rome at Easter and found that their celebrations differed by a month compared with a Greek, a Hebrew, a Scythian, and an Egyptian with whom they shared lodgings.⁸⁰ He also noted that people in Gaul, Britain, Africa, Persia, the East,

---

75 The episode is discussed in Ireland, "Whitby *Life* of Gregory," 152–53.
76 Walsh and Ó Cróinín, *Cummian's Letter*, 56–57, line 4. See also Ó Corráin, *Clavis*, ii, 696–97 §544; Lapidge and Sharpe, *Bibliography of Celtic-Latin*, 78 §289; Sharpe, *Handlist*, 93 §208.
77 This Cummian may be the same person as Cuimmíne Fota *sapiens* discussed below.
78 Walsh and Ó Cróinín, *Cummian's Letter*, 90–91 and notes.
79 See Archibald Duncan's comments on Bede's tendency to create artificial north/south divisions: Duncan, "Bede, Iona, and the Picts," 31–32.
80 Walsh and Ó Cróinín, *Cummian's Letter*, 94–95, lines 281–83.

and India all adored the one Christ.[81] Note that when he wrote (632), there were no compelling reasons for Cummian to mention an incipient Anglo-Saxon conversion in southeast Britain, and an inchoate mission in Northumbria under Paulinus. Cummian asked rhetorically, why should certain Britons and Gaels, who are almost at the end of the earth, separate themselves from universal practice?[82] Cummian applied an exegetical argument against particularism with a long history in the Church.[83] He defended a universal and, hence, orthodox approach that was to be repeated by Bede a century later.[84]

Cummian operated in a world widely exposed to the science of computus. His letter to Ségéne and Beccán is full of scriptural citations with reference to the timing of Christ's passion, resurrection, and ascension. He reported that over a year he had thoroughly examined the Scriptures and ten different computistical cycles. The first cycle he mentioned was the one that "holy Patrick, our bishop, brought and made."[85] Already by 630 we note the primacy assigned to St. Patrick and his association with orthodox practice, implying the rising importance of Armagh.[86] The second cycle listed was that of Anatolius who, Cummian observed, said that a "cycle of eighty-four years can never arrive" at the correct reckoning of Easter.[87] Cummian referred to the *latercus* and denigrated it. Other named cycles included Theophilus, Dionysius, Cyril, Morinus, Augustine, Victorius, Pacomius, and, finally, the nineteen-year cycle of the three hundred and eighteen bishops from the council of Nicaea.[88] This latter cycle was the one cited by Stephen of Ripon in *Vita Wilfridi* (*VW* c. 10).[89] The cycles of Dionysius Exiguus and Victorius of Aquitaine, both cited in Cummian's list, were the two most frequently used throughout the seventh century, in both the insular world and on the Continent. The Dionysiac practices eventually dominated by the eighth century as the orthodox observance promoted by Rome in the western Church (Figure 6.a).[90]

---

81 Walsh and Ó Cróinín, *Cummian's Letter*, 76–77, lines 138–40.
82 Walsh and Ó Cróinín, *Cummian's Letter*, 72–75.
83 Bracken, "Rome and the Isles," 80–81, 87–88, 90–94.
84 Bede's use of this argument is usually put in the mouth of Wilfrid at the "synod" of Whitby: Bracken, "Rome and the Isles," 80–81, 88, 90, 92, 94.
85 "sanctus Patricius papa noster tulit et fecit": Walsh and Ó Cróinín, *Cummian's Letter*, 84; Sharpe, *Handlist*, 413 §1154. For a full discussion, see Mc Carthy, "Paschal Cycle of St Patrick."
86 Swift, "Patrick's Conversion of Ireland."
87 Walsh and Ó Cróinín, *Cummian's Letter*, 84–85; see Mc Carthy and Breen, *Ante-Nicene Christian Pasch*.
88 Walsh and Ó Cróinín, *Cummian's Letter*, 86–87.
89 Colgrave, *Life of Bishop Wilfrid*, 20–21; Sharpe, *Handlist*, 633 §1672.
90 For the earliest firmly dated insular example of the Dionysiac chronological tradition identified so far, see Ireland, "Lutting of Lindisfarne."

We see in Cummian's letter characteristics of Gaelic exegesis such as its emphasis on the "three sacred languages" (tres linguae sacrae): Hebrew, Greek, and Latin.[91] The emphasis on three sacred languages is found in the seventh-century *De origine Scoticae linguae*, now known as O'Mulconry's Glossary.[92] Cummian's arguments reveal a deep reading of Holy Scripture. The sophistication of his challenge to particularism and support of universality reflects a familiarity with the writings of Church fathers over previous controversies.[93] Features common to seventh-century Gaelic exegesis are discussed by Dáibhí Ó Cróinín in a commentary on Genesis.[94]

Cummian's letter contains the first instance of Pope Gregory being referred to as "golden mouth."[95] That epithet applied to Gregory appears roughly eighty years later in *Vita Gregorii* by an anonymous Whitby hagiographer.[96] Cummian praised Gregory declaring that he was "accepted by all of us."[97] He elaborated stating that "although he [Gregory] wrote after everyone, nevertheless he is deservedly to be preferred to all."[98] Cummian recognized Gregory as coming at the end of a long line of Church fathers but who, nevertheless, deserved special esteem. The conclusion of Cummian's letter draws directly from Gregory's *Moralia in Iob* without acknowledgement.[99] Cummian's respectful tone shows that Gregory's prestige among the Gaels had continued to grow since Columbanus had written to him. Although Gregory and Columbanus disagreed openly over Paschal matters, nevertheless Columbanus had read and appreciated Gregory's works and had requested copies. Respect for Gregory among Gaelic scholars will be evident in the following discussions.

Cummian's letter should be seen against external insular events. It was written after Bishop Paulinus of the Gregorian mission converted King Edwin of

---

[91] Walsh and Ó Cróinín, *Cummian's Letter*, 56–57; Bischoff, "Turning-Points," 85–86; Howlett, "'Tres Linguae Sacrae'."
[92] The oldest stratum is seventh century, later additions were made in the ninth and tenth centuries: Moran, *De origine Scoticae linguae*, 76–77. For the emphasis on Greek and Hebrew, see Moran, "Pronunciation of Greek"; Moran, "Hebrew in Early Irish Glossaries."
[93] Bracken, "Rome and the Isles."
[94] Ó Cróinín, "Commentary on Genesis." See further Ó Néill, *Biblical Study*; Stansbury, "Irish Biblical Exegesis."
[95] "et oris aurei appellatione donati": Walsh and Ó Cróinín, *Cummian's Letter*, 82–83, line 191.
[96] "ut a gente Romana . . . os aureum appellatur": Colgrave, *Life of Gregory*, 116–19 and 155n99; Ireland, "Whitby *Life* of Gregory," 143–47.
[97] "a nobis in commune suscepti": Walsh and Ó Cróinín, *Cummian's Letter*, 82–83, lines 190–91.
[98] "Qui etsi post omnes scripsit, tamen est merito omnibus preferendus": Walsh and Ó Cróinín, *Cummian's Letter*, 82–83, lines 191–92.
[99] Stancliffe, "Creator and Creation," 14–15.

Northumbria ca. 627 (*HE* ii 14). Edwin proved a reluctant subject for conversion in Bede's account (*HE* ii 9, 12–13), in contrast to the rapid conversion described in *Vita Gregorii*.[100] The remainder of Edwin's reign marked six years when Northumbria claimed to be Christian based on orthodox teachings from Canterbury. Those six years were followed by thirty active, successful years of the Iona mission.

Both Edwin's conversion and Cummian's letter fall within the early years of Ségéne's long abbacy of Iona (623–652). The accession to the Northumbrian throne by Oswald (634), shortly after Edwin's death (633), marked a growth in influence for Ségéne and Iona. Paulinus (d. 644) abandoned Northumbria after Edwin's death and retired to Rochester (*HE* ii 20), leaving Northumbria to be controlled by bishops from Iona working out of Lindisfarne.

King Oswald (634–642) invited missionaries from Iona into his kingdom. Bishop Aidan (634–651) founded Lindisfarne in 635. Oswald and his half-brother Oswiu (642–670) had been baptized and educated among the Gaels of Dál Ríata. Oswald sometimes acted as Aidan's interpreter (*HE* iii 3). Since Aidan's bishopric falls within the abbacy of Ségéne we can assume a regular intercourse between the two and their institutions.

Oswald worked closely with Iona and its personnel. Nevertheless, as soon as he was king he visited King Cynegisl of Wessex and the newly arrived Bishop Birinus (634–ca. 650) sent by Pope Honorius. Birinus baptized Cynegisl with Oswald serving as the latter's sponsor, and the two kings established Dorchester as the episcopal see for Birinus (*HE* iii 7). As soon as his reign began we see Oswald diligently promoting Christianity, in both Northumbria and Southumbria, and cooperating closely with bishops from different Paschal traditions.

Sometime in the 630s and into the 640s Fursa, famous for his vision (*HE* iii 19), and his named companions enjoyed the patronage of Sigeberht (*HE* iii 19) and Anna (*HE* iii 7), kings of the East Angles. This was during the bishopric of Felix (ca. 631–ca. 648; *HE* ii 15) who cooperated with Bishop Aidan of Lindisfarne (*HE* iii 25). Fursa and his companions eventually made an impact on the Continent which continued to have repercussions back in Britain among the East Angles.

Cummian's letter also falls within the reign of Domnall mac Áedo meic Ainmirig of Cenél Conaill (628–642), the first king to be described as "king of Ireland" (rex Hiberniae) in Gaelic annals.[101] The title implies he was Ireland's first officially recognized high-king, a contested title as noted below, but it also

---

100 Colgrave, *Life of Gregory*, 98–101, c. 16.
101 Mac Airt and Mac Niocaill, *Annals of Ulster*, 122–23 s.a. 642; Stokes, "Annals of Tigernach," 186 [Felinfach i 146]; Byrne, *Irish Kings*, 112–14, 256–58; Charles-Edwards, *Early Christian Ireland*, 484–85, 494, 503–4; Mac Shamhráin and Byrne, "Kings Named," 197–98.

suggests a growing sense of *natio* among the Gaels.[102] Domnall's reign overlapped that period of Edwin's rule (627–633) when Northumbria claimed conversion by Paulinus of the Gregorian mission, and it overlapped the reign of Oswald (634–642), who introduced missionaries from Iona into Northumbria.

A major battle occurred during Domnall's reign, over which serious political issues were fought, and around which three Middle Gaelic legends evolved.[103] The historical Battle of Mag Roth (Moira, Co. Down; 639) involved Cenél Conaill, Cenél nÉogain, Dál nAraidi, and Dál Riata, septs of northern Ireland and northwest Britain.[104] The first two named represent the northern Uí Néill. One purpose for the battle was to control access to the high-kingship.

One Middle Gaelic legend that evolved around the battle involves the historical Cenn Fáelad *sapiens*, as noted in chapters two and three, and the syncretism of major branches of learning: *légend*, *fénechas*, and *filidecht*. According to the legend, after the battle Cenn Fáelad lost his "brain of forgetting" (inchinn dermait), remembered everything he heard, and preserved it all in poetry.[105] The historical Cenn Fáelad *sapiens* (d. 679) will be discussed presently.[106]

An event during Domnall's reign recorded by Bede was the letter that pope-elect John IV (640) wrote to various Gaelic churchmen concerning the Paschal controversy. This letter only names the addressees so there is ambiguity as to which ecclesiastical establishments received the letter, but most have northern locations. Among likely recipients are the following churches: Armagh, Clonard, Nendrum, Connor, Bangor, Moville, Tory Island, Old Leighlin, Devenish, Iona, and Emly (*HE* ii 19).[107] Old Leighlin and Emly are located in Bede's "southern provinces." Clonard is in the midlands. Armagh appears at the head of the list which implies its primacy over the other establishments. By the end of the seventh century, as the seat of St. Patrick, Armagh had confirmed that primacy. This papal letter of 640 almost certainly came into Bede's possession from a Gaelic source.[108]

---

[102] It has been argued that one aim of the "pseudo-historical prologue" to the *Senchas Már* is to express a sense of *natio*: Wadden, "Pseudo-Historical Origins."
[103] The three Middle Gaelic legends were *Fled Dúin na nGéd*, *Buile Suibne*, *Cath Maige Roth*: Carney, "Language and Literature," 478–79. The latter included the legend of Cenn Fáelad.
[104] Byrne, *Irish Kings*, 112–14; Charles-Edwards, *Early Christian Ireland*, 57 (map), 494–98; Ó Cróinín, "Ireland, 400–800," 217–18.
[105] Ireland, "Case of Cenn Fáelad," 68–70.
[106] Ireland, "Learning of a *Sapiens*," 68–71; Ireland, "Case of Cenn Fáelad."
[107] Plummer, *Venerabilis Baedae opera*, ii, 112–14; Colgrave and Mynors, *Ecclesiastical History*, 198–203; Charles-Edwards, *Early Christian Ireland*, 277, 409; Warntjes, *Munich Computus*, lxix, lxxvii–lxxviii.
[108] Herren, "'Papal letters to the Irish'."

An anonymous Hiberno-Latin poet of the mid seventh century wrote about the Six Ages of the World as reflected in the Eusebio-Hieronimian chronicle. Dáibhí Ó Cróinín used this poem, *Deus a quo facta fuit*, to argue that early annal entries could originate from marginal notes in chronological and computistical texts.[109] The poem established a relative chronology from Biblical events and synchronized events from pagan history in such places as Assyria, Greece, Persia, and Rome. The poet then designated his own time by noting the number of years from the baptism of Christ to the death of a local king "*Domnalus rex Scotorum*," that is, Domnall mac Áedo *rex Hiberniae* (628–642).[110] The poet mistakenly calculated the date as 645 A.D. The three year discrepancy for Domnall's death is caused by calculating from Christ's passion rather than his baptism – a three year difference.[111] Septuagint chronology, also used by Isidore of Seville, was utilized by the author of *Deus a quo facta fuit* which implies that he wrote from an orthodox stance that eschewed the *latercus*.[112]

It was during Domnall's reign that: 1) Cummian (632) wrote against the *latercus* citing ten computistical cycles and applying exegesis in his arguments; 2) Oswald (634) invited Ionan missionaries into Northumbria and worked with Bishop Birinus in Wessex; 3) Fursa and his companions (ca. 640) worked among the East Angles before moving onto the Continent; 4) the Battle of Moira (639) helped ensure the prominence of the Uí Néill; 5) pope-elect John IV wrote (640) to Gaelic churchmen urging conformity with Rome in matters of Easter (*HE* ii 19); and 6) an anonymous poet wrote (645) on the Six Ages of the World and placed contemporary Gaels into that larger picture.

This period of intense intellectual activity among the Gaels spilled over into the world of the Anglo-Saxons, north and south, as seen in Oswald's accomplishments, and Fursa's presence. Growing numbers of Gaelic scholars were in sympathy with Rome and orthodox Easter observance, as attested by Cummian and the anonymous poet of *Deus a quo facta fuit*. The abbacy of Iona, which followed the *latercus*, was dominated by members of Cenél Conaill. Domnall mac Áedo, *rex Hiberniae*, was a member of Cenél Conaill. Nevertheless, neither

---

**109** Ó Cróinín, "Annals from Easter Tables." The evolution of annalistic and chronicling traditions in Francia have been explained in similar ways: Story, "Frankish Annals," 73–74. For an edition and translation of the poem, see Howlett, "Seven Studies," 1–6.
**110** Howlett, "Seven Studies," 1–6.
**111** Ó Cróinín, "Annals from Easter Tables," 79–80.
**112** Chronicles that relied on Vulgate chronology (*Hebraica veritas*) were introduced into the insular world with the *latercus* in the fifth century: Mc Carthy, *Irish Annals*, 120–23; Mc Carthy, "Vulgate Chronology," 163–70; Mc Carthy, "Recovering Years Lost," 268–71.

family affiliations nor ethnic identity were determinants for orthodoxy in matters of Easter observance.

## Gaelic *Sapientes* in the Time of Peripatetic Anglo-Saxon Students

Bede noted that Anglo-Saxons of every social class benefited from free schooling in the Gaelic world (*HE* iii 27). He specifically cited the timeframe of 651–664, the middle of Oswiu's reign, a king who admired Gaelic learning (*HE* iii 25) and would have encouraged such an educational project. Agilberht (*HE* iii 7) and Trumhere (*HE* iii 24), who each served as bishops, had studied in Ireland in the 640s. Around 658, or shortly after, the main computistical texts used by Bede would have entered Northumbria from Ireland.[113] Those named by Bede who studied at Rath Melsigi (*HE* iii 27, 37; iv 3; v 9–11) did so after 664 and the "synod" of Whitby. Those who attended Mayo of the Saxons (*HE* iv 4) did so after the early 670s. Aldhelm wrote to Wihtfrith and Heahfrith in the last quarter of the century.[114] The descriptions in *Hisperica Famina* help to fill out the portrayals of student life among the Gaels as painted by Bede and Aldhelm.[115]

Cross-cultural study of computus involving Anglo-Saxon students is seen in the Munich Computus, a text firmly dated to 719. It contains a handful of Gaelic vocabulary used in the Latin text. But among the vernacular terms is the Old English *gerīm* used in the meaning "number" of days. It implies the presence of Anglo-Saxons among the students being taught.[116] It is in this context of cross-cultural educational opportunities that the following section examines the learning available to those peripatetic students by examining the products of Gaelic *sapientes*.

Beginning in the seventh century individual scholars in Ireland were referred to by the epithet *sapiens*.[117] It is unclear whether or not the term was used as a title or as an honorific adjective. *Sapientes* were respected for superior

---

113 Ó Cróinín, "Irish Provenance"; Ó Cróinín, "Bede's Irish Computus"; Wallis, *Reckoning of Time*, lxxii–lxxix. For an edition and discussion of the introductory materials, see Howlett, "Computus in Hiberno-Latin," 268–79.
114 Lapidge and Herren, *Aldhelm*, 139–40, 154–55 (Wihtfrith); 143–46, 160–64 (Heahfrith); Herren, "Scholarly Contacts," 30–35 (Heahfrith), 35–36 (Wihtfrith). For another edition and discussion of the letter to Heahfrith, see Howlett, *British Books*, 106–124.
115 Herren, *Hisperica Famina: I*, 32–39, 79–87; Ireland, "Study Abroad Destination," 68–71.
116 Warntjes, "Old English *gerīm*"; Warntjes, *Munich Computus*, 188–89.
117 Richter, "Personnel of Learning"; Ireland, "Learning of a *Sapiens*"; Charles-Edwards, *Early Christian Ireland*, 264–71; Johnston, *Literacy and Identity*, 102–12.

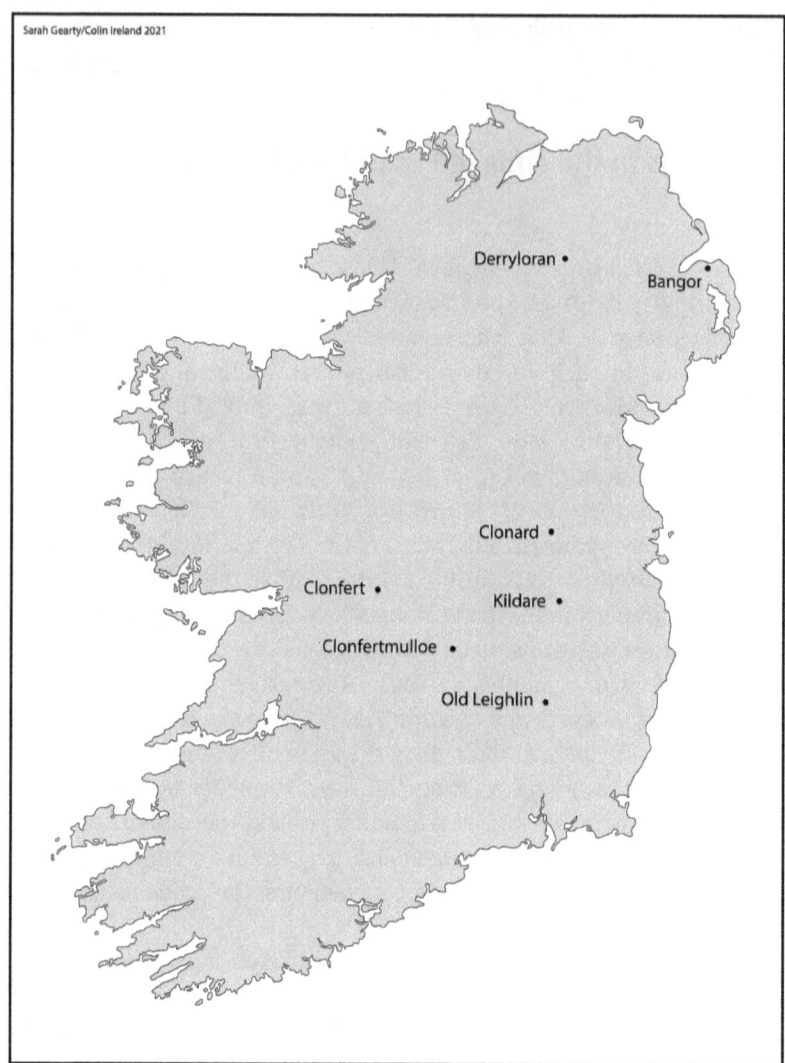

**Figure 4.b:** This map shows the locations associated with the six seventh-century *sapientes* to whom surviving texts, in either Latin or Old Gaelic, can be attributed.
Laidcenn *sapiens* mac Baíth Bannaig (d. 661) of Clonfertmulloe (*Cluain Ferta Mo-Lua*; Kyle, Co. Laois)
Cuimmíne Fota *sapiens* (d. 662) of Clonfert (*Cluain Ferta Brénainn*; Co. Galway)
Ailerán *sapiens* (d. 665) of Clonard (*Cluain Iraird*; Co. Meath)
Cenn Fáelad *sapiens* mac Ailello (d. 679) of Derryloran (*Daire Lúráin*; Co. Tyrone)
Banbán *sapiens* (d. 686) is associated with Kildare (*Cill Dara*; Co. Kildare) and possibly Old Leighlin (*Lethglenn*; Co. Carlow, in the Barrow valley near Rath Melsigi)
Aldfrith *sapiens* mac Ossu (son of Oswiu), king of Northumbria (d. 704) is associated with Bangor (*Bennchor*; Co. Down).

learning attested in their surviving writings in both Latin and Gaelic. The *floruit* for three named *sapientes* coincides with the period Bede highlighted, the bishoprics of Fínán and Colmán, as the time that Anglo-Saxon students frequented Ireland for free education. Michael Herren, in his edition, identified this period as most likely for the composition of the *Hisperica Famina*.[118] The section *Lex diei* (rule of the day) provides a graphic description of seventh-century student life.[119]

## Laidcenn

Laidcenn mac Baíth Bannaig (d. 661) of Clonfertmulloe (*Cluain Ferta Mo-Lua*; Kyle, Co. Laois) is the earliest *sapiens* recorded in the annals.[120] Laidcenn composed a famous *lorica*.[121] It was widely distributed and copied into Anglo-Saxon prayer books, a clear expression of appreciation.[122] *Loricae* were intended to have prophylactic qualities, as seen in vernacular poems by Bécán mac Luigdech and a short poem attributed to Adomnán, as noted in chapter two. Laidcenn's schematized recitation of body parts from head to feet suggests that knowledge of human anatomy, coupled with a more than rudimentary medical science, was practiced among the Gaels.[123] While no equivalent medical texts to the Old English *Læcboc* (Leechbook) or *Lacnunga* survive in Early Gaelic, the fact that Laidcenn's *Lorica* was copied into *Lacnunga*, and that healing or prophylactic charms in Old Gaelic are preserved in these same Old English medical texts, shows that the Anglo-Saxons consciously adopted Gaelic practices into their knowledge base.[124]

---

118 Herren, *Hisperica Famina: I*, 32–39.
119 Herren, *Hisperica Famina: I*, 74–91; Ireland, "Study Abroad Destination," 68–71.
120 Mac Airt and Mac Niocaill, *Annals of Ulster*, 132–33; Stokes, "Annals of Tigernach," 196 [Felinfach i 156]. Ireland, "Learning of a *Sapiens*," 64–65.
121 Ó Corráin, *Clavis*, ii, 725–27 §567; Sharpe, *Handlist*, 357 §998; Lapidge and Sharpe, *Bibliography of Celtic-Latin*, 80 §294; Kenney, *Sources*, 270–72 §100; Herren, "So-called *Lorica Gildae*." For editions, see Herren, *Hisperica Famina: II*, 76–89; Howlett, "Five Experiments," 6–18.
122 The *Lorica* is found in seven manuscripts including the Books of Cerne (Cambridge, University Library, MS Ll.1.10) and Nunnaminster (London, British Library, Harley MS 2965), and in a copy of the *Lacnunga*: Herren, *Hisperica Famina: II*, 4. See further Gneuss, *Handlist*, 29 §28, 75 §421, 76 §432. For discussions, see Hughes, "Irish Influence," 51–53; Brown, *Book of Cerne*, 19, 46, 48, 63, 68–70, 130, 140–41, 154; Raw, "Book of Nunnaminster," 153 (appendix); Hill, "Invocation of the Trinity," 266.
123 This has not been a widely held view. See Davies, "Place of Healing."
124 Meroney, "Old English Charms." For illustrations of manuscripts with Old English medical texts, see Breay and Story, *Anglo-Saxon Kingdoms*, 276–77 (Leechbook), 278–79 (*Lacnunga*).

Law-tracts such as *Bretha Crólige* (Judgements on Blood-lyings)[125] and *Bretha Déin Chécht* (Judgements of Dían Cécht),[126] the latter a mythical physician of the Tuatha Dé Danann, deal with responsibility for sick maintenance and physician's fees.[127] Both vernacular texts are part of the legal collection *Senchas Már* and date to the seventh century in Armagh.[128] These two law-tracts, along with others on status, demonstrate the existence of professional physicians among the Gaels at this early period.[129]

Laidcenn also abridged Pope Gregory's *Moralia in Iob*. Gregory's work investigated moral questions and the formation of the Christian soul. It was composed near the end of the sixth century and comprised a total of thirty-five books in six volumes. Laidcenn's epitome is referred to as *Ecloga de Moralibus in Iob*,[130] and reflects the respect bestowed by the Gaels on this favorite pope of the Anglo-Saxons.[131] Nevertheless, seventh-century Gaels tended to privilege the exegesis on Job of Philippus presbyter whose work is more condensed than that by Gregory.[132] Philippus's work was even shorter than Laidcenn's epitome in the *Ecloga*, and was known to the authors of *De mirabilibus sacrae scripturae* from southern Ireland, the *Altus Prosator* from Iona, as well as by Ailerán *sapiens* in the midlands.[133]

Laidcenn seems to have produced hagiography. A Life of St. Mo-Lua, which displays a great interest in Gregory the Great, is likely to have been written by him.[134] This Life of Mo-Lua may be one of the earliest surviving in the Gaelic hagiographical tradition. The monastery associated with Laidcenn, Clonfertmulloe, was founded by and named for this Mo-Lua (Lugaid maccu Óchae) of the Life. Mo-Lua also founded *Druimm Snechtai* (Drumsnat, Co. Cavan), the site where *Cín Dromma*

---

125  Binchy, "*Bretha Crólige*."
126  Binchy, "Bretha Déin Chécht."
127  For Dian Cécht, see Gray, *Cath Maige Tuired*, 122–23.
128  Breatnach, *Senchas Már*, 2 §§33, 34, 41–42 (dating).
129  Kelly, *Guide*, 57–59.
130  Ó Corráin, *Clavis*, ii, 723–25 §566; Lapidge and Sharpe, *Bibliography of Celtic-Latin*, 80 §293; Kenney, *Sources*, 278–79 §106; see also Ganz, "Earliest Manuscript."
131  For a contrast in the reception of Gregory's works in the seventh century, see Ireland, "Whitby *Life* of Gregory," 143–47.
132  Richter, *Ireland and Her Neighbours*, 190, 231–32; Ó Cróinín, "Commentary on Genesis," 250–51.
133  Richter, *Ireland and Her Neighbours*, 231–32; Stevenson, "Altus Prosator," 356; Ó Cróinín, "Commentary on Genesis," 252.
134  Byrne, "Life of St Molua," 103–7. For an edition, see Plummer, *Vitae Sanctorum Hiberniae*, ii, 206–25.

*Snechtai* was produced.[135] The *Cín*, and its early texts, was discussed in chapter three. Genealogical materials suggest that a certain Bicgu *abb sruithe* (Bicgu abbot of the seniors) of Clonmacnoise may have been Laidcenn's teacher.[136]

### Cuimmíne Fota

Cuimmíne Fota *sapiens* of Clonfert (*Cluain Ferta Brénainn*; Co. Galway) died in 662 at the age of seventy-two according to early annals.[137] He may have been abbot or bishop at the monastery.[138] Some *sapientes* had rich vernacular traditions develop around them, and Cuimmíne is one such. His Munster origins and broad learning are eulogized, and he is described as worthy to fill the seat vacated by Gregory, in an early vernacular lament.[139] An entry in the Fragmentary Annals repeats quatrains of the "lament" and attributes them to a certain Colmán úa Clúasaig who is described as Cuimmíne's tutor (*aite*).[140] Later vernacular texts associate Cuimmíne Fota with the wise fool Mac dá Cherda (literally, son of two crafts) during the seventh-century reign of King Guaire Aidni of Connacht. The two are described as half-brothers conceived incestuously.[141] Guaire Aidni was the king in an etiology involving Senchán Torpéist, as seen in chapter three.

A comprehensive penitential is attributed to Cuimmíne.[142] It begins by stressing penance as medicine for the salvation of souls, a common *topos* among the Gaels and repeated in *Vita Gregorii*.[143] In the main section "penances are grouped

---

135 Ó Corráin, *Clavis*, ii, 1053–54 §815; Ní Dhonnchadha, "Irish Vernacular Literary Tradition," 574–75.
136 Ó Corráin, "Creating the Past," 200.
137 Mac Airt and Mac Niocaill, *Annals of Ulster*, 132–33; Stokes, "Annals of Tigernach," 196 [Felinfach i 156]; Sharpe, *Handlist*, 94 §210. Cummíne Fota is cited as an authority in many Gaelic texts, both Latin and vernacular, and many vernacular stories developed about him: Ireland, "Learning of a *Sapiens*," 65–66.
138 One set of annals describe him as *comarbae Brénainn*: Mac Airt, *Annals of Inisfallen*, 94–95 s.a. 661. See further references at Ireland, "Learning of a *Sapiens*," 65.
139 Byrne, "Lament for Cummíne Foto" argued that the "lament" may be ca. 700, in contrast to Gearóid Mac Eoin who felt the poem was Middle Gaelic: Mac Eoin, "Lament for Cuimíne Fota."
140 Radner, *Fragmentary Annals*, 12–13 s.a. 662. This Colmán and his school in Cork have a long vernacular poem, with qualities of a *lorica*, as protection against the plague of ca. 664 attributed to them: Stokes and Strachan, *Thesaurus*, ii, 298–306.
141 For references, see Ireland, "Learning of a *Sapiens*," 66.
142 Bieler, *Irish Penitentials*, 5–7, 108–35; Ó Corráin, *Clavis*, ii, 763–64 §581; Lapidge and Sharpe, *Bibliography of Celtic-Latin*, 154 §601; Kenney, *Sources*, 241 §73.
143 Ireland, "Whitby *Life* of Gregory," 165–67.

according to the eight capital sins as formulated by Cassian."[144] Cuimmíne's penitential was known at Theodore's school in Canterbury and would have helped develop a tradition of penance among the Anglo-Saxons.[145]

Cuimmíne Fota is credited with the descriptive list *De figuris apostolorum* written, perhaps, as early as the 630s.[146] The text described each apostle in a consistently recognizable fashion. The iconic descriptions would have aided in the didactic purposes of painted pictures, panels, and wall-hangings in early churches as noted, for example, in Cogitosus's descriptions (ca. 680) of the church at Kildare.[147] Bede had noted that Augustine and his comrades carried panels with images of the Lord when they preached to the court of Æthelberht of Kent in the open air (*HE* i 25).[148] Benedict Biscop is credited with bringing painted illustrations back to Wearmouth-Jarrow from Rome. Bede's *Historia abbatum* stated that on his fourth journey (fifth trip to Rome, ca. 680) Benedict Biscop brought paintings of holy images, including ones of Mary and the twelve apostles.[149] On his fifth journey (sixth, and last, trip to Rome, ca. 686) he brought pictures relating the story of the Lord and others about the agreement of the Old and New Testaments.[150] The anonymous Life of Ceolfrith noted that Benedict brought from Rome "a painting of Bible stories" along with holy books, relics, and masters of singing for the church services.[151] In his homily on Benedict Biscop, Bede repeated the list of holy books, relics, masons, glaziers, and pictures brought from Rome for use in local churches.[152]

Cuimmíne composed a hymn, *Celebra Iuda*, in praise of the apostles.[153] The order of eleven apostles named in the hymn follows the order as found in Mat-

---

144 Bieler, *Irish Penitentials*, 5.
145 See Frantzen, *Literature of Penance*, 130–37; Charles-Edwards, "Penitential of Theodore," 147–58; Stancliffe, "Disputed Episcopacy," 18 and notes.
146 Ó Cróinín, "Iconography of Christ and the Apostles"; Ó Corráin, *Clavis*, ii, 713–14 §560; Lapidge and Sharpe, *Bibliography of Celtic-Latin*, 79–80 §292; Howlett, "Seven Studies," 46–47.
147 Connolly, "*Life of St Brigit*," 25–27 §32; Bitel, "Ekphrasis at Kildare."
148 Colgrave and Mynors, *Ecclesiastical History*, 74–75.
149 Grocock and Wood, *Abbots of Wearmouth*, 36–37 §6 (*Historia abbatum*).
150 Grocock and Wood, *Abbots of Wearmouth*, 44–45 §9 (*Historia abbatum*).
151 Grocock and Wood, *Abbots of Wearmouth*, 86–89 §9 (*Vita Ceolfridi*).
152 Grocock and Wood, *Abbots of Wearmouth*, 16–17 §12 (*Homilia in natale S. Benedicti*).
153 Bernard and Atkinson, *Liber Hymnorum*, i, 16–21; Ó Corráin, *Clavis*, ii, 714 §561; Lapidge and Sharpe, *Bibliography of Celtic-Latin*, 148–49 §582; Kenney, *Sources*, 266 §93; Howlett, "Seven studies," 40–46.

thew 10:1–4.[154] Both Cuimmíne's hymn and Cynewulf's *Fates* highlight the apostle John's special relationship with Christ.[155]

It has been suggested that Cuimmíne Fota is the same Cummianus who wrote the letter *De controversia Paschali* (ca. 632), as discussed above. The ten named Paschal cycles demonstrate that issues of Easter observance, so crucial in the careers of Wilfrid and Bede, were already intensely debated by the Gaels before either of the two Anglo-Saxons had been born. A majority of Gaelic churches had already decided in favor of Rome in matters of Paschal observance before the "synod" of Whitby.

Cummian's reference to Pope Gregory as "golden mouth" was repeated at Whitby in *Vita Gregorii*.[156] In his letter Cummian specified as a "whited wall" (*paries dealbatus*) a certain Gaelic cleric, still not identified, who rejected orthodox Paschal observance in favor of the old tradition.[157] Disagreement about the transition from older to newer Easter traditions existed in the early seventh century but only Iona, and monasteries under its influence, persisted in the older tradition for any length of time. The term "whited wall" comes from Acts 23:3, but its explanation is clarified by reference to Ephesians 2:14. Its use demonstrates Cummian's facility with, and depth of knowledge in, exegetical argumentation.[158] It is also likely that a "Commentary on the Gospel of Mark" is another example of exegesis by Cuimmíne/Cummianus.[159]

---

**154** Howlett, "Seven Studies," 44. For the structure of the Old English poem, see Howlett, "*Se giddes begang*." The order of apostles in Cynewulf follows that in *Celebra Iuda*, with the pairs James and John and Thaddeus and Simon being reversed. Cynewulf wrote to emphasize their "fates": For the orders, see Howlett, "Seven Studies," 40 §5 (James), 41 §6 (John), 41 §12 (Thaddeus), 41 §13 (Simon); Krapp, *Vercelli Book*, 51, line 23b (John); 52, line 35b (James); 53, line 77b (Simon and Thaddeus).
**155** For Cuimmíne, see Howlett, "Seven Studies," 41, 43 §6; for Cynewulf, see Krapp, *Vercelli Book*, 51–52, lines 25–27a which state that John was "most beloved of Christ in human form."
**156** Walsh and Ó Cróinín, *Cummian's Letter*, 82–83 and notes; Colgrave, *Life of Gregory*, 116–19, c. 24. See further, Ireland, "Whitby *Life* of Gregory," 43–44.
**157** Walsh and Ó Cróinín, *Cummian's Letter*, 92, line 271; for suggestion that the "whited wall" was Fintan of Taghmon, Co. Wexford: Walsh and Ó Cróinín, *Cummian's Letter*, 49–50 and notes.
**158** For the depth of exegesis, see O'Brien, "Exegesis as Argument."
**159** Ó Corráin, *Clavis*, ii, 711–13 §559. For an edition of the preface and arguments of its Gaelic provenance, see Howlett, "Seven Studies," 36–40. An edition of the full text was noncommittal about its Gaelic origins: Cahill, *Expositio evangelii*.

## Ailerán

Ailerán *sapiens* (d. 665) of Clonard (*Cluain Iraird*; Co. Meath) died of the plague, called in Gaelic *buide Chonaill*,[160] which devastated much of Britain and Ireland at the time. Early records do not assign ecclesiastical titles to him, but rather refer to him as either *sapiens* or *ecnae* (wise man, sage).[161] He composed a text on the allegorical interpretations of the names in the genealogy of Jesus found in Matthew's gospel, *Interpretatio Mystica Progenitorum Domini Iesu Christi*.[162] It is an exegetical work that relies on Jerome's etymological works on Biblical names, but also on works by Pope Gregory.[163] Among the text's Gaelic features is the use of the triad "thought, word, and deed."[164] The influence of Aileán's text extended to the Anglo-Saxons, in the works of Alcuin,[165] and onto the continent, in works by Walahfrid Strabo and Hrabanus Maurus.[166]

Also attributed to Aileán is the *Carmen in Eusebii canones*, known as the *Kanon euangeliorum rhythmica*, which "sets forth in riming Latin verse the number of agreements found by the canons to exist between the different gospels."[167] All the information is concisely presented in forty-two lines of verse. As David Howlett has noted: "One aspect of the astonishing density of phenomena packed into this poem . . . is that Aileán has made it unobtrusive. In reading this limpid verse nothing gets in the way of the expression of plain sense. . . . [I]n presenting the data as conversations among the symbols [of the Gospels] . . . Aileán has converted mere numbers into mythological narrative."[168]

---

160 Mac Airt and Mac Niocaill, *Annals of Ulster*, 136–37.
161 The *scholia* in *Félire Óengusso* (December 29) in the Franciscan ms. refer to him as *fer léigind*: Stokes, *Félire Óengusso*, 262; Ireland, "Learning of a *Sapiens*," 67.
162 Breen, *Ailerani Interpretatio mystica*; Ó Corráin, *Clavis*, ii, 714–16 §562; Lapidge and Sharpe, *Bibliography of Celtic-Latin*, 82–83 §299; Kenney, *Sources*, 279–80 §107(i). For a study of its opening paragraph, see Howlett, "Seven Studies," 6–11.
163 The works of Gregory appear to have been *Moralia in Iob* and "Homilies in Ezekiel," see Breen, *Ailerani Interpretatio mystica*, 111, 160–61, 178.
164 Breen, *Ailerani Interpretatio mystica*, 32 (Latin), 55 (translation), 61–62 (notes).
165 Sharpe, *Handlist*, 36–46 §87.
166 Breen, *Ailerani Interpretatio mystica*, 69.
167 Kenney, *Sources*, 280–81 §107(ii). See further, Ó Corráin, *Clavis*, ii, 716–17 §563; Lapidge and Sharpe, *Bibliography of Celtic-Latin*, 83 §300. For editions and studies of the text, see Howlett, "Seven Studies," 11–20; Howlett, "Aileán's *Canon euangeliorum*"; Howlett, "Eusebian Canons," 162–66.
168 Howlett, "Eusebian Canons," 166.

Ailerán may have written hagiographical materials on St. Brigit and his work was incorporated into what became known as *Vita prima Brigitae*.[169] An interesting feature of this Life is that Brigit's mother, while pregnant with the future saint, was sold as a slave to a *poeta*. The reference is a reminder of the high social status achieved by the professional poetic class. While at the poet's household a holy man, who arrived as a guest, saw a ball of fire in the place where Brigit's pregnant mother slept.[170] Shortly thereafter a druid prophesied that a child born at daybreak the next day "would have no equal on earth." Brigit was born at the time prophesied by the druid.[171]

The *floruit*s of the three *sapientes* just discussed all fall within the timeframe noted by Bede as attracting Anglo-Saxon students of all social classes to study among the Gaels (*HE* iii 27). All three *sapientes* relied on works by Pope Gregory, which implies their orthodox sympathies and predilections.[172] They reflect the Latinate learning freely available to those Anglo-Saxon students who crossed the Irish Sea.

The *Hisperica Famina*, a Bangor text, paints the most detailed picture of a student's life among the Gaels in the mid seventh century.[173] Bede commented on the free tuition available to students of every social rank (*HE* iii 27). The flow of Anglo-Saxon students to Ireland continued for many decades, as seen in those named by Bede at Rath Melsigi, those who traveled to "Mayo of the Saxons" with Bishop Colmán, in addition to Aldhelm's letters to Wihtfrith and Heahfrith. The *Hisperica Famina* were arranged as lessons for students and reveal how competition and disputation formed part of their pedagogical methods. Competition among Gaelic vernacular poets was common, as noted in chapters one and three.[174] The grammarian Virgilius Maro Grammaticus favored disputation as a pedagogical style.[175] The rich vocabulary of the hisperic texts reflects much of his playful linguistic practices.[176]

---

169 McCone, "Brigit in the Seventh Century," 134–41; Connolly, "Vita Prima," 6–7; Ó Corráin, *Clavis*, i, 274–75 §227. Extended arguments have been made about which is older, the so-called *vita prima* or the *vita* by Cogitosus. Many of these arguments have been rehearsed in Sharpe, "Vitae S Brigidae"; Connolly, "Vita Prima"; Mc Carthy, "Chronology of St Brigit."
170 Connolly, "Vita Prima," 15 §4.
171 Connolly, "Vita Prima," 15 §6. See McKenna, "Between Two Worlds."
172 Ó Néill, "*Romani* Influences"; Ireland, "Whitby *Life* of Gregory," 145–47.
173 For the text's connections to Bangor, see Stevenson, "Bangor and the *Hisperica Famina*." For the array of sources used, see Herren, *Hisperica Famina I*, 19–32.
174 See discussion in Carey, "Obscure Styles."
175 Law, *Wisdom, Authority and Grammar*, 29–30.
176 Harvey, "Blood, Dust and Cucumbers."

## *Sapientes* in a Bilingual World

Three seventh-century *sapientes* have only vernacular texts attributed to them. Nevertheless, the contents of their texts and their personal backgrounds reveal Latinate training. They confirm the extent of the bilingual intellectual world of the Gaels by the second half of the seventh century. Given the extended sojourns of certain Anglo-Saxons in Ireland, such as Ecgberht and Willibrord at Rath Melsigi, it is only natural that many learned Gaelic as part of their educations. The kings, Oswald and Oswiu, had done just that in an earlier period. Bilingual learning in Latin and Gaelic, whether ecclesiastical or secular, would have been available to those inclined to access it.

### Cenn Fáelad

Cenn Fáelad *sapiens* mac Ailello (d. 679) of Derryloran (*Daire Lúráin*; Co. Tyrone) belonged to Cenél nEogain, the same Uí Néill family to which the poet Bécán mac Luigdech, Bishop Fínán of Lindisfarne, and King Aldfrith *sapiens* belonged. The Middle Gaelic etiological legend that evolved around him, in which he lost his "brain of forgetting" and wove all that he learned of "Latinate, ecclesiastical learning," "native law," and "poetry and native lore," into poetic form is a later narrative elaboration of the syncretic, synthesizing processes of the seventh century.[177] His feat of creative memory and poetic exposition suggests the notion of "university" in the etymological sense of forming "one out of many" by turning "joint knowledge" into "all-embracing knowledge."[178] The historical Cenn Fáelad initiated his career in the time of Domnall mac Áedo (628–642), as discussed above.[179]

All texts associated with Cenn Fáelad are in the vernacular but none can be attributed with confidence to the seventh century on linguistic dating, though most are clearly eighth century. Cenn Fáelad is cited as an authority in contexts that show his Latinate and ecclesiastical education. For example, he is cited in the eighth-century law-tract *Míadšlechtae* (Sections on Rank) on a point concerning the *suí canóine* (professor of canon law or scriptures).[180] Similarly, in a law-tract of the second quarter of the eighth century, *Bretha Nemed Toísech*

---

177 Ireland, "Learning of a *Sapiens*," 68–71; Ireland, "Case of Cenn Fáelad." For the date of the battle of Moira, see Mc Carthy, http://www.irish-annals.cs.tcd.ie/, s.a. 639.
178 See discussion in Moran, "Vernacular Origin Stories."
179 Ireland, "Case of Cenn Fáelad."
180 MacNeill, "Ancient Irish Law," 313; Ireland, "Case of Cenn Fáelad," 73.

(First Judgement of Privileged Persons), Cenn Fáelad is quoted concerning the place of the church in legal judgements which should rely on 1) *fír aicnid* (truth of nature),[181] 2) similar cases for precedence, and 3) testimony (*teistemain*), frequently in the form of scriptural quotations.[182] Both citations above imply his training in ecclesiastical and legal matters.

His reputation was such that portions of an Old Gaelic law-tract, *Bretha Étgid* (Judgements concerning Irresponsible Acts), were attributed to him.[183] The attribution is stated so as to reflect the syncretism in its composition. Certain canonical statements are attributed to the legendary king Cormac mac Airt, and Cenn Fáelad provided the learned commentary.[184] The poem ascribed to Cenn Fáelad in the eighth-century death tale of Cú Chulainn ties him to the secular narrative tradition about Ulster heroes, and suggests his rôle in its preservation and dissemination.[185] The poem has linguistic features that point to the late seventh century.[186]

The first early medieval attempt to create a grammar for a vernacular language, the early eighth-century *Auraicept na nÉces* (The Scholars' Primer), is attributed, in part, to Cenn Fáelad.[187] The text as preserved, however, cannot be firmly dated to the seventh century on linguistic grounds.[188] It is important, nonetheless, as a grammar of a vernacular language based on late Antique grammarians of Latin, such as Donatus and Priscian, and it draws on the Biblical story of the Tower of Babel to explain how the Gaelic language was formed and gained pre-eminence among the world's languages.[189] *Auraicept na nÉces*

---

**181** This citation of Cenn Fáelad's work is too cryptic to be fully interpreted, but the vague reference to *fír aicnid* (truth of nature) appears to parallel *recht aicnid* (law of nature; *lex naturae*) and may imply the inclusion of *naturale bonum* in Church judgements. For discussions of the natural good, see Donahue, "Beowulf, Ireland," 267–71, 273; Ó Corráin, Breatnach, Breen, "Laws of the Irish," 385–86, 428–29; McCone, "Dubthach maccu Lugair," 10–12; Carey, "Dubthach's Judgment," 2, 9–12; Scowcroft, "*Recht Fáide*," 147–50; Cronan, "'Beowulf', the Gaels," 148, 160–61, 179; O'Sullivan, "Anti-Pelagian Motif."
**182** Breatnach, "*Bretha Nemed Toísech*," 5, 12–13 §8; Ireland, "Case of Cenn Fáelad," 73–74.
**183** Kelly, *Guide*, 149–50, 246, 272 (Appendix 1 no. 33); Breatnach, *Companion*, 176–82.
**184** Breatnach, *Companion*, 176–82 §5.12 (*Bretha Étgid*).
**185** Kimpton, *Death of Cú Chulainn*, 24–25 §24 (Gaelic), 43–44 (English). See arguments for an "anthology" of death tales: Clancy, "Die Like a Man?"
**186** Kimpton, *Death of Cú Chulainn*, 61.
**187** Calder, *Auraicept na n-Éces*, 6–9; Ahlqvist, *Early Irish Linguist*, 14–16 (source grammarians), 18–19 (authorship); Ó Corráin, *Clavis*, ii, 1130–34 §850. It is more accurate to describe the *Auraicept* as a primer for poets that required a basis in grammar: Acken, *Structure and Interpretation*. For discussion of the methods of the schools, see Burnyeat, "Irish *Grammaticus*?"
**188** Ahlqvist, *Early Irish Linguist*, 36.
**189** See Poppe, "Latin Quotations"; Hayden, "Anatomical Metaphor."

uses Biblical and Latinate materials to promote the status of a vernacular language.[190] As such it is an expression of the cultural sense of *natio* among the Gaels by the early eighth century. It also depicts how teaching in the schools may have been conducted.[191]

This first grammar of a vernacular language in Western Europe is a reminder of other Hiberno-Latin grammars produced at this period.[192] Among them are the works of Virgilius Maro Grammaticus, noted for his enigmatic observations on philosophy and Latin grammar.[193] The author of *Anonymus ad Cuimnanum* was familiar with Virgilius, as well as Donatus. The anonymous author quoted Gregory the Great in an attempt to open debate for introducing non-Christian works into ecclesiastical teaching.[194] Others who were familiar with Donatus included *Ars Ambrosiana*[195] and the grammarian Malsachanus, and this latter also used Isidore of Seville and knew his Virgilius.[196] The early glossary *De origine Scoticae linguae* reflects these grammatical concerns, as well as the interest in the "three sacred languages."[197]

Virgilius Maro Grammaticus composed the *Epistolae* and *Epitomae* presented as grammar that contains much philosophy.[198] His work was popular in his own time and its popularity continued for several centuries.[199] There are frequently moral or ethical messages in his work which relies on word play and is often presented in the form of maxims, precepts, or riddles.[200] Virgilius was quite inventive in his interpretations of grammar and the derivation of words, much of which seems overly abstruse, if not downright perverse. Nevertheless, close study reveals

---

**190** See discussion of the *Auraceipt* and Gaelic language in Russell, "'What was best of every language'," 405–6, 448–50.
**191** Burnyeat, "Irish *Grammaticus*?" See further Moran, "Vernacular Origin Stories."
**192** Richter, *Ireland and Her Neighbours*, 163–69.
**193** See, for example, Law, *Wisdom, Authority and Grammar*; Bracken, "Virgilius Grammaticus."
**194** Richter, *Ireland and Her Neighbours*, 167–68; Ó Corráin, *Clavis*, ii, 653–54 §503.
**195** Ó Corráin, *Clavis*, ii, 654–55 §504.
**196** Löfstedt, *Malsachanus*; Ó Corráin, *Clavis*, ii, 658–59 §511; Richter, *Ireland and Her Neighbours*, 168–69.
**197** Moran, *De origine Scoticae linguae*; Ó Corráin, *Clavis*, ii, 1176 §890. For a larger context, see Russell, 'Read it in a Glossary.'
**198** Ó Corráin, *Clavis*, ii, 717–23 §564 (*Epitomae & Epistulae*), §565 (*Fragmentum Incertum*); Lapidge and Sharpe, *Bibliography of Celtic-Latin*, 81–82 §§295–97.
**199** Richter, *Ireland and Her Neighbours*, 159, 166–67.
**200** For comparisons of his works to other wisdom literatures, see Law, *Wisdom, Authority and Grammar*, 22–40 (The Wisdom Tradition), 41–46 (Avarice and the Four Keys to Wisdom), 47–56 (The Multifarious Nature of Wisdom). An example was cited in chapter two in the discussion of what is known as Bede's "Death Song."

more methodical thought than previously assumed.[201] Many scholars, both medieval and modern, frequently overlook the humor Virgilius intended.[202]

Aldhelm quoted Virgilius in his letter to Heahfrith,[203] and Bede cited etymologies from Virgilius in *De temporum ratione* ca. 725[204] and in *De orthographia*.[205] David Howlett proposed that the Iona text *Altus Prosator* was composed by Virgilius.[206] Aldhelm, working in Wessex, was familiar with both *Altus Prosator* and the works of Virgilius.[207]

### Banbán

Banbán *sapiens* (d. 686) is associated with Kildare (*Cill Dara*; Co. Kildare)[208] and, possibly, Old Leighlin (*Lethglenn*; Co. Carlow), in the Barrow valley near Rath Melsigi.[209] Banbán was a contemporary of the hagiographer Cogitosus who wrote a *Vita Brigitae* ca. 680 which is full of information about Kildare. The vernacular law-tract *Cáin Fhuithirbe*, which survives only in fragments, is said to have been written by Banbán *sapiens* as part of a team.[210] A certain Díblíne instituted the law and Amairgen mac Amloingid arranged it.[211] *Cáin Fhuithirbe* can be dated on linguistic and internal evidence to ca. 680.[212] It is, therefore,

---

**201** Harvey, "Linguistic Method," 92–101. For an exposition of Virgilius's methods, see Harvey, "Varia I."
**202** For an overview of Virgilius, see Ó Cróinín, "Works of Virgilius Maro Grammaticus." For examples of his work methods, see Harvey, "Linguistic Method"; Harvey, "Blood, Dust and Cucumbers," 359–62; Harvey, "Varia I."
**203** Lapidge and Herren, *Aldhelm*, 164, 202n37; Howlett, *British Books*, 114, 119–20; Orchard, *Poetic Art of Aldhelm*, 96; Barker, "Carmen rhythmicum," 255.
**204** Bracken, "Virgil the Grammarian and Bede"; Warntjes, *Munich Computus*, xlvii–li, lxixn176.
**205** Picard, "Bede and Irish Scholarship," 144–47; Brown and Biggs, *Bede*, i, 63–73.
**206** Howlett, "'Altus Prosator'."
**207** Aldhelm's use of both the *Altus Prosator* and Virgilius is found in his letter to Heahfrith: Lapidge and Herren, *Aldhelm*, 143–46 (discussion), 160–64 (translation).
**208** Mac Airt and Mac Niocaill, *Annals of Ulster*, 148–49 s.a. 686 (*ōs cāch sapientis*); Stokes, "Annals of Tigernach," 209 [Felinfach i 169] (*fer léigind*).
**209** A certain "Banbán, a sparkling mass of gold" is cited at November 26 in *Félire Óengusso*. The *scholia* in Oxford, Bodleian Library, MS Rawlinson B.505 identify him as *epscop Lethglindi* (bishop of Leighlin): Stokes, *Félire Óengusso*.
**210** Breatnach, "*Cáin Fhuithirbe*."
**211** Breatnach, "*Cáin Fhuithirbe*," 43–44, line 17 (Díblíne) and line 21 (Amairgen); 46–48 (discussion).
**212** Binchy, "*Uraicecht Becc*," 53; Breatnach, "*Cáin Fhuithirbe*," 46; Breatnach, *Companion*, 216–18 §5.24.4.

roughly contemporary with the production of the *Senchas Már*. Although the text is fragmentary, the ecclesiastical background is clear from the contents and its associations with Munster in style and content are evident.[213]

*Cáin Fhuithirbe* is concerned with cooperation between secular kingship and the Church. It contains the following important line: "ro dilsiged la dub in dícubus" (that which is contrary to conscience has been made forfeit by ink).[214] The line implies that this law, despite its emphasis on secular ruling practices, contains nothing that contradicts Christian teaching because it is the result of collaboration between secular and ecclesiastical authorities.[215] It shows that the team who promulgated the law were conscious of syncretizing indigenous practices of the native ruling classes with the teachings and doctrines of the Church.

*Cáin Fhuithirbe* shows familiarity with the legend of Patrick's conversion of Lóegaire mac Néill at Tara, which is given fuller expression in Muirchú's *Vita Patricii* (ca. 695). The legend is expanded in the "pseudo-historical prologue" to the *Senchas Már* and explains the syncretism of Church teachings with native traditions, in which the poet Dubthach maccu Lugair and his pupil Fiacc Finn played prominent parts.[216] The text shows that Banbán and his co-workers were familiar with the etiologies about syncretism and were consciously working to achieve their aims.

An anonymous mid seventh-century law-tract, *Bechbretha* (Bee Judgements), "deals with trespass by bees, bee-stings and ownership of swarms."[217] It is among the oldest of the currently edited law-tracts and is part of the *Senchas Már*.[218] Just as *Cáin Fhuithirbe* showed an awareness of King Lóegaire mac Néill of Tara, *Bechbretha* referred to King Congal of the Dál nAraidi of Co. Antrim and described him as a king of Tara,[219] the only surviving source to do so. Most sources attribute that title only to members of the Uí Néill. Both law-tracts deal with the Tara kingship and the notion of *natio* that it implies. *Bechbretha*'s citation of a king of Dál

---

213 Ó Coileáin, "Mag Fuithirbe Revisited."
214 Breatnach, "*Cáin Fhuithirbe*," 43–44 (from recension C line 15) where the gloss to this line reads: "i.e. that which was contrary to conscience, they did not allow into this law"; Ó Corráin, "Church and Secular Society," 300–302.
215 Breatnach, "*Cáin Fhuithirbe*," 48. In the context of other *sapientes*, see Ireland, "Case of Cenn Fáelad," 74–75.
216 McCone, "Dubthach Maccu Lugair"; Carey, "Dubthach's Judgment"; Carey, "Pseudo-Historical Prologue." For discussion in a context related to early poets, see Ireland, "Vernacular Poets," 51, 55–56.
217 Kelly, *Guide*, 274. For an edition, see Charles-Edwards and Kelly, *Bechbretha*; Breatnach, *Companion*, 296.
218 Breatnach, *Senchas Már*, 2 §21, 41–42 (dating).
219 For a discussion, see the notes in Charles-Edwards and Kelly, *Bechbretha*, 123–31 §§31, 32.

nAraidi suggests its origins in a region associated with the evolution of vernacular literature in the northeast of Ireland.

Several early texts are concerned with kingship: the earliest vernacular *speculum principum Audacht Morainn*;[220] the political prophecy *Baile Chuinn Chétchathaig*;[221] the ritual *tarbfeis*[222] for predicting a future king; the Hiberno-Latin *De duodecim abusivis*,[223] which may have been composed ca. 630–650.[224] This latter text may have left its mark on the *Vita prima* of St. Brigit.[225] Centuries later the Anglo-Saxon homilist Ælfric discussed *De duodecim abusivis* and translated it into Old English.[226]

## Aldfrith

Aldfrith *sapiens*, son of Oswiu (*mac Ossu*), king of Northumbria (685–704) earned a reputation for learning among both the Anglo-Saxons and Gaels. Bede described him as "in scripturis doctissimus" (most learned in the scriptures; *HE* iv 26) and "undecumque doctissimus" (most learned in all respects; *HE* v 12).[227] Aldhelm sent the arcane and eclectic *Epistola ad Acircium* to him shortly after he became king, addressed to the one "who governs the kingdom of the northern empire."[228] The personal references in Aldhelm's exordium and epilogue show that the two had studied together at an unidentified time and place, perhaps in Ireland itself. Roughly a century later, Alcuin referred to him as "rex simul atque magister" (a king and a teacher at the same time).[229] Aldfrith's rôle as *magister* is revealed in his interactions with Witmer (*HA* §15) and Dryhthelm (*HE* v 12).

---

220  Kelly, *Audacht Morainn*; Ó Corráin, *Clavis*, ii, 1188–90 §908.
221  Bhreathnach, "Political Context"; Bhreathnach and Murray, "*Baile Chuinn Chétchathaig*"; Ó Corráin, *Clavis*, iii, 1525–26 §1135.
222  Knott, *Togail Bruidne Da Derga*; Ó Corráin, *Clavis*, iii, 1488–93 §1120; O'Connor, *Destruction of Da Derga's Hostel*.
223  Ó Corráin, *Clavis*, ii, 745–48 §576; Lapidge and Sharpe, *Bibliography of Celtic-Latin*, 96–97 §339.
224  Breen, "Irish Exegesis," 76; Clayton, *Two Ælfric Texts*, 41–48. For its exegesis, see Breen, "Irish Exegesis"; Breen, "*De Duodecim Abusivis*."
225  Johnson, "*Vita I S Brigitae*."
226  Clayton, *Two Ælfric Texts*. For the influence of this text in a broad insular context, see Grigg, "Just King."
227  For Anglo-Saxon records on Aldfrith's learning, including Alcuin's reference to him as *magister*, see Ireland, "Where Was King Aldfrith Educated?" 35–40.
228  Lapidge and Herren, *Aldhelm*, 34, 31–47 (introduction and translation); Ireland, "Where Was King Aldfrith Educated?" 37–40.
229  Godman, *Alcuin*, 70–71, line 864.

Bangor (*Bennchor*; Co. Down) is the most likely place for Aldfrith *sapiens* to have sojourned among the Gaels, not Iona as has frequently been stated.[230] The ninth-century *Félire Óengusso* lists Aldfrith, using his Gaelic name Flann, at December 15.[231] The quatrain calls Faustus, the Latin name of Comgall founder of Bangor, and the fine clergy of his church, to "the feast of Flann the honourable emperor, the enduring heir of Bangor."[232] Calling Aldfrith/Flann "emperor" (*imper*) follows Bede's descriptions of Oswald and Oswiu, and Aldhelm's salutation in *Epistola ad Acircium*. The "enduring heir of Bangor" (*comarbae búan Bennchoir*) stresses the wealth of knowledge Aldfrith inherited from Bangor and implies Bangor's allegiance to him.[233]

The only texts ascribed to Aldfrith are in Gaelic and use his Gaelic name. *Bríathra Flainn Fhína maic Ossu* (The Sayings of Flann Fína [Aldfrith] son of Oswiu) is an Old Gaelic wisdom text comprised of long series of three-word maxims as well as other sententious pieces.[234] Wisdom literature was popular among the Gaels, in Hiberno-Latin as well as in Gaelic, as noted for *De duodecim abusivis* and works of Virgilius Maro Grammaticus.[235] No texts attributed to Aldfrith/Flann Fína can be firmly dated linguistically to the seventh-century.[236] One must remain circumspect, therefore, about the ascription of this Old Gaelic text to a seventh-century Northumbrian king.

The tone of these wisdom texts, however, coincides with what we know of Aldfrith's predilections. They may reflect what he taught as *magister*. The three-word maxims emphasize "considerate behaviour in interpersonal relationships"; they promote "respect for skills and learning achieved through diligence and hard work"; and they encourage "humility and non-violence."[237] The *Bríathra Flainn Fhína* do not constitute a *speculum principum*, despite a strong tradition of such texts among the Gaels.[238] The *Bríathra* have an egalitarian tone, which

---

230 Ireland, "Where Was King Aldfrith Educated?" 48–52 and notes (Iona), 63–69 (Bangor).
231 Aldfrith's death is listed as December 14 at Driffield in the Peterborough Chronicle: Swanton, *Anglo-Saxon Chronicles*, 41. Discrepancies in dates for minor saints are common.
232 Stokes, *Félire Óengusso*, 251; Ireland, "Where was King Aldfrith Educated?" 64–65.
233 Ireland, "Where Was King Aldfrith Educated?" 63–72.
234 Ireland, *Bríathra Flainn Fhína maic Ossu*; Ó Corráin, *Clavis*, ii, 1190–92 §909.
235 Law, *Wisdom, Authority and Grammar*, 32–33. For a list of Gaelic wisdom texts, see Kelly, *Guide*, 284–86 (Appendix 2); Yocum, "Wisdom Literature."
236 For the Old Gaelic dating of *Bríathra Flainn Fhína*, see Ireland, *Bríathra Flainn Fhína maic Ossu*, 34–38.
237 Ireland, *Bríathra Flainn Fhína maic Ossu*, 20, but see the full section "Contents and Intent," 13–20.
238 For examples of early Gaelic *specula*, see Kelly, *Audacht Morainn*; Meyer, *Instructions of King Cormac*; Smith, "Briatharthecosc Conculaind"; Yocum, "Wisdom Literature."

contrasts with the hierarchical nature of Early Gaelic society,[239] implying that this wisdom text deliberately entered new territory aimed at a wider audience beyond the elites. These texts appear to reflect a school of thought, the social and educational philosophy, to which Aldfrith *sapiens* himself ascribed.[240]

| | |
|---|---|
| Maith dán ecnae | Learning is a beneficial occupation |
| Do·gní ríg di bocht | It makes a king of a poor person |
| Do·gní ánṡruth di esirt | It makes an accomplished person of a landless one |
| Do·gní sochenél di docheníul | It makes an exalted family of a lowly one |
| Do·gní gáeth di báeth | It makes a wise person of a fool |
| Maith a thosach | Its commencement is good |
| Ferr a deired | Its end is better |
| Airmitnech isin cenntur | It is respected in this world |
| Lógmar isin alltur | It is precious in the next world |
| Ní derchoíntech fri deired | It is not despairing concerning the end |
| Doilig dán láechdacht | The martial life is a distressful occupation |
| Ní airdirc | It is not renowned |
| ₇ is dérgnae a duí | And its unskilled practitioner is undistinguished |
| Gnímach duthain a suí | Its expert is toiling [and] transitory |
| It tregtaig a bí | Its living [practitioners] are pierced through |
| It ifernaig a mairb | Its dead are bound for hell |
| Mairg dán láechdacht | The martial life is a woeful occupation. |

This Old Gaelic text, in its surviving form, may not have been composed by King Aldfrith *sapiens* himself. But it reflects accurately his personal philosophy and the school of thought promoted by this "king as well as teacher" (*rex simul atque magister*, quoting Alcuin). It stresses *ecnae* (learning, wisdom; *sapientia*) over *láechdacht* (lay life; martial occupation).

(Based on edition in Ireland, *Bríathra Flainn Fhína maic Ossu*, 90–93 §7).

**Figure 4.c:** *Maith dán ecnae*, attributed to Flann Fína mac Ossu (Aldfrith *sapiens* son of Oswiu).

One section contrasts the good "occupation" (*dán*) of *ecnae* (learning; *sapientia*) with the distressful occupation of *láechdacht* (the lay state; martial life) (Figure 4.c).[241] The text enumerates the benefits of *ecnae*, whose rewards accrue not only in this world (*cenntar*) but also in the next (*alltar*). *Ecnae* can elevate the

---

**239** Kelly, *Guide*, 7–12 (Rank); Patterson, *Cattle Lords & Clansmen*, 181–206 (Rank).
**240** Yorke, *Rex Doctissimus*, 12–13.
**241** Ireland, *Bríathra Flainn Fhína maic Ossu*, 90–93 §7, and notes 155–61.

status of a poor person (*bocht*) and create an accomplished person (*ánṡruth*).²⁴² The pursuit of *ecnae* can also exalt one's extended family (*sochenél*). Implicit in the preoccupation with elevating one's rank, is the concern that one may also fall in social standing. There was fluidity in social status depending on professional accomplishment and accumulation of wealth, or their opposites.²⁴³ While *ecnae* implies the pursuit of Latinate learning (*sapientia*), it does not require the commitment of religious vows and its study can help elevate one's social standing. On the other hand, the deficiencies of *láechdacht* (the lay life) are noted. Its practitioners are "toiling" (*gnímach*) and "transitory" (*duthain*). *Láechdacht* entails a social obligation to military service, if not a commitment to it, and implies indulgence in licentious behavior, at least from the early Church's perspective.²⁴⁴

By contrast, *Vita Wilfridi* implies an obligation to military service from those who do not enter religious life. Stephen of Ripon reported that many secular leaders gave their sons to be instructed, as they chose, either for life in religion or for armed service when they were grown (*VW* c. 21).²⁴⁵ In the Wilfridian *schola* no preference was stated for religious training over armed service. The choice, apparently, was left to those who entrusted their sons to Wilfrid's care. *Vita Wilfridi* describes his retinue being accompanied by armed forces (*VW* cc. 12, 13, 24, 28).

All Northumbrian kings before Aldfrith *sapiens* were noted for their expansion of territory at the expense of their neighbors, whether other Anglo-Saxons, Britons, Picts, or Gaels. Once Aldfrith assumed kingship, that aggressive expansion was curtailed. Bede stated that "He [Aldfrith] ably restored the shattered state of the kingdom although within narrower bounds" (*HE* iv 26 [24]).²⁴⁶ The only reference that associated Aldfrith with the use of force comes from *Vita Wilfridi* when Stephen claimed that Aldfrith proposed to compel Wilfrid by force to accept his and Archbishop (of Canterbury) Berhtwald's decision, if so desired by Berhtwald,

---

**242** The term *ánṡruth* may denote someone who has reached the highest levels in a profession, such as poetry, but who cannot be awarded the highest title of *ollam* for some reason, whether due to deficiencies in family background or lack of available positions in the highest grade. See Breatnach, *Uraicecht na Ríar*, 94.
**243** Persons could fall in rank as well as rise: Patterson, *Cattle Lords & Clansmen*, 181–206 (Rank).
**244** *Láechdacht* for the early Church implied indulgence in bloodletting and licentious sexual behavior. See Sharpe, "Hiberno-Latin *laicus*"; Ireland, *Bríathra Flainn Fhína maic Ossu*, 157–60 §7.12.
**245** Colgrave, *Life of Bishop Wilfrid*, 44–45.
**246** "destructumque regni statum, quamuis intra fines angustiores, nobiliter recuperauit": Colgrave and Mynors, *Ecclesiastical History*, 430–31.

rather than allow Wilfrid to appeal once again to the pope (*VW* c. 47).[247] The only hint of warfare during Aldfrith's reign is the cryptic entry in the recapitulation at the end of Bede's *Historia* (s.a. 698) where it says that a *dux* of the Northumbrian king, named Berhtred, was killed by the Picts.[248]

*Cáin Adomnáin*, or *Lex innocentium* (law of the innocents), promulgated in 697 by Abbot Adomnán, is important in this context. Adomnán and Aldfrith were in agreement regarding warfare and violence. *Lex innocentium* protected "innocents," women, children, and clerics, from violence in war.[249] Children were to be under the law's protection "until they are capable of slaying a man" (co mbat ingnīma fri guin duine),[250] that is, until they were old enough to fulfill their military obligations. Adomnán's law was enforced throughout Gaelic and Pictish lands.

An *athláech* (ex-layman) is someone who has voluntarily exchanged the lay state (*láechdacht*) for a life in religion.[251] The *famulus Christi* Witmer, "a man as learned in the knowledge of worldly subjects as of the Scriptures,"[252] joined the monastery at Wearmouth, gifting it with ten hides of land that he had received from Aldfrith *sapiens*.[253] The existence of Witmer *eruditus* suggests that Aldfrith *sapiens* functioned as *magister*, or ensured that others did, for the local lay population. Witmer's death was noted along with the translations of abbots Eosterwine and Sicgfrith on August 22, 716.[254]

---

**247** Aldfrith would only use force if Archbishop Berhtwald so desired: Colgrave, *Life of Bishop Wilfrid*, 98–99, but see notes on 180 where the editor stated "It is difficult to believe that the account of the transactions at this conference has not been highly coloured by Eddius (i.e. Stephen)."
**248** Colgrave and Mynors, *Ecclesiastical History*, 564–65. It seems likely that Bede derived this information from Gaelic sources, "A battle between the Saxons and the Picts, in which fell Bernith's son, called Brectrid/Brechtraidh [Berhtred]": Mac Airt and Mac Niocaill, *Annals of Ulster*, 158–59 s.a. 698; Stokes, "Annals of Tigernach," 216 [Felinfach i 176].
**249** Meyer, *Cáin Adamnáin*; Ní Dhonnchadha, "Law of Adomnán"; Houlihan, *Adomnán's Lex Innocentium*.
**250** Meyer, *Cáin Adamnáin*, 24–25 §34; Ní Dhonnchadha, "Law of Adomnán," 62.
**251** For discussion, see Etchingham, *Church Organization*, 296–98. Four are listed in Hull, "Conall Corc," 900; they are entered in Ó Riain, *Dictionary*, 136–37 (Mo-Chammóc (Caimín) of Inis Celtra in Loch Derg), 185–86 (Colmán mac Lénéni, d. 606), 281–83 (Énna of the Árann islands), 285–86 (Bishop Ercc of Sláne in Mag Breg). Bishop Ercc's *obit* is given as 513: Mac Airt and Mac Niocaill, *Annals of Ulster*, 62–63 s.a. 513; Stokes, "Annals of Tigernach," 126 [Felinfach i 86].
**252** "in omni tam saeculari quam scripturarum scientia eruditus": Grocock and Wood, *Abbots of Wearmouth*, 60–61 §15 (*Historia abbatum*).
**253** Grocock and Wood, *Abbots of Wearmouth*, 60–61 §15 (*Historia abbatum*); Plummer, *Venerabilis Baedae opera*, ii, 365–66.
**254** Grocock and Wood, *Abbots of Wearmouth*, 70–71 §20 (*Historia abbatum*); Plummer, *Venerabilis Baedae opera*, ii, 369.

Bede cited instances that imply he sympathized with the benefits of *ecnae* over *láechdacht*. He observed that "many of the Northumbrian race, both noble and simple, have laid aside their weapons and taken the tonsure, preferring that they and their children should take monastic vows rather than train themselves in the art of war" (*HE* v 23).[255] Bede noted those who opted to leave the "lay-state (*láechdacht*)" in order to pursue learning or life in religion.

Dryhthelm was a married man with a family. He was stricken ill, apparently died, but recovered and declared that he had returned from the dead. He became famous for relating his experiences of the afterlife which paralleled Fursa's vision (*HE* iii 19). Aldfrith *sapiens* visited Dryhthelm frequently and listened to his experiences. At Aldfrith's request Dryhthelm entered Melrose and accepted the tonsure (*HE* v 12).[256]

Seventh-century Gaels and Anglo-Saxons were concerned with the larger world and how it was ordered. Aldfrith *sapiens*, acting as royal patron, exchanged eight hides of land along the River Fresca for a *codex cosmographiorum* recently brought back to Northumbria from Rome by Benedict Biscop shortly before he died (ca. 689).[257] No information on the contents of this "book of cosmographies" survives. But ca. 687 Aldfrith *sapiens* received a copy of *De locis sanctis* from Adomnán when the abbot visited *Aldfridus amicus* for a second time in Northumbria. Aldfrith richly rewarded Adomnán for the work. Aldfrith *sapiens*, through his *largitio* (generosity), again acting as *magister*, saw that *De locis sanctis* was dispensed widely for "lesser" or "younger" folk to read (*HE* v 15).[258] Recent research has expanded our appreciation of its intellectual depth.[259]

---

**255** "plures in gente Nordanhymbrorum, tam nobilis quam priuati, se suosque liberos depositis armis satagunt magis, accepta tonsura, monasterialibus adscribere uotis quam bellicis exercere studiis": Colgrave and Mynors, *Ecclesiastical History*, 560–61. It is possible to read this in light of the negative treatment the question received in Bede's "Letter to Bishop Ecgberht," where he decried the establishment of hereditary monasteries by nobles with no religious calling: Grocock and Wood, *Abbots of Wearmouth*, liii–lvii, 140–51 §§10–13.
**256** King Offa's and Dryhthelm's cases are discussed by Lapidge, "Debate Poem on Divorce," 14–15.
**257** Grocock and Wood, *Abbots of Wearmouth*, 58–59 §15 (*Historia abbatum*).
**258** Colgrave and Mynors translated *minoribus* as "lesser" but Richard Sharpe suggested that "younger" was more appropriate. Given Adlfrith's reputation as *magister* and *sapiens* either translation is applicable: Colgrave and Mynors, *Ecclesiastical History*, 508–9; Sharpe, "Books from Ireland," 5n16.
**259** O'Loughlin, "Adomnán's *De locis sanctis*"; O'Loughlin, *Adomnán and the Holy Places*; Loughlin, "*De locis sanctis* as a Liturgical Text"; Aist, "Adomnán, Arculf"; Hoyland and Waidler, "Adomnán's *De Locis Sanctis*."

Bede created an epitome of *De locis sanctis* ca. 703 and devoted two chapters of *Historia ecclesiastica* to topics from the text (*HE* v 16–17).[260] References to *De locis sanctis* are common throughout the Old English *Martyrology*.[261] Despite the Anglo-Saxon Church's emphasis on Rome from its earliest records, Adomnán's work does not cite the city of Rome among the "holy places."[262] Neither Bede's epitome nor the two chapters in *Historia ecclesiastica* mention Rome. Yet Bede included these chapters "for the benefit of readers" and encouraged them to consult either Adomnán's original or his own epitome of *De locis sanctis* (*HE* v 17).

The *Hisperica Famina*, the text that best portrays the world of Anglo-Saxon students among the Gaels, demonstrated an interest in the physical world, as shown by titles of discrete sections: "on the sky" (*de caelo*), "on the sea" (*incipit de mari*), "about the field" (*de campo*), "about the wind" (*de uento*).[263] Marina Smyth has noted that a preliminary reading of *de caelo* suggests "the secular cosmological views of late antiquity."[264] The text derives from a fully Christian milieu with a mix of sources including Isidore and Vergil.[265] The *Hisperica Famina* are associated with Bangor,[266] the place where Aldfrith *sapiens* most likely trained and taught.[267]

Several texts from the Gaelic world reflect the desire to understand the physical world. Among the earliest datable is *De mirabilibus sacrae scripturae* which can be firmly dated to 655 on internal evidence. It came from the monastery of Lismore in Co. Waterford.[268] The author, referred to as Pseudo-Augustine or Augustinus Hibernicus, "sets out to provide 'natural' explanations for all of the miracles in the Bible" and supports "his vision of nature as a harmonious whole whose integrity not even God will violate."[269]

---

260 For Bede's epitome, see Foley and Holder, *Biblical Miscellany*, 1–25 (*De locis sanctis*).
261 Rauer, *Old English Martyrology*, §§1, 52, 53, 56, 58, 67, 79, 111a, 200.
262 Meehan, *De Locis Sanctis*, 106–7 (3.1 Concerning the City of Constantinople), 118–19 (3.5 Concerning the Image of the Holy Mary).
263 Herren, *Hisperica Famina: I*, 90–93 (*de caelo*), 92–97 (*incipit de mari*), 98–101 (*de campo*), 102–3 (*de uento*).
264 Smyth, *Understanding the Universe*, 114.
265 Smyth, *Understanding the Universe*, 114–34; Smyth, "Physical World," 207–8.
266 Stevenson, "Bangor and the *Hisperica Famina*."
267 Ireland, "Where Was King Aldfrith Educated?" 63–69.
268 Ó Corráin, *Clavis*, ii, 738–41 §574; Lapidge and Sharpe, *Bibliography of Celtic-Latin*, 79 §291; Kenney, *Sources*, 275–77 §104.
269 Carey, *King of Mysteries*, 51. For the author, see Sharpe, *Handlist*, 165 §138. For discussions of contents, see Smyth, "Physical World"; Smyth, *Understanding the Universe*, 18–46, 59–71, 163–70, 208–15, 229–36; Smyth, "From Observation to Scientific Speculation"; Willis, "Mythologizing Thought."

The provenance of *Liber de ordine creaturarum* is also southern Ireland. It was composed sometime between 655 and ca. 680.[270] This text drew on the works of Gregory the Great, Jerome, Augustine, Columbanus, Caesarius of Arles, and others.[271] Bede used *Liber de ordine creaturarm* in his *De natura rerum* (ca. 703) and the author of the Old English *Martyrology* referred to it.[272]

The abecedarian poem *Altus Prosator* is about the Creator and his creation.[273] David Howlett called it the "earliest cosmological and eschatological poem extant in Insular literature."[274] This Hiberno-Latin text from northern Britain became known in Southumbria. Shared vocabulary with early glossaries such as Épinal-Erfurt, Corpus, and Erfurt II imply that it may have been known at Theodore's and Hadrian's school in Canterbury.[275] Aldhelm's short sojourn at the Canterbury school may be where he became familiar with it.[276] *Altus Prosator* has been proposed as a model for Aldhelm's *Carmen rhythmicum*.[277] References to Classical mythology in *Altus Prosator* come from Vergil.[278]

The involvement of Aldfrith *sapiens* in the intellectual life of late seventh-century Northumbria is clear from this discussion. His participation in the lives of Witmer and Dryhthelm reflects his predilections as *magister* and his promotion of *ecnae* or *sapientia*, including entrance to religious life, as opposed to *láechdacht*. His help in distributing such works as Adomnán's *De locis sanctis*, his generous payment for a *codex cosmographiorum*, and his reception of Aldhelm's *Epistola ad Acircium* help clarify how the world of Gaelic *sapientes* could spread into Northumbria, and Anglo-Saxon Britain generally, as a result of the free schooling available in Gaelic Ireland.

---

270 Díaz y Díaz, *Liber de ordine creaturarum*; Smyth, "*Liber de ordine creaturarum*"; Ó Corráin, *Clavis*, ii, 742–45 §575; Lapidge and Sharpe, *Bibliography of Celtic-Latin*, 98 §342.

271 Díaz y Díaz, *Liber de ordine creaturarum*, 32–38.

272 For Bede's use, see Picard, "Bede and Irish Scholarship," 139–44. For the Old English *Martyrology*, see Rauer, *Old English Martyrology*, §§46, 48, 50, 52, 53 (Pseudo-Isidore).

273 Ó Corráin, *Clavis*, i, 174–76 §267; Lapidge and Sharpe, *Bibliography of Celtic-Latin*, 148 §580; Stevenson, "Altus Prosator."

274 Howlett, "'Altus Prosator'," 363.

275 Orchard, *Poetic Art of Aldhelm*, 55–57; Stevenson, "Altus Prosator," 359–61. For an overview of early Gaelic glossaries, see Russell, *'Read it in a Glossary'*.

276 Orchard, *Poetic Art of Aldhelm*, 57.

277 Orchard, *Poetic Art of Aldhelm*, 55; Barker, "*Usque Domnoniam*," 17–18; Lapidge, "Career of Aldhelm," 28.

278 Lapidge, "'Epinal-Erfurt Glossary'," 147. For an earlier source of Classical mythology transmitted by the Gaels, see Holford-Strevens, *Disputatio Chori*.

## The Shared World of Insular Hagiography

The second half of the seventh century and the first half of the eighth experienced a florescence of hagiography written in the insular world.[279] Ironically, among the earliest surviving hagiographies were those written on the Continent by continentals about Gaelic *peregrini*.[280] Jonas of Bobbio composed ca. 640 a Life of Columbanus (d. 615) and, as a member of the monastery, was able to consult those who had personally known the saint.[281] Similarly, an anonymous Life of Fursa (d. ca. 649) was created within decades of the visionary saint's death.[282] These continental *vitae* about Gaelic saints written within living memory of their subjects is a feature common to the earliest Anglo-Saxon *vitae* with, perhaps, the exception of *Vita Gregorii* by an anonymous monk from Whitby.[283] While some Gaelic hagiographers may have been able to consult eyewitnesses whose lives overlapped with their subjects, surviving works about Patrick, Brigit, and Columba are retrospective looks back to an earlier age of saints.[284]

While most seventh-century Gaelic hagiographers are known, some are anonymous. Having named hagiographers permits us to establish somewhat the backgrounds of those who undertook to commemorate the saints. The earliest Gaelic hagiographers were active in the period designated by Bede as that time when Anglo-Saxons of every social class flocked to Gaelic schools for free education (*HE* iii 27). Among those early hagiographers were the *sapientes* Laidcenn mac Baíth (d. 661) and Ailerán (d. 665), both discussed above.

Laidcenn mac Baíth (d. 661) of Clonfertmulloe may have composed the *Vita* of St. Mo-Lua (d. ca. 612).[285] Laidcenn *sapiens* was commemorating the person who founded the monastery with which he was most closely associated. Mo-Lua,

---

279 For a discussion of the networks, see Gramsch, MacCarron, MacCarron, Yose, "Biographical Networks."
280 Sharpe, *Irish Saints' Lives*, 8.
281 For a translation, see O'Hara and Wood, *Jonas of Bobbio*; Ó Corráin, *Clavis*, i, 447–51 §339.
282 For a translation, see Rackham, *Transitus Beati Fursei*. For Fursa's *obit*, see Mc Carthy, http://www.irish-annals.cs.tcd.ie/, s.a. 649. Some Gaelic annals have doublets for his death: Mac Airt and Mac Niocaill, *Annals of Ulster*, 124–27 s.a. 648, 649; Stokes, "Annals of Tigernach," 190, 193–94 [Felinfach i 150, 153–54]. For his *vita* and *visio*, see Ó Corráin, *Clavis*, i, 308–10 §236.
283 Colgrave, *Life of Gregory*, 128–35, c. 30.
284 Sharpe, *Irish Saints' Lives*, 10.
285 Mc Carthy, http://www.irish-annals.cs.tcd.ie/, s.a. 607; Mac Airt and Mac Niocaill, *Annals of Ulster*, 104–5 s.a. 609; Mac Airt, *Annals of Inisfallen*, 84–85 s.a. 612; Sharpe, *Handlist*, 357 §998. For the Life of Mo-lua and its contexts, see Kenney, *Sources*, 390–99 §191; Lapidge and Sharpe, *Bibliography of Celtic-Latin*, 112 §394; Ó Corráin, *Clavis*, i, 311–14 §239 (*Codex Salmanticensis*).

the hypocoristic form of Lugaid (maccu Óchae), also founded the establishment at Druimm Snechtai (Drumsnat, Co. Monaghan) which gave its name to the *Cín Dromma Snechtai*, the manuscript collection of early vernacular narratives and poems discussed in chapter three. Given the timelines of their lives, Laidcenn could have consulted with people who had known the saint. Considerable attention is paid to Gregory the Great in the Life and Laidcenn *sapiens* is noted for his epitome of Gregory's *Moralia in Iob*. This concentration on Gregory, a favorite pope of the Anglo-Saxons, helps sustain the argument that Laidcenn composed the Life.[286]

It is plausible that Ailerán *sapiens* (d. 665) composed, at least portions of, what came to be called the *Vita prima* of Brigit of Kildare.[287] Arguments vary as to whether the text as we have it should be dated to the mid seventh or mid eighth century.[288] A feature of the text is that many of the pagan characters, specifically *magi* (druids), are portrayed in a positive light with some able to foretell the future success of the unborn saint.[289] The text also portrays the saint as sending emissaries to Rome to report to her on changes there as though the hagiographer was showing her foundation's compliance with orthodoxy as promoted by Rome.[290] In the *Vita prima* the mother of the yet-unborn Brigit is sold to a *poeta*, a recognition of their social rank and professional status. This particular poet entertained as a guest a certain holy man who saw a ball of fire over Brigit's sleeping mother and reported it to the poet.[291]

The *Vita prima* portrays Brigit engaging in two circuits of Ireland. The first circuit happens before she is veiled and is undertaken in the company of a druid. The second circuit takes place after she is veiled and in the company of St. Patrick or his associates. Although Brigit is associated with Leinster, specifically with Kildare, the two circuits allow her influence to be portrayed as island-wide. The first, and shorter, circuit allows her sanctity to be widely previewed before she takes the veil. The second circuit portrays Brigit as cooperating with, but not subordinated to, St. Patrick, Armagh, and the eventual Uí Néill hegemony. In fact,

---

286 Byrne, "Life of St Molua," 103–7.
287 For the variety of works on Brigit, see Kenney, *Sources*, 356–63 §§147–155. For the *Vita prima*, see Lapidge and Sharpe, *Bibliography of Celtic-Latin*, 102 §352; Ó Corráin, *Clavis*, i, 274–75 §227; Sharpe, "*Vita S Brigidae*," 100–101. For Ailerán, see Sharpe, *Handlist*, 31–32 §71.
288 For a summary of dating arguments, see Sharpe, *Irish Saints' Lives*, 15n51. Subsequent arguments for an early date have been made by Dan Mc Carthy who discussed competing chronologies for Brigit's life and career: Mc Carthy, "Chronology of St Brigit."
289 Charles-Edwards, *Early Christian Ireland*, 198; McKenna, "Between Two Worlds."
290 Connolly, "Vita Prima," 41 §90.4–5.
291 Connolly, "Vita Prima," 15 §4.1–2; McKenna, "Between Two Worlds," 67.

most of the Life takes place outside Leinster.[292] In a manner similar to Tírechán's *Collectanea* of Patrick, the *Vita prima* uses the travels of the saint throughout the territories of Ireland as a way to claim influence and jurisdiction over those regions.

Bishop Ultán maccu Chonchobair (d. 657)[293] of Ardbraccan (*Ard Breccáin*; Co. Meath), apparently instituted hagiographies, or at least created dossiers, on both St. Patrick and St. Brigit. For example, hagiographers of St. Patrick from later in the century, Tírechán of Tirawley and, less certainly, Muirchú maccu Machtheni, acknowledged Bishop Ultán as their source for information on the four names of Patrick and their meanings.[294] Tírechán is even more explicit about his debt to Bishop Ultán when he says that he learned much from him, along with other elders (*senioribus multis*), because Ultán had fostered him (*qui nutriuit me*).[295] Surviving abecedarian verses about St. Brigit suggest that Ultán may have created a hagiographical dossier on her. Only three verses are preserved, representing the end of the alphabet (x, y, z), but the lines *Xpistus in nostra insula que uocatur Hibernia* and the naming of Brigit, leave no doubt of the provenance. Bishop Ultán is among those credited with composition of the verses in prefaces from two of three manuscripts.[296]

In the context of dossiers and poetic fragments devoted to saints, the abecedarian hymn beginning *Audite omnes amantes Deum*, and commonly referred to as Sechnall's *Hymn* on St. Patrick, deserves mention. Sechnall is the Gaelic name of Secundinus,[297] one of three early missionaries, Auxilius and Iserninus being the other two, associated with St. Patrick.[298] Arguments have also been advanced to attribute the hymn to Colmán Elo (d. 611). The work is found in the Antiphonary of Bangor (680x691) but it is certainly earlier than the late seventh century.[299] While the hymn in praise of Patrick might not qualify as hagiography, it is rich in biblical language and diction. It borrows wording and phrasing from St. Patrick's own writings, much as subsequent hagiography on Patrick did, reflecting a continuity of tradition. In the hymn Patrick is equated with

---

**292** Dawson, "Brigit and Patrick."
**293** Sharpe, *Handlist*, 699 §1875.
**294** Mac Eoin, "Four Names of St Patrick"; Bieler, *Patrician Texts*, 62–63 (Muirchú), 124–25 (Tírechán).
**295** Bieler, *Patrician Texts*, 138–39, §18 (1).
**296** Sharpe, *Irish Saints' Lives*, 62–63 and notes. For an edition, see Howlett, "*Xpistus in nostra insula*."
**297** Sharpe, *Handlist*, 601 §1605.
**298** Dumville et al., *Saint Patrick*, 89–105 (Auxilius, Iserninus, Secundinus, and Benignus).
**299** Ó Corráin, *Clavis*, i, 376–78 §268. For editions, see Orchard, "'Audite omnes amantes'"; Howlett, *Celtic Latin Tradition*, 138–52.

saints Peter and Paul, and the second last stanza makes a strong Trinitarian statement.

Cuimmíne Find (Cummeneus Albus),[300] abbot of Iona (657–669), had gathered material for a hagiography of St. Columba. What survives is called *De virtutibus sancti Columbae*. It has been incorporated into the oldest extant copy of Adomnán's *Vita sancti Columbae* which was written several decades later (ca. 688x704).[301] *De virtutibus* survives only in a continental manuscript now in Schaffhausen, transcribed by the scribe Dorbbéne (d. 713) who may have served as abbot of Iona for a short time before his death (Figure 2.b).[302]

Cuimmíne Find was abbot of Iona at the time of the "synod" of Whitby (664) which saw a bishop originally from Iona depart from and relinquish authority over Lindisfarne and Northumbria. The decision at Whitby must have seemed a disruptive blow to the prestige of Iona and its founder. Cuimmíne was abbot when Bishop Colmán returned from Lindisfarne after the "synod" with thirty Anglo-Saxon monks accompanying him. He was still abbot when Colmán and those same monks established a monastery on Inishboffin off the west coast of Ireland in 668, discussed in chapter six. *De virtutibus* may have been written as part of a project in defense of Columban tradition in northern Britain, but it is impossible to be certain based on what survives of Cuimmíne's work. Two vernacular poems in praise of Columba by Bécán mac Luigdech from the same period were discussed in chapter two. The poems confirm the prestige accruing to Columba and Iona after the rejection at Whitby.

Cogitosus wrote *Vita S. Brigitae* at Kildare (*Cill Dara*) in the late seventh century.[303] Although not preserved in any insular manuscripts, his work is found in over sixty continental manuscripts.[304] The preface to his work also shows the influence of continental writers on this early insular hagiography. Echoes of the works of Jerome, Sulpicius Severus, and of Athanasius's *Vita Antonii* have been identified.[305] These three late Antique hagiographers were also noted chronographers, stressing the importance of chronology and chronicles to the Gaels

---

300 Sharpe, *Handlist*, 93 §209.
301 Anderson and Anderson, *Life of Columba*, 188–91, iii 5 and n214; Bullough, "Columba, Adomnan: Part I," 114.
302 Kenney, *Sources*, 428–29 §213; Sharpe, *Irish Saints' Lives*, 14; Graff, "Report on the Codex," 19–21; Picard, "Schaffhausen"; Stansbury, "Schaffhausen Manuscript," 70–76.
303 Ó Corráin, *Clavis*, i, 276–78 §228; Sharpe, *Handlist*, 89 §197; Lapidge and Sharpe, *Bibliography of Celtic-Latin*, 84 §302.
304 Sharpe, *Irish Saints' Lives*, 14.
305 Bullough, "Columba, Adomnan: Part II," 19–20. Note the importance of these three hagiographers in subsequent early Anglo-Latin saints' lives: Jones, *Saints' Lives and Chronicles*, 54–55.

from their earliest acquaintance with Continental sources in the fifth and sixth centuries.[306] Importantly for the Easter controversy of the seventh century, parts of the prologue from Victorius of Aquitaine have been identified in the preface and demonstrate that Cogitosus wrote from a stance that rejected the *latercus*.[307]

Cogitosus used Biblical themes to elevate Kildare. At both the beginning and particularly at the end of the Life Cogitosus emphasized Kildare's church buildings, with their decorations and paintings, as a city of refuge and as a New Jerusalem.[308] The physical descriptions can be compared with Bede's reports in *Historia Abbatum* and in his ecclesiastical history (*HE* i 25) about pictures and painted panels, mostly those brought back to Northumbria by Benedict Biscop after his visits to Rome. Cogitosus wrote in the Biblical style and the Life, when divided into thematic clusters, can be seen to have been presented in chiastic form.[309]

Cogitosus was a contemporary of Banbán *sapiens*, also associated with Kildare. The *Cáin Fhuithirbe*, associated with Banbán, reveals an awareness of the legends of St. Patrick and the syncretism of indigenous practices and the Church's teachings. Both Cogitosus and Banbán *sapiens* were working in a heightened intellectual atmosphere that was promoting the production of hagiography. Cogitosus's Kildare would have been known among Anglo-Saxons at such establishments as Ripon, Whitby, and Lindisfarne.[310] The orthodoxy of Cogitosus's work, as noted above, is shown by his brief citation from Victorius of Aquitaine's letter to Hilary, who subsequently became pope.[311] In the insular world of the late seventh century both Dionysiac and Victorian traditions appear to have been accepted as orthodox with regard to Easter practices, although the Dionysiac practices dominated and won out by the eighth century.

Tírechán of Tirawley[312] (*Tír Amolngaid*; Co. Mayo) gathered materials that were intended for a Life of Patrick and are referred to as *Collectanea Patricii*.[313] As noted he had acquired materials "from the mouth or book of Bishop Ultán (d. 657), whose pupil and fosterling he was" (ex ore uel libro Ultani episcopi,

---

**306** Jones, *Saints' Lives and Chronicles*, 57.
**307** Bullough, "Columba, Adomnan: Part II," 20.
**308** Krajewski, "Kildare and the Kingdom of God," 94–98.
**309** Howlett, *Celtic Latin Tradition*, 243–49; Krajewski, "Kildare and the Kingdom of God," 98–111.
**310** Stancliffe, "Irish Tradition in Northumbria," 41–42.
**311** Stancliffe, "Disputed Episcopacy," 12–14.
**312** Sharpe, *Handlist*, 697 §1871.
**313** Swift, "Tírechán's Motives." For an overview of the Patrician dossier, see Ó Corráin, *Clavis*, i, 261–66 §217.

cuius ipse alumnus uel discipulus fuit).[314] The four names for Patrick were derived from such a book. It is difficult to date this text precisely, partly because of its compilatory nature. Tírechán may have begun this work before the death of Ultán and completed it by the mid 680s. A period from 671–683 seems likely.[315] It is clear that Tírechán accepted the supremacy of Patrick with Armagh as his see, implying that the Uí Néill were the dominant political entity. But he emphasized the special relationship of Patrick with the descendants of Conall Cremthainne from Mayo rather than with other Uí Néill polities. Unlike his near contemporary Muirchú, he had Patrick fail to convert King Lóegaire at Tara.[316] According to Tírechán, Lóegaire's father, the eponymous Niall of the Uí Néill, forbade his son accept the faith, but rather he should be buried fully armed in the walls of Tara in order to face his traditional enemies in Leinster, a custom assumed to reflect pagan practice.

In a manner similar to the *Vita prima* of St. Brigit, Tírechán portrayed Patrick as making a circuit of Ireland as a way of claiming each area visited for his own jurisdiction. Such claims for the cult of Patrick imply the orthodoxy of the establishments.[317] For example, in Co. Tyrone, Patrick was said to have baptized the Uí Thuirtri in whose territory Cenn Fáeled *sapiens* (d. 679), the relative of Aldfrith *sapiens*, established his reputation as a scholar at Derryloran (*Daire Lúráin*).[318] Patrick is said to have had a church built at Bile Torten which then passed to the *familia* at Ardbraccan, Co. Meath in the see of Bishop Ultán (d. 657) discussed above.[319] In Leinster he consecrated Fiacc Finn Sléibte, who established the see at Sleaty. It was Bishop Áed of Sleaty (d. 700) who commissioned Muirchú to write a Life of Patrick. Fiacc Finn was the student poet companion of the chief poet Dubthach maccu Lugair at King Lóegaire's court.[320] Tírechán also has Patrick baptize the sons of Dúnlang in Leinster, the traditional enemies of King Lóegaire of Tara who refused to convert.[321] Not alone does Tírechán seem to be claiming these regions for Patrick, but his techniques weave together a network of social and political relationships in the evolving intellectual world of seventh-century Gaeldom.

---

314 Bieler, *Patrician Texts*, 124–25 [III.1].
315 Swift, "Tírechán's Motives," 80; but see Charles-Edwards, *Early Christian Ireland*, 439–40.
316 Bieler, *Patrician Texts*, 132–33, §12 (1–2).
317 For the orthodoxy of the Patrician cult, see Mc Carthy, "Paschal Cycle of St Patrick."
318 Bieler, *Patrician Texts*, 162–63, §50 (2); Ireland, "Case of Cenn Fáelad," 68–70.
319 Bieler, *Patrician Texts*, 162–63, §51 (1).
320 Ireland, "Vernacular Poets," 49–52.
321 Bieler, *Patrician Texts*, 162–63, §51 (4).

Muirchú maccu Machtheni produced *Vita Patricii* probably ca. 690.[322] The broadest range for the dates would be from 661, the start of Ségéne's bishopric at Armagh (not to be confused with Abbot Ségéne of Iona, 623–652), and the death of Bishop Áed of Sleaty in 700.[323] It used to be accepted that Muirchú had been a member of the Tuath Mochtaine, a people of the Plain of Machae (*Mag Machae*) found to the south and east of Armagh (*Ard Machae*; Co. Armagh).[324] However, there is strong evidence of his Leinster origins, perhaps at a place called Clane (*Clóenad*; Co. Kildare), only a few miles from the cult center of St. Brigit.[325] In his preface Muirchú refers to Cogitosus, author of the *Vita S. Brigitae*, as his (spiritual) father whom he is striving to emulate in his efforts at hagiography.[326] We see clearly the prestige of the Patrick cult when churchmen from Leinster and nearby Brigit's Kildare undertake the hagiography of Patrick. At a slightly earlier period Banbán *sapiens*, in *Cáin Fhuithirbe* ca. 680, shows familiarity with the evolving Patrick legend and cult. One manuscript of *Vita Patricii* suggests that, like Tírechán before him, Muirchú had relied upon Bishop Ultán's dossier to report the four names of Patrick.[327]

It was Bishop Áed of Sleaty (*Sléibte*) who commissioned Muirchú to write Patrick's *Vita*.[328] Sleaty, Co. Laois is in the Barrow River valley a few kilometers north of Rath Melsigi. Bishop Áed submitted a testament (*audacht*) to Bishop Ségéne of Armagh sometime probably in the 680s which committed his church to Patrick forever.[329] Áed died as an anchorite in 700, probably at Armagh rather than in Sleaty.[330] Both Bishop Áed and Muirchú are named as guarantors for the *Cáin Adomnáin* (*Lex innocentium*) promulgated by Abbot Adomnán of Iona in 697.[331]

---

322 Sharpe, *Handlist*, 381 §1068. For discussions of his vocabulary and style, see Harvey, "Muirchú and his *remi cymba*"; Howlett, *Muirchú Moccu Macthéni's*, 133–80. For an overview of the Patrician dossier, see Ó Corráin, *Clavis*, i, 261–66 §217.
323 David Howlett suggested the period from 686 to 700: Howlett, *Muirchú Moccu Macthéni's*, 182; T. M. Charles-Edwards argued for the decade of the 690s, i.e., ca. 695: Charles-Edwards, *Early Christian Ireland*, 439–40.
324 Kenney, *Sources*, 331; Hogan, *Onomasticon*, 652; Sharpe, "St Patrick and the see of Armagh."
325 Harvey, "Muirchú and his *remi cymba*," 44–45; Hogan, *Onomasticon*, 540.
326 Bieler, *Patrician Texts*, 62–63; Howlett, *Muirchú Moccu Macthéni's*, 40–41.
327 Bieler, *Patrician Texts*, 62–63; Mac Eoin, "Four Names of St Patrick."
328 Bieler, *Patrician Texts*, 62–63; Howlett, *Muirchú Moccu Macthéni's*, 40–41.
329 Bieler, *Patrician Texts*, 178–79, §16 (1–2) (Additamenta); Charles-Edwards, *Early Christian Ireland*, 439–40.
330 Ó Cróinín, *Early Medieval Ireland*, 157.
331 Ní Dhonnchadha, "Guarantor List," 180, 192–93 §25 (Áed), 180, 196 §36 (Muirchú).

A world of churchmen and scholars were coalescing around hagiographical and legal projects in the second half of the seventh century, many involving the syncretism of Latinate and indigenous traditions. It was a time when the growth of Patrick's cult reflected the steady elevation of Armagh to primatial status. It also coincides with the time when Anglo-Saxon students flocked to Ireland in "fleet loads" to take advantage of free education.

A short but significant episode of Muirchú's *Vita Patricii* reflects early written evidence of an etiological legend about the syncretism of the Church's teachings with indigenous custom and practice. The episode relates how a *poeta optimus* Dubthach maccu Lugair, who was present at the pagan court of King Lóegaire in Tara, was the first to rise in respect of Patrick, accept the faith, and be baptized. Dubthach was accompanied by a young poet named Fiacc Finn Sléibte who was to become the founding bishop of Sleaty (*Sléibte*) from which Bishop Áed commissioned Muirchú to write *Vita Patricii*.[332] Muirchú had Patrick succeed in converting King Lóegaire.

Both poets, Dubthach and Fiacc, have etiological legends associated with them and intertextual references are frequent.[333] According to the legend expressed in the eighth-century "pseudo-historical prologue" of the *Senchas Már*, Dubthach oversaw a nine-man committee comprised of secular rulers, religious authorities, and men learned in native lore which examined the customs and practices of the Gaels against the Church's teachings and declared that those Gaelic customs that did not conflict with Christian conscience should continue to be practiced in conjunction with the new faith.[334]

Adomnán, abbot of Iona (679–704), produced *Vita Columbae* sometime toward the end of the century.[335] Vernacular poets and poetry figure prominently in the cultural milieu of Columba and his times. The episode about Crónán (*poeta scoticus*) has been discussed in chapter one.[336] Another episode from the Life told how vernacular songs about the saint, with the quality of *loricae*, protected his kinsmen.[337] The survival of vernacular praise poems to Columba validates the episode. *Amrae Choluim Chille*, whose original core may be from ca.

---

**332** Bieler, *Patrician Texts*, 92–93; Howlett, *Muirchú Moccu Macthéni's*, 80–83.
**333** Ireland, "Vernacular Poets," 52–58.
**334** McCone, "Dubthach Maccu Lugair"; Carey, "Dubthach's Judgment"; Carey, "Pseudo-Historical Prologue."
**335** Ó Corráin, *Clavis*, i, 280–90 §230; Sharpe, *Handlist*, 25 §49; Kenney, *Sources*, 429–33 §214; Lapidge and Sharpe, *Bibliography of Celtic-Latin*, 86 §305.
**336** Anderson and Anderson, *Life of Columba*, 76–77, i 42 (43a–b).
**337** Anderson and Anderson, *Life of Columba*, 16–17, i 1 (9b).

600, praises Columba.[338] Two seventh-century vernacular poems by Bécán mac Luigdech, discussed in chapter two, praised the saint.

Although Columba was of the Cenél Conaill of the northern Uí Néill, as was Adomnán and most early abbots of Iona, the *Vita Columbae* does not mention Tara as did Tírechán and Muirchú in their depictions of King Lóegaire's court.[339] Adomnán was, nevertheless, concerned about legitimate kingship. For example he referred to King Oswald as emperor of all Britain "ordained by God" (a deo ordinatus),[340] and he discussed Diarmait mac Cerbaill (d. ca. 565) a king of Ireland "ordained by God's will" (deo auctore ordinatum).[341]

Adomnán manipulated Columba's chronology to extend his death by four years from 593 to 597.[342] Part of Adomnán's purpose was to have Columba's death occur on a Sunday. But it had the added advantage of making the year coincide with the arrival of the Gregorian mission at Canterbury. Columba's vision telling him of the divine extension of his earthly life was witnessed by Luigne maccu Blaí[343] and Pilu *Saxo* (the Saxon).[344] Bede reported that Columba came to Iona in 565 and died about 32 years later, agreeing with the revised *obit* for Columba of 597 (*HE* iii 4). Since more reliable Gaelic records do not report that date, Bede must have taken the revised dating from Adomnán's *Vita Columbae*.[345]

Adomnán wrote to celebrate Iona's founder whose Easter traditions were considered schismatic by the second half of the seventh century. Nevertheless, Iona had successfully evangelized much of Britain, with the greatest successes in Pictland and Northumbria. Bede claimed that Adomnán had been converted to orthodox Paschal practices on a visit (ca. 687) to Aldfrith *sapiens* during which he visited some unnamed Northumbrian monasteries (*HE* v 15).[346] Abbot Ceolfrith, in his letter to King Nechtán of the Picts, mentioned Adomnán's visit to Wearmouth-Jarrow but cited only tonsure as a topic of their conversation (*HE* v 21). Based on Bede's argument it is reasonable that Adomnán wished to portray

---

**338** Bisagni, *Amrae Coluimb Chille*, 156–57, 250–57.
**339** Lóegaire's father Niall was the eponymous ancestor of the Uí Néill.
**340** Anderson and Anderson, *Life of Columba*, 16–17, i 1.
**341** Anderson and Anderson, *Life of Columba*, 64–65, i 36.
**342** Mc Carthy, "Chronology of St Columba's Life."
**343** This person witnessed another vision of Columba's which helped rescue a monk miles away in Durrow: Anderson and Anderson, *Life of Columba*, 202–3, iii 15. The maccu Blaí may have originated in Leinster: Hogan, *Onomasticon*, 539.
**344** Anderson and Anderson, *Life of Columba*, 214–15, iii 22.
**345** Mc Carthy, "Chronology of St Columba's Life," 4–6.
**346** For the argument that Lindisfarne was most likely, see Ireland, "Lutting of Lindisfarne."

Columba and his foundation as orthodox too, even though records set the date for Iona's transition to orthodoxy at 716 (*HE* iii 4; v 22).[347]

Adomnán followed the style of previous hagiographers, both continental and insular, as seen in his two prefaces.[348] Like Cogitosus before him, Adomnán inserted echoes of Athanasius's *Vita S. Antonii* and Sulpicius Severus's *Vita S. Martini*.[349] A passage on Columba's gift of spiritual vision is borrowed from Pope Gregory's account of St. Benedict. He included quotations from *Acts of Sylvester*, he quoted from Victorius of Aquitaine's prologue to Hilarius, as well as echoing Dionysius Exiguus's dedicatory letter to Bishop Petronius which prefaced his Easter table.[350]

Adomnán implicitly acknowledged the primacy of the growing Patrician cult when he stated that a "disciple of the holy bishop Patrick" (*sancti Patricii episcopi discipulus*), a certain pious Briton named Maucte (*Mochtae*), had prophesied the greatness of Columba and the future cooperation between their two monasteries.[351] By the time Adomnán wrote, the cult of Patrick and his see at Armagh represented orthodoxy among the Gaels. When Columba left this world his fame spread from Iona, a small, remote island, throughout all Ireland, Britain, Spain, Gaul, Italy, and to Rome itself which is the "chief of all cities" (*caput est omnium ciuitatum*).[352]

### Early Anglo-Saxon Contributions to Hagiography

Among the earliest datable writings by a named Anglo-Saxon are three short poems by a certain Lutting dedicated to his teacher, Baeda *magister*, who died in 681. Michael Lapidge edited the poems and argued that Lindisfarne was the most likely location for Baeda *magister* to have taught and for his pupil Lutting to have composed at so early a period, although Ripon and Wearmouth-Jarrow cannot be ruled out.[353] Two aspects of these poems must be noted. Firstly, they

---

[347] Mac Airt and Mac Niocaill, *Annals of Ulster*, 172–73; Stokes, "Annals of Tigernach," 225 [Felinfach i 185].
[348] For example, see Picard, "Purpose of Adomnán's *Vita Columbae*"; Picard, "Tailoring the Sources"; Picard, "Cult of Colum Cille."
[349] Bullough, "Columba, Adomnan: Part I," 125–28; Sharpe, *Adomnán of Iona*, 57–59.
[350] Bullough, "Columba, Adomnan: Part I," 129; Bullough, "Columba, Adomnan: Part II," 22–24; Stancliffe, "'Charity with Peace'," 53–54; Stancliffe, "Disputed Episcopacy," 14.
[351] Anderson and Anderson, *Life of Columba*, 4–5, 2nd preface (3a).
[352] Anderson and Anderson, *Life of Columba*, 232–33, iii 23 (135b).
[353] Lapidge, "Lutting of Lindisfarne."

display unequivocal Hiberno-Latin style in their composition.[354] Lapidge noted that Baeda *magister* taught a curriculum that included Vergil, Juvencus, Paulinus of Nola, Caelius Sedulius, and Arator as likely sources.[355] Given the Gaelic influence at Lindisfarne through the mission from Iona, poems in a Hiberno-Latin style are natural. It would be harder to explain the promotion of an overtly Hiberno-Latin style in the Wilfridian establishment at Ripon (established ca. 663), or the contemporaneously founded Wearmouth-Jarrow (673x681).

The second aspect, not noted by Lapidge, is that the *annus Domini* dating used in the first of Lutting's three poems is the earliest firmly dated use of Dionysiac chronological reckoning in Northumbria, if not in the insular world.[356] If the retrospective eighth-century accounts of the "synod" of Whitby portrayed in Stephen of Ripon's *Vita Wilfridi* (712–714) and in Bede's *Historia ecclesiastica* (731) can be taken at face value, it was the Dionysiac traditions that were promoted by the Wilfridians at Whitby (664) and which won out in Oswiu's final decision. Bede's earliest datable use of Dionysiac reckoning is found in *De temporibus* (ca. 703). Yet, Lutting's use of Dionysiac chronology appeared at Lindisfarne, not at Ripon or Wearmouth-Jarrow, according to Lapidge. If Bede's arguments that Adomnán was converted to Dionysiac tradition while on a visit ca. 687 to Aldfrith *sapiens* are accurate, then the most likely of the unnamed Northumbrian establishments that Adomnán visited would have been Lindisfarne with its early links to Iona (*HE* v 15).

The anonymous *Vita Cuthberti* (698–705), the first of the Anglo-Saxon hagiographies, was created during the reign of Aldfrith *sapiens* and may be contemporary with Adomnán's *Vita Columbae*. Like the hagiography of Cogitosus and Admonán the anonymous hagiographer seeks to highlight in his preface the continuity with continental traditions and presents an orthodox stance with regard to Paschal practices. The recording of Dionysiac tradition by Lutting at Lindisfarne roughly two decades before the composition of the anonymous *Vita Cuthberti* makes the portrayal of Cuthbert's orthodoxy in the Life a natural reflection of the practice of Lindisfarne's monks at the time of its writing.

The anonymous Life has two prefaces, which quote verbatim from Evagrius's translation of Athanasius's *Vita Antonii* and Sulpicius Severus's *Vita Martini*. There is also a substantial quotation from Victorius of Aquitaine's dedicatory letter to Hilary, archdeacon of Rome at the time, but subsequently pope, which served as a preface to Victorius's Easter tables. These appeared in the

---

354 For a fuller discussion, see Howlett, "Lutting, Bede."
355 Lapidge, "Lutting of Lindisfarne," 20.
356 Ireland, "Lutting of Lindisfarne."

anonymous hagiographer's first preface. There are citations from the *Acts of Sylvester*, the pope credited with baptizing the emperor Constantine at York, as well as a long citation from Isidore's *De ecclesiasticis officiis* on the qualities for a bishop. Also when Cuthbert saw the soul of Aidan ascending to heaven, the anonymous hagiographer used the words of Pope Gregory's *Dialogues* where St. Benedict saw the soul of Germanus ascending to heaven.[357]

Like the Hiberno-Latin style of the poems of Lutting, the anonymous *Vita Cuthberti* revealed its debt to the Gaelic intellectual milieu as recorded in the prefaces to the hagiographies by Cogitosus and Adomnán. Just as Lutting demonstrated his orthodoxy in dating clauses, orthodoxy can be shown by Cogitosus in the sources for his arguments about Brigit and Kildare.[358] Whereas Lutting and Cogitosus, near contemporaries, were both legitimately orthodox, Adomnán and Cuthbert's anonymous hagiographer present their saints as having been so, despite the fact that neither Columba nor Cuthbert would have originally worn the coronal tonsure nor followed Paschal traditions considered orthodox at the time their hagiographies were written. Bede's claims for Admonán's conversion to orthodoxy are reflected in Adomnán's allusive suggestions for the orthodoxy of Columba's Iona.[359] And the anonymous hagiographer of Cuthbert could describe the saint as "orthodox in faith" (fide catholicus) with "the Petrine tonsure after the shape of the crown of thorns that bound the head of Christ" (tonsuraeque Petri formam in modum corone spineae capud Christi cingentis).[360] Lutting's poem confirms that Lindisfarne had been following orthodox Paschal traditions for roughly two decades by the time Cuthbert's anonymous Life was written.

Just as Brigit's *Vita prima* and the *Collectanea* of Patrick by Tírechán portray both saints as making circuits of Ireland as a way of demonstrating their territorial influence, so does the anonymous Life of Cuthbert name places the saint visited throughout the north of Britain, as if attempting to establish a far-flung *paruchia*.[361] Bede's revisions in the prose Life of Cuthbert (ca. 720) omit many of these place names, suggesting that he understood the motives of the anonymous hagiographer, and intended to eliminate some of its Gaelic characteristics. Bede produced a verse Life of Cuthbert (ca. 705)[362] in addition to his later

---

[357] Colgrave, *Lives of Saint Cuthbert*, 11–13; Bullough, "Columba, Adomnan: Part I," 129–30; Bullough, "Columba, Adomnan: Part II," 19–20, 26–27; Thacker, "Cult of St Cuthbert," 112–13; Stancliffe, "Disputed Episcopacy," 12–14.
[358] Stancliffe, "Disputed Episcopacy," 13–14.
[359] See observations by Stancliffe, "'Charity with Peace'," 53–54.
[360] Colgrave, *Lives of Saint Cuthbert*, 76–77, bk. ii, c. 1 (orthodoxy); bk. ii, c. 2 (tonsure).
[361] McMullen, "Ecclesiastical Landscape."
[362] Lapidge, *Bede's Latin Poetry*, 70–91, 184–313 (text and translation), 457–505.

prose Life which may have been written to respond to implicit criticisms of Cuthbert made in *Vita Wilfridi*.[363] All of the Lives of Cuthbert were produced during the abbacy of Eadfrith of Lindisfarne (flourished after 698). Ironically, Bede enhanced certain Gaelic features in Cuthbert's prose Life such as the practice of penance and prayer in water.[364] In both of Bede's versions he introduced the important character Boisil, prior of Melrose, who formed one point on the influential triangle that connected Iona, Melrose, and Rath Melsigi through the figure of Ecgberht.[365]

An anonymous Whitby monk produced a Life of Gregory the Great, *Vita Gregorii*, sometime near the end of Abbess Ælfflæd's rule (ca. 704–714).[366] It was the first Life ever written of this important pope who instituted the Roman mission to the Anglo-Saxons in 597. Its influence is suggested by the fact that the Old English *Martyrology* cites an episode from the Life in its entry for Pope Gregory.[367] With regard to Anglo-Saxon affairs *Vita Gregorii* emphasizes the conversion of King Edwin ca. 627 by Paulinus of the Gregorian mission. The text is full of Gaelic *topoi* and characteristics but is written from an orthodox stance. It remains to be answered why it should have been produced at Whitby rather than Canterbury. *Vita Gregorii* is an example of early Anglo-Saxon hagiography that could not rely on eyewitnesses, as the anonymous hagiographer clearly stated that none alive knew the great pope.[368] Likewise, in discussing King Edwin (616–633), the hagiographer stated that no eyewitnesses survived for what was related.[369]

The anonymous hagiographer referred to Pope Gregory by the term "Golden Mouth," an epithet first used to refer to that pope in Cummian's Paschal letter of 632.[370] The anonymous author used etymological word play to advance the narrative, a feature common in seventh-century Gaelic hagiography and in vernacular narratives.[371] The episode about posthumously baptizing the long-deceased Roman emperor Trajan through the pope's tears has parallels in Gaelic tradition and fits into the *topos* of the *naturale bonum*.[372] Such episodes suggest how the *Beowulf*

---

363 Stancliffe, "Disputed Episcopacy," 14–17.
364 Ireland, "Penance and Prayer in Water," 62–63.
365 Lapidge, *Bede's Latin Poetry*, 248–51 §20 (*Vita Cuthberti metrica*); Colgrave, *Lives of Saint Cuthbert*, 172–75, c. 6; 180–85, c. 8 (*Vita Cuthberti prosa*); McCann, "Cuthbert and Boisil."
366 Sharpe, *Handlist*, 25 §51.
367 Rauer, *Old English Martyrology*, 64–65 §42.
368 Colgrave, *Life of Gregory*, 76–77, c. 3; 132–33, c. 30.
369 Colgrave, *Life of Gregory*, 98–99, c. 16.
370 Ireland, "Whitby *Life* of Gregory," 143–47.
371 Ireland, "Whitby *Life* of Gregory," 147–53.
372 Ireland, "Whitby *Life* of Gregory," 153–59 and notes.

poet could portray a pagan ancestor as being a monotheist.[373] The way rivals are dealt with in the Life can again be paralleled in seventh-century Gaelic hagiography.[374] This text, along with the three Lives of Cuthbert, reproduces a version of the "secret watcher" motif most highly developed in Adomnán's *Vita Columbae*.[375] Other motifs, such as treating penance as medicine for wounded souls and a reluctant actor being whipped or scourged in a dream to impel him into action, while not unique to insular texts, are found in earlier Gaelic texts which are the likely sources for the anonymous Whitby hagiographer.[376]

Stephen of Ripon[377] wrote the *Vita Wilfridi* sometime between 712 and 714, just a few years after Wilfrid's death in 710.[378] While Wilfrid held the rank of bishop for roughly forty-five years (ca. 665–710) his career was divisive and fraught with contention in both secular and ecclesiastical spheres. He served, in total, only about twenty years in his capacity as bishop, experienced long periods of exile from Northumbria, and made two trips to Rome to appeal directly to the pope for reinstatement to his posts with negligible success.[379] Wilfrid's contentiousness ensured difficult relations with the Northumbrian kings Oswiu (d. 670), Ecgfrith (d. 685), and Aldfrith (d. 704). He fared no better with the ecclesiastics Benedict Biscop of Wearmouth-Jarrow (d. 689), Abbess Hild of Whitby (d. 680), or the two archbishops of Canterbury, Theodore (d. 690) and Berhtwald (d. 731).

There is much in Wilfrid's career and lifestyle that resembles that of a secular prince.[380] It has been argued that he exerted his authority over territory under his control as though it were his ecclesiastical empire.[381] One way he accomplished this was to link his authority to that of a secular ruler. For example, during the first half of King Ecgfrith's reign Wilfrid claimed the churches, together with their lands, of the Brittonic clergy and their populations conquered by Ecgfrith (*VW* c. 17).[382] *Vita Wilfridi* revels in the conquest by Ecgfrith of Pictish territories and the slaughter of the Picts so that conquering troops were able

---

373 Hill, "*Beowulf* and Conversion History"; Fulk, Bjork, Niles, *Klaeber's Beowulf*, lxxviii–lxxix (The Pagan Hero as Spiritual Warrior).
374 Ireland, "Whitby *Life* of Gregory," 159–61.
375 Ireland, "Whitby *Life* of Gregory," 161–65.
376 Ireland, "Whitby *Life* of Gregory," 165–67 (Doctor of Souls), 168–71 (Whipped in a Dream).
377 Sharpe, *Handlist*, 633–34 §1672.
378 Stancliffe, "Dating Wilfrid's Death."
379 Goffart, *Narrators of Barbarian History*, 258 and notes. For a chronology of his career, see Cubitt, "Appendix 2."
380 Tyler, "Wilfrid and the Mercians," 282.
381 Foot, "Wilfrid's Monastic Empire," 33; Fouracre, "Wilfrid on the Continent," 186.
382 Colgrave, *Life of Bishop Wilfrid*, 36–37; Jones, "Donations to Bishop Wilfrid."

to cross rivers by treading on Pictish slain bodies (*VW* c. 19).³⁸³ Wilfrid's large retinue included an armed force (*auxilia hominum*; *VW* c. 12)³⁸⁴ which was utilized in the slaughter of South Saxon pagans ca. 666 (*strage non modica*; *VW* c. 13)³⁸⁵ whom, it is claimed, Wilfrid converted roughly two decades later in the early 680s (*VW* c. 41; *HE* iv 13).³⁸⁶

Stephen's *Vita Wilfridi* copied extensively from the first and second prefaces of the anonymous *Vita Cuthberti* (*VW* preface), a clear indication that Stephen was reliant on his insular predecessors for arguments and models. This copying included a citation from Victorius of Aquitaine's preface to his Easter tables despite the fact that, in his description of the "synod" of Whitby, Stephen implied that Wilfrid promoted the Dionysiac Paschal traditions (*VW* preface; c. 10).³⁸⁷ The Dionysiac tradition came to dominate by the early eighth century, and the poet Lutting showed that it had been in use in Northumbria, probably at Lindisfarne, by 681.³⁸⁸ Other passages in *Vita Wilfridi* echo the anonymous Life of Cuthbert and Clare Stancliffe has shown that Stephen had altered the scenes dealing with the Petrine tonsure and their elevations to the bishopric in order to present Wilfrid in a superior light to Cuthbert.³⁸⁹

Stephen had Wilfrid claim for himself, in a sort of four plank manifesto (*VW* c. 47),³⁹⁰ that 1) he had stamped out the poisonous weeds planted by the *Scotti*, 2) he had made Northumbria orthodox,³⁹¹ 3) he had introduced proper musical practice,³⁹² and 4) he had introduced the Benedictine Rule.³⁹³ It is not clear what was meant by the first claim. It may be intended to complement the second. Nevertheless, no single claim can be convincingly substantiated. Stephen's *Vita Wilfridi* is the only surviving text to emanate from the Wilfridian *schola*. No other

---

**383** Colgrave, *Life of Bishop Wilfrid*, 40–43.
**384** Colgrave, *Life of Bishop Wilfrid*, 26–27.
**385** Colgrave, *Life of Bishop Wilfrid*, 28–29.
**386** Colgrave, *Life of Bishop Wilfrid*, 80–85.
**387** Colgrave, *Life of Bishop Wilfrid*, 2–3 (preface), 20–23 (c.10); Stancliffe, "Disputed Episcopacy," 14n31.
**388** Ireland, "Lutting of Lindisfarne."
**389** Stancliffe, "Disputed Episcopacy," 14–17.
**390** Colgrave, *Life of Bishop Wilfrid*, 98–99.
**391** The "synod" of Whitby was as much a political as an ecclesiastical council and, as such, King Oswiu deserves credit for the final decision: Ireland, "Social and Political Background."
**392** This claim cannot be substantiated based on surviving records: Billett, "Wilfrid and Music."
**393** The evidence of *Vita Wilfridi* in the appointment of abbots contradicts the Benedictine Rule. The earliest clear references to the Rule are found in the anonymous *Vita Cuthberti*: Álvarez-López, "Rule of St Benedict."

texts have been firmly identified that can be attributed to his circle or *schola*, if one existed.[394] There are no *computistica*, musical texts, or monastic rules that can be associated with Ripon or Hexham that might support the "manifesto."[395] Throughout the Life, Wilfrid relied on his knowledge of and adherence to canon law to demonstrate his orthodoxy.[396] This basis in canon law as portrayed for Wilfrid by Stephen agrees with the conclusion by Sandra Duncan that Wilfrid's "was a legalistic view of the Christian life; in the end obedience to the true Church was all that was needful."[397] Stephen's *Vita Wilfridi* portrayed Wilfrid as the one authoritative representative in Britain of that "true Church."

Shortly after the appearance of *Vita Wilfridi*, Bede[398] produced his *Historia abbatum* ca. 716 which was followed shortly by the anonymous *Vita Ceolfridi*.[399] Although treated as hagiography, these latter two texts share in common with *Vita Wilfridi* the qualities of ecclesiastical chronicles, a genre brought to its apex in an Anglo-Saxon context by Bede with his *Historia ecclesiastica* ca. 731.[400] Both *Historia abbatum* and *Vita Ceolfridi* provide valuable information about Wearmouth-Jarrow, its early development, and its personnel.

Bede's *Historia abbatum* concentrates on such founding fathers of Wearmouth-Jarrow as Benedict Biscop, Ceolfrith, and Eosterwine. Much of the information about Benedict Biscop revolves around his many trips to Rome and his efforts to bring skilled craftsmen and their work to Northumbria in order to create monastic buildings with interiors that would resemble those on the continent. A major purpose of Benedict Biscop was to build up the libraries at his monasteries in Northumbria. Two episodes from *Historia abbatum* reveal aspects of his success. Wearmouth-Jarrow came into existence through the patronage of King Ecgfrith, and his half-brother Aldfrith *sapiens* helped carry on that royal patronage. Aldfrith purchased a *codex cosmographiorum* that Benedict Biscop had recently brought from the continent.[401] Ceolfrith received a papal privilege which the *magnificus rex* Aldfrith, along with assembled bishops, confirmed in a synod.[402]

---

[394] Foot, "Wilfrid's Monastic Empire," 35–37.
[395] Lapidge, *Anglo-Saxon Library*, 42–43 (Hexham and Ripon).
[396] Stancliffe, "Disputed Episcopacy," 17–18.
[397] Duncan, "Prophets Shining in Dark Places," 92.
[398] Sharpe, *Handlist*, 70–76 §152.
[399] Grocock and Wood, *Abbots of Wearmouth*, xxi. It has been argued that Bede also wrote *Vita Ceolfridi*: McClure, "Life of Ceolfrid."
[400] For arguments that these works be treated as hagiography, see Grocock and Wood, *Abbots of Wearmouth*, xxii–xxiii.
[401] Grocock and Wood, *Abbots of Wearmouth*, 58–59 §15 (*Historia abbatum*).
[402] Grocock and Wood, *Abbots of Wearmouth*, 58–61 §15 (*Historia abbatum*).

At this time the *famulus Christi* Witmer entered St. Peter and bequeathed ten hides to the monastery.[403]

The anonymous *Vita Ceolfridi* was produced at roughly the same time but almost certainly after Bede's *Historia abbatum*. It concentrates on Ceolfrith and his contribution to the twin monasteries. Sometime near the death of Benedict Biscop (ca. 689) Ceolfrith was made abbot of Wearmouth-Jarrow. He resigned the abbacy in 716 and undertook a pilgrimage to Rome but died en route at Langres in Burgundy. Ceolfrith first entered religious life ca. 660 at the monastery of Gilling which had been established in 651 by King Oswiu. The first abbot of Gilling was Trumhere, a kinsman of Eanflæd, queen of Oswiu (*HE* iii 24). Trumhere had been trained among the Gaels, sometime in the 640s, at about the same time as Agilberht. No location was specified for where they trained, although it has been suggested that Agilberht was at Bangor.[404] When Ceolfrith entered Gilling his brother Cynefrith was in charge, but Cynefrith soon chose to depart Gilling in order to study the Scriptures and serve the Lord in Ireland (*Hibernia*).[405] No location is given, but it could not have been "Mayo of the Saxons" which was not founded until early in the decade of the 670s.[406]

Felix of Crowland (*Crugland*)[407] wrote a Life of Guthlac sometime in the 740s. Guthlac (ca. 672–715), son of Penwalh, came from Mercia. After a youth spent fighting and plundering the contiguous Britons, he became a hermit and settled in the Anglian Fenlands.[408] It has been noted that although Wilfrid benefited greatly from Mercian royal patronage during his exiles from Northumbria, he does not seem to have figured in Mercian traditions.[409] For example, neither Wilfrid nor Guthlac figures in the Life of the other. Guthlac was evidently a popular saint and twelve manuscripts of his Life survive, with several lost copies known to have existed.[410] By comparison, only two manuscripts survive of *Vita Wilfridi*. Guthlac is cited in the Old English Martyrology[411] and two

---

402 Grocock and Wood, *Abbots of Wearmouth*, 58–61 §15 (*Historia abbatum*).
403 Grocock and Wood, *Abbots of Wearmouth*, 60–61 §15 (*Historia abbatum*).
404 Hammer, "'Holy Entrepreneur'," 62.
405 Grocock and Wood, *Abbots of Wearmouth*, 80–81 §2 (*Vita Ceolfridi*).
406 As was suggested in the latest edition: Grocock and Wood, *Abbots of Wearmouth*, 80n14 (*Vita Ceolfridi*).
407 Sharpe, *Handlist*, 116 §296.
408 Brady, *Welsh Borderlands*, 53–59.
409 For discussion, see Capper, "Prelates and Politics."
410 Colgrave, *Life of Saint Guthlac*, 26–46. For manuscript illustrations that accompany a late copy of his life, see Breay and Story, *Anglo-Saxon Kingdoms*, 138.
411 Rauer, *Old English Martyrology*, 80–81 §63, 252 (commentary). He does not figure, however, in either Willibrord's Calendar or in Bede's Martyrology.

Old English Lives of Guthlac survive.[412] It has been argued that one of these vernacular poems about Guthlac can be attributed to Cynewulf.[413]

Felix relied on many of the same sources that other insular hagiographers used such as Suplicius Severus's *Vita Martini*, Evagrius's translation of Athanasius's *Vita Antonii*, Pope Gregory's *Dialogues* among his other works, and he cited frequently from Vergil. He also relied on insular works such as Aldhelm's *De virginitate* and *Epistola ad Acircium*, and he knew works about the Gaelic saint Fursa.[414] Felix's knowledge of Vergil and Aldhelm, and his use of arcane, and sometimes invented, vocabulary reveal his familiarity with the world encompassed by Iona, Canterbury, and Malmesbury, the points of an intellectual triangle represented in surviving glossaries.[415]

Guthlac understood the Brittonic language having spent a period of "exile" among the Britons.[416] It seems a natural outcome of his martial youth and, like Wilfrid's claiming churches and lands from conquered Britons, suggests a greater proximity of Brittonic and Anglo-Saxon settlement in the second half of the seventh century than typically assumed.

A certain *librarius* of Bishop Headda, named Wigfrith, had spent time among the Gaels (*inter Scottorum populos*). When Headda and Wigfrith were on a visit to Guthlac, which resulted in the saint accepting the office of priest (*officium sacerdotale*), Wigfrith stated to his companions that he would be able to discern the nature and source of Guthlac's wondrous powers. This was because among the Gaels he had seen "false hermits" (*pseudo-anachoritas*) as well as those who followed the true religion and "abounded in many signs and miracles."[417] Wigfrith's claims about what he learned of "signs and miracles" while among the Gaels is a reminder that Old English *drȳ* (magician, sorcerer) is borrowed from Old Gaelic *druí* (druid; plural *druid*). Note the positive portrayal of druids and their divinatory skills as found in the *Vita prima* of St. Brigit. The survival of pre-Christian beliefs among both Gaels and Anglo-Saxons is no surprise. When an Abbess Ecgburh asked who would follow him after his death, Guthlac answered that his successor, Cissa, was still among the pagans and had not yet accepted baptism.[418]

---

412 Krapp and Dobbie, *Exeter Book*, 49–88.
413 Bjork, *Poems of Cynewulf*, 33–75 (translation), 239, 246–47 (notes).
414 Colgrave, *Life of Saint Guthlac*, 16–17.
415 Lapidge, "School of Theodore"; Lapidge, "Career of Aldhelm"; Lapidge, "'Epinal-Erfurt Glossary'."
416 Colgrave, *Life of Saint Guthlac*, 108–111, c. 34; Brady, *Welsh Borderlands*, 53–59.
417 Colgrave, *Life of Saint Guthlac*, 142–45, c. 46.
418 Colgrave, *Life of Saint Guthlac*, 146–49, c. 48.

Guthlac's answer to Abbess Ecgburh is a reminder that the Anglo-Saxon conversion was an incomplete process as late as the early eighth century. Churchmen like Aldhelm, Theodore, Hadrian, and Bede, may have thoroughly adapted themselves and the texts they wrote to a Christianized context. But while they worked in a social environment that was largely Christian in name, it was not yet thoroughly so in practice.[419] It is also clear from the earliest Anglo-Latin hagiography that the Gaels continued to shape Anglo-Saxon intellectual models.

---

[419] Compare the situation in eighth-century Rome: Smith, "Cursing and Curing."

## Appendix 4.a: Aldhelm in a Gaelic World

Already before Aldhelm was born it is possible to trace Gaelic influence in the religious and intellectual life of Wessex. Once King Oswald (634–642) assumed the Northumbrian throne he established a relationship with King Cynegisl (611–642[?]) of Wessex (Gewisse). Oswald married Cynegisl's daughter, Cyneburh, helped with the conversion of the Gewisse, and stood sponsor at Cynegisl's baptism.[420] This was achieved with the aid of Bishop Birinus (634–ca. 650) who had been sent to Wessex by Pope Honorius (625–638).[421] The two kings gave Dorchester (*Dorcic*) to Birinus as his episcopal see (*HE* iii 7). By the mid 630s we see, outside of Northumbria, cooperation between clerics sent from Rome with those who followed the traditions of Iona.

Bede says that Gaelic missionaries appeared in all the lands ruled by Oswald, but this example shows that Gaelic influence extended to wherever Oswald developed relationships (*HE* iii 7). It suggests how channels of communication from Iona, as seen in Aldhelm's familiarity with *Altus Prosator*, could appear in Southumbria later in the century. From our earliest evidence of Christianity in Wessex we see Gaels active in the process.

The bishopric of the Frank Agilberht provides another conduit for Gaelic influence in Wessex in the 650s. Although his dates are uncertain, he had previously spent *non paruo tempore* in Ireland sometime in the 640s for the purpose of "studying the scriptures" (*HE* iii 7). Given Agilberht's later relationship with Wilfrid, and his rôle at the "synod" of Whitby, wherever he studied in Ireland offered education and training deemed orthodox. Agilberht's period of study in Ireland and his bishopric of Wessex allowed for a substantial period of contact that opened communications in Wessex with Gaelic establishments that followed orthodox practices.

No specific evidence survives for how Gaels first appeared in western Southumbria, but a certain Colmán had established himself at Hanbury (Worcestershire) sometime during the reign of Wulfhere of Mercia (ca. 658–675). It is possible that Colmán arrived while King Oswiu was involved in the conversion of Mercia.[422] Oswiu's involvement began ca. 653 when a son and daughter of his each married a daughter and son of King Penda's. Part of the marriage pact was the conversion of Penda's children which he allowed although remaining a pagan himself (*HE* iii 21). With Penda's defeat and death in 655 the conversion began in earnest. Bishop

---

[420] For a summary of contacts between Bernicia and Wessex in the seventh century, see Yorke, "Competition for the Solent," 39.
[421] Yorke, *Wessex*, 171–72.
[422] Yorke, "Irish and British Connections," 166.

Fínán appointed the Gael Diuma (Dímma) as first bishop (655–658), followed by another Gael Ceollach (Cellach) who did not remain long in the post (*HE* iii 21). Ceollach's early departure was probably due to the fact that when Wulfhere, a younger son of Penda, took over Mercia in 658 he expelled those associated with Oswiu and the Northumbrians. However, Wulfhere put Trumhere (ca. 659–ca. 662) in place as bishop. Trumhere had been educated and consecrated among the Gaels (*HE* iii 24) in the 640s and had served as the first abbot at Gilling (651–ca. 659). With Trumhere as bishop of Mercia, and Agilberht as bishop of Wessex in the 650s, Gaelic missionaries and teachers, such as Colmán at Hanbury, had opportunities to establish themselves throughout Wessex and Mercia.

It is possible that Gaels destined for the continent, or other parts of Britain, would pass through the Bristol Channel. It suggests how someone like Máeldub may have arrived in the area of Malmesbury.[423] Bede had called Malmesbury *Maildubi urbs* (Máeldub's city) (*HE* v 18).[424] Colmán of Hanbury and Máeldub of Malmesbury were apparently contemporaries.[425] It cannot be proven that Máeldub was, in fact, Aldhelm's teacher, but Aldhelm's writing style leaves little doubt that he was familiar with, and had been influenced by, Gaelic tradition that he acquired from an early age.[426] A letter to Aldhelm from an anonymous Gaelic student reminded Aldhelm that "you were nourished by a certain holy man of our race."[427] The student praised Aldhelm's erudition because he had been to Rome and requested the loan of a book for two weeks. The student stated that he would obtain a messenger and horse to complete the transaction. The short period of the loan indicates that the Gaelic student was living relatively close by Malmesbury.

The *Epistola ad Acircium*, sent to Aldfrith *sapiens* soon after he assumed the throne, indicates that he and Aldhelm had studied together roughly two decades previously. Aldhelm leaves no hints as to where that may have happened.[428] However, it seems most likely that their time together was among the Gaels, most

---

**423** Yorke, "Irish and British Connections," 165–66.
**424** For the likely derivation of the name, see Yorke, "Irish and British Connections," 164–65.
**425** Sims-Williams, *Religion and Literature*, 109.
**426** Discussions of Aldhelm's Gaelic influences have been traced in such works as Howlett, "Aldhelm and Irish Learning"; Herren, "Scholarly Contacts," 29–30; Dempsey, "Aldhelm and the Irish." For a discussion of Aldhelm's library that reveals Gaelic influence, see Orchard, "Aldhelm's Library." Not everyone sees Gaelic influence in Aldhelm's writing style, see Winterbottom, "Aldhelm's Prose Style."
**427** Lapidge and Herren, *Aldhelm*, 166; Yorke, "Irish and British Connections," 172–73; Dempsey, "High Ecclesiasticism in a Barbarian Kingdom," 50n13.
**428** Aldfrith married into Aldhelm's extended family which may have helped ensure a continuing relationship between them: Brooks, "Introduction," 4–5; Lapidge, "Career of Aldhelm," 22–26; Yorke, *Rex Doctissimus*, 9–10.

probably in Ireland itself, perhaps at Bangor.[429] In a study of the Épinal-Erfurt Glossary Michael Lapidge suggested that, based on vocabulary pertinent to the works of Vergil, and known to both Abbot Adomnán and to Aldhelm, that location must have been Iona in the mid to late 660s.[430] Lapidge proposed that Adomnán would have taught both Aldhelm and Aldfrith there. There are, however, serious shortcomings to such a scenario. Adomnán cannot be placed at Iona until he assumed the abbacy in 679, and indications are that his career previous to Iona was spent in Ireland.[431] Since the time that Aldhelm and Aldfrith studied together was likely after 664 and the "synod" of Whitby, Iona seems an even less probable location given the accounts by Stephen of Ripon and Bede that never hint that either Aldfrith *sapiens* or Aldhelm followed anything other than orthodox Paschal practices.[432]

If these three had shared an educational experience at a Columban institution in Ireland in the second half of the decade of the 660s, then Iona is improbable but Durrow seems a possibility. It is a place well known to Adomnán, as attested by references in *Vita Columbae*. However, external references do not link Adomnán to Durrow, and so any connection linking Adomnán, Aldhelm, and Aldfrith there is tenuous at best.[433]

Bangor, Co. Down appears to be the primary location for Aldfrith's training and education among the Gaels.[434] Bangor has also been suggested as the place in Ireland where Agilberht studied before he became bishop of Wessex, based on his family's connections with Columbanian foundations on the continent.[435] Bangor is not a location where Adomnán could have acted as mentor to Aldhelm and Aldfrith, despite his portrayal of close interactions between St. Columba and Comgall of Bangor in *Vita Columbae*.[436] Nevertheless, Bangor has a proven record for bilingual learning. Bangor is the source of the *Hisperica Famina*, a text that shows knowledge of Vergil, as well as the life of wandering students.[437] Circumstantial evidence is strong enough to argue that Bangor should be on a short list of places where Aldhelm and Aldfrith *sapiens* studied together.

---

[429] Barbara Yorke does not mention Bangor, but favors Ireland: "Irish and British Connections," 172.
[430] Lapidge, "Career of Aldhelm," 22–30, 47–48; Lapidge, "'Epinal-Erfurt Glossary'," 147–57.
[431] Herbert, *Iona, Kells, and Derry*, 48; Herbert, "World of Adomnán," 36.
[432] Ireland, "Where Was King Aldfrith Educated?" 48–52.
[433] Ireland, "Where Was King Aldfrith Educated?" 52–53.
[434] Ireland, "Where Was King Aldfrith Educated?" 63–69.
[435] Hammer, "'Holy Entrepreneur'," 62.
[436] Anderson and Anderson, *Life of Columba*, 88–91 (49b–50b), 200–201 (114a), 206–7 (118ab).
[437] Stevenson, "Bangor and the *Hisperica Famina*." For Vergil as a source, see Herren, *Hisperica Famina: I*, 20, 24–26.

Aldhelm was familiar with *Altus Prosator*, the abecedarian poem from Iona.[438] The poem contains much of the obscure vocabulary used by Aldhelm and noted elsewhere by Lapidge from the early glossaries. It is not clear how Aldhelm came to know this Ionan text in Southumbria, particularly since it was most likely composed in the second half of the century.[439] Aldhlem would have had to learn of this text soon after its composition and dissemination. But *Altus Prosator* may well have influenced the final form of Aldhelm's own *Carmen rhythmicum*.[440] Aldhelm knew the work of Virgilius Maro Grammaticus and quoted from it in his letter to Heahfrith.[441] David Howlett proposed that *Altus Prosator* had been composed by Virgilius Maro Grammaticus, a suggestion that, based on vocabulary alone, has much to recommend it.[442] It has also been noted that Aldhelm and Virgilius were each very different in temperament and outlook.[443]

Aldhelm's letter to Wihtfrith must have been written after his sojourn at the Canterbury school but sometime during his abbacy, that is, between ca. 675 and 706. The letter demonstrates the continuing desire of Anglo-Saxon students to travel to Ireland to advance their studies. Wihtfrith, it seems, was not satisfied with the study of the Old and New Testaments and opted for what "philosophers" might teach him.[444] What those "philosophers" taught, or who they may have been, has not been clarified.[445] A hint is contained in a text that was excerpted from the *Saturnalia* of Macrobius (ca. 400) by Gaels, most likely from southeast Ireland around 600. The excerpted parts were about the history of the Roman calendar and, therefore, would have interested anyone working on chronology and computistics. Bede acquired this work from Gaelic sources and labelled it with the name by which it is now known, *Disputatio Chori et Praetextati*.[446] He cited it in his own works on time. The excerpts contain a surprising amount of references to pagan gods and festivals.

---

**438** Orchard, *Poetic Art of Aldhelm*, 54–60.
**439** "These narrow limits require a date for writing of the poem between 650 and 700": Stevenson, "Altus Prosator," 364.
**440** Orchard, *Poetic Art of Aldhelm*, 55; Lapidge, "Career of Aldhelm," 28; Barker, "*Usque Domnoniam*," 17–18; Lapidge, "'Epinal-Erfurt Glossary'," 151.
**441** Lapidge and Herren, *Aldhelm*, 164, 202n37; Howlett, *British Books*, 111, lines 181–82, 114.
**442** Howlett, "'Altus Prosator'."
**443** Law, *Wisdom, Authority and Grammar*, 101–4.
**444** Herren, "Scholarly Contacts," 35–36.
**445** Vivien Law suggested that for Aldhelm these "philosophers" might include the anonymous author of *De mirabilibus sacrae scripturae* and Virgilius Maro Grammaticus: Law, *Wisdom, Authority and Grammar*, 103–4.
**446** Holford-Strevens, *Disputatio Chori*.

In his letter to Wihtfrith Aldhelm launched into admonitory examples from Classical myth and legend naming characters who are found in Vergil's *Aeneid*. Aldhelm may have been showing off knowledge acquired at Canterbury. What becomes clear in the course of the letter, as one might expect from the author of the prose and verse *De virginitate*, is Aldhelm's concern with sexual transgressions frowned upon by the Church.[447] Wihtfrith is warned against consorting with prostitutes and succumbing to their baubles and adornment which, Aldhelm implies, Wihtfrith will find in abundance in Ireland. It is these concerns that help clarify the earlier Classical references in the letter. Proserpina was abducted by the god of the underworld and became his consort; Hermione, daughter of Menelaus and Helen, was betrothed originally to Orestes but married Neoptolemus instead. Aldhelm impugned the ancient priests known as *Luperci* for conducting rites that sacrificed to Priapus known for his permanent erection.

The contemporary Gaelic penitential literature shows a similar preoccupation with sexual transgression.[448] Early Gaelic law recognized many forms of marriage, several of which did not meet with the approval of all churchmen.[449] There are many examples of the Church attempting to curtail the activities, particularly of young men, that were considered outside the norms of settled society. *Láechdacht* (lay state; martial life) implied sexual license and bloodletting, both serious transgressions for the early Church.[450] Before achieving full status in society by acquiring property and marrying, many young men engaged in *díberg* (brigandage) which involved them frequently in raiding, rapine, and other forms of impropriety.[451] Such activities are represented in *Togail Bruidne Da Derga*, discussed in chapter three. An Old Gaelic text attributed to Aldfrith *sapiens* contrasts the benefits of *ecnae* (learning; *sapientia*) with the deficiencies of *láechdacht* (Figure 4.c).[452]

It is ironic that Aldhelm should have impugned the Gaels for being preoccupied with philosophers and myths and then showed off his own knowledge. As noted above, Michael Lapidge used the evidence of early glossaries to suggest that familiarity with Vergil, specifically of the *Aeneid*, was shared by Aldhelm

---

[447] For arguments about the extremes of Aldhelm's views, see Dempsey, "Social Theology."
[448] Bieler, *Irish Penitentials*.
[449] For brief discussions, see Kelly, *Guide*, 70–73 (marriage), 73–75 (divorce), 134–37 (rape); Eska, *Cáin Lánamna*, 13 (rape), 13–18 (marriage), 20–24 (divorce); Kelly, *Marriage Disputes*, 1–4 (marriage), 4–6 (divorce).
[450] Ireland, *Bríathra Flainn Fhína maic Ossu*, 157–60, §7.12 (*láechdacht*).
[451] See discussions in Sharpe, "Hiberno-Latin *laicus*"; McCone, "Juvenile Delinquency." The young Guthlac lived a similar lifestyle: Colgrave, *Life of Saint Guthlac*, 80–83, cc. 16–18.
[452] Ireland, *Bríathra Flainn Fhína maic Ossu*, 90–93 §7 and notes 155–61.

and Adomnán. It is possible that Aldhelm used Classical figures to serve as ciphers for characters from secular tales in the vernacular.[453] There is evidence of Gaelic influence in the early glossaries that contain words used by Aldhelm.[454]

Aldhelm was familiar with the poetic traditions of his own people. If he had studied among the Gaels, as seems likely, he would have known that they too had a rich vernacular lore. Aldhelm's Latin poetry suggests influence from Old English poetry.[455] Preoccupations with secular traditions in the vernacular are hinted at in Aldhelm's letter to Heahfrith which begins with a reference to panegyric and poems to the Creator (*prosator*) of princes and commanders, and then evolves into one of the few surviving descriptions of Anglo-Saxon paganism, according to its translator.[456]

Aldhelm's pupil Heahfrith had just returned from the "northwest part of the island of Ireland"[457] having spent six years "sucking the teat of wisdom."[458] Aldhelm would have derived the metaphor "teat of wisdom" from the Gaels.[459] Michael Herren suggested that the location was "Mayo of the Saxons."[460] It was founded with Anglo-Saxon monks who departed after the "synod" (664), traveled to Iona with Bishop Colmán, then onto Inishboffin (*Inis Bó Finne*; 668), and finally to *Mag nÉo na Saxan* where Bishop Colmán negotiated with a local chieftain their new location (*HE* iv 4). Bishop Colmán died in 676, so "Mayo of the Saxons" was established early in the 670s, as discussed in chapter six.[461] If Heahfrith had spent six years at Mayo, Aldhelm's letter is not likely to have been written until well into the decade of the 680s, if not later.[462]

Bede acknowledged that the monastery at Mayo remained active and had grown large in his own day. Towards the end of the century Alcuin corresponded

---

**453** References and arcane vocabulary in the *Hisperica Famina* suggest they may derive from indigenous Gaelic traditions: Carey, "Obscurantists."
**454** Pheifer, *Épinal-Erfurt Glossary*, lv–lvii; Orchard, *Poetic Art of Aldhelm*, 58–59.
**455** Lapidge, "Aldhelm's Latin Poetry."
**456** Michael Herren argues that it ranks along with three descriptions of Anglo-Saxon paganism by Bede: Lapidge and Herren, *Aldhelm*, 160–61, 201n25.
**457** "ex Hiberniae brumosis circionis insulae": Ehwald, "Epistolae," 489, line 8; Lapidge and Herren, *Aldhelm*, 161 (translation); Howlett, *British Books*, 107, line 21; 111 (translation).
**458** "uber sofiae sugens": Ehwald, "Epistolae," 489, line 9; Lapidge and Herren, *Aldhelm*, 161 (translation); Howlett, *British Books*, 107, line 21, 111 (translation); 107, line 23, 111 (translation).
**459** See Bayless and Lapidge, *Collectanea Pseudo-Bedae*, 122–23 §1, 199n1; Richter, *Ireland and Her Neighbours*, 159–60; Orchard, "Hisperica Famina as Literature," 30–32.
**460** Lapidge and Herren, *Aldhelm*, 145.
**461** Mac Airt and Mac Niocaill, *Annals of Ulster*, 142–43; Stokes, "Annals of Tigernach," 203 [Felinfach i, 163].
**462** For a manuscript that contains the letter to Heahfrith, see Breay and Story, *Anglo-Saxon Kingdoms*, 102–3.

with the still thriving community of Anglo-Saxon monks there. Did *Mag nÉo na Saxan*, as a daughter house of Iona, follow the *latercus* until 716? Aldhelm described the learning acquired by Heahfrith as "orthodox."[463] Bede stated that, by his time of writing, the monks at Mayo had "adopted a better Rule" (*HE* iv 4).[464] Just what that "better Rule" meant and when it was adopted remain open questions. Those questions would have mattered to Aldhelm and his pupil Heahfrith. If *Mag nÉo na Saxan* is the location for Heahfrith's studies, did it change to orthodox practice before its mother house Iona? If it hadn't, we need to ask where else in northwest Ireland Heahfrith may have studied and acquired an "orthodox" education.

The letter to Heahfrith acknowledged the high reputation of Gaelic learning among Anglo-Saxon students.[465] Aldhelm asked why was "Ireland, whither assemble the thronging students by the fleetload, exalted with a sort of ineffable privilege."[466] He then answered his own rhetorical question by stating that the "country of Ireland is adorned, so to speak, with a browsing crowd of scholars, just as the hinges of heaven are decorated with stellar flashings of twinkling stars."[467] He acknowledged that Ireland's "browsing crowd of scholars" seemed numerous beyond counting. As is well known, Aldhelm was setting up the scenario to introduce the school of Theodore and Hadrian at Canterbury as an alternative to education in Ireland. Bede praised Theodore's Canterbury as providing instruction in Latin and Greek, as well as sacred and secular learning (*HE* iv 2). Although Bede praised the school at Canterbury, he never mentioned Aldhelm's presence there. The Canterbury school is a reminder of how late seventh-century Anglo-Saxon society relied on foreign impetus to impel its learned culture forward.

Aldhelm described Theodore being "hemmed in by a mass of Irish students"[468] who challenged their instructor who, in turn, defended his teaching like a wild boar surrounded by a pack of hounds, or like a bowman in battle

---

**463** Ehwald, "Epistolae," 491, lines 12–14; Lapidge and Herren, *Aldhelm*, 162 (translation); Howlett, *British Books*, 109, lines 94–97; 113 (translation).
**464** See a full discussion in Orschel, "Mag nEó na Sacsan"; Orschel, "Early History of Mayo."
**465** Herren, "Scholarly Contacts," 30–35.
**466** "Cur, inquam, Hibernia, quo catervatim istinc lectitantes classibus advecti confluunt, ineffabili quodam privilegio efferatur": Ehwald, "Epistolae," 492, lines 9–10; Lapidge and Herren, *Aldhelm*, 163 (translation); Howlett, *British Books*, 109, lines 124–26; 113 (translation).
**467** "Quamvis enim praedictum Hiberniae rus discentium opulans vernansque, ut ita dixerim, pascuosa numerositate lectorum, quemadmodum poli cardines astriferis micantium vibraminibus siderum, ornetur": Ehwald, "Epistolae," 492, lines 12–15; Lapidge and Herren, *Aldhelm*, 163 (translation); Howlett, *British Books*, 109, lines 124–26; 113 (translation).
**468** "Hibernensium globo discipulorum": Ehwald, "Epistolae," 493, line 4; Lapidge and Herren, *Aldhelm*, 163 (translation); Howlett, *British Books*, 110, line 153; 114 (translation).

surrounded by enemy formations. Yet Theodore repelled those who challenged him by his superior knowledge, "with the filed tooth of the grammarian."[469] One is reminded of competition among the rhetors in the *Hisperica Famina*.[470] Secular poets as related in Gaelic narratives, discussed in chapters one and three, competed with each other for patronage. An eighth-century tale tells how Eochu *rígéces* (royal poet) was bested at knowledge of local sites (*dindšenchas*) by clerical students and youths.[471] Even a pope may be challenged, as seen in the letter of Columbanus to Pope Gregory where Columbanus defended his views on Easter.[472] As we will see presently, Aldhelm was familiar with the "cut and thrust" of Gaelic repartee and participated efficiently in it himself.

Aldhelm intended to promote the Canterbury school as a destination for Anglo-Saxon students, but he described only Gaelic students as being present there. Bede's description of Anglo-Saxon students in Ireland enjoying instruction told how some "preferred to travel round to the cells of various teachers and apply themselves to study" (*HE* iii 27).[473] Education in the seventh century was frequently peripatetic. Aldhelm himself started locally in Wessex, spent time among the Gaels, probably in Ireland, took advantage of the school at Canterbury for a few years, and also traveled to Rome. Aldhelm's description demonstrates that substantial numbers of Gaelic students took advantage of the presence of Theodore and Hadrian at Canterbury.

In the last prose paragraph of his letter Aldhelm is nearly apologetic for his comments on the Gaels and their methods, stating that his comments are meant to be witty and fraternal jests. Aldhelm is careful not to offend Heahfrith for having partaken so successfully of Gaelic learning. He stated that "I meant to busy myself with building and forging in good humour the reputation of our own [scholars], not with heaping derisive and scornful abuse on yours!"[474] Aldhelm claimed the Greek Theodore and the North African Hadrian for the Anglo-Saxons but placed his own pupil Heahfrith among the Gaels.

The letters to Wihtfrith and Heahfrith rely on images of seafaring. Several students named by Bede crossed the Irish Sea to study at Rath Melsigi. Those

---

**469** "limato . . . grammatico dente": Ehwald, "Epistolae," 493, lines 5–6; Lapidge and Herren, *Aldhelm*, 163 (translation); Howlett, *British Books*, 110, line 156; 114 (translation).
**470** Herren, *Hisperica Famina: I*, 13–19.
**471** Knott, "Why Mongán was Deprived."
**472** Walker, *Sancti Columbani Opera*, 8, lines 6–18 (Latin); 9, lines 9–22 (English).
**473** "alii magis circueundo per cellas magistrorum lectioni operam dare gaudebant": Colgrave and Mynors, *Ecclesiastical History*, 312–13.
**474** "quippe cum satagerem praeconium cudens affabiliter texere nostrorum, non sugillationem ridiculose cachinnans rumigerare vestrorum": Ehwald, "Epistolae," 493, lines 13–15; Lapidge and Herren, *Aldhelm*, 163 (translation); Howlett, *British Books*, 111, lines 173–74; 114 (translation).

who followed Bishop Colmán to the west of Ireland and *Mag nÉo na Saxan*, all undertook a sea voyage. Students from Rath Melsigi, such as Wihtberht, Willibrord, the two Hewalds, undertook additional voyages onto the continent to work as missionaries. It is appropriate to paraphrase the Old English *Seafarer* for these Anglo-Saxons who felt compelled by the heart's desire to seek a land of strangers because the joys of the Lord meant more to them than a dead, transitory life at home.[475]

Later in his career Aldhelm received a letter from the Gael Cellán of Péronne, where St. Fursa had been interred. Cellán praised Aldhelm's learning and requested that he send some little sermons to refresh a pilgrim.[476] Cellán's style is deliberately Aldhelmian and it is clear from his letter that he is familiar with Aldhelm's *Epistola ad Acircium, Epistola ad Heahfridum*, and the prose *De virginitate*. Cellán was imitating Aldhelm in order to mock him implying that he found his work mannered and derivative. Interestingly, Aldhelm's self-depreciating response to Cellán demonstrates that he understood Cellán's playful gibes, reminiscent of Aldhelm's own jests with Heahfrith, and is able to respond in kind.[477]

It is possible to see Gaelic influence at nearly every turn in Aldhelm's career. His early relationship with Aldfrith *sapiens* recalls a period of time among the Gaels, most likely in Ireland. His knowledge of *Altus Prosator* and the works of Virgilius Maro Grammaticus imply a depth and range of contact that allowed some among the Gaels to acquire an appreciation for his own works as shown by the requests from the anonymous Gaelic student and from Cellán in Péronne.

---

[475] For the Old English poem in the context of these wandering scholars, see Ireland, "*Seafarer*."
[476] "paucos transmitte sermunculos": Ehwald, "Epistolae," 499, line 1; Howlett, *Celtic Latin Tradition*, 109, 110 (translation). For Cellán, see Sharpe, *Handlist*, 84, §182.
[477] Howlett, *Celtic Latin Tradition*, 108–13; Lapidge and Herren, *Aldhelm*, 167.

## Appendix 4.b: Bede in a Gaelic World

Bede's *Historia ecclesiastica* is the most significant external source for our knowledge of seventh-century Gaelic cultural history.[478] Ironically, for someone who informed us so well about the insular world, we know little about Bede's personal background beyond what he chose to tell us himself (*HE* v 24).[479] Some have argued that Bede was of noble social background.[480] While others have assumed that he was of low social status, as suggested by the fact that he never achieved any rank above priest.[481] These are intriguing questions, but will remain unresolved for present purposes.

Bede sometimes mentioned persons and locations that are either rarely or never cited in Gaelic records. His consciousness of the Gaels' contribution to early Anglo-Saxon culture is reflected in his description of the successful Iona mission to Northumbria. It is contrasted with the slow progress of the Canterbury missions and their occasional failures. He outlined the biography of Bishop Aidan (634–651) founder of Lindisfarne, and miracles performed by him (*HE* iii 3, 5, 15–17). Bede also related how Aidan's friendship with King Oswine of Deira roused the jealousy of King Oswiu (*HE* iii 14). The relationship between Aidan and Oswine undermines the notion of a Northumbrian dichotomy dividing an Iona-leaning Bernicia from a Deira sympathetic to Canterbury through Paulinus's conversion of King Edwin.

Bede told of the schooling available in Ireland throughout the seventh century. During the bishoprics of Fínán (651–ca. 661) and Colmán (661–664) at Lindisfarne many Anglo-Saxon students of every social class pursued learning opportunities in Ireland. They were offered religious and secular subjects of study, many moving about from teacher to teacher, for free (*HE* iii 27). That period coincides with the *floruits* of *sapientes* like Laidcenn, Cuimmíne Fota, and Ailerán who represent the teaching available to them. But even before this period, Bishop Agilberht, present at the "synod" of Whitby, had spent time in the 640s studying scripture in Ireland (*HE* iii 7). Trumhere, founding abbot of Gilling (651), had been educated and consecrated among the Gaels in the 640s (*HE* iii 24).

---

[478] For a useful survey of Gaels in Bede's *Historia ecclesiastica*, see Thacker, "Bede and the Irish"; McCann, *"Plures de Scottorum regione."* For recognition of Bede's debt to the Gaels, see Love, "Library of the Venerable Bede." For a cautionary approach to Bede as source, see Wickham, *Framing the Early Middle Ages*, 343.
[479] Charles Plummer discussed Bede's background without judging what his social status may have been: Plummer, *Venerabilis Baedae opera*, ix–xi.
[480] Campbell, "Bede"; Thacker, "Ordering of Understanding," 40–41.
[481] Brown, *Bede the Venerable*, 15; Grocock and Wood, *Abbots*, xiv–xvii; Ireland, "Vernacular Poets," 59.

Bede noted thirty Anglo-Saxon monks who departed Northumbria, accompanied by Bishop Colmán, after the "synod" of Whitby (664). They first went to Iona. That group then established a monastery on Inishboffin in 668 (*HE* iv 4).[482] Bede gave a good approximation of the name, *Inisboufinde* (Inis bó finne), and its meaning "island of the white heifer" (insula uitulae albae). Before his death in 676,[483] Colmán negotiated with a local chieftain another establishment on the mainland at *mag éo* or *muig éo* (Mayo; *HE* iv 4). Bede did not translate the name, which means "plain of yews," but the establishment thrived. Decades later Alcuin wrote to the monks there.[484] The Old Gaelic name, *Mag nÉo na Saxan* (Mayo of the Saxons), recognizes the Anglo-Saxon connection.[485] This foundation is discussed in chapter six.

Bede named many Anglo-Saxons who trained at Rath Melsigi (*HE* iii 27, 37; iv 3; v 9–11) in the Barrow Valley in the "southern provinces." The name as recorded by Bede, but not translated, is recognizably Gaelic but its individual elements cannot be unambiguously explained.[486] A prominent member was Wihtberht who, after an unsuccessful mission to the Frisians, returned to Ireland to work with his brothers there (*HE* v 9). An Ichtbricht (Wihtberht) is included on the guarantor list of *Cáin Adomnáin* (697) and in *Félire Óengusso*.[487] The successful Frisian mission of Willibrord (Wilbrord; 690–737) was undertaken after he had spent twelve years (678–690) training at Rath Melsigi.[488] Willibrord participated in perpetuating the growing cult of King Oswald among the Gaels (*HE* iii 13). The missions to the Frisians undertaken by those trained at Rath Melsigi suggest conduits for the transmission of traditions about the one verifiable historical event in *Beowulf*.[489]

---

482 Mac Airt and Mac Niocaill, *Annals of Ulster*, 138–39; Stokes, "Annals of Tigernach," 200 [Felinfach i 160].
483 Mac Airt and Mac Niocaill, *Annals of Ulster*, 142–43; Stokes, "Annals of Tigernach," 203 [Felinfach i 163].
484 Allott, *Alcuin of York*, 44–45 §33; Duemmler, "Alcvini Epistolae," 445–46.
485 For Bede's sense of Gaelic names, see Duncan, "Bede, Iona, and the Picts," 19–20. For the importance of the Gaelic language in his works, see Hall, "Interlinguistic Communications."
486 Bede recorded the name as one-word *Rathmelsigi*. For discussion of possible derivations for the name, see Ireland, "Where Was King Aldfrith Educated?" 59–60n175.
487 For *Cáin Adomnáin*, see Ní Dhonnchadha, "Guarantor List," 180, 193–94 §29, although she confuses him with Ecgberht. For the example in *Félire Óengusso*, see Stokes, *Félire Óengusso*, 250, December 8, who also confuses him with Ecgberht.
488 This is based on the timeframe given in Alcuin's Life of Willibrord: Albertson, *Anglo-Saxon Saints*, 280–82 §§4–5.
489 Frederick Biggs discussed the possible sources for the historical Frisian events in *Beowulf* but did not mention Willibrord: Biggs, "Frisian Raids."

**Rathmelsigi** (*HE* iii 27) *quod lingua Scottorum Rathmelsigi appellatur*
   The name is not clearly attested in Gaelic sources, but Bede's form is reasonably transparent. It appears to be made up of *ráth* (fort, rampart) + *máel* (tonsured one; devotee) + *Sige* (?) a personal name. Names formed with *máel* are common. For example, Máel Umai occurs in the genealogy with Flann Fína/Aldfrith; Máel Muru (d. 887) was a poet; Máel Inmain was one of three Gaels who set themselves adrift and were brought to the court of King Alfred in 891 (A.S. Chronicle).

**Inishboffin** (*HE* iv 4) *sermone Scottico Inisboufinde, id est Insula uitulae albae*
   Bede gives a close version of the Old Gaelic name of the island, *Inis bó finne*, and translates the name accurately, "island of the white heifer." The island is off the west coast of Co. Galway.

**Mayo** (*HE* iv 4) *qui lingua Scottorum Mag éo nominator; Muig éo consuete uocatur*
   Bede did not translate this name which means the "plain of yews," but he lists it twice, the first time using a nominative singular form of *mag* (plain), and the second time using a dative singular form *muig*, which is common in designating places. The location is on the mainland in Co. Mayo. Its full Gaelic name reveals its relationship with the Anglo-Saxon monks who continued to inhabit the site beyond the ninth century, *Mag nÉo na Saxan* (Mayo of the Saxans).

**Durrow** (*HE* iii 4) *quod a copia roborum Dearmach lingua Scottorum, hoc est Campus Roborum, cognominator*
   Bede gave a form of the Gaelic name, Dearmach, that suggests that it was influenced by the Latinized form, e.g., Codex Durmachensis (Book of Durrow), an early illuminated manuscript. Adomnán, in *Vita Columbae*, tended to use Latin forms that equated with *Campus Roborum* but once used the Gaelic form *Dairmag* (oak plain).

**Dál Ríata/Dalriada** (*HE* i 1) *qui duce Reuda de Hibernia progressi . . . a quo uidelicet duce usque hodie Dalreudini uocantur, nam lingua eorum daal partem significat*
   Dál Ríata is named after an ancestor of the sept (Ríata; Bede's *Reuda*). *Dál* has a long vowel represented by Bede's doubling of the vowel. *Dál* can mean "part, share" but also "division, tribe, sept." Two important contemporary septs in northeast Ulster are Dál nAraidi and Dál Fiatach.

**Columba/Colum Cille** (*HE* v 9) *Qui uidelicet Columba nunc a nonnullis conposito a cella et Columba nomine Columcelli uocatur.*
   Bede here indicated that Colum is the Gaelicized form of Columba "dove," and implied that *cill* (church; genitive singular *cille*) is derived from Latin *cella*. So that the Gaelicized name Colum Cille means "dove of the church."

**Figure 4.d:** Gaelic Names in Bede.

Ecgberht, the most influential person named at Rath Melsigi, functioned at the upper levels of administration (*HE* v 9). Some modern scholars see him as Bede's chief informant on Gaelic affairs.[490] Bede is our only source for Boisil of Melrose who was prior at this daughter house of Iona (*HE* iv 27–28, v 9).[491] The name Boisil is a Gaelic form of Basil of Caesarea, remembered as a father of monasticism.[492] Boisil may have been Ecgberht's mentor before he traveled to Ireland.[493] Boisil died of plague sometime between 661 and 664.[494] Ecgberht survived the plague of 664 and pledged to remain in "exile" (*HE* iii 27). The year 664 saw the triumph of the Wilfridian party at the "synod" of Whitby. Boisil later intervened through dreams to encourage Ecgberht to convert Iona to orthodox Easter traditions which, according to Bede, Ecgberht accomplished in 716 (*HE* v 9). Rath Melsigi is discussed in chapter six.

Bede recorded the "vision" of St. Fursa from a *libellus*, most likely the seventh-century Life written on the continent (*HE* iii 19).[495] Fursa had arrived in East Anglia sometime in the 630s or early 640s before proceeding to Lagny, near Chelles. He arrived from Ireland, probably Co. Louth. Four of his companions were named by Bede. It is not clear which East Anglian king Fursa first established relationships with, but his monastic site was probably Cnobheresburg.[496] The chronological sequence of the foundations of Lindisfarne and Cnobheresburg cannot be certainly established. Nevertheless, within a decade, two significant Gaelic missions were active in Anglo-Saxon Britain, one in Northumbria, the other in East Anglia.

Abbess Hild may have encountered Fursa and his *peregrini* during her sojourn in East Anglia in the 640s, when she planned to join her sister Hereswith on the continent, somewhere near Chelles (*HE* iv 23). She was, however, called back to Northumbria by Bishop Aidan sometime before 647.[497] The prominence

---

[490] Archibald Duncan suggested Ecgberht as Bede's source but placed him in Mayo: Duncan, "Bede, Iona, and the Picts," 23; Henderson, *From Durrow to Kells*, 93–97.
[491] Colgrave, *Lives of Saint Cuthbert*, 173, 175, 181, 183, 185, 187, 231. The most thorough discussion of Boisil is found in McCann, "Cuthbert and Boisil."
[492] Ireland, "Boisil"; McCann, "Cuthbert and Boisil."
[493] Kirby, "Cuthbert, Boisil."
[494] Plummer, *Venerabilis Baedae opera*, ii, xxi; Thacker, "Boisil," 452.
[495] Kenney, *Sources*, 501–2 §296; Sharpe, *Irish Saints' Lives*, 8, 34, 287–88. For comparison of passages from the *libellus*, that is *Vita Fursei*, and Bede's treatment in the *Historia*, see Picard, "Bède et ses sources irlandaises," Fig. 1 and 2; Rackham, *Transitus Beati Fursei*. For its influence on religious thought, see Hamann, "Religious Thought."
[496] Whitelock, "Church in East Anglia."
[497] The fact that she was "called back" (*reuocata*) by Bishop Aidan implies that they, too, already had a working relationship (*HE* iv 23).

of Fursa's vision in Bede's *Historia* shows that he recognized its importance for the Christian world. *Fís Fursa* (the vision of Fursa) is included in the tenth-century tale lists, discussed in chapter three.[498] Gaelic annals record Fursa's vision ca. 629.[499] After Fursa's death (ca. 649) his cult was developed at Péronne (*Perrona Scottorum*) in Picardy. The Gael Cellán from Péronne corresponded with Aldhelm whose response shows that he understood and appreciated Cellán's word play.[500] Their correspondence suggests a route by which Bede may have learned about Fursa.

Patrick Sims-Williams noted that the triad "thought, word, deed," although not originating among the Gaels, had become a characteristic of their exegesis by the second half of the seventh century. It appears in Anglo-Latin literature in Gaelic contexts. Sims-Williams noted its presence in an eighth-century Mercian private prayer-book (London, British Library, Royal 2 A. xx) where it is attributed to a Hygebald, likely the abbot of Lindsey who visited Rath Melsigi (*HE* iv 3).[501] It is also found in the Book of Cerne (Cambridge, University Library, MS Ll.1.10).[502]

Bede used the triad three times in relation to visions. It appears in the "vision" of Fursa (*HE* iii 19), but Sims-Williams noted that it was not in Bede's source, implying that it was not known to Fursa's continental hagiographer but was added by Bede himself.[503] A second vision was told to Bede by Pehthelm of Whithorn who related that during the time of King Cenred of Mercia (704–709) an unrepentant layman had a vision warning him to change his ways. The triad was part of the unsuccessful urgings in the vision (*HE* v 13).[504]

Dryhthelm returned from the dead, apparently, after a serious illness when all had assumed he had died (*HE* v 12). His vision of the afterlife has parallels with Fursa's vision. Dryhthelm's angelic guide told him that any souls that "are perfect in every word and deed and thought" went directly to heaven once they had left the body.[505] King Aldfrith used to visit Dryhthelm to hear about his vision (ca. 695). Aldfrith helped him gain admittance to Melrose as a monk. Bede's eyewitness source was Hæmgisl who later retired to Ireland to lead a more ascetic life (*HE* v 12).

---

**498** Mac Cana, *Learned Tales*, 48, 58.
**499** Mc Carthy, http://www.irish-annals.cs.tcd.ie/, s.a. 629; Mac Airt and Mac Niocaill, *Annals of Ulster*, 114–15, s.a. 627; Stokes, "Annals of Tigernach," 180 [Felinfach i 140].
**500** Howlett, *Celtic Latin Tradition*, 108–13.
**501** Sims-Williams, "Thought, Word and Deed," 94, 99.
**502** Sims-Williams, "Thought, Word and Deed," 101.
**503** Sims-Williams, "Thought, Word and Deed," 109n185.
**504** Sims-Williams, "Thought, Word and Deed," 109.
**505** "in omni uerbo et opere et cogitatione perfecti sunt": Colgrave and Mynors, *Ecclesiastical History*, 494–95; Sims-Williams, "Thought, Word and Deed," 109.

The triad "thought, word, deed" occurs in *Beowulf*, where King Hrothgar described Beowulf as being "strong in might and intelligent in mind, a wise wordspeaker."[506] Another example is where Hrothgar lamented the violent death of his counselor Æschere at the hands of Grendel's mother. Æschere is described as *rūnwita* (confidant, trusted advisor), *rǣdbora* (counselor), *eaxlġestealla* (shoulder-companion, fellow, associate).[507] Both examples in *Beowulf* are spoken by the wise, old king Hrothgar of the Scyldings, noted for a possible poetic performance in chapter one. It is not improbable that Bede and the *Beowulf* poet acquired the triad through similar channels.

Bede rarely cited his sources by name and often altered those sources so as to give the text his own stylistic imprint.[508] Emily Thornbury stated that Bede was likely to change material "for the sake of not quoting directly from a predecessor."[509] Bede's writing style has complicated the task for modern scholars of identifying his immediate sources.

An exception to this rule was Bede's use of *De locis sanctis* by Adomnán (*HE* v 15). Bede wrote his own epitome (ca. 703) and devoted two chapters in *Historia ecclesiastica* to topics from the work (*HE* v 16–17). While Bede acknowledged his debt to Adomnán, he nevertheless altered the original to suit his needs, as seen when he reduced Adomnán's original text of approximately 12,500 words to roughly 3,700 words.[510] Bede appreciated Adomnán and called him "a good and wise man with an excellent knowledge of the scriptures" (*HE* v 15).[511]

Adomnán's *De locis sanctis* discussed significant locations of the Christian world while mentioning Rome only as a transit point and in juxtaposition to the grandeur of Constantinople "metropolis of the Roman Empire" (*Romani est*

---

**506** The discussion and translation is by Orchard, *Companion to Beowulf*, 55, 218. The Old English reads, "þū eart mæġenes strang ond on mōde frōd, wīs wordcwida": Fulk, Bjork, Niles, *Klaeber's Beowulf*, 62, lines 1844–45a.
**507** Passage discussed by Orchard, *Companion to Beowulf*, 73, lines 1323b–28a.
**508** See, for example, Jones, *Saints' Lives and Chronicles*, 75; Duncan, "Bede, Iona, and the Picts," 1; Picard, "Bède et ses sources irlandaises"; and Bracken, "Virgil the Grammarian and Bede." Andy Orchard made similar observations about Bede: Orchard, *Poetic Art of Aldhelm*, 259–60.
**509** Thornbury, *Becoming a Poet*, 192. Thornbury was repeating observations made by Michael Lapidge about Bede's practice of self-editing in his metrical *Life* of St. Cuthbert: Lapidge, "Metrical *Vita S. Cuthberti*," 82.
**510** Picard, "Bède et ses sources irlandaises," §8, Fig. 4 and 5.
**511** "Erat enim uir bonus et sapiens et scientia scripturarum nobilissime instructus": Colgrave and Mynors, *Ecclesiastical History*, 506–7. For arguments that Adomnán is *magister* and Bede is *discipulus*, see O'Loughlin, *Adomnán and the Holy Places*, 188–97 (Adomnán and Bede: *Magister* and *Discipulus*).

*metropolis imperii*).⁵¹² Bede's epitome and the chapters in his *Historia* do not mention Rome at all, even in the context of Constantinople. This is surprising given the centrality of Rome in arguments against the Gaels about the Easter controversy.

In Bede's epitome, in the second last paragraph, he referred to Adomnán as "most learned in the scriptures" (eruditissimus in scripturis).⁵¹³ He used a similar phrase (*in scripturis doctissimus*) to describe both Ecgberht of Rath Melsigi (*HE* iii 4) and King Aldfrith (*HE* iv 26).⁵¹⁴ Aldfrith *sapiens* helped disseminate *De locis sanctis* throughout Northumbria after receiving it from Adomnán (ca. 687).⁵¹⁵

Peter Hunter Blair proposed that Bede's *De locis sanctis* had been dedicated to King Aldfrith, although no dedication survives.⁵¹⁶ The conclusion of Bede's epitome suggests that it was intended for someone whose secular duties might distract him from ecclesiastical study. As Bede said, "we pass along to you what should be read, praying that in all respects you take pains to temper your toil in the present age not with the leisure of idle amusement, but with a zeal for reading and prayer."⁵¹⁷ Bede was about thirty years old when he wrote and recently ordained priest by John of Beverley (*HE* iv 23 [21], v 24). Bede may have relied on Aldhelm for a precedent.⁵¹⁸ Aldhelm, in his *Epistola ad Acircium*, had encouraged Aldfrith, despite the responsibilities and "cares of secular administration," not to neglect "the mellifluous studies of the Holy Scriptures," nor to allow himself to be distracted by that which is unimportant.⁵¹⁹

Since the 1940s it has been acknowledged that Bede relied on Gaelic sources for his work in computus.⁵²⁰ A variety of computistical knowledge was studied and disseminated among Gaels from early in the seventh century.⁵²¹ As noted in chapter four, Cummian (ca. 632) named ten different computistical cycles that

---

512 Meehan, *De Locis Sanctis*, 106–7 (iii 1)," 118–19 (iii 5).
513 Fraipont, "Bedae De locis sanctis," 280; Foley and Holder, *Biblical Miscellany*, 25, xix 4 (translation). For the relationship between Adomnán and Bede, see O'Loughlin, *Adomnán and the Holy Places*, 188–97 (Adomnán and Bede: *Magister* and *Discipulus*).
514 Ireland, "Where Was King Aldfrith Educated?" 63–69.
515 Anderson and Anderson, *Life of Columba*, 178–79 (103b).
516 Hunter Blair, *World of Bede*, 185–86.
517 The original reads: "tibi legenda transmittimus, obsecrantes per omnia, ut praesentis saeculi laborem non otio lasciui torporis, sed lectionis orationisque studio tibi temperare satagas": Fraipont, "Bedae De locis sanctis," 280; Foley and Holder, *Biblical Miscellany*, 25, xix 5 (translation).
518 For discussions of Aldhelm's influence on Bede's Latin poetry, see, for example: Orchard, *Poetic Art of Aldhelm*, 254–60; Thornbury, *Becoming a Poet*, 187–91.
519 Lapidge and Herren, *Aldhelm*, 46–47; "mundanae dispensationis curis . . . melliflua divinarum studia scripturarum": Ehwald, "De Metris," 203, lines 11–13.
520 Jones, *Bedae opera*, 131; Ó Cróinín, "Irish Provenance"; Ó Cróinín, "Bede's Irish Computus"; Wallis, *Reckoning of Time*, lxxii–lxxix; Warntjes, *Munich Computus*, xlvii–li, liii–liv.
521 For a survey, see Warntjes, *Munich Computus*, cvii–clviii.

were known and studied by the Gaels at a time when most Anglo-Saxons had yet to be converted.[522] Bede had noted that the Gaels in the "southern provinces" followed Paschal customs favored by Rome, while Gaels in the northern province and the Pictish nation followed an older custom (*HE* iii 3). With the exception of Iona, both Bede and Gaelic sources are vague about which Gaelic *paruchia* were orthodox and when they became so.[523]

Bede is our source for a letter from Pope John IV, who was pope-elect at the time (ca. 640), written to certain churches in more northerly regions of the Gaels. The letter named certain bishops, priests, teachers, and abbots, without naming their establishments, making it uncertain in some cases which churches were addressed. Armagh, Clonard, Nendrum, Bangor, Moville, Devenish, and Iona were among the addressees (*HE* ii 19).[524] The implication is that these were "northern" churches that needed to change their observation of Easter. Neither Bede nor surviving Gaelic sources indicate how the churches responded to the letter. Michael Herren has argued that this letter, and others on the Easter controversy, was acquired by Bede through Gaelic sources.[525]

Three models existed for Paschal observance in the seventh-century insular world.[526] The Gaels of northern Britain, Picts, and many Britons observed Easter according to the *latercus* with lunar limits of *luna* 14 to 20.[527] They derived their scriptural authority from the Gospel of John. Throughout the seventh and eighth centuries, on the continent as well as in the insular world, two other practices vied for dominance. Victorius of Aquitaine compiled tables ca. 457 that offered a choice between Alexandrian lunar limits of *luna* 15 to 21 and an older Roman table of lunar limits of *luna* 16 to 22. The cycle translated by Dionysius Exiguus (d. 544) observed Alexandrian lunar limits of *luna* 15 to 21.[528] Both the Victorian and the Dionysiac Paschal observances relied on the Synoptic Gospels for their authority.[529] The Dionysiac tradition eventually dominated Western Christianity. It

---

522 Walsh and Ó Cróinín, *Cummian's Letter*, 82–87.
523 For a discussion of the evolution of Paschal observance among the Gaels, see Warntjes, "Victorius vs Dionysius."
524 Plummer, *Venerabilis Baedae opera*, ii, 112–13; Charles-Edwards, *Early Christian Ireland*, 277, 409; Warntjes, *Munich Computus*, lxix, lxxvii–lxxxvii.
525 Herren, "'Papal letters to the Irish'."
526 Dailey, "One Easter from Three."
527 The *latercus* was created by Sulpicius Severus in Aquitaine and introduced into the insular world in the fifth century: Mc Carthy, "Arrival of the *Latercus*."
528 In the *Historia ecclesiastica* Bede silently seems to accept both Victorian and Dionysiac reckonings as being "orthodox," while clearly favoring the Dionysiac reckoning, which eventually won out, in his own writings on time.
529 Pelteret, "Apostolic Authority."

was favored by Bede and, apparently, by Wilfrid as portrayed in *Vita Wilfridi*.[530] The two parties at the "synod" of Whitby each cited scriptural authority to back their positions which made the conflict more intractable.[531] In *Vita Wilfridi* Stephen made Bishop Colmán of Lindisfarne defend the Evangelist John "who leaned on the breast of the Lord at supper" and who was considered the Lord's most "beloved" (*VW* c. 10).[532] Bede reproduced similar arguments in his account of the "synod" of Whitby (*HE* iii 25).[533]

In Bede's prose *Vita Cuthberti* he described Boisil's death and told how Cuthbert spent the last week of Boisil's life with him reading through the Gospel of John.[534] The scene is indicative of the ethos of Melrose ca. 661–664. However, the two concentrated on "faith which worketh by love" (Galatians 5:6) and they avoided "deep matters of dispute" which referred to the Paschal controversy.[535] This story must have resonated with Cuthbert's community because the small, beautifully crafted gospel book preserved in his coffin at Durham Cathedral is a copy of John's Gospel.[536] It is even more significant that at Bede's own death, as depicted in Cuthbert's *Epistola de obitu Bedae*, one of the last projects undertaken by Bede himself was to translate part of the Gospel of John into the Old English vernacular (euangelii sancti Iohannis . . . in nostram linguam ad utilitatem ecclesiae Dei conuertit).[537] Bede implicitly argued for rapprochement between the two parties in the Easter controversy and a unity in belief.

Bede revealed Gaelic influence in his earliest writings as well. For example, his *De orthographia* (ca. 691–703),[538] in which he created a compendium of earlier grammatical works, shows that he was familiar with Virgilius Maro Grammaticus, specifically his *Epitomae*.[539] Traces of this same work by Virgilius can be sourced, at least indirectly, in etymologies of the chapter headings in Bede's later *De*

---

[530] The arguments in *Vita Wilfridi* are vague and attempt to leave the impression that they support Dionysiac observance of Easter with lunar limits of *luna* 15 to 21 without being specific: Colgrave, *Life of Bishop Wilfrid*, 20–23; Ireland, "Lutting of Lindisfarne."
[531] Pelteret, "Apostolic Authority."
[532] Colgrave, *Life of Bishop Wilfrid*, 20–21.
[533] Colgrave and Mynors, *Ecclesiastical History*, 300–301.
[534] For an illustration of a manuscript that contains both Bede's prose and verse Life of Cuthbert, see Breay and Story, *Anglo-Saxon Kingdoms*, 196–97.
[535] Colgrave, *Lives of Saint Cuthbert*, 182–83, c. 8.
[536] Breay and Story, *Anglo-Saxon Kingdoms*, 122–23.
[537] Plummer, *Venerabilis Baedae opera*, i, clxii; Colgrave and Mynors, *Ecclesiastical History*, 582–83.
[538] See dating arguments in Brown and Biggs, *Bede*, i, 63–73.
[539] Picard, "Bede and Irish Scholarship," 144–47; Picard, "Bède et ses sources irlandaises," Fig. 9 and 10.

*temporum ratione* (ca. 725).⁵⁴⁰ Virgilius's emphasis on Christ as the *logos*, the Word of God, as found at the beginning of the Gospel of John, would not have been missed by Bede.⁵⁴¹ However, it is clear that Bede sometimes overlooked or simply missed the humor intended by Virgilius.⁵⁴²

In *De temporum ratione* Bede used a text by Philippus presbyter that he acquired through Gaelic sources. The work by Philippus was known by Gaelic scholars such as the author of *De mirabilibus sacrae scripturae*, the author of *Altus Prosator* from Iona, and the *sapiens* Ailerán of Clonard.⁵⁴³ The peculiar use of the word *dodrans* by the Gaels makes this text stand out. Bede, however, understood its original usage and clarified the terminology.⁵⁴⁴

The monk Trumberht taught Bede the scriptures (*HE* iv 3). Trumberht had himself been taught by Chad, who had been among the original pupils of Bishop Aidan (*HE* iii 28). Chad later studied with Ecgberht at Rath Melsigi (*HE* iv 3). John of Beverley ordained Bede deacon (ca. 692) and then priest (ca. 703; *HE* v 24). John was one of six persons trained at Whitby who attained the position of bishop (*HE* iv 23 [21]).⁵⁴⁵ The Gaelic ethos of Whitby is clear throughout Hild's abbacy (Hild abbatissa cum suis in parte Scottorum: *HE* iii 25) and continued until the end of Abbess Ælfflæd's tenure (680–714) as shown by Gaelic characteristics of *Vita Gregorii*.⁵⁴⁶ Bede's two mentors, Trumberht and John of Beverley, both benefited from Gaelic learning.

The pedigree of Bede's education helps explain Gaelic influences in sourcing the origins of his Biblical exegesis.⁵⁴⁷ Bede's interest in exegesis can be seen in his selections from *De locis sanctis*. But this latter work also highlights his preoccupations with understanding the physical world. Faith Wallis noted that "Bede was also heir to an Irish intellectual culture that regarded the study of nature as a key to validating the miracles of the Bible (cf. *De mirabilibus sacrae scripturae*) or of

---

**540** Bracken, "Virgil the Grammarian and Bede." For an illustration of one of the manuscripts, see Breay and Joanna Story, *Anglo-Saxon Kingdoms*, 268–69.
**541** For Virgilius's emphasis, see Law, *Wisdom, Authority and Grammar*, 25, 36, 39, 73.
**542** Picard, "Bede and Irish Scholarship," 146–47; Picard, "Bède et ses sources irlandaises," §§18, 19.
**543** Richter, *Ireland and Her Neighbours*, 190, 231–33; Stevenson, "Altus Prosator," 351, 356; Breen, *Ailerani interpretatio mystica*, 181.
**544** For *dodrans*, see Wallis, *Reckoning of Time*, 270. For references to Philippus and his work, see Wallis, *Reckoning of Time*, lxxxiv, 17–18 §4 (text), 270 (discussion), 82–85 §29 (text), 307–10 (discussion).
**545** John may have been one of Bede's informants for events at Whitby such as the "synod" and for Cædmon's composition of poetry: Cronan, "Cædmon's Audience," 353, 355–56.
**546** Ireland, "Whitby *Life* of Gregory."
**547** For further examples of exegesis, see Picard, "Bède et ses sources irlandaises," Fig. 11 and 12.

penetrating God's own creative processes (cf. *De ordine creaturarum*)."[548] The influence of this latter treatise can be found in Bede's *De natura rerum* (701–703).[549] Bede's other sources for *De natura rerum* include Isidore, Pliny, Augustine, and Ambrose, but he also used the anonymous *De ordine creaturarum*.[550]

A disturbing event in Bede's life was to have been publicly accused of heresy by a member of the Wilfridian party in the presence of the bishop himself.[551] Bede described his accuser as having been in his cups and requested that his letter of exoneration, addressed to his friend Plegwine, be presented by a certain David to Bishop Wilfrid.[552] We know that Bede was personally acquainted with Wilfrid, having discussed with him the delicate topic of Queen Æthelthryth's virginity (*HE* iv 19). The fact that Wilfrid was present when Bede was accused of heresy, but did not refute the accusation, concerned Bede deeply.

According to his letter to Plegwine, Bede had been accused of denying that Christ had come into the world in the Sixth Age. Bede explained that in *De temporibus* he had relied not on Septuagint chronology but rather on Vulgate chronology derived from Jerome's translation of the Bible known as the *hebraica veritas*.[553] He had once shown *De temporibus* to a member of the Wilfridian party.[554] This event took place around 708, about five years after he had written *De temporibus*.

The letter presents technical detail to justify his arguments and choice of chronological apparatus. But it seems that his concern was based on his accuser knowing the channel of transmission for his sources. Bede used Vulgate chronology in both *De temporibus* (703) and *De temporum ratione* (725) and he most likely acquired his chronological apparatus from Gaelic chronicling traditions.[555] Among the calendrical materials obtained through Gaelic sources, and cited by Bede in

---

548 Wallis, *Reckoning of Time*, lxxxv.
549 Kendall and Wallis, *Bede*.
550 Picard, "Bede and Irish Scholarship," 139–44; Picard, "Bède et ses sources irlandaises"; Fig. 6, 7, and 8.
551 See discussion, Darby, *Bede and the End of Time*, 35–64 (The *Epistola ad Plegwinum* and Its Contemporary Setting); MacCarron, "Bede, *Annus Domini*," 121–23.
552 As Roger Ray states, "Bede's response was anything but deferential and conciliatory": Ray, "Who Did Bede Think He Was?" 21. Faith Wallis argues that "there is no contemporary evidence that the charge of heresy was taken seriously by anyone save Bede himself": Wallis, *Reckoning of Time*, xxxi. For a translation, see Wallis, *Reckoning of Time*, 405–15, §§1, 17. Nevertheless, it is clear that Bede worried about the consequences of heresy and schism in others: Holder, "Hunting Snakes"; Thacker, "Why did Heresy Matter."
553 Mc Carthy, *Irish Annals*, 138–39; MacCarron, "Bede, Irish *computistica*," 300–303.
554 Wallis, *Reckoning of Time*, 406, §3.
555 Mc Carthy, "Vulgate Chronology"; MacCarron, "Christology and the Future."

his two works on time, is the text he named *Disputatio Chori et Praetextati*.⁵⁵⁶ This text was excerpted from the *Saturnalia* of Macrobius (ca. 400) by Gaels sometime around 600 working somewhere in southeast Ireland.⁵⁵⁷

Bede's choice of chronologies was influenced by interpretations of scripture which could prove controversial.⁵⁵⁸ Bede used Isidore to structure his chronology in *De temporibus*, a source that he did not overtly acknowledge. But Bede also derived information from Iona, a center for Gaelic chronicling until ca. 740. When he diverged from the Iona Chronicle his information coincides with Isidore.⁵⁵⁹ Given the attitude of Bishop Wilfrid to the Gaels, as expressed in *Vita Wilfridi*, it is likely that many in his party reflected Wilfrid's sentiments. Bede felt the need to be cautious about his sources (*VW* c. 47).⁵⁶⁰

Northumbria could have acquired the Iona Chronicle, and other chronological and computistical texts from Iona, any time after the foundation of Lindisfarne. However, a most logical time was early in the reign of Aldfrith *sapiens* when Adomnán visited on two occasions (ca. 687). That is the time when Bede acknowledged receipt of *De locis sanctis* by Aldfrith and its dissemination throughout Northumbria.⁵⁶¹ There is every reason to believe that materials from Gaelic sources were welcomed by Aldfrith *sapiens* and made available to those in Northumbria who could profit from their use.⁵⁶² Bede's library at Wearmouth-Jarrow would have been a natural recipient of such materials.

Few Anglo-Latin or Old English scholars accept that Bede knew Adomnán's *Vita Columbae*. Bede's tendency to obscure his immediate sources makes them difficult to trace. He did, however, know the Gaelic form of Columba's name, Colum Cille, derived from *columba* (dove) and *cill* (church; from Latin *cella*), hence "dove of the church" (*HE* v 9). In his description of Iona's foundation by Columba he stated, "Some written records of his [Columba's] life and teachings are said to have been preserved by his disciples" (*HE* iii 4).⁵⁶³ The statement is

---

556 Holford-Strevens, *Disputatio Chori*.
557 Holford-Strevens, *Disputatio Chori*, 5–6.
558 MacCarron, "Bede, Irish *computistica*."
559 Mc Carthy, *Irish Annals*, 123–25.
560 Wilfrid is made to enquire, "Was I not the first . . . to root out the poisonous weeds planted by the Scots? Did I not change and convert the whole Northumbrian race to the true Easter?": Colgrave, *Life of Bishop Wilfrid*, 98–99.
561 Mc Carthy, "Vulgate Chronology."
562 For Aldfrith's learning, see Ireland, "Where Was King Aldfrith Educated?" 35–48. For Aldfrith as the channel for reception of material from Iona, see Mc Carthy, *Irish Annals*, 137–38; Mc Carthy, "Vulgate Chronology," 185–86.
563 "de cuius uita et uerbis nonnulla a discipulis eius feruntur scripta haberi": Colgrave and Mynors, *Ecclesiastical History*, 224–25.

true. The poems of Bécán mac Luigdech were reviewed in chapter two. Adomnán wrote *Vita Columbae* sometime between 688–704, but he also relied on an earlier text *De virtutibus Columbae* by Cuimmíne Find seventh abbot of Iona (657–669). Bede's statement is framed to make it appear that he does not know these records, but it is possible to identify *Vita Columbae* as a source.

The discovery of the Easter table known as the *latercus* has allowed accurate reconstruction of the chronology of the Early Gaelic annals by analyzing the ferial data as used by the annalists.[564] This discovery demonstrated that contemporaneous chronicling was taking place at Iona during the lifetime of Columba which makes those records more than a century older than the writings of Adomnán or Bede. Annalistic ferial data allowed Daniel Mc Carthy to establish 593 as the year of Columba's death.[565] The traditionally accepted date has been 597,[566] but the chronology of the Gaelic annals suggests an earlier date.[567]

The second last chapter of *Vita Columbae* presents Columba as having a vision that foretold the extension of his earthly life by four years. The extension caused Columba much sorrow since he eagerly anticipated joining the Lord. Two eyewitnesses were present, Luigne maccu Blaí and Pilu Saxo (the Saxon).[568] The four-year extension, a hagiographical necessity created by Adomnán, ensured that Columba departed the physical world on Sunday June 9, 597.[569] The long final chapter of *Vita Columbae* stresses Columba dying on a Sunday.[570] Pilu is only the second Anglo-Saxon named by Adomnán for the Iona fraternity. Having an Anglo-Saxon witness the extension of Columba's life to 597 allowed Adomnán to contrast Columba's death with Pope Gregory's mission to Canterbury in that year.[571] Although Bede did not give a specific date, his statement

---

[564] Mc Carthy, "Chronology of the Irish Annals." For a deeper discussion of Gaelic chronological traditions, see Mc Carthy, "Genesis and Evolution."
[565] Mc Carthy, "Chronology of St Columba's Life," 12 (Fig. 2), 16 (Fig. 5).
[566] Mc Carthy, "Chronology of St Columba's Life," 5 (Fig. 1).
[567] Mac Airt and Mac Niocaill, *Annals of Ulster*, 96–97 s.a. 595 (594); Stokes, "Annals of Tigernach," 160 [Felinfach i 120]. The translation of the so-called "Chronicle of Ireland" enters his *obit* at 595 but notes the discrepancies and that having Columba die on Sunday June 9 had to happen in 597, not in 595: Charles-Edwards, *Chronicle of Ireland*, i, 118. The Annals of Inisfallen seem to have followed a source that was aware of Bede: Mac Airt, *Annals of Inisfallen*, 80–81 s.a. 597.
[568] Anderson and Anderson, *Life of Columba*, 214–17, iii 22. For arguments about Adomnán's reliance on named informants, see Picard, "Bede, Adomnán," 52–54.
[569] June 9 was a Tuesday in 593: Mc Carthy, "Chronology of St Columba's Life," 20–27.
[570] Anderson and Anderson, *Life of Columba*, 216–35, iii 23.
[571] Bede's chronology for Columba places his death thirty-two years after 565, his date for the foundation of Iona, and thus at 597.

that Columba arrived in Iona in 565 and died about 32 years later means he set that date at 597 and reveals his knowledge of Adomnán's hagiography.[572]

Another indication of Bede's knowledge of Iona and its *familia* is his familiarity with Durrow in Ireland's midlands. Bede called it *Dearmach*, a form that suggests he learned the name *Dairmag* from Latinized sources. Nevertheless, he knew its meaning, literally "oak plain," and reported it as *campus roborum* (*HE* iii 4). Adomnán discussed Durrow numerous times in *Vita Columbae* but used the Gaelic form only once, while naming it in Latin several times.[573]

Bede's habit of altering texts to obscure his original sources was at work in his prose *Vita Cuthberti*. The anonymous hagiographer described how Cuthbert, while still a layman, saw the soul of Bishop Aidan being borne to heaven as if in a "globe of fire."[574] This phrase has an honorable pedigree. Gregory the Great used it in his *Dialogues*, but the topos originated with Athanasius in his Life of St. Anthony.[575] When Bede wrote his prose Life of Cuthbert he altered this phrase. There is no obvious reason why. Bede respected Bishop Aidan, as made clear in *Historia ecclesiastica* (*HE* iii 3, 5, 14–17), so the change is not intended to reflect negatively on him. Clare Stancliffe has suggested that Bede changed the phrase because Adomnán had applied it to Columba as a child in *Vita Columbae*.[576] The change offers further evidence that Bede knew Adomnán's hagiography.

Gaelic influence in Bede's prose *Vita Cuthberti* is found in scenes of Cuthbert's prayer and vigils while immersed in water. Bede elaborated those scenes from the anonymous Life in ways that reflect the practice as described in Gaelic sources and show his familiarity with the practice.[577] Confirmation comes from Bede's account of Dryhthelm and his vision (*HE* v 12). Dryhthelm performed prayers and vigils and recited psalms immersing himself in the river at Melrose, even in winter.

Bede framed the *Historia ecclesiastica* within an acknowledgement of Anglo-Saxon debt to the Gaelic world. Chapter one of book one discussed the islands of Britain and Ireland. It noted Gaelic as one of five languages spoken in Britain. Each language is devoted to setting forth knowledge of sublime truth. Bede also noted that a Gaelic kingdom, Dál Riata, existed in northwest Britain.

---

572 Mc Carthy, "Chronology of St Columba's Life," 4–6.
573 Anderson and Anderson, *Life of Columba*, 24 (*Dairmag*), 56, 88–90, 96, 162, 202.
574 Colgrave, *Lives of Saint Cuthbert*, bk. 1, c. 5 (*quasi in globo igneo*).
575 Stancliffe, "Disputed Episcopacy," 13n25; Stancliffe, "Polarity between Pastor and Solitary," 26, 43–44 (appendix).
576 Anderson and Anderson, *Life of Columba*, 184–85, iii 2; Stancliffe, "Disputed Episcopacy," 23n78.
577 Ireland, "Penance and Prayer in Water," 62–63.

Bede understood that the region was named for an eponymous ancestor, which he recorded as Reuda. He correctly noted that *dál*, which he Latinized as *daal* to show the long syllable, meant "a part" (*HE* i 1). The word can designate a sept or tribe and the lands they inhabit. Dál nAraidi and Dál Fiatach are in close proximity in northeast Ireland. Dál Riata stretched across the Irish Sea and occupied lands both in Ireland, along the Glens of Antrim, and in Britain, in the Argyll and Bute region. Its existence reinforces the concept of an Irish Sea culture-province, discussed in chapter three.

This first chapter of Bede's *Historia* included "folkloric" information about Ireland that Bede may have known from his youth. The island was abundant in "milk and honey," as well as fish, birds, and deer for hunting. Winters are milder in Ireland so that hay need not be cut in summer to feed to cattle in winter, nor need the cattle be kept in stables. He also noted that snakes cannot live there. In fact, if a serpent were brought from Britain to Ireland, it would die once it caught the scent of the air. Anything produced in Ireland was effective against poison. He noted that snake bite could be cured by drinking water that contained scrapings from manuscripts produced in Ireland (*HE* i 1).

A concluding theme of *Historia ecclesiastica* is the repayment to the Gaels of the debt incurred by the Anglo-Saxons for having brought them the faith. For Bede this took the form of Ecgberht overseeing Iona's adoption of orthodox Easter observance in 716 (*HE* iii 4, 27; v 9, 22, 24). Ecgberht, aged twenty-five, was living in "exile" at Rath Melsigi during the plague of 664 (*HE* iii 27). He died in 729 at the age of ninety having spent his entire adult life among the Gaels (*HE* v 22). Bede referred to Ecgberht as *sanctus* at his death in the historical recapitulation (*HE* v 24). Rath Melsigi and Iona are the only two locations named for where Ecgberht had lived and worked. Bede portrayed Ecgberht as the agent by which the Anglo-Saxon debt was repaid to Iona, but Ecgberht was himself a product of Gaelic learning. Gaelic annals acknowledge the conversion of Iona in 716 but do not credit Ecgberht or any specific person.[578]

Bede began his *Historia ecclesiastica* with "folkloric" anecdotes about Ireland, its climate, and environmental virtues. He concluded by claiming that a Gaelic-trained Anglo-Saxon from Rath Melsigi converted Iona to orthodoxy thus repaying the Anglo-Saxon debt. But the facts are plain. Bede's purpose was to explain the debt owed to the Gaels.

---

[578] Mac Airt and Mac Niocaill, *Annals of Ulster*, 172–73 s.a. 716.4; Stokes, "Annals of Tigernach," 225 [Felinfach i 185]. Ecgberht is not named in the Gaelic annals in 716 at the conversion of Iona to the orthodox Easter. Only Bede provides that information. Ecgberht is named in the Gaelic annals at his death in Iona in 729.

# Chapter Five
# The Ethnic Mix of Anglo-Saxon Empire

A historical survey of the late sixth through early eighth centuries reveals that there was never a time when kings of Northumbria did not interact with their Brittonic, Pictish, and Gaelic neighbors. While their expansionist policies meant that military conflict was how Anglo-Saxons frequently confronted their neighbors, there are examples of alliance, refuge, and intermarriage. King Edwin's interactions with Britons, for example, have been understated. More tellingly, during the crucial century from 635 to 735, Northumbria was ruled for fifty-five years by fluent Gaelic-speaking kings. Their contributions to the success of Gaelic clerics and missionaries working throughout Britain, and for Anglo-Saxon students benefiting from free education in Ireland, should not be underestimated. Where Anglo-Saxon hegemony was enforced on Britons, Picts, and Gaels, their influence still manifested as a substratum whose languages, social customs, and cultural habits did not instantly disappear because of Anglo-Saxon rule. Where Gaels were active in Britain as clerics and missionaries, their influence would appear as a superstratum through their direct input, and through the high-ranking Anglo-Saxons that they had trained. Gaelic-speaking kings Oswald, Oswiu, and Aldfrith were bilingual, bicultural influencers.

Bede, in his *Historia ecclesiastica*, is concerned with kingship and aristocratic power. "[I]t is kings and their *duces, fideles, milites,* or *viri nobilissimi* who fight the wars that are the main secular political activities in his narrative."[1] Bede named seven Anglo-Saxon kings who ruled over *imperia* by which he implied that their rule subsumed diverse peoples, whether other Anglo-Saxon kingdoms of Southumbria or Northumbria, or the other peoples of Britain: Picts, Britons, or Gaels (*HE* ii 5). As rulers of an *imperium* each of these seven kings was an *imperator*. In Old English each came to be called a *brytenwalda* (wide ruler) or a *bretwalda* (ruler of Britain).[2] Bede, of course, did not use either of these two terms. They are found in later texts such as the *Anglo-Saxon Chronicles*.

---

[1] Wickham, *Framing the Early Middle Ages*, 343. For a survey of kingship in Britain and Ireland in this period, see Yorke, "Kings and Kingship."
[2] Wormald, "Bede, the *Bretwaldas*"; Fanning, "Bede, *Imperium*"; Yorke, "Origins of Overlordship"; Higham, *Ecgfrith*, 17–24.

Rule over various peoples must be understood in the context of Britain's ethnic diversity.³ As discussed in chapter one, the Britons and Gaels preserved rich vernacular literatures that included the practice of encomium. In their interrelationships with Britons, Gaels, and Picts the Anglo-Saxons must have learned something of these neighboring poetic traditions which paralleled their own.⁴

A salient feature for four fifths of the seventh century is the constant encroachment of Anglo-Saxon kingdoms upon the territories of their multi-ethnic neighbors.⁵ Rosemary Cramp argued that similarities in social organization during this period "facilitated the interchange of members of ruling groups by exile, hostage taking, and intermarriage."⁶ Exile and intermarriage will be prominent in the following discussion.

For more than fifty years, a full half of the seventh century, Northumbria was ruled by Gaelic-speaking kings: Oswald (634–642), Oswiu (642–670), and Aldfrith (685–704).⁷ All three were bilingual in Old English and Old Gaelic, and Aldfrith *sapiens* knew Latin. For five decades kings familiar with Gaelic traditions, customs, laws, and lore oversaw the development of Northumbria. There was ample opportunity for exchange of ideas and practice as transmitted through vernacular as well as Latinate sources.

The first four *imperatores* named by Bede were Southumbrians and the first two of these, Ælle of the South Saxons and Ceawlin of the West Saxons, cannot be firmly placed in time or location. With Æthelberht of Kent (d. ca. 616) we are on firmer ground. He had a Christian wife from the continent and was ruling when Gregorian missionaries arrived at Canterbury. He was baptized by them and is noted by Bede as the first Christian king among the Anglo-Saxons (*HE* i 26).⁸ The fourth imperial king was Rædwald of the East Angles (d. ca. 625), probably during the time of the Sutton Hoo ship burial. Shortly after his death we can mark the arrivals in East Anglia of both Bishop Felix (ca. 630–ca. 647) from Francia and the

---

3 For an overview of Britain before the period under discussion, see Yorke, "Britain and Ireland." For changing views on contacts between Anglo-Saxons and Britons, see Lucy, "From Pots to People"; Thomas, Stumpf, and Härke, "Apartheid-like Social Structure."
4 The inter-ethnic mix of Mercians and Britons is attested throughout the seventh century: Brady, *Welsh Borderlands*, 29–32, 53–59.
5 Aldfrith apparently did not attempt to expand the territory of Northumbria but, rather, ruled well the various peoples under his authority.
6 Cramp, "Whithorn," 2. For the ethnic and social mix, see Thornton, "Communities and Kinship."
7 These three kings had been educated among the Gaels. For a survey of Gaels in Bede's *Historia ecclesiastica*, see McCann, "*Plures de Scottorum regione*."
8 Bede painted a picture of conversion and a Christian kingdom in Kent that may not have been as straightforward as he presents: North, *Heathen Gods*, 313–21. Alex Woolf discussed the complexities of Anglo-Saxon ethnic origins: Woolf, "Imagining English Origins."

Gaelic *peregrinus* Fursa and his companions from Ireland. The three remaining *imperatores* named by Bede were Northumbrians: Edwin, Oswald, and Oswiu.

The Britons were divided into several groupings and did not constitute a unified whole on the island of Britain.[9] There were major populations in Devon, Cornwall, Strathclyde, Cumbria, Lancashire, and Wales, with lesser populations in remote areas of the Yorkshire Moors and Dales, and throughout the Pennines. Recorded contacts between Britons and Anglo-Saxons tended toward hostility, though not consistently. The contacts occurred at every social level and in various capacities, most thoroughly recorded in Anglo-Saxon sources between Britons and their Mercian allies (*HE* ii 14, 20; iii 1, 9, 18, 21, 24) and West Saxon neighbors, as described in the Laws of Ine in this latter case.[10] The example of Mercians allying with Britons shows the unrealized potential for cooperation (e.g., *HE* ii 20). The most sustained contacts occurred when Anglo-Saxons conquered Brittonic territories (e.g., *VW* c. 17). Thus, the major avenue for influence by the Britons on the Anglo-Saxons is as a large substratum in recently acquired lands.[11] Anglo-Saxon contact with the Picts, primarily in what is now eastern Scotland, would have been of a similarly confrontational nature (e.g., *VW* c. 19).

By contrast, contacts between the Gaels and Anglo-Saxons during this period were more culturally interactive. While Anglo-Saxons certainly waged war against Gaelic kingdoms in Britain (e.g., *HE* i 34), the prevailing productive intercourse between the two was through the Gaelic mission from Iona into Northumbria and from Ireland into other regions of Anglo-Saxon Britain.[12] Since many early Anglo-Saxon converts were among the nobility, Gaelic influence in Anglo-Saxon society would tend to appear as a superstratum among the higher social ranks. It would have profound effects on intellectual and cultural development as noted for the kings Oswald, Oswiu, and Aldfrith *sapiens*.

The poetic traditions of both Britons and Gaels with regard to praising the deeds of ancestors and contemporary chieftains were potential sources of influence on the Anglo-Saxons' own traditions of praise and encomium.

---

**9** For an overview of how these groups transitioned through the post-Roman period and survived intact into the seventh century, see Charles-Edwards, *Wales and the Britons*, 75–115; White, "Managing Transition."
**10** For a facing page translation, see Attenborough, *Laws of the Earliest English Kings*, 36–61.
**11** Loyn, "Conversion of the English."
**12** Edmonds, *Gaelic Influence*, 5–10.

## Ida (ca. 547)

In his historical recapitulation, not in the body of his narrative, Bede noted that King Ida, from whom the Northumbrian royal family descends, began to reign in 547 for twelve years (*HE* v 24).[13] The *Historia Brittonum* stated that Ida joined Bernicia (Berneich) and Deira (Deur) into a single country and named the stronghold Din Guayrdi,[14] which the Gaels called Dún Guaire and the Anglo-Saxons Bamburgh, named from Bebba, one of King Æthelfrith's wives (*HE* iii 6).[15]

In the context of the Britons' wars against the pagan Anglo-Saxons five poets are named, as discussed in chapter one.[16] Subsequent paragraphs of *Historia Brittonum* tell how the sons of Ida fought against such Brittonic heroes as Urien Rheged, Rhydderch Hen, Gwallawg, and Morcant, and that these struggles continued into the time of the Gregorian mission to Kent.[17]

One son of Ida, Theodoric, fought against Urien Rheged and his sons with martial fortunes shifting back and forth between the opposing sides. At one time Urien blockaded the Anglo-Saxons on the island of Lindisfarne for three days and nights, but Urien was assassinated by a faction on his own side out of jealousy during this campaign.[18] For the Britons, the sixth and early seventh centuries constitute a legendary heroic age lauded by named poets. The poems attributed to Taliesin and Aneirin, which depict the conflict against encroaching Anglo-Saxons, must be kept in mind when analyzing Anglo-Saxon traditions of a heroic past.

## Æthelfrith (ca. 592–617)

Another Northumbrian, Æthelfrith, ravaged the Britons more than any previous Anglo-Saxon king, according to Bede (*HE* i 34),[19] who implied that he be compared

---

[13] Charles-Edwards, *Wales and the Britons*, 343–59. It is sometimes argued that a unified Northumbria can be traced to the Roman presence: Wood, "Roman Origins"; Hall, "A gente Anglorum appellatur."

[14] Morris, *Nennius*, 36, 78 §61. Another Brittonic form of the name is Din Guoaroy: Morris, *Nennius*, 38, 79 §63.

[15] Morris, *Nennius*, 38, 79 §63.

[16] Morris, *Nennius*, 37, 78 §62.

[17] These events coincide with Columbanus's early career: Ó Cróinín, "Political Background," 63. For notes on interpreting these early events, see Clancy, "The Kingdoms of the North," 161–65.

[18] Morris, *Nennius*, 38, 79 §63.

[19] "qui plus omnibus Anglorum primatibus gentem uastauit Brettonum": Colgrave and Mynors, *Ecclesiastical History*, 116–17.

to Saul, king of Israel, except that he was "ignorant of the divine religion" (quod diuinae erat religionis ignarus: *HE* i 34). Bede wrote about his conquests and referred to him as "most eager for glory," a phrase appropriate to encomiastic verse and paralleled in vernacular usage.[20] Bede apparently viewed Æthelfrith as an instrument of divine retribution.

During Æthelfrith's reign the Gregorian mission was established at Canterbury in Kent. According to Bede, Archbishop Augustine and his followers summoned a conference with Brittonic bishops and learned men at Augustine's Oak (*Augustinæs Āc*) on the borders of the Hwicce and the West Saxons, ostensibly to encourage cooperation between them as long as the Britons would recognize the supremacy of the mission from Rome (*HE* ii 2). A second meeting was called and seven bishops and many learned men (*uiri doctissimi*) of the Britons came, chiefly from the monastery at Bangor-is-y-coed (North Wales). However, the Britons perceived Augustine's and his followers' attitude as one of arrogance based on the advice of an anchorite who was "holy and prudent" (uirum sanctum ac prudentem: *HE* ii 2). When the Britons refused to accept Augustine as their archbishop he berated them and declared that they would suffer vengeance at the hands of their enemies.

A number of years later, but not later than ca. 616, Æthelfrith defeated the Britons and slaughtered a large number of monks from Bangor-is-y-coed at what Bede called the Battle of Chester (*Legacaestir*; *Caerlegion*). He reported that a large number of monks had gathered to pray for the success of the Brittonic forces and Æthelfrith, therefore, ordered that the monks be attacked and hundreds were slain (*HE* ii 2). Thus, an indeterminate number of years after Augustine's death, his prophetic threat was carried out against the Brittonic ecclesiastics by the pagan Æthelfrith.

Several years before the Battle of Chester a king of Dál Riata, Áedán mac Gabráin, moved to check Æthelfrith's successes against the Britons and expansion of Anglo-Saxon territory (*HE* i 34).[21] Substantial Gaelic lore developed around these events. According to Bede, Áedán was defeated by Æthelfrith and had to flee with a few survivors from the Battle of Degsastan, ca. 603.[22] Gaelic sources put

---

**20** "gloriae cupidissimus": Colgrave and Mynors, *Ecclesiastical History*, 116. Beowulf is described as *lofgeornost* (most eager for praise): Fulk, Bjork, Niles, *Klaeber's Beowulf*, 109, line 3182b.
**21** For arguments that Bede confused his sources on these two events, see Duncan, "Bede, Iona, and the Picts," 17–18.
**22** Edmonds, *Gaelic Influence*, 33–35. These events overlap with Columbanus's career: Ó Cróinín, "Political Background," 60–62.

the battle a few years earlier,[23] and Áedán's death a few years later.[24] The Annals of Tigernach report that Áedán died at the age of seventy-four after a reign of thirty-eight years.[25] Bede reported the death of Æthelfrith's brother, Theobald, and the loss of all his army (*HE* i 34).[26] The Annals of Tigernach state that Æthelfrith's brother was slain by Máel Umai *rígféinnid* (royal champion).[27] Máel Umai was of the Cenél nÉogain[28] and died ca. 610.[29] A tale title about his adventures, and *Compert Mongáin*, a tale from *Cín Dromma Snechtai*, both discussed in chapter three, revolve around the wars of Áedán mac Gabráin against the Anglo-Saxons.[30]

Dál Ríata was home to two Anglo-Saxons in the late sixth century. In *Vita Columbae* they are portrayed as eyewitnesses when St. Columba experienced angelic apparitions. Genereus *saxo*, a baker at Iona, was present when the saint observed the soul of a virtuous woman ascend to heaven.[31] When Columba received the divine revelation that he must remain in the flesh for four more years Pilu *saxo* was present.[32]

Acha, daughter of King Ælle of Deira, was one of Æthelfrith's wives. She was sister of Edwin, a rival of Æthelfrith who succeeded him to the Northumbrian throne. Bede noted that King Oswald, son of Æthelfrith and Acha, united the two Northumbrian kingdoms, Bernicia and Deira, in his bloodlines (*HE* iii 6). Edwin was forced to spend Æthelfrith's reign in exile seeking refuge in various kingdoms throughout Britain (*HE* ii 12).

---

[23] Mc Carthy, http://www.irish-annals.cs.tcd.ie/, s.a. 600: Mac Airt and Mac Niocaill, *Annals of Ulster*, 98–99; Stokes, "Annals of Tigernach," 163 [Felinfach, i, 123].

[24] Mc Carthy, http://www.irish-annals.cs.tcd.ie/, s.a. 606: Mac Airt and Mac Niocaill, *Annals of Ulster*, 104–5; Stokes, "Annals of Tigernach," 167 [Felinfach, i, 127].

[25] Stokes, "Annals of Tigernach," 167 [Felinfach, i, 127].

[26] Bede is our only source for Theodbald whose appearance in the Anglo-Saxon Chronicle is drawn from Bede.

[27] Stokes, "Annals of Tigernach," 163 [Felinfach, i, 123].

[28] O'Brien, *Corpus genealogiarum Hiberniae*, 135 (140 a 37–40). He was related to Bishop Fínán of Lindisfarne, Cenn Fáelad *sapiens*, and Aldfrith *sapiens*: Ireland, "Irish Genealogies," 69, 74.

[29] Mc Carthy, http://www.irish-annals.cs.tcd.ie/, s.a. 610: Mac Airt and Mac Niocaill, *Annals of Ulster*, 104–5; Stokes, "Annals of Tigernach," 169 [Felinfach, i, 129].

[30] White, *Compert Mongáin*, 71, 78–79.

[31] Anderson and Anderson, *Life of Columba*, 196–97, iii 10.

[32] Anderson and Anderson, *Life of Columba*, 214–17, iii 22. This is the context in which Adomnán changes the *obit* of Columba from 593 to 597 with the latter date being reported by Bede and suggesting his knowledge of *Vita S. Columbae*: Mc Carthy, "Chronology of St Columba's Life."

## Edwin (ca. 617–633)

The defeat and death of the Bernician Æthelfrith allowed the Deiran Edwin (*Eadwine*) to achieve rule over Northumbria. Edwin was son of Ælle, made famous by the comment attributed to Pope Gregory about "angelic" Anglian slave boys on sale in Rome (*HE* ii 1).[33] Bede depicted an imperial reign for Edwin once he gained power. Edwin was the first Northumbrian king to convert and be baptized, an achievement credited to Paulinus of the Gregorian mission. His conversion is first told in *Vita Gregorii* written ca. 704–714 (*Vita Gregorii*, c. 16). Edwin's conversion is elaborately described by Bede (*HE* ii 9–13). Despite the versions in Anglo-Saxon sources for Edwin's conversion by Paulinus, there is evidence for his previous exposure to Christianity through Britons.

Edwin endured political exile among various hosts throughout Britain during the reign of his rival Æthelfrith. Once Edwin came to power Æthelfrith's seven named sons,[34] along with other Anglo-Saxon nobles, were forced into exile among the Gaels and Picts. Their exile included sojourns in Ireland, not just northern Britain, for some of Æthelfrith's offspring and those who joined them (*HE* iii 1).[35] Two sons of Æthelfrith, Oswald and Oswiu, ensured that indelible Gaelic cultural traits were woven into the fabric of Northumbrian society after their political exiles enforced by Edwin.

### Exile among the Britons

Edwin spent much of his youth in political exile among a variety of hosts throughout Britain during Æthelfrith's reign (*HE* ii 12).[36] Bede named only an Anglo-Saxon

---

[33] Colgrave, *Life of Gregory*, 90–91, c. 9; Colgrave and Mynors, *Ecclesiastical History*, 132–35. See discussion in Ireland, "Whitby *Life* of Gregory," 147–53.

[34] Some sources name the seven brothers: Morris, *Nennius*, 36, 77 (*Historia Brittonum* §57); Plummer, *Chronicles Parallel*, s.a. 617, version E; Swanton, *Anglo-Saxon Chronicles*, 24 s.a. 617, version E. These two sources do not agree in all of the names of the seven brothers.

[35] Moisl, "Bernician Royal Dynasty." Bede said that the sons of Æthelfrith spent time "among the Irish and Picts" (apud Scottos siue Pictos exulabant): Colgrave and Mynors, *Ecclesiastical History*, 212–13. Eanfrith spent time among the Picts. His son Talorcan eventually became king of the Picts in mid 650s: Kirby, *Earliest English Kings*, 87, 94 and notes; Charles-Edwards, *Early Christian Ireland*, 302. The Annals of Ulster enter Talorcan's *obit* at 657: Mac Airt and Mac Niocaill, *Annals of Ulster*, 130–31. Aldfrith's maternal background shows that Oswiu spent time among the Cenél nÉogain: Ireland, "Irish Genealogies," 68–69, 72–73.

[36] Bede says, "he [Edwin] wandered secretly as a fugitive for many years through many places and kingdoms" (per diuersa occultus loca uel regna multo annorum tempore profugus uagaretur)

host for Edwin, Rædwald (d. ca. 625) of East Anglia (*HE* ii 12).[37] Bede portrayed Edwin as under threat of death from Æthelfrith before Rædwald saved him by defeating and killing Æthelfrith in battle on the River Idle (616; *HE* ii 12). Both the anonymous *Vita Gregorii* and Bede's account portray Æthelfrith as urging Rædwald to have Edwin killed while under his protection, offering Rædwald monetary reward (*HE* ii 12).[38] Bede made Edwin exclaim in his exile, "Whither am I now to fly seeing that I have been wandering for long years throughout all the kingdoms of Britain, trying to avoid the snares of my enemies?" (*HE* ii 12).[39]

It is significant that Edwin said the "kingdoms of Britain" and did not specify Anglo-Saxon kingdoms only. A body of evidence indicates relationships with Britons for Edwin. He must have been fostered, as part of his exile, at the Brittonic court of King Cadfan on Anglesey. Bede claimed that Edwin came to control territory that originally belonged to Cadfan (*HE* ii 5, 9). Such evidence helps explain why Cadwallon, Cadfan's son, became a deadly rival of Edwin and the Anglo-Saxons generally (*HE* ii 20, iii 1).[40]

With the death of Æthelfrith Edwin was able to control a vast area of Britain, not just Northumbria. Bede said that he ruled all peoples in Britain and the islands between Ireland and Britain, except for the Kentish folk (*HE* ii 5, 9). Bede used the term Mevanian islands, that is Man and Anglesey, to describe some of the Brittonic territory formerly ruled by Cadfan and now controlled by Edwin.[41]

Bede described the safety of Edwin's "empire" by stating that a woman could carry her new-born child from coast to coast without fear (*HE* ii 16).[42] Bede's description owes more to idealized stereotypes than to reality (*in prouerbio dicitur*).

---

due to the persecution of Æthelfrith, until he finally found refuge with Rædwald: Colgrave and Mynors, *Ecclesiastical History*, 176–77. Bede's description is consistent with Edwin spending time in exile among Britons as well as Anglo-Saxons.

**37** Colgrave, *Life of Gregory*, 98–101, c. 16; Colgrave and Mynors, *Ecclesiastical History*, 174–83.

**38** Colgrave, *Life of Gregory*, 98–101, c. 16; Colgrave and Mynors, *Ecclesiastical History*, 174–83. All three kings involved are evidently still pagan, but Rædwald is honorable enough to refuse to be brided.

**39** "Quo enim nunc fugiam, qui per omnes Brittaniae prouincias tot annorum temporumque curriculis uagabundus hostium uitabam insidias?": Colgrave and Mynors, *Ecclesiastical History*, 178–79.

**40** Edmonds, *Gaelic Influence*, 35–37.

**41** "Meuanias Brettonum insulas": *HE* ii 5. Bede even describes these islands belonging to the Britons and their relative sizes: *HE* ii 9.

**42** Charles-Edwards said that Bede may have intended a comparison between Edwin's reign and imperial Roman rule: Charles-Edwards, *Wales and the Britons*, 390.

The notion of ruling from coast to coast (wave to wave) is also found in Early Gaelic law.[43] There are suggestions from the Gaelic tale lists and annal entries that not all was peaceful during Edwin's reign. A tale title about a military expedition led by Fiachnae mac Báetáin to Bamburgh (Dún Guaire), supported by an annal entry ca. 623, were discussed in chapter three.[44]

Bede repeated the motif of the king placing bronze drinking cups at springs in the countryside for the refreshment of travelers. Out of respect for him no one dared abuse Edwin's liberality by stealing the cups (*HE* ii 16). The motif was also attested in "Cormac's Glossary." The obscure word *ána* was described as a silver cup (*stáb*) left at a well or spring for use by passersby. These vessels were placed for public use as a way of testing adherence to the king's laws.[45] A quatrain in the entry claims that the practice is as old as Fiachu Muillethan, a legendary contemporary of Cormac mac Airt of the third or fourth centuries, whose lineage produced the Éoganacht dynasties of Munster.[46]

Contrary to Bede's depiction of Edwin's peaceful *imperium* (*HE* ii 16), Brittonic poetic records describe Edwin as ungrateful, deceitful, and avaricious having been fostered by King Cadfan of Anglesey amongst a Christian people.[47] *Trioedd Ynys Prydein* (Triads of the Island of Britain) describe Edwin as "one of the three chief oppressions of Môn [Anglesey] nurtured therein" (vn o Deir Prif Ormes Mon a uagwyt yndi).[48] Fosterage or political exile in Anglesey at Cadfan's court fits easily in Bede's description of Edwin's wanderings throughout

---

**43** Etchingham, "Early Medieval Irish History," 131; Bhreathnach, "Temoria," 85; Ó Cathasaigh, "Aspects of Identity and Memory," 212–13; Breatnach, "Law and Literature," 217.
**44** An entry in the Annals of Ulster s.a. 623 reads, "Expugnatio Ratho Guali la Fiachna m. Baetain" (The storming of Ráth Guala [Dún Guaire?] by Fiachnae mac Báetáin): Mac Airt and Mac Niocaill, *Annals of Ulster*, 112–13; Stokes, "Annals of Tigernach," 176 [Felinfach i 136]. Both annals contain an accompanying quatrain. Since Ráth Guala has never been identified, some have suggested it is intended for Dún Guaire: Edmonds, *Gaelic Influence*, 36. If this is accurate, it contradicts Bede's assertion that the battle at Degsastan ca. 603 represents the last time a Gaelic king in Britain dared wage war against the Anglo-Saxons (*HE* i 34).
**45** "ba ō rīgaib dobertis forra do promad a cāna": Meyer, "*Sanas Cormaic*," 5–6 §48; Flower, *Irish Tradition*, 53–54.
**46** Byrne, *Irish Kings*, 67, 200, 291.
**47** Anglesey was the royal seat of King Cadfan whose son, Cadwallon, became an implacable foe of Edwin and the Anglo-Saxons generally (*HE* ii 20). In her introduction Bromwich remarked that the normally unreliable Geoffrey of Monmouth accurately reflected Brittonic tradition when he stated that Edwin and Cadwallon were raised as foster-brothers and that Cadwallon was forced into exile in Ireland by Edwin: Bromwich, *Trioedd Ynys Prydein*, xcvii–xcviii. See also Plummer, *Venerabilis Baedae opera*, ii, 93; Cook, "Oswy and Cædmon's Hymn," 72n2; Rowland, *Early Welsh Saga Poetry*, 123; Charles-Edwards, *Wales and the Britons*, 345.
**48** Bromwich, *Trioedd Ynys Prydein*, 47–48. See further, Brady, *Welsh Borderlands*, 27–28.

Britain. There is much in Edwin's biography to support extensive relationships with Britons.[49] The later triads and poetic records help explain the fierce rivalry between Edwin and Cadwallon, Cadfan's son.[50] By contrast, Bede portrayed Cadwallon as an enemy of Northumbria who had "rebelled" against Edwin (*HE* ii 20), without providing other explanations for their rivalry.[51]

Edwin's dealings with Britons involved the kingdom of Elmet (Modern Welsh *Elfed*), in the Leeds area, which brought him into contact with the infant Hild, who became abbess of Whitby. Hild was born ca. 614. Her father, Hereric, a relative of Edwin's, was living in exile in Elmet under the protection of the Brittonic king Ceredig (*HE* iv 23).[52] Bede reported that Hereric was poisoned but did not say by whom (*HE* iv 23).[53] The *Historia Brittonum* states that Edwin occupied Elmet and expelled Ceredig.[54] The *Annales Cambriae* note that Ceredig died in 616 without giving a cause of death.[55] Hild was a child of two or three years of age when her father was poisoned and Ceredig was expelled by Edwin. Hild was apparently adopted by Edwin's retinue because she was baptized ca. 627

---

49 Rowland, *Early Welsh Saga Poetry*, 127–29; Koch, *Gododdin of Aneirin*, xx–xxiii, xxxiii–xxxiv; Charles-Edwards, *Wales and the Britons*, 345, 389–90.
50 Koch, *Gododdin of Aneirin*, xx–xxiii; Brady, *Welsh Borderlands*, 34–36. For translations of Brittonic poems celebrating Cadwallon as a warrior against the Anglo-Saxon enemy, with one poem, *Moliant Cadwallon*, specifically naming Edwin as an opponent, see Koch, *Celtic Heroic Age*, 372–77. For arguments against the early date of this poem, see Woolf, "Caedualla *Rex Brettonum*," 15–18. These poems were first edited in modern Welsh translations by Gruffydd, "Canu Cadwallon."
51 "rebellauit": Colgrave and Mynors, *Ecclesiastical History*, 202. Bede's choice of verbs reflects his political bias, making Edwin the rightful ruler. Brittonic poetic tradition portrays Edwin in antithetical terms.
52 Koch, *Gododdin of Aneirin*, xxxiii–xxxiv. Hild's father Hereric seems to have been living among the British of Elmet in a political exile much as Edwin had lived among the Britons on Anglesey and with Rædwald in East Anglia during the reign of Æthelfrith.
53 "Hereric exularet sub rege Brettonum Cerdice, ubi ut ueneno periit": Colgrave and Mynors, *Ecclesiastical History*, 410.
54 Morris, *Nennius*, 38, 79 §63 (*Historia Brittonum*); Rowland, *Early Welsh Saga Poetry*, 100–101. Colgrave and Mynors speculate that Edwin conquered Elmet in revenge for Hereric's being poisoned, but given the nature of dynastic rivalries, it seems as likely that Hereric had been poisoned on Edwin's orders. One need only recall the rivalry between Æthelfrith and Edwin, and how Æthelfrith tried to persuade Rædwald of the East Angles either to have Edwin killed when he sought refuge in East Anglia or hand him over (*HE* ii 12). Æthelfrith's own sons had to seek refuge among the Gaels and Picts during Edwin's reign implying that their lives would have been endangered had they remained in Northumbria. Edwin's conquest of Brittonic Elmet fits in with his gaining control over the Mevanian Islands once controlled by Cadfan (*HE* ii 5, 9).
55 Morris, *Nennius*, 46, 86.

by Bishop Paulinus, along with King Edwin, at approximately thirteen years of age (*HE* iv 23).

Bishop Paulinus first came to Edwin's court in 625 when he accompanied Æthelburh, daughter of the Christian king Æthelberht of Kent, who was betrothed to Edwin (*HE* ii 9).[56] Since Edwin was described as a pagan, despite having lived among Christian Britons, the marriage agreement stipulated that Æthelburh and her retinue be allowed to practice their Christian faith (*HE* ii 9).[57]

When Cadwallon killed Edwin (633), Bishop Paulinus fled back to Kent. James the deacon was left in charge of York and was credited with good works in Paulinus's absence (*HE* ii 20). Brittonic poetic tradition is explicit that York was burned by Cadwallon.[58] Bede said only that Cadwallon and Penda ravaged vast areas of Northumbria, but did not refer to York as having been burned (*HE* ii 14, iii 1). Whether or not York was burned, Paulinus left the region to the deacon James and occupied the vacant bishopric at Rochester, remaining there until his death in 644 (*HE* ii 20).

Edwin died at Hatfield (Hæthfelth; *HE* ii 20) in 633, at the age of forty-eight, fighting the allied forces of Cadwallon and the pagan Mercian Penda.[59] Edwin and his army suffered a crushing defeat in the battle. His death, along with his two sons, marked the end of the Deiran line as primary players in Northumbrian royal politics.[60] Bede described Cadwallon, despite the acknowledged presence of his pagan Mercian allies, as "meaning to wipe out the whole English nation from the land of Britain" (*HE* ii 20).[61] Brittonic tradition, on the other hand, implies that Edwin had turned against those who had fostered him in his exile.

With Edwin's death his wife Æthelburh fled with their children, first to Kent, then ultimately to Dagobert,[62] king of the Franks, since he was her kin and protector (*HE* ii 20).[63] Eanflæd, a daughter of Edwin, was baptized by Bishop Paulinus

---

[56] Edwin had a previous marriage to a daughter of the king of the Mercians.
[57] For the possibility of paganism in Kent, Essex, and among East Angles, see North, *Heathen Gods*, 312–23.
[58] For example, see translation of *Moliant Cadwallon*, lines 36–37: Koch, *Celtic Heroic Age*, 376; and also Koch, *Four Welsh Poems*, 161–229.
[59] The *Annales Cambriae* and *Historia Brittonum* name the site as Meicen: Morris, *Nennius*, 37, 78 §61 (*Historia Brittonum*), 46, 86 s.a. 630 (*Annales Cambriae*).
[60] *Historia Brittonum* states that his two sons died with him in the battle and their deaths marked the end of his line: Morris, *Nennius*, 37, 78 §61; Yorke, *Kings and Kingdoms*, 169.
[61] "ac totum genus Anglorum Brittaniae finibus erasurum se esse deliberans": Colgrave and Mynors, *Ecclesiastical History*, 204.
[62] His own son, Dagobert II, would be sent into exile in Ireland and, after twenty years, returned to Francia by Wilfrid; Picard, "Church and Politics."
[63] Wallace-Hadrill, *Historical Commentary*, 85.

along with her father when she was still an infant (ca. 627), and was raised in Kent (*HE* iii 15). Eanflæd became the wife of King Oswiu recognized by Bede. The *Vita Gregorii* explains how Edwin's bones came to be buried at Whitby in the time of abbess Ælfflæd, daughter of Oswiu and Eanflæd.[64]

The early seventh century was a time of frequent Anglo-Saxon contact with Britons, often through aggressive attempts to subdue them and take their lands. Unassimilated Britons can be identified throughout territories allegedly controlled by Edwin. His fosterage on Anglesey among Britons helps explain the bitter rivalry with Cadwallon as reflected in the Brittonic poetic traditions, and as noted by Bede. As will be discussed in chapter six, Brittonic traditions reveal that Bishop Paulinus can either be equated with the cleric Rhun mab Urien, or that Paulinus and Rhun cooperated to achieve Northumbria's conversion as described by Bede (*HE* ii 14).

Despite the depiction of Paulinus's successful conversion of Northumbria (*HE* ii 14), Bede reported widespread apostasy in both Bernicia and Deira upon Edwin's death. For the year 634, two kings apostasized: Eanfrith, son of Æthelfrith, king of Bernicia, and Osric king of Deira (*HE* iii 1). Eanfrith had, apparently, spent his exile among the Picts.[65] Both kings were slain by the allied forces of Cadwallon and Penda.[66] Bede declared that due to their apostasy the reigns of these two kings were not reckoned in the history of Northumbria (*HE* iii 1).

## Oswald (634–642)

Oswald, Eanfrith's brother, overcame Cadwallon and his much larger army at Denisesburn in 634 (*HE* iii 1). Adomnán, writing in *Vita Columbae* several decades before Bede, related how St. Columba appeared in a vision to Oswald before the battle. The saint's imposing, angelic figure dressed in radiant clothing seemed to reach the clouds. Columba identified himself to Oswald and prophesied victory.[67] Oswald's people were greatly encouraged by the vision and promised to accept baptism. Adomnán named the witnesses who handed down the account of the vision as related originally by Oswald himself.[68]

---

64 Colgrave, *Life of Gregory*, 100–105, cc. 18, 19.
65 See Miller, "Eanfrith's Pictish Son."
66 For the larger context of the Brittonic and Mercian alliance, see Charles-Edwards, *Wales and the Britons*, 387–96.
67 Anderson and Anderson, *Life of Columba*, 14–15, i 1 (8a–b).
68 Anderson and Anderson, *Life of Columba*, 16–17, i 1 (9b).

Bede must have been aware of Adomnán's earlier account. Bede's version had Oswald hold in place a hastily made cross as his soldiers secured it in the hole prepared for it. His army, after prayer, fought under the sign of the cross and gained their great victory. Bede's version complements Adomnán's. The place where they prayed before battle, called Heavenfield (*Hefenfeld*; *Caelestis campus*), became famous for its healing miracles with people taking splinters from the wooden cross (*HE* iii 2). Willibrord declared that he had a piece of the cross with him in Ireland in the 680s (*HE* iii 13). A saint's cult evolved around Oswald.

Adomnán stated of Northumbria, "up to that time all the land of the English was shadowed by the darkness of heathenism and ignorance, excepting the king Oswald himself, and twelve men who had been baptized with him" during their exile among the Gaels.[69] Adomnán contradicted Bede's description of Paulinus's success at converting and baptizing near Yeavering, in Bernicia, and Catterick, in Deira. But Bede seems to concur with Adomnán when he stated "for as far as we know, no symbol of the Christian faith, no church, and no altar had been erected in the whole of Bernicia before that new leader of the host [Oswald], inspired by his devotion to the faith, set up the standard of the holy cross" (*HE* iii 2).[70]

## The Growth of a Saint's Cult

Adomnán stated that after his victory over Cadwallon, Oswald was "ordained by God as emperor of the whole of Britain."[71] Describing Oswald as *imperator* of Britain, ordained by God, presages Bede's pronouncements about Oswald and other *bretwaldas* (*HE* ii 5). *Vita Columbae* shows Oswald's cult forming among the Gaels before it can be firmly identified among the Anglo-Saxons.

---

[69] "Nam usque in id temporis tota illa Saxonia gentilitatis et ignorantiae tenebris obscurata erat, excepto ipso rege Ossualdo cum xii. uiris qui cum eo Scotos inter exsolante babtizati sunt": Anderson and Anderson, *Life of Columba*, 14–16, i 1 (9a).
[70] "Nec inmerito, quia nullum, ut conperimus, fidei Christianae signum, nulla ecclesia, nullum altare in tota Berniciorum gente erectum est, priusquam hoc sacrae crucis uexillum nouus militae ductor, dictante fidei deuotione": Colgrave and Mynors, *Ecclesiastical History*, 216–17.
[71] "totius Brittanniae imperator a deo ordinatus est": Anderson and Anderson, *Life of Columba*, 16–17, i 1 (9a).

*Oswald 634–642* (born 604 = 38 years)
   Exiled among the Gaels during Edwin's reign, 617–633:
      Oswald was aged roughly 13–30 during his exile.

Oswald introduced Bishop Aidan to Northumbria and translated for him:
"It was indeed a beautiful sight when the bishop [Aidan] was preaching the gospel, to see the king acting as interpreter of the heavenly word for his ealdormen and thegns, for the bishop was not completely at home in the English tongue, while the king had gained a perfect knowledge of Irish during the long period of his exile" (*HE* iii 3).

A saint's cult developed around Oswald at Hexham, probably under Bishop Eata (678–681), described by Willibrord while at Rath Melsigi (678–690; *HE* iii 13).
Adomnán in *Vita Columbae* referred to Oswald as *totius Brittanniae imperator a deo ordinatus* (emperor of all Britain ordained by God).

*Oswiu 642–670* (born 612 = 58 years)
   Exiled among the Gaels during Edwin's reign, 617–633:
      Oswiu was aged roughly 5–21 during his exile.

"Oswiu, who had been educated and baptized by the Irish and was well versed in their language, considered that nothing was better than what they had taught" (*HE* iii 25).

Oswiu's liaison with a woman of Cenél nEógain produced his son Aldfrith/Flann Fína. His interactions with Cenél nEógain would have exposed him to the vernacular intellectual world of poets represented by Bécán mac Luigdech and *sapientes* such as Cenn Fáelad mac Ailella and his own son Aldfrith/Flann Fína.

Oswiu established Gilling 651 whose first abbot, Trumhere, had been educated and consecrated among the Gaels in the 640s (*HE* iii 24). Oswiu had good relations with Bishops Fínán and Colmán and oversaw proceedings at the "synod" of Whitby 664 (*HE* iii 25). Pope Vitalian communicated with Oswiu to establish the Canterbury school of Theodore and Hadrian in 669 (*HE* iii 29).

*Aldfrith sapiens 685–704* (born ca. 639 = 65 years)
   Aldfrith was a close contemporary of Aldhelm of Malmesbury and Ecgberht of Rath Melsigi. He appears, as Flann Fína, in the same Cenél nEógain genealogy as his illustrious kinsman Cenn Fáelad *sapiens*.

   Gaelic annals describe Aldfrith mac Ossu (son of Oswiu) as *sapiens*. Several Gaelic texts are attributed to Aldfrith/Flann Fína, but only *Bríathra Flainn Fhína maic Ossu* are firmly dateable to the Old Gaelic period.

   Aldfrith and Aldhelm received part of their early educations together, probably among the Gaels. Aldfrith also had a personal relationship with Adomnán of Iona, who presented him with a copy of *De locis sanctis* and referred to him as *Aldfridus amicus* (friend Aldfrith).

**Figure 5.a:** Three Gaelic-Speaking Northumbrian Kings.

Bede reported that the monks of Hexham, founded in the 670s by Wilfrid, kept a vigil at Heavenfield on the night before each anniversary of Oswald's death (*HE* iii 2). At a later period Bishop Acca of Hexham (709-731) encouraged a cult of Oswald.[72] Bede did not specify when this custom began, but Eata, first trained by Aidan at Lindisfarne, served as bishop of Hexham ca. 678-ca. 681 and 685/686 (*HE* iv 12).[73] Eata was succeeded at Hexham by John of Beverley who had been trained at Abbess Hild's Whitby (*HE* iv 23; v 2, 6). Vigils to commemorate Oswald likely began in Eata's time, were continued by John of Beverley and then, once established, were maintained by Acca. Based on Bede's evidence, Oswald was remembered for having introduced the Gaels from Iona into the cultural and religious life of Northumbria. Given the negative statements about the Gaels attributed to Wilfrid in *Vita Wilfridi*, a cult celebrating Oswald seems unlikely to have originated with members of the Wilfridian party.[74]

Early evidence for Oswald's cult is related by Willibrord to Wilfrid and Acca when they visited him in Frisia on their way to Rome ca. 703. Willibrord told how Oswald's reputation was known in Ireland, and how a local Gaelic scholar sought Oswald's healing relics from Willibrord, which Willibrord provided (*HE* iii 13). Such an incident must have happened in the 680s, perhaps during the plague of 685. Oswald's reputation had grown enough, probably through Eata, that it had already spread to Ireland. Willibrord himself possessed some of the stake on which Oswald's head had been impaled (*HE* iii 13).

## A Missionary King

Once Oswald had secured the throne, he worked to have the people adopt the Christian faith that he and his thegns had accepted during their exile among the Gaels. He invited missionaries into his kingdom and Iona sent Bishop Aidan who established the monastery of Lindisfarne within view of the royal site at Bamburgh. Bede spoke highly of Aidan, his character, his pastoral style, his

---

**72** Stancliffe, "Disputed Episcopacy," 32-35.
**73** Bede is vague about the jurisdictions of the bishoprics at this time, stating that Eata was "at Hexham or else in Lindisfarne" (ille in Hagustaldensi siue in Lindisfarnensi ecclesia cathedram habens episcopalem): Colgrave and Mynors, *Ecclesiastical History*, 370-71. There seems to have been a short period, 685/686, when Hexham was again in his charge.
**74** "Was I not the first . . . to root out the poisonous weeds planted by the Scots?" (Necnon et ego . . . Scotticae virulenta plantationis germina eradicarem): Colgrave, *Life of Bishop Wilfrid*, 98-99, c. 47.

success as a missionary (*HE* iii 5), and attributed many miracles to him (*HE* iii 15–17). Oswald, who had a perfect command of Gaelic, was enthusiastic about spreading the faith, and sometimes interpreted for his thegns and aldermen because Aidan had not yet mastered Old English (*HE* iii 3).[75]

Many Gaelic teachers and preachers (*de Scottorum regione*) came into every part of Britain ruled by Oswald. Bede's phrase implies that the Gaels came not just from Iona, but from wider afield in the Gaelic world. For example, Fursa, likely from Co. Louth, along with his companions, established themselves in East Anglia soon after Aidan established Lindisfarne (*HE* iii 19).[76] Oswald gave lands and funded churches and schools so that children and their elders might be instructed and have the opportunity to live by a Rule (*HE* iii 3).[77]

Shortly after Oswald's victory over Cadwallon, he established a relationship with King Cynegisl (611–642[?]) in Wessex and married his daughter, apparently named Cyneburh.[78] But Oswald first assisted with the king's conversion to Christianity. Pope Honorius (625–638) had sent Bishop Birinus (634–ca. 650) to Wessex. Bishop Birinus baptized Cynegisl with Oswald standing in as his sponsor (*HE* iii 7). The two kings gave Dorchester (*Dorcic*) to Birinus as his episcopal see. Oswald cooperated with representatives of two different ecclesiastical traditions, the Ionan Aidan, and Birinus sent by a pope in Rome, that would come into contention a few decades later at the "synod" of Whitby (664).

Surviving records do not identify the Gaels who came to Wessex in Oswald's time, but we have indications. Agilberht, from Francia, was one of Birinus's successors in the bishopric of Wessex. However, before Agilberht became bishop there he "had spent a long time in Ireland for the purpose of studying the scriptures" (*HE* iii 7).[79] The dates of Agilberht's bishopric were roughly in the 650s. King Cenwealh removed Agilberht from the bishopric and replaced him with a Gaul named Wine sometime before 664. Agilberht subsequently served as the

---

[75] "Vbi pulcherrimo saepe spectaculo contigit, ut euangelizante antistite, qui Anglorum linguam perfecte non nouerat, ipse rex suis ducibus ac ministris interpres uerbi existeret caelestis, quia nimirum tam longo exilii sui tempore linguam Scottorum iam plene didicerat": Colgrave and Mynors, *Ecclesiastical History*, 220–21.

[76] Hamann, "St Fursa."

[77] "donabantur munere regio possessiones et territoria ad instituenda monasteria, inbuebantur praeceptoribus Scottis paruuli Anglorum una cum maioribus studiis et obseruatione disciplinae regularis": Colgrave and Mynors, *Ecclesiastical History*, 220.

[78] Kirby, *Earliest English Kings*, 58, 89; Brooks, "Introduction," 5; Lapidge, "'Epinal-Erfurt Glossary'," 148.

[79] "sed tunc legendarum gratia scripturarum in Hibernia non paruo tempore demoratus": Colgrave and Mynors, *Ecclesiastical History*, 234–35.

senior cleric on the Wilfridian side at the "synod" of Whitby. Wherever Agilberht studied in Ireland, his scriptural training had prepared him to support Wilfrid's orthodox stance at Whitby. Agilberht's family connections in Francia were with Columbanus's missions.[80] It has been suggested, therefore, that he had studied in Bangor.[81] Agilberht's period as bishop provided a sustained period of contact between the Gaels and Wessex. He would have served as a natural conduit for intercultural exchange.

Aldhelm served as abbot of Malmesbury in Wessex for several decades. Bede named the place as "Máeldub's city" (*Maildubi urbs*; *HE* v 18). Máeldub apparently founded Malmesbury and taught Aldhelm in his early years. Aldhelm was born ca. 639. The time of Máeldub's arrival and foundation of Malmesbury are not known. However, Máeldub's influence in Wessex recalls Oswald's relationship with King Cynegisl, the presence of the Gaelic-trained Bishop Agilberht in the 650s, and the Gregorian mission's lack of success outside of Britain's southeast corner. Aldhelm's knowledge of *Altus Prosator*,[82] his familiarity with Virgilius Maro Grammaticus,[83] his personal acquaintance with Aldfrith *sapiens*,[84] and his correspondence with Cellán of Péronne,[85] all reflect a Gaelic influence in Wessex, first noted in Oswald's presence there by 634.

Oswald was killed, aged thirty-eight, by the pagan Mercian king Penda at Maserfelth on August 5, 642 (*HE* iii 9).[86] Penda was acting in coalition with his Brittonic ally Cadwallon.

The *Vita Columbae* provided an early indication of a cult forming around Oswald. His presence in the *Calendar* of Willibrord, the *peregrinus* who trained at Rath Melsigi, reinforces Adomnán's focus on Oswald.[87] Willibrord's anecdote told to Wilfrid and Acca about a Gaelic scholar seeking a cure through Oswald's relics reflects that growing cult in Ireland in the 680s (*HE* iii 13). Monks at Hexham commemorated Oswald's death at Heavenfield beginning, perhaps, with

---

**80** Wood, "Ripon, Francia and the Franks Casket," 11.
**81** Hammer, "'Holy Entrepreneur'," 62.
**82** Orchard, *Poetic Art of Aldhelm*, 54–60.
**83** Lapidge and Herren, *Aldhelm*, 140, 164, 202n37; see also Law, *Wisdom, Authority and Grammar*, 101–4.
**84** Lapidge and Herren, *Aldhelm*, 32; Ireland, "Where Was King Aldfrith Educated?" 37–40, 55–58.
**85** Howlett, *Celtic Latin Tradition*, 108–13.
**86** The Annals of Tigernach state, "Cath Osuailt contra Panta in quo Osualt cecidit" (Battle of Oswald against Penda in which Oswald fell): Stokes, "Annals of Tigernach," 185 [Felinfach, i 145]; Mc Carthy, http://www.irish-annals.cs.tcd.ie/, s.a. 641; Morris, *Nennius*, s.a. 644 at Cogfry (*Annales Cambriae*).
**87** Wilson, *Calendar of St Willibrord*, 10, 36, folio 38.

Bishop Eata (ca. 678–681; *HE* iv 12).[88] Oswald appears under the appropriate date in the *Félire Óengusso* (ca. 830) as follows: "with holy Oswald whom we implore, the noble overking of the Saxons."[89] Later in the century the Old English *Martyrology* stated of Oswald that "God gave him greater authority than any of his predecessors. Subjected to him were the four nations which are in Britain, namely the Britons and the Picts and the Gaels and the English."[90] But the Old English *Martyrology* also credited Oswald with bringing Aidan to Northumbria, that is, with introducing what *Vita Wilfridi* referred to as the "poisonous weeds planted by the Scots."[91] Oswald's story is told as a saint's life by Ælfric,[92] and his fame continued among the Anglo-Saxons into the early modern period.[93] Bishop Acca of Hexham (709–731) has been credited with promoting Oswald's cult.[94] While Acca may have helped spread the practice, Oswald's cult was already well established and may have been as strong among the Gaels as among the Anglo-Saxons.

## Oswiu (642–670)

Oswiu was thirty years of age when he succeeded his half-brother Oswald to the kingship in 642. His reign, which Bede described as "troublesome" (*laboriosissime*; *HE* iii 14), lasted for twenty-eight years until 670 when Oswiu was fifty-eight. He had a fierce rival in the Mercian king Penda. A nephew, Œthelwald son of Oswald, sided with Penda at a crucial stage. A son, Ealhfrith, apparently rebelled against him (*HE* iii 14). A highlight of Oswiu's reign was his controlling presence at the "synod" of Whitby which scrutinized the thorny issues of Easter observance, involving the complexities of ecclesiastical politics and the machinations

---

88 Clare Stancliffe sees Bishop Acca of Hexham (709–731) as a clever strategist, promoting Oswald and trying to bridge the gap between Lindisfarne with its supporters of Cuthbert and the Wilfridian party: Stancliffe, "Disputed Episcopacy," 32–39.
89 "la hOsualt nóeb náilme, ardrí Saxan sóerdae": Stokes, *Félire Óengusso*, 174, at August 5. An *ardrí*, while not equivalent to *imperator*, implies rule of one king over others. See discussion in Higham, *Ecgfrith*, 20–21.
90 "ond him sealde God mare rice þonne ænigum hys forgengum. Him wæron underðeodde ða feowera þeoda þe syndon on Bretene, þæt syndon Brytwalas ond Peohtas ond Scottas ond Ongle": Rauer, *Old English Martyrology*, 154–55 §146, 279 (commentary).
91 At the entry for Bishop Aidan, August 31, Oswald is credited with bringing him to England: Rauer, *Old English Martyrology*, 172–73 §171, 287 (commentary).
92 Lazzari, "Kingship and Sainthood."
93 Bassi, "St Oswald."
94 Stancliffe, "Disputed Episcopacy," 32–35; Thacker, "*Membra Disjecta*."

of the synod's participants. Oswiu's command of proceedings at the "synod" suggests how and why he was successful socially, politically, intellectually, and militarily in controlling his *imperium*.

Oswiu is the seventh *bretwalda* named by Bede (*HE* ii 5). Along with his half-brother Oswald, Oswiu had spent the reign of Edwin (616–633) in exile among the Gaels, from roughly age five to twenty-two. He spoke Gaelic fluently and thought highly of their learning (*HE* iii 25). His multiple marital liaisons reflect his rule over an ethnically mixed "empire." Each liaison produced a son who served as a king. His three liaisons suggest his astuteness at dealing with political and social issues within the ethnic patchwork of seventh-century Northumbria.

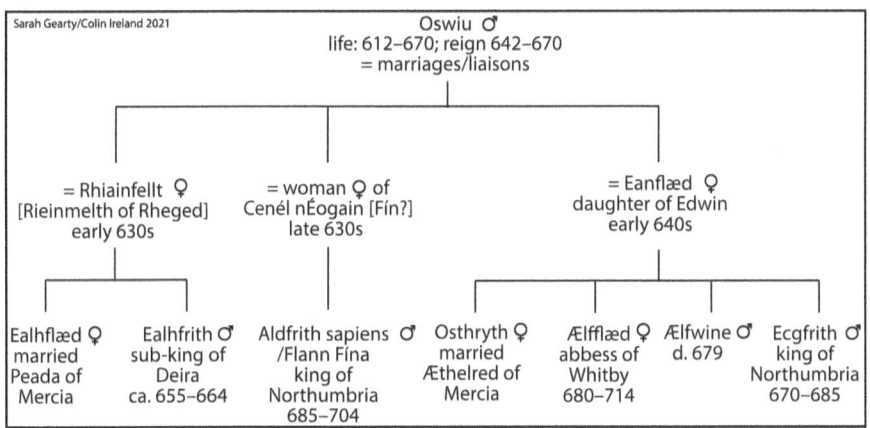

**Figure 5.b:** Chart of Oswiu's Liaisons and Offspring.
Oswiu's *imperium* was multi-ethnic. He had three liaisons that produced sons who served as kings. Rhiainfellt of Rheged, a Briton, was the mother of Ealhfrith, sub-king of Deira (ca. 655–664). The mother of Aldfrith *sapiens*, king of Northumbria (685–704), was a Gael of the Cenél nÉogain in the Inishowen peninsula. An Anglo-Saxon woman Eanflæd, daughter of Edwin, was mother of Ecgfrith, king of Northumbria (670–685).

## Marital Liaisons

Shortly after he came to the throne, Oswiu married Eanflæd daughter of Edwin (ca. 643), in what was his third recognized liaison. Eanflæd had been baptized as an infant, ca. 625, by Bishop Paulinus of the Gregorian mission. Eanflæd was raised in Kent after her father Edwin was killed by Cadwallon in 633. Her upbringing followed orthodox practice with regard to Easter observance. Four offspring are known from this liaison (Figure 5.b).

Ecgfrith (670–684) was the best known of the sons of Oswiu and Eanflæd. He acceded to the Northumbrian throne after his father. His younger brother Ælfwine was killed at eighteen years of age in a battle between Ecgfrith and Æthelred, king of the Mercians, in 679 on the river Trent (*HE* iv 21). The battle reflects tragic elements of early medieval societies known from Old English epic where women are pawns in the quarrels of men.[95] Not alone did Ecgfrith's younger brother Ælfwine lose his life, but their sister Osthryth was married to Æthelred, the opposing Mercian king (*HE* iv 21).[96]

Ælfflæd was the most famous daughter of Oswiu and Eanflæd.[97] She was born ca. 654 and dedicated to the church by Oswiu in thanksgiving for his victory (655) over the Mercian Penda. Ælfflæd was raised by Abbess Hild who, at the time, was at Hereuteu.[98] Two years later Hild was given Whitby (*Strēanæshalh*) to "set in order."[99] Ælfflæd eventually replaced Hild (d. 680) in the abbacy and served her tenure as abbess (680–714), along with her mother Eanflæd while the latter lived.

Oswiu's first marital liaison helps explain his success at bringing neighboring Britons into the orbit of his empire. The *Historia Brittonum* named Oswiu's first wife (*uxor*) as Rhiainfellt, daughter of Rhoyth son of Rhun (son of Urien Rheged).[100] It would thus appear that she was the great granddaughter of Urien Rheged.[101] Rhun is associated with Paulinus of the Gregorian mission in *Historia Brittonum* and *Annales Cambriae*. Kenneth Jackson argued that such a marriage made it "quite possible that he [Oswiu] acquired Rheged by marriage and not by conquest."[102] The importance of Rhiainfellt is shown in the ninth-century core of the Durham *Liber Vitae* where her name, in Anglicized form *Rægenmæld*, appears

---

[95] For editions and discussions of the Finn episode and Finnsburg Fragment, see Fulk, Bjork, Niles, *Klaeber's Beowulf*, 273–90; Hill, *Minor Heroic Poems*, 27–29, 42–43, 52–56.
[96] Colgrave, *Life of Bishop Wilfrid*, 80–81, c. 40. Bede, in his chronological summary, added the detail that Osthryth was murdered in 697 by her Mercian nobles: Colgrave and Mynors, *Ecclesiastical History*, 564–65 (*HE* v 24).
[97] A letter by Ælfflæd survives: Sharpe, *Handlist*, 25 §51.
[98] For some archaeologicial studies of Hartlepool, see Daniels, "Monastery at Hartlepool"; Okasha, "Inscribed Stones." For arguments placing Hereuteu in the context of *Beowulf*, see Harris, "Note on the Other Heorot."
[99] "construendum siue ordinandum monasterium": Colgrave and Mynors, *Ecclesiastical History*, 408.
[100] "Rieinmelth, filia Royth, filii Rum": Morris, *Nennius*, 36, 77 §57.
[101] This follows a suggestion by Nora Chadwick, "Celtic Background," 329. For complications with this identification, see Clancy, "The Kingdoms of the North," 158, 164.
[102] Jackson, "Angles and Britons," 71.

first in the list under the rubric *Nomina reginarum et abbatissarum*.[103] Her name appears in prominent letters and is followed by Eanflæd, Oswiu's wife recognized by Bede.

Two children have been identified from this liaison (Figure 5.b). They had a daughter, Ealhflæd (Alhflæd/Alchfled), who was married to Peada son of the Mercian king Penda, the fierce rival of her father Oswiu (*HE* iii 21). Peada ruled the Middle Angles, serving as a sub-king for his father. According to Bede, the marriage agreement involved Peada's acceptance of the Christian faith (653; *HE* v 24), two years before the death of Penda who remained pagan. Peada's baptism, along with his retinue's, was performed by Bishop Finán of Lindisfarne (*HE* iii 21).

Ealhfrith (Alhfridus/Alchfridus) was the son of Oswiu and Rhiainfellt.[104] Ealhfrith married Cyneburh, daughter of Penda (*HE* iii 21). Despite the murderous rivalry between their fathers, Oswiu and Penda, marriage alliances were intended to form relationships between Northumbria and Mercia, since Ealhfrith and Peada had married each other's sisters. Ealhfrith served his father Oswiu as sub-king of Deira (ca. 655–664). Given the alliance between the Mercians, under Penda, and the Britons, under Cadwallon, it appears that Oswiu's children with Brittonic background were useful in forging marriage pacts.[105]

Ealhfrith developed a friendship with the young cleric Wilfrid and granted the monastery at Ripon to him (661x663), putting Eata and Cuthbert out because they persisted in the practices of Melrose and Iona. Ealhfrith and Wilfrid worked in consort to initiate the "synod" of Whitby (664). However, the resulting contention between father, Oswiu, and son, Ealhfrith, did not end well for the latter.[106] Bede mentioned that Oswiu was attacked (*inpugnatus*) by Ealhfrith (*HE* iii 14) and we never hear of him again after the "synod."[107] Powerful kings

---

[103] Rollason and Rollason, *Durham Liber Vitae*, i, 93 (Folio 16R1 (1)); ii, 42 A.1.81 (for linguistic discussion of name).

[104] Kirby argued that Oswiu had a son, Ealhfrith, and daughter, Ealhflæd, with Rhiainfellt, granddaughter of Rhun of Rheged in the 630s: Kirby, *Earliest English Kings*, 90; Smyth, *Warlords and Holy Men*, 24–25. See the genealogical chart in Stancliffe and Cambridge, *Oswald*, 13; Koch, "Why Was Welsh Literature First Written Down?" 28–29; Grimmer, "Exogamous Marriages," §§29–31.

[105] Brady, *Welsh Borderlands*, 31–32. For Penda's reliance on Brittonic allies, see Brady, *Welsh Borderlands*, 23–52; Tyler, "Early Mercia and the Britons."

[106] James Campbell suggested that Ealhfrith's willingness to side with Wilfrid in a bid against Gaelic influence in Northumbria was his knowledge of the potential rivalry from his half-brother Aldfrith: Campbell, "Debt of the Early English," 336–37.

[107] Mayr-Harting, *Coming of Christianity*, 107–8; Yorke, *Kings and Kingdoms*, 79. As Richard Abels succinctly put it, "Alhfrith had destroyed himself at Whitby": Abels, "Council of Whitby," 20. Abels argued that Ealhfrith (son of Oswiu and Rhiainfellt) felt pressure from his younger

sometimes used close relatives, in this case a son, to help rule.[108] It is a practice that can work against, as well as for, the original goal.

A third liaison, but probably Oswiu's second in sequence, was to a Gaelic woman of Cenél nÉogain. In the seventh century the main Cenél nÉogain territory was the Inishowen (*Inis Éogain*) peninsula, the northernmost part of Ireland. This liaison suggests that Oswiu spent time in Ireland itself, and not only among the Gaels of Northern Britain. Aldfrith *sapiens* (685–704) was Oswiu's son with the woman of Cenél nÉogain (Figure 5.b).[109] The timing of this liaison was most likely in the late 630s.[110] Aldfrith *sapiens* was a close contemporary of Aldhelm of Malmesbury and of Ecgberht of Rath Melsigi, and he knew Aldhelm and Adomnán of Iona personally.

Bede considered Aldfrith illegitimate (*nothus*),[111] but Early Gaelic law accepted a variety of liaisons as legitimate.[112] Given the social standing Aldfrith *sapiens* achieved, the Gaels did not consider him *nothus*. Such issues were matters for intellectual debate among the Gaels and reflect their syncretic preoccupations. An eighth-century law-tract on sick-maintenance, *Bretha Crólige*, discussed the *díre* (honour price) due to each person in a couple based on their type of marriage. The jurist stated, "For there is a dispute in Irish law as to which is more proper, whether many sexual unions or a single one: for the chosen [people] of God lived in plurality of unions, so that it is not easier to condemn it than to praise it."[113] Indigenous marital customs that contravened the Church's official views were defended by reference to the Old Testament.[114] Oswiu admired Gaelic learning. His son Aldfrith was a respected *sapiens*. They were aware of Gaelic customary law.

---

half-brother Ecgfrith, son of Eanflæd, who had, therefore, a claim to both Deiran and Bernician ancestry. Ecgfrith would have been about nineteen years old at the time of the "synod": Abels, "Council of Whitby," 7–8.

108 Jaski, *Irish Kingship*, 140–42.
109 It is possible that her name was Fín, but this may also have been an epithet implying excellence: Ireland, "Irish Genealogies," 70–74. For a survey of some of the evidence, see Grimmer, "Exogamous Marriages," §§16–27.
110 Ireland, "Irish Genealogies"; Kirby, *Earliest English Kings*, 143; Yorke, *Rex Doctissimus*, 7–9.
111 Lapidge, *Bede's Latin Poetry*, 256–57 §21; Colgrave, *Lives of Saint Cuthbert*, 238–39, c. 24; Yorke, "Irish and British Connections," 171.
112 For a sense of the varieties of recognized marriages and liaisons, see Kelly, *Guide*, 70–75; Eska, *Cáin Lánamna*, 13–24; Ireland, "Irish Genealogies," 67, 76–77.
113 "ar ata forcosnam la Fēne cia de as techtta in nilar comperta fa huathad. Ar robattar tuiccsi de i (n)nilar lanamnusa, connach airissa a caithiugud oldas a molad": Binchy, "*Bretha Crólige*," 44–45 §57; Kelly, *Marriage Disputes*, 3.
114 For a larger context, see Jaski, "Marriage Laws." A fragmentary Latin poem on divorce shows that personal issues of union and separation were a serious topic: Lapidge, "Debate Poem on Divorce."

Oswiu's multiple marriage liaisons helped him secure control over the ethnically disparate *imperium* of Northumbria and beyond. Each of his known liaisons produced a king: Rhiainfellt was mother of Ealhfrith (ca. 655–664) sub-king of Deira; a woman of Cenél nÉogain was mother of Aldfrith (685–704) king of Northumbria; and Eanflæd was mother of Ecgfrith (670–685) king of Northumbria. Oswiu's political and social acuity is shown in his intercultural marriages, his treatment of friends, his efforts to convert allies, his military success against enemies, and in his control of ecclesiastical politics in the Easter controversy.

## Military Difficulties

Oswiu's struggles against the Mercian Penda, who had killed his half-brother Oswald, and against Penda's Brittonic allies lasted for thirteen years. Bede said that Oswiu was forced to pay a vast treasure on condition that Penda cease his depredations. But the pagan Mercian would not accept the conditions and continued his raids with a desire to destroy Northumbria (*HE* iii 24). The *Historia Brittonum*, in a convoluted account, suggests a somewhat different scenario. Part of the account states that Oswiu paid over vast amounts of riches to Penda who, in turn, distributed them to his Brittonic allies. This dispersal of wealth is called *Atbret Iudeu* (Restitution of Iudeu) in *Historia Brittonum*.[115] The name implies that the Britons viewed this payment as recompense for what had been taken from them by Northumbrians, and suggests that their alliance with Penda was an attempt to reclaim what had been lost.[116]

According to Bede, Oswiu's failure to purchase peace forced him to dedicate his infant daughter Ælfflæd as a "holy virgin." She was given to Hild to be raised and ended her life in 714 as abbess of Whitby. Oswiu also donated twelve estates to become monasteries, six in Deira and six in Bernicia, to be "freed from any concern about earthly military service," these were places that "might be provided for the monks to wage heavenly warfare and to pray with unceasing devotion that the race might win eternal peace" (*HE* iii 24).[117] Bede implied

---

[115] Morris, *Nennius*, 38, 79 §65. The editor translates *atbret* as "distribution," but a modern Welsh reflex *edfryd* (to restore) shows the meaning is closer to "restitution." The placename *Iudeu* has been identified as the site of the Roman fort *Habitancum* near Risingham, Northumberland: Jackson, "Bede's *Urbs Giudi*."

[116] Higham, *Ecgfrith*, 99–102; Brady, *Writing the Welsh Borderlands*, 39–41.

[117] Colgrave and Mynors, *Ecclesiastical History*, 290–93. It would seem that Whitby had been one of the estates donated by Oswiu to become monasteries. In 657 Hild was asked to set Whitby in order.

that, because of these commitments, Oswiu and Ealhfrith, with a much smaller force, were able to defeat and kill Penda (655) in battle near the River Winwæd (*HE* iii 24).[118] A nephew of Oswiu, Œthelwald, sided with Penda, while Oswiu's son Ecgfrith, as a youngster, was held hostage among the Mercians (*HE* iii 24).[119] With the defeat and death of Penda, Oswiu began the conversion of the Mercians.

### Converting Friends and Enemies

Bede appears to condemn Oswiu for certain actions early in his reign.[120] One example was Oswiu's rivalry with Oswine, king of Deira. Oswine and Bishop Aidan had developed a close relationship (*HE* iii 14), and Oswiu had Oswine killed in 651, apparently eliminating a rival (*HE* iii 14).[121] In order to atone for the murder, Oswiu, at the instigation of his wife Eanflæd (*HE* iii 24), established the monastery of Gilling where prayers could be said for both kings. The murder of Oswine and the establishment of Gilling seem to have caused Oswiu to focus on positive actions as shown in the conversion of both friends and former enemies. Wherever Oswiu worked to convert neighbors, Gaelic monks and clergy, or those trained and consecrated by the Gaels, arrived in the territories.

Oswiu was active in the re-conversion of the East Saxons, where the mission of Mellitus of Canterbury had failed (*HE* iii 22). King Sigeberht (d. ca. 653) of the East Saxons had a friendship with Oswiu, according to Bede, and would visit Northumbria where Oswiu encouraged him to give up pagan beliefs. Oswiu's arguments were against belief in man-made idols of wood or stone, and for belief in God the creator of the world and mankind. Sigeberht was eventually baptized by Bishop Fínán. Sigeberht asked that Oswiu send teachers (*doctores*). Among them was Cedd who had served as a priest for the Middle Angles after Peada's conversion (*HE* iii 21). Because of Cedd's success among Sigeberht's East Saxons he was later consecrated bishop by Fínán (*HE* iii 22). Cedd would subsequently serve as "interpreter" at the "synod" of Whitby.

---

**118** Swanton, *Anglo-Saxon Chronicles*, 29 s.a. 654 in version E; Mac Airt and Mac Niocaill, *Annals of Ulster*, 130–31 s.a. 656; Morris, *Nennius*, 46, 87 s.a. 656/7 (*Annales Cambriae*). The location of Winwæd has not been identified. *Historia Brittonum* describes the battle as taking place at "campus Gaii," but no one has identified "Gaius's field": Morris, *Nennius*, 38, 79 §64. See recent discussions in Charles-Edwards, *Wales and the Britons*, 393–96; Dunshea, "Road to *Winwæd*?"; Higham, *Ecgfrith*, 100–102; Brady, *Welsh Borderlands*, 39–42.
**119** Œthelwald was the son of Oswald and, at the time, king of Deira (*HE* iii 24).
**120** For example, see the arguments in Higham, *(Re-)Reading Bede*, 155–59.
**121** Gunn, *Bede's Historiae*, 169–72.

Two years before Penda's death, Oswiu had given his daughter Ealhflæd (daughter of Rhiainfellt) in marriage to Peada son of Penda, on the condition of his (Peada's) conversion (ca. 653; *HE* iii 21). Bishop Fínán baptized Peada. Oswiu's son Ealhfrith had married Cyneburh, daughter of Penda and sister of Peada (*HE* iii 21). Bede said that Penda, although pagan himself, allowed preaching in his kingdom (*HE* iii 21). Penda's *laissez faire* attitude to Christianity may have been a product of his alliances with Christian Britons.

After the death of Penda (655), Oswiu became active in the conversion of the Mercians. A Gael, Diuma (*Dímma*), became bishop (ca. 656–ca. 658) of the Middle Angles and Mercians for a time, and was consecrated by Bishop Fínán (*HE* iii 21). When Diuma died he was followed by another Gael named Ceollach (*Cellach*). At this time, however, a group of Mercian lords rebelled against Oswiu and established a younger son of Penda's, Wulfhere (ca. 658–674), as king of Mercia. Perhaps due to Wulfhere's accession, Ceollach returned to be among the Gaels (*HE* iii 21).[122] But the Mercians remained Christian and Trumhere (ca. 659–ca. 662), educated and consecrated by Gaels, followed Ceollach as bishop. Trumhere, a relative of both Oswine and Eanflæd, had initially served as first abbot at Gilling (*HE* iii 24). Chad, who had spent time with Ecgberht at Rath Melsigi, was eventually consecrated bishop of Mercia (669–672) by Theodore of Canterbury (*HE* iv 2).

**Straddling the Divide**

Oswiu's commanding rôle at the "synod" of Whitby must be understood in the context of his personal history. While his intellectual comprehension of the controversy should not be underestimated, his political and social experiences alone were enough to ensure that he grasped the issues of the "synod." He did not need to be schooled in scripture and computistics in order to appreciate the advantages to him and his kingdom of championing one side over the other.

During his reign up until the "synod" (664), the bishopric at Lindisfarne was filled by bishops from Iona. Oswiu and his retinue followed the Easter practices of Iona. His wife, Eanflæd and her household observed Easter as she had learned in Kent. Bede noted the difficulties caused at court when Easter celebra-

---

[122] Bede specifically says Ceollach returned to Iona: *reuersus est ad insulam Hii*: Colgrave and Mynors, *Ecclesiastical History*, 280. Bede later uses a different phrase which seems to imply that Ceollach may have returned to Ireland: *ad Scottiam rediit*: Colgrave and Mynors, *Ecclesiastical History*, 292.

tions by Oswiu and Eanflæd differed in their timing (*HE* iii 25).[123] Oswiu thus had at least twenty years to observe and comprehend the disjunctions caused by the contrasting traditions on Easter observance.

Gilling was established by Oswiu (651), at the urging of his wife Eanflæd, to atone for the murder of his rival King Oswine of Deira. Gilling was where Ceolfrith, Bede's own abbot, began his life in religion. It is not clear what practices were followed at Gilling and arguments can be made for either Ionan or Kentish practices, as discussed in chapter six. Trumhere, a relative of Eanflæd, was its first abbot, followed by Cynefrith, brother of Ceolfrith. Trumhere had trained in Ireland (*HE* iii 24), and Cynefrith withdrew from the abbacy and lived an ascetic life in Ireland with other nobles.[124] Trumhere later served as bishop among the Mercians (ca. 659–ca. 662). It has not been established which ecclesiastical foundation in Ireland attracted Cynefrith and his companions (*cum aliis quoque Anglorum nobilibus*) away from Gilling by the late 650s or early 660s.[125] These dates coincide with those Bede highlighted for Anglo-Saxon students accessing free Gaelic education. Since Gilling was established by Oswiu, the actions of Cynefrith and other nobles suggest they had the king's implicit approval and were following his educational policies.

These records about Gilling are likely to have been preserved and transmitted to Bede through the Gaels.[126] It seems less likely that Ceolfrith was Bede's source since Bede never mentioned Cynefrith. The close relationship between Bishop Aidan and Deira's King Oswine (*HE* iii 14) contravenes the stereotype that Deira favored Kent and Canterbury, and that Bernicia followed Iona.

Bishop Aidan died (August 31, 651; *HE* iii 14, 17) shortly after the murder of King Oswine (August 20, 651; *HE* iii 14). Vicky Gunn argued that Aidan and Oswiu did not have a good relationship.[127] That may or may not be true. Oswiu must have viewed the relationship between Aidan and Oswine as a threat. Oswiu worked closely with Bishop Fínán, as noted above, and had great respect for Bishop Colmán (*HE* iii 26). Lindisfarne's first bishops came from Iona, a monastery whose hierarchy was dominated by the Cenél Conaill. Oswiu's relationships

---

123 See an excellent discussion, which shows how frequently there would have been discrepancies in the dates for Easter, in Holford-Strevens, "Marital Discord."
124 Grocock and Wood, *Abbots of Wearmouth*, 80–81 §§2–3 (*Vita Ceolfridi*); Hunter Blair, *World of Bede*, 101.
125 Grocock and Wood, *Abbots of Wearmouth*, 80 §3.
126 Dáibhí Ó Cróinín argued that this Cynefrith is likely the one who appears in Willibrord's *Calendar* and, if so, suggests that it was Gaelic tradition and not Northumbrian that preserved this information: "Rath Melsigi, Willibrord," 31–32; Wilson, *Calendar of St Willibrord*, 40 (17 Setpember); Richter, *Ireland and Her Neighbours*, 143–44.
127 Gunn, *Bede's Historiae*, 38.

in Ireland were firmest with Cenél nÉogain. Cenél Conaill and Cenél nÉogain were political rivals throughout the seventh century.[128] Fínán, the bishop with whom Oswiu worked most closely, was likely from Cenél nÉogain.[129] If Oswiu was unafraid to oppose Cenél Conaill, even indirectly, through its representatives from Iona, it was because he understood the political dynamics throughout Gaeldom. If he offended Iona, Oswiu knew the alternatives that existed for himself and his kingdom elsewhere among the Gaels.[130]

Oswiu appreciated Gaelic learning and "considered that nothing was better than what they had taught" (*HE* iii 25).[131] His relationships with Cenél nÉogain helped confirm his opinion: the education acquired by his son Aldfrith *sapiens*; the intellectual reputation of Cenn Fáelad *sapiens* (d. 679); the achievements of Bécán mac Luigdech (fl. 670). All contrasted sharply with the incipient learning available in Oswiu's Northumbria and Anglo-Saxon Britain generally. The period Bede highlighted (651–664) of Anglo-Saxons availing themselves of free education among the Gaels (*HE* iii 27) occurred in the middle of Oswiu's reign, with two Lindisfarne bishops, Fínán and Colmán, that he esteemed and worked well with. That increased traffic of Anglo-Saxons students abroad in Ireland must reflect Oswiu's deliberate educational policy.

The future bishop Wilfrid gained recognition as a teenager for his talents in the household of Oswiu's queen Eanflæd. The *Vita Wilfridi* stated that he "found grace in her sight" (*VW* c. 2),[132] and began his rise in ecclesiastical politics.[133] Wilfrid had entered Lindisfarne ca. 648, giving him time to have met Bishop Aidan. Eanflæd sent Wilfrid to Kent by ca. 652, and Wilfrid made his first trip to the continent ca. 654 with Benedict Biscop, although they parted ways before visiting Rome. Wilfrid remained away for several years. Upon his return to Northumbria, Wilfrid formed a relationship with Oswiu's son Ealhfrith, sub-king of Deira. Wilfrid

---

**128** Lacey, *Cenél Conaill*, 31–32, 43–46, 165–66, 285–86, 289–308.
**129** Ireland, "Irish Genealogies," 74 and notes.
**130** Conall Cóel mac Máele Cobo (d. 654) and his brother Cellach mac Máele Cobo (d. 658) of Cenél Conaill apparently shared the "high-kingship" of Ireland at the time: Byrne, *Irish Kings*, 275; Mac Shamhráin and Byrne, "Prosopography," 198–99 (Conall Cóel), 199, 315 (Cellach). The era of the 630s would have seen a lot of internal strife for Cenél nÉogain and the subsequent decades, through ca. 658, saw Cenél Conaill dominate the high-kingship, followed by a protracted period where Síl nÁedo Sláine were dominant (to ca. 695).
**131** "nil melius quam quod illi docuissent autumabat": Colgrave and Mynors, *Ecclesiastical History*, 296–97.
**132** "invenit gratiam in conspectu illius"; Colgrave, *Life of Bishop Wilfrid*, 6, quoting Esther 2:9.
**133** For a reliable chronology of Wilfrid's life and career, see Cubitt, "Appendix 2."

received from Ealhfrith the monastery of Ripon (661x663).[134] Wilfrid and Ealhfrith together initiated the "synod" of Whitby. As Oswiu oversaw the proceedings, he must have been aware of the cooperation between his son Ealhfrith and Wilfrid, and Wilfrid's background in his wife's household.

About 653 a twenty-five-year-old thegn (*minister*) named Baducing (Benedict Biscop) had received land from Oswiu according to his rank. But Baducing put aside the ways of the world, including a wife, and became famous as Benedict Biscop and his trips to Rome.[135] Baducing and Wilfrid made their first trip to the continent as companions ca. 654. Baducing was six years older than Wilfrid, and neither had yet been to Rome, but Stephen described Baducing as Wilfrid's "guide" in the *Vita Wilfridi* (*VW* c. 3).[136] The two parted company on the trip, apparently discordantly.[137] Bede, in *Historia Abbatum*, related that Ealhfrith intended to visit the tombs of the apostles in Rome with Benedict Biscop after the "synod" (i.e., ca. 665), but Oswiu forbade them from making the journey.[138] Both Benedict Biscop and Wilfrid began their lives within Oswiu's sphere of influence, both were committed to Rome and its authority, and both formed relationships with Oswiu's son Ealhfrith.

Oswiu had every opportunity to understand the implications of rejecting Iona at the "synod." In his marriage and court life Oswiu had twenty years to experience the contrast between the traditions of Iona and Kent. His knowledge of Gaelic polity made him aware of the deficits of relying solely on a monastic *familia* dominated by Cenél Conaill. His trusted bishop Fínán was likely a member of Cenél nÉogain.

The two Northumbrians who did most to cultivate relationships with Rome, Benedict Biscop and Wilfrid, both began their careers as members of Oswiu's extended retinue. Oswiu did not have to be a scholar, theologian, or computist to negotiate the intricacies of the "synod" or to anticipate the advantages of favoring Rome; he simply had to be an astute *imperator* of a diverse *imperium*.

---

134 Colgrave, *Lives of Saint Cuthbert*, 174–81, cc. 7–8 (*VCProsa*). Bede says that Wilfrid received Ripon and forty hides of land (*HE* iii 25), but Stephen of Ripon says that Wilfrid previously had received from Ealhfrith ten hides at *Stanforda* and then thirty hides at Ripon when Eata and Cuthbert refused to change their practices (*VW* c. 8).
135 Grocock and Wood, *Abbots of Wearmouth*, 22–25 §1 (*Historia abbatum*). On Benedict Biscop giving up a wife for life in religion, see Lapidge, "Debate Poem on Divorcem," 14–15.
136 Colgrave, *Life of Bishop Wilfrid*, 8–9.
137 Grocock, "Monk who Knew too Much?"; Ó Carragáin and Thacker, "Wilfrid in Rome"; Wood, "Journeys of Wilfrid and Biscop."
138 Grocock and Wood, *Abbots of Wearmouth*, 24–27 §2 (*Historia abbatum*); Stancliffe, "Kings who Opted Out," 156, 170.

## Whitby and Its Aftermath

The "synod" of Whitby (664) saw the end of bishops coming to Lindisfarne from Iona and ensured the abandonment of the *latercus*. Northumbria became orthodox with regard to Easter and tonsure. Three bishops were present at the "synod" but, in both Stephen of Ripon's and Bede's accounts, it was King Oswiu who oversaw proceedings and pronounced the final decision.[139] A total solar eclipse on the first of May in that year, and a plague that ravaged both Britain and Ireland subsequently, may well have helped impel implementation of the "synod." Whitby sat directly in the path of totality of the eclipse, as did other sites donated for monasteries by Oswiu less than a decade previously.[140] Ealhfrith in consort with Wilfrid, who had just been ordained priest by Bishop Agilberht (*HE* iii 25), instigated the "synod."

Prior to the "synod" Oswiu experienced persons and institutions who sympathized with Kent and Canterbury, including his wife Eanflæd, Wilfrid who participated in her household, and Benedict Biscop as a thegn of Oswiu's who chose life in religion. Both Wilfrid and Benedict Biscop supported Roman orthodoxy and developed relationships with Oswiu's son Ealhfrith. Oswiu's establishment of Gilling implies his acquaintance with its early abbots Trumhere and Cynefrith, brother of Ceolfrith. It is not known which Easter practices were followed at Gilling,[141] but family relations of named personnel suggest Kentish practices. Oswiu could not have arrived at the "synod" without a practical working knowledge of the Easter controversy.

The immediate aftermath of the "synod" must be reconstructed giving due notice to each party's biased viewpoint. Bede stated that Oswiu was attacked (*inpugnatus*) by his son Ealhfrith (*HE* iii 14), but provided no details. Since Ealhfrith is not mentioned again after the "synod," it has been assumed that Ealhfrith lost his life in a confrontation, perhaps an open rebellion, against his father.[142] Stephen of Ripon, in the *Vita Wilfridi*, is completely silent about what happened to Ealhfrith. After the "synod" Oswiu forbade Benedict Biscop and Eahlfrith from visiting Rome together. We can only speculate about Ealhfrith's fate, but Benedict Biscop made his second visit to Rome (ca. 665) without him.

---

**139** Ireland, "Social and Political Background."
**140** Mc Carthy and Breen, "Astronomical Observations," 12, 24–30, 43 (with map showing Whitby in the middle of the path of totality of the eclipse).
**141** See the arguments presented by Higham, *Ecgfrith*, 141.
**142** Mayr-Harting, *Coming of Christianity*, 107–8; Yorke, *Kings and Kingdoms*, 79. As Abels succinctly put it, "Alhfrith had destroyed himself at Whitby": Abels, "Council of Whitby," 20.

After Oswiu's decision to reject Iona at the "synod," Tuda, ordained by Gaels in a catholic manner, was appointed bishop over Northumbria, working from Lindisfarne, but he soon died in the plague (*HE* iii 26). Wilfrid was then chosen by Ealhfrith to become bishop, at the age of thirty, having only recently been ordained priest (*HE* iii 28).[143] Wilfrid insisted on going to Gaul, ostensibly to ensure the orthodoxy of his consecration but, perhaps, to avoid confrontation with authorities at home given the absence of his patron Ealhfrith. Stephen claimed that the kings "prepared him a ship and a force of men as well as a large sum of money" (*VW* c. 11; *HE* iii 28).[144] Stephen described the elaborate consecration of Wilfrid at Compiègne with twelve bishops officiating and with Agilberht participating (*VW* c. 12; *HE* iii 28). Wilfrid delayed his return to Northumbria for roughly two years (ca. 666).[145] Although Wilfrid appears in the Old English *Martyrology*, he is not in Willibrord's *Calendar* nor in Bede's *Martyrology*.[146]

In Wilfrid's absence Oswiu had Chad appointed bishop of York (*HE* iii 28). When Wilfrid returned to Northumbria (ca. 666) he retired to Ripon as abbot. When Theodore arrived at Canterbury he re-assigned the see at York to Wilfrid (669). Chad was removed from York and became bishop of Mercia (669–672). It would seem, with Wilfrid now in the bishopric at York, that he had achieved his goals. However, although Wilfrid was a bishop for forty-four years, he served officially for less than half that time.[147]

The thirty years dominated by the mission from Iona helped consolidate Anglo-Saxon rule over Brittonic neighbors. The agreement in Paschal practice of Brittonic clerics and those from Iona eased relations.[148] Orthodox clerics in Northumbria after the "synod" suggests a return to contentious relationships with local Britons during Ecgfrith's reign and Wilfrid's bishopric, as revealed in the dedication ceremony of Ripon in the 670s (*VW* c. 17).[149]

---

[143] Stephen of Ripon stated that this plan met with the "cordial" approval of the kings, but Bede said only that Ealhfrith chose Wilfrid as bishop (*VW* c. 11; *HE* iii 28). For the order of Tuda first, then Wilfrid, see Cubitt, "Wilfrid's 'Usurping Bishops'," 18.

[144] "praeparantes ei navem et auxilia hominum et pecuniae multitudinem": Colgrave, *Life of Bishop Wilfrid*, 26–27, c. 12.

[145] Cubitt, "Appendix 2," 342.

[146] It is not clear where the information in the entry came from: Rauer, *Old English Martyrology*, 84–87 §68, 254 (commentary). For a study in the growth of Bede's Martyrology, see Biggs, "Bede's *Martyrologium*."

[147] Goffart, *Narrators of Barbarian History*, 258n115 for an overview. For a chronology of Wilfrid's career, see Cubitt, "Appendix 2."

[148] Higham, *Ecgfrith*, 67.

[149] Colgrave, *Life of Bishop Wilfrid*, 36–37; Higham, *Ecgfrith*, 144–47.

In the year of the "synod" and plague Deusdedit, bishop of Canterbury, died leaving the bishopric empty. Oswiu and King Ecgberht of Kent (664–673) consulted together and sent a delegation with many gifts to Rome requesting an archbishop for Canterbury (*HE* iv 1).[150] They included their candidate for archbishop, Wigheard, but he died of plague in Rome (*HE* iii 29; iv 1). The wealth of the delegation implies that Oswiu, as *imperator*, undertook the major expense. The answer from Pope Vitalian, cited by Bede, is written only to Oswiu (*HE* iii 29). It suggests the pope's recognition of Oswiu's greater power over an *imperium* in the north of Britain, and the pope's desire to spread his own influence there.[151]

The pope praised Oswiu for having adopted the "true and apostolic faith,"[152] and commended his efforts at converting his people (*HE* iii 29). The pagan Penda, for example, had killed two Christian kings from East Anglia, Sigeberht and Anna (*HE* iii 18), so Oswiu's conversion of Mercia would be appreciated.

The pope explained that he could not immediately send a replacement for Canterbury, but that once it could be arranged a suitable candidate, fully instructed, would be sent. In response to the gifts sent by Oswiu and Ecgberht, the pope reciprocated with an array of holy relics and a special gift for Queen Eanflæd. Among the relics were some from Gregory the Great. The reception of these relics of Pope Gregory appears to be the earliest indication of his cult among Anglo-Saxons.[153]

Pope Vitalian's candidates were Theodore of Tarsus and Hadrian from North Africa. They arrived in Canterbury by 669 and established their famous school with Theodore assuming the archbishopric. But before their arrival in Britain, Theodore had to delay his departure to allow his hair to grow so that he might receive the coronal tonsure, and Hadrian was to accompany him to see that he did not introduce any Greek customs that might not be orthodox (*HE* iv 1). Theodore presented the Anglo-Saxon Church with parallel problems to those introduced by Iona: tonsure and doctrine. But the arrival of Theodore and Hadrian,

---

150 In the *Historia Abbatum*, written after 716, Bede says that only Ecgberht, king of Kent, was responsible for sending Wigheard to Rome: Grocock and Wood, *Abbots of Wearmouth*, 26–29 §3 (*Historia abbatum*).
151 Charles-Edwards argued that this letter from the pope to Oswiu has implications for control over northern Britain and the islands "to bring his power to bear on Iona in the interests of orthodoxy": Charles-Edwards, *Early Christian Ireland*, 434.
152 "ueram et apostolicam fidem": Colgrave and Mynors, *Ecclesiastical History*, 318–19.
153 See the arguments in Thacker, "Memorializing Gregory."

who were able to teach Latin and Greek, like the Gaels among the Anglo-Saxons, provided vigorous foreign stimulus to an incipient Christian culture.[154]

Oswiu would have appreciated a school where students could learn Latin and Greek and be exposed to texts from the Mediterranean world. Given his social rank, Oswiu's education among the Gaels would have exposed him to reading and writing in both Latin and Gaelic, if he had chosen to pursue them.[155] Oswiu appreciated the superior learning of seventh-century Gaeldom when compared to that of his contemporary Anglo-Saxons. The educational opportunities presented by Theodore and Hadrian would not have been underestimated by Oswiu.

Oswiu died after suffering an illness at age fifty-eight on February 15, 670, about two years after the arrival of Theodore at Canterbury, and three years after Benedict Biscop's third visit to Rome. Oswiu had reconciled with Wilfrid who, by now, had returned to Northumbria from Francia. Oswiu intended to visit Rome if he recovered from his illness. He would have been accompanied by a well-remunerated (non parua pecuniarum) Wilfrid as his guide (*HE* iv 5).[156] Bede said of Oswiu that "he was so greatly attached to the Roman and apostolic customs that he had intended . . . to go to Rome and end his life there among the holy places" (*HE* iv 5).[157] Had he been able to fulfil his intentions as outlined by Bede, Oswiu would have been among the earliest of Anglo-Saxon kings to "opt out" of secular power and responsibility to take up religious life.[158]

## Ecgfrith (670–685)

Ecgfrith (670–685) became king of Northumbria after the death of his father in 670. As the son of Oswiu and Eanflæd, and the grandson on his paternal side of

---

[154] In order to appreciate the breadth of the school at Canterbury, see Lapidge, "School of Theodore"; Bischoff and Lapidge, *Biblical Commentaries*. For an edition of a specific work from the Canterbury school, see Stevenson, *"Laterculus Malalianus."*

[155] It is worth reviewing Bede's statement that Oswiu was educated (*edoctus*) by the Gaels and that he thought that nothing was better than what they taught: "Quia nimirum Osuiu a Scottis edoctus ac baptizatus, illorum etiam lingua optime inbutus, nil melius quam quod illi docuissent, autumabat": Colgrave and Mynors, *Ecclesiastical History*, 296.

[156] "Uilfridumque episcopum ducem sibi itineris fieri promissa non parua pecuniarum donatione rogaret": Colgrave and Mynors, *Ecclesiastical History*, 348–49. Previously, Stephen, in *Vita Wilfridi* had described Benedict Biscop (Baducing) as guide for Wilfrid, six years younger of the two, when they made their first trip to Rome ca. 654: Colgrave, *Life of Bishop Wilfrid*, 8–9, c. 3.

[157] "tenebatur amore Romanae et apostolicae institutionis ut . . . etiam Romam uenire ibique ad loca sancta uitam finire disponeret": Colgrave and Mynors, *Ecclesiastical History*, 348–49.

[158] Stancliffe, "Kings who Opted Out," 156.

Æthelfrith, and on his maternal side of Edwin, Ecgfrith confirmed the unification of Bernicia and Deira in his bloodlines.[159] Ecgfrith was an active patron to both Benedict Biscop and Wilfrid, churchmen committed to orthodox Roman practices. Ecgfrith also helped ensure the success of Theodore's archbishopric at Canterbury. A characteristic of his reign, and one that persisted for kings of his lineage, was a fraught relationship veering between cooperation and hostility with Bishop Wilfrid. Ecgfrith continued the military expansion of Northumbria so that his interactions with Britons, Picts, Gaels, and other Anglo-Saxons was typically grasping and aggressive.

Ecgfrith's first wife was Æthelthryth, daughter of the Christian king Anna (d. 654) of East Anglia. Æthelthryth had been raised in an East Anglia that experienced the presence of Fursa and his companions, as well as continued contacts with the continent (*HE* iii 19). Æthelthryth, although previously married to Tondberht of the South Gyrwe, preserved her virginity for twelve years.[160] Ecgfrith entreated Wilfrid to convince her to consummate the marriage, but Wilfrid cultivated his relationship with the virgin queen, thus helping to aggravate his relationship with Ecgfrith (*HE* iv 19).[161] Æthelthryth granted Hexham to Wilfrid (*VW* c. 22),[162] probably about the same time that she received the veil from him (*HE* iv 19). Hexham became Wilfrid's second most important ecclesiastical site after Ripon.

Æthelthryth eventually separated from Ecgfrith and entered the monastery at Coldingham (Berwickshire, Scotland) which was overseen by Æbbe, sister of Oswiu and aunt of Ecgfrith (*HE* iv 19). As daughter of Æthelfrith, Æbbe would have entered into exile among the Gaels and Picts of northern Britain during the reign of Edwin (616–633).[163] Like her brothers, she too would be a fluent Gaelic speaker. Æbbe had once requested that Cuthbert visit her monastery to exhort her nuns, which he did.[164] While there Cuthbert continued his habit of ascetic immersions in the sea.[165] Coldingham was noted for its destruction by

---

[159] Bede implied that Oswald had already unified Northumbria and that under him Bernicia and Deira "were peacefully united and became one people" (in unam sunt pacem et uelut unum conpaginatae in populum): Colgrave and Mynors, "Ecclesiastical History," 230 (*HE* iii 6); McClure, "Life of Ceolfrid," 79; Thacker, "Bede's Ideal of Reform," 147–48.
[160] The chronology is not clear here. Æthelthryth became abbess of Ely in 673.
[161] Foley, "*Imitatio Apostoli*," 20–28.
[162] Colgrave, *Life of Bishop Wilfrid*, 44–47, c. 22.
[163] Farmer, *Dictionary of Saints*, 157, s.n. Ebbe.
[164] Colgrave, *Lives of Saint Cuthbert*, 80–81, bk. ii, c. 3 (Anonymous *Life*); 188–89, c. 10 (Bede's Prose *Life*).
[165] Ireland, "Penance and Prayer in Water," 61–63.

fire, ostensibly because of its laxness, and this disaster was foreseen by a Gaelic monk named Adamnanus (*HE* iv 25).[166] Æthelthryth was at Coldingham only for a short time when she was made abbess in 673 at Ely in her home among the East Angles (*HE* iv 19). She died in 679. Bede wrote an abecedarian poem celebrating her virginity (*HE* iv 20 [18]).

Ecgfrith's second wife was Iurminburg (Eormenburg). She was not mentioned by Bede, but Stephen of Ripon spoke disparagingly of her accusing Iurminburg of turning Ecgfrith against Wilfrid when Wilfrid was first expelled from his see in 678 (*VW* c. 24).[167] Stephen referred to her as a she-wolf (*lupa*), a sorceress (*venifica*), and a wicked Jezebel (*impiissima Gezabel*).[168] It would seem that Iurminburg objected to the vast wealth accumulated by Wilfrid as displayed in the dedication of Ripon in the 670s (*VW* c. 17).[169]

## A Patron for Wilfrid and for Benedict Biscop

The *Vita Wilfridi* shows clearly that Ecgfrith and Wilfrid worked together initially. Stephen described Ripon's dedication, organized by Wilfrid, roughly a decade after he had received it from Oswiu's son Ealhfrith (*HE* iii 25). Wilfrid had the church built with dressed stone and elaborately decorated "with gold and silver and varied purple" (*VW* c. 17).[170] At the dedication were King Ecgfrith, his brother Ælfwine, many other nobles, functionaries, and abbots. Wilfrid stood before the assembled audience and read out a list of lands which the kings, then present, had donated to him, including a list of the consecrated places which "the British clergy had deserted when fleeing from the hostile sword wielded by the warriors of our own nation."[171] The text then names a number of

---

**166** Some versions of the Anglo-Saxon Chronicle give the date of the fire as 679 which seems too early since Æbbe didn't die until 683: Swanton, *Anglo-Saxon Chronicles*, 39 s.a. 679, version E. Wallace-Haddrill says the fire took place in 680s: Wallace-Hadrill, *Historical Commentary*, 167–68. See further Kirby, "Bede's Native Sources," 355.
**167** Colgrave, *Life of Bishop Wilfrid*, 48–51, c. 24; Foley, "Imitatio Apostoli," 26–27.
**168** Colgrave, *Life of Bishop Wilfrid*, 49.
**169** Foley, "Imitatio Apostoli," 26–27.
**170** "auro et argento purpuraque varia mirifice decoravit": Colgrave, *Life of Bishop Wilfrid*, 34–35, c. 17. For a discussion of the archaeological evidence, see Cambridge, "Wilfrid's Architecture."
**171** "quae clerus Bryttannus, aciem gladii hostilis manu gentis nostrae fugiens, deseruit": Colgrave, *Life of Bishop Wilfrid*, 36–37, c. 17. The extravagant dedication of Ripon can be compared to the elaborate ordination, including display of wealth and power, of Wilfrid at Compiègne (*VW* c. 12).

the places in question, confirming the existence of formerly viable Brittonic communities in the midst of their Anglo-Saxon neighbors (*VW* c. 17).[172]

*Vita Wilfridi* described campaigns against the Picts in which so many were slain that two rivers filled with their corpses and the victors were able to cross the rivers on their slain bodies to pursue and kill those who fled. Stephen said of the defeated Picts that "the tribes were reduced to slavery and remained subject under the yoke of captivity until the time when the king [Ecgfrith] was slain" (*VW* c. 19).[173]

Stephen further stated that the Mercian king Wulfhere gathered other southern peoples against Northumbria but that Ecgfrith, with a smaller force, was able to overcome the Mercians. According to Stephen "[C]ountless numbers were slain, the king [Wulfhere] put to flight and his kingdom laid under tribute" (*VW* c. 20).[174]

Ecgfrith's victories meant that his kingdom extended south, bringing other Anglo-Saxon peoples under his rule, as well as north, encompassing Britons, Picts, and Gaels. But with the expansion of Ecgfrith's reign, so it was that Wilfrid's own "ecclesiastical kingdom" grew (regnum ecclesiarum multiplicabatur; *VW* c. 21).[175] Many abbots and abbesses dedicated their resources to Wilfrid, and many secular leaders gave their sons to be instructed, as they chose, either for life in religion or for armed service when they were grown (*VW* c. 21). During this time Wilfrid saw to the building of Hexham on land bequeathed to him by Queen Æthelthryth. This act of patronage happened, apparently, against the wishes of Ecgfrith, in collusion between Wilfrid and Æthelthryth. According to Stephen, Hexham was elaborately built of dressed stone and finely decorated, especially later by Bishop Acca (709–731; *VW* c. 22).[176]

Royal relations begun by King Oswiu with Wilfrid and Benedict Biscop were continued by Ecgfrith, as seen in other acts of patronage. Queen Iurminburg seems not to have had the same issues with Benedict Biscop that she had with Wilfrid. In the year that Bede was born, 673, Ecgfrith granted Wearmouth to Benedict Biscop.[177] Eight years later, in 681, Ecgfrith donated Jarrow. The year

---

[172] For examples of lands taken from Britons, see Jones, "Donations to Bishop Wilfrid"; Tyler, "Early Mercia and the Britons."
[173] "populi usque ad diem occisionis regis captivitatis iugo subiecti iacebant": Colgrave, *Life of Bishop Wilfrid*, 42–43, c. 19.
[174] "occisis innumeris, regem fugavit regnumque eius sub tributo distribuit": Colgrave, *Life of Bishop Wilfrid*, 42–43, c. 20.
[175] Colgrave, *Life of Bishop Wilfrid*, 42–43, c. 21.
[176] Bidwell, "Wilfrid and Hexham"; Cambridge, "Wilfrid's Architecture."
[177] Grocock and Wood, *Abbots of Wearmouth*, 22–25, c. 1 (*Historia abbatum*); Plummer, *Venerabilis Baedae opera*, i, 364–65.

before, in 680, Bede's relatives had left him as a seven-year-old boy in the charge of Benedict Biscop. Ceolfrith, who had begun his life in religion at Gilling with his brother Cynefrith, and who had spent time at Ripon with Wilfrid, now became abbot at Jarrow.

Ecgfrith, apparently with the aid of Iurminburg, expelled Wilfrid from his see at York ca. 678 (*VW* c. 24; *HE* iv 12). Archbishop Theodore of Canterbury and Abbess Hild of Whitby were among those who testified against Wilfrid at the council as portrayed by Stephen (*VW* c. 24). It is significant that Hild, who had opposed the Wilfridian party at the "synod" of Whitby (664), should have continued to oppose Wilfrid so near the end of her life (680).[178]

In hagiography about Cuthbert, Ecgfrith is portrayed as trying to entice the saint to accept the bishopric of Lindisfarne.[179] Cuthbert was elected in 684 and consecrated March 26, 685. Although Cuthbert had been raised in the traditions of Iona, he had twenty years to adapt to orthodox practices after Whitby in 664. If Lutting had come from Lindisfarne, the *annus Domini* dating for 681 in his poem praising *magister* Baeda demonstrates that Lindisfarne had successfully made the transition to orthodox practice.[180] Cuthbert took much persuading to undertake the bishopric, and then only did so reluctantly. The sharp contrast in pastoral styles between Cuthbert and Wilfrid helps explain why Wilfrid's short sojourn as bishop of Lindisfarne (687–688) after Cuthbert's death was so discordant (*HE* iv 16).

## Political and Military Overreach

In June 684 Ecgfrith sent his general (*dux*) Berht with an army into Ireland (*Mag Breg*; *Brega*) and many churches and peoples suffered (*HE* iv 26). The Gaelic annals provide fuller accounts than is typical for their laconic style. The Annals of Ulster reported: "The Saxons lay waste Mag Breg, and many churches, in the month of June."[181] Ecgfrith carried out this campaign against the advice of Ecgberht of Rath Melsigi. Ecgberht's advisory rôle to the Northumbrian king shows that communication between Rath Melsigi and Northumbria could operate at

---

[178] Plummer had noted the significance of Hild's continued opposition to Wilfrid throughout her life: Plummer, *Venerabilis Baedae opera*, ii, 189–90.
[179] Colgrave, *Lives of Saint Cuthbert*, 110–13, bk. iv, c. 1 (Anonymous Life); 234–39, c. 24 (Bede's *Vita prosa*).
[180] Ireland, "Lutting of Lindisfarne."
[181] "Saxones Campum Bregh uastant 7 aeclesias plurimas in mense Iuni": Mac Airt and Mac Niocaill, *Annals of Ulster*, 148–49 s.a. 685; Stokes, "Annals of Tigernach," 208 [Felinfach i 168].

the highest levels (*HE* iv 26 [24]).¹⁸² This military campaign reveals a consciousness of Gaelic affairs on Ecgfrith's part. Bede described the Gaels as an inoffensive people and clearly regretted the attack.¹⁸³ *Críth Gablach*, an early eighth century law-tract, cited an ordinance (*rechtgae*) enforced by local kings "for expelling a foreign race, i.e. against the Saxons."¹⁸⁴ This ordinance can only refer to the attack on Mag Breg ordered by Ecgfrith and carried out by Berht.

The raid took place during the reign of King Fínsnechta Fledach (675–695).¹⁸⁵ Fínsnechta is identified in the seventh-century political prophecy *Baile Chuinn Chétchathaig*, discussed in chapter three. The attack "wretchedly devastated a harmless race" (uastauit misere gentem innoxiam: *HE* iv 26 [24]). The vocabulary of the Gaelic annal entries supports the interpretation that the raid's purpose was to finance Ecgfrith's more ambitious campaign against the Picts.¹⁸⁶

Ecgfrith then opened a campaign against the Picts who were ruled by his cousin Bruide mac Bili of Fortriu.¹⁸⁷ This Pictish campaign was undertaken against the advice of Cuthbert (*HE* iv 26), who had recently been made bishop of Lindisfarne at Ecgfrith's urging. The counsel of the ecclesiastics, Ecgberht of Rath Melsigi and Cuthbert of Lindisfarne, to Ecgfrith on matters dealing with Northumbria's non-Anglo-Saxon neighbors highlights the intercultural network provided by the Church to the Anglo-Saxons throughout the seventh century.

Ecgfrith fell in battle against the Picts along with the might of his army which suffered a great slaughter and left Northumbria militarily weakened. The Annals of Ulster reported: "The battle of Dún Neachtáin was fought on Saturday, May 20th, and Ecgfrith son of Oswiu, king of the Saxons, who had completed the 15th year of his reign, was slain therein with a great body of his soldiers."¹⁸⁸ The Annals of Tigernach added that Ecgfrtih was defeated "by Bruide son of Bile,

---

182 Yorke, "Court of King Aldfrith," 39.
183 The best explanation yet offered sees the attack as the exploitation of a soft target to gain booty to pay for the more pressing campaign against the Picts: Pelteret, "Attack on Brega."
184 "do indarbbu echtarchiníuil .i. fri Saxanu": Binchy, *Críth Gablach*, 20–21, lines 522–23. For discussions of the ramifications of this attack, see Wadden, "First English Invasion."
185 For discussions of this important king, see Bhreathnach, *Ireland in the Medieval World*, 60–64; Byrne, *Irish Kings*, 91, 104, 146, 276–77, 281; Ó Cróinín, "Ireland, 400–800," 208, 210.
186 Pelteret, "Attack on Brega." Another interpretation sees the raid in terms of Irish Sea politics: Edmonds, *Gaelic Influence*, 41–42.
187 Smyth, *Warlords and Holy Men*, 66; see further Miller, "Eanfrith's Pictish Son."
188 "Bellum Duin Nechtain uicisimo die mensis Maii, Sabbati die, factum est, in quo Etfrith m. Ossu, rex Saxonum, .x.u. anno regni sui consummata magna cum caterua militum suorum interfectus est": Mac Airt and Mac Niocaill, *Annals of Ulster*, 148–49, s.a. 686.

king of Fortriu."[189] In contrast to what Stephen had said in *Vita Wilfridi* about Ecgfrith's earlier successes against the Picts, Bede reported that after Ecgfrith's defeat Gaels, Picts, and Britons attained, and maintained, their freedom from Northumbrian rule (*HE* iv 26).

The raid on Mag Breg and the disastrous campaign against the Picts highlight cross cultural contacts crucial to Northumbria. Cuthbert counseled against the Pictish war which greatly weakened the Northumbrian polity. Ecgberht advised against the raid on Mag Breg and Fínsnechta Fledach, which resulted in the transactions (ca. 685) between Adomnán of Iona and Aldfrith *sapiens* on behalf of Síl nÁedo Sláine. Adomnán's return of sixty captives from Northumbria demonstrates his interactions with both Fínsnechta and Aldfrith.[190] Shortly after their three-way transaction, Fínsnechta entered clerical life (688) but the following year he resumed his kingship (689).[191]

There is a tradition that Ecgfrith was buried at Iona.[192] This is plausible since Iona was the mother church for the Picts at this time. As victors in the battle, the Picts would have controlled what happened to Ecgfrith's body. There is no record of Ecgfrith's burial among the Anglo-Saxons as there is for Oswald at Bardney, and for Oswiu and Edwin at Whitby. Aldfrith's presence at Iona before the battle, and Adomnán's visits to Northumbria shortly after the battle, suggest Iona's political control of the situation. In the *scholia* for the ninth-century *Félire Óengusso* (Martyrology of Óengus), but not in the main text, Echfritán mac Ossa (Ecgfrith + diminutive) son of Oswiu) is listed at May 27, a week later than Bede's record of his death at May 20, 685 (*HE* iv 26).[193] The later date in the *scholia* of the *Félire* likely reflects the day of Ecgfrith's burial at Iona after the battle.

---

189 "la Bruidhi mac Bili, regis Fortrenn": Stokes, "Annals of Tigernach," 209 [Felinfach i 169]. For discussions of the likely location of the battle, see Woolf, "Dún Nechtain"; Higham, *Ecgfrith*, 210–13.
190 Mac Airt and Mac Niocaill, *Annals of Ulster*, 150–51, s.a. 687. One of the wisdom texts attributed to Aldfrith/Flann Fína praises Síl nÁedo Sláine, the sept that Fínsnechta belonged to: Ireland, *Bríathra Flainn Fhína maic Ossu*, 164–65, lines 8.19–22.
191 Mac Airt and Mac Niocaill, *Annals of Ulster*, 150–51 s.a. 688, 152–52 s.a. 689. Stancliffe, "Kings who Opted Out," 163; Bhreathnach, *Ireland in the Medieval World*, 61–62.
192 In the Fragmentary Annals the entry for the *obit* of Aldfrith/Flann Fína has three quatrains that can only refer to Ecgfrith: Radner, *Fragmentary Annals*, 54–55. See further discussion in Yorke, "Court of King Aldfrith," 29–40; Higham, *Ecgfrith*, 210; Edmonds, *Gaelic Influence*, 43.
193 Stokes, *Félire Óengusso*, 136–37.

## Aldfrith (685–704)

Aldfrith *sapiens* succeeded his half-brother Ecgfrith after his disastrous defeat and death at the hands of the Picts in inaccessible mountain passes. Aldfrith seems to have been overlooked by those who wielded power, whether secular or ecclesiastical, in Northumbria.[194] He had lived among the Gaels, most likely at Bangor, and gained a reputation as a scholar, earning the epithet *sapiens*, discussed in chapter four.

### Saint Cuthbert's Prophecy

According to hagiography about Cuthbert, Abbess Ælfflæd of Whitby organized a meeting with the saint on Coquet Island off the Northumberland coast (ca. 684). Ælfflæd wanted to tap Cuthbert's prophetic abilities to satisfy her concern about the future of her brother Ecgfrith's kingship and its succession because he had no heirs.[195] Prophecies predicting future rulers were common in both secular and ecclesiastical traditions among the Gaels as noted in chapter three. This episode, found in hagiography, with Cuthbert foretelling Aldfrith's accession, has been cited as an example of political prophecy.[196]

Ælfflæd learned from Cuthbert that Ecgfrith had but a short time left, which saddened the abbess. Ecgfrith was killed in battle by the Picts within a year. When Ælfflæd asked about Ecgfrith's successor, Cuthbert replied that her answer could be found on an island in the sea, by which she understood that he referred to Aldfrith, her father's son by a woman of the Cenél nÉogain.[197] The anonymous Life stated that Aldfrith was then on the island of Iona.[198] The political ramifications of Aldfrith's presence at Iona are more important than the ecclesiastical ones. Bede's prose Life used vaguer terms and stated that Aldfrith was either *in insulis Scottorum* or *in regionibus Scottorum*, expanding the possibilities to

---

**194** See the brief discussion in Edmonds, *Gaelic Influence*, 42–44.
**195** See varying discussions of Aldfrith's accession: Moisl, "Bernician Royal Dynasty," 120–24; Kirby, *Earliest English Kings*, 142–47; Yorke, *Rex Doctissimus*, 7–8, 20–23; Warntjes, "Early Irish Regnal Succession," 178–82.
**196** Colgrave, *Lives of Saint Cuthbert*, 329 and notes. Colgrave cited the discussion by the Chadwicks who concluded for this example from Cuthbert, "The story was presumably put into shape by someone who . . . may have been familiar with the conventions of Irish and British poetry": Chadwick and Chadwick, *Growth of Literature*, 472.
**197** Colgrave, *Lives of Saint Cuthbert*, 102–5, bk. 3, c. 6 (Anonymous *Life*), 236–37, c. 24 (Bede's Prose *Life*).
**198** Colgrave, *Lives of Saint Cuthbert*, 104–5.

include the island of Ireland.[199] Cuthbert assured Ælfflæd that she would find her half-brother Aldfrith no less a brother than Ecgfrith, implying that their relationship would be a good one, as it proved to be.[200] Ælfflæd played an active rôle in Aldfrith's succession and reign.[201] *Vita Wilfridi* testifies that the relationship lasted until Aldfrith's death (*VW* c. 60).

### Inheriting a Shattered Kingdom

Since Bangor is most closely associated with Aldfrith *sapiens,* his presence at Iona shortly before Ecgfrith's defeat should be interpreted in political terms. Despite an apparent delay in taking power, once in place Aldfrith does not seem to have met any serious resistance.[202]

Ecgfrith's defeat was deeply disruptive to the Northumbrian polity as it had evolved under previous kings. The weakened state of Northumbria would have required drastic readjustments in governance no matter who took over. Ecgfrith was killed "with the greater part of the forces he had taken with him."[203] Many in his forces "were either slain by the sword or enslaved or escaped by flight from Pictish territory."[204] Even Trumwine, who had been assigned the bishopric at Abercorn (West Lothian) had to flee with companions back to Northumbria. Trumwine settled at Whitby where he was said to have been a help to the community overseen by Abbess Ælfflæd (*HE* iv 26). Under Ælfflæd Whitby continued to be prominent in political and cultural matters.

After Ecgfrith's defeat Bede stated, quoting Vergil's *Aeneid,* that "the hopes and strength of the English kingdom began to 'ebb and fall away'."[205] The Picts recovered their land held by Northumbrians, and many Gaels in northern Britain, as well as many Britons, regained their independence. These remarks by Bede confirm the expansionist policies of Aldfrith's predecessors. The ninth-century *Historia Brittonum* stated that after Ecgfrith's defeat the *Saxones ambronum* (Saxon

---

199 Colgrave, *Lives of Saint Cuthbert,* 236, 238.
200 Colgrave, *Lives of Saint Cuthbert,* 104–5 (Anonymous *Life*), 236–37 (Bede's Prose *Life*).
201 Yorke, "Court of King Aldfrith," 36–40.
202 Yorke, *Rex Doctissimus,* 8–11.
203 "et cum maxima parte copiarum, quas secum adduxerat": Colgrave and Mynors, *Ecclesiastical History,* 428–29.
204 "inter plurimos gentis Anglorum uel interemtos gladio uel seruitio addictos uel de terra Pictorum fuga lapsos": Colgrave and Mynors, *Ecclesiastical History,* 428–29.
205 "spes coepit et uirtus regni Anglorum 'fluere ac retro sublapsa referri'": Colgrave and Mynors, *Ecclesiastical History,* 428–29.

gluttons) were never strong enough again to exact tribute from the Picts.[206] Chris Wickham observed that "Bede was unenthusiastic about unwarlike kings . . . even if their policies had Christian motivation."[207] Bede had more to say about kings who expanded the *imperium* of Northumbria than he did about Aldfrith,[208] although Bede would have agreed with the Christian ideals that motivated Aldfrith.[209]

Bede stated that, as a result of Ecgfrith's defeat, the independence recovered by Britons, Picts, and Gaels obtained for forty-six years, that is, until the time of Bede's writing in 731 (*HE* iv 26). It is significant that Bede should be so precise as to the duration of this situation. He was emphasizing that from Ecgfrith's death Northumbrian political and military hegemony had receded. Bede's statement is a reminder that the Anglo-Saxon expansion throughout Britain took place at the expense of peoples and communities with strong identities distinct from the Anglo-Saxons. Military conquest did not immediately alter their languages, their social customs, their cultural practices, or their political allegiances. At this period when the Anglo-Saxons were still undergoing conversion to Christianity, Anglo-Saxon culture could not dominate that of their learned Christian neighbors. Anglo-Saxon political hegemony, where it existed, could only subsume, and then gradually amalgamate, Britain's rich ethnic and cultural diversity.

Bede referred to Aldfrith as *nothus* (illegitimate) in both the metrical and prose versions of his Life of Cuthbert and stated that he "was said to be the brother of Ecgfrith and the son of King Oswiu" (*HE* iv 26).[210] Bede's words suggest a disparaging attitude toward Aldfrith's family background. In order for Bede to maintain that attitude he had to overlook the common conjugal practices, and the resultant offspring, of insular nobility regardless of ethnic origins. His words reveal his ignorance, perhaps willful, of Gaelic laws on marriage and the rearing of offspring from various kinds of legally recognized, and therefore legitimate, liaisons.[211]

Although Bede's tone toward Aldfrith *sapiens* may be interpreted as demeaning, nevertheless, he stated that once Aldfrith succeeded to the throne he

---

**206** Morris, *Nennius*, 36 §57 (English), 77 (Latin).
**207** Wickham, *Framing the Early Middle Ages*, 343.
**208** Higham, *(Re-)Reading Bede*, 167–69; Grocock and Wood, *Abbots of Wearmouth*, lii.
**209** See comments about Aldfrith's teachings and writings in Yorke, *Rex Doctissimus*, 12.
**210** "qui frater eius et filius Osuiu regis esse dicebatur": Colgrave and Mynors, *Ecclesiastical History*, 430–31; Colgrave, *Lives of Saint Cuthbert*, 238–39, c. 24 (*Vita prosa*); Lapidge, *Bede's Latin Poetry*, 256, c. 21 (*Vita metrica*).
**211** Kelly, *Guide*, 70–73; Eska, *Cáin Lánamna*, 13–18 (Marriage), 19–20 (Affiliation and Raising of Children); Patterson, *Cattle Lords & Clansmen*, 288–327 (Marriage, Sexual Relations, and the Affiliation of Children).

"ably restored the shattered state of the kingdom although within narrower bounds."[212] After the devastation of Ecgfrith's defeat and destruction of his army, the restoration of Northumbria's weakened polity was no small feat.

We get indications that Aldfrith *sapiens* was an able administrator burdened with responsibilities that he carried out well. In the epilogue to the *Epistola ad Acircium*, sent early in his reign, Aldhelm encouraged Aldfrith not to neglect the study of the Holy Scriptures, despite being worn down by the responsibilities of secular administration.[213] Bede himself, earlier in his career, may have encouraged Aldfrith in a similar manner. Peter Hunter Blair had suggested that Bede's epitome of Adomnán's *De locis sanctis* had been dedicated to Aldfrith (ca. 703).[214] Although no evidence survives to prove Hunter Blair's suggestion, Bede concluded his epitome with the following words: "we pass along to you what should be read, praying that in all respects you take pains to temper your toil in the present age not with leisure of idle amusement but with a zeal for reading and prayer."[215] The conclusion of Bede's epitome was addressed to an unnamed someone in the second person singular. It was intended, much as Aldhelm's *epistola* was, to encourage a person distracted by worldly duties to continue with pious pursuits.

It has never been adequately explained what forces brought Aldfrith to the throne of Northumbria, particularly since it is clear that he had spent most of his life among the Gaels. There may well have been an alliance with the Picts, between Picts and Cenél Conaill, and later between Picts and Cenél nEogain, but this is by no means certain.[216] There are good indications that Iona played a significant rôle in securing the Northumbrian kingship for Aldfrith.[217] Iona's rôle is suggested by Adomnán's two visits to Northumbria shortly after Aldfrith's accession. Adomnán's return of the captives taken in Berht's raid on Brega shows that he not only had the necessary contacts in Northumbria, but that he was acting on behalf of Síl nÁedo Sláine and King Fínsnectha Fledach.

---

212 "destructumque regni statum, quamuis intra fines angustiores, nobiliter recuperauit": Colgrave and Mynors, *Ecclesiastical History*, 430–31.
213 For a translation, see Lapidge and Herren, *Aldhelm*, 46–47.
214 Blair, *World of Bede*, 185–86. Note that 703 is when Aldfrith expelled Wilfrid from Northumbria.
215 "[T]ibi legenda transmittimus, obsecrantes per omnia, ut praesentis saeculi laborem non otio lasciui torporis, sed lectionis orationisque studio tibi temperare satagas": Fraipont, "Bedae De locis sanctis," 280. For a translation, see Foley and Holder, *Biblical Miscellany*, 25, xix 5.
216 Moisl, "Bernician Royal Dynasty," 120–24; Yorke, *Rex Doctissimus*, 7–8; Yorke, "Court of King Aldfrith," 37.
217 Warntjes, "Early Irish Regnal Succession," 176–82; Yorke, *Rex Doctissimus*, 7–11; Yorke, "Court of King Aldfrith," 37–39.

One Old Gaelic text attributed to Aldfrith *sapiens* names septs of the southeast quadrant of Ireland. The text reserves particular praise for Síl nÁedo Sláine, the sept that suffered the raid on Brega in 684 led by Berht.[218]

Adomnán presented *De locis sanctis* to Aldfrith *sapiens* on one of his Northumbrian trips. He also visited monastic establishments which, according to Bede, were instrumental in his conversion to orthodox Paschal practices (*HE* v 15). These included a visit to Ceolfrith, as reported in Ceolfrith's letter (ca. 710) to King Nechtan of the Picts (*HE* v 21). More importantly Adomnán must have visited Lindisfarne where Lutting's use of *annus Domini* dating by 681 proves that Dionysiac Easter traditions were understood and implemented.[219]

Although Bede seemed to equivocate in his attitude towards Aldfrith *sapiens*, there is one important statement made by Bede toward the end of his life in circumstances that reflect sincerity. In his letter (734) to Bishop Ecgberht of York (*Epistola ad Ecgbertum*), Bede complained of the practice whereby local rulers established monasteries, sometimes installing themselves or their spouses as abbots or abbesses.[220] Bede encouraged Bishop Ecgberht to rescind and prevent these practices which had been common for the past "thirty years, since King Aldfrith was taken from the world of men."[221] Bede's comments show that throughout his reign, Aldfrith *sapiens* not only "ably restored" (nobiliter recuperauit) a shattered Northumbria (*HE* iv 26), but his experience at Bangor had prepared him as a judicious and efficient ecclesiastical administrator as well.[222]

## Contentions with Wilfrid

Bede's grudging comments about this learned king are difficult to understand. They have inhibited a fair assessment of Aldfrith's contribution to the cultural flowering of Northumbria. It has been suggested that one reason for Bede's reticence has to do with Aldfrith's apparent neglect of Wearmouth-Jarrow. This topic will be discussed presently. Another possible set of circumstances revolve

---

[218] Ireland, *Bríathra Flainn Fhína maic Ossu*, 162–68 §8.19–22.
[219] Ireland, "Lutting of Lindisfarne."
[220] See comments in this regard by Yorke, *Kings and Kingdoms*, 92–93.
[221] "Sic per annos circiter triginta, hoc est ex quo Aldfrid rex humanis rebus ablatus est": Grocock and Wood, *Abbots of Wearmouth*, 148–49 §13 (*Epistola ad Ecgbertum*).
[222] Aldfrith may have served as *comarbae ecalsa* at Bangor, making him the presiding authority over the church without being in ecclesiastical orders: Ireland, "Where Was King Aldfrith Educated?" 66. See further Etchingham, *Church Organization*, 67–68.

around Wilfrid and his partisans who contended with both Aldfrith and Bede and may have made it difficult for Bede to praise Aldfrith, even in later years.

Aldfrith expelled Wilfrid from his bishopric and out of Northumbria ca. 703, about the time that Bede completed his epitome of *De locis sanctis*. Wilfrid, for a second time, traveled to Rome to appeal to the pope to be re-instated. When Wilfrid returned from Rome, having acquired a favorable papal judgment, Aldfrith *sapiens*, now near the end of his life, refused to meet with Wilfrid and obey the papal mandate to reinstate Wilfrid in his bishopric (*VW* c. 58; *HE* v 19). *Vita Wilfridi* claims that Aldfrith, on his death bed, repented his treatment of Wilfrid in front of Abbess Ælfflæd and a certain Abbess Æthelburg who has not been positively identified (*VW* cc. 58, 59).[223] Aldfrith died on December 14 or 15 without meeting again with Wilfrid, but desiring that his successor make amends for the sake of his soul (*VW* c. 59). According to *Vita Wilfridi* Aldfrith had "softened" his position towards Wilfrid but died, nevertheless, without being able to reconcile in person.[224]

Bede had his own problems with followers of Wilfrid who in 708 had accused him [Bede] of heresy in the presence of Wilfrid at a time when he [Wilfrid] was bishop over Wearmouth-Jarrow.[225] Although Bede knew Wilfrid personally (*HE* iv 19), Wilfrid had not defended Bede against the charge of heresy. Bede felt compelled to answer the charge in his *Epistola ad Plegwinum*.[226] It is plausible that Bede believed, when writing years later, that he had to self-censor his comments about Aldfrith for fear of the attitude of partisans of Wilfrid.[227]

Aldfrith could not have been a favorite among the Wilfridians, having exiled the bishop ca. 703 and then having refused to meet with him (*VW* c. 58). Stephen of Ripon portrayed Aldfrith as having fallen ill after his refusal to meet Wilfrid and having repented in the presence of Abbess Ælfflæd. Aldfrith purportedly committed his heir to make amends with Bishop Wilfrid (*VW* c. 59). Ælfflæd was described in glowing terms by Stephen and through her figure Aldfrith's repentance was repeated and his commitment to have his son and heir

---

[223] Æthelburg may have been daughter of King Anna and sister of Æthelthryth, Wilfrid's virgin friend. She may have become abbess of Faremoutier-en-Brie, but the chronology is not clear: Colgrave, *Life of Bishop Wilfrid*, 184.

[224] D. P. Kirby argued that Stephen wrote two contradictory accounts of Aldfrith's death so the *Vita Wilfridi* must be used cautiously as evidence in this case: Kirby, "Bede, Eddius Stephanus," 106–8.

[225] Bede took a charge of heresy seriously. See Holder, "Hunting Snakes"; Thacker, "Why did Heresy Matter."

[226] For a translation, see Wallis, *Reckoning of Time*, 405–15. See discussion in Darby, *Bede and the End of Time*, 35–64.

[227] See comments by Goffart, "Bede's History," 214–18.

reinstate Wilfrid was carried out (*VW* c. 60). There is evidence that Stephen rewrote these parts of *Vita Wilfridi* at a later date.[228] Stephen described Aldfrith's illness and death as "divine vengeance" (ultio divina; *VW* c. 59).

The relationship between Aldfrith and Ælfflæd encompassed all of Aldfrith's reign. It is portrayed in two early Anglo-Saxon hagiographies: the anonymous *Vita Cuthberti*, that prophesied his kingship, and Stephen of Ripon's *Vita Wilfridi*, that portrayed Ælfflæd's presence at his death. Alcuin of York indicated that Aldfrith was buried at Whitby, which seems certain given his relationship with Ælfflæd. Against her positive portrayal in *Vita Wilfridi*, there is no indication that feelings were reciprocal. The anonymous *Vita Gregorii*, produced at Whitby in the final decade of her abbacy (704–714), after Aldfrith's death, and most likely before the completion of *Vita Wilfridi* (712–714), promoted Rome and the Gregorian mission to the Anglo-Saxons. Although promoting Roman orthodoxy in Northumbria through Paulinus's conversion of King Edwin (ca. 627), the *Vita Gregorii* never referenced the "synod" of Whitby (664) and thus never mentioned Wilfrid and the rôle claimed by his party.[229]

**Deira and Beyond**

Alcuin of York had stated that Aldfrith "passed away in a time of peace and was at last laid to rest beside his fathers" which can only mean at Whitby with his father Oswiu and with Edwin, maternal grandfather of Abbess Ælfflæd and King Ecgfrith.[230] The relationship between Aldfrith and Ælfflæd makes burial at Whitby nearly certain. Alcuin of York, himself a Deiran, praised Aldfrith *sapiens* as "a man from the earliest years of his life imbued with love of sacred learning, a scholar with great power of eloquence, of piercing intellect."[231]

The northern versions of the Anglo-Saxon Chronicle state that King Aldfrith died in Driffield, Yorkshire.[232] The Driffield area had significant iron deposits which emphasizes the economic importance of the region.[233] The location suggests Aldfrith's emphasis on Deira over Bernicia. The distribution of royal coins throughout eastern Yorkshire and northern Lindsey suggests that Aldfrith *sapiens*

---

**228** Kirby, "Bede, Eddius Stephanus," 106–8.
**229** See Ireland, "Whitby *Life* of Gregory," 172–73.
**230** Godman, *Alcuin*, 86–87, lines 1082–83; Yorke, *Rex Doctissimus*, 17.
**231** "qui sacris fuerat studiis imbutus ab annis aetatis primae, valido sermone sophista, acer et ingenio": Godman, *Alcuin*, 70–71, lines 844–46.
**232** Swanton, *Anglo-Saxon Chronicles*, 41.
**233** For the importance of this region over time, see Loveluck, "Anglo-Saxon Landscape."

**Figure 5.c:** Aldfrith's Network of Influence.
Aldfrith *sapiens* is associated with places named on this map.
Inishowen Peninsula: This is the homeland of Cenél nÉogain, his mother's people.
Bangor: Aldfrith was "heir" (*comarbae*) of Bangor's learning. Rath Melsigi: One point on the likely triangulation with Bangor and Anglo-Saxon Britain. Iona: Aldfrith was friend of Adomnán and was present at Iona in 684. Malmesbury: Aldfrith was personally acquainted with Aldhelm. Wessex: Aldfrith's wife Cuthburh was sister of King Ine of Wessex. Melrose: The visionary Dryhthelm was admitted here under Aldfrith's auspices. Lindisfarne: St. Cuthbert foretold Aldfrith's kingship (ca. 684). The anonymous *Vita Cuthberti* was written during Aldfrith's reign.
Wearmouth-Jarrow: Aldfrith bought a *codex cosmographiorum* brought by Benedict Biscop; Bede acquired *De locis sanctis* through Aldfrith's largesse; Witmer *eruditus*, a thegn of Aldfrith's, was buried at St. Peter's Church.
Whitby: Aldfrith's relationship with Abbess Ælfflæd of Whitby lasted from the beginning to the end of his reign. Aldfrith was buried at Whitby. Driffield: Aldfrith died at Driffield and his coinage spread into Southumbria from there.

maintained a royal seat, or at least an important estate, near Driffield and concentrated his efforts in developing the economy around Deira and the Humber estuary.[234] Aldfrith would have nurtured pre-existing links between Lindsey and Rath Melsigi established by Chad (*HE* iv 3), and maintained by Hygebald (*HE* iv 3) and Æthelwine (*HE* iii 11, 27; iv 12) (Figure 6.b).

King Aldfrith concentrated his efforts on Deira and the Humber region, but he did not disregard Bernicia. The Gaelic background of Lindisfarne and the influential cult of Cuthbert, coupled with its intellectual engagement with Dionysiac computistical practices, as shown by Lutting's use of *annus Domini*, would have appealed to Aldfrith. His interest in Dryhthelm, who entered Melrose under his auspices (*HE* v 12), and the reputation of Witmer *eruditus* at Wearmouth show his continued interest as *magister* and *sapiens* in the affairs of wider Bernicia. Aldfrith's purchase of the *codex cosmographiorum* brought by Benedict Biscop, and his confirmation of the papal privileges granted Wearmouth-Jarrow by Pope Sergius earned him the epithet "splendid king" (magnificus rex; *HA* §15).[235]

If Bede resented Aldfrith's purported neglect of his monastic home it is difficult to understand why.[236] During Aldfrith's reign the dual monasteries founded by his half-brother Ecgfrith, Wearmouth in 673 and Jarrow in 681, were mere newcomers when compared with the establishments of Lindisfarne in 635 and Whitby in 657. Bede himself was only born in 673, when Wearmouth was founded, and did not begin writing texts until sometime in the 690s.

Aldfrith *sapiens* also had relationships in Wessex. He and Aldhelm of Malmesbury had studied together somewhere among the Gaels, as shown in Aldhelm's *Epistola ad Acircium*. Aldfrith married Cuthburh, sister of King Ine of Wessex, so there were opportunities and reasons for lasting exchanges with the southwest of Britain, and further afield in Southumbria.[237] The school at Canterbury had been established at the end of his father's reign. Aldfrith *sapiens* would not have overlooked its importance.

Aldfrith's ties to Bangor may have extended south to Rath Melsigi. In the late sixth century King Cormac mac Diarmata of Uí Bairrche in Leinster gave up his kingship and retired to Bangor as one of the earliest examples of a king who "opted out" of secular for religious life.[238] Later hagiography states that King Cormac bequeathed three strongholds (*cum tribus castellis*) along the River Barrow

---

**234** Yorke, *Rex Doctissimus*, 14–15.
**235** Grocock and Wood, *Abbots of Wearmouth*, 58–61.
**236** For Bede's concerns about the future of his monastery, see Grocock, "Separation Anxiety."
**237** Kirby, *Earliest English Kings*, 143; Lapidge, "The Career of Aldhelm," 17–19, 22–23; Lapidge, "'Epinal-Erfurt Glossary'," 149.
**238** Stancliffe, "Kings who Opted Out," 161.

near Carlow to Abbot Comgall of Bangor.[239] The evidence is only circumstantial, but the *ráth* (fort, rampart) at Rath Melsigi may have been one of the three strongholds thereby making Rath Melsigi a daughter house of Bangor. Contact with personnel at Rath Melsigi would be natural for Aldfrith *sapiens* as *comarbae* (heir) at Bangor.[240] Aldfrith's dual heritage would have made him a natural liaison in a triangulation of Bangor, Rath Melsigi, and Anglo-Saxon Britain.[241]

The friendship between Adomnán and Aldfrith *amicus* drew on the intellectual backgrounds of both Iona and Bangor. In *Vita Columbae* Adomnán portrayed a connection between the two monasteries by highlighting the bond between Columba of Iona and Comgall of Bangor.[242] If Rath Melsigi were a daughter house of Bangor, then the relationship that Adomnán portrayed between Bangor and Iona forms the groundwork for Bangor's personnel to be involved in Iona's internal affairs. In such a case, one could see how someone like Ecgberht, who by 716 had gained seniority in the ranks, could participate in a delegation from Bangor to Iona. Nevertheless, no records have yet been identified that assign a rôle for Bangor in the conversion of Iona.

The other well-known monastery of Anglo-Saxon students, Mayo of the Saxons, was a daughter house of Iona.[243] The significance of its history would not have been lost on Adomnán. It will be discussed further in chapter six. Again, based on the relationship between Aldfrith and Adomnán, one can see how Aldfrith's influence, through his dual heritage and learning, would have contributed to maintaining the viability of an establishment populated largely by Anglo-Saxons in the far west of Ireland.

## The Achievements of a Bastard

In the realm of secular duties, Aldfrith *sapiens* was the first Northumbrian king to utilize coins. Their existence implies that he endeavored to restore the economy of his shattered kingdom.[244] The coins have a wide distribution in Deira, Lindsey, and points further south, but are not found in Bernicia. They appear primarily in

---

239 Ireland, "Where Was King Aldfrith Educated?" 71–72 and notes.
240 For a discussion of the term *comarbae* in the context of Aldfrith *sapiens* at Bangor, see Ireland, "Where Was King Aldfrith Educated?" 66–67; Etchingham, *Church Organization*, 67–68.
241 For more on Rath Melsigi, see Ireland, "Where Was King Aldfrith Educated?" 59–63.
242 Anderson and Anderson, *Life of Columba*, 88–89 (i 49), 200–201 (iii 13), 206–7 (iii 17).
243 Ireland, "Where Was King Aldfrith Educated?" 58–59.
244 Kirby, *Earliest English Kings*, 146; Yorke, *Rex Doctissimus*, 14–15. For illustrations of the coins, see Webster and Backhouse, *Making of England*, 63, 66 §54.

"rural locations which may have functioned as markets, assembly sites or centres for collection of royal payments."[245] Such descriptions are reminiscent of the Gaelic *oenach* (gathering; fair) and *airecht* (assembly; court) which would have been familiar to Aldfrith. One side of the coin displays a crude image of a *lion courant*.[246] These early coins included Aldfrith's name on the obverse which suggests two important points: 1) the coinage was controlled by the king, and 2) many who used the coins could read. As *magister* Aldfrith *sapiens* promoted literacy among his subjects. The continental custom of producing royal coinage by a Gaelic-educated king reflects Aldfrith's cross-cultural, outward-looking approach to governance.

It was in the context of secular responsibilities that Bede first described Aldfrith *sapiens* as "very learned [*doctissimus*] in the scriptures." He used this particular phrase twice about Aldfrith (*HE* iv 26; *HA* §15). Bede applied the same phrase to Ecgberht of Rath Melsigi, the person he credited with the pivotal rôle of converting Iona to the orthodox Easter (*HE* iii 4; v 9). Bede used a similar phrase "a man most learned [*eruditissimus*] in the scriptures," to describe Adomnán in his epitome of *De locis sanctis*.[247] Bede elsewhere described Adomnán as "a good and wise man with an excellent knowledge of the scriptures" (*HE* v 15). Bede used the phrase "most learned in all respects [*undecumque doctissimus*]" to describe both Aldfrith (*HE* v 12) and Aldhelm (*HE* v 18), for the latter when discussing the breadth of his learning.[248] For Bede, then, Aldfrith's learned background put him in the same league with Ecgberht *antistes* of Rath Melsigi, Adomnán abbot of Iona, and Aldhelm abbot of Malmesbury and bishop of Sherborne.

As noted in chapter four, Aldfrith *sapiens* was personally acquainted with both Adomnán and Aldhelm. He received substantial writings from both and understood and appreciated their contents.[249] It is also possible that he knew Ecgberht of Rath Melsigi. The bishops of Lindsey maintained contacts with Ecgberht and Rath Melsigi at this time (Figure 6.b). Furthermore, if Bangor were the mother house for Rath Melsigi, then Aldfrith's dual heritage made him the

---

**245** Yorke, *Rex Doctissimus*, 14–15.
**246** Gannon, *Anglo-Saxon Coinage*, 125–27. In style the lion has been compared to the lion symbol for Mark in the Book of Durrow.
**247** Fraipont, "Bedae De locis sanctis," 280; Foley and Holder, *Biblical Miscellany*, 25, xix 4; Ireland, "Where Was King Aldfrith Educated?" 45–48. The traditional view has been that Adomnán presented the text to Aldfrith on a visit ca. 687. In recent years it has been argued that Adomnán visited Aldfrith ca. 702/3 which is when Adomnán presented him with *De locis sanctis*: Woods, "Adomnán's Composition."
**248** For some insight into their relationship, see Thornbury, *Becoming a Poet*, 153–54. See also Dempsey, "Aldhelm and the Irish."
**249** For an assessment of the learning reflected in these works, see Yorke, "Court of King Aldfrith," 45–46.

natural liaison between the two. His close relationship with Adomnán of Iona helps explain the unusual circumstances claimed by Bede that Ecgberht converted Iona to catholic Easter practices (*HE* iii 4; v 9). Except for the fact that Bede himself had said it, few Anglo-Latin or Old English scholars appreciate how improbable the circumstances are in a Gaelic context, that a minor character of unknown rank and family origin (Ecgberht) from an establishment whose affiliations are not clear (Rath Melsigi) should arrive at a major monastery with an illustrious history (Iona) and claim to oversee its transition in the hotly debated matter of orthodox Paschal practice.[250]

The ecclesiastical relationships of Oswald (634–642) and Oswiu (642–670) focused on Iona and its representatives at Lindisfarne. But the potential for Gaelic influence would have naturally shifted towards Bangor during Aldfrith's reign. Nevertheless, Aldfrith's relationship with Adomnán shows that the Gaelic presence in Anglo-Saxon Britain would not have simply emphasized one monastery over the other, and would not have eliminated other Gaelic sources.

Two anonymous hagiographies reflect Gaelic influence inspired, at least in part, by Aldfrith in Northumbrian intellectual culture. Cuthbert was still bishop of Lindisfarne, which had by then adopted orthodox Dionysiac practices, when Aldfrith assumed the kingship.[251] The pastoral style and eremitic impulse in *Vita Cuthberti* are Gaelic characteristics.[252] The *Vita Gregorii* from Whitby adopts an orthodox stance but emphasizes *naturale bonum* and the worthy pagan, among other Gaelic features.[253] It has yet to be explained why Whitby, rather than Canterbury or a continental monastery, first honored Pope Gregory in this way.

The impact of King Aldfrith on incipient Anglo-Saxon bilingual cultural history must be understood in the context of Gaelic *sapientes*, discussed in chapter four, and the contribution of Bangor, the place where Aldfrith most likely sojourned *ob studium litterarum* (for the study of letters) and *ob amorem sapientiae* (for the love of wisdom).[254] The *sapientes* Laidcenn mac Báith (d. 661), Cuimmíne Fota (d. 662), and Ailerán (d. 665) all flourished during Oswiu's reign when Anglo-Saxons of every social rank frequented the free schooling offered

---

[250] For a more complex rôle for Ecgberht than that portrayed by Bede, see Duncan, "Bede, Iona, and the Picts," 26–27.
[251] Ireland, "Lutting of Lindisfarne."
[252] For the practice of praying in water, see Ireland, "Penance and Prayer in Water." For the notion of making a circuit to claim territory, see McMullen, "Ecclesiastical Landscape."
[253] Ireland, "Whitby *Life* of Gregory."
[254] "et tunc in insulis Scottorum ob studium litterarum exulabat": Colgrave, *Lives of Saint Cuthbert*, 236–37, c. 24; "qui non paucis ante temporibus in regionibus Scottorum lectioni operam dabat, ibi ob amorem sapientiae spontaneum passus exilium": Colgrave, *Lives of Saint Cuthbert*, 238–39, c. 24. See further Ireland, "Where Was King Aldfrith Educated?" 63–69.

by the Gaels (*HE* iii 27). Aldfrith is among those *sapientes*, Cenn Fáelad (d. 679) and Banbán (d. 686) are two others, who composed in Gaelic. The writings of Columbanus, reviewed in chapter four, and the contents of the Antiphonary reflect the Latinate learning of Bangor. The *Hisperica Famina*, with sections describing student life, were likely composed at Bangor (651–664).[255] The early prose narrative, *Táin Bó Fraích*, has Bangor associations, as do certain texts from *Cín Dromma Snechtai*, as noted in chapter three.[256]

The products of Gaelic bilingual intellectual culture should concentrate the attention of those interested in the contents of *Beowulf*, *Deor*, and *Widsith*, or the iconography of the Franks Casket. If *Beowulf*, with its Christian coloring, was composed ca. 700 in an Anglian-speaking region of Southumbria,[257] then the *Weltanschauung* of Aldfrith *sapiens* must be considered. The concentration of his coins in Deira, Lindsey, and points south, delineates his influence around the Humber estuary and beyond. If *Widsith* is early, then its historical and geographical program can be compared to the anonymous Hiberno-Latin poem on the Six Ages of the World, noted in chapter four.[258] Images from the Franks Casket reflect a bewildering array of traditions without any clear interpretation.[259] Its allegorical messages are as baffling as those found in *Immram Brain* or *Echtrae Chonnlai*, discussed in chapter three. The production of Anglo-Saxon literature, either in Latin or Old English, must consider the precedence of bilingual Gaelic intellectual life and Anglo-Saxon students' exposure to it.

The involvement of St. Cuthbert and Abbess Ælfflæd in the career of Aldfrith *sapiens* emphasizes his influence from Lindisfarne to Whitby. His death at Driffield, a region known for its iron deposits and agricultural potential, suggests that he kept an estate there and, along with his burial at Whitby, reflects

---

**255** Herren, *Hisperica Famina: I*, 32–39; Stevenson, "Bangor and the *Hisperica Famina*."
**256** *Táin Bó Fraích* was discussed in the context of *Beowulf* by James Carney, *Literature and History*, 114–28; for edition and translation, see Meid, *Romance of Froech*.
**257** For a survey on issues of dating, see Fulk, Bjork, Niles, *Klaeber's Beowulf*, clxii–clxxx. For a volume of essays that argues for an earlier, rather than later, date, see Neidorf, *Dating of Beowulf*. The most thorough survey involving possible Gaelic influence is Donahue, "*Beowulf* and the Christian Tradition."
**258** For arguments for the early dating of *Widsith*, see Neidorf, "Dating of *Widsið*." For a survey of its breadth, see Niles, "Anthropology of the Past." For a translation of *Deus a quo facta fuit*, see Howlett, "Seven Studies," 1–6.
**259** Webster, "Franks Casket." For matters of acculturation, see Abels, "What Has Weland to Do with Christ?" For a discussion in the context of other Old English poems, see Dobbie, *Anglo-Saxon Minor Poems*, cxxv–cxxx, 116–17, 204–7. For Biblical style in its texts, see Howlett, *British Books*, 275–84.

his concentration on Deira.²⁶⁰ The wide distribution, particularly into Southumbria, of the first Northumbrian coins, reflects Aldfrith's concerns to energize the economy and create a trading network across Anglo-Saxon Britain. The intellectual potential brought by a regal *sapiens* into Northumbrian life is reflected by Adomnán's *De locis sanctis* and Aldhelm's *Epistola ad Acircium*. The products of that intellectual input are represented by two anonymous hagiographies, *Vita Cuthberti* from Lindisfarne and *Vita Gregorii* from Whitby.

## Osred (705–716)

After the death of Aldfrith *sapiens* there was a short interregnum of a few months when a certain Eadwulf, of unknown descent, became king. He was soon replaced by Osred (705–716), a son of Aldfrith but whose mother is not known.²⁶¹ Osred was a boy of only eight years. Bede, initially, spoke hopefully of Osred referring to him as the "new Josiah" in his verse *Vita Cuthberti*.²⁶² His respectful tone suggests an early composition date soon after Osred's accession.²⁶³ Josiah became king of Judah at eight years of age in 639 B.C. and instituted religious reforms (2 Kings 22–23). Unfortunately, Bede's optimistic assessment of the young Osred was not fulfilled.

The early ninth-century judgment of Osred's character by Æthelwulf in *De abbatibus* is quite negative. Æthelwulf wrote from a monastery of uncertain location that had been established during the reign of Osred, probably by someone who had been forcibly tonsured.²⁶⁴ Æthelwulf described Osred as someone who "knew not how to subdue the wanton sense through the mind." Osred "did not honour the nobles, or even fittingly worship Christ, but . . . devoted his whole life to empty acts." Osred "destroyed many by a pitiable death, but forced others to serve their parents above, and to live in monastic enclosures after receiving tonsure."²⁶⁵

---

260 Loveluck, "Anglo-Saxon Landscape."
261 Osred seems to have come to the kingship through an alliance against Eadwulf that comprised high-ranking nobles including Berhtfrith, Bishop Wilfrid, and his partisans, and Abbess Ælfflæd: Goffart, *Narrators of Barbarian History*, 271–72; Yorke, *Kings and Kingdoms*, 92–93; Kirby, *Earliest English Kings*, 145–47.
262 Lapidge, *Bede's Latin Poetry*, 256–57, c. 21.
263 Lapidge, "Metrical *Vita S. Cuthberti*," 78.
264 For the possible location at Bywell, Northumberland, see Howlett, "*De abbatibus*."
265 Campbell, *Æthelwulf*, 4–7 §2.

In the mid eighth century (ca. 746) Boniface wrote to King Æthelbald of Mercia (d. 757) urging reforms. In his letter Boniface noted that two previous kings, the first being Æthelbald's immediate predecessor Ceolred of Mercia, who had come to the throne at a young age,[266] and the second Osred of Northumbria, had violated the privileges of churches in their kingdoms. Boniface accused both young kings of "debauchery and adultery with nuns." He claimed that Osred "was driven by the spirit of wantonness, fornicating, and in his frenzy debauching throughout the nunneries virgins consecrated to God."[267] Osred was murdered in 716, and Ceolred died in the same year apparently driven "mad by a malign spirit" (*HE* v 24).[268] The reigns of these young kings marked low points in the early eighth century for both Northumbria and Mercia.[269]

Despite the negative reputation of Osred reported by these two later sources, the *Vita Wilfridi* claims that Osred, son of Aldfrith, became the adoptive son of Bishop Wilfrid (*filius adoptivus factus est*; *VW* c. 59). Some have commented that Bede equated the reign of Osred with the increase in spurious monasteries that he decried in his *Epistola ad Ecgbertum* (734).[270] Among the last acts of Bishop Wilfrid recorded by Stephen of Ripon was for a visit to the young King Ceolred to look after the position of his monasteries in Mercia. Wilfrid declared his intention to establish a relationship with Ceolred "for he promises to order his whole life after my instruction" (*VW* c. 64).[271] On his trip to his Mercian monasteries shortly before his death Wilfrid "either increased the livelihood of their monks by gifts of land or rejoiced their hearts with money" (*VW* c. 65).[272]

Stephen wrote *Vita Wilfridi* sometime in the period 712–714 and rewrote parts years later. Wilfrid's hagiographer Stephen had ample opportunity to know of Osred's and Ceolred's negative reputations yet maintained the claim of a close relationship between Wilfrid and the two young kings.

It may seem odd to conclude a chapter on Anglo-Saxon empire by discussing Bishop Wilfrid. But there is ample evidence to show his desire to expand

---

266 For some background on Ceolred, see Kirby, *Earliest English Kings*, 128; Yorke, *Kings and Kingdoms*, 111–12.
267 Whitelock, *English Historical Documents*, 820–21 §177; Duemmler, "Bonafatii Epistolae," 343–44; Tangl, *Die Briefe*, letter no. 73.
268 Whitelock, *English Historical Documents*, 820 §177.
269 See comments by Yorke, *Kings and Kingdoms*, 111–12.
270 Grocock and Wood, *Abbots of Wearmouth*, lvi.
271 "qui enim omnem vitam suam meo iudicio disponere promittit": Colgrave, *Life of Bishop Wilfrid*, 138–39.
272 "aut cum terris vitam monachorum suorum augmentavit aut cum pecunia corda eorum laetificavit": Colgrave, *Life of Bishop Wilfrid*, 140–41.

his own ecclesiastical empire.[273] *Vita Wilfridi* gives clear examples of Wilfrid's predilections for empire in the description of Ripon's dedication ceremony sometime before 678. Wilfrid read out, in the presence of authenticating bishops, the lands granted to him by various kings, as well as lands and riches he acquired through the conquest by King Ecgfrith of local Brittonic kingdoms (*VW* c. 17).[274] Furthermore, Bede reported that while Wilfrid was in Rome seeking redress for his expulsion from Northumbria (678) by King Ecgfrith in the time of Pope Agatho (ca. 679), the following declaration was added to the acts of a synod he attended there: "[Wilfrid] has confessed the true and catholic faith on behalf of the whole northern part of Britain and Ireland, together with the islands inhabited by the English and British races, as well as the Irish and Picts, and has confirmed it with his signature" (*HE* v 19).

Some commentators have seen this unsubstantiated claim by Wilfrid in Rome as a natural extension of the northern campaigns against Gaels, Britons, and Picts by Oswiu and Ecgfrith, but also as an expression of desire for control in northern Britain, and in Ireland, by the papacy.[275] If the papal authorities in Rome were looking for an agent among the newly converted Anglo-Saxons to help them extend their own ecclesiastical empire further into the insular world, they had found an enthusiastic, if not always efficacious, accomplice in Wilfrid.

---

**273** Many commentators have noted Wilfrid's predilections for "empire" building: Foot, "Wilfrid's Monastic Empire"; Fouracre, "Wilfrid on the Continent," 186; Tyler, "Wilfrid and the Mercians," 282.

**274** For examples of lands taken from Britons, see Jones, "Donations to Bishop Wilfrid"; Tyler, "Mercia and the Britons."

**275** Charles-Edwards, *Early Christian Ireland*, 416–17, 432–35. It has also been argued that some late seventh-century Hiberno-Latin hagiography was a response to this attempted expansion of papal influence through Anglo-Saxon churchmen rather than through Gaels: Howlett, *Muirchú Moccu Macthéni's*, 180–86.

# Chapter Six
# The Long Century of Anglo-Saxon Conversion

Ecclesiastical contacts between Gaels and Anglo-Saxons are abundantly recorded and the present chapter investigates some of their consequences. This chapter attempts to dispel the false dichotomy, encouraged by differing Easter practices throughout Britain at the time, of a "heterodox" Gaelic Christianity being replaced by an "orthodox" Anglo-Saxon movement, inspired to a degree from Canterbury. The lasting successes of the Iona mission to Northumbria are outlined. An important monastery, "Mayo of the Saxons," was established as a direct result of the "synod" of Whitby. Another foundation, Rath Melsigi, trained Anglo-Saxon clerics who returned to work among their kin in Britain, and others who joined missions to their pagan Germanic kinsmen on the Continent. Neither of these two productive training centers for Anglo-Saxons could exist without a Gaelic "mother" house, nor without the approval and contributions of the local secular polity and its population. Gaelic contacts, including from Iona, throughout Anglo-Saxon Britain can be recorded for the full century from the foundation of Lindisfarne to the death of Bede.

The "long" century of the Anglo-Saxons' conversion began before any mission was undertaken from Rome by Pope Gregory.[1] The Anglo-Saxons were in contact with Christian Britons and Germanic peoples of Francia after their migration to Britain.[2] Once settled in Britain Anglo-Saxons interacted with Christian Britons and Gaels whose vernacular poetic cultures had adapted to, and complemented, the agendas of the Church.[3]

Many Britons had been Christian since Roman times and the conversion of many Anglo-Saxons began with their early social and cultural interactions.[4] There was Christian influence in Kent from contiguous Germanic kinsmen on the continent. By the second third of the seventh century that influence had extended to East Anglia and Wessex. On the other hand, *Vita Guthlaci* suggests that early in the eighth century there were still pagans in Anglo-Saxon Britain

---

**1** Some have argued that the conversion took nearly ninety years: Mayr-Harting, *Coming of Christianity*, 13–68, especially 29–30; North, *Heathen Gods*, 312.
**2** For a broad survey of conversion on both islands, see Pryce, "Conversions to Christianity."
**3** Yorke, "From Pagan to Christian." But see the state of affairs implied by Thomas, Stumpf, and Härke, "Apartheid-like Social Structure."
**4** Brooks, "From British to English," and for the broad context of the Anglo-Saxon conversions and their relationship to the papacy, see Ortenberg, "Anglo-Saxon Church and the Papacy," 31–42.

as Guthlac (ca. 674–716) stated, prophetically, that his own replacement was still among pagans and had not yet been baptized.[5]

The conversion of the Picts describes Ninian as the great missionary to the "southern" Picts. According to Bede, Ninian operated in the early fifth century from Whithorn (*Candida Casa*) and had been trained in Rome (*HE* iii 4).[6] The evangelist of the "northern" Picts was Columba who founded Iona in the second half of the sixth century (*HE* iii 4).[7] The conversion of the Gaels of Ireland is attributed to Patrick, working in the fifth century. There is evidence, however, for pre-Patrician missionaries in Ireland.[8] The *Chronicon* of Prosper of Aquitaine stated that in 431 Pope Celestine sent Bishop Palladius to Ireland "to the Gaels believing in Christ," the year before Patrick's traditional arrival date.[9] Columbanus, writing on the continent, accepted the primacy of this earliest papal mission.[10] The Gaels were Christian for five or six generations by the time Augustine arrived at Canterbury. They played a prominent rôle in Bede's *Historia ecclesiastica*.[11]

Augustine led the mission instituted by Pope Gregory the Great. It arrived at Canterbury in Kent sometime in 597.[12] The mission's success was muted in Bede's account in *Historia ecclesiastica*, despite two successive waves of missionaries.[13] Augustine was accompanied by Laurentius among others, and was supplemented, ca. 601, by Mellitus, Paulinus, Rufinianus, and Justus (*HE* i 29). Its greatest influence was in Kent and East Anglia, although the conversion progressed in fits and starts.[14] Christians from the continent married into local ruling families and helped with the conversion. King Æthelberht of Kent was said to be married to a Frankish Christian woman named Bertha (*HE* i 25). Æthelberht had welcomed the Gregorian

---

5 Colgrave, *Life of Saint Guthlac*, 146–49, c. 48, 175 and notes.
6 For a more nuanced take on Bede's use of sources here, see Duncan, "Bede, Iona, and the Picts," 27–31.
7 Mc Carthy, http://www.irish-annals.cs.tcd.ie/, ca. 563; Bede says 565: Colgrave and Mynors, *Ecclesiastical History*, 562–63.
8 For discussion of possible pre-Patrician bishops and missionaries in Ireland, see, Sharpe, "*Quatuor Sanctissimi Episcopi*."
9 "*Ad Scottos in Christum credentes ordinatus a papa Caelestino Palladius primus episcopus mittitur*": Mommsen, "Prosperi Chronicon," 473. For discussion, see Ó Cróinín, *Early Medieval Ireland*, 35–36, 47–48, 74–75.
10 Walker, *Sancti Columbani Opera*, 38–39, lines 21–27 (Epistula 5).
11 For a survey, see McCann, "*Plures de Scottorum regione*."
12 Mayr-Harting, *Coming of Christianity*, 57–68.
13 Augustine of Canterbury is noted in the Old English *Martyrology* at May 26. Bede seems to have been the primary source: Rauer, *Old English Martyrology*, 108–9 §92, 262.
14 Kirby, *Earliest English Kings*, 31–42; North, *Heathen Gods*, 312–23. See study concerning St. Augustine and Gregorian missionaries which suggests that the Anglo-Saxons had little consideration for Augustine and his companions: Lendinara, "Forgotten Missionaries."

missionaries to Kent in Bede's account and is considered the first Christian king among the Anglo-Saxons (*HE* i 25).[15]

The *Vita Gregorii* described a brief success in Northumbria with the baptism of King Edwin by Paulinus.[16] Bede portrayed a reluctant Edwin whom Paulinus worked persistently to convert (*HE* ii 9, 12–13). Ironically, Edwin had probably already been introduced to Christianity through British fosterers.[17] Upon Edwin's death (633), six years after his conversion, Paulinus abandoned Northumbria for Rochester (*HE* ii 20). When Oswald ascended the Northumbrian throne (634) the dynamic mission from Iona began, spearheaded by Bishop Aidan.

## The Gregorian Mission in Northumbria

Edwin was exiled during the reign of the Bernician king Æthelfrith (ca. 592–ca. 617). He wandered throughout Britain and sought refuge in various courts of which Rædwald of East Anglia is the only one named by Bede (*HE* ii 12).[18] Edwin received a vision that promised success over his enemies should he recognize certain signs. *Vita Gregorii* (ca. 704–714) asserted that Paulinus had appeared to Edwin in the vision.[19] Bede's version portrayed Edwin agonizing for years over his decision to convert (*HE* ii 12). The anonymous Whitby account is reminiscent of the vision received by Oswald before he fought Cadwallon, as related in *Vita Columbae*, where Columba appeared to Oswald, identified himself, and assured him of success.[20] Adomnán named a string of witnesses to his account.[21]

Paulinus, as portrayed by Bede, had difficulty converting Edwin who claimed he would convert once he had achieved certain goals, and only with the approval

---

**15** North, *Heathen Gods*, 313–21.
**16** Kirby, *Earliest English Kings*, 78–79 for Rhun; North, *Heathen Gods*, 312–23.
**17** See comments about the conversion by North, *Heathen Gods*, 323–40.
**18** Colgrave, *Life of Gregory*, 98–101, c. 16; Colgrave and Mynors, *Ecclesiastical History*, 174–83.
**19** "Sub hac igitur specię dicunt illi Paulinum prefatum episcopum primo apparuisse": Colgrave, *Life of Gregory*, 98–101, c. 16, quotation at 100.
**20** This may have been Adomnán's way of reminding Northumbria of its debt to Iona and Columba. See comments by Picard, "Purpose of Adomnán's *Vita Columbae*," 175.
**21** Adomnán relates that he had himself heard this account from his predecessor abbot Fáilbe who had heard Oswald telling his vision to abbot Ségéne: Anderson and Anderson, *Life of Columba*, 14–17, i 1 (8a–9b). It seems plausible that the "vision" episode in the anonymous *Vita Gregorii* relies on the similar episode involving Oswald in the *Vita Columbae*.

of his counselors.[22] Coifi, a pagan priest, made the most dramatic move in favor of the new religion. Coifi advised Edwin to accept the new faith and reject the old (*HE* ii 13).[23] And so, in the eleventh year of his reign, Edwin, his nobles, and many common people received the faith in 627 (*HE* ii 14).[24]

According to *Historia Brittonum* and the *Annales Cambriae* Edwin was baptized by Rhun mab Urien, identifying this Rhun (son of Urien Rheged) with Paulinus.[25] Urien Rheged had been a fierce rival of the Bernicians.[26] There is no reason why Urien Rheged could not have had a son who became a cleric.[27] Neither in the *Vita Gregorii* nor in Bede's *Historia*, however, is there any equation, or suggestion of cooperation, between Paulinus and any Briton. Bede made much of Paulinus's success at catechizing and baptizing at Yeavering in Bernicia,[28] and in Deira along the River Swale at Catterick (*HE* ii 14). The *Historia Brittonum*, while acknowledging the success of Paulinus or Rhun, described those he baptized as *gens ambronum* (a race of gluttons).[29]

---

[22] Chronological difficulties of this period and the relationships of the people named here are discussed briefly by Wallace-Hadrill, *Historical Commentary*, 65. Bede's account of Edwin's conversion by Paulinus suggests that Edwin was a reluctant convert and took a lot of persuading, including promises of future success (*HE* ii 9, 12–13); see also comments by Butler, "Doctor of Souls," 178. The anonymous Whitby *Life* of Gregory gives a more favorable account of Edwin's conversion: Colgrave, *Life of Gregory*, 98–101, c. 16. See comments about the conversion by North, *Heathen Gods*, 323–40.

[23] For Coifi, see North, *Heathen Gods*, 332–38.

[24] It should be noted against the background of the evolving Anglo-Saxon myth of their own origins, that York (*Eboracum*) was where Constantine was proclaimed Roman emperor in 306. Constantine's mother, Helena, is credited with the discovery of the "true cross."

[25] Morris, *Nennius*, 38, 79 §63 (*Historia Brittonum*), 46, 86 s.a. 626 (*Annales Cambriae*); but see Rowland, *Early Welsh Saga Poetry*, 86, 92; and Koch, *Gododdin of Aneirin*, xxxiii and n4; Koch "Why Was Welsh Literature First Written Down?" 22–23; Clancy, "The Kingdoms of the North," 158, 164. The *Historia Brittonum* equates the two identities and applies the name Rhun mab Urien to Paulinus, archbishop of York: Lot, *Nennius*, 203–4. Welsh genealogies attest to Urien Rheged having a son named Rhun: Williams, *Canu Llywarch Hen*, 137 n39c. The name Paulinus occurs commonly in Welsh ecclesiastical tradition, for example, as the name of Dewi Sant's teacher: Evans, *Buched Dewi*, 5; see other examples of Paulinus in early Welsh tradition at Howlett, "Insular Latin Poetry," 66–67.

[26] Rowland, *Early Welsh Saga Poetry*, 89–92; Charles-Edwards, *Wales and the Britons*, 384.

[27] Chadwick, "Celtic Background," 329.

[28] Bede calls this place *Gefrin*, but based on archaeological finds of goat remains, the proposed Brythonic etymology of "goat-hill" (*gefr bryn*) seems very likely. For continued presence of Britons throughout Northumbria, see Koch, "Why Was Welsh Literature First Written Down?" 20–22, 26; Higham, *Ecgfrith*, 51–52, 54 (for Yeavering); North, "Singing Welsh Bishop."

[29] Morris, *Nennius*, 38, 79 §63.

Paulinus's possible Brittonic identity helps explain his success at baptizing large crowds in regions that had large Brittonic and, therefore, Christian populations (*HE* ii 14).[30] It is possible that a charismatic Brittonic cleric was working in the region at the same time as Paulinus.[31] The success of Paulinus at Yeavering and Catterick, as described by Bede, contrasts sharply with the slow pace of conversion, and notable setbacks, by the Gregorian mission in the south and with Paulinus's own subsequent subdued, low-profile sojourn at Rochester (633–644; *HE* ii 20).

Many scenarios have been proposed to solve this dilemma. Kenneth Jackson suggested that the successful baptism of so many was a joint effort between Paulinus, emissary of Rome, and a cleric descended from the royal family of Rheged.[32] Large populations of Britons existed in remote areas of Bernicia and Deira and were already Christian. The success claimed for Paulinus may reflect a population of Anglo-Saxons already prepared for conversion.[33] Caitlin Corning suggested that Rhun had sponsored Edwin at his baptism by Paulinus.[34] A. P. Smyth suggested that Edwin had been baptized at the court of Rhun son of Urien while Edwin lived in exile among the Britons of Rheged.[35] Edwin's associations with Britons, including his likely refuge with King Cadfan of Anglesey, were noted in chapter five. If that were the case, then Paulinus's conversion of Edwin, as related in *Vita Gregorii* and by Bede, is better explained as Edwin's "re-confirmation" of faith by a member of the mission from Canterbury.[36]

The name Paulinus occurs in Welsh hagiographical tradition as well as in Brittonic poetry and inscriptions of the sixth and seventh centuries. In the Life of St. David (*obit* 588), *Buched Dewi Sant* of perhaps the twelfth century, one of

---

30 Hunter Blair, *World of Bede*, 94.
31 Bede told of Ninian (Ninias/Nynias), "a Briton who had received orthodox instruction at Rome" and whose episcopal see was at Whithorn, within the region presumed to have included Rheged (*HE* iii 4). Bede also described Rónán, a Gael who supported the *Romani* during the time of Bishop Fínán of Lindisfarne (*HE* iii 25).
32 Jackson, "Northern British Section," 33.
33 Molly Miller had suggested, based on the equation of Rhun and Paulinus and on Bede's statement that Ninian of Whithorn was orthodox, that Rhun and Rhiainfellt (Oswiu's Brittonic wife) may have been Roman in their practices: Miller, "Dates of Deira," 47n3.
34 Corning, "Baptism of Edwin."
35 Smyth, *Warlords and Holy Men*, 22–24.
36 This interpretation accepts Bede's view that Brittonic clergy were "unorthodox." But notice that Bede says the Brittonic bishop Ninian, based at Whithorn (Candida Casa), was "orthodox" and trained in Rome (*HE* iii 4).

the saint's teachers was named Paulinus, a disciple of a bishop in Rome.[37] Many clerics and scholars took names in Latin. For example, Crimthann is the Gaelic name of Columba of Iona;[38] Comgall, founding abbot of Bangor, was known as Faustus; Baducing became Benedict (Benedictus) Biscop; Willibrord, missionary to Frisia, was known as Clemens; and Wynfrith was the name of Boniface (Bonifatius), the West Saxon missionary in eighth-century Francia. The equation of Rhun mab Urien with Paulinus awaits full explanation, but it cannot be dismissed out of hand.

Paulinus served as bishop of York from 625–633. He baptized Edwin in 627 which means that Northumbria had six years when it was overseen by a member of the Gregorian mission. Paulinus's tenure at Rochester lasted from 633 to 644. It overlaps with the bishoprics of Honorius of Kent (Canterbury; ca. 630–653), Felix of East Anglia (ca. 631–ca. 648), Birinus of Wessex (ca. 635–649), and Aidan of Lindisfarne (634–651).[39] However, there is little evidence of his cooperation with these other bishops. Despite appearing in *Vita Gregorii* and in Bede, Paulinus does not appear in the Old English *Martyrology*.[40]

## Differing Easter Observances

The picture Bede created of Paulinus's success at converting Northumbria, however short-lived, has become symptomatic of a larger tendency. The Anglo-Saxon conversion is frequently presented as an imperial "orthodox" church, originating with the Gregorian mission to Canterbury, expanding inexorably throughout Britain at the expense of non-Anglo-Saxon "heterodox" Christians.[41] A misleading dichotomy has frequently been drawn between an ill-defined unorthodox "Celtic" Christianity, comprised of Britons, Picts, and Gaels, and a properly

---

**37** "Odyna yd aeth Dewi hyt att athro a elwit Paulinus, a disgybyl oed hwnnw y esgob sant a oed yn Ryfein" (From there David went to a teacher named Paulinus, the latter had been a disciple to the holy bishop who was in Rome): Evans, *Buched Dewi*, 5.
**38** Colum Cille "dove of the church" is a Gaelicized form of his Latin name, Columba (dove) and the gen. sg. of *cill* (church) from Lat. *cella*.
**39** Paulinus's successor at Rochester was Ithamar (*HE* iii 14), described by Bede as a "man of Kentish extraction." However, Richard Sharpe has noted that the practice of choosing Hebrew names from the Old Testament is most common among the Britons and suggests that Ithamar may have been Brittonic, or that Brittonic influence continued beyond the identification of Rhun map Urien with Paulinus: Sharp, "Naming of Bishop Ithamar."
**40** Rauer, *Old English Martyrology*. See also Lendinara, "Forgotten Missionaries."
**41** For an imperial Northumbrian Church, see Higham, *Ecgfrith*, 4, 133–35, 140, 147–48, 193, 200–201, 234–35.

orthodox Christianity practiced by Anglo-Saxons that had the *imprimatur* of papal authority through the mission sent by Gregory the Great.[42]

---

*Latercus*: provenance Gaul, composed by Sulpicius Severus in the early fifth century. It was brought to Britain and Ireland ca. 425 and continued in use among many Britons, Picts, and at Iona and some monasteries under Iona's control into the eighth century.
- 84–year Paschal cycle based on an 84–year lunar cycle
- Lunar limits: *luna* 14–20

*Victorian*: provenance Gaul, composed by Victorius of Aquitaine in 457 at the request of Archdeacon Hilarius, pope from 461–468. His table accommodated both Latin and Alexandrian (Greek) lunar limits. Victorian tables were used in the insular world and on the Continent through the seventh and eighth centuries.
- 532–year Paschal cycle based upon a 19–year cycle
- Lunar limits: choice between *luna* 16–22 (Latin); or *luna* 15–21 (Greek)

*Dionysiac*: provenance Rome, translated by Dionysius Exiguus in 525 from an Alexandrian table used in the eastern Mediterranean. The Dionysiac table was adopted by Rome sometime in middle of the seventh century but was not accepted by all Western churches until after the eighth century. It was the Dionysiac table that instituted *annus Domini* dating.
- 532–year Paschal cycle based upon a 19–year cycle
- Lunar limits: *luna* 15–21

Cummian's letter of 632, *De controversia Paschali*, addressed to Abbot Ségéne of Iona (623–652), challenged Iona's continued use of the *latercus* and represented that it had been unanimously rejected by important Gaelic churches at the synod of Mag Léne. Cummian named ten computistical systems that he had studied, including both the Victorian and Dionysiac tables.

---

**Figure 6.a:** Differing Paschal Cycles.

A more nuanced picture is required. There were, to be sure, local differences in religious observance which occurred all across Europe, not merely in the insular world.[43] Columbanus could, for example, contend with Pope Gregory the Great (590–604), in a letter of ca. 603, about the celebration of Easter decades before Rome itself had committed to what it would promote as universal practice.[44] Yet a decade later Columbanus could declare to Pope Boniface IV, ca.

---

[42] Questions about the validity of a separate "Celtic" Christianity and Church have been discussed in Hughes, "Celtic Church," Davies, "Myth of the Celtic Church."

[43] See, for example, arguments in O'Loughlin, *Celtic Theology*, 1–24 (Celtic Theology?); O'Loughlin, "'A Celtic Theology'."

[44] Walker, *Sancti Columbani Opera*, 8–9 (Epistola I). See discussion in Corning, "Columbanus and the Easter Controversy."

613, that the Gaels were "disciples of Saints Peter and Paul and of all the disciples who wrote the sacred canon . . . and we accept nothing outside the evangelical and apostolic teaching . . . but the Catholic Faith, as it was delivered by you first, who are the successors of the holy apostles, is maintained unbroken."[45] The "you" of this latter statement by Columbanus is plural, making it refer to the papal succession and, therefore, implicitly acknowledging the mission of Palladius sent by Pope Celestine from Rome in 431.[46] Columbanus, like Bede more than a century later, was eager to show the unity of the Christian world which, for Columbanus of course, included the Gaels.[47]

Throughout Christendom in the sixth and seventh centuries differences existed in matters of tonsure and the celebration of Easter, a movable holy day not assigned a fixed calendar date. Columbanus was defending the *latercus* when he wrote to Gregory. Rome under Gregory's tutelage, however, was still in the process of identifying a universal Paschal celebration.

In the insular world of the seventh century, there were three sets of competing Paschal tables (Figure 6.a). The *latercus* was commonly used by most Britons, Picts, and the Gaels of Iona and its associated monasteries. Two other computational tables, one developed by Victorius of Aquitaine (ca. 457) and the other written by Dionysius Exiguus (ca. 525), were used throughout Gaul and the insular world. Dating based on *annus Domini* is derived from the system of Dionysius.

The *latercus* had been composed by Sulpicius Severus, author of a chronicle on sacred history and hagiographer of St. Martin of Tours, and was introduced into the insular world ca. 425 from Gaul.[48] Those who followed the *latercus* could be identified by their tonsure which differed from the coronal "crown of Peter" (*HE* iii 26, v 21) promoted by Rome and so worn at Canterbury and in the "southern provinces" of the Gaels.[49] Christ's crucifixion and resurrection were always associated in Scripture with the Jewish Passover celebrated on the fourteenth day of the lunar month of Nisan. Passover had no fixed date in the solar calendar and neither did Easter.

Early Christians, particularly those of Jewish descent, often celebrated Easter on Passover, *luna* 14, regardless of the day of the week. They came to be known as "Quartodecimans." Other early Christians, emphasizing the resurrection, felt

---

45 Walker, *Sancti Columbani Opera*, 38–39 (Epistola V), line 25 (*vobis*).
46 Walker, *Sancti Columbani Opera*, 39n1.
47 Bracken, "Rome and the Isles."
48 Mc Carthy, "Arrival of the *Latercus*."
49 See Mc Carthy, "Insular Tonsure." Matters of tonsure cannot always be firmly coupled with Easter practice as differing tonsures existed around the Christian world, as seen in the case of Archbishop Theodore (*HE* iv 1).

Easter should always fall on a Sunday.[50] Those who followed the *latercus* always celebrated Easter on a Sunday, but didn't object if Easter also fell on Passover as long as it was a Sunday.[51] It was, therefore, inaccurate to accuse them of being Quartodecimans, as members of the Wilfridian party often did.[52] Easter tables accepted as orthodox applied lunar limits that could never coincide with Passover. Having Easter always fall on a Sunday became standard in the Christian world, but how to determine which Sunday remained a contentious problem.

Easter tables developed by Victorius of Aquitaine (ca. 457) became popular throughout Gaul and the insular world in the seventh century. Victorius used lunar limits of *luna* 16 to 22 but for certain years allowed for a choice between a "Latin" date, derived from an earlier Roman table, and a "Greek" date, based on the Alexandrian tables of the Eastern Church. The Victorian observances remained popular in parts of Gaul well into the eighth century. Victorius's scriptural authorities were the Synoptic Gospels.

Dionysius Exiguus (d. 544) wrote Paschal tables based on the Alexandrian practices of the Eastern Church which applied lunar limits of *luna* 15 to 21.[53] The Dionysiac method eventually became the universal practice promoted by Rome. It is not clear when Rome confirmed "orthodox" practice. It was most likely the decade of the 640s. Like for Victorius, the Dionysiac practices used the Synoptic Gospels as scriptural authority. Bede endorsed the Dionysiac traditions, as made clear in *De temporibus* (ca. 703) and *De temporum ratione* (ca. 725), and helped popularize the use of *annus Domini* dating practices.[54]

The scriptural authority cited by followers of the *latercus* pitted the Gospel of John against the Synoptic Gospels.[55] A consequence of privileging the Gospel of John, the disciple most beloved of Jesus, was to question the primacy of Peter, who thrice denied the Lord. By implication, this tainted the "rock" upon which the Church of Rome was built. The Synoptic Gospels present a different chronology for the passion of Christ from the Gospel of John. Both parties justified their practices with arguments extracted from the New Testament, and highlighted differences which could not be legislated out of existence.

---

**50** Jones, *Bedae opera*, 7–9; Mc Carthy, "*Latercus* Paschal Cycle."
**51** Mc Carthy, "*Latercus* Paschal Cycle," 27–37.
**52** Laynesmith, "Anti-Jewish Rhetoric."
**53** Mc Carthy, "*Latercus* Paschal Cycle," 26. For a summary of the above, see Mayr-Harting, *Coming of Christianity*, 103–4; Dailey, "One Easter from Three."
**54** For translations, see Kendall and Wallis, *Bede*, 21, 24–25, 115, 130, 169, 177; Wallis, *Reckoning of Time*, liii–lv, lxxv, lxxvii. For a survey of Gaelic texts on time that preceded and influenced Bede's *De temporum ratione*, see Bisagni, *From Atoms to the Cosmos*.
**55** Pelteret, "Apostolic Authority."

The Gaels who privileged the *latercus* called the evangelist John *Eoin bruinne* (John of the breast) because he had leaned against the Lord's breast at the last supper.[56] In *Vita Wilfridi* Stephen has Wilfrid, at the "synod" of Whitby, refer to the "Evangelist John 'who leaned on the breast of the Lord at supper' and was called the friend of the Lord."[57] The implication was that the apostle John was Jesus's favorite, and highlights a contrast with the apostle Peter. In both accounts of the "synod" of Whitby the rôle of the apostle John is prominent in the arguments against those who sided with Lindisfarne and Iona.

The "synod" of Whitby is often portrayed as a culminating victory by the "orthodox" Anglo-Saxon Church over a major "heterodox" Church operating in Northumbria. The evidence for that view comes from two retrospective eighth-century accounts: Stephen of Ripon's account in *Vita Wilfridi* (712–714; *VW* c. 10),[58] and Bede's account in *Historia ecclesiastica* (731; *HE* iii 25).[59] *Vita Wilfridi* is the only product of the Wilfridian *schola*. Despite Wilfrid's more than four decades as a bishop, no other verifiable texts survive.[60] A single short, ambiguous chapter in the *Vita* by Stephen offers the only hint of what Wilfrid may have taught with regard to computistics. Bede's works on time, from 703 and 725, demonstrate that he privileged Dionysiac practices and denigrated the *latercus*. At present, the earliest confirmation of Dionysiac practices in Northumbria comes from a Hiberno-Latin poem written in 681 by Lutting of Lindisfarne praising his *magister* Baeda.[61]

It is not certain when Rome officially instituted the Dionysiac Paschal tradition, but most likely several decades after Gregory's death. Each system, Victorian and Dionysiac, was favored in different regions of the Christian west. From some of Bede's statements it appears that both traditions could be considered "orthodox" in the seventh-century insular world. Although Victorian methods might offer two different dates for Easter in the same year, one of those dates would coincide with Dionysiac practice.[62]

Issues of tonsure and theology are not black and white. Theodore of Canterbury came originally from the Greek Church. He can be presumed to have known well the Alexandrian tables which formed the basis of the Dionysiac traditions

---

[56] For *Eoin bruinne*, see Walsh and Ó Cróinín, *Cummian's Letter*, 69n89; Monge Allen, "Metamorphosis of *Eoin Bruinne*."
[57] Colgrave, *Life of Bishop Wilfrid*, 20–21, c. 10, quoting John 21:20.
[58] Colgrave, *Life of Bishop Wilfrid*, 20–23, c. 10.
[59] Colgrave and Mynors, *Ecclesiastical History*, 294–309. Bede's works on time prove that he privileged the Dionysiac cycle.
[60] Foot, "Wilfrid's Monastic Empire," 35–37.
[61] Ireland, "Lutting of Lindisfarne."
[62] Ohashi, "Victorius of Aquitaine"; Warntjes, "Victorius vs Dionysius."

which became Rome's orthodoxy. Yet Theodore had to delay his departure for Britain for four months in order to change his own tonsure. He was also accompanied by Abbot Hadrian who was to ensure that Theodore did not introduce at Canterbury any "Greek customs which might be contrary to the true faith" (*HE* iv 1).[63]

The *latercus* already had a long history in Britain and Ireland by the time the Gregorian mission arrived at Canterbury. It would persist in some parts of Britain until the middle of the eighth century. For Britons, Picts, and Gaels who followed the *latercus*, seventh-century decisions made in Rome about Paschal celebration required them to overturn long-standing traditions that they had observed for generations. For Anglo-Saxons who had only begun the process of conversion, to accept without question Paschal observances promoted as universal by Rome in the mid seventh century was only natural.[64]

Bede regularly remarked on clerics, both Anglo-Saxons and Gaels, who, throughout the seventh century, had trained or been ordained in "southern provinces" of Ireland in an "orthodox" or "catholic" manner. The letter of Cummian (ca. 632), *De controversia Paschali*, discussed in chapter four, confirms that many Gaelic churches had rejected the *latercus* and aligned themselves with Rome. Cummian's letter also provided evidence that a computus employed by St. Patrick was derived from the Alexandrian tradition which formed the basis of the Dionysiac practices championed by Roman orthodoxy.[65] By the time of Paulinus's bishopric at York (626–633), before the Ionan mission to Northumbria (634), and before either Wilfrid or Bede were born, a substantial portion of ecclesiastical foundations in Ireland had aligned themselves with Rome. Cummian's letter demonstrates that those who supported the *latercus* faced ineluctable forces of change. Whichever Paschal tradition was finally chosen by Rome would prevail in the Christian West.

The significance of John's Gospel is displayed in Boisil's death scene, in Bede's prose *Vita Cuthberti*, when he and Cuthbert read it together during Boisil's final days yet avoided "deep matters of dispute."[66] The harsh tone against the Gaels in *Vita Wilfridi*[67] seems more pronounced when it is noted that among

---

**63** "ne quid ille contrarium ueritati fidei Graecorum more in ecclesiam cui praesset introduceret": Colgrave and Mynors, *Ecclesiastical History*, 330–31.
**64** The desire to defend long-standing tradition can be seen in the willingness of Columbanus to contend with Pope Gregory concerning Paschal matters several decades before Rome itself confirmed a specific practice: Walker, *Sancti Columbani Opera*, 2–13 (Epistola I).
**65** Mc Carthy, "Paschal Cycle of St Patrick."
**66** Colgrave, *Lives of Saint Cuthbert*, 180–85, c. 8.
**67** Colgrave, *Life of Bishop Wilfrid*, 98–99, c. 47.

Bede's last acts, recorded in Cuthbert's *Epistola de obitu Bedae*, was to translate into Old English part of the Gospel of John "to the great profit of the Church."[68]

Seventh- and eighth-century texts show that the Gaels recognized differences of interpretation and suggest how they dealt with them. *De ordine creaturarum*, an orthodox text composed between 655 and 680,[69] stated that in order to resolve ambiguities and differing opinions priority must be given to Holy Scripture and what "most catholic believers have reconciled with their faith."[70] The eighth-century *Collectio canonum Hibernensis* recognized that Scripture and the Church fathers may disagree and contradict each other. These issues of difference were faced squarely in the *Hibernensis* in its final book *De contrariis causis*.[71]

The convening of the "synod" of Whitby represented a growing intolerance on the part of some Anglo-Saxon clerics. The success of the Lindisfarne bishops who came from Iona and worked with Kent, East Anglia, and the West Saxons reveals a greater level of tolerance, as suggested by Peter Hunter Blair, among the Gaels and in the early Northumbrian church.[72] The Lindisfarne bishops from Iona were demonstrably more effective than their Canterbury counterparts in converting the Anglo-Saxons.

Bede implied that Abbot Adomnán of Iona had been converted to Roman orthodoxy after a trip to Northumbria. Adomnán visited King Aldfrith ca. 687 and stayed to observe local churches. Bede declared that Adomnán "altered his opinion" (*mutatus mente est*) so greatly that he preferred what he saw and heard in Northumbria. Nevertheless, he was not able to convert his own monastery of Iona (*HE* v 15, 21). Abbot Ceolfrith's letter to King Nechtán of the Picts (ca. 710) stated specifically that Adomnán visited ca. 687. However, while Ceolfrith's letter to Nechtán shows that Wearmouth-Jarrow followed Dionysiac practices by the eighth century, Ceolfrith's reported conversation with Adomnán was about matters of tonsure and not about Easter tables (*HE* v 21).[73]

The only person Bede named in Northumbria for Adomnán's visit was Aldfrith *sapiens*, whom Adomnán described as *Aldfridus amicus*.[74] Most seventh-century *sapientes* were orthodox and canonical as shown by their writings.[75] Aldfrith's

---

68 Colgrave and Mynors, *Ecclesiastical History*, 582–83.
69 Smyth, "Date and Origin."
70 Díaz y Díaz, *Liber de ordine creaturarum*, 118–19 §5.11; see translation by Smyth, "*Liber de ordine creaturarum*," 177.
71 Flechner, "Problem of Originality"; Flechner, *Hibernensis*, i, 466–74 §66 (text); ii, 825–31 (translation).
72 Hunter Blair, *World of Bede*, 100–101.
73 Ireland, "Lutting of Lindisfarne."
74 Anderson and Anderson, *Life of Columba*, 178–79 (103b).
75 Ó Néill, "*Romani* Influences"; Ireland, "Whitby *Life* of Gregory," 143–47 (Golden Mouth).

orthodoxy has never been questioned in any surviving sources. If Adomnán converted to orthodoxy due to what he encountered in a Northumbrian monastery ca. 687, then Lindisfarne is the most likely site. It would have the greatest appeal to an abbot from Iona. Michael Lapidge favored Lindisfarne as the location for Lutting and *magister* Baeda.[76] Lutting's poem noted the death of his teacher in 681, the earliest surviving record of Dionysiac *annus Domini* chronology in Northumbria.[77] A visit to Aldfrith *sapiens* and to Lindisfarne offered Adomnán exposure to "orthodoxy" in a Northumbrian context.

The conflict between what Adomnán came to believe and what his monastery continued to practice is reflected in one of the vernacular poems attributed to him, as noted in chapter two.
That stanza is worth repeating here:

> Ciped cruth nond·ráidet Scuitt
>    a scél n-amra n-aitt,
> sruith a n-aithne ad·noär duitt,
>    'Ba idan, a maicc.'
>
> (Whatever be the manner in which the Scotti [Gaels] relate that strange and wonderful tale, wise is the injunction that is given to you: Be worthy (*idan*), my son.)[78]

That "strange and wonderful tale" was the crucifixion and resurrection of Christ which lies at the heart of the Easter controversy. Adomnán apparently continued to work productively with his fellow monks at Iona.[79] His diplomatic success at instituting *Cáin Adomnáin* (*Lex innocentium*) in 697, securing the support of both ecclesiastical and secular leaders throughout Ireland and Northern Britain, reveals tolerance among clerics and secular leaders who may have disagreed over Easter observances.[80] It must be recalled that the arrival of Theodore at Canterbury had the potential to present similar dilemmas of tonsure, local practice, and theology as had previously existed at Lindisfarne, Melrose, and other Ionan foundations in Northumbria, and which came to a head at the "synod" of Whitby.

Nick Higham has observed that political benefits would have accrued to the Northumbrian polity from following the Ionan Paschal observances for thirty years. Having a Gaelic clergy operating throughout Northumbria who followed the practices of the surrounding Brittonic population and clergy helps explain

---

[76] Lapidge, "Lutting of Lindisfarne."
[77] Ireland, "Lutting of Lindisfarne."
[78] Carney, "A maccucáin," 36 §19.
[79] Stancliffe, "'Charity with Peace'."
[80] See the impressive list of guarantors: Ní Dhonnchadha, "Guarantor List"; Ní Dhonnchadha, "Law of Adomnán."

their greater success at conversion, and those years from 634–664 with Ionan bishops in charge of Northumbria from Lindisfarne must have helped Oswald and Oswiu to consolidate their power over indigenous populations, whether Brittonic, Gaelic, or Pictish, who followed the *latercus*.[81]

## Gaelic Missions and Missionaries

In the same year that Gregory the Great became pope (590), and a few years before the Gregorian mission arrived in Kent, a Gaelic monk named Columbanus departed Bangor for the continent with twelve companions.[82] Although not the first *peregrinus pro amore Dei* among the Gaels, Columbanus became one of the most influential.[83] Three ecclesiastical foundations were established by Columbanus and his monks in the Burgundy region: Luxeuil, Fontaines, and Annegray. Eventually Columbanus, intending to journey on to Rome, established Bobbio in Italy under the patronage of the Lombard king Agilulf. Columbanus died at Bobbio in 615.

The quality of Columbanus's education received at Bangor in the late sixth century can be gauged by the texts reliably attributed to him which include poems, sermons, letters (some to popes), penitentials, and monastic rules, as discussed in chapter four. Two Latin poems are from early in his career, before he departed Bangor. One poem deals with the transitory nature of the world, appropriate to a *peregrinus*.[84] A second poem is found in the Antiphonary of Bangor (680–691).[85]

His hagiographer Jonas wrote *Vita Columbani* ca. 640.[86] Jonas entered Bobbio ca. 618 within a few years of the saint's death and was able to interview persons who had known Columbanus well.[87] The Life is short on detail with regard to Columbanus's life in Ireland, but its existence attests to the early growth of

---

81 Higham, *Ecgfrith*, 67, 94.
82 For a survey of the interrelationships across both islands and onto the continent, see Fouracre, "Britain, Ireland, and Europe."
83 For a discussion of the varieties of Gaelic *peregrinatio*, see Johnston, "Exiles from the Edge?"
84 Walker, *Sancti Columbani Opera*, 182–85. See discussions in Schaller, "'De mundi transitu'"; Howlett, *Celtic Latin Tradition*, 156–69.
85 Lapidge, "Columbanus and the 'Antiphonary'"; Lapidge, "'Precamur patrem'"; Stancliffe, "Ventantius Fortunatus." For editions and further discussion, see Howlett, "Earliest Irish Writers"; Howlett, *Celtic Latin Tradition*, 169–77. For arguments that the poem is later, ca. 630–ca. 680, and may be classified as a *Romani* text, see Herren and Brown, *Christ in Celtic Christianity*, 284–88.
86 Kenney, *Sources*, 203–5 §48; Richter, *Bobbio*, 24–32 (Columbanus), 50–53 (Jonas).
87 O'Hara and Wood, *Jonas of Bobbio*.

the saint's influence on the continent; similarly for the Life of St. Fursa written on the continent soon after his death (ca. 650).

The impact of the Columbanian missions in Burgundy is reflected in Agilberht's history. He became bishop of the West Saxons during the 650s.[88] Previous to his bishopric Agilberht "had spent a long time in Ireland for the purpose of studying the Scriptures" (*HE* iii 7).[89] Based on his relationship with the Columbanian establishments in Francia, then Bangor seems a likely place for him to have studied.[90] Wherever he studied in Ireland, Agilberht played a key rôle on the Wilfridian side at the "synod" of Whitby (664). He attained the bishopric of Paris by 668.[91] Agilberht's study in Ireland must have been considered properly orthodox by the young Wilfrid who was ordained priest by Agilberht before the "synod."

The bishopric of Felix of East Anglia (ca. 631–ca. 648; *HE* ii 15) is another example of Columbanian foundations in Burgundy helping secure Christianity among the Anglo-Saxons.[92] Felix, from Burgundy, benefited from the Gaelic presence in his homeland. His bishopric overlapped closely with Aidan's of Lindisfarne (634–651) and Bede had noted that the two cooperated well (*HE* iii 25). During Felix's bishopric Hild arrived in East Anglia in anticipation of joining her sister on the continent. It is not known how long Hild was there before being called back to Northumbria by Bishop Aidan (647; *HE* iv 23). Her story suggests the nature of the working relationship between Aidan and Felix. Hild's time in East Anglia overlapped with Fursa's presence there. Even if she had never met Fursa himself, there were other named companions of his, Fáelán (Fullanus), Gobbán (Gobbanus), Dícuill (Dicullus), and Ultán (Ultanus), working in East Anglia at the time (*HE* iii 19).

Fursa represents the connection between Ireland and the Continent with East Anglia serving to link the two. He came from Ireland's northeast coast, perhaps Co. Louth or Co. Down.[93] The time of Fursa's group in East Anglia overlaps

---

**88** Wormald, "Bede and Benedict Biscop," 143, 145, 149; Wood, "Ripon, Francia and the Franks Casket," 10–11, 13.
**89** "sed tunc legendarum gratia scripturarum in Hibernia non paruo tempore demoratus": Colgrave and Mynors, *Ecclesiastical History*, 234–35.
**90** Hammer, "'Holy Entrepreneur,'" 62.
**91** Hunter Blair, *World of Bede*, 111–12; Hammer, "'Holy Entrepreneur'."
**92** Campbell, "First Century." See also Whitelock, "Church in East Anglia," 5; Stancliffe, "Kings who Opted Out," 169–70.
**93** Later traditions connect Fursa to Connacht: Ó Riain, "Sanctity and Politics." He originated in East Ulster: Ó Riain, *Dictionary*, 357–59. This is also the area where Cuanu and the *Táin* likely originated: Kelleher, "*Táin* and the Annals"; Ó hUiginn, "Development of *Táin Bó Cúailnge*," 57–62.

with Bishop Felix (ca. 631–ca. 648; *HE* ii 15, iii 18, 20, 25) who had connections with the Columbanian missions in Burgundy (*HE* ii 15).[94] Fursa's group extended their contacts onto the Continent at Nivelles in Flanders during the time of Abbess Gertrude (ca. 626–659). Both Fáelán (d. 655) and Ultán (d. 680) were at Nivelles.[95]

Precise dating for Fursa's presence in East Anglia is unclear.[96] But with Fursa and members of his group as intermediaries, the good working relationship between Bishops Felix and Aidan is easier to understand (*HE* iii 25). Those relationships extended onto the Continent.

Sigeberht of East Anglia (630/1–[?]) was an early convert. He had gone into exile in Francia and, apparently, was converted on the continent. When he took the East Anglian throne, he supported Bishop Felix's efforts to convert and educate his people (*HE* ii 15, iii 18). Fursa and his companions arrived during Sigeberht's reign and worked diligently to convert and instruct his subjects (*HE* iii 19). Sigeberht is the first recorded Anglo-Saxon king to "opt out" and relinquish his throne for a monastic life.[97]

King Anna (d. 654) of East Anglia was known for his piety. He ruled for roughly nineteen years. Anna and his nobles endowed Fursa's monastery at Cnobheresburg (Burgh Castle) with gifts and enhanced the buildings. King Anna's daughters were also known for their piety (*HE* iii 7). Æthelthryth married King Ecgfrith of Northumbria, as discussed in chapter five (*HE* iv 20 [18]). Fursa and his companions in East Anglia in the 630s and 640s provide a context for Hild's presence in East Anglia pre-647 when she intended to join her sister on the continent.[98]

Fursa arrived on the continent ca. 649 and founded a monastery at Lagny, east of Paris near Chelles, not far from Faremoutiers. Upon his death ca. 650[99] his body was taken for burial to a chapel in Péronne (*Peronna Scottorum*) in Picardy north of Paris by Eorcenwold.[100] His cult developed there and the site became an important center for the Gaels on the continent.[101] A Gael named Cellán (d. 706)[102]

---

[94] Campbell, "First Century."
[95] Richter, *Ireland and Her Neighbours*, 126–31.
[96] Charles-Edwards, *Early Christian Ireland*, 317–18 for dating arguments; Whitelock, "Church in East Anglia," 2–6; Wood, "Irish in England: Part I," 184–85 and notes.
[97] Stancliffe, "Kings who Opted Out," 154, 169.
[98] Whitelock, "Church in East Anglia," 2–6, 8.
[99] See synchronisms, Mc Carthy, www.irish-annals.cs.tcd.ie; Mac Airt and Mac Niocaill, *Annals of Ulster*, 124–25 s.a. 648 (*obit*), 126–27 s.a. 649 (Péronne); Stokes, "Annals of Tigernach," 190 (Péronne) [Felinfach i 150].
[100] Colgrave and Mynors, *Ecclesiastical History*, 276–77.
[101] For an overview of Fursa's career, see Richter, *Ireland and Her Neighbours*, 126–33.
[102] Sharpe, *Handlist*, 84 §182.

from Péronne exchanged letters with Aldhelm requesting certain of the latter's "little sermons."[103] Their exchange suggests how Bede came to know about Fursa who recorded an account of Fursa's vision (*HE* iii 19) which he found in a *libellus* written on the continent.[104] Bede's account contains an example of the Gaelic triad "thought, word and deed" not found in his continental source, as discussed in Appendix 4.b.[105]

The monastic memoir "Monastery of Tallaght" (830s) relates that the daughter of a king in the eastern country (ingen ind rig isna tirib thair) granted Fursa land where he could rest his "anvil of devotion" (indeuin crábid).[106] It is possible that a daughter of King Anna is intended, but the eastern land could refer either to East Anglia or to Francia.[107] Fursa is entered in the Old English *Martyrology* at January 16, just as he is in the *Félire Óengusso*.[108]

The residents of Würzburg recognize Kilian (Cellán/Celléne) as founder of an influential monastery among the pagans of central Germany in the seventh century. Kilian had gone to Rome to secure Pope Conon's (686/7) approval for his foundation and returned as bishop. However, upon his return he found that the local ruler, Duke Gozbert, had married his brother's widow. When Kilian condemned the marriage the duke's new wife had Kilian and two of his monks killed, a rare example of martyrdom among early Gaelic missionary churchmen.[109]

In his study of the Anglo-Saxon library, Michael Lapidge discussed the surviving book inventory for Würzburg.[110] Lapidge cited Würzburg as an Anglo-Saxon foundation, noting that it was "established as a bishopric by Boniface and occupied first by the Anglo-Saxon bishop Burghard in 742."[111] Whatever about the Anglo-Saxon presence by the mid eighth century, Würzburg never lost its Gaelic associations. An important collection of Early Gaelic glosses, made in the mid eighth century, comes from Würzburg in the extensively glossed

---

**103** Lapidge and Herren, *Aldhelm*, 149, 167 and notes; Howlett, "Aldhelm and Irish Learning"; Howlett, *Celtic Latin Tradition*, 108–113; Lapidge and Sharpe, *Bibliography of Celtic-Latin*, 168 §643; Orchard, *Poetic Art of Aldhelm*, 240–41; Sims-Williams, *Religion and Literature*, 346, 351; Wood, "Irish in England: Part I," 185.
**104** Rackham, *Transitus Beati Fursei*.
**105** Sims-Williams, "Thought, Word, Deed."
**106** Gwynn and Purton, "Monastery of Tallaght," 134 §19.
**107** Whitelock, "Church in East Anglia," 8.
**108** Rauer, *Old English Martyrology*, 48–49 §21, 237 (commentary); Stokes, *Félire Óengusso*, 36, 44–47 (notes).
**109** Richter, *Ireland and Her Neighbours*, 133–34; Wood, "Irish in England: Part I," 185 and notes.
**110** Lapidge, *Anglo-Saxon Library*, 148–51.
**111** Lapidge, *Anglo-Saxon Library*, 78.

Pauline Epistles.[112] The glosses helped early linguists create a grammar for Old Gaelic.[113] Jacopo Bisagni studied Gaelic and Latin code-switching based on the Würzburg glosses and demonstrated the depth of bilingual linguistic competence of early Gaelic *literati*.[114] After its foundation by a Gael, the next firm references to Würzburg's personnel may be to Anglo-Saxons in the mid eighth century, but the Gaelic glossing of the Pauline Epistles in the same period proves the continued contribution of Gaelic monks there.

One of the most influential missionaries from Ireland never made it to the continent. Columba, known in the Gaelicized form as Colum Cille (Dove of the Church), founded Iona ca. 562 (*HE* iii 4).[115] He was a prominent member of the Cenél Conaill branch of the northern Uí Néill federation from Donegal. Columba evangelized the northern Picts and furthered the work of Ninian (Nynias) of Whithorn according to Bede (*HE* iii 4).[116] Columba's prominence is reflected by his mention in the Old English *Martyrology* which drew on some unidentified sources.[117]

Iona bequeathed a rich poetic heritage and produced an eclectic literature in both Latin and Gaelic in the course of the seventh century, as outlined in chapter four.[118] *Altus Prosator*, known to Aldhelm, is a poem from Iona. The vernacular poems by Bécán mac Luigdech in praise of Columba, discussed in chapter two, reflect the cooperation between the poets and the Church. Abbot Adomnán composed poems in both Latin and Gaelic. *Vita Columbae* has an episode about lay people who chanted songs about Columba which acted as *loricae* and protected them from enemies.[119] Another anecdote was about the poet Crónán and how Columba's monks expected to be entertained by him *ex more*.[120] Iona's greatest contribution to Northumbria was through the thirty-year mission (634–664) operating from Lindisfarne, to be discussed below.

---

112 Stokes and Strachan, *Thesaurus*, i, xxiii–xxv, 499–712; Kavanagh, *Lexicon*; Thurneysen, *Grammar of Old Irish*, 4–5 §5.
113 Thurneysen, *Grammar of Old Irish*, 4–8.
114 Bisagni, "Study of Code-Switching."
115 Mc Carthy, http://www.irish-annals.cs.tcd.ie/, s.a. 562; Mac Airt and Mac Niocaill, *Annals of Ulster*, 82–83, s.a. 563; Stokes, "Annals of Tigernach," 144 [Felinfach i 104].
116 "qui erat Romae regulariter fidem et mysteria ueritatis edoctus": Colgrave and Mynors, *Ecclesiastical History*, 222. For Columba's relationship with the Picts, see Charles-Edwards, *Early Christian Ireland*, 299–308. For a brief discussion of Whithorn, see Edmonds, *Gaelic Influence*, 120–26.
117 Rauer, *Old English Martyrology*, 114–15 §100 (June 9), 265 (commentary).
118 Clancy and Márkus, *Iona*.
119 Anderson and Anderson, *Life of Columba*, 16–17, i 1.
120 Anderson and Anderson, *Life of Columba*, 76–77, i 42.

## Iona's Mission to Northumbria

After the death of Edwin (633), the first Christian king of Northumbria, Oswald ascended the throne. He had spent the reign of Edwin in exile, along with his brothers, in Northern Britain among the Gaels and Picts, where he was educated, baptized, and became fluent in Gaelic. Once Oswald was on the throne he invited missionaries from Iona to convert his kingdom. Although Bede had described Paulinus's great success at converting both the Bernicians and Deirans (*HE* ii 14), Adomnán declared Oswald's newly acquired kingdom to be largely pagan.[121] The first missionary to come from Iona soon returned complaining of the barbaric Anglo-Saxons, but the second to come, Aidan, was very successful (*HE* iii 5).

Shortly after his victory over Cadwallon, who had defeated and killed Edwin, Oswald established a relationship with King Cynegisl of Wessex (Gewisse) and married his daughter Cyneburh. But Oswald first assisted with King Cynegisl's conversion to Christianity. Pope Honorius (625–638) had sent Bishop Birinus (634–ca. 650) to Wessex. He found that the Gewisse were "all completely heathen."[122] Birinus baptized Cynegisl with Oswald standing in as sponsor. The two kings gave Birinus Dorchester (Dorcic) in the Thames Valley as his episcopal see (*HE* iii 7). We see here Oswald cooperating with both the Ionan bishop, Aidan, and the bishop sent by Rome, Birinus, to establish the Christian faith in Wessex. Oswald is commemorated as a saint by the Anglo-Saxons and the Gaels at August 5.[123]

Cynegisl's son Cenwealh repudiated the faith. Cenwealh had been married to the Mercian king Penda's sister and suffered attacks from Penda when he divorced her and married another. Cenwealh sought refuge with the Christian king Anna of East Anglia. Although we have no firm dates for when this occurred, Cenwealh was in East Anglia during that period when Fursa and his companions were active there. His sojourn in East Anglia apparently recommitted Cenwealh to the Christian faith. When Cenwealh regained the throne of Wessex he installed Agilberht as bishop during the decade of the 650s (*HE* iii 7). Agilberht had been educated in Ireland in the 640s, perhaps at Bangor.[124] It

---

[121] "Nam usque in id temporis tota illa Saxonia gentilitatis et ignorantiae tenebris obscurata erat": Anderson and Anderson, *Life of Columba*, 14–17, i 1.
[122] "cum omnes ibidem paganissimos inueniret": Colgrave and Mynors, *Ecclesiastical History*, 232–33.
[123] The Old English martyrology notes that his relics are found in Bamburgh, Lindisfarne, and in Lindsey at Bardney: Rauer, *Old English Martyrology*, 154–55 §146, 279 (commentary). He occurs at the same date in *Félire Óengusso*: Stokes, *Félire Óengusso*, 124, 182–83 where the *scholia* confuse him with Aldfrith, here called Flann Fína mac Ossu.
[124] Hammer, "'Holy Entrepreneur'," 62.

appears that Cenwealh's time in East Anglia with the Christian king Anna, nurtured further by Fursa and his companions, encouraged him to restore Christianity to Wessex in the 650s and to install the Gaelic-trained Frankish bishop Agilberht.

## Bishop Aidan (634–651)

Bishop Aidan was sent from Iona by Abbot Ségéne (623–652) at the request of King Oswald. Aidan founded the monastery at Lindisfarne (635), within view of the royal site of Bamburgh. The Old English *Martyrology*, at August 31, states that King Oswald brought Aidan to Northumbria and that his bones (relics) lie "partly with the Gaels, partly in St. Cuthbert's monastery."[125] Bede relates several miracles attributed to Aidan (*HE* iii 15–17) and is fulsome in his description of Aidan's pastoral style. Bede stated that Aidan "taught them no other way of life than that which he himself practised among his fellows." For example, "he neither sought after nor cared for worldly possessions but he rejoiced to hand over at once, to any poor man he met, the gifts which he had received from kings or rich men of the world" (*HE* iii 5). Aidan rarely traveled by horse, but usually went on foot. All who accompanied him, whether secular or religious, were expected to engage in study of the scriptures and memorization of psalms. Such practices imply that Aidan encouraged those around him to become literate. Bede stated that Aidan's life was "in great contrast to our modern slothfulness" (*HE* iii 5).

Upon his arrival Aidan took in twelve Anglo-Saxon boys to be trained by the Church. Among the twelve was Eata who became abbot of Melrose. Eata's abbacy overlapped with Boisil's time as prior at Melrose when Cuthbert entered the monastery there (*HE* iv 27). Eata eventually became bishop of Hexham 678–681 and again for a short time ca. 685–685/6. He served as bishop of Lindisfarne, but it is difficult to know just how that post overlapped with his time at Hexham (*HE* iv 27). Another boy was Chad who became bishop of Mercia and Lindsey at Lichfield, 669–672, having previously served as abbot at Lastingham, a monastery originally established by Cedd (*HE* iii 23). Chad also trained at Rath Melsigi with Ecgberht (*HE* iv 3). Chad's brother Cedd became bishop of the East Saxons. He served as interpreter for all parties at the "synod" of Whitby. Although he supported the Ionan party, along with Hild and her community, he accepted the decision and followed the universal, orthodox practices for Easter (*HE* iii 26). Unfortunately, he died in 664 shortly afterwards. Cedd is listed in the Old English *Martyrology*

---

[125] Rauer, *Old English Martyrology*, 172–73 §171, 287 (commentary). The Gaels commemorate him on the same date: Stokes, *Félire Óengusso*, 179, 190–91.

at October 26.[126] Bede has Ecgberht relate a miraculous story to Hygebald, abbot of Lindsey, while on a visit to Rath Melsigi late in the seventh century, about Chad's death and how Cedd's soul descended "from the sky with a host of angels" and returned to heaven taking Chad's soul with them (*HE* iv 3). Chad is named at March 2 in the Old English *Martyrology*.[127]

Bishop Aidan developed good working relations with Bishop Felix of East Anglia (ca. 631–ca. 648) and with Bishop Honorius of Kent (627x631–653; *HE* iii 25). Their bishoprics all overlap closely. However, Bede never mentioned Paulinus, bishop of Rochester (633–644), in this context despite his reported successes in converting Northumbria before Aidan's arrival. Fursa and his companions were in East Anglia during the bishoprics of Felix and Aidan. A recently converted East Anglia had opportunities for cooperation with two Gaelic sources. Hild, who was abbess of Whitby during Cædmon's time, arrived in East Anglia prior to 647, intending to follow her sister Hereswith to the continent (*HE* iv 23). But Bishop Aidan, who had developed a working relationship with her, recalled (reuocata) her to Northumbria to take charge of Heruteu (Hartlepool). This early monastic site was founded by a woman named Heiu, ordained by Bishop Aidan probably ca. 640 (*HE* iv 23), and seems, according to archaeological evidence, to have been more important than written records reveal in the period prior to 800.[128]

The name Heruteu, as Bede explained, means "island of the hart" (insula cerui: *HE* iii 24). Much of the argumentation for an early dating of *Beowulf* has been based on onomastics and the fact that proper names from *Beowulf* have been preserved in various early Anglo-Saxon records.[129] Joseph Harris has suggested that there may be a similar connection to the great hall *Heorot* (Hart), mentioned several times in *Beowulf* and once in *Widsith*, and the early institutional name Heruteu in Northumbria.[130]

After King Oswiu defeated Penda of Mercia (655) he dedicated to the Church his infant daughter Ælfflæd, who had been born the year before, in gratitude for his victory. Ælfflæd was given into Hild's care at Heruteu. Ælfflæd remained in Hild's care and moved with her two years later to Whitby. When Hild died in 680, Ælfflæd took over as abbess and, with the assistance of her mother Eanflæd while she lived, ruled Whitby until her death in 714.[131] Cædmon most likely performed at Whitby during Hild's time, but his career may have extended into

---

126 Rauer, *Old English Martyrology*, 206–7 §214, 302 (commentary).
127 Rauer, *Old English Martyrology*, 60–61 §37, 243 (commentary).
128 Daniels, "Monastery at Hartlepool"; Okasha, "Inscribed Stones."
129 Shippey, "Names in *Beowulf*."
130 Harris, "Note on the Other Heorot."
131 It is not known when Eanflæd died, but probably sometime after ca. 685.

Ælfflæd's abbacy.[132] It was towards the end of Ælfflæd's abbacy, ca. 704–714, that an anonymous author of Whitby produced *Vita Gregorii*. This first ever Life of such an important pope is written from an orthodox, catholic viewpoint, yet the text is replete with features that reflect the continuing Gaelic ethos at Whitby.[133] Ælfflæd was prominent enough among the Gaels for her death to be noted in their annals ca. 713, although she is not named.[134]

Five bishops were named by Bede as having been trained at Whitby during Hild's tenure. One of them, Oftfor, began his life in religion at Heruteu with Hild and was said to have "devoted himself to the reading and observance of the Scriptures" at both of Hild's monasteries (*HE* iv 23 [21]),[135] that is, at Heruteu and at Whitby. His career included further schooling at Canterbury with Archbishop Theodore, as well as a trip to Rome. When he returned to Britain he settled among the Hwicce, assisting the bishop there for a long time (*multo tempore*). He was eventually appointed bishop ca. 691–693, being consecrated by Bishop Wilfrid, who was acting bishop for the Middle Angles, because Archbishop Theodore had died by that time.[136] Thus Oftfor had a career that paralleled Aldhelm's with a firm foundation in Gaelic influenced education, its expansion at Theodore's school in Canterbury, and a sojourn in Rome before settling into a bishopric in Wessex.

Bishop Aidan developed a close relationship with King Oswine of Deira, who was a rival of King Oswiu of Bernicia (*HE* iii 14). The piety of Oswine and his devotion to Bishop Aidan demonstrate the inroads of the Iona mission into the polity of Deira. It contradicts the supposition that Deira maintained the Canterbury traditions of Paulinus and Edwin in contrast to the Ionan practices of Aidan and Oswald in Bernicia. The personal and pastoral characteristics described for Aidan by Bede influenced Oswine and, apparently, helped strengthen the jealousy in Oswiu who had his rival murdered.

Bishop Paulinus is not mentioned in the Old English *Martyrology* whereas Bishop Aidan is cited there. Bede gave Aidan's death date as August 31, 651, in the seventeenth year of his bishopric (*HE* iii 17). The *Félire Óengusso*, on the

---

132 For arguments on dating, see Cronan, "Cædmon's *Hymn*"; and O'Donnell, *Cædmon's Hymn*, 10n6.
133 For the larger cultural context, see Ireland, "Whitby *Life* of Gregory."
134 The annal entry states that Oswiu's daughter died at Hild's monastery: Mac Airt and Mac Niocaill, *Annals of Ulster*, 68–69 s.a. 713; Stokes, "Annals of Tigernach," 223 [Felinfach i 183].
135 "lectioni et obseruationi scripturarum operam dedisset": Colgrave and Mynors, *Ecclesiastical History*, 408–9.
136 For a review of his career among the Hwicce, see Sims-Williams, *Religion and Literature*, 184–94.

same date, describes him as "Aidan the brilliant sun of Inis Medcoit [Lindisfarne] whom we praise."[137]

## Bishop Fínán (651–ca. 661)

Bishop Fínán[138] replaced Aidan and had only recently been in the bishopric when Oswiu established the monastery at Gilling (*HE* iii 14, 24), discussed in chapter five. Trumhere, "educated and consecrated by the Irish" (*HE* iii 24),[139] a relative of Oswiu's wife Eanflæd, became Gilling's first abbot. Trumhere later became bishop at Lindsey (ca. 659–ca. 662). The second abbot of Gilling was Cynefrith, brother of Ceolfrith. Cynefrith withdrew to Ireland, with other nobles, where he died of plague.[140] Charles Plummer suggested that the plague that killed Cynefrith occurred ca. 661, about the time that Ceolfrith moved to Ripon, and the editors of *Vita Ceolfridi* concurred.[141] The editors suggested that the location in Ireland sought by Cynefrith and "other noble Angles" may have been "Mayo of the Saxons."[142] However, Bede's narrative makes it clear that *Mag nÉo na Saxan* was not established until a decade later, ca. 673. The location in Ireland where Trumhere, Cynefrith, and the "other noble Angles" studied the scriptures or sought an ascetic life, like that for Bishop Agilberht, remains to be identified.

Modern scholars have varied opinions about the practices followed at Gilling. Dorothy Whitelock considered that Gilling was an Ionan establishment which, for her, explained Ceolfrith's decision to leave it and join Wilfrid at Ripon.[143] Nick Higham stated that Gilling "was an Ionan house, which accommodated Catholic practices only in or after 664."[144] But the arguments for Gilling's orthodox sympathies are also strong. To start with, Gilling was established at the urging of

---

137 "Áedán in grían geldae, Inse Medcoit molmae": Stokes, *Félire Óengusso*, 179.
138 Fínán's dates are based on the chronology as established by Bede in *Historia ecclesiastica*. Gaelic and Frankish annals cite an *obit* of ca. 659 for Fínán: Mc Carthy, http://www.irishannals.cs.tcd.ie/, s.a. 659; Mac Airt and Mac Niocaill, *Annals of Ulster*, 132–33 s.a. 660; Stokes, "Annals of Tigernach," 195 [Felinfach i 155]; Story, "Frankish Annals," 108 s.a. 658.
139 "edoctus et ordinatus a Scottis": Colgrave and Mynors, *Ecclesiastical History*, 292–93.
140 "ipse discendarum studio scripturarum Hiberniam secedens simul et desiderio liberius Domino in lacrimis precibusque seruiendi": Grocock and Wood, *Abbots of Wearmouth*, 80–81 §§2–3 (*Vita Ceolfridi*); Plummer, *Venerabilis Baedae opera*, i, 388; Hunter Blair, *World of Bede*, 101.
141 Plummer, *Venerabilis Baedae opera*, ii, 196; Grocock and Wood, *Abbots of Wearmouth*, 81n17 (*Vita Ceolfridi*).
142 Grocock and Wood, *Abbots of Wearmouth*, 80n14 (*Vita Ceolfridi*).
143 Whitelock, "Church in East Anglia," 10–11.
144 Higham, *Ecgfrith*, 141.

Oswiu's wife Eanflæd who was raised in Kent and followed orthodox practices at Oswiu's court (*HE* iii 25).[145] Trumhere, her relative, served as Gilling's first abbot at Eanflæd's request and later as a bishop among the Mercians. None of our sources suggest that Trumhere had anything but an orthodox background. Like Agilberht before him, he must have been trained and ordained at an orthodox establishment among the Gaels. Cynefrith and the "other noble Angles" likely attended orthodox monasteries in Ireland. Ceolfrith, at Wearmouth-Jarrow, would have remembered several decades later, ca. 716, Cynefrith's and others' choices to undertake self-imposed exile and study in Ireland. Bede did not mention Cynefrith in his writings. It is likely that Ceolfrith was the direct source for narratives about Anglo-Saxon monks and students who studied among the Gaels during the time of Bishops Fínán and Colmán since Bede had not yet been born (*HE* iii 27).[146] The history of Gilling also suggests Fínán's tolerance and willingness to work with those who followed different practices.

Fínán may have been from Cenél nÉogain, the sept from which Oswiu's son Aldfrith *sapiens* descended.[147] Fínán is described as "mac Rímedo" in two sets of annals, implying that he was son of Colmán Rímid (d. 604) who purportedly shared the high-kingship of Tara with Áed Sláine.[148] There is the likelihood, therefore, that Bishop Fínán was Aldfrith's maternal uncle.[149]

Fínán's membership of Cenél nÉogain helps explain the good working relationship between himself and Oswiu.[150] Fínán played an active part in Oswiu's strategy of converting defeated enemies, as in the case of the Mercians (*HE* iii 21), or re-introducing the faith where the Augustinian mission under Mellitus had failed, as among the East Saxons and King Sigeberht (*HE* iii 22).[151] Fínán worked

---

145 "ut bis in anno uno pascha celebraretur, et cum rex pascha dominicum solutis ieiuniis faceret, tum regina cum suis persistens adthuc in ieiunio diem palmarum celebraret": Colgrave and Mynors, *Ecclesiastical History*, 296–97.
146 Richter, *Ireland and Her Neighbours*, 143–44.
147 Plummer, *Venerabilis Baedae opera*, ii, 189; Ireland, "Irish Genealogies," 74; Higham, *Ecgfrith*, 92–93.
148 For the *obit* of Bishop Fínán mac Rímedo, see Mac Airt and Mac Niocaill, *Annals of Ulster*, 132–33 s.a. 660; Stokes, "Annals of Tigernach," 195 [Felinfach i 155]; discussed at Ireland, "Irish Genealogies," 74.
149 Aldfrith's mother, according to the genealogies, was Fín, daughter of Colmán Rímid. Bishop Fínán may well have been her brother and Aldfrith's uncle. Etymologically related names are sometimes found in the same family: Ireland, "Irish Genealogies," 74; Higham, *Ecgfrith*, 92–93.
150 It has been suggested that Oswiu did not get along that well with Bishop Aidan. The relationship with Fínán seems to be an improvement, perhaps because of the Cenél nÉogain connection. See Gunn, *Bede's Historiae*, 38.
151 Whitelock, "Church in East Anglia," 2–6, 9.

closely with Cedd to whom he assigned key rôles among the Mercians and East Saxons.

Sometime during Fínán's bishopric there appeared a "violent defender" of the "orthodox" Easter (acerrimus ueri paschae defensor), a Gael named Rónán who had acquired his learning either in Gaul or Italy (*HE* iii 25).[152] It is said that he succeeded in convincing some and encouraging others into deeper inquiry into the matter of Easter reckoning. However, due to his vehemence, Fínán was not one of his converts. The presence of Rónán in Northumbria at this time is a reminder that the Paschal controversy was actively disputed, just as it had been in Ireland as shown by Cummian's letter (632). The fact that Rónán had succeeded in converting some people reflects the state of flux in Northumbria and Ireland on the Easter issues. Bishop Fínán had to work in that fluctuating state of affairs, as noted for the establishment and early operation of Gilling.

It is against this eclectic, fluid background of Fínán's bishopric that we must see the appearance of Wilfrid and Benedict Biscop.[153] The younger man Wilfrid had been placed in the household of Oswiu's queen Eanflæd ca. 648 at the age of fourteen, after which he was placed for four years at Lindisfarne in the service of an infirm thegn.[154] Benedict Biscop started as a thegn of Oswiu and had received land from the king but, around the age of twenty-five, chose a life in religion over a secular one.[155] Both went to Kent early in the 650s, and by ca. 654 they departed together from Kent for Rome but separated during the journey at Lyon. Each eventually reached Rome but not as companions and, although both became leading proponents for orthodox practice and loyalty to Rome among their countrymen, they never worked together or cooperated again.[156]

In 657 Fínán asked Hild to leave Heruteu and take over at *Strēanæshalh* (Whitby). Bede's language is ambiguous and it is not certain whether he meant that she was to "found" a new monastery or to "set in order" a pre-existing establishment. Whichever alternative was intended, Whitby under Abbess Hild became one of Northumbria's most important monasteries. Hild already had a working relationship with Bishop Aidan when, at least ten years previously, he

---

[152] Ian Wood has suggested that this Rónán and the Romanus of Poitou were one and the same person: Wood, "Irish in England: Part II," 210.
[153] Rauer, *Old English Martyrology*, 46–47 §17, 235 (commentary). Although the martyrologist seems to have relied on Bede's *Historia abbatum* for his information about Benedict Biscop, January 12, he only mentioned one trip to Rome.
[154] Colgrave, *Life of Bishop Wilfrid*, 6–7, c. 2.
[155] Grocock and Wood, *Abbots of Wearmouth*, 21–25 §1 (*Historia abbatum*).
[156] Grocock, "Monk who Knew too Much?"; Ó Carragáin and Thacker, "Wilfrid in Rome," 216–17.

brought her back from East Anglia to oversee Heruteu. Hild's importance is shown by the stories that developed around her (*HE* iv 23) and her inclusion, at November 17, in the Old English *Martyrology*.[157]

Whitby developed a prolific cultural record for a foundation with such humble origins. Within seven years of Hild's arrival, the "synod" of Whitby (*HE* iii 25) made its name synonymous with the Paschal controversy, the heart of seventh-century Northumbrian cultural history, a focal point of Bede's *Historia ecclesiastica*, and the basis for Bishop Wilfrid's career. Significantly, Abbess Hild and her community sided with Bishop Colmán and the Ionan party (*HE* iii 25).[158] It is clear that orthodox, catholic practice was accepted by all of the Ionan party who remained in Northumbria, including Hild and her community. But while Hild eschewed Ionan Paschal observances, her opposition to Wilfrid continued to the end of her life (*VW* c. 54).[159] Hild's pastoral style as described by Bede closely resembled the customs of Bishops Aidan and Colmán, and differed markedly from Wilfrid's.

One of Whitby's lay brothers, Cædmon, became the first recorded poet in the Old English vernacular (*HE* iv 24 [22]).[160] Hild's successors continued to ensure Whitby's prominence. In the last decade of Abbess Ælfflæd's tenure, ca. 704–714, an anonymous monk of Whitby composed the first hagiography of Pope Gregory the Great.[161] The *Vita Gregorii* adopts an orthodox point of view, yet is replete with features that confirm the Gaelic milieu in which it was created.[162]

Bede named six men educated and trained at Whitby who became bishops (*HE* iv 23 [21]) although the sixth, Tatfrith, died soon after his appointment among the Hwicce. The other five are more prominent in Bede's *Historia ecclesiastica*. Offor, as mentioned earlier, began his monastic career with Hild at Heruteu and Whitby. He studied at Canterbury with Theodore before going to Rome. He settled among the Hwicce where he was consecrated bishop ca. 692.[163] Bosa was consecrated bishop of York (ca. 678–706) by Archbishop Theodore in 678. John of Beverley became bishop of Hexham ca. 688 and then succeeded Bosa at York (706–714[?]). John of Beverley ordained Bede as deacon (ca. 692) and

---

157 Rauer, *Old English Martyrology*, 216–17 §226, 306 (commentary).
158 "Hild abbatissa cum suis in parte Scottorum": Colgrave and Mynors, *Ecclesiastical History*, 298.
159 In the dispute of 678 that split the diocese of York and expelled Wilfrid from Northumbria, Hild is listed, along with Theodore of Canterbury, as among Wilfrid's accusers: Colgrave, *Life of Bishop Wilfrid*, 116–17.
160 For a thorough, wide-ranging study, see O'Donnell, *Cædmon's Hymn*.
161 Colgrave, *Life of Gregory the Great*.
162 Ireland, "Whitby *Life* of Gregory."
163 Sims-Williams, *Religion and Literature*, 184–94.

then as priest (ca. 703; *HE* v 24). The two apparently had a close relationship. John was a likely source for Bede on matters concerning Whitby's personnel and its history.[164] Another person, referred to as Wilfrid II, succeeded John of Beverley as bishop of York (718–732). The last of the group, Ætla, became bishop of Dorchester-on-Thames (675x685) but little is known of him.

In addition to the citations in annals noted above, Fínán is listed in the Martyrology of Tallaght at January 9.[165] In a list of cognomina for saints, there is a certain Fínán whose cognomen (*comainm*) is given as Fínán Daire Chalgaig.[166] What came to be called Daire Choluim Cille (the oakwood of St. Columba) was a Columban monastery located in modern Derry at the southern end of the Inishowen peninsula, the traditional territory of Cenél nÉogain.[167] Its earliest name was Daire Chalgaig, and is referred to as such by Adomnán in the *Vita Columbae*.[168] It served as a harbor in Ireland for voyages to Britain and Iona. Daire Chalgaig is a fitting cognomen for a bishop of Northumbria from Iona with a Cenél nÉogain background representing a Columban monastery.

### Bishop Colmán (661–664)

Colmán[169] was bishop at Lindisfarne when the "synod" of Whitby was held in 664. A solar eclipse and devastating plague in both Britain and Ireland may have helped precipitate the "synod" initiated by King Ealhfrith of Deira, son of Oswiu, and the ambitious monk Wilfrid.[170] Issues about Easter reckoning arose because Iona and its establishments continued to use the *latercus* and wear a different tonsure. Whereas Rome, by this time, was promoting Dionysiac Easter practices.[171] Only retrospective accounts of the "synod" survive, that in *Vita Wilfridi* (*VW* c. 10) and in Bede's *Historia ecclesiastica* (*HE* iii 25).

Agilberht, who had studied scripture in Ireland before becoming bishop of the West Saxons in the 650s, was the senior cleric for the Wilfridian party. Bede

---

164 See Biggs, "Bede and John of Beverley."
165 Best and Lawlor, *Martyrology of Tallaght*, 6.
166 Ó Riain, *Corpus Genealogiarum Sanctorum Hiberniae*, 146 (707.447).
167 Lacey, "Founder of the Monastery of Derry?"; Lacey, "Derry."
168 Anderson and Anderson, *Life of Columba*, 20 (11b), 46 (26a), 158 (90a).
169 Colmán's dates are based on Bede's chronology. But if Fínán died ca. 659, as recorded in Gaelic and Frankish annals, then it is not certain that we should trust the accuracy of these dates for Colmán's bishopric.
170 Mc Carthy and Breen, "Astronomical Observations," 12, 24–30.
171 We have no firm date for when Rome itself converted to the Dionysiac method for calculating Easter.

proffered the peculiar story that, after roughly a decade, the Wessex king Cenwealh tired of Agilberht's "barbarous speech" and had him replaced as bishop (*HE* iii 7). He came to Northumbria early in the 660s before the "synod" and became friendly with King Ealhfrith and Wilfrid, recently installed at Ripon. At Ealhfrith's request Agilberht ordained Wilfrid priest prior to the "synod." Bishop Colmán came from Lindisfarne to represent the Ionan party. Cedd, bishop of the East Saxons, trained by the Gaels, acted as interpreter for the proceedings. Abbess Hild and her community hosted the gathering. King Oswiu oversaw proceedings and was responsible for the final decision.

In surviving accounts, Oswiu was presented with the choice of following Columba of Iona or Peter, founding bishop of Rome. Oswiu opted for Peter. Those who sided with the Ionan party were expected either to change their practices or depart. Bishop Cedd and Abbess Hild and her community had sided with the Ionan party but, according to Bede, were willing to adapt to catholic practices. Those not willing to change departed with Bishop Colmán and returned to Iona. In *Vita Wilfridi* Colmán was told to leave if he would not change. In Bede's account the tone is softer and states that Colmán chose to leave, with those who wished to follow him, since his teachings were no longer accepted.

Oswiu was said to have respected Colmán "for his innate prudence,"[172] so when Colmán requested that Eata, who had been abbot of Melrose, should be made abbot of Lindisfarne, Oswiu complied. In this same chapter Bede also described in a positive way Colmán's pastoral practices and habits (*HE* iii 26). Tuda, educated among the southern Gaels and consecrated bishop by them, was chosen to replace Colmán. Bede assured his readers that Tuda wore the Petrine tonsure and "observed the catholic rules for the date of Easter."[173] He had arrived back in Britain during Colmán's bishopric and had taught the true faith by word and example (*HE* iii 26).

## Mayo of the Saxons

When Bishop Colmán left Lindisfarne at least thirty Anglo-Saxon monks departed Northumbria for Iona with him (*HE* iv 4). Colmán brought some of the bones of Bishop Aidan as relics (*HE* iii 26). By 668 Colmán had taken his monks, including the Anglo-Saxons, and settled on the island of Inishboffin (*Inis bó*

---

[172] "pro insita illi prudentia": Colgrave and Mynors, *Ecclesiastical History*, 308.
[173] "et catholicam temporis paschalis regulam obseruans": Colgrave and Mynors, *Ecclesiastical History*, 308.

*finne*) off the west coast of Ireland (*HE* iv 4).[174] Gaelic annal entries state that they arrived with relics, presumably those of Aidan brought from Lindisfarne, and founded a church.[175] Bede stated that the island monastery had both Gaels and Anglo-Saxons, but that disputes arose between them with regard to summer work. To settle the cultural differences Colmán organized with a local chieftain (*comes*) a site on the mainland at *Mag éo* (plain of yews (Mayo)) for his Anglo-Saxon monks.[176] Its Gaelic name, *Mag nÉo na Saxan* (Mayo of the Saxons), reflects more fully the history of its foundation. The monastery was built with the "help of the chief and all the neighbours."[177] Colmán died in 676,[178] so Mayo of the Saxons must have been founded in the early 670s, sometime ca. 673. Bede's narrative about Mayo's foundation demonstrates that both Mayo of the Saxons and Rath Melsigi, even if populated largely by Anglo-Saxons, could not have been established and operated without the authority of a Gaelic mother church and the cooperation of the local secular polity. They reflect Bede's comments that Gaels provided free tuition and books for Anglo-Saxon students (*HE* iii 27). Monasteries like Mayo of the Saxons and Rath Melsigi could not have been established, run, and maintained from sources or authorities in Anglo-Saxon Britain.

In a manner that seems deliberately obfuscating, Bede noted that, by the time of his writing, the monks of Mayo had adopted a "better Rule" (*meliora instituta*) without explaining what that meant or when it happened.[179] Given that the "mother house" of Mayo of the Saxons was Iona and its founder was Bishop Colmán, it may imply that it had turned to orthodox Paschal practices which Iona adopted in 716, well before Bede wrote. Tírechán's late seventh-century *Collectanea* of St. Patrick has sections that concentrate on the area in Co. Mayo to the north of Mayo of the Saxons along the River Moy.[180] This concentration implies that by the time of Tírechán's writing, that area followed the Patrician cult and

---

174 Bede gave an acceptably accurate form of the Gaelic name, *Inisboufinde*, and knew its meaning, *Insula uitulae albae*: Colgrave and Mynors, *Ecclesiastical History*, 346. Its foundation is noted in some of the annals: Mac Airt and Mac Niocaill, *Annals of Ulster*, 138–39 s.a. 668; Stokes, "Annals of Tigernach," 200 [Felinfach i 160].
175 Mac Airt and Mac Niocaill, *Annals of Ulster*, 138–39 s.a. 668; Stokes, "Annals of Tigernach," 200 [Felinfach i 160]. See discussion in Wycherley, *Cult of Relics*, 95, 113.
176 Orschel, "Mag nEó na Sacsan."
177 "iuuante etiam comite ac uicinis omnibus": Colgrave and Mynors, *Ecclesiastical History*, 348. For a discussion of its foundation and possible local affiliations, see Ní Mhaonaigh, "Colmán, Gerald and the Monastery of Mayo," 413–19.
178 Mac Airt and Mac Niocaill, *Annals of Ulster*, 142–42 s.a. 676; Stokes, "Annals of Tigernach," 203 [Felinfach i 163].
179 Colgrave and Mynors, *Ecclesiastical History*, 348–49.
180 Bieler, *Patrician Texts*, 156–59, §§42–45.

was, therefore, orthodox. Bede's vague "better Rule" may imply Mayo's conversion to orthodoxy prior to Iona's conversion.

The monastery continued to grow. New Anglo-Saxon recruits arrived and Bede related that "after the example of the venerable fathers" (ad exemplum uenerabilium patrum) the community lived "under a Rule, having an abbot elected canonically" (sub regula et abbate canonico).[181] Whether or not Bede wanted his readers to believe that they had adopted the Benedictine Rule, an ideal claimed by Wilfrid, is not clear. The lack of clarity leaves two interpretations: 1) Bede wanted his audience to believe that *Mag nEó na Saxan* operated according to his ideals, or 2) Bede really didn't know and had less firm information than he intimated.

Bede noted that in his own time the monastery was still occupied by Anglo-Saxons and had grown quite large (*HE* iv 4).[182] Mayo of the Saxons seems to have been known to Aldhelm. His letter to Heahfrith who was returning from "the north-west part of the island of Ireland" implies that Heahfrith may have studied there.[183] Aldhelm described his pupil as having received "orthodox teaching."[184] The time frame is vague from both Aldhelm and Bede. If Heahfrith had spent six years in Ireland, and he was indeed at Mayo of the Saxons, Aldhelm's letter could not have been written before the 680s given Mayo's foundation ca. 673.

More than a century later Alcuin, who corresponded with various houses in Ireland, wrote to its still growing numbers of Anglo-Saxon monks, and praised them for the knowledge that had spread from them back to their own country.[185] Various Gaelic annal entries give a sense of its history between its founding to the time of Alcuin. One notes the death of a bishop (*pontifex*) named Garalt in 732.[186] The entry for 773 cites the death of a Bishop Áedán (Eadwine/Hadwine).[187] At 783 the Annals of Ulster note, without explanation, the burning of both Armagh and Mayo of the Saxons.[188] This seems to have occurred during the bishopric of Leothfrith, another correspondent of Alcuin.[189]

---

181 Colgrave and Mynors, *Ecclesiastical History*, 348–49.
182 Orschel, "Mag nEó na Sacsan," 98–99.
183 "ex Hiberniae brumosis circionis insulae climatibus": Ehwald, "Epistolae," 489, line 8; Lapidge and Herren, *Aldhelm*, 145 (discussion), 161 (translation).
184 Lapidge and Herren, *Aldhelm*, 162 (translation); Ehwald, "Epistolae," 491, lines 12–14.
185 Duemmler, "Alcvini Epistolae," 445–46 §287; Allott, *Alcuin of York*, 44–45 §33; Edmonds, *Gaelic Influence*, 117–20.
186 Mac Airt and Mac Niocaill, *Annals of Ulster*, 184–85 s.a. 732; Stokes, "Annals of Tigernach," 236 [Felinfach i 196].
187 Mac Airt and Mac Niocaill, *Annals of Ulster*, 226–27 s.a. 773.
188 Mac Airt and Mac Niocaill, *Annals of Ulster*, 238–39 s.a. 783. The juxtaposition of these two establishments suggests their connection through the Patrician cult.
189 Duemmler, "Alcvini Epistolae," 19 §2; Allott, *Alcuin of York*, 43–44 §32.

A conundrum for Anglo-Latin and Old English scholars is that *Mag nÉo na Saxan*, of the handful of clearly identified destinations for Anglo-Saxon students in seventh- and eighth-century Ireland, was founded by the very establishment and personnel that had been rejected at the "synod" of Whitby in 664. Yet its continued growth and success had positive ramifications for the homeland of the Anglo-Saxon monks there at least until the time of Alcuin and the Carolingian cultural florescence.

## Gaelic Influence in Southumbria and Northumbria

While on the one hand it can be argued that the "synod" of Whitby resulted in an important west of Ireland monastery frequented by Anglo-Saxons, a second significant outcome was the establishment of the Canterbury school of Theodore and Hadrian. Bishop Deusdedit of Canterbury had died in the same year as the "synod." King Oswiu and King Ecgberht of Kent sent a delegation to Rome with their candidate for archbishop, Wigheard (*HE* iv 1). Unfortunately, he died of plague in Rome. Pope Vitalian, responding only to Oswiu ca. 668, provided the first clear reference to relics of Pope Gregory brought to Britain (*HE* iii 29). The pope sent replacements for Wigheard in Theodore of Tarsus and Hadrian from North Africa. Theodore presently became archbishop. Theodore and Hadrian established the school at Canterbury in 669 noted for teaching Latin and Greek.[190] One of its most famous early students was Aldhelm of Malmesbury who was there sometime in the first half of the 670s.[191] From Aldhelm's letters we know that the Canterbury school also attracted Gaelic students.[192]

Seventh-century insular learning was peripatetic. Bede noted the many people *de gente Anglorum* of all social ranks who left their own country to apply themselves to a monastic life. Some "preferred to travel round to the cells of various teachers and apply themselves to study."[193] The Gaels welcomed them, fed them, and provided them with free books and tuition. Peripatetic teaching and study are seen in the varied forms of Gaelic influence manifested among early Anglo-Saxon churchmen and their texts. That influence was not restricted

---

**190** Lapidge, "School of Theodore"; Bischoff and Lapidge, *Biblical Commentaries*.
**191** See Aldhelm's letter to Hadrian: Lapidge and Herren, *Aldhelm*, 138–39 (discussion), 153–54 (translation).
**192** See Aldhelm's letter to Heahfrith: Lapidge and Herren, *Aldhelm*, 163 (translation).
**193** "alii magis circueundo per cellas magistrorum lectioni operam dare gaudebant": Colgrave and Mynors, *Ecclesiastical History*, 312–13.

by any means to Northumbria and the thirty years that bishops from Iona ruled from Lindisfarne.

In 634 when Bishop Aidan first arrived in Northumbria, as Bede related, he took a dozen boys as trainees, among them were Eata and Chad. Eata was abbot of Melrose by the time Cuthbert entered monastic life, shortly after the death of Aidan in 651.[194] Cuthbert was mentored by Boisil (*HE* iv 27), the Gaelic prior of Melrose who subsequently exerted persuasive influence over Ecgberht of Rath Melsigi (*HE* v 9).[195] Cuthbert is the first Anglo-Saxon to have hagiography about him, written by an anonymous author. Bede wrote both a verse and prose Life of Cuthbert.[196] Regardless of the version of the Life, Cuthbert reflects the teachings of his Gaelic-educated abbot and the Gaelic prior at Melrose. A clear example is his habit of nocturnal immersions in water to pray and as a form of penance.[197] Bede repeated the motif of immersion in water in the episode about Dryhthelm and his vision (ca. 696), just prior to the writing of Cuthbert's anonymous Life (*HE* v 12). The nature of Dryhthelm's otherworldly vision is reminiscent of Fursa's vision (*HE* iii 19). King Aldfrith *sapiens* used to visit Dryhthelm to hear accounts of his vision and helped Dryhthelm eventually to enter Melrose. Bede's eyewitness source for the stories of Dryhthelm, a certain Hæmgisl, retired to Ireland to pursue an ascetic life (*HE* v 12).

By 664 and the "synod" of Whitby, Bishop Cedd had founded the monastery at Lastingham, had helped with the conversion of the Mercians, and with the re-introduction of the faith among the East Saxons where the Gregorian mission had failed (*HE* preface, iii 22). Cedd sided with the Ionan party at the "synod" (*HE* iii 25) although Bede assured us that he gave up the practices he learned from Iona and Lindisfarne and "accepted the catholic method of keeping Easter" (*HE* iii 26).[198] Cedd served as "interpreter" at the "synod,"[199] which provides evi-

---

**194** Cuthbert is frequently mentioned in the Old English *Martyrology* with his main entry at March 20: Rauer, *Old English Martyrology*, 68–69 §49, 246–47 (commentary); 82–85 §66, 253 (Æthelwald); 98–101 §80, 258 (Eadberht); 172–72 §171, 287 (Aidan).
**195** McCann, "Cuthbert and Boisil," 41–68.
**196** Colgrave, *Lives of Saint Cuthbert*; Lapidge, *Bede's Latin Poetry*, 181–313.
**197** Ireland, "Penance and Prayer in Water," 61–63.
**198** "Cedd, relictis Scottorum uestigiis, . . . utpote agnita obseruatione catholici paschae": Colgrave and Mynors, *Ecclesiastical History*, 308.
**199** "qui et interpres in eo concilio uigilantissimus utriusque partis extitit": Colgrave and Mynors, *Ecclesiastical History*, 298.

dence that Anglo-Saxon churchmen of the mid seventh century learned Gaelic without, apparently, having spent time in Ireland or Gaelic-speaking Britain.[200]

Abbess Hild worked with all three Northumbrian bishops from Iona and had also been in East Anglia during Fursa's time there. So, although Hild was baptized as a teenager ca. 627 by Bishop Paulinus as part of King Edwin's retinue, the fact that "Abbess Hild and her followers were on the side of the Irish" at the "synod" is pertinent to the argument here (*HE* iii 25).[201] Bede explicitly stated that the community of Whitby sided with the Ionan party, which does not necessarily mean that they favored the *latercus* over orthodox Paschal practices. It is more likely that they preferred the pastoral methods of the Gaels as opposed to Wilfrid's style. Bede described Hild's pastoral style in terms reminiscent of those for Aidan and Colmán (*HE* iv 23). Near the end of her life ca. 678, Hild was described by Stephen of Ripon as an accuser of Wilfrid, along with Archbishop Theodore of Canterbury, when Wilfrid was expelled from York and the Northumbrian diocese was partitioned (*VW* c. 54).[202] This latter incident, however, suggests more about the personality and character of Wilfrid than it does about Hild's Gaelic sympathies.[203]

Upon Wilfrid's return from his exile of 678, *Vita Wilfridi* claims that he converted the pagan South Saxons to the faith sometime in the first half of the 680s (*VW* c. 41).[204] When Bede recounted the story, however, he noted that a Gael named Dícuill, along with five or six brothers, had "served the Lord in humility and poverty" at Bosham in the same region (*HE* iv 13).[205]

The Whitby community's sympathy for the Ionan party suggests a larger appreciation of Gaelic cultural practices and norms. The story of Cædmon and the first recorded composition of Old English poetry at Whitby must be seen against the background of Gaelic vernacular poets cooperating with the Church (*HE* iv 24 [22]).[206] The success of six members of the community in attaining bishop-

---

**200** For arguments that Latin was not used as a *lingua franca* at the "synod," see Herren, "Scholarly Contacts," 38.
**201** "Hild abbatissa cum suis in parte Scottorum": Colgrave and Mynors, *Ecclesiastical History*, 298.
**202** Colgrave, *Life of Bishop Wilfrid*, 116–17.
**203** Charles Plummer had pointed out that Hild's continued opposition to Wilfrid so long after 664 must be kept in mind when considering Wilfrid's conduct and character: Plummer, *Venerabilis Baedae opera*, ii, 189–90.
**204** Colgrave, *Life of Bishop Wilfrid*, 80–85.
**205** Colgrave and Mynors, *Ecclesiastical History*, 372–73.
**206** Ireland, "Cædmon and Colmán"; Ireland, "Vernacular Poets."

rics, and the fact that one of them, John of Beverley, ordained Bede as deacon and later priest (*HE* v 24), highlight their community's achievements in pedagogy and ecclesiastical politics and shows that communal sympathy for Gaelic customs and traditions were not inimical to orthodoxy (*HE* iv 23 [21]). The imprint of Gaelic *topoi* and narrative features are evident decades after Hild's death, and towards the end of Ælfflæd's abbacy, in the anonymous *Vita Gregorii* by a monk of Whitby (ca. 704–ca. 714), a text that takes an orthodox stance. The reference to Pope Gregory as "golden mouth," the reliance on etymological wordplay to advance the narrative, sympathy for the notion of *naturale bonum*, are among the features that indicate a Gaelic milieu for the Life.[207]

The schooling available to young Anglo-Saxons eager for learning is highlighted by the foundation of Gilling in 651. It was established at the urging of Queen Eanflæd, who had been raised in Kent, to expiate the killing of her kinsman, King Oswine, by her husband King Oswiu (*HE* iii 14, 24). Gilling's first abbot, Trumhere, was another relative of the queen and he had been educated and consecrated among the Gaels (*HE* iii 24). This means that Trumhere had been educated, most likely in Ireland, during the 640s. Agilberht was also educated in Ireland in the same decade (*HE* iii 7). Agilberht was bishop of the West Saxons in the 650s, overlapping with Trumhere's abbacy at Gilling. Agilberht's education among the Gaels was acceptably orthodox for Wilfrid and Ealhfrith at the "synod" of Whitby. Similar educational opportunities were available to Trumhere. By implication, when Trumhere's successor at Gilling, Cynefrith, relinquished his duties as abbot and retired to Ireland, he sought orthodox options, as did the "other noble Angles" who followed him. In fact, Cynefrith may be listed in Willibrord's calendar.[208] Several of the manuscripts used by Willibrord and his circle originated at the orthodox training center at Rath Melsigi.[209]

The arrival among the pagan West Saxons (ca. 634) of Bishop Birinus, sent by Pope Honorius, coincided with King Oswald's presence there to form a marriage alliance with King Cynegisl. Oswald sponsored Cynegisl at his baptism by Birinus and the two kings established Dorchester as his bishopric (*HE* iii 7). Bede noted that from Oswald's time many Gaels came into Britain, preaching and instructing, and that young and old were instructed "in advanced studies

---

207 Ireland, "Whitby *Life* of Gregory."
208 Ó Cróinín, "Rath Melsigi, Willibrord," 31–32.
209 For the manuscripts used by Willibrord and his circle, see Ó Cróinín, "Rath Melsigi, Willibrord"; Warntjes, "*Computus Cottonianus*"; Pelteret, "Willibrord's Autobiography"; Ó Cróinín, "Willibrord."

and in the observance of the discipline of a Rule" (*HE* iii 3).²¹⁰ Against this background, we see Agilberht as bishop of the West Saxons (650s) under King Cenwealh, before he moved to Northumbria to support Wilfrid as the senior cleric at the "synod" of Whitby. Agilberht had studied *non paruo tempore* (*HE* iii 7) beforehand (640s) in Ireland, probably at Bangor.²¹¹ Agilberht's episcopacy of the West Saxons formed a natural conduit for a Gaelic presence in Wessex and western Mercia and helps explain the presence of Máeldub at Malmesbury (*HE* v 18) and, further north, Colmán at Hanbury.²¹²

How or when Máeldub arrived at Malmesbury is not known, but the Gaelic characteristics in Aldhelm's writing should be attributed to the educational framework constructed by Máeldub.²¹³ An anonymous letter from a student requesting the loan of a book confirms the Gaelic identity of Aldhelm's teacher.²¹⁴ Aldhelm's personal relationship with Aldfrith *sapiens* indicates that the two had studied together as young men, probably somewhere in Ireland.²¹⁵ The erudition of neither man is disputed. Aldhelm knew *Altus Prosator*, a poem on the Creator and creation that appealed to the author of the *Enigmata*, and helped shape his *Carmen rhythmicum*.²¹⁶ But it has not yet been fully explained how *Altus Prosator* got from Iona to Southumbria.²¹⁷ The letter from Cellán of Péronne to Aldhelm requesting some of his writings at once praised and teased Aldhelm for his Latinity. Aldhelm's response indicated his understanding of, if not appreciation for, Cellán's word play.²¹⁸

Two letters by Aldhelm to students indicate that they had either studied in Ireland or were about to. Aldhelm described Heahfrith as having returned from an unidentified location in Ireland where he had spent six years "sucking the teat of wisdom," a metaphor that Aldhelm learned from Gaelic sources.²¹⁹ If, as

---

210 "cum maioribus studiis et obseruatione disciplinae regularis": Colgrave and Mynors, *Ecclesiastical History*, 220–21.
211 Hammer, "'Holy Entrepreneur,'" 61–62.
212 Sims-Williams, *Religion and Literature*, 106–8 (Colmán), 108–9 (Máeldub).
213 Orchard, *Poetic Art of Aldhelm*, 4, 58–59; Dempsey, "Aldhelm and the Irish," 5–9.
214 Lapidge and Herren, *Aldhelm*, 146–47 (discussion), 164 (translation).
215 Yorke, "Irish and British Connections," 169–75; Ireland, "Where Was King Aldfrith Educated?" 39–40, 48–52, 55–59, 73.
216 Orchard, *Poetic Art of Aldhelm*, 55; Lapidge, "Career of Aldhelm," 28; Barker, "*Usque Domnoniam*," 17–18; Lapidge, "'Epinal-Erfurt Glossary'," 151.
217 Orchard, *Poetic Art of Aldhelm*, 54–55, 57.
218 Howlett, *Celtic Latin Tradition*, 108–113; Lapidge and Herren, *Aldhelm*, 149 (discussion), 167 (translations).
219 "uber sofiae sugens": Ehwald, "Epistolae," 489 §5; Lapidge and Herren, *Aldhelm*, 161 (translation). Aldhelm would have derived the metaphor "teat of wisdom" from the Gaels: see

has been suggested, Heahfrith had just returned from Mayo of the Saxons, then that institution's affiliations with Iona must be acknowledged.[220] In his letter to Wihtfrith, who intended to study in Ireland, Aldhelm stressed the foolishness of spurning Scriptural study in favor of worldly philosophers. To illustrate his point, he cited examples from Classical mythology – probably to show off – of inappropriate marriages and sexual liaisons before warning Wihtfrith against the temptations of the flesh. Research into Classical mythology known by the Gaels continues to grow.[221] It is equally probable that Aldhelm intended it as a cipher for vernacular secular traditions being recorded then among the Gaels.[222]

In the twelfth century William of Malmesbury related traditions that Aldhelm was a renowned vernacular poet.[223] Evidence from his Latin hexameters show that he was familiar with the style, formulaic quality, and alliterative patterns of Old English verse.[224] Those arguing for an early dating for *Beowulf* have noted the similar conceptions of the dragons as portrayed in that vernacular poem and in Aldhelm's *De Virginitate*.[225] The *Liber monstrorum* is another local text from Aldhelm's time that emphasizes fantastic monsters and their progeny as enemies.[226] Anglo-Saxon coins from the seventh and eighth centuries tend to have some sort of "dragon-like" figure on one side.[227] The circumstances found in Aldhelm's Wessex provide the necessary background, including details of West Saxon genealogical tradition,[228] to nurture secular poetry in the vernacular similar to what was preserved in *Beowulf*. The practice of the Gaels in preserving secular, vernacular traditions must have helped shape the scholar Aldhelm.[229]

---

Bayless and Lapidge, *Collectanea Pseudo-Bedae*, 122–23 §1, 199n1; Richter, *Ireland and Her Neighbours*, 159–60; Orchard, "*Hisperica Famina* as Literature," 30–32.
**220** Lapidge and Herren, *Aldhelm*, 145.
**221** For evidence of Classical mythology among the Gaels, see Howlett, "Hellenic Learning"; Herren, "Classical Mythology in Ireland"; Herren, "Study of Greek in Ireland." See the references to Classical mythology in Holford-Strevens, *The Disputatio Chori*.
**222** The lost *Cín Dromma Snechtai*, discussed in previous chapters, contained texts that have been dated to the late seventh and early eighth centuries.
**223** Lapidge, "'Beowulf', Aldhelm," 157–58; Frank, "Anglo-Saxon Oral Poet," 30–34; Niles, "Anglo-Saxon Oral Poet," 7.
**224** Lapidge, "Aldhelm's Latin Poetry."
**225** Pascual, "Material Monsters," 214–17; Lapidge, "'Beowulf', Aldhelm," 158–62.
**226** Lapidge, "'Beowulf', Aldhelm," 163–77; Orchard, *Companion to Beowulf*, 133–37; Pascual, "Material Monsters," 215–17.
**227** Clemoes, *Interactions*, 17–18.
**228** Lapidge, "'Beowulf', Aldhelm," 184–88; Cronan, "Scyld in the West Saxon Royal Genealogy."
**229** Cronan, "'Beowulf', the Gaels."

## Training Missionaries at Rath Melsigi

*Rathmelsigi* (*Ráth Máelsige* [?]) was the location in Ireland that attracted the greatest number of Anglo-Saxons named by Bede (*HE* iii 27).[230] The major function of this monastic site was to train students for positions in the incipient Anglo-Saxon Church back in Britain, and as missionaries to Germanic pagans on the continent. Scripture was the main subject taught. Rath Melsigi was located in the Barrow (*Berba*) river valley in Co. Carlow, a few kilometers south of Carlow town.[231] Unfortunately the physical site cannot be studied because it has been consumed by a gravel quarry. Bede never suggested any Gaelic ecclesiastical affiliations or associations for Rath Melsigi, and Gaelic sources provide no firm evidence. Nevertheless, Rath Melsigi had to have a Gaelic mother house.

Rath Melsigi was located in what was then Uí Bairrche territory and could not have survived without their consent and participation.[232] Late in the sixth century, or very early in the seventh, the Uí Bairrche developed relationships with St. Comgall's church at Bangor, Co. Down when their king Cormac mac Diarmata ceded a local site on the River Barrow near Carlow (*Cetharlach*) to Comgall.[233] Cormac of the Uí Bairrche was one of the earliest insular examples of a king "opting out" of his secular responsibilities for the religious life.[234] It is possible, therefore, that Bangor was the mother house of Rath Melsigi as it sat in Uí Bairrche territory and that sept had a close relationship with Bangor.

Sleaty (*Sléibte*), just north of Carlow town, was another important religious foundation in Uí Bairrche territory. Its founding bishop was Fiacc Finn, the *adoliscens poeta* present at King Lóegaire's pagan court as related by Muirchú in *Vita*

---

229 Cronan, "'Beowulf', the Gaels."
230 For this important establishment and its network of influence, sees Ó Cróinín, "Rath Melsigi, Willibrord." *Rathmelsigi* is the form that Bede cited. For possible original Gaelic forms of the name, see Ireland, "Where Was King Aldfrith Educated?" 59–60n175.
231 Ó Cróinín, "Rath Melsigi, Willibrord," 41–49 (appendix by Thomas Fanning). Subsequent surveys suggest that the archaeological remains are more extensive than previously thought: Barrett, "County Carlow," 46–48.
232 For background on Uí Bairrche, see Smyth, *Celtic Leinster*, 59–61; Byrne, *Irish Kings*, 136–37, 145–46; Ó Cróinín, "Ireland, 400–800," 193–94; Charles-Edwards, *Early Christian Ireland*, 236 (map).
233 Bhreathnach, "Genealogies of Leinster," 263–64; Ireland, "Where Was King Aldfrith Educated?" 71–72.
234 Stancliffe, "Kings who Opted Out," 161. For a larger context for Cormac, see Ó Cróinín, "Ireland, 400–800," 193–94. These events can also be viewed against the career of Columbanus: Ó Cróinín, "Political Background," 54–58.

**Figure 6.b:** Map of Rath Melsigi's Networks in Ireland, Britain, and the Continent. Rath Melsigi is connected to the following places through the following personnel:

Melrose through Boisil (*HE* v 9)
Iona through Ecgberht (*HE* iii 4; v 22, 24)
Lindsey through Chad (*HE* iv 3), Hygebald (*HE* iv 3), and Æthelwine (*HE* iii 11, 27; iv 12)
Lastingham through Chad (*HE* iv 3)
York through Chad (*HE* iv 2; *VW* cc. 14, 15)
Ripon through Willibrord (*VW* c. 26)
Echternach through Willibrord (*Vita Willibrordi*)
Frisia through Wihtberht (*HE* v 9) and Willibrord (*HE* iii 13, v 10–11)
Birr through Wihtberht (*Cáin Adomnáin*)
Rhine River through Black and White Hewald (*HE* v 10).

*Patricii*.²³⁵ Fiacc Finn was the pupil of the *poeta optimus* Dubthach maccu Lugair, also from a Leinster family, famous in the Patrick legend for helping to syncretize indigenous traditions and Church teachings, as related in the "pseudo-historical prologue" to the *Senchas Már*.²³⁶ A relationship between Sleaty and Armagh had evolved no later than 688, and probably earlier, as seen in the testament (*audacht*) of Bishop Áed of Sleaty submitted to Bishop Ségéne of Armagh (ca. 661–d. 688). Bishop Áed commissioned Muirchú to write the *Vita Patricii*.²³⁷ The Uí Bairrche territory of Leinster had been orthodox for decades by 664, the time of Bede's first mention of Rath Melsigi. The Uí Bairrche and other Leinster septs were intertwined with the growing cult of St. Patrick. In other words, the mother house of Rath Melsigi may, but need not, have been a local Leinster foundation.²³⁸

Rath Melsigi was a foreign site to which Anglo-Saxons had to cross the sea, and from which many voyaged, to serve as missionaries to their pagan relatives on the continent. The training site at Rath Melsigi may represent the iconic center for the Old English *Seafarer* poem from the Exeter Book. Whether the poem is interpreted literally or allegorically, it reflects the penitential or exilic state of mind required of *peregrini*.²³⁹

|  |  |
|---|---|
| heortan geþohtas, | Forþon cnyssað nu<br>Þæt ic hean streams,<br> |
| sealtyþa gelac | sylf cunnige; (Lines 33b–35b) |
| ferð to feran,<br>elþeodigra | Þæt ic feor heonan<br>eard gesece (Lines 37a–38b). |
| Forþon me hatran sind<br>dryhtnes dreamas<br>læne on londe. | þonne þis deade lif,<br>(Lines 64b–66a)²⁴⁰ |

---

235 Bieler, *Patrician Texts*, 92–93. Fiacc Finn's connection to the Uí Bairrche, and Leinster generally, can be seen in O'Brien, *Corpus genealogiarum Hiberniae*, 46 (121 a 39), 50 (121 BC 44). See further, Ó Cróinín, "Ireland, 400–800," 194.
236 Ireland, "Vernacular Poets," 52–55 (Fiacc Finn Sléibte), 55–58 (Dubthach maccu Lugair). See further, McCone, "Dubthach Maccu Lugair"; Carey, "Dubthach's Judgment"; Carey, "Pseudo-Historical Prologue." For discussion in context of the origins of *Beowulf*, see Cronan, "'Beowulf', the Gaels," 159–62.
237 Bieler, *Patrician Texts*, 1, 62–63 (preface); Charles-Edwards, *Early Christian Ireland*, 428, 439.
238 Ireland, "Where Was King Aldfrith Educated?" 59–63 (Rath Melsigi), 63–72 (Bangor).
239 Ireland, "*Seafarer*." See also Mullins, "*Herimum in mari*."
240 Krapp and Dobbie, *Exeter Book*, 144–45.

> (Indeed the heart's thoughts urge, that I should know the high streams, the play of salt waves (Lines 33b–35b)
>
> [the heart's thoughts urge] the spirit to travel, that far hence I should seek a land of foreigners (Lines 37a–38b)
>
> Indeed the Lord's joys are more fervent to me than this dead, transitory life on land.) (Lines 64b–66a)

The *Seafarer* cannot be firmly dated, and no specific locations are named in the text, but the homiletic conclusion suggests a monastic environment frequented by Anglo-Saxons for its composition and dissemination, like those found in Ireland.

Ecgberht is the most important person at Rath Melsigi named by Bede. He occupied a pivotal rôle in the *Historia ecclesiastica*, being credited with overseeing the training of many named Anglo-Saxons but, most importantly, with converting Iona to orthodoxy in 716 (*HE* iii 4; v 22). Gaelic sources also note the important change at Iona in that year. But no named person is credited with the change in the Annals of Ulster, the Annals of Tigernach, or the Chronicum Scotorum.[241] Bede stated that Dúnchad was Iona's abbot at the time (*HE* v 22). Gaelic records concerning Iona's abbacy are uncertain for this crucial period. It is possible that Dúnchad, a close relative of Adomnán, supported the Dionysiac traditions and so encouraged the change.[242] The Annals of Tigernach state that Fáelchú mac Dorbbéni undertook the "seat of Columba" at the end of summer that same year.[243]

Bede stated that Ecgberht remained at Iona for another thirteen years, until his death at ninety years of age on Easter day in 729 (*HE* v 22, 24).[244] Gaelic annals, naming him Eicbericht, note his death at the same date.[245] The Annals of Tigernach note allusively in the same entry that "the bearded foreigner, the shrewdest man in his time" (in Gall Ulcach, fear as glicca bai 'na aimsir) died on the same day. Ecgberht would have been seventy-seven years

---

[241] Mac Airt and Mac Niocaill, *Annals of Ulster*, 172–73 s.a. 716; Stokes, "Annals of Tigernach," 225 [Felinfach i 185]; Hennessy, *Chronicum Scotorum*, 118–19 s.a. 714 (referring only to the tonsure).
[242] Herbert, *Iona, Kells, and Derry*, 57–59.
[243] "Pasc[h]a in Eó[a] ciuitate commotatur. Faelchu mac Doirbeni cathedram Columbe .lxxx. uii. etatis [sue] anno in .iiii.kl. Septimbris die sabati suscepit": Stokes, "Annals of Tigernach," 225 [Felinfach i 185].
[244] Ó Cróinín, "First Century of Anglo-Irish Relations," 9–16. For an interpretation of these events that posits Ecgberht as having come from Mayo of the Saxons, see Duncan, "Bede, Iona, and the Picts," 25–27.
[245] Mac Airt and Mac Niocaill, *Annals of Ulster*, 182–83 s.a. 729. The *Annals of Tigernach* refer to him as *ridire Crist* the equivalent of *miles Christi*: Stokes, "Annals of Tigernach," 234 [Felinfach i 194].

old in 716. It is improbable that he traveled alone. It is more likely that he served in a delegation. Bede offered no explanation of how delegates from an orthodox ecclesiastical establishment in Leinster should decamp to Iona and remain there. Gaelic sources have not yet offered a solution to the conundrum.

Bede stated that the monks at Iona, "together with the monasteries under their rule, were brought by the Lord's guidance to canonical usages in the matter of Easter and of the form of the tonsure (*HE* v 22).".[246] When Ecgberht came to Iona in 716 he was "most honourably and joyfully received" (honorifice ab eis et multo cum gaudio susceptus est; *HE* v 22). Bede noted of the monks at Iona that "through the English nation, they are brought to a more perfect way of life in matters wherein they were lacking (*HE* v 22)."[247] But this achievement in the person of Ecgberht of bringing Iona, and other Gaels, to a *perfectam uiuendi normam*, in fact reflects the deep debt of the Anglo-Saxons to the Gaels. For "that race [the Gaels] had willingly and ungrudgingly taken pains to communicate its own knowledge and understanding of God to the English nation (*HE* v 22)."[248] The Gaelic missions to Northumbria, East Anglia, Wessex, Mercia, Sussex, and countless unnamed regions, as well as the Anglo-Saxons who came to *Ráth Máelsige*, *Mag nÉo na Saxan*, and many other unacknowledged sites in Northern Britain and Ireland, all attest to the debt that Ecgberht allegedly repaid.

Ecgberht's own history reveals how indebted he was personally to the Gaels. If he died in 729 at the age of ninety then he was born ca. 639. He was a close contemporary of Aldhelm and Aldfrith *sapiens*. Aldhelm's debt to Gaelic teachers is well known and his writings reflect their learning. Bede described Ecgberht as *doctissimus in scripturis*, a phrase he twice used of Aldfrith's learning (*HE* iii 4). Ecgberht's earliest mention was the plague year 664 when he was twenty-five years old. He spent a minimum of sixty-five years living, working, and studying among the Gaels.

During the plague of 664 Ecgberht and a companion named Æthelhun became ill. Most of their fellow monks either died or were scattered to other places. Ecgberht vowed to live in exile if he survived. Æthelhun died. Ecgberht lived, fulfilled his vow, and remained among the Gaels for the rest of his long life (*HE* iii 27).

Ecgberht was involved in both Gaelic and Anglo-Saxon politics when he advised King Ecgfrith against his raid into Síl nÁedo Sláine territory in Mag Breg

---

[246] "cum his quae sibi erant subdita monasteriis, ad ritum paschae ac tonsurae canonicum Domino procurante perducti sunt.": Colgrave and Mynors, *Ecclesiastical History*, 552–53.
[247] "ipsa quoque postmodum per gentem Anglorum in eis minus habuerat ad perfectam uiuendi normam perueniret": Colgrave and Mynors, *Ecclesiastical History*, 554–55.
[248] "ut quoniam gens illa quam nouerat scientiam diuinae cognitionis libenter ac sine inuidia populis Anglorum communicare curauit": Colgrave and Mynors, *Ecclesiastical History*, 554–55.

in 684. Bede stated that the raid "wretchedly devastated a harmless race that had always been most friendly to the English" (*HE* iv 26 [24]).[249] Bede was upset that they attacked churches and monasteries.[250] The king of the region, Fínsnechta Fledach (675–695), was high-king at the time.[251] The prophetic poem on kingship, *Baile Chuinn*, was written during Fínsnechta's reign.[252] Gaelic annals note that Adomnán returned the captives taken in the raid back to Ireland from Aldfrith's Northumbria in 687.[253] The following year Fínsnechta entered clerical life, but one year later resumed the kingship and remained king until his death in 695.[254]

Ecgberht had desired to undertake a mission to his Germanic brethren on the continent, listed by Bede as Frisians, Rugians, Danes, Old Saxons, and more.[255] Failing that, he wanted to go to Rome to worship at the shrines there, an aspiration that helps confirm the orthodox background of Rath Melsigi. Bede portrayed pilgrimage to Rome as the apex of spiritual aspiration and achievement. However, Ecgberht was dissuaded from his continental mission through the visions received by a monastic brother who had once been a servant to Boisil, the prior at Melrose and mentor of St. Cuthbert. Previously Boisil's prophetic abilities had persuaded Cuthbert to accept the bishopric at Lindisfarne in 685 (*HE* iv 28).[256] The brother at Rath Melsigi received two visions from Boisil who warned that Iona ploughed a crooked furrow and urged that Ecgberht must "call them back to the true line" (*HE* v 9).[257]

---

249 "uastauit misere gentem innoxiam et nationi Anglorum semper amicissiman": Colgrave and Mynors, *Ecclesiastical History*, 426. For discussions of the raid, see Higham, *Ecgfrith*, 206–7; Pelteret, "Attack on Brega."
250 See discussion of the concept of high-kingship in Higham, *Ecgfrith*, 17–24. It has been argued that the effect of this raid was to change the concepts of kingship for the island of Ireland and the sense of *natio* on the island: Wadden, "First English Invasion."
251 For fuller contexts, see Ó Cróinín, "Ireland, 400–800," 208, 210; Bhreathnach, *Ireland in the Medieval World*, 60–64.
252 Murphy, "Dates of Two Sources," 145–51; Carey, "*Cín Dromma Snechtai* Texts," 74–77; Bhreathnach and Murray, "*Baile Chuinn Chétchathaig*."
253 Mac Airt and Mac Niocaill, *Annals of Ulster*, 150–51 s.a. 687; Stokes, "Annals of Tigernach," 210–11 [Felinfach i 170–71].
254 Mac Airt and Mac Niocaill, *Annals of Ulster*, 150–51 s.a. 688 (*clericatum suscepit*), 152–53 s.a. 689 (*reuertitur ad regnum*); Stokes, "Annals of Tigernach," 210 [Felinfach i 170]. Clare Stancliffe noted this example, but did not discuss it: Stancliffe, "Kings who Opted Out," 163; Bhreathnach, *Ireland in the Medieval World*, 62.
255 Bede's list of Germanic peoples is a reminder of the knowledge among the Anglo-Saxons of their continental relatives as reflected in Old English poems like *Beowulf* and *Widsith*. See Niles, "Anthropology of the Past."
256 For arguments about Boisil's Gaelic ethnicity, see McCann, "Cuthbert and Boisil."
257 "eum ad rectum haec tramitem reuocare": Colgrave and Mynors, *Ecclesiastical History*, 478.

Bede is vague as to when any of these events happened. Boisil died in the early 660s, a victim of plague. Melrose was established from Iona and followed the practices of Lindisfarne before 664. Bede seems to be having it both ways, therefore, when he inducted Boisil as the instrument by which Ecgberht became the agent for change to orthodox practice at Iona. Bede is our best source for Boisil who appears in *Historia ecclesiastica* (*HE* iv 27, 28 [26]; v 9) and in both the metrical and prose *Vita Cuthberti*. He is not in Cuthbert's anonymous Life.[258] Boisil's introduction into Bede's Lives of Cuthbert helped the saint's transition to orthodoxy in Anglo-Saxon eyes, despite his "heterodox" beginnings. Based on his relationship to Boisil, Melrose seems to be Ecgberht's most likely "home" monastery back in Britain.[259]

Bede named several others who were with Ecgberht at Rath Melsigi during his long career. Some of them held important positions in Britain. For example, Chad, who became a saint, was abbot of Lastingham and bishop among the Mercians at Lindsey. Others from Lindsey, Bishop Æthelwine and Abbot Hygebald, maintained the connection to Rath Melsigi and Ecgberht, as will be shown. Although Ecgberht never went on mission to the continent, he was instrumental in preparing others named by Bede such as Wihtberht, Willibrord, and the two Hewalds. Willibrord enjoyed great success, including visits to Rome. Each of these will be discussed below. Later in the eighth century, Alcuin of York, relying on Bede's narrative, referred to Ecgberht as *antistes* (overseer) and said that he had "set the Irish an example of how to live."[260] Despite his important rôle in the *Historia ecclesiastica*, Ecgberht is not listed as a saint in the Old English *Martyrology*, although he does appear in the entry for St. Chad.[261]

Chad and his brother Cedd were credited with helping convert Mercia, where the faith had not been known, and with reviving it among the East Saxons, who had rejected it after the failure of Mellitus's mission (*HE* preface). They also had two brothers, Cælin and Cynebill, who were involved in religious life (*HE* iii 23).

Chad and Eata had been among Bishop Aidan's original twelve boys trained when his mission began (*HE* iii 28). Chad had also studied and lived the monastic life in Ireland with Ecgberht when they were both youths (*adulescens*; *HE* iv 3).

---

**258** Cuthbert was portrayed as "orthodox" in the anonymous *Life*. Bede used Boisil as the vehicle by which Cuthbert was brought into the correct Christian life: Colgrave, *Lives of Saint Cuthbert*, 172–75, c. 6; 180–85, c. 8; 185–87, c. 9.
**259** Kirby, "Cuthbert, Boisil."
**260** "Scotis iam maxima vitae tunc exempla dabat": Godman, *Alcuin*, 82–83, lines 1016–17.
**261** Ecgberht appears only in the context of St. Chad's entry, at March 2, when he and Hygebald related the anecdote about Cedd's soul retrieving the soul of his brother Chad: Rauer, *Old English Martyrology*, 60–61 §37, 243 (commentary).

Bede is vague about the timing and location of these events but says that Chad returned to Britain while Ecgberht remained in Ireland. Nevertheless, it appears that Chad had been introduced to the traditions of Iona and Lindisfarne with Aidan yet received orthodox training with Ecgberht in Ireland. A certain Trumberht related stories to Bede about Chad's piety. This same Trumberht had taught Bede scripture. Trumberht had been educated and lived under the Rule of Chad's monastery (*HE* iv 3).

Chad was selected by King Oswiu to become bishop of York after the "synod" of Whitby when Wilfrid delayed in his return from Gaul (*HE* iii 28; v 19). But Chad relied on Brittonic bishops for his consecration so that when Theodore arrived he removed Chad from York and re-consecrated him in the "catholic" tradition (*HE* iv 2; *VW* cc. 14, 15). According to Bede, Theodore subsequently requested that King Oswiu call Chad out of retirement at Lastingham to become bishop of the Mercians because he was impressed with his humility (669–672; *HE* iv 3). However, Stephen of Ripon implied that King Wulfhere had already appointed Chad as bishop ([?]667–669; *VW* c. 15). According to Bede, Wulfhere granted Chad fifty hides of land at Barrow in the province of Lindsey to establish a monastery "where up to the present-day traces of the monastic Rule which he established still survive" (*HE* iv 3).[262]

Chad showed saintly characteristics throughout his life. His pastoral style reflected the humility and simplicity described for Bishops Aidan and Colmán, and for Abbess Hild. He was able to foresee his own impending death seven days in advance. This prophetic feature marked the lives of holy men such as Columba, Boisil, Cædmon, and Wilfrid. Chad called certain chosen monks to him and urged them to follow "the Rule of life which he had taught them" (*HE* iv 3).[263] Chad is listed in the Old English Martyrology at March 2, 672 and is buried at Lichfield.[264] His relics cure (*HE* iv 3). The links Chad established between Lindsey and Ireland continued.

Æthelwine became bishop of Mercia at Lindsey, ca. 680–[?]692 (*HE* iii 11, 27; iv 12). He had studied in Ireland, like his brother Æthelhun, who was the companion of Ecgberht at Rath Melsigi but who died in the plague of 664 (*HE* iii 27). Bede did not state where in Ireland Æthelwine had studied, although Rath Melsigi seems a natural option given his brother's relationship with Ecgberht. The two brothers had a sister named Æthelhild who became abbess of a house in Lincolnshire (*HE* iii 11).

---

[262] "in quo usque hodie instituta ab ipso regularis uitae uestigia permanent": Colgrave and Mynors, *Ecclesiastical History*, 336–37.
[263] Colgrave and Mynors, *Ecclesiastical History*, 340–41.
[264] Rauer, *Old English Martyrology*, 60–61 §37, 243.

Abbot Hygebald, from the province of Lindsey, visited Ecgberht at Rath Melsigi sometime in the late seventh or early eighth century. The two discussed the lives of early fathers and Ecgberht related an anecdote stating that he knew a man, still in the flesh (possibly himself), who had seen Cedd (d. 664) and a band of angels descend from the sky to collect Chad's soul and bring it to heaven (*HE* iv 3). The ongoing relationship between Lindsey and Rath Melsigi, and the topic of conversation between Hygebald and Ecgberht, reflect the links between the Anglo-Saxons and the Gaels into the eighth century.

Patrick Sims-Williams identified a penitential prayer which may be attributed to Abbot Hygebald (Hygbaldus).[265] It refers to God as Creator and has characteristics of *loricae*. The prayer used the triad "thought, word, deed" which was most frequent in Gaelic texts. Hygebald referred to himself as *homunculus*, a term Aldhelm used to describe himself in his correspondence with Cellán of Péronne, but used most frequently by Adomnán self-referentially.[266] We have no firm dates for Hygebald, but he appears in the Old English *Martyrology* at December 14.[267]

## Continental Missions from Rath Melsigi

Wihtberht, an understudy to Ecgberht, lived as an anchorite and was known for his learning. He undertook a mission to the Frisians, sometime in the 680s during the reign of King Radbod (ca. 680–719), but returned to Ireland after two years when he had no success (*HE* v 9).[268] Bede indicated that he resumed his former anchoritic life.[269] Although his foreign mission failed, when he returned "he took care to help his own people more" implying that he worked with Anglo-Saxons in Ireland.[270] Alcuin called Wihtberht a "fitting companion" for Ecgberht, though they later separated. Wihtberht lead a life of solitude and

---

265 Sims-Williams, *Religion and Literature*, 322–23.
266 For the example for Aldhelm, see his response to Cellán: Howlett, *Celtic Latin Tradition*, 113. For its wide use in Gaelic contexts and Adomnán's use of the term to refer to himself, see Márkus, "*Adiutor laborantium*."
267 Rauer, *Old English Martyrology*, 226–27 §237, 309–10 (commentary).
268 Based on paschal tables used by Willibrord's mission, it is possible that Wihtberht's mission was begun before 684: Ó Cróinín, "Rath Melsigi, Willibrord," 30.
269 "solito in silentio uacare Domino coepit": Colgrave and Mynors, *Ecclesiastical History*, 480–81.
270 "suis amplius ex uirtutum exemplis prodesse curabat": Colgrave and Mynors, *Ecclesiastical History*, 480–81.

contemplation yet built an excellent shelter for monks of his own race and was a sterling example for them.²⁷¹

Wihtberht's name appears in Gaelic sources which supports the claim that he became influential in Ireland after his failed continental mission. The guarantor list for *Cáin Adomnáin* (697) names among the ecclesiastics a certain *Ichtbricht epscop* (Bishop Wihtberht).²⁷² Unfortunately, no other sources assign him the title of bishop, and the guarantor list provides no ecclesiastical affiliations. The ninth-century *Félire Óengusso* names Wihtberht at December 8, as cited in Appendix 2.a. The entry reads:

| | |
|---|---|
| Buaid nIchtbrichtáin umail | (The triumph of humble Wihtberht |
| darrala tar romuir | who came over the great sea |
| do Chríst cachain figil | for Christ he performed a vigil |
| hi curchán cen choduil.²⁷³ | in a curragh without hides.) |

The quatrain confirms that Anglo-Saxon *peregrini* were "seafarers" by virtue of coming to Ireland from Britain, whether or not they continued on as missionaries to the continent as Wihtberht had done. Alcuin derived his information from Bede, and neither source provides a sense of where Wihtberht established himself to work with his fellow countrymen. He may have remained at or near Rath Melsigi. The *scholia* for the *Félire Óengusso* suggest other locations, but none provide convincing leads.²⁷⁴ Most frequently mentioned is *Mag nÉo na Saxan* affiliated with Iona.²⁷⁵ Tullylease (*Tulach Léis*, Co. Cork) has several inscribed and carved stones with what appear to be Anglo-Saxon names.²⁷⁶ Yet another possibility is Tisaxon (*Tech Saxan*; house of the Saxons), near Kinsale, Co. Cork.²⁷⁷ The Munster location of both Tullylease and Tisaxon are both in Bede's "southern provinces" and, therefore, orthodox. More research remains to be done on these sites, but they provide tantalizing hints for places where Anglo-Saxons came to study.

---

271 Godman, *Alcuin*, 82–83, lines 1022–33.
272 Ní Dhonnchadha, "Guarantor List," 180, 193–94 §29, where he is mistakenly identified as Ecgberht, but Ó Cróinín correctly identified Wihtberht: "Rath Melsigi, Willibrord," 25 and notes.
273 Stokes, *Félire Óengusso*, 250 (my translation). For a comparison of this description of Wihtberht with the Old English *Seafarer*, see Ireland, "Seafarer," 9.
274 Stokes, *Félire Óengusso*, 256–59.
275 See the cogent discussion by Ó Cróinín, "Rath Melsigi, Willibrord," 26n1.
276 See Henderson and Okasha, "Inscribed and Carved Stones."
277 For a discussion of locations in Ireland which Anglo-Saxons may have frequented, see Edmunds, "Practicalities of Communication," 135 (map); Ó Cróinín, "Willibrord."

Willibrord was the most successful missionary who trained with Ecgberht. His mission to Frisia began in 690 and six years later (696), he became archbishop and had established his see at Echternach. After a long, productive career, including visits to Rome, he died in 739.[278] He had studied at Rath Melsigi for at least a dozen years, from 678–690 (*HE* iii 13, v 10–11).[279] The manuscripts produced for Willibrord's mission were of Gaelic provenance. They were not the products of his Northumbrian homeland.[280] The autobiographical note in Willibrord's Calendar shows eclectic influence from Anglo-Saxon, Frankish, and Gaelic sources.[281] Specific works like the *Computus Cottonianus* of 689 were compiled at Rath Melsigi for his use.[282]

Willibrord began his monastic life at Ripon. The year that he transferred to Rath Melsigi (678) is the same year that Bishop Wilfrid was exiled under pressure from King Ecgfrith, Archbishop Theodore, and Abbess Hild, among others (*VW* cc. 24, 54).[283] Wilfrid left for the continent and Rome, going first to King Aldgisl of the Frisians where, Stephen claimed, he successfully preached to the pagans. In this context Stephen intimated that Willibrord "his [Wilfrid's] son, brought up in Ripon" (*filius eius, Inhripis nutritus*) had built his mission on the foundations first laid by Wilfrid in the conversion of the Frisians.[284] Despite the claim made in *Vita Wilfridi* for closeness with Willibrord, Wilfrid is not named in Willibrord's Calendar.[285] Alcuin's Life of Willibrord provides fuller information than his "Bishops, Kings, and Saints of York" which simply synopsizes Bede.[286]

---

278 For a survey of his career, see Levison, *England and the Continent*, 53–69. Note further, Wood, "Irish in England: Part I," 185–86 and notes. Dionysiac Paschal traditions are most likely to have entered Frankish kingdoms through Willibrord's mission: Palmer, "Adoption of Dionysian Easter."
279 These dates are based on Alcuin's Life of Willibrord: Albertson, *Anglo-Saxon Saints and Heroes*, 280–82, cc. 4–5 (translation); Krusch and Levison, "Vita Willibrordi," 118–21.
280 Ó Cróinín, "Pride and Prejudice," 358–62; Ó Cróinín, "Rath Melsigi, Willibrord," 26–42; Ó Cróinín, "Willibrord"; Breay and Story, *Anglo-Saxon Kingdoms*, 111–13 (Echternach Gospels), 130–31 (Willibrord's Calendar). For hints at the relationship between Willibrord's "mission" and Northumbria, see Story, "Bede, Willibrord."
281 Pelteret, "Willibrord's Autobiography"; Howlett, "Wilbrord's Autobiographical Note," 154–61. For his autobiographical note in the calendar, see Breay and Story, *Anglo-Saxon Kingdoms*, 130–31.
282 Warntjes, "*Computus Cottonianus*."
283 Colgrave, *Life of Bishop Wilfrid*, 48–51, c. 24; 116–17, c. 54.
284 Colgrave, *Life of Bishop Wilfrid*, 52–53, c. 26.
285 Wilson, *Calendar of St Willibrord*.
286 For Alcuin's Life, see Albertson, *Anglo-Saxon Saints and Heroes*, 275–95 (translation); Krusch and Levison, "Vita Willibrordi." For mention in "Bishops, Kings, and Saints of York," see Godman, *Alcuin*, 82–85, lines 1034–43.

Willibrord helped disseminate the cult of Oswald. When he was visited (ca. 703) by Wilfrid and Acca in Frisia, Willibrord related a tale about how Oswald's relics cured a Gaelic scholar. The scholar fell ill and beseeched Willibrord to help him because he had heard of Oswald's healing power. Willibrord had a piece of the stake upon which Oswald's head had been impaled. By dipping a splinter into water for a drink, Willibrord was able to cure the scholar (*HE* iii 13). The events in this anecdote occurred in the 680s. Willibrord, by that time, already had some of Oswald's curative relics with him. The anecdote provides evidence that Rath Melsigi was a mixed institution with both Anglo-Saxon and Gaelic members.

If *Beowulf* is from the late seventh or early eighth century then Willibrord's successful Frisian mission (690–739) suggests how the one identifiable historical event in the poem, the Frisian raid, had been transmitted to, and kept alive among, the Anglo-Saxons.[287] The connections between Lindsey, in the Anglian linguistic territory, and Rath Melsigi should also be noted in the context of *Beowulf*. Among the Gaels the preservation of secular vernacular tales and lore occurred in conjunction with ecclesiastical establishments. Peripatetic Anglo-Saxon students training at Gaelic establishments were capable of replicating such literary practices.

Despite the failure of Wihtberht's mission, and building on the success of Willibrord's, two priests who shared the same name determined to undertake a mission to the Old Saxons on the continent. Black Hewald and White Hewald were distinguished by the color of their hair. They both had "long lived in exile in Ireland for the sake of their eternal fatherland" (*HE* v 10).[288] Bede was vague about the timeframe, but their mission must have occurred in the last decade of the seventh century or, perhaps, in the early eighth. Both were devout, but Black Hewald was the more knowledgeable in the scriptures. Both were martyred (*HE* v 10). White Hewald was put to death quickly, but Black Hewald was tortured and suffered an agonizing death. Their bodies were thrown into the Rhine but, miraculously, traveled for miles against the current to where their companions were. Their martyrdoms resulted in miracles. Tilmon, a companion who had lived as a soldier before becoming a monk, identified through a vision where their martyred bodies could be found (*HE* v 10). Tilmon must have trained at Rath Melsigi along

---

[287] For discussion of the episode involving Hygelac and his death in Frisia, see Biggs, "Frisian Raids." Biggs does not discuss how this information may have been transferred to Anglo-Saxon England.

[288] "qui in Hibernia multo tempore pro aeterna patria exulauerant": Colgrave and Mynors, *Ecclesiastical History*, 480–81.

with the two Hewalds. Alcuin synopsized details from Bede's account about the two including their martyrdoms and miracles.[289]

## Establishments in the Barrow Valley

Rath Melsigi cannot be viewed in isolation. Ecclesiastical establishments throughout Gaeldom engaged Anglo-Saxon students of varied social rank and intellectual ambition. The Barrow (*Berba*) River Valley formed an active corridor in the ecclesiastical and intellectual activities of the seventh century. It is a region that was orthodox for decades before the "synod" of Whitby. The brief survey of sites that follows progresses from south to north (Figure 6.c).

The monastery at St. Mullins was established in the seventh century. Its founder and namesake, Mo-Ling, became famous in later legend for his interactions with Suibne *geilt* and his rich legacy of nature poetry.[290] Mo-Ling is credited with composing poetry, but surviving attributions are later than his period.[291] According to tradition he helped remit an onerous tax called the *bórama* levied on the Leinstermen by the Uí Néill. An eighth-century Gospel prayer book is associated with his monastery.[292] Mo-ling was a guarantor for *Cáin Adomnáin* (697).[293] His *obit* appears in the Annals of Ulster for the same year.[294]

Abbot Laisrén (hypocoristic form Mo-Laise) of Old Leighlin (*Lethglenn*, Co. Carlow), on the opposite side of the river from Rath Melsigi, was an advocate for orthodoxy and a visitor to Rome in later hagiography. In one tradition he debated the Paschal controversy with Munnu (St. Fintan) who supported the *latercus*.[295] Mo-Laise's *obit* is recorded at 639.[296] Old Leighlin is associated with Banbán *sapiens* (d. 686). An abbot of Old Leighlin named Manchéne (d. 726) was a guarantor for the *Cáin Adomnáin*.[297] The Old Gaelic "Triads" list Old Leighlin as "one of the three prayer houses (*dairthech*)" of Ireland.[298]

---

289 Godman, *Alcuin*, 84–87, lines 1044–71.
290 O'Keeffe, *Buile Suibhne*; Nagy, Introduction to *Buile Suibhne*.
291 Stokes and Strachan, *Thesaurus*, ii, 294. See further Ó Corráin, *Clavis*, ii, 1156 §869.
292 Ó Corráin, *Clavis*, i, 48–50 §§14, 15.
293 Ní Dhonnchadha, "Guarantor List," 180, 188–89 §18.
294 Mac Airt and Mac Niocaill, *Annals of Ulster*, 158–59 s.a. 697; Stokes, "Annals of Tigernach," 215 [Felinfach i 175].
295 Walsh and Ó Cróinín, *Cummian's Letter*, 49–51.
296 Mac Airt and Mac Niocaill, *Annals of Ulster*, 120–21 s.a. 639; Stokes, "Annals of Tigernach," 185 [Felinfach i 145].
297 Ní Dhonnchadha, "Guarantor List," 180, 188 §14.
298 Meyer, *Triads of Ireland*, 14–15 §108.

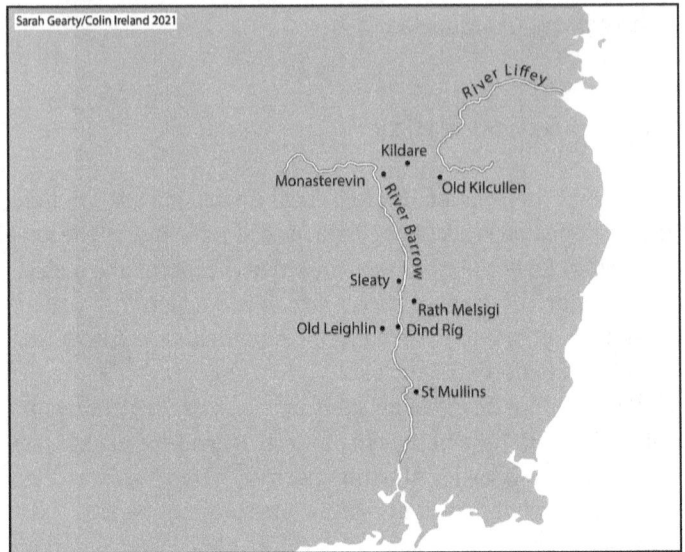

**Figure 6.c:** Map of locations in the Barrow Valley.
This map of the southeast corner of Ireland shows Rath Melsigi in the middle of the Barrow Valley corridor with important ecclesiastical sites, such as Kildare, Monasterevin, and Old Kilcullen on the north end, St. Mullins in the south, and Sleaty and Old Leighlin in the middle near Rath Melsigi. Seventh-century hagiography includes *Vita Brigitae* by Cogitosus from Kildare and *Vita Patricii* by Muirchú maccu Machtheni commissioned from Sleaty. The ancient inaugural site of *Cnoc Ailinne* (Hill of Ailenn), mentioned in poems by Óengus mac Óengobann (Figure 2.d) and Orthanach úa Cóellámae (Figure 2.e), sits between Kildare and Old Kilcullen, the latter monastic site associated with the early Patrician cult. Dind Ríg, discussed in the first three chapters, sits near Rath Melsigi. It is referred to in early dynastic poetry, prosimetric narrative, and Orthanach's poem (Figure 2.e).

On the west bank of the river near Leighlinbridge are earthworks thought to be Dind Ríg.[299] It was the site of a deadly conflict over Leinster dynastic succession as noted in one of the "rhymeless Leinster poems," cited in chapter one.[300] A poem by Orthanach úa Cóellámae (d. ca. 839) named Dind Ríg and key players in the events there (Figure 2.e). The tenth-century prosimetrum *Orgain Denna Ríg* (The Destruction of Dind Ríg), discussed in chapter three, is the fullest surviving account of the conflict.[301] The "Iron house motif" from *Orgain Denna Ríg* reappears

---

[299] Carney, "Language and Literature," 480–81.
[300] Corthals, "Observations on the Versification," 117 §1 (*Dind ríg | ruad Tuaim Tenbad*).
[301] Greene, *Fingal Rónáin*, 16–26 (*Orgain Denna Ríg*); O'Rahilly, *Early Irish History and Mythology*, 101–17.

in the Old English Vercelli Homily IX.[302] The geographical proximity of Rath Melsigi and Dind Ríg suggests routes of transmission for the motif.

Sleaty (*Sléibte*, Co. Laois) lies a few miles north of Rath Melsigi, on the banks of the Barrow. Its founding bishop was Fiacc Finn Sléibte of Uí Bairrche cited in seventh-century documents such as *Vita Patricii*, the Patrician *Collectanea*, and the *Additamenta*.[303] In *Vita Patricii* Fiacc Finn was the *adoliscens poeta* present with Dubthach maccu Lugair at Lóegaire's pagan court.[304] One of his successors, Bishop Áed, commissioned Muirchú to write the Life of Patrick. Both Bishop Áed and Muirchú were guarantors for the *Cáin Adomnáin* (697).[305] Áed died as an anchorite, probably at Armagh, in 700.[306] Fiacc Finn and Dubthach represent the rôle of poets in promoting the Church and in syncretizing indigenous and ecclesiastical world views.

Further north on the Barrow was the establishment of Monasterevin (*Mainister Éimíne*; Co. Kildare), founded by Éimíne. The Old Gaelic *Cáin Éimíne Báin* was an early charter intended to ensure privileges from the king Bran úa Fáeláin (d. 693).[307] Éimíne is associated with St. Fursa at Lagny and with a local saint named Mac Táil of Kilcullen of early Patrician traditions.[308] The hilltop site of Old Kilcullen looks across to Knockaulinn (*Cnoc Ailinne*; Hill of Ailenn), an ancient inauguration site celebrated in verse in the prologue of *Félire Óengusso* (Figure 2.d), and by Orthanach úa Cóellámae (Figure 2.e), bishop of nearby Kildare, the cult center of St. Brigit.

The Barrow Valley locations noted above represent the intellectual, literary, and social environments that seventh- and eighth-century Anglo-Saxon students at Rath Melsigi encountered as part of their sojourns. All of these establishments are in the southern, orthodox regions of Ireland as identified by Bede.

---

302 Wright, *Irish Tradition*, 194–206.
303 Bieler, *Patrician Texts*, 92–93, I 19 (18) (Muirchú), 162–63, 51.4 (Tírechán), 176–77, 13.3–5 (*Additamenta*).
304 Ireland, "Vernacular Poets," 49–55.
305 Ní Dhonnchadha, "Guarantor List," 180, 192–93 §25 (Áed), 180, 196 §36 (Muirchú).
306 Mac Airt and Mac Niocaill, *Annals of Ulster*, 158–59 s.a. 700; Stokes, "Annals of Tigernach," 216 [Felinfach i 176].
307 For the *cáin*, see Poppe, "*Cáin Éimíne Báin*"; Poppe, "List of Sureties." For the *obit* of the king, see Mac Airt and Mac Niocaill, *Annals of Ulster*, 154–55 s.a. 693; Stokes, "Annals of Tigernach," 213 [Felinfach i 173].
308 Ó Riain, *Dictionary*, 291–92 (Éimíne), 423–24 (Mac Táil).

## The Uninterrupted Influence of Iona

Gaelic influence on Anglo-Saxon ecclesiastical and intellectual culture came from many sources and lasted throughout the period under discussion. That influence was disseminated by Gaels active in Anglo-Saxon Britain, as well as by Anglo-Saxons who studied and trained among the Gaels. In fact, that influence cannot be shown to have abated.

Two major sources, Bede's *Historia ecclesiastica* and Stephen of Ripon's *Vita Wilfridi*, share the themes either of overcoming Gaelic influence, or of repaying the debt for it. Both sources pivot on the resolution of the Paschal controversy at the "synod" of Whitby opting for Roman "orthodoxy" which allowed most Britons, Picts, and Gaels associated with Iona to be branded as "schismatic" or, at best, "heterodox." Despite the "synod" putting an end to bishops from Iona officiating in Northumbria, it did not end the influence of Iona, or interactions with it, in Anglo-Saxon cultural affairs.

The intellectual and literary power of Iona is manifested in the influence of *Altus Prosator* which was known to Aldhelm in Southumbria.[309] It may well have influenced his description of the cosmos in his *Carmen rhythmicum*.[310] Some of its erudite vocabulary circulated throughout Aldhelm's world and was dispersed widely.[311] The paths of transmission have yet to be clearly identified but may well lead through Theodore's school at Canterbury.[312]

The success of Mayo of the Saxons, established by Bishop Colmán (ca. 673), cannot be underestimated. Colmán's departure, with thirty Anglo-Saxon monks and others, from Northumbria in 664, their sojourn in Iona, and journey to Inishboffin in 668, attest to their determination to succeed. Bede acknowledged the growing numbers of Anglo-Saxons there in his day and Alcuin corresponded with them and praised their influence on their homeland in Britain. Their success lasted well into the ninth century and beyond.[313]

Abbot Adomnán and Aldfrith *sapiens* had a close relationship whose origins cannot be precisely traced. Adomnán described Aldfrith as *Aldfridus amicus*. Aldfrith was present at Iona ca. 684, before Ecgfrith's defeat at Nechtansmere and subsequent burial at Iona. The return back to Ireland of captives from Northumbria after the raid into Mag Breg reveals a cooperative triangle from Iona into

---

309 Orchard, *Poetic Art of Aldhelm*, 54–60.
310 Barker, "*Usque Domnoniam*," 17–18, 51.
311 Lapidge, "'Epinal-Erfurt Glossary'," 152–56.
312 Orchard, *Poetic Art of Aldhelm*, 54–60.
313 See Orschel, "Mag nEó na Sacsan"; Orschel, "Early History of Mayo."

Northumbria and with Síl nÁedo Sláine. During Adomnán's 687 visit to Northumbria he presented Aldfrith with *De locis sanctis* for which he was richly rewarded.[314] Bede created an epitome of *De locis sanctis* and included two chapters in *Historia ecclesiastica* based on it. According to Bede, Adomnán adopted orthodox practices during his visit to Aldfrith *sapiens* ca. 687 (*HE* v 15).

Boisil, the prior of Melrose (d. ca. 664), followed the traditions of Iona and Lindisfarne before the "synod" of Whitby.[315] He was the mentor of Cuthbert in the 650s and responsible for his training. Boisil prophesied that Cuthbert would become bishop. Years later, it was Boisil's prophecy that convinced Cuthbert to accept the bishopric reluctantly (*HE* iv 27, 28).

Boisil influenced Ecgberht through prophecy, according to Bede. Through the dreams of a monastic brother, Boisil encouraged Ecgberht to convert Iona to orthodoxy (*HE* v 9). No explanations have yet been advanced, beyond the account by Bede, for how Ecgberht single-handedly could have converted the powerful Columban monastery of Iona.

The cult of Oswald, who introduced the "schismatic" mission from Iona into Northumbria, reflects continuing ties.[316] *Vita Columbae* (688–704) described how Columba appeared to Oswald in a vision and predicted victory at Hefenfeld.[317] Adomnán designated Oswald as *totius Brittanniae imperator a deo ordinatus*.[318] The custom of keeping a vigil at Hefenfeld to commemorate Oswald's death originated at Hexham (*HE* iii 2), most likely under Bishop Eata (ca. 678), one of the original disciples of Bishop Aidan (*HE* iv 12). Willibrord's anecdote about Oswald's relics curing a Gaelic scholar occurred in the 680s at Rath Melsigi (*HE* iii 13), and Willibrord already possessed some of Oswald's healing relics.[319]

---

[314] Adomnán is not mentioned in the Old English Martyrology, but Arculf is cited numerous times which shows that *De locis sanctis* was well known in Anglo-Saxon England as a text, and that Arculf as witness is given priority over Adomnán as author: Rauer, *Old English Martyrology*, 84–85 §67 (St George), 96–97 §79 (Ascension of Christ), 124–25 §111a (Summer Solstice), 194–95 §200 (Jerome).
[315] McCann, "Cuthbert and Boisil."
[316] Rauer, *Old English Martyrology*, 155 §146, 279; Stokes, *Félire Óengusso*, 175 (August 5).
[317] Anderson and Anderson, *Life of Columba*, 14–15, i 1 (8a–b).
[318] Anderson and Anderson, *Life of Columba*, 16–17, i 1 (9a).
[319] Acca may have been Bede's intermediary in the transmission of stories from Whitby, such as Cædmon's poem, with Bosa, trained at Whitby, serving as the primary source: Cronan, "Cædmon's Audience," 353–55.

The latest datable Old English poem *Durham*, an *encomium urbis* written ca. 1100, harkens back to a "golden age" when Iona first established Lindisfarne.[320] It is roughly contemporary with Gilla in Choimded's retrospective poem about iconic figures of Gaelic poetry and law.[321] The *Durham* poem emphasizes holy relics contained in that city, not unlike in Adomnán's poem "*Sruith in tíag*," where naming the contents opens space for reflection and meditation. The first named relic is St. Cuthbert himself, followed by the head of King Oswald, and then Bishop Aidan. Then follow three bishops at Lindisfarne, although only one is given that title. Eadberht was bishop when Cuthbert's remains were exhumed and found incorrupt. The Lives of Cuthbert, by both the anonymous hagiographer and by Bede, were dedicated to Bishop Eadfrith, mentioned in tandem with Eadberht, as "worthy companions" (æðele gefēres). Bishop Æthelwold was probably in office when Bede died. Finally Bede and Boisil, here called abbot, are named.

At the end of the Anglo-Saxon period the *Durham* poem hearkens back to an age when a Gaelic-educated, Gaelic-speaking king, Oswald, introduced from Iona a Gaelic bishop, Aidan, who founded Lindisfarne and began the successful conversion in Northumbria. Cuthbert, the first Northumbrian saint, benefited from the learning and training of his Gaelic mentor Boisil. The scholar Bede recorded the most thorough evidence for these events. Three bishops of Lindisfarne, Eadberht, Eadfrith, and Æthelwold, ensured the growth of St. Cuthbert's cult, established and made possible by the Gaelic mission from Iona.

---

**320** Evan, "Word-Play"; O'Donnell, "Old English *Durham*"; Bailey and Cambridge, "Dating 'Durham'."
**321** Smith, "Aimirgein Glúngel Tuir Tend."

# Chapter Seven
# Cædmon's World at Whitby

This chapter gathers evidence presented in previous chapters to identify the "Gaelic background" in one example of Old English poetic composition. Bede's account of Cædmon is the earliest and the most complete description of how a poet worked in the Anglo-Saxon world (*HE* iv 24).[1] Critics use it as the leading example of the methods and techniques employed by Old English poets.[2] It has, however, close analogues from contemporary Brittonic and Gaelic poetic cultures, both represented at Whitby and its environs. Bede's account of Cædmon can be fully explained in the context of Gaelic poetic practices.

The majority of members in the Whitby community were probably Anglo-Saxons. But linguistic evidence shows that a local Brittonic substratum was present in the region at the time. The personal histories of the abbesses Hild (657–680) and Ælfflæd (680–714) demonstrate a Gaelic superstratum at Whitby of Gaelic-educated "more learned men" (*viri doctiores*), like those who approved Cædmon's performances.[3]

## The Ethnic Mix and Gaelic Ethos of Whitby

Hild was born ca. 614 while her father was living under the protection of a Brittonic king in Elmet (Modern Welsh *Elfed*), western Yorkshire. She was raised in King Edwin's retinue and baptized, at about the age of thirteen, by Paulinus of the Gregorian mission ca. 627. The identity of Paulinus is intertwined with Rhun mab Urien as discussed in chapter six.

---

[1] See also, Wallace-Hadrill, *Historical Commentary*, 165–67. Plummer, *Venerabilis Baedae Opera*, i, 258–62; ii, 248–58. For the most comprehensive study yet done, see O'Donnell, *Cædmon's Hymn*. Charles Jones argued for the authenticity of Bede's sources for the story of Cædmon: *Saints' Lives and Chronicles*, 185.
[2] For some discussions of Cædmon in the larger context of poetic and literary culture, see Schrader, "Caedmon and the Monks"; Opland, *Anglo-Saxon Oral Poetry*, 106–20, 124–29; Frantzen, *Desire for Origins*, 130–67. Bede's list of topics covered by Cædmon's poetic output suggests the catechetical *narratio* as promoted by St. Augustine: Day, "Catechetical *narratio*," 51–53, 55.
[3] For an overview of the monastery at Whitby, and its relationship with Hartlepool and Hackness, see Cramp, "Monastic Site of Whitby."

> 1) Hild had a personal relationship with Bishop Aidan of Lindisfarne (*HE* iv 23)
> 2) Hild was in East Anglia at the time of Fursa and his companions (pre-647; *HE* iv 23)
> 3) At the "synod" of 664 Hild and her community sided with the "Iona/Lindisfarne party" (*HE* iii 25)
> 4) Cædmon's poetic composition in Bede's account reflects Gaelic practices (*HE* iv 24)
> 5) Abbess Ælfflæd's relationship with Aldfrith *sapiens* lasted throughout his reign (anonymous *Vita Cuthberti*, iii 6; *VW* c. 59)
> 6) Kings buried at Whitby: Oswiu (*HE* iii 24), Edwin (*HE* iii 24; *Vita Gregorii*, cc. 18, 19), Aldfrith (Alcuin)
> 7) *Vita Gregorii*, produced in Ælfflæd's time, shows Gaelic characteristics.

**Figure 7.a:** The Gaelic Ethos of Whitby.

Hild's baptism by Paulinus cannot be interpreted as a commitment to orthodoxy as purveyed by Rome. Sometime before 647 Hild went to East Anglia intending to follow her sister Hereswith to a monastery on the continent (*HE* iv 23). Her East Anglian sojourn overlapped with the presence there of Fursa and his named companions (*HE* iii 19). Like Hild and her sister, they were destined for the same region on the continent (*HE* iii 19).

Hild's time in East Anglia overlapped with Bishop Felix's tenure (ca. 631–ca. 648) who had a respectful relationship with Bishop Aidan of Lindisfarne (634–651; *HE* iii 25). Hild was called back to Northumbria in 647 by Bishop Aidan. Within a year Hild was put in charge of Heruteu (Hartlepool). Bishop Aidan and other devout men visited her often, instructed her, and appreciated her wisdom and devotion (*HE* iv 23). King Oswiu submitted his daughter Ælfflæd into Hild's care around 655 (*HE* iii 24). Ælfflæd remained with Hild all her life and succeeded her as abbess when Hild died in 680.

Hild continued her good relations with succeeding bishops of Lindisfarne, Fínán and Colmán. In 657 Bishop Fínán put Hild in charge of Whitby (*Streanæshalh*). Hild's pastoral style (*HE* iv 23) compares closely with those of bishops Aidan (*HE* iii 5) and Colmán (*HE* iii 26).

After seven years, in 664, the "synod" of Whitby was held (*HE* iii 25). It was overseen by the Gaelic-speaking, Gaelic-educated King Oswiu (*HE* iii 25). There were three bishops at the "synod," all of whom had received Gaelic training. Bishop Colmán of Lindisfarne must have traveled with a contingent but neither account names any of his companions. Bishop Cedd of the East Saxons acted as interpreter for the proceedings. Cedd's brother Chad was one of the original twelve boys trained by Bishop Aidan. Cedd sought to emulate them both (*HE* iii 28). Cedd's rôle as interpreter implies that he had learned Gaelic although no records show him having studied outside of Northumbria. The third bishop was Agilberht, a Gaul, who in the 640s "had spent a long time in Ireland for the purpose of studying the Scriptures" (*HE* iii 7).

At the "synod" Abbess Hild and her community, as well as Bishop Cedd, supported the Ionan party (Hild abbatissa cum suis in parte Scottorum; HE iii 25). Bede's description of Hild's pastoral practices and administrative style imply that she and her community preferred the *modus vivendi* of the Gaels. Hild is frequently cited as Bede's ideal teaching nun.[4] Among Whitby's achievements are five men trained at Whitby who became bishops (*HE* iv 23). One of them, John of Beverley, ordained Bede as deacon (ca. 692) and then as priest (ca. 703; *HE* v 24).

At Hild's death in 680 Ælfflæd took over as abbess at Whitby and was assisted by her mother Eanflæd. Ælfflæd and Aldfrith *sapiens* had a good relationship throughout his reign (685–704). Alcuin of York provided evidence that Aldfrith was buried at Whitby.[5] The *Vita Gregorii* was completed at Whitby during the last decade of Ælfflæd's abbacy. It is filled with Gaelic *topoi* and literary devices.[6]

Cædmon likely performed during Hild's abbacy (657–680), but he may have lived on beyond those years.[7] The ethos during Ælfflæd's abbacy would have helped transmit traditions about Cædmon. Bede could not have been more than a young boy, if he were even born, when Cædmon performed and stories about him began to be repeated. There would have been one to two generations of transmission for stories about Cædmon before Bede heard about them, let alone recorded them. In his autobiographical note at the end of the *Historia*, Bede stated that he gleaned information from ancient documents (*ex litteris antiquorum*), from his own knowledge (*ex mea ipse cognitione*), but also from the tradition of elders (*ex traditione maiorum*; *HE* v 24). John of Beverley is a likely candidate as "elder" who informed Bede of events and personnel at Whitby.[8]

---

[4] See, for example, Fell, "Hild, Abbess of Streonæshalch"; Hunter Blair, "Whitby as a Centre of Learning"; Ward, "'To my dearest sister'"; Wormald, "St. Hilda, Saint and Scholar"; Lees and Overing, "Birthing Bishops"; Bauer, "Hilda of Whitby"; Gunn, *Bede's Historiae*, 176–77. For a more critical view, see Hollis, *Women and the Church*, 243–70.
[5] Yorke, *Rex Doctissimus*, 17.
[6] Ireland, "Whitby *Life* of Gregory."
[7] O'Donnell, *Cædmon's Hymn*, 10 and n6; Cronan, "Cædmon's *Hymn*."
[8] Cronan, "Cædmon's Audience," 353, 355–56. Charles Jones expressed surprise that Bede did not credit his Whitby sources in his Preface: *Saints' Lives and Chronicles*, 185.

## Cædmon as a Briton

Since at least 1934 it has been known that Cædmon is a Brittonic name.[9] It is not an Old English name. Kenneth Jackson noted that Cædmon derives from Primitive Welsh *Cadμan which itself derives from Common British *Catumandos.[10] The form of the name in Middle Welsh was Cadfan, the same name as the king of Anglesey who fostered Edwin, and whose son Cadwallon became a fierce rival of the Anglo-Saxons. Large populations of Britons flourished throughout Britain as noted at Wilfrid's dedication of Ripon in the 670s when he cited the lands he acquired from the Brittonic kingdoms conquered by King Ecgfrith (VW c. 17).[11]

Basing his arguments largely on river and place names, Jackson argued that "isolated communities of Britons must have existed in the Pennines and Yorkshire Moors, still speaking British, after the English had absorbed the lower lands around them."[12] Within living memory Abbess Hild had been hosted in the Brittonic kingdom of Elmet. Jackson also noted that "there is evidence in the forms of some of the British place-names adopted into English in the Yorkshire Moors that a British-speaking population was by-passed in the Cleveland area and left undisturbed for over a century."[13] The Yorkshire Moors and Cleveland Hills lie immediately to the west and slightly to the south of Whitby. Jackson's evidence shows that a viable Brittonic population continued in existence near Whitby for several decades beyond Cædmon's floruit. Brittonic names in the genealogies of the royal families of Wessex and of Lindsey suggest intermarriage at high social levels.[14] Hild's father Hereric living in Elmet under Ceredig's protection, Edwin's likely fosterage with Cadfan on Anglesey, Oswiu's marriage to Rhiainfellt, all support such a conclusion.

The Laws of King Ine of Wessex, in the late seventh century, accurately portray the interactions between Anglo-Saxons and Britons.[15] Generations of conflict

---

**9** Holthausen, *Etymologisches Wörterbuch*. Cædmon's name only merits a footnote in O'Donnell, *Cædmon's Hymn*, 3n2. But for possible contributions of Britons to Old English poetry, see North, "Singing Welsh Bishop."
**10** Jackson, *Language and History*, 554.
**11** For examples of lands taken from Britons, see Jones, "Donations to Bishop Wilfrid." Bede did not have a positive view of the Britons: Hall, "Interlinguistic Communications," 37–43. St. Guthlac had lived among Britons and understood their language: Colgrave, *Life of Saint Guthlac*, 108–11, c. 34; Tyler, "Mercia and the Britons."
**12** Jackson, *Language and History*, 197.
**13** Jackson, "Angles and Britons," 67.
**14** Jackson, *Language and History*, 244.
**15** Attenborough, *Laws of the Earliest English Kings*, 34–61; see further Thomas, Stumpf, and Härke, "Apartheid-like Social Structure."

resulted in lower status for Britons wherever Anglo-Saxons dominated. The Laws of Ine describe an inferior status for Britons living under Anglo-Saxon rule, including where Britons continued to own land. Charles-Edwards called it a parallel hierarchy and stated: "The same standards apply to English and to Welsh; the difference comes in the lower status which the same wealth provides for a Welshman."[16] The language of the politically dominant people would eventually become the *lingua franca* of both groups. However, Britons would have experienced a period of bilingualism as their language and culture were subsumed under Anglo-Saxon hegemony.[17]

In the second half of the seventh century many of Whitby's members would be low status, bilingual Britons. Bede intimated as much when he stated that Cædmon produced delightful verse *in sua, id est Anglorum, lingua* (in his own, that is in the Old English, language; *HE* iv 24).[18] Bede differentiated Old English from some other language, in this case Brittonic, due to Cædmon's Brittonic name. The other language was not Latin since whatever Cædmon learned of scripture or divine writings (*ex divinis litteris*) was learned through translators (*per interpretes*). At this early stage of conversion, Latin was not likely to have been a living, spoken language at Whitby except, perhaps, among a minority of learned members (*viri doctiores*).[19] After Cædmon others among the Anglo-Saxons attempted to make religious verse, but none could equal him (et quidem et alii post illum in gente Anglorum religiosa poemata facere temtabant, sed nullus eum aequiperare potuit; *HE* iv 24). If the cultural and social milieu at Whitby was dominated by Old English-speaking Anglo-Saxons, the phrase *in gente Anglorum* would be superfluous, unless Bede had in mind Britons and Gaels whose poets composed vernacular religious verse.[20]

Critics have proposed various reasons for Cædmon's inability, or unwillingness, to perform before an audience. C. L. Wrenn suggested that the Alfredian translation of Bede's account of Cædmon, which included the phrase *for sceome* (for shame) as an explanation for his departure from the *convivium*, was a "distinctive English tradition."[21] Francis Magoun stated that Cædmon's "real and

---

16 Charles-Edwards, "Origins of the Hide." The inevitable result of this second-class citizenship for Britons under Anglo-Saxon rule is discussed by Woof, "Apartheid and Economics."
17 Jackson, *Language and History*, 241–46.
18 For Bede's multiple meanings for *lingua*, see Major, "Words, Wit, and Wordplay," 204–6.
19 For example, Latin was probably not used at the "synod" of Whitby: Herren, "Scholarly Contacts," 37–39.
20 Early chapters noted Gaelic poetry that Bede may have considered. For the possibility of Brittonic poetry, see Koch, "Why Was Welsh Literature First Written Down?"
21 Wrenn, "Poetry of Cædmon," 281.

sole difficulty would seem then to have been only an unconquerable fear and consequent inability to sing before an audience, to have suffered in effect a kind of stage-fright; he may have been like a stammerer who can speak quite clearly when alone."[22] Similar difficulties with speech and performance have been noted in both Gaelic and Brittonic poetic traditions.[23] Ute Schwab argued that Cædmon's unwillingness to perform was because Old English was not his mother tongue but rather a second language.[24]

Bilingualism as the explanation for Cædmon's hesitancy to perform is reinforced if the Old English translation *for sceome* reflects an accurate tradition about Cædmon. Bede was sensitive to the multi-lingual character of Britain. The prevalence of bilingualism, and multi-lingualism, must be noted in three Gaelic-speaking kings, in Bishop Cedd as interpreter, missionaries from Iona learning Old English, and poor language skills attributed to Bishop Agilberht for deferring to Wilfrid as spokesperson at the "synod."

Bilingualism is compatible with arguments for oral-formulaic composition by Cædmon. Bede stated that he had never received training in poetry. A bilingual individual could learn the formulae and poetic diction in the same way that a native speaker would, simply by attending *convivia*.[25] By listening to others perform a bilingual of advanced years could have absorbed Old English formulaic diction.[26]

## An Untrained Poet?

The formal training required of Gaelic professional poets as outlined in *Uraicecht na Ríar* helped justify the poets' *sóernemed* social status (p. 106, c.3). Gaelic student poets could be referred to as *daltae* (fosterling; pupil, disciple) or *deiscipul* (disciple, pupil),[27] but *éicsíne* (learner of *éicse*; student of poetry) was

---

22 Magoun, "Bede's Story of Cædmon," 59.
23 Ford, "Blind, the Dumb, and the Ugly."
24 "che probabilmente per il poeta, visto che il suo nome è celtico, l'inglese non fosse la lingua materna, bensí la seconda": Schwab, *Caedmon*, 48. The point is reiterated in a later article arguing for the miraculous nature of Cædmon's story: Schwab, "Miracles of Cædmon," 11.
25 Magoun, "Bede's Story of Cædmon," 59.
26 Fry, "Formulaic Poet," 233.
27 eDIL: http://www.dil.ie, s.v. *daltae* or dil.ie/14451; eDIL: http://www.dil.ie, s.v. *deiscipul* or dil.ie/15268. Both of these terms were used of Fiacc Finn Sléibte, the student poet of Dubthach maccu Lugair: Ireland, "Vernacular Poets," 54.

a specific word for those undertaking formal training.[28] There is no equivalent for historical Old English poets.[29] *Widsith* and *Deor* demonstrate that poets (*scopas*; *gleomen*) relied on chieftains to act as patrons and provide a living. There is no evidence for systematized training.[30] The most detailed model proposed for poetic training is the oral-formulaic model which Donald Fry described, based on the research of Albert Lord, as 1) listening, 2) singing to himself, 3) public performance.[31] Such a model implies that Old English poets were either self-taught or received informal lessons from more experienced poets. Opening formulae for Old English poems, which rely on terms like *gefricgan* (to learn by asking or by inquiry; to hear of) and *gefrignan* (to ask; to learn by asking, hear of), support an emphasis on oral transmission of poetic tradition.[32]

Bede claimed that Cædmon did not learn poetry from men nor through human intervention (namque ipse non ab hominibus neque per hominem institutus canendi artem didicit; *HE* iv 24). Furthermore, Cædmon was advanced in years without ever having learned anything about poetry (usque ad tempora prouectioris aetatis constitutus, nil carminum aliquando didicerat; *HE* iv 24). Bede deliberately separated Cædmon from the Germanic poetic tradition as it existed in Anglo-Saxon Britain.[33] But consider the source. Bede was himself proficient in Latin poetry, a discipline that required formalized learning. He displayed his skills in the hymn Æthelthryth (*HE* iv 20), and in the substantial verse Life of St. Cuthbert (*HE* v 24).[34] After stating that Cædmon composed "in his own, that is in the Old English, language" (*HE* iv 24) why did Bede translate the hymn into Latin? Having done so, he explained how a translation can never capture the elegance and dignity of the original. By translating the hymn, was Bede implying that Latin was the proper medium for poetry, or was he anticipating that his *Historia* would circulate on the Continent beyond Anglo-Saxon Britain?[35] Latin poetry required formal training. Old English poetry did not. Bede's interest in Cædmon, apparently,

---

**28** eDIL: http://www.dil.ie, s.v. *éicsíne* or dil.ie/19734. The word is used in an early eighth-century text *Scél Mongáin*: White, *Compert Mongáin*, 75 (Gaelic), 81–82 (English) §§1–2.
**29** Thornbury, *Becoming a Poet*, 34–36.
**30** "No reliable study of Anglo-Saxon schools exists": Lendinara, "Anglo-Saxon Learning," 279n1.
**31** Fry, "Formulaic Poet," 233; based on Lord, *Singer of Tales*, 21–26.
**32** Ireland, "Visionary Poets," 126.
**33** For a summation, see O'Donnell, *Cædmon's Hymn*, 23–24 §1.33.
**34** Lapidge, *Bede's Latin Poetry*.
**35** Dennis Cronan noted that a major audience for Bede's *Historia* resided on the continent and was not familiar with insular vernacular cultures: Cronan, "Cædmon's Audience," 361; Bredehoft, *Authors, Audiences*, 19–20.

was not as an Old English poet, but rather as someone whose life and poetry were exemplary for his monastic audience.

Bilingual learning was already the norm in Gaelic monastic schools by the second half of the seventh century. Anecdotes about poets from *Vita Columbae*[36] and the poems of Bécán mac Luigdech, discussed in chapter two, highlight the vernacular. The "more learned men" who judged Cædmon's verses had been trained in that bilingual Gaelic tradition, whether they were themselves Gaels or Gaelic-trained Anglo-Saxons.

Bede's account of Cædmon is too well known to reproduce in detail (*HE* iv 24). The following synopsis allows for comparison with Gaelic practices. Cædmon used to attend *convivia* at the monastery where members sang and entertained themselves, sometimes to the accompaniment of the harp (*cithara*). Cædmon habitually absented himself when the harp approached him. On one occasion he left the *convivium* and settled into a stable (*stabula iumentorum*) where it was his duty to tend the animals. As he lay down to sleep a certain something (*quidam*) spoke to him and requested a song about the creation. Cædmon composed his famous hymn that night.

The next morning Cædmon went to the reeve (*vilicus*) in charge who took him to the abbess who, in turn, had him perform before the *viri doctiores* who judged his poem. They determined that Cædmon's hymn was the product of divine grace. The *viri doctiores* then provided Cædmon with a passage from sacred history or doctrine (sacrae historiae siue doctrinae sermonem; *HE* iv 24) and bid him turn it into verse. Cædmon returned the next morning having completed the task. Cædmon was able to do this better than any of his contemporaries. He memorized passages, "ruminated" over them, and turned them into the most delightful songs (in carmen dulcissimum conuertebat; *HE* iv 24).[37]

In the following discussion Bede's description of Cædmon's methods will be compared to Gaelic traditions. The closest comparisons in detail are found in seventeenth-century descriptions of Gaelic bardic schools in the *Memoirs of the Marquis of Clanricarde*, published in 1722, and in Martin's *Description of the Western Islands of Scotland*, published in 1703.[38] However, for purposes of this study, despite the closeness of these late analogues, material from the Old and Middle Gaelic period will be cited for pertinent comparisons.

---

36 Anderson and Anderson, *Life of Columba*, 16–17, i 1; 76–77, i 42.
37 The metaphor of rumination for cogitation is common in Biblical and patristic writings. In the description of *imbas for·osnai* from *Sanas Cormaic*, the diviner chews a piece of red meat but does not swallow it (p. 145, c. 3).
38 Relevant sections of the descriptions can be found in Bergin, *Irish Bardic Poetry*, 5–8 (Clanricarde), 8–9 (Martin).

Cædmon's avoidance of the harp may have other reasons besides ignorance of song, or the insecurity of a low status bilingual Briton. In Gaelic tradition high-ranking poets did not accompany themselves on the harp. As noted in the law-tracts, harpers had their own status distinct from that of the poets (p. 107, c.3). Cædmon was of low status within the monastery, as befits his likely Brittonic ethnicity. Nevertheless, his advanced years and secular status imply that Cædmon was familiar with poetic traditions of Britons and Gaels who eschewed accompanying themselves on the harp.

The practice of lying down in a darkened space, in a snug structure or darkened room, in order to compose through sleep or trance, is represented in Gaelic and Brittonic traditions. Cædmon departed the *convivium* for the stables (*stabula iumentorum*) where it was his duty to look after the animals.[39] Nevertheless, he entered a structure to lie down to sleep.[40]

The description of *imbas for·osnai* from *Sanas Cormaic* portrays the *fili* as entering a structure, lying down, and covering his face with his palms to create a darkened aspect (p. 145, c.3). Likewise, in *Togail Bruidne Da Derga* when Ingcél spies Conaire Mór arising out of his sleep to recite a cryptic poem, Conaire is in his chamber within Da Derga's hostel (p. 159, c.3). The stereotype of a darkened chamber for poetic composition is seen in the prose preface to *Altus Prosator* preserved in the tenth-century *Liber Hymnorum*.[41] The preface states, anachronistically, that St. Columba composed the poem to honor Pope Gregory and that "for seven years he worked at this hymn in a dark cell without light" (per septem annos hunc hymnum scrutans in nigra cellula sine lumine).[42] Gaelic poets are often portrayed as lying on their beds in a structure before rising from their sleep to recite poems.[43]

The purpose of the ritual *tarbfeis* (bull sleep or bull feast) was to divine a future king (p. 157, c. 3). *Tarb* (bull) and the dual meanings of *feis* (feast or sleep) are reflected in Cædmon's account because he left a *convivium* (*gebeorscipe* in Old English), and settled down to sleep in a stable. In chapter three examples were noted, from both Brittonic and Gaelic thirteenth- through seventeenth-century sources, of

---

**39** It has always been assumed that Cædmon was tending cattle even though *iumentum* refers to beasts of burden, typically equine.

**40** Descriptions of later Gaelic bardic schools all portray the students entering darkened rooms to lie in their beds overnight to compose on their assigned topics: Bergin, *Irish Bardic Poetry*, 5–8 (Clanricarde), 8–9 (Martin).

**41** Ó Corráin, *Clavis*, i, 364–66 §265.

**42** Bernard and Atkinson, *Liber Hymnorum*, ii, 23.

**43** The late sixteenth-century poet Fear Flatha Ó Gnímh criticized another poet Fearghal Óg for composing on horseback in the open air rather than on his bed in a darkened room, see Bergin, *Irish Bardic Poetry*, 118–19 (Gaelic), 265–66 (translation).

divinations taking place on the hide of a cow, bull, or ox on which the diviner slept overnight (pp. 158–59, c. 3). Entering a darkened structure to compose, bovine references, sleeping and feasting, are all found in Gaelic poetic practices, most specifically in *tarbfeis*.

The fragment by Colmán mac Lénéni (d. 606), discussed in chapter two, portrayed the poet awakening to a "worthy" poem "after beautiful and sweet-dreamed sleep" (pp. 54–55, c. 2). Just as Colmán awoke to a poem, Cædmon did likewise, but the Gaelic example is from several generations previous.[44] In the narrative tale *Togail Bruidne Da Derga* Conaire Mór rose from his sleep to recite a cryptic poem (p. 159, c. 3). In *Táin Bó Cúailnge* Dubthach Dóel chanted, through his *cotlud* (sleep; trance), a prophetic poem that described the ensuing battle (p. 160, c. 3). When compared with the Gaelic, and Brittonic, poetic traditions Cædmon has not done anything unique.

The *viri doctiores* (more learned men) who approved Cædmon's compositions have parallels in Gaelic tradition. In *Uraicecht na Ríar*, the *ollam filed* (chief poet) had to approve the aspiring poet's progress and declare the rank he acquired through training (p. 109, c. 3; Figure 3.a). In the description of *tarbfeis* from *Serglige Con Culainn*, four druids chant an *ór fírindi* (incantation of truth) over the man performing the divination (pp. 157, c. 3). Their incantation ensured the truthfulness of the diviner and pre-empted the need for "more learned men" to confirm the worthiness of the divination after the fact.

After Cædmon's initial verse had been approved by the *viri doctiores* they assigned further subjects and requested that Cædmon return the next morning with compositions based on the assigned topics.[45] Cædmon successfully completed the assignment. Composing a poem through sleep, and then repeating the process, was recorded in *Togail Bruidne Da Derga* where Conaire Mór was described as sleeping, then awakening from his sleep, rising, and chanting a lay (*laíd*). At least one manuscript version had him repeat the process (pp. 159–60, c. 3).

Bede described Caedmon as memorizing assigned topics and then ruminating over them "like some clean animal chewing the cud."[46] The metaphor of rumination was common in Late Antiquity though not in Hiberno-Latin. It was used by Aldhelm in the epilogue of his *Epistola ad Acircium* where he encouraged

---

[44] These comparisons have been made before: Ireland, "Precursor of Cædmon"; Ireland, "Cædmon and Colmán."

[45] In descriptions of the seventeenth-century Gaelic bardic schools students are assigned topics overnight and go off into their darkened rooms to compose their verses: Bergin, *Irish Bardic Poetry*, 5–8 (Clanricarde), 8–9 (Martin).

[46] "quasi mundum animal ruminando": Colgrave and Mynors, *Ecclesiastical History*, 418–19; West, "Rumination"; Wieland, "Caedmon, the Clean Animal."

Aldfrith *sapiens* "to chew [*masticare*] a bit and ruminate [*ruminare*] on that which was not repugnant to me."[47] The imaginative description of *imbas for·osna* from *Sanas Cormaic*, has the diviner chew red meat but not swallow it (p. 145, c. 3). The divinatory practice that allowed Fionn mac Cumhaill to access hidden knowledge, and express it in verse, *teinm láeda* (the chewing of the pith), involved Fionn putting his finger or thumb into his mouth, or sometimes chewing with his "tooth of knowledge" (p. 144, c. 3). The latter examples show that the Gaels understood the metaphor of "chewing" or "ruminating" on a difficult subject.

## Poetic Inspiration and Divine Grace

Instances of poetic inspiration among the Britons and Gaels are common. The Britons designated it as *awen*, while the Gaels called it *aí* (p. 12, c. 1). In the *Historia Brittonum* a noted sixth-century poet was Talhaearn Tad Awen "Talhaearn father of the poetic muse [*awen*]" (p. 11, c. 1). Bécán mac Luigdech described Columba as *dún mo üad* "fort of my poetic art [*aí*]" (p. 63, c. 2).[48] In the same poem Columba was to be praised *ríaraib imbaiss* (according to the demands of poetic knowledge; p. 63, c. 2). Poetic inspiration, through *imbas* (encompassing (poetic) knowledge), could be enhanced through continuous study and practice. *Imbas* allowed Fedelm *banfili* to predict the outcome of Ailill's and Medb's military expedition and to foresee the martial feats of Cú Chulainn (pp. 17, 154–55, cc. 1, 3). *Imbas* allowed the female martial arts instructor Scáthach to prophesy Cú Chulainn's future and foretell the outcome of the *Táin* (p. 115, c. 3).

The fanciful entry for *imbas for·osna* in *Sanas Cormaic* seems to have borrowed from descriptions of *tarbfeis*. Nevertheless, *imbas for·osna*, *tarbfeis*, and *teinm láeda* as depicted in the literature, whether or not they reflect actual practice, emphasize the prestige and aura of superior knowledge that the *filid* had created around their profession. *Vita Guthlaci* shows that early Anglo-Saxons recognized such practices among the Gaels (p. 151, c. 3; Figure 3.b).

The "Caldron of Poesy" proclaimed that either sorrow or joy can inspire poetic outbursts, even in those with no apparent poetic skills. The example of King Hrothgar in *Beowulf* appears to be an extempore outpouring brought on by sorrow and angst (pp. 32–33, c. 1). The "Caldron of Poesy" stated that poetry-inspiring joy was of two kinds: "divine joy" (*fáilte déoda*) and "human joy" (*fáilte dóenda*). "Divine joy" is caused by the arrival of "divine grace" (*rath déoda*) and can lead

---

[47] Lapidge and Herren, *Aldhelm*, 46.
[48] Poetic art or "inspiration" (*aí*) appears in the genitive singular as *üad*.

to an outburst of poetry because, metaphorically, it causes the "caldron" within a person to be turned upright, as happened to Cædmon through *gratia divina* (p. 151, c. 3).[49]

Creating a darkened aspect for composition is part of the stereotype of the proficient poet.[50] Entering a darkened structure and inducing sleep or a trance in order to compose, allows poems to be described as the result of dream-filled sleep. This is reflected in religious poems of the tenth or eleventh centuries, as noted in chapter three, when the poet can request "may you be what I behold always in my sleep,"[51] or "may they [angels] reveal true visions to us in our sleep."[52] Sleep resulting in a poem survives in the fragment by Colmán mac Lénéni (pp. 54–55, c. 2). There is nothing unusual in Cædmon's method of composition when compared to Brittonic or, especially, Gaelic sources.[53]

## Cædmon as *Athláech*

Cædmon would have been considered an *athláech* (ex-layman) among the Gaels (pp. 51, 197, c. 2, 4).[54] The term defines someone who had given up secular life for a religious vocation.[55] Its significance would be greatest during the early stages of a society's conversion.[56] Colmán mac Lénéni was a famous *athláech*.[57] In addition

---

49 Early Christian poets tended to attribute their "inspiration" to God or the holy spirit: Ziolkowski, "Classical Influence," 22–26.
50 In the tenth-century *Cath Almaine* (Battle of Allen), the severed head of a *fer airfitid* (entertainer) Donn Bó is brought from the battlefield to entertain the victors. Donn Bó's head was set on a pillar and "Donn Bó turned his face to the wall of the house so that it might be dark for him" (impóis Donn Bó a aigidh fri fraigid in tichi ar dáig comadh dorcha dó): Ó Riain, *Cath Almaine*, 28, lines 114–15 (Book of Fermoy). The "severed head" that speaks is found often in Gaelic and Brittonic narratives that predate the Middle English example in *Sir Gawain and the Green Knight*.
51 Murphy, *Early Irish Metrics*, 42–43 §18 verse 2.
52 Murphy, *Early Irish Metrics*, 46–47 §19 verse 2.
53 O'Donnell, *Cædmon's Hymn*, 63 §3.9.
54 For Colmán mac Lénéni as *athláech*, see Hull, "Conall Corc," 900; Ní Dhonnchadha, "Irish Vernacular Literary Tradition," 556–57.
55 Etchingham, *Church Organization*, 296–98.
56 The *Lebor Brecc* preface to *Félire Óengusso* tells how Óengus observed angels hovering over the grave of an *athláech* which inspired him to compose the versified martyrology: Stokes, *Félire Óengusso*, 6–9.
57 For Colmán and other ex-laymen, see Ó Riain, *Dictionary*, 136–37 (Caimín), 185–86 (Colmán), 281–83 (É[a]nna), 285–86 (E[a]rc).

to Cædmon's poetic skills applied to benefit the Church, his exemplary life and death marked him out for emulation.

Cædmon's worthiness is seen in the "foreknowledge of his death" (praescius sui obitus; *HE* iv 24).[58] Saintly contemporaries include Columba of Iona who foreknew his own death.[59] Chad, bishop of Lindsey, had foreknowledge of his death and prepared his monks ahead of time (*HE* iv 3). In Bede's prose *Vita Cuthberti*, Cuthbert's mentor Boisil foreknew his impending death. The two read the Gospel of John together during Boisil's remaining days.[60] Bede was eager to show Cædmon's piety and faith. He stressed the divine nature of Cædmon's poetic gift, how his gift was used to bring others to the faith, and how this pious ex-layman met an exemplary death.[61]

## Creator/Creation Theme

The theme of the Creator and His creation is pertinent in the context of any society's conversion. It is the central theme of Genesis, and elsewhere in the Bible, and would have been a natural topic in catechetical *narratio* as promoted by St. Augustine.[62] As Ernst Curtius noted, "The Christian poet knows, of course, that nature was created by God."[63] Venantius Fortunatus, in the second half of the sixth century, while serving in his youth as a court poet, also delighted in the natural world in his later life as a religious.[64] Dracontius, a North African poet of the fifth century, wrote of Genesis and how the creation bears witness to the omnipotence of God.[65] Eugenius, bishop of Toledo (646–658), revised and added to that part of Dracontius's poem that dealt with creation.[66] Isidore of Seville, the most influential writer from Visigothic Spain, showed his preoccupation with the

---

58 For parallelism of Bede's description of Cædmon's "vision" and his request for the Eucharist at his death, see Beechy, "Consumption, Purgation," 164.
59 Anderson and Anderson, *Life of Columba*, 214–35, iii 22–23. For Bede's knowledge of it, see Mc Carthy, "Chronology of St Columba's Life."
60 Colgrave, *Lives of Saint Cuthbert*, 182–83, c. 8.
61 Later traditions attempted to sanctify Cædmon: Stanley, "St Cædmon." See further entries for Cædmon and Colmán in Farmer, *Dictionary of Saints*, 83–84 (Cædmon), 113 (Colmán of Cloyne).
62 Day, "Catechetical *narratio*."
63 Curtius, *European Literature*, 92.
64 Raby, *Christian-Latin Poetry*, 86–95.
65 Raby, *Christian-Latin Poetry*, 97–98.
66 Raby, *Christian-Latin Poetry*, 127.

natural world in *De natura rerum*.[67] His most famous work, the *Etymologiae*, showed the same interest in God's creation.[68]

Creation is well represented in early insular literatures generally.[69] Bede portrayed it as a natural subject for King Oswiu to use in his efforts to convert King Sigeberht of the East Saxons (*HE* iii 22).[70] The *Beowulf* poet, at lines 90b–98, found the creation story an appropriate topic for his audience's Continental ancestors to hear at Heorot.[71] In the Brittonic tradition the theme is present among the Juvencus *englynion*, some of the earliest datable Welsh verse.[72]

The Creator and His creation are found in Early Gaelic literature, in both Latin and the vernacular.[73] Varied opinions about the nature of the created world existed among the Gaelic *intelligentsia*. No single view prevailed, which reveals the level of debate and discussion among the Gaels in the seventh century.[74] *De mirabilibus sacrae Scripturae* (655) attempted to explain Biblical "miracles" from the perspective that God, having created a perfect world, withdrew from direct intervention in order to allow it to function as a harmonious whole.[75] *De ordine creaturarum* (before 680) drew on *De mirabilibus*. It was known to Bede[76] and describes the creation in descending order.[77] The *Epitomae* and *Epistolae* of Virgilius Maro Grammaticus make frequent allusions to the creation.[78] Tírechán's dossier on St. Patrick, the *Collectanea* (ca. 680), related an episode in which Patrick explained to two daughters of a pagan king that his God was "the God of heaven and earth,

---

67 See a translation, Kendall and Wallis, *Isidore of Seville*, 105–76.
68 Oroz Reta and Marcos Casquero, *Etimologías*, ii, bk. 12 (*De animalibus*), bk. 13 (*De mundo et partibus*), bk. 14 (*De terra et partibus*).
69 For the early insular interest in Genesis, see Ó Cróinín, "Commentary on Genesis."
70 "qui caelum et terram et humanum genus creasset": Colgrave and Mynors, *Ecclesiastical History*, 282. For similar wording, see Hygebald's prayer, which may reflect Gaelic influence: Sims-Williams, *Religion and Literature*, 322–23.
71 Fulk, Bjork, Niles, *Klaeber's Beowulf*, 6, lines 90b–98. See the wider discussion in Neville, *Representations*, 62–69.
72 "Omnipotens auctor tidicones" (Almighty Creator, thou hast made): Williams, "Juvencus Poems," 101–3.
73 For an example in the vernacular, see Carey, "Tract on Creation."
74 See, for example, Smyth, *Understanding the Universe*; Mac Mathúna, "Perceptions of the Cosmos": Stancliffe, "Creator and Creation"; Smyth, "Early Medieval Irish Cosmology," 133–43.
75 For some translations, see Carey, *King of Mysteries*, 51–74.
76 Smyth, "Date and Origin."
77 Stancliffe, "Creator and Creation," 10. For an edition, see Díaz y Díaz, *Liber de ordine creaturarum*; for an English translation, see Smyth, "*Liber de ordine creaturarum*."
78 Law, *Wisdom, Authority and Grammar*, 38–40.

of the sea and the rivers, God of the sun and moon and all the stars, the God of high mountains and low valleys."[79]

The subjects of the Creator and His creation were taught and debated in schools. The *Hisperica Famina* includes sections "on the sky" (*de caelo*), "on the sea" (*de mari*), "concerning fire" (*de igne*), "about the field" (*de campo*), "about the wind" (*de uento*).[80] We have no indication of the contents of the *codex cosmographiorum* acquired by Aldfrith *sapiens* except for how it is described. *Altus Prosator* (High Creator) leaves no doubt of its contents. This text from Iona was known to Aldhelm who may have learned of it while at Canterbury.[81] Several decades ago Donald Fritz had proposed that "Cædmon's whole program suggests the contemporaneous *Altus Prosator*."[82] The contents of Cædmon's *Hymn* is in keeping with the intellectual preoccupations of the insular world and followed Late Antique precedence on the Continent.

## Eulogy and Encomium

Cædmon's *Hymn* is noted for its encomiastic diction. Arguments have varied as to whether or not that diction was innovative, deriving from traditional Germanic usage and then applied to the new Christian dispensation.[83] Precedents for such semantic shifts and metaphorical usage in vocabulary are found in the Bible itself as, for example, in the Psalms and the Deus/Dominus equation. *Adiutor laborantium* (Helper of Workers), attributed to Adomnán, contains a list of epithets for God reminiscent of Cædmon's short *Hymn*.[84] Its translators stated: "God is addressed in the kind of language with which a client might praise or flatter a powerful patron" (p. 76, c. 2).[85] Scholars of Old English recognize that no prior tradition of eulogy survives from Old English, or any other early Germanic languages. Given the Gaelic ethos of Whitby, the "body of contemporary material against which to compare Cædmon's poem" can be found in the Brittonic and Gaelic poetic traditions.[86]

---

[79] "Deus caeli ac terrae, maris et fluminum, Deus solis ac lunae <et> omium siderum, Deus montium sublimium ualliumque humilium": Bieler, *Patrician Texts*, 142–43, §26.8–9, lines 26–8.
[80] Herren, *Hisperica Famina: I*, 90–103.
[81] Orchard, *Poetic Art of Aldhelm*, 54–60.
[82] Fritz, "Monastic Exegete," 360.
[83] See the survey in chapter three of O'Donnell, *Cædmon's Hymn*, 60–77 (*Cædmon's Hymn* and Germanic Convention).
[84] For an edition and translation, see Clancy and Márkus, *Iona*, 69–80.
[85] Clancy and Márkus, *Iona*, 69–70 (manuscript), 74 (quote). The poem is now attributed to Adomnán: Márkus, "*Adiutor laborantium*."
[86] The quotation is from O'Donnell, *Cædmon's Hymn*, 62 §3.7.

Poems attributed to Aneirin and Taliesin reflect the heroic age ethos of the late sixth to early seventh centuries. The *Gododdin* describes warriors who fought against the Anglo-Saxon kingdoms of Deira and Bernicia (pp. 12–13, c. 1). Poems attributed to Taliesin praise Urien Rheged and his son Owain and their combats against Anglo-Saxon and Pictish enemies (pp. 13–14, c. 1). Cadwallon was a noted enemy of Northumbrians but ally of Mercians (*HE* ii 20, iii 1). A poem, *Moliant Cadwallon* (Praise of Cadwallon), survives.[87] Peter Hunter Blair noted cogently: "We have become so accustomed to regarding this period of history as part of the Dark Ages that we have perhaps tended to envelop those whom we study in the darkness through which we ourselves move, to forget that this was indeed the British Heroic Age."[88]

Gaelic poetic fragments from the seventh century and earlier confirm the existence of encomium. Poems in the Leinster genealogies praise illustrious ancestors (p. 15, c. 1). The tenth-century *Orgain Denna Ríg* expands on events recorded in a cryptic encomium from the genealogies that reputedly took place around 300 B.C. (pp. 28, 37–38, 94, 137–38, cc. 1, 2, 3).

Fragments by Colmán mac Lénéni reflect his rôle as praise poet: his poem on the gift of a sword from Domnall Ilchelgach has been noted (pp. 52–53, c. 2); a fragment about Fergus Tuile king of Uí Liatháin implies that Colmán formally praised his royal patron (pp. 53–54, c. 2); he also praised Áed Sláine (d. ca. 604), eponymous ancestor of Síl nÁedo Sláine (p. 41, c. 1), the sept that occupied Brega when it was attacked by *dux* Berht in the reign of King Ecgfrith (*HE* iv 26). Two substantial poems by Bécán mac Luigdech praise Columba, as discussed in chapter two. Bécán converted secular encomiastic diction for ecclesiastical purposes. That process was not unique to Cædmon.

*Tarbfeis* predicted a future king (p. 157, c. 3). *Baile Chuinn* prophesied persons who would claim the "kingship of Tara" (pp. 120–21, c. 3). *Audacht Morainn* is western Europe's first vernacular *speculum principum* (pp. 17–19, 121, cc. 1, 3). The law-tract *Cáin Fhuithirbe* (ca. 680) harmonized indigenous kingship practices with the ideals of the Church (pp. 191–92, c. 4). The diction emphasizing kingship in Cædmon's *Hymn* had ample precedence in the literatures of the contiguous Britons and Gaels. Neither the encomiastic diction of Cædmon's *Hymn*, nor his reliance on inspiration to produce it, are unique or unusual when compared to contemporary Brittonic and Gaelic traditions.[89]

---

87 Koch, *Four Welsh Poems*, 161–229.
88 Hunter Blair, "Origins of Northumbria," 51; Yorke, "Anglo-Saxon Kingdoms," 76–79. The most likely early Brittonic poems were panegyrics and eulogies: Koch, "Waiting for Gododdin."
89 O'Donnell described Cædmon's methods as "unusual" several times: O'Donnell, *Cædmon's Hymn*, 60 §3.2, 63 §3.9, 76 §3.36.

Although Bede described Cædmon as untrained in poetry, his methods of composition are duplicated in contemporary Gaelic and, to a lesser extent, Brittonic sources. The origins of poetic inspiration, including the reception of divine grace and resultant poems, are explained in Gaelic records. Bede's description of Cædmon's transition from lay into religious life has parallels in the Gaelic *athláech*. Bede's Latin paraphrase of the *Hymn*, rather than a vernacular version, and his emphasis on divine grace, rather than "poetic inspiration," served to "soften" what was radical for a conservative, newly converted *ecclesia gentis Anglorum*, and helped to disguise what was "foreign" for both continental and later Anglo-Saxon audiences of the *Historia ecclesiastica*.[90]

In his account of Cædmon, Bede was describing, whether consciously or not, poetic practices that reflected both a Brittonic substratum and a Gaelic superstratum among the personnel at the monastery of Whitby. The closest analogues, if not the direct sources, for Bede's description of Cædmon's methods are found in the Gaelic poetic tradition.

---

[90] A major audience for Bede resided on the continent and would not be familiar with insular vernacular cultures: Cronan, "Cædmon's Audience," 361.

# Afterword

Old English literature is widely known and studied. For many medievalists it epitomizes early vernacular literature and has become the model for how those literatures should be studied. Familiarity with Early Gaelic literary culture, however, provides a broader perspective and encourages the search for a more informed understanding of the nature of insular vernacular literatures.

Old English and Early (Old and Middle) Gaelic literatures are remarkably dissimilar. Both societies embraced Christianity and adopted the vast intellectual edifice introduced through Latin. Their literatures responded to the priorities of the Church and produced saints' lives, homilies, litanies, martyrologies; in general, texts sourced in the Latinate tradition. But the Old English corpus preserves little else. The few Old English poems that deal with native lore represent the larger Germanic world, with characters and events on the Continent, and not with Anglo-Saxon lore and tradition in Britain. Only a handful of Old English texts can be located on the island of Britain (e.g., Battle of Maldon, Battle of Brunanburh, Durham poem). Old English literature is, largely, a literature of translation, an extension of the learning recorded elsewhere in the Christian world. As a result, the preoccupations of Old English and Anglo-Latin scholars are consumed with source study, that is, with identifying texts from that larger Christian world that explain the plot or that elucidate motifs in Old English texts.

By contrast Early Gaelic literature is full of narratives that treat indigenous peoples and their traditions. Story cycles can be identified through consistent intertextual cross-referencing of characters and events. Most texts identify recognizable locations, typically in Ireland, but many in Britain. Place lore (*dindśenchas*) was an important genre. Gaelic textual scholars can establish relationships across tales, through fore-tales, or through sub-tales of longer narratives. The "digressions" in *Beowulf* can only hint at such narrative richness.

The study of named Old English poets, whether mythico-legendary or historical, is a narrow field. Gaelic poets were professionals and achieved high social standing. Named poets appear in hagiography, law-tracts, genealogies, annals, poems, prose prefaces to poems, and narrative literature. Their self-assurance as professionals and self-awareness as poets encouraged the production of vernacular texts on "poetics," a unique achievement so early in the Middle Ages.

Anglo-Latin and Hiberno-Latin literatures, in contrast to the vernacular literatures, shared much. Both traditions drank deeply from the wells of Biblical, late Antique, and patristic learning. Gaels and Anglo-Saxons shared the same sources. Latin texts by scholars like Columbanus (d. 615) and Cummian (fl. 632) give a sense of the learning controlled by Gaels of the late sixth and early seventh centuries. Latinate learning did not arrive among the Anglo-Saxons directly from the Continent only. Gaelic missionaries and teachers worked throughout Britain, and Anglo-Saxons acquired free education in Ireland among the Gaels. Already in the mid seventh century, decades before Aldhelm became an abbot, and before Bede was even born, Anglo-Saxon students were being taught by Gaelic teachers from Latinate sources that would later appear in Old English and Anglo-Latin texts.

By the late sixth and early seventh centuries Gaelic poems and named poets were being recorded. By the last quarter of the seventh century Gaelic intellectual life was thoroughly bilingual. Ecclesiastically affiliated *sapientes* wrote in either Gaelic or Latin. By the eighth century the Gaels had created etiological legends, most specifically the "pseudo-historical prologue" to the *Senchas Már*, to explain the cooperation between the ecclesiastical orders and professional poets in helping to build that bilingual intellectual edifice.

Early Anglo-Latin authors – Aldhelm, Bede, Stephen of Ripon, Felix of Crowland, and several anonymous writers – all evinced Gaelic influence in Anglo-Saxon society, whether or not they embraced it or rebuffed it. But contacts with Gaels, and reliance on texts they provided, did not stop in the early eighth century. Alcuin (d. 804), in his Life of Willibrord, told how he spent twelve years at Rath Melsigi before undertaking his successful mission to the Continent and his archbishopric of Echternach. Alcuin also corresponded with Anglo-Saxon monks then at *Mag nÉo na Saxan* which continued to thrive. His letters naming Colcu and Joseph, both apparently from Clonmacnoise, connected Ireland and the Continent through York and Mercia, and informed Colcu of contention between Offa and Charlemagne. Early in the ninth century Æthelwulf's *De abbatibus* (803x821) praised Ultán, scribe and illuminator, for his holy life and teachings. King Alfred (d. 899) the Great's court, busy with translation work, welcomed three Gaelic *peregrini* who had set themselves adrift *pro amore Dei*. The same chronicle entry noted the death of the Gaelic teacher Suibne (d. 891), to be identified with the *scriba optimus* of Clonmacnoise. In his youth Dunstan (d. 988) entered Glastonbury, which the Gaels called *Glastimbir na nGáedel* (Glastonbury of the Gaels), and carefully studied books left by Gaelic *peregrini*. The influential seventh-century Gaelic text *De duodecim abusivis* resurfaced in the works of both Ælfric (d. ca. 1012) and Wulfstan (d. ca. 1023). The latest datable Old English poem *Durham* (ca. 1100) reverted to the age of Cuthbert described by Bede and named the Gaels Aidan and Boisil. A consciousness of Gaelic contributions is identifiable in all periods of Anglo-Saxon cultural history.

It was natural that Bede should describe acts of poetic composition by Cædmon at Whitby that so accurately reflected Gaelic practices. Scholars of Old English and Anglo-Latin literatures need only turn to Anglo-Latin authors as their primary sources to begin the discovery of that "Gaelic background."

# Bibliography

Abels, Richard. "The Council of Whitby: A Study in Early Anglo-Saxon Politics." *Journal of British Studies* 23, no. 1 (1983): 1–25.
Abels, Richard. "What Has Weland to Do with Christ? The Franks Casket and the Acculturation of Christianity in Early Anglo-Saxon England." *Speculum* 84, no.3 (July 2009): 549–81.
Acken, James. *Structure and Interpretation in the* Auraicept na nÉces. Saarbrücken: VDM Verlag, 2010.
Ahlqvist, Anders, ed. *The Early Irish Linguist: An Edition of the Canonical Part of the "Auraicept na nÉces."* Helsinki: Societas Scientiarum Fennica, 1983.
Aist, Rodney. "Adomnán, Arculf and the Source Material of *De locis sanctis*." In *Adomnán of Iona: Theologian, lawmake peacemaker*, edited by Jonathan Wooding, with Rodney Aist, Thomas Owen Clancy, and Thomas O'Loughlin, 162–80. Dublin: Four Courts Press, 2010.
Albertson, Clinton, SJ, ed. and trans. *Anglo-Saxon Saints and Heroes*. New York: Fordham University Press, 1967.
Allott, Stephen, comp. *Alcuin of York, c. A.D. 732 to 804 – His Life and Letters*. York: William Sessions Ltd., 1974.
Álvarez-López, Francisco José. "The Rule of St Benedict in England at the Time of Wilfrid." In *Wilfrid: Abbot, Bishop, Saint: Papers from the 1300th Anniversary Conferences*, edited by Nicholas J. Higham, 40–53. Donington: Shaun Tyas, 2013.
Anderson, Alan Orr and Marjorie Ogilvie Anderson, ed. and trans. *Adomnán's Life of Columba*. Oxford: Clarendon Press, 1991.
Anderson, Earl R. *Cynewulf: Structure, Style, and Theme in his Poetry*. London: Associated University Press, 1983.
Attenborough, F. L., ed. and trans. *The Laws of the Earliest English Kings*. Cambridge: Cambridge University Press, 1922. Reprint, Felinfach: Llanerch Publishers, 2000.
Backhaus, Norbert. "The Structure of the List of *Remscéla Tána Bó Cualngi* in the Book of Leinster." *Cambridge Medieval Celtic Studies* 19 (Summer 1990): 19–26.
Bailey, Richard N. and Eric Cambridge. "Dating the Old English Poem 'Durham'." *Medium Ævum* 85, no. 1 (2016): 1–14.
Baker, Peter S. *Introduction to Old English*. Oxford: Blackwell Publishing, 2003.
Baker, Peter S. and Michael Lapidge, eds. *Byrhtferth's Enchiridion*. Early English Text Society SS 15. Oxford: Oxford University Press, 1995.
Barker, Katherine. "*Usque Domnoniam*: The Setting of Aldhelm's *Carmen rhythmicum*, Literature, Language and the Liminal." In *Aldhelm and Sherborne: Essays to Celebrate the Founding of the Bishopric*, edited by Katherine Barker with Nicholas Brooks, 15–54. Oxford & Oakville: Oxbow Books, 2010.
Barker, Katherine. "The *Carmen rhythmicum*: Aldhelm, Poet and Composer of *Carmina*." In *Aldhelm and Sherborne: Essays to Celebrate the Founding of the Bishopric*, edited by Katherine Barker with Nicholas Brooks, 233–70. Oxford & Oakville: Oxbow Books, 2010.
Barker, Katherine with Nicholas Brooks, ed. *Aldhelm and Sherborne: Essays to Celebrate the Founding of the Bishopric*. Oxford and Oakville: Oxbow Books, 2010.
Barrett, Gillian F. "The Archaeology of County Carlow: An Aerial Perspective." In *Carlow: History and Society: Interdisciplinary Essays on the History of an Irish County*, edited by Thomas McGrath, 31–51. Dublin: Geography Publications, 2008.

Bassi, Roberta. "St. Oswald in Early English Chronicles and Narratives." In *Hagiography in Anglo-Saxon England: Adopting and Adapting Saints' Lives into Old English Prose (c.950–1150)*, edited by Loredana Lazzari, Patrizia Lendinara, and Claudia Di Sciacca, 535–55. Textes et Études du Moyen Âge 73. Madrid and Barcelona: Fédération Internationale des Instituts d´Études Médiévales, 2014.

Bauer, Nancy. "Abbess Hilda of Whitby: All Britain Was Lit by Her Splendor." In *Medieval Women Monastics: Wisdom's Wellsprings*, edited by Miriam Schmitt and Linda Kulzer, 13–31. Collegeville: Liturgical Press, 1996.

Bayless, Martha and Michael Lapidge, eds. *Collectanea Pseudo-Bedae*. Scriptores Latini Hiberniae 14. Dublin: Dublin Institute for Advanced Studies, 1998.

Beechy, Tiffany. "Consumption, Purgation, Poetry, Divinity: Incarnational Poetics and the Indo-European Tradition." *Modern Philology* 114, no.2 (November 2016): 149–69.

Bergin, Osborn. *Irish Bardic Poetry: Texts and Translations, together with an Introductory Lecture*, edited and compiled by David Greene and Fergus Kelly. Dublin: Dublin Institute for Advanced Studies, 1970.

Bergin, Osborn and Richard Irvine Best. "Tochmarc Étaíne." *Ériu* 12 (1934–1938): 137–96.

Bernard, J. H. and Robert Atkinson, ed. and trans. *The Irish Liber Hymnorum*. 2 vols. London: Henry Bradshaw Society, 1898.

Bessinger, Jess B. "Homage to Cædmon and Others: A Beowulfian Praise Song." In *Old English Studies in Honour of John C. Pope*, edited by Robert B. Burlin and Edward B. Irving, Jr., 91–106. Toronto: University of Toronto Press, 1974.

Best, Richard Irvine. "The Settling of the Manor of Tara." *Ériu* 4 (1908–1910): 121–72.

Best, Richard Irvine and Osborn Bergin, eds. *Lebor na Huidre: Book of the Dun Cow*. Dublin: Royal Irish Academy, 1929.

Best, Richard Irvine and H. J. Lawlor, eds. *The Martyrology of Tallaght: from the Book of Leinster and MS. 5100–4 in the Royal Library, Brussels*. London: Henry Bradshaw Society, 1931.

Best, Richard I. and Michael A. O'Brien, eds. *The Book of Leinster formerly Lebar na Núachongbála*. Vol. 4. Dublin: Dublin Institute for Advanced Studies, 1965.

Best, Richard I. and Michael A. O'Brien, eds. *The Book of Leinster formerly Lebar na Núachongbála*. Vol. 5. Dublin: Dublin Institute for Advanced Studies, 1967.

Bhreathnach, Edel. "Temoria: Caput Scotorum?" *Ériu* 47 (1996): 67–88.

Bhreathnach, Edel. "Kings, the Kingship of Leinster and the Regnal Poems of *Laídshenchas Laigen*: A Reflection of Dynastic Politics in Leinster, 650–1150." In *Seanchas: Studies in Early and Medieval Irish Archaeology, History and Literature in Honour of Francis J. Byrne*, edited by Alfred P. Smyth, 299–312. Dublin: Four Courts Press, 2000.

Bhreathnach, Edel. "The Genealogies of Leinster as a Source for Local Cults." In *Studies in Irish Hagiography: Saints and Scholars*, edited by John Carey, Máire Herbert, and Pádraig Ó Riain, 250–67. Dublin: Four Courts Press, 2001.

Bhreathnach, Edel. "*Níell cáich úa Néill nasctar géill:* the Political Context of *Baile Chuinn Chétchathaig*." In *The Kingship and Landscape of Tara*, edited by Edel Bhreathnach, 49–68. Dublin: Four Courts Press for the Discovery Programme, 2005.

Bhreathnach, Edel. "The Airgíalla Charter Poem: The Political Context." In *The Kingship and Landscape of Tara*, edited by Edel Bhreathnach, 95–99. Dublin: Four Courts Press for the Discovery Programme, 2005.

Bhreathnach, Edel. *Ireland in the Medieval World AD 400–1000: Landscape, Kingship and Religion*. Dublin: Four Courts Press, 2014.

Bhreathnach, Edel and Kevin Murray. "*Baile Chuinn Chétchathaig*: Edition." In *The Kingship and Landscape of Tara*, edited by Edel Bhreathnach, 73–94. Dublin: Four Courts Press for the Discovery Programme, 2005.
Bhreathnach, Edel and Kevin Murray. "The Airgíalla Charter Poem: Edition." In *The Kingship and Landscape of Tara*, edited by Edel Bhreathnach, 124–58. Dublin: Four Courts Press for the Discovery Programme, 2005.
Bidwell, Paul. "Wilfrid and Hexham: The Anglo-Saxon Crypt." In *Wilfrid: Abbot, Bishop, Saint*, edited by Nicholas J. Higham, 152–62. Donington: Shaun Tyas, 2013.
Bieler, Ludwig, ed. *The Irish Penitentials*. Dublin: Dublin Institute for Advanced Studies, 1963.
Bieler, Ludwig, ed. "Adamnani De locis sanctis." In *Itineraria et Alia Geographica*. Corpus Christianorum Series Latina 175 (CCSL 175), 175–234. Turnhout: Brepols, 1965.
Bieler, Ludwig, ed. *The Patrician Texts in the Book of Armagh*. Dublin: Dublin Institute for Advanced Studies, 1979.
Biggs, Frederick M. "Deor's Threatened 'Blame Poem'." *Studies in Philology* 94, no.3 (1997): 297–320.
Biggs, Frederick M. *Sources of Anglo-Saxon Literary Culture: The Apocrypha*. Instrumenta Anglistica Mediaevalia I. Kalamazoo, MI: Medieval Institute Publications, 2007.
Biggs, Frederick M. "History and Fiction in the Frisian Raids." In *The Dating of Beowulf: A Reassessment*, edited by Leonard Neidorf, 138–56. Cambridge: D. S. Brewer, 2014.
Biggs, Frederick M. "*Domino in domino dominorum*: Bede and John of Beverley." *Anglo-Saxon England* 44 (2015): 17–30.
Biggs, Frederick M. "Bede's *Martyrologium* and the *Martyrologium Hieronymianum*." *Analecta Bollandiana* 134 (2016): 241–78.
Biggs, Frederick M. "Two Scribal Additions Concerning *Capitula* in Bede's List of His Works." *Revue Bénédictine* 128 (2018): 84–94.
Billett, Jesse D. "Wilfrid and Music." In *Wilfrid: Abbot, Bishop, Saint*, edited by Nicholas J. Higham, 163–85. Donington: Shaun Tyas, 2013.
Binchy, Daniel. A. "*Bretha Crólige*." *Ériu* 12 (1934–1938): 1–77.
Binchy, Daniel A., ed. *Críth Gablach*. Mediaeval and Modern Irish Series XI. Dublin: Dublin Institute for Advanced Studies, 1941.
Binchy, Daniel A. "The Date and Provenance of *Uraicecht Becc*." *Ériu* 18 (1958): 44–54.
Binchy, Daniel A., ed. *Scéla Cano meic Gartnáin*. Mediaeval and Modern Irish Series XVIII. Dublin: Dublin Institute for Advanced Studies, 1963.
Binchy, Daniel A. "Bretha Déin Chécht." *Ériu* 20 (1966): 1–66.
Bisagni, Jacopo. "Prolegomena to the Study of Code-Switching in the Old Irish Glosses." *Peritia* 24–25 (2013–2014): 1–58.
Bisagni, Jacopo. "Flutes, Pipes, or Bagpipes? Observations on the Terminology of Woodwind Instruments in Old and Middle Irish." In *Early Medieval Ireland and Europe: Chronology, Contacts, Scholarship – A Festschrift for Dáibhí Ó Cróinín*, edited by Pádraic Moran and Immo Warntjes, 343–94. Turnhout: Brepols, 2015.
Bisagni, Jacopo, ed. *Amrae Coluimb Chille: A Critical Edition*. Early Irish Text Series I. Dublin: Dublin Institute for Advanced Studies, 2019.
Bisagni, Jacopo. *From Atoms to the Cosmos: The Irish Tradition of the Divisions of Time in the Early Middle Ages*. Kathleen Hughes Memorial Lectures 18. Cambridge: Department of Anglo-Saxon, Norse and Celtic, 2020.
Bisagni, Jacopo and Immo Warntjes. "Latin and Old Irish in the Munich Computus: A Reassessment and Further Evidence." *Ériu* 57 (2007): 1–33.

Bisagni, Jacopo and Immo Warntjes. "The Early Old Irish Material in the Newly Discovered *Computus Einsidlensis* (c.AD 700)." *Ériu* 58 (2008): 77–105.

Bitel, Lisa M. "Ekphrasis at Kildare: The Imaginative Architecture of a Seventh-Century Hagiographer." *Speculum* 79, no.3 (2004): 605–27.

Bischoff, Bernard. "Turning-Points in the History of Latin Exegesis in the Early Middle Ages." In *Biblical Studies: The Medieval Irish Contribution*, edited by Martin McNamara M.C.S., 74–160. Dublin: Dominican Publications, 1976.

Bischoff, Bernard and Michael Lapidge, eds. *Biblical Commentaries from the Canterbury School of Theodore and Hadrian*. Cambridge: Cambridge University Press, 1994.

Bjork, Robert E. *The Old English Verse Saints' Lives: A Study in Direct Discourse and the Iconography of Style*. Toronto: University of Toronto Press, 1985.

Bjork, Robert E., ed. *The Cynewulf Reader*. London and New York: Routledge, 2001.

Bjork, Robert E. *The Old English Poems of Cynewulf*. Dumbarton Oaks Medieval Library 23. Cambridge, MA: Harvard University Press, 2013.

Bjork, Robert E. and John D. Niles, eds. *A Beowulf Handbook*. Exeter: University of Exeter Press, 1996.

Bjork, Robert E. and Anita Obermeier. "Date, Provenance, Author, Audience." In *A Beowulf Handbook*, edited by Robert E. Bjork and John D. Niles, 13–34. Exeter: University of Exeter Press, 1996.

Bloomfield, Morton and Charles W. Dunn, *The Role of the Poet in Early Societies*. Cambridge: Boydell and Brewer, 1989.

Bolton, W. F. "*Epistola Cuthberti de Obitu Bedae*: A Caveat." *Medievalia et Humanistica* 1 (1970): 140–55.

Bonner, Gerald, ed. *Famulus Christi: Essays in Commemoration of the Thirteenth Centenary of the Birth of the Venerable Bede*. London: Society for Promoting Christian Knowledge, 1976.

Bonner, Gerald, David Rollason, and Clare Stancliffe, eds. *St Cuthbert, His Cult and His Community to AD 1200*. Woodbridge: Boydell Press, 1989.

Borsje, Jacqueline. "Approaching Danger: *Togail Bruidne Da Derga* and the Motif of Being One-Eyed." In *Identifying the 'Celtic,'* edited by Joseph Falaky Nagy, 75–99. CSANA Yearbook 2. Dublin: Four Courts Press, 2002.

Borsje, Jacqueline and Fergus Kelly. "'The Evil Eye' in Early Irish Literature and Law." *Celtica* 24 (2003): 1–39.

Bracken, Damian. "Authority and Duty: Columbanus and the Primacy of Rome." *Peritia* 16 (2002): 168–213.

Bracken, Damian. "Virgilius Grammaticus and the Earliest Hiberno-Latin Literature." In *Ogma: Essays in Celtic Studies in Honour of Próinséas Ní Chatháin*, edited by Michael Richter and Jean-Michel Picard, 251–61. Dublin: Four Courts Press, 2002.

Bracken, Damian. "Virgil the Grammarian and Bede: A Preliminary Study." *Anglo-Saxon England* 35 (2006): 7–21.

Bracken, Damian. "Rome and the Isles: Ireland, England and the Rhetoric of Orthodoxy." In *Anglo-Saxon/Irish Relations before the Vikings*, edited by James Graham-Campbell and Michael Ryan, 75–97. Proceedings of the British Academy 157. Oxford: Oxford University Press, 2009.

Brady, Lindy. *Writing the Welsh Borderlands in Anglo-Saxon England*. Artes Liberales Ser. Manchester: Manchester University Press, 2017.

Breatnach, Liam. "The Caldron of Poesy." *Ériu* 32 (1981): 45–93.

Breatnach, Liam. "Canon Law and Secular Law in Early Ireland: The Significance of *Bretha Nemed*." *Peritia* 3 (1984): 439–59.
Breatnach, Liam. "The Ecclesiastical Element in the Old-Irish Legal Tract *Cáin Fhuithirbe*." *Peritia* 5 (1986): 36–52.
Breatnach, Liam, ed. *Uraicecht na Ríar: The Poetic Grades in Early Irish Law*. Early Irish Law Series II. Dublin: Dublin Institute for Advanced Studies, 1987.
Breatnach, Liam. "The First Third of *Bretha Nemed Toísech*." *Ériu* 40 (1989): 1–40.
Breatnach, Liam. "An Edition of *Amra Senáin*." In *Sages, Saints and Storytellers: Celtic Studies in Honour of Professor James Carney*, edited by Donnchadh Ó Corráin, Liam Breatnach, and Kim McCone, 7–31. Maynooth Monographs 2. Maynooth: An Sagart, 1989.
Breatnach, Liam. "Zur Frage der *Roscada* im Irischen." In *Metrik und Medienwechsel – Metrics and Media*, edited by Hildegard L. C. Tristram, 197–205. ScriptOralia 35. Tübingen: Gunter Narr Verlag, 1991.
Breatnach, Liam. "An Mheán-Ghaeilge." In *Stair na Gaeilge, in Ómos do Pádraig Ó Fiannachta*, edited by Kim McCone, Damian McManus, Cathal Ó Háinle, Nicholas Williams, Liam Breatnach, 221–333. Maigh Nuad [Maynooth]: Roinn na Sean-Ghaeilge, 1994.
Breatnach, Liam. "Poets and Poetry." In *Progress in Medieval Irish Studies*, edited by Kim McCone and Katharine Simms, 65–77. Maynooth: Department of Old Irish, 1996.
Breatnach, Liam. *A Companion to the Corpus iuris Hibernici*. Early Irish Law Series V. Dublin: Dublin Institute for Advanced Studies, 2005.
Breatnach, Liam. "Satire, Praise and the Early Irish Poet." *Ériu* 56 (2006): 63–84.
Breatnach, Liam. "Law and Literature in Early Mediaeval Ireland." In *L'Irlanda e gli Irlandesi nell'Alto Medioevo*, 215–38. Settimane di Studio della Fondazione Centro Italiano di Studi sull'Alto Medioevo LVII. Spoleto: Presso la Sede della Fondazione, 2010.
Breatnach, Liam. *The Early Irish Law Text Senchas Már and the Question of its Date*. E. C. Quiggin Memorial Lecture 13. Cambridge: Department of Anglo-Saxon, Norse and Celtic, 2011.
Breatnach, Liam. "Varia: III. The Meaning of *Nómad*." *Ériu* 62 (2012): 197–205.
Breatnach, Liam, ed. *Córus Bésgnai: An Old Irish Law Tract on the Church and Society*. Early Irish Law Series VII. Dublin: Dublin Institute for Advanced Studies, 2017.
Breay, Claire and Joanna Story, eds. *Anglo-Saxon Kingdoms: Art, Word, War*. London: British Library, 2018.
Bredehoft, Thomas A. *Authors, Audiences and Old English Verse*. Toronto: University of Toronto Press, 2009.
Bredehoft, Thomas A. "The Date of Composition of *Beowulf* and the Evidence of Metrical Evolution." In *The Dating of Beowulf: A Reassessment*, edited by Leonard Neidorf, 97–111. Cambridge: D. S. Brewer, 2014.
Breen, Aidan. "Some Seventh-Century Hiberno-Latin Texts and their Relationships." *Peritia* 3 (1984): 204–14.
Breen, Aidan. "Pseudo-Cyprian *De Duodecim Abusivis Saeculi* and the Bible." In *Irland und die Christenheit: Bibelstudien und Mission/Ireland and Christendom: the Bible and the Missions*, edited by Proinséas Ní Chatháin and Michael Richter, 230–45. Stuttgart: Klett-Cotta, 1987.
Breen, Aidan. "The Evidence of Antique Irish Exegesis in Pseudo-Cyprian, *De Duodecim Abusivis Saeculi*." *Proceedings of the Royal Irish Academy* 87, no. 4 (1987): 71–101.
Breen, Aidan, ed. *Ailerani interpretatio mystica et moralis progenitorvm Domini Iesv Christi*. Blackrock: Four Courts Press, 1995.

Breen, Aidan. "Columbanus' Monastic Life and Education in Ireland." *Seanchas Ard Mhacha* 23, no. 2 (2011): 1–21.

Breeze, Andrew. "A Celtic Etymology for Old English *Deor* 'Brave'." In *Alfred the Wise: Studies in Honour of Janet Bately*, edited by Jane Roberts and Janet L. Nelson with Malcolm Godden, 1–4. Cambridge: D. S. Brewer, 1997.

Bromwich, Rachel, ed. and trans. *Trioedd Ynys Prydein: The Welsh Triads*. 2nd ed. Cardiff: University of Wales Press, 1978.

Brooks, Kenneth R., ed. *Andreas and The Fates of the Apostles*. Oxford: Clarendon Press, 1961.

Brooks, Nicholas. "From British to English Christianity: Deconstructing Bede's Interpretation of the Conversion." In *Conversion and Colonization in Anglo-Saxon England*, edited by Catherine E. Karkov and Nicholas Howe, 1–30. Tempe, AZ: Arizona Center for Medieval and Renaissance Studies, 2006.

Brooks, Nicholas. "Introduction." In *Aldhelm and Sherborne: Essays to Celebrate the Founding of the Bishopric*, edited by Katherine Barker with Nicholas Brooks, 1–14. Oxford and Oakville, CT: Oxbow Books, 2010.

Brown, George Hardin. *Bede the Venerable*. Boston: Twayne Publishers, 1987.

Brown, George Hardin and Frederick M. Biggs. *Bede: Part i-ii, Fascicles 1–4*. The Sources of Anglo-Saxon Literary Culture. Amsterdam: Amsterdam University Press, 2017–2018.

Brown, Michelle P. *The Book of Cerne: Prayer, Patronage and Power in Ninth-Century England*. Toronto: University of Toronto Press, 1996.

Brown, Michelle P. "From Columba to Cormac: The Contribution of the Irish Scribes to the Insular System of Scripts." In *L'Irlanda e gli Irlandesi nell'Alto Medioevo*, 623–46. Settimane di Studio della Fondazione Centro Italiano di Studi sull'Alto Medioevo LVII. Spoleto: Presso la Sede della Fondazione, 2010.

Buckley, Ann. "Music in Ireland to c.1500." In *A New History of Ireland I: Prehistory and Early Ireland*, edited by Dáibhí Ó Cróinín, 744–813. Oxford: Oxford University Press, 2005.

Bullough, Donald A. "Columba, Adomnan and the Achievement of Iona: Part I." *Scottish Historical Review* 43 (1964): 111–30.

Bullough, Donald A. "Columba, Adomnan and the Achievement of Iona: Part II." *Scottish Historical Review* 44 (1965): 17–33.

Bullough, Donald A. "The Career of Columbanus." In *Columbanus: Studies on the Latin Writings*, edited by Michael Lapidge, 1–28. Studies in Celtic History XVII. Woodbridge: Boydell Press, 1997.

Burnyeat, Abigail. "The Early Irish *Grammaticus*?" *Aiste* 1 (2007): 181–217.

Butler, Brian. "Doctor of Souls, Doctor of the Body: Whitby *Vita Gregorii* 23 and Its Exegetical Context." In *Listen, O Isles, unto Me: Studies in Medieval Word and Image in Honour of Jennifer O'Reilly*, edited by Elizabeth Mullins and Diarmuid Scully, 168–80. Cork: Cork University Press, 2011.

Butler, Robert M. "Glastonbury and the Early History of the Exeter Book." In *Old English Literature in its Manuscript Context*, edited by Joyce Tally Lionarons, 173–215. Morgantown: West Virginia University Press, 2004.

Byrne, Francis John. "The Lament for Cummíne Foto." *Ériu* 31 (1980): 111–22.

Byrne, Francis John. *Irish Kings and High-Kings*. 2nd ed. Dublin: Four Courts Press, 2001.

Byrne, Francis John. "Church and Politics, c.750–c.1100." In *A New History of Ireland: I Prehistoric and Early Ireland*, edited by Dáibhí Ó Cróinín, 656–79. Oxford: Oxford University Press, 2005.

Byrne, Francis John. "Ireland and Her Neighbours, c.1014–c.1072." In *A New History of Ireland: I Prehistoric and Early Ireland*, edited by Dáibhí Ó Cróinín, 862–98. Oxford: Oxford University Press, 2005.

Byrne, Paul. "Life of St Molua: Date and Authorship." *Peritia* 24–25 (2013–2014): 90–107.

Cahill, Michael, ed. *Expositio evangelii secundum Marcum*. Scriptores Celtigenae 2. Corpus Christianorum Series Latina 82. Turnhout: Brepols Publishers, 1997.

Calder, Daniel. G. *Cynewulf*. Boston: Twayne Publishers, 1981.

Calder, Daniel G. and Michael J. B. Allen, trans. *Sources and Analogues of Old English Poetry: The Major Latin Texts in Translation*. Cambridge: D. S. Brewer; Totowa, NJ: Rowman and Littlefield, 1976.

Calder, Daniel G., Robert E. Bjork, Patrick K. Ford, and Daniel F. Melia, trans. *Sources and Analogues of Old English Poetry II: The Major Germanic and Celtic Texts in Translation*. Cambridge: D. S. Brewer; Totowa, NJ: Barnes & Noble, 1983.

Calder, George, ed. *Auraicept na n-Éces: The Scholars' Primer: Being the Texts of the Ogham Tract from the Book of Ballymote and the Yellow Book of Lecan and the Text of the Trefhocul from the Book of Leinster*. Edinburgh: John Grant, 1917. Reprint, Dublin: Four Courts Press, 1995.

Cambridge, Eric. "The Sources and Functions of Wilfrid's Architecture at Ripon and Hexham." In *Wilfrid: Abbot, Bishop, Saint*, edited by Nicholas J. Higham, 136–51. Donington: Shaun Tyas, 2013.

Cameron, M. L. "Aldhelm as Naturalist: A Re-examination of Some of his *Enigmata*." *Peritia* 4 (1985): 117–33.

Campbell, Alistair, ed. *Æthelwulf: De abbatibus*. Oxford: Clarendon Press, 1967.

Campbell, James. "The First Century of Christianity in England." *Ampleforth Journal* 76 (1971): 16–29.

Campbell, James. "The Debt of the Early English Church to Ireland." In *Irland und die Christenheit: Bibelstudien und Mission/Ireland and Christendom: The Bible and the Missions*, edited by Próinéas Ní Chatháin and Michael Richter, 332–46. Stuttgart: Klett-Cotta, 1987.

Campbell, James. "Bede." In *Oxford Dictionary of National Biography*, edited by H. C. G. Matthew and Brian Harrison, 758–65. Oxford: Oxford University Press, 2004.

Capper, Morn. "Prelates and Politics: Wilfrid, Oundle and the 'Middle Angles'." In *Wilfrid: Abbot, Bishop, Saint*, edited by Nicholas J. Higham, 260–74. Donington: Shaun Tyas, 2013.

Carella, Bryan. "The Source of the Prologue to the Laws of Alfred." *Peritia* 19 (2005): 91–118.

Carey, John. "*Scél Tuáin meic Cairill*." *Ériu* 35 (1984): 93–111.

Carey, John. "A Tract on the Creation." *Éigse* 21 (1986): 1–9.

Carey, John. "The Two Laws of Dubthach's Judgment." *Cambridge Medieval Celtic Studies* 19 (1990): 1–18.

Carey, John. "An Edition of the Pseudo-Historical Prologue to the *Senchas Már*." *Ériu* 45 (1994): 1–32.

Carey, John. *The Irish National Origin-Legend: Synthetic Pseudohistory*. E. C. Quiggin Memorial Lecture 1. Cambridge: Department of Anglo-Saxon, Norse, and Celtic, 1994.

Carey, John. "On the Interrelationships of Some *Cín Dromma Snechtai* Texts." *Ériu* 46 (1995): 71–92.

Carey, John. "The Rhetoric of *Echtrae Chonlai*." *Cambrian Medieval Celtic Studies* 30 (1995): 41–65.

Carey, John. "Obscure Styles in Medieval Ireland." *Mediaevalia* 19 (1996): 23–39.
Carey, John. "The Three Things Required of a Poet." *Ériu* 48 (1997): 41–58.
Carey, John. *King of Mysteries: Early Irish Religious Writings*. Dublin: Four Courts Press, 1998.
Carey, John. *A Single Ray of the Sun: Religious Speculation in Early Ireland: Three Essays*. Andover, MA and Aberystwyth: Celtic Studies Publications, Inc., 1999.
Carey, John. "Varia II: The Address to Fergus's Stone." *Ériu* 51 (2000): 183–87.
Carey, John. "The Lough Foyle Colloquy Texts: *Immacaldam Choluim Chille 7 ind Óglaig oc Carraig Eolairg* and *Immacaldam in Druad Brain 7 inna Banfátho Febuil ós Loch Febuil*." *Ériu* 52 (2002): 53–87.
Carey, John. "The Obscurantists and the Sea-Monsters: Reflections on the *Hisperica Famina*." *Peritia* 17–18 (2003–2004): 40–60.
Carey, John. "From David to Labraid: Sacral Kingship in the Emergence of Monotheism in Israel and Ireland." In *Approaches to Mythology and Religion in Celtic Studies*, edited by Katja Ritari and Alexandra Bergholm, 2–27. Newcastle: Cambridge Scholars Publishing, 2008.
Carey, John. "In Search of Mael Muru Othna." In *Clerics, Kings and Vikings: Essays on Medieval Ireland in Honour of Donnchadh Ó Corráin*, edited by Emer Purcell, Paul MacCotter, Julianne Nyhan, and John Sheehan, 429–39. Dublin: Four Courts Press, 2015.
Carey, John. "Learning, Imagination and Belief." In *The Cambridge History of Ireland: Vol. 1 600–1550*, edited by Brendan Smith, 47–75. Cambridge: Cambridge University Press, 2018.
Carey, John. *The Mythological Cycle of Medieval Irish Literature*. Cork Studies in Celtic Literatures 3. Cork: Cork Studies in Celtic Literature, 2018.
Carney, James. "*De Scriptoribus Hibernicis*." *Celtica* 1 (1946–50): 86–110.
Carney, James. *Studies in Irish Literature and History*. Dublin: Dublin Institute for Advanced Studies, 1955. Reprint, 1979.
Carney, James, ed. *The Poems of Blathmac son of Cú Brettan together with the Irish Gospel of Thomas and a Poem on the Virgin Mary*. Dublin: Irish Texts Society, 1964.
Carney, James. "The Deeper Level of Early Irish Literature." *Capuchin Annual* (1969): 160–71.
Carney, James. "Three Old Irish Accentual Poems." *Ériu* 22 (1971): 23–80.
Carney, James. "The Earliest Bran Material." In *Latin Script and Letters A.D. 400–900*, edited by John J. O'Meara and Bernd Naumann, 174–93. Leiden: E. J. Brill, 1976.
Carney, James. "The Dating of Early Irish Verse Texts, 500–1100." *Éigse* 19 (1982–1983): 177–216.
Carney, James. "*A maccucáin sruith in tíag*." *Celtica* 15 (1983): 25–41.
Carney, James. "The Dating of Archaic Irish Verse." In *Early Irish Literature, Media and Communication: Mündlichkeit und Schriftlichkeit in der frühen irischen Literatur*, edited by Stephen Tranter and Hildegard L. C. Tristram, 39–55. ScriptOralia 10. Tübingen: Gunter Narr Verlag, 1989.
Carney, James. "Language and Literature to 1169." In *A New History of Ireland I: Prehistoric and Early Ireland*, edited by Dáibhí Ó Cróinín, 451–510. Oxford: Oxford University Press, 2005.
Chadwick, Nora K. "Imbas Forosnai." *Scottish Gaelic Studies* 4 (1935): 97–135.
Chadwick, Nora K. "The Celtic Background of Anglo-Saxon England." In *Celt and Saxon: Studies in the Early British Border*, edited by Kenneth H. Jackson, Peter Hunter Blair, Bertram Colgrave, Bruce Dickins, Joan and Harold Taylor, Christopher Brooke, and Nora K. Chadwick, 323–52. Cambridge: Cambridge University Press, 1963.

Chadwick, H. Munro and Nora Kershaw Chadwick. *The Growth of Literature, vol. 1: The Ancient Literatures of Europe*. Cambridge: Cambridge University Press, 1932.
Chadwin, Tom. "The *Remscéla Tána Bó Cualngi*." *Cambrian Medieval Celtic Studies* 34 (Winter 1997): 67–75.
Chapman-Stacey, Robin. "Law and Literature in Medieval Ireland and Wales." In *Medieval Celtic Literature and Society*, edited by Helen Fulton, 65–82. Four Courts Press: Dublin, 2005.
Charles-Edwards, Thomas M. "Kingship, Status and the Origins of the Hide." *Past and Present* 56 (1972): 3–33.
Charles-Edwards, Thomas M. "The Penitential of Theodore and the *Indicia Theodori*." In *Archbishop Theodore: Commemorative Studies on his Life and Influence*, edited by Michael Lapidge, 141–74. Cambridge Studies in Anglo-Saxon England. Cambridge: Cambridge University Press, 1995.
Charles-Edwards, Thomas M. "The Penitential of Columbanus." In *Columbanus: Studies on the Latin Writings*, edited by Michael Lapidge, 217–39. Woodbridge: Boydell Press, 1997.
Charles-Edwards, Thomas M. *Early Christian Ireland*. Cambridge: Cambridge University Press, 2000.
Charles-Edwards, Thomas M., trans. *The Chronicle of Ireland*. 2 vols. Translated Texts for Historians 44. Liverpool: Liverpool University Press, 2006.
Charles-Edwards, Thomas M. *Wales and the Britons 350–1064*. Oxford: Oxford University Press, 2013.
Charles-Edwards, Thomas M. and Fergus Kelly, eds. *Bechbretha*. Early Irish Law Series I. Dublin: Dublin Institute for Advanced Studies, 1983.
Clancy, Thomas Owen. "Women Poets in Early Medieval Ireland: Stating the Case." In *"The Fragility of her Sex?" Medieval Irishwomen in their European Context*, edited by Christine Meek and Katharine Simms, 43–72. Blackrock: Four Courts Press, 1996.
Clancy, Thomas Owen. "Die Like a Man? The Ulster Cycle Death-Tale Anthology." *Aiste* 2 (2008): 70–93.
Clancy, Thomas Own. "The Kingdoms of the North: Poetry, Places, Politics." In *Beyond the Gododdin: Dark Age Scotland in Medieval Wales, Proceedings of a Day Conference held on 19 February 2005*, edited by Alex Woolf, 153–75. St. John's House Papers 13. St. Andrews: The Committee for Dark Age Studies, 2013.
Clancy, Thomas Owen and Gilbert Márkus, OP, trans. *Iona: The Earliest Poetry of a Celtic Monastery*. Edinburgh: Edinburgh University Press, 1995.
Clarke, Michael. "Demonology, Allegory and Translation: The Furies and the Morrígan." In *Classical Literature and Learning in Medieval Irish Narrative*, edited by Ralph O'Connor, 101–22. Cambridge: D. S. Brewer, 2014.
Clarke, Michael. "Reconstructing the Medieval Irish Bookshelf: A Case Study of *Fingal Rónáin* and the Horse-Eared King." In *Classical Literature and Learning in Medieval Irish Narrative*, edited by Ralph O'Connor, 123–39. Cambridge: D. S. Brewer, 2014.
Clayton, Mary, ed. and trans. *Two Ælfric Texts: The Twelve Abuses and the Vices and Virtues, an Edition and Translation of Ælfric's Old English Versions of "De Duodecim Abusivis" and "De Octo Vitiis et de Duodecim Abusivi."* Cambridge: D. S. Brewer, 2013.
Clayton, Mary and Juliet Mullins, ed. and trans. *Old English Lives of Saints: Ælfric*. 3 vols. Dumbarton Oaks Medieval Library, 58–60. Cambridge, MA: Harvard University Press, 2019.

Clemoes, Peter. *Interactions of Thought and Language in Old English Poetry*. Cambridge: Cambridge University Press, 1995.
Clemoes, Peter, ed. *Aelfric's Catholic Homilies: The First Series*. Early English Texts Society Supplementary Series 17. Oxford: Oxford University Press, 1997.
CODECS: Collaborative Online Database and e-Resource for Celtic Studies. https://www.vanhamel.nl/codecs/.
Colgrave, Bertram, ed. and trans. *The Life of Bishop Wilfrid by Eddius Stephanus*. Cambridge: Cambridge University Press, 1927. Reprint, 1985.
Colgrave, Bertram, ed. and trans. *Two Lives of Saint Cuthbert: A Life by an Anonymous Monk of Lindisfarne and Bede's Prose Life*. New York: Greenwood Press, 1969. Reissued, Cambridge University Press, 1985.
Colgrave, Bertram, ed. and trans. *Felix's Life of Saint Guthlac*. Cambridge: Cambridge University Press, 1956. Reprint, 1985.
Colgrave, Bertram. "Bede's Miracle Stories." In *Bede: His Life, Times and Writings. Essays in Commemoration of the Twelfth Century of his Death*, edited by Alexander H. Thompson, 201–29. New York: Oxford University Press, 1935. Reissued, Russell & Russell, 1966.
Colgrave, Bertram, ed. and trans. *The Earliest Life of Gregory the Great, by an Anonymous Monk of Whitby*. Cambridge: Cambridge University Press, 1968.
Colgrave, Bertram and R. A. B. Mynors, eds. *Bede's Ecclesiastical History of the English People*. Oxford: Clarendon Press, 1969.
Connellan, Owen. *Imtheacht na Tromdhaimhe: The Proceedings of the Great Bardic Institution*. Transactions of the Ossianic Society 5. Dublin: John O'Daly, 1857.
Connolly, Seán. "Cogitosus's *Life of St Brigit*: Content and Value." *Journal of the Royal Society of Antiquaries of Ireland* 117 (1987): 5–27.
Connolly, Seán. "Vita Prima Sanctae Brigitae: Background and Historical Value." *Journal of the Royal Society of Antiquaries of Ireland* 119 (1989): 5–49.
Cook, Albert S. "King Oswy and Cædmon's Hymn." *Speculum* 2 (1927): 67–72.
Corning, Caitlin. "The Baptism of Edwin, King of Northumbria: A New Analysis of the British Tradition." *Northern History* 36, no. 1 (2000): 5–15.
Corning, Caitlin. "Columbanus and the Easter Controversy: Theological, Social and Political Contexts." In *The Irish in Early Medieval Europe: Identity, Culture and Religion*, edited by Roy Flechner and Sven Meeder, 101–15. London: Palgrave, 2016.
Corthals, Johan. "The *Retoiric* in *Aided Chonchobuir*." *Ériu* 40 (1989): 41–59.
Corthals, Johan. "Some Observations on the Versification of the Rhymeless 'Leinster Poems'." *Celtica* 21 (1990): 113–25.
Corthals, Johan. "Early Irish *Retoirics* and their Late Antique Background." *Cambrian Medieval Celtic Studies* 31 (Summer 1996): 17–36.
Corthals, Johan. "The Rhymeless 'Leinster Poems': Diplomatic Texts." *Celtica* 24 (2003): 79–100.
Corthals, Johan. "Why Did Fergus Rise from his Grave?" *Cambrian Medieval Celtic Studies* 55 (Summer 2008): 1–9.
Corthals, Johan. "The *Áiliu* Poems in *Bretha Nemed Dédenach*." *Éigse* 37 (2010): 59–91.
Corthals, Johan. "Decoding the 'Caldron of Poesy'." *Peritia* 24–25 (2013–2014): 74–89.
Cramp, Rosemary. "A Reconsideration of the Monastic Site of Whitby." In *The Age of Migrating Ideas: Early Medieval Art in Northern Britain and Ireland*, edited by R. Michael Spearman and John Higgitt, 64–73. Edinburgh: Alan Sutton Publishing, 1993.

Cramp, Rosemary. *Whithorn and the Northumbrian Expansion Westwards*. Third Whithorn Lecture. Whithorn: Friends of the Whithorn Trust, 1995.
Cronan, Dennis. "'Beowulf', the Gaels, and the Recovery of the Pre-Conversion Past." *Anglo-Saxon* 1 (2007): 137–80.
Cronan, Dennis. "Cædmon's *Hymn*: Context and Dating." *English Studies* 91 (2010): 817–25.
Cronan, Dennis. "Cædmon's Audience." *Studies in Philology* 109, no. 4 (Summer 2012): 333–63.
Cronan, Dennis. "*Beowulf* and the Containment of Scyld in the West Saxon Royal Genealogy." In *The Dating of "Beowulf": A Reassessment*, edited by Leonard Neidorf, 112–37. Cambridge: D. S. Brewer, 2014.
Cubitt, Catherine. "Wilfrid's 'Usurping Bishops': Episcopal Elections in Anglo-Saxon England, c.600–c.800." *Northern History* 25 (1989): 18–38.
Cubitt, Catherine. *Anglo-Saxon Church Councils c. 650–c.850*. London and New York: Leicester University, 1995.
Cubitt, Catherine. "Appendix 2: The Chronology of Stephen's Life of Wilfrid." In *Wilfrid: Abbot, Bishop, Saint*, edited by Nicholas J. Higham, 334–47. Donington: Shaun Tyas, 2013.
Curran, Michael. *The Antiphonary of Bangor and the Early Irish Monastic Liturgy*. Dublin: Irish Academic Press, 1984.
Curtius, Ernst Robert. *European Literature and the Latin Middle Ages*. Translated by Willard R. Trask. London and Henley: Routledge & Kegan Paul, 1953.
Dailey, Erin T. "To Choose One Easter from Three: Oswiu's Decision and the Northumbrian Synod of AD 664." *Peritia* 26 (2015): 47–64.
Daniels, Robin. "The Anglo-Saxon Monastery at Hartlepool, England." In *Northumbria's Golden Age*, edited by Jane Hawkes and Susan Mills, 105–12. Thrupp: Sutton Publishing, 1999.
Darby, Peter. *Bede and the End of Time*. Studies in Early Medieval Britain. Farnham: Ashgate, 2012.
Davies, Luned Mair. "The 'mouth of gold': Gregorian Texts in the *Collectio canonum Hibernensis*." In *Ireland and Europe in the Early Middle Ages: Texts and Transmission / Irland und Europa im früheren Mittelalter: Texte und Überlieferung*, edited by Próinséas Ní Chatháin and Michael Richter, 249–67. Dublin: Four Courts Press, 2002.
Davies, Morgan Thomas. "Protocols of Reading in Early Irish Literature: Notes on Some Notes to *Orgain Denna Ríg* and *Amra Coluim Cille*." *Cambrian Medieval Celtic Studies* 32 (1996): 1–23.
Davies, Morgan Thomas. "Cultural Memory, the Finding of the *Táin*, and the Canonical Process in Early Irish Literature." In *Medieval Irish Perspectives on Cultural Memory*, edited by Jan Erik Rekdal and Erich Poppe, 81–108. Studien und Texte zur Keltologie 11. Münster: Nodus Publikationen, 2014.
Davies, Morgan Thomas. "Warrior Time." In *Kings and Warriors in Early North-West Europe*, edited by Jan Erik Rekdal and Charles Doherty, 237–309. Dublin: Four Courts Press, 2016.
Davies, Wendy. "The Place of Healing in Early Irish Society." In *Sages, Saints and Storytellers, Celtic Studies in Honour of Professor James Carney*, edited by Donnchadh Ó Corráin, Liam Breatnach, and Kim McCone, 43–55. Maynooth: An Sagart, 1989.
Davies, Wendy. "The Myth of the Celtic Church." In *The Early Church in Wales and the West. Recent Work in Early Christian Archaeology, History and Place-names*, edited by Nancy Edwards and Alan Lane, 12–21. Oxbow Monograph 17. Oxford: Oxbow Books, 1992.
Dawson, Elizabeth. "Brigit and Patrick in *Vita Prima Santae Brigitae*: Veneration and Jurisdiction." *Peritia* 28 (2017): 35–50.

Day, Virginia. "The Influence of the Catechetical *narratio* on Old English and Some Other Medieval Literature." *Anglo-Saxon England* 3 (1974): 51–61.
Dempsey, G. T. "Aldhelm of Malmesbury and the Irish." *Proceedings of the Royal Irish Academy* 99C (1999): 1–22.
Dempsey, G. T. "Aldhelm of Malmesbury's Social Theology: The Barbaric Heroic Ideal Christianised." *Peritia* 15 (2001): 58–80.
Dempsey, G. T. "Aldhelm of Malmesbury and High Ecclesiasticism in a Barbarian Kingdom." *Traditio* 63 (2008): 47–88.
Díaz y Díaz, Manuel C., ed. and trans. *Liber de ordine creaturarum: Un Anónimo Irlandés del Siglo VII*. Monografias de la Universidad de Santiago de Compostela. Santiago de Compostela: Secretariado de Publicaciones de la Universidad de Santiago, 1972.
Dillon, Myles. "Stories from the Law-Tracts." *Ériu* 11 (1931–1932): 42–65.
Dillon, Myles. *The Cycles of the Kings*. London and New York: Geoffrey Cumberlege, Oxford University Press, 1946.
Dillon, Myles. *Early Irish Literature*. Chicago: University of Chicago Press, 1948. Reprint, Dublin, 1994.
Dillon, Myles, ed. *Serglige Con Culainn*. Mediaeval and Modern Irish Series XIV. Dublin: Dublin Institute for Advanced Studies, 1953.
Discenza, Nicole G. and Paul E. Szarmach, eds. *A Companion to Alfred the Great*. Brill's Companions to the Christian Tradition 58. Leiden: Brill, 2015.
Dobbie, Elliott van Kirk, ed. *The Manuscripts of Cædmon's Hymn and Bede's Death Song: With a Critical Text of the Epistola Cuthberti de obitu Bedae*. New York: Columbia University Press, 1937.
Dobbie, Elliott van Kirk, ed. *The Anglo-Saxon Minor Poems*. Anglo-Saxon Poetic Records VI. New York: Columbia University Press, 1942.
Dobbs, Margaret. "Nínine Écess." *Études Celtique* 5 (1949): 148–53.
Dobbs, Margaret. "A Poem Ascribed to Flann mac Lonáin." *Ériu* 17 (1955): 16–34.
Donahue, Charles. "Beowulf, Ireland and the Natural Good." *Traditio* 7 (1949–1951): 263–77.
Donahue, Charles. "*Beowulf* and Christian Tradition: A Reconsideration from a Celtic Stance." *Traditio* 21 (1965): 55–116.
Dooley, Ann. "Early Irish Literature and Contemporary Scholarly Disciplines." In *Medieval and Modern Ireland*, edited by Richard Wall, 60–74. Totowa, NJ: Barnes and Noble Books, 1988.
Downey, Clodagh. "The Life and Work of Cúán Ó Lothcháin." *Ríocht na Midhe* 19 (2008): 55–78.
Duemmler, Ernst, ed. "Bonafatii et Lullii Epistolae." In *Monumenta Germaniae Historica*, 215–431. Epistolae Merowingici et Karolini Aevi I. Berlin: Weidmann, 1892.
Duemmler, Ernst, ed. "Alcvini sive Albini Epistolae." In *Monumenta Germaniae Historica*, 1–481. Epistolae Karolini Aevi II. Berlin: Weidmann, 1895.
Dumville, David N. "Ulster Heroes in the Early Irish Annals: a Caveat." *Éigse* 17 (1977–1979): 47–54.
Dumville, David N. "Ireland and Britain in *Táin Bó Fraích*." *Études Celtiques* 32 (1996): 175–87.
Dumville, David N. "*Félire Óengusso*: Problems of Dating a Monument of Old Irish." *Éigse* 33 (2002): 19–48.
Dumville, David N., with Lesley Abrams, T. M. Charles-Edwards, Alicia Corrêa, K. R. Dark, K. L. Maund, and A. P. McD. Orchard, eds. *Saint Patrick*. Woodbridge: Boydell Press, 1993.

Duncan, Archibald A. M. "Bede, Iona, and the Picts." In *The Writing of History in the Middle Ages, Essays Presented to Richard William Southern*, edited by R. H. C. Davis and J. M. Wallace-Hadrill, 1–42. Oxford: Clarendon Press, 1981.

Duncan, Sandra. "Prophets Shining in Dark Places: Biblical Themes and Theological Motifs in the *Vita Sancti Wilfridi*." In *Wilfrid: Abbot, Bishop, Saint*, edited by Nicholas J. Higham, 80–92. Donington: Shaun Tyas, 2013.

Dunn, Marilyn. "Columbanus, Charisma and the Revolt of the Monks of Bobbio." *Peritia* 20 (2008): 1–27.

Dunshea, Philip. "The Meaning of Catraeth: A Revised Early Context for Y Gododdin." In *Beyond the Gododdin: Dark Age Scotland in Medieval Wales, Proceedings of a Day Conference held on 19 February 2005*, edited by Alex Woolf, 81–114. St. John's House Papers, 13. St. Andrews: The Committee for Dark Age Studies, 2013.

Dunshea, Philip. "The Road to *Winwæd*? Penda's Wars against Oswiu of Bernicia, c. 642 to c. 655." *Anglo-Saxon England* 44 (2015): 1–16.

eDIL: Dictionary of the Irish Language. http://www.dil.ie.

Edmonds, Fiona. "The Practicalities of Communication between Northumbrian and Irish Churches c.635–735." In *Anglo-Saxon/Irish Relations before the Vikings*, edited by James Graham-Campbell and Michael Ryan, 129–47. Proceedings of the British Academy, 157. Oxford: Oxford University Press, 2009.

Edmonds, Fiona. *Gaelic Influence in the Northumbrian Kingdom: The Golden Age and the Viking Age*. Woodbridge: The Boydell Press, 2019.

Ehwald, Rudolf, ed. "Epistolae." In *Monumenta Germaniae Historica*, 475–503. Auctores Antiquissimi 15. Aldhelmi Opera. Berlin: Weidmann, 1919.

Ehwald, Rudolf, ed. "De Metris et Enigmatibus ac Pedum Regulis." In *Monumenta Germaniae Historica*, 61–204. Auctores Antiquissimi 15. Aldhelmi Opera. Berlin: Weidmann, 1919.

Eska, Charlene M. *Cáin Lánamna: An Old Irish Tract on Marriage and Divorce Law*. Leiden and Boston: Brill, 2010.

Etchingham, Colmán. "Early Medieval Irish History." In *Progress in Medieval Irish Studies*, edited by Kim McCone and Katharine Simms, 123–53. Maynooth: Department of Old Irish, St. Patrick's College, 1996.

Etchingham, Colmán. *Church Organization in Ireland A.D. 650 to 1000*. Naas: Laigin Publications, 1999.

Evan, Peter D. "Word-Play as Evidence for the Date of *Durham*." *Medium Ævum* 82 (2013): 314–17.

Evans, D. Simon. *Buched Dewi: O Lawysgrif Llanstephan 27*. Caerdydd [Cardiff]: Gwasg Pryfysgol Cymry, 1965.

Fanning, Steven. "Bede, *Imperium*, and the Bretwaldas." *Speculum* 66/1 (1991): 1–26.

Farmer, David Hugh. *The Oxford Dictionary of Saints*. 5th edition. Oxford: Oxford University Press, 2003.

Fell, Christine E. "Hild, Abbess of Streonæshalch." In *Hagiography and Medieval Literature: a Symposium*, edited by Hans Bekker-Nielsen, 76–99. Odense: Odense University Press, 1981.

Findon, Joanne. *A Woman's Words: Emer and Female Speech in the Ulster Cycle*. Toronto: University of Toronto Press, 1997.

Findon, Joanne. "Dangerous Siren or Abandoned Wife? Gloss Versus Text on an Early Irish Manuscript Page." In *Signs on the Edge: Space, Text and Margin in Medieval Manuscripts*, edited by Rolf H. Bremmer and Sarah Larratt Keefer, 187–202. Mediaevalia Groningana, NS, 10. Louvain: Peeters, 2007.

Flechner, Roy. "The Problem of Originality in Early Medieval Canon Law: Legislating by Means of Contradictions in the *Colletio Hibernensis*." *Viator* 43, no. 2 (2012): 29–47.

Flechner, Roy, ed. and trans. *The Hibernensis*. 2 vols. Washington, DC: The Catholic University of America Press, 2019.

Flower, Robin. *The Irish Tradition*. Oxford: Clarendon Press, 1947.

Foley, William Trent. "*Imitatio Apostoli*: St. Wilfrid of York and the Andrew Script." *The American Benedictine Review* 40, no. 1 (March 1989): 13–31.

Foley, William Trent and Arthur G. Holder, trans. *Bede: A Biblical Miscellany*. Translated Texts for Historians 28. Liverpool: Liverpool University Press, 1999.

Follet, Westley. "*Céli Dé" in Ireland: Monastic Writing and Identity in the Early Middle Ages*. Studies in Celtic History 23. Woodbridge: Boydell Press, 2006.

Foot, Sarah. "Wilfrid's Monastic Empire." In *Wilfrid: Abbot, Bishop, Saint*, edited by Nicholas J. Higham, 27–39. Donington: Shaun Tyas, 2013.

Ford, Patrick K, trans. *The Mabinogi and Other Medieval Welsh Tales*. Berkeley, Los Angeles, London: University of California Press, 1977.

Ford, Patrick K. "The Blind, the Dumb, and the Ugly: Aspects of Poets and their Craft in Early Ireland and Wales." *Cambridge Medieval Celtic Studies* 19 (Summer 1990): 27–40.

Ford, Patrick K. *The Celtic Poets: Songs and Tales from Early Ireland and Wales*. Belmont, MA: Ford & Bailie Publishers, 1999.

Fouracre, Paul. "Britain, Ireland, and Europe, c.500–c.750." In *A Companion to the Early Middle Ages: Britain and Ireland, c.500–c.1100*, edited by Pauline Stafford, 126–42. Chichester: Blackwell Publishing, 2009.

Fouracre, Paul. "Wilfrid on the Continent." In *Wilfrid: Abbot, Bishop, Saint*, edited by Nicholas J. Higham, 186–99. Donington: Shaun Tyas, 2013.

Fraipont, J., ed. "Bedae De locis sanctis." In *Itineraria et Alia Geographica*. Corpus Christianorum Series Latina 175 (CCSL 175), 245–80. Turnhout: Brepols, 1965.

Frank, Roberta. "Germanic Legend in Old English Literature." In *The Cambridge Companion to Old English Literature*, edited by Malcolm Godden and Michael Lapidge, 88–106. Cambridge: Cambridge University Press, 1991.

Frank, Roberta. "The Search for the Anglo-Saxon Oral Poet." *Bulletin of the John Rylands University Library of Manchester* 75 (1993): 11–36.

Frantzen, Allen J. *The Literature of Penance in Anglo-Saxon England*. New Brunswick, NJ: Rutgers University Press, 1983.

Frantzen, Allen J. *Desire for Origins: New Language, Old English, and Teaching the Tradition*. New Brunswick, NJ: Rutgers University Press, 1990.

Fraser, James E. "Adomnán and the Morality of War." In *Adomnán of Iona: Theologian, Lawmaker, Peacemaker*, edited by Jonathan M. Wooding, with Rodney Aist, Thomas Owen Clancy, and Thomas O'Loughlin, 95–111. Dublin: Four Courts Press, 2010.

Frese, Dolores Warwick. "The Art of Cynewulf's Runic Signatures." In *Anglo-Saxon Poetry: Essays in Appreciation for John C. McGalliard*, edited by Lewis E. Nicholson and Dolores Warwick Frese, 312–34. Notre Dame, IN: University of Notre Dame Press, 1975.

Fritz, Donald. "Caedmon: A Monastic Exegete." *American Benedictine Review* 25 (1974): 351–63.

Fry, Donald. "Caedmon as a Formulaic Poet." *Forum for Modern Language Studies* 10 (1974): 227–47.

Fulk, Robert D. "*Beowulf* and Language History." In *The Dating of Beowulf: A Reassessment*, edited by Leonard Neidorf, 19–36. Cambridge: D. S. Brewer, 2014.
Fulk, Robert D., Robert E. Bjork, John D. Niles, eds. *Klaeber's Beowulf and the Fight at Finnsburg*. 4th ed. Toronto: University of Toronto Press, 2008.
Gannon, Anna. *The Iconography of Early Anglo-Saxon Coinage: Sixth to Eighth Centuries*. Oxford: Oxford University Press, 2003.
Gantz, Jeffrey, trans. *Early Irish Myths and Sagas*. Harmondsworth: Penguin Books, 1981.
Ganz, David. "The Earliest Manuscript of Lathcen's *Eclogae Moralium Gregorii* and the Dating of Irish Cursive Minuscule Script." In *Early Medieval Ireland and Europe: Chronology, Contacts, Scholarship – A Festschrift for Dáibhí Ó Cróinín*, edited by Pádraic Moran and Immo Warntjes, 597–624. Turnhout: Brepols, 2015.
Garde, Judith N. *Old English Poetry in Medieval Christian Perspective, a Doctrinal Approach*. Cambridge: Boydell and Brewer, 1991.
*Geiriadur Prifysgol Cymru: A Dictionary of the Welsh Language*. Cyfrol [Volume] 1. Caerdydd [Cardiff]: Gwasg Prifysgol Cymru, 1950–1967.
Gneuss, Helmut. *Handlist of Anglo-Saxon Manuscripts: A List of Manuscripts and Manuscripts Fragments Written or Owned in England up to 1100*. Tempe: Arizona Center for Medieval and Renaissance Studies, 2001.
Gneuss, Helmut and Michael Lapidge. *Anglo-Saxon Manuscripts: A Bibliography Handlist of Anglo-Saxon Manuscripts and Manuscript Fragments Written or Owned in England up to 1100*. Toronto Anglo-Saxon Series. Toronto: University of Toronto Press, 2014.
Godden, Malcolm, ed. *Aelfric's Catholic Homilies, the Second Series Text*. Early English Texts Society 5. Oxford: Oxford University Press, 1979.
Godden, Malcolm. "Wærferth and King Alfred: the Fate of the Old English *Dialogues*." In *Alfred the Wise: Studies in Honour of Janet Bately on the Occasion of her Sixty-fifth Birthday*, edited by Jane Roberts and Janet L. Nelson with Malcolm Godden, 35–51. Cambridge: D. S. Brewer, 1997.
Godden, Malcolm. "Did King Alfred Write Anything?" *Medium Ævum* 71, no. 1 (2007): 1–23.
Godman, Peter, ed. *Alcuin: The Bishops, Kings, and Saints of York*. Oxford: Clarendon Press, 1982.
Goffart, Walter. *The Narrators of Barbarian History (A.D. 550–800): Jordanes, Gregory of Tours, Bede, and Paul the Deacon*. Notre Dame, IN: University of Notre Dame Press, 1988.
Goffart, Walter. "Bede's History in a Harsher Climate." In *Innovation and Tradition in the Writings of The Venerable Bede*, edited by Scott DeGregorio, 203–26. Medieval European Studies VII. Morgantown, WV: West Virginia University Press, 2006.
Gordon, Ida L., ed. *The Seafarer*. Old and Middle English Texts. Manchester: Manchester University Press, 1979.
Graff, Eric. "Report on the Codex: Schaffhausen, Stadtbibliothek, Generalia 1." In *The Schaffhausen Adomnán (Schaffhausen, Stadtbibliothek, MS Generalia 1) Part II Commentary*, edited by Damian Bracken and Eric Graff, 17–55. Irish Manuscripts in Facsimile I. Cork: Cork University Press, 2014.
Gramsch, Robert, Máirín MacCarron, Pádraig MacCarron, and Joseph Yose. "Medieval Historical, Hagiographical and Biographical Networks." In *Maths Meets Myths: Quantitative Approaches to Ancient Narratives*, edited by Ralph Kenna, Máirín MacCarron, and Pádraig MacCarron, 45–69. Switzerland: Springer International Publishing, 2017.
Gray, Elizabeth A., ed. *Cath Maige Tuired: The Second Battle of Mag Tuired*. Irish Texts Society LII. Naas: Irish Texts Society, 1982.

Greene, David, ed. *Fingal Rónáin and Other Stories*. Mediaeval and Modern Irish Series XVI. Dublin: Dublin Institute for Advanced Studies, 1955.

Greenfield, Stanley B. and Daniel G. Calder. *A New Critical History of Old English Literature*. New York and London: New York University Press, 1986.

Grigg, Julianna. "The Just King and *De Duodecim Abusiuis Saeculi*." *Parergon* 27, no.1 (2010): 27–51.

Grimmer, Martin. "The Exogamous Marriages of Oswiu of Northumbria." *The Heroic Age: A Journal of Early Medieval Northwestern Europe* 9, October, 2006. http://www.heroicage.org/issues/9/grimmer.html

Grocock, Christopher. Review of *The Celtic Latin Tradition in Biblical Style*, by David R. Howlett. *Peritia* 12 (1998): 379–89.

Grocock, Christopher. "Wilfrid, Benedict Biscop and Bede – the Monk who Knew too Much?" In *Wilfrid: Abbot, Bishop, Saint*, edited by Nicholas Higham, 93–111. Donington: Shaun Tyas, 2013.

Grocock, Christopher. "Separation Anxiety: Bede and Threats to Wearmouth and Jarrow." In *Bede and the Future*, edited by Peter Darby and Faith Wallis, 67–92. London and New York: Routledge, 2014.

Grocock, Christopher and Ian N. Wood, ed. and trans. *Abbots of Wearmouth and Jarrow: Bede's "Homily" i.13 on Benedict Biscop, Bede's "History of the Abbots of Wearmouth and Jarrow," The Anonymous "Life of Ceolfrith," Bede's "Letter to Ecgbert, Bishop of York."* Oxford: Clarendon Press, 2013.

Grosjean, Paul. "Sur quelques exégètes irlandais du VIIe siècle." *Sacris Erudiri* 7 (1955): 67–98.

Gruffydd, R. Geraint. "Canu Cadwallon ap Cadfan." In *Astudiaethau ar yr Hengerdd*, edited by Rachel Bromwich and R. Brinley Jones, 25–43. Gwasg Prifysgol Cymru: Caerdydd [Cardiff], 1978.

Gunn, Vicky. *Bede's* Historiae*: Genre, Rhetoric, and the Construction of Anglo-Saxon Church History*. Woodbridge: The Boydell Press, 2009.

Gwynn, Edward J. *The Metrical Dindshenchas*. 5 vols. Dublin: Royal Irish Academy, 1903–1935. Reprint, Dublin Institute for Advanced Studies, 1991.

Gwynn, Edward J. "An Old-Irish Tract on the Privileges and Responsibilities of Poets." *Ériu* 13, no. 1–2 (1942): 1–60, 220–36.

Gwynn, Edward J. and W. J. Purton. "The Monastery of Tallaght." *Proceedings of the Royal Irish Academy* 29C (1911–1912): 115–79.

Hall, Alaric. "Interlinguistic Communication in Bede's *Historia Ecclesiastica Gentis Anglorum*." In *Interfaces between Language and Culture in Medieval England: A Festschrift for Matti Kilpiö*, edited by Alaric Hall, Agnes Kiricsi, and Olga Timofeeva with Bethany Fox, 37–80. The Northern World 48. Brill: Leiden, 2010.

Hall, Alaric. "*A gente Anglorum appellatur*: The Evidence of Bede's *Historia Ecclesiastica Gentis Anglorum* for the Replacement of Roman Names by English Ones during the Early Anglo-Saxon Period." In *Words in Dictionaries and History: Essays in Honour of R. W. McConchie*, edited by Olga Timofeeva and Tanja Säily, 219–32. Amsterdam: John Benjamins, 2011.

Hamann, Stefanie. "St. Fursa, the Genealogy of an Irish Saint – The Historical Person and his Cult." *Proceedings of the Royal Irish Academy* 112 C (2012): 147–87.

Hamann, Stefanie. "Religious Thought in the Early Seventh Century as Reflected in the *Visio Fursei*." *Peritia* 30 (2019): 123–44.

Hammer, Carl I. "'Holy Entrepreneur': Agilbert, a Merovingian Bishop between Ireland, England and Francia." *Peritia* 22–23 (2011–2012): 53–82.
Harris, Joseph. "A Note on the Other Heorot." In *The Dating of "Beowulf: "A Reassessment*, edited by Leonard Neidorf, 178–90. Cambridge: D. S. Brewer, 2014.
Harvey, Anthony. "The Cambridge Juvencus Glosses – Evidence of Hiberno-Welsh Literary Interaction?" In *Language Contact in the British Isles*, edited by Per Sture Ureland and George Broderick, 181–98. Tübingen: De Gruyter, 1991.
Harvey, Anthony. "Reading the Genetic Code of Early Medieval Celtic Orthography." In *LautSchriftSprache: Beiträge zur vergleichenden historischen Graphematik*, edited by Elvira Glaser, Annina Seiler, and Michelle Waldispühl, 155–66. Zürich: Chronos Verlag, 2011.
Harvey, Anthony. "Linguistic Method in his Literary Madness? The Word-coinings of Virgilius Maro Grammaticus." In *Linguistic and Philological Studies in Early Irish*, edited by Elisa Roma and David Stifter, 79–104. Lewiston and Lampeter: Edwin Mellen Press, 2014.
Harvey, Anthony. "Blood, Dust and Cucumbers: Constructing the World of Hisperic Latinity." In *Clerics, Kings and Vikings: Essays on Medieval Ireland in Honour of Donnchadh Ó Corráin*, edited by Emer Purcell, Paul MacCotter, Julianne Nyhan, and John Sheehan, 352–62. Dublin: Four Courts Press, 2015.
Harvey, Anthony. "Muirchú and his *remi cymba*: Whence his Latin and its Wordstore?" *Peritia* 27 (2016): 43–62.
Harvey, Anthony. "Varia I: Hiberno-Latin *quantotus, tantotus*." *Ériu* 66 (2016): 191–94.
Hawkes, Jane. "*Iuxta morem Romanorum*: Stone and Sculpture in Anglo-Saxon England." In *Anglo-Saxon Styles*, edited by Catherine E. Karkov and George Hardin Brown, 69–99. Albany: State University of New York Press, 2003.
Haycock, Marged. "Early Welsh Poets Look North." In *Beyond the Gododdin: Dark Age Scotland in Medieval Wales, Proceedings of a Day Conference held on 19 February 2005*, edited by Alex Woolf, 9–39. St. John's House Papers, 13. St. Andrews: The Committee for Dark Age Studies, 2013.
Hayden, Deborah. "Anatomical Metaphor in *Auraicept na nÉces*." In *Authorities and Adaptations: The Reworking and Transmission of Textual Sources in Medieval Ireland*, edited by Elizabeth Boyle and Deborah Hayden, 23–61. Dublin Institute for Advanced Studies: Dublin, 2014.
Henderson, George. *From Durrow to Kells: The Insular Gospel-books 650–800*. London: Thames and Hudson, 1987.
Henderson, Isabel and Elisabeth Okasha. "The Early Christian Inscribed and Carved Stones of Tullylease, Co. Cork." *Cambridge Medieval Celtic Studies* 24 (Winter 1992): 1–36.
Hennessy, William M., ed. and trans. *Chronicum Scotorum: A Chronicle of Irish Affairs from the Earliest Time to A.D. 1135*. London: Longmans, Green, Reader, and Dyer, 1866.
Henry, Patrick L. *The Early English and Celtic Lyric*. London: George Allen & Unwin Ltd, 1966.
Henry, Patrick L. *Saoithiúlacht na Sean-Ghaeilge: Bunú an Traidisiúin*. Baile Átha Cliath [Dublin]: Oifig an tSoláthair, 1978.
Henry, Patrick L. "The Caldron of Poesy." *Studia Celtica* 14–15 (1979–1980): 114–28.
Henry, Patrick L. "*Verba Scáthaige*." *Celtica* 21 (1990): 191–207.
Henry, Patrick L. "*Conailla Medb Míchuru* and the Tradition of Fiacc Son of Fergus." In *Miscellanea Celtica in Memoriam Heinrich Wagner*, edited by Séamus Mac Mathúna and Ailbhe Ó Corráin, 53–70. Uppsala: Uppsala University, 1997.

Herbert, Máire. *Iona, Kells, and Derry: The History and Hagiography of the Monastic* Familia *of Columba*. Oxford: Clarendon Press, 1988.
Herbert, Máire. "The Preface to *Amra Coluim Cille*." In *Sages, Saints and Storytellers: Celtic Studies in Honour of Professor James Carney*, edited by Donnchadh Ó Corráin, Liam Breatnach, and Kim McCone, 67–75. Maynooth: An Sagart, 1989.
Herbert, Máire. "The World of Adomnán." In *Adomnán at Birr, AD 697: Essays in Commemoration of the Law of the Innocents*, edited by Thomas O'Loughlin, 33–39. Dublin: Four Courts Press, 2001.
Herbert, Máire. "The Representation of Gregory the Great in Irish Sources of the Pre-Viking Era." In *Listen, O Isles, unto Me: Studies in Medieval Word and Image in Honour of Jennifer O'Reilly*, edited by Elizabeth Mullins and Diarmuid Scully, 181–90. Cork: Cork University Press, 2011.
Herbert, Máire and Martin McNamara, trans. *Irish Biblical Apocrypha: Selected Texts in Translation*. Edinburgh: T & T Clark, 1989.
Herity, Michael and Aidan Breen. *The* Cathach *of Colum Cille: An Introduction*. Dublin: Royal Irish Academy, 2002.
Herren, Michael W. "The Authorship, Date of Composition and Provenance of the So-called *Lorica Gildae*." *Ériu* 24 (1973): 35–51.
Herren, Michael W. *The Hisperica Famina: I. The A-Text*. Toronto: Pontifical Institute of Mediaeval Studies, 1974.
Herren, Michael W. "Some New Light on the Life of Virgilius Maro Grammaticus." *Proceedings of the Royal Irish Academy* 79C (1979): 27–71.
Herren, Michael W. *The Hisperica Famina: II. Related Poems, A Critical Edition with English Translation and Philological Commentary*. Toronto: Pontifical Institute of Mediaeval Studies, 1987.
Herren, Michael W. "Scholarly Contacts between the Irish and the Southern English in the Seventh Century." *Peritia* 12 (1998): 24–53.
Herren, Michael W. "Literary and Glossarial Evidence for the Study of Classical Mythology in Ireland A.D. 600–800." In *Text and Gloss: Studies in Insular Learning and Literature Presented to Joseph Donovan Pheifer*, edited by Helen Conrad-O'Briain, Anne Marie D'Arcy, John Scattergood, 49–67. Dublin: Four Courts Press, 1999.
Herren, Michael W. "The Study of Greek in Ireland in the Early Middle Ages." In *L'Irlanda e gli Irlandesi nell'Alto Medioevo*, 511–32. Settimane di Studio della Fondazione Centro Italiano di Studi sull'Alto Medioevo LVII. Spoleto: Presso la Sede della Fondazione, 2010.
Herren, Michael W. "The 'Papal Letters to the Irish' Cited by Bede: How Did He Get Them?" In *Clerics, Kings and Vikings: Essays on Medieval Ireland in Honour of Donnchadh Ó Corráin*, edited by Emer Purcell, Paul MacCotter, Julianne Nyhan, and John Sheehan, 3–10. Dublin: Four Courts Press, 2015.
Herren, Michael W. and Shirley Ann Brown. *Christ in Celtic Christianity: Britain and Ireland from the Fifth to the Tenth Century*. Woodbridge: Boydell Press, 2002.
Higham, Nicholas J. *(Re-)Reading Bede: The 'Ecclesiastical History' in Context*. London and New York: Routledge, 2006.
Higham, Nicholas J., ed. *Britons in Anglo-Saxon England*. Woodbridge: Boydell Press, 2007.
Higham, Nicholas J. *Ecgfrith: King of the Northumbrians, High-King of Britain*. Donington: Shaun Tyas, 2015.
Hill, Joyce, ed. *Old English Minor Heroic Poems*. 3rd ed. Durham: Centre for Medieval and Renaissance Studies and Toronto: Pontifical Institute of Mediaeval Studies, 2009.

Hill, Thomas D. "Invocation of the Trinity and the Tradition of the *Lorica* in Old English Poetry." *Speculum* 56/2 (1981): 259–67.
Hill, Thomas D. "*Beowulf* and Conversion History." In *The Dating of Beowulf: A Reassessment*, edited by Leonard Neidorf, 191–201. Cambridge: D. S. Brewer, 2014.
Hillgarth, J. N. "Ireland and Spain in the Seventh Century." *Peritia* 3 (1984): 1–16.
Hogan, Edmund, SJ. *Onomasticon Goedelicum Locorum et Tribuum Hiberniae et Scotiae: An Index, with Identifications, to the Gaelic Names of Places and Tribes*. Dublin: Hodges Figgis, 1910. Reprint, Dublin: Four Courts Press, 1993.
Holder, Arthur G. "Hunting Snakes in the Grass: Bede as Heresiologist." In *Listen, O Isles, unto Me: Studies in Medieval Word and Image in Honour of Jennifer O'Reilly*, edited by Elizabeth Mullins and Diarmuid Scully, 105–14. Cork: Cork University Press, 2011.
Holford-Strevens, Leofranc. "Marital Discord in Northumbria: Lent and Easter, His and Hers." In *Computus and its Cultural Context in the Latin West, AD 300–1200*, edited by Immo Warntjes and Dáibhí Ó Cróinín, 143–58. Turnhout: Brepols, 2010.
Holford-Strevens, Leofranc. "Church Politics and the Computus: From Milan to the Ends of the Earth." In *The Easter Controversy of Late Antiquity and the Early Middle Ages, Its Manuscripts, Texts, and Tables*, edited by Immo Warntjes and Dáibhí Ó Cróinín, 1–20. Turnhout: Brepols, 2011.
Holford-Strevens, Leofranc, ed. and trans. *The* Disputatio Chori et Praetextati: *The Roman Calendar for Beginners*. Studia Traditionis Theologiae 32. Turnhout: Brepols, 2019.
Hollis, Stephanie. *Anglo-Saxon Women and the Church: Sharing a Common Fate*. Woodbridge: Boydell & Brewer, 1992.
Hollo, Kaarina. "The Ulster Cycle, the Law-tracts, and the Medieval Court: The Depiction of Senchae mac Ailella, *Aurlabraid Ulad*." *Aiste* 1 (2007): 170–80.
Hollo, Kaarina. "Allegoresis and Literary Creativity in Eighth-Century Ireland: The Case of *Echtrae Chonnlai*." In *Narrative in Celtic Tradition: Essays in Honor of Edgar M. Slotkin*, edited by Joseph F. Eska, 117–28. CSANA Yearbook 8–9. Hamilton, NY: Colgate University Press, 2011.
Holthausen, Ferdinand. *Altenglisches Etymologisches Wörterbuch*. Heidelberg: Carl Winters, 1934.
Houlihan, James W. *Adomnán's Lex Innocentium and the Laws of War*. Dublin: Four Courts Press, 2020.
Howe, Nicholas. *Migration and Mythmaking in Anglo-Saxon England*. Notre Dame, IN: University of Notre Dame Press, 2001.
Howlett, David R. "The Theology of Caedmon's Hymn." *Leeds Studies in English* 7 (1974): 1–12.
Howlett, David R. "*Se giddes begang* of The Fates of the Apostles." *English Studies* 56 (1975): 385–89.
Howlett, David R. "The Provenance, Date, and Structure of *De abbatibus*." *Archaeologia Aeliana* 3, 5th series (1975): 121–30.
Howlett, David R. "The Earliest Irish Writers at Home and Abroad." *Peritia* 8 (1994): 1–17.
Howlett, David R. *The Book of Letters of Saint Patrick the Bishop*. Dublin: Four Courts Press, 1994.
Howlett, David R. "Aldhelm and Irish Learning." *Archivum Latinitatis Medii Aevi* 52 (1994–1995): 37–75.
Howlett, David R. "Five Experiments in Textual Reconstruction and Analysis." *Peritia* 9 (1995): 1–50.

Howlett, David R. *The Celtic Latin Tradition of Biblical Style*. Blackrock: Four Courts Press, 1995.
Howlett, David R. "Seven Studies in Seventh-Century Texts." *Peritia* 10 (1996): 1–70.
Howlett, David R. *British Books in Biblical Style*. Dublin: Four Courts Press, 1997.
Howlett, David R. "Hellenic Learning in Insular Latin: An Essay on Supported Claims." *Peritia* 12 (1998): 54–78.
Howlett, David R. "The Brigitine Hymn *Xpistus in nostra insula*." *Peritia* 12 (1998): 79–86.
Howlett, David R. "Further Manuscripts of Ailerán's *Canon euangeliorum*." *Peritia* 15 (2001): 22–26.
Howlett, David R. "'Tres Linguae Sacrae' and Threefold Play in Insular Latin." *Peritia* 16 (2002): 94–115.
Howlett, David R. "Early Insular Latin Poetry." *Peritia* 17–18 (2003–2004): 61–109.
Howlett, David R. "Hibero-Latin, Hiberno-Latin, and the Irish Foundation Legend." *Peritia* 19 (2005): 44–60.
Howlett, David R. *Muirchú Moccu Macthéni's 'Vita Sancti Patricii' Life of Saint Patrick*. Dublin: Four Courts Press, 2006.
Howlett, David R. "Wilbrord's Autobiographical Note and the 'Versus Sybillae de Iudicio Dei'." *Peritia* 20 (2008): 154–64.
Howlett, David R. "Hiberno-Latin Poems on the Eusebian Canons." *Peritia* 21 (2010): 162–71.
Howlett, David R. "Computus in Hiberno-Latin Literature." In *Computus and Its Cultural Context in the Latin West, AD 300–1200: Proceedings of the 1st International Conference on the Science of Computus in Ireland and Europe, Galway, 14–16 July, 2006*, edited by Immo Warntjes and Dáibhí Ó Cróinín, 259–323. Turnhout: Brepols, 2010.
Howlett, David R. "Music and the Stars in Early Irish Compositions." In *Music and the Stars: Mathematics in Medieval Ireland*, edited by Mary Kelly and Charles Doherty, 111–28. Dublin: Four Courts Press, 2013.
Howlett, David R. "The 'Altus Prosator' of Virgilius Maro Grammaticus." In *Clerics, Kings and Vikings: Essays on Medieval Ireland in Honour of Donnchadh Ó Corráin*, edited by Emer Purcell, Paul MacCotter, Julianne Nyhan, and John Sheehan, 363–88. Dublin: Four Courts Press, 2015.
Howlett, David R. "Lutting, Bede, and Hiberno-Latin Tradition." *Peritia* 31 (2020): 107–24.
Hoyland, Robert and Sarah Waidler. "Adomnán's *De Locis Sanctis* and the Seventh-Century Near East." *English Historical Review* 129, no. 539 (2014): 787–807.
Hughes, Kathleen. "Some Aspects of Irish Influence on Early English Private Prayer." *Studia Celtica* 5 (1970): 48–61.
Hughes, Kathleen. "The Celtic Church: Is This a Valid Concept?" *Cambridge Medieval Celtic Studies* 1 (Summer 1981): 1–20.
Hughes, Kathleen. "The Irish Church, 800–c.1050." In *A New History of Ireland: I Prehistoric and Early Ireland*, edited by Dáibhí Ó Cróinín, 635–55. Oxford: Oxford University Press, 2005.
Hull, Vernam E. "The Conception of Conchobor." In *Irish Texts, Fasciculus IV*, edited by J. Fraser, Paul Grosjean, J. G. O'Keeffe, 4–12. London: Sheed and Ward, 1934.
Hull, Vernam E. "Conall Corc and the Corco Luigde." *Proceedings of the Modern Language Association* 62 (1947): 887–909.
Hull, Vernam E., ed. *Longes mac n-Uislenn: The Exile of the sons of Uilsiu*. New York: The Modern Language Association of North America, 1949.

Hunter Blair, Peter. "The Origins of Northumbria." In *Archaeologia Aeliana*, edited by Peter Hunter Blair, 1–51. Newcastle upon Tyne: Society of Antiquaries, 1947.
Hunter Blair, Peter. *The World of Bede*. Cambridge: Cambridge University Press, 1970.
Hunter Blair, Peter. "Whitby as a Centre of Learning in the Seventh Century." In *Learning and Literature in Anglo-Saxon England: Studies Presented to Peter Clemoes*, edited by Michael Lapidge and Helmut Gneuss, 3–32. Cambridge: Cambridge University Press, 1985.
Ireland, Colin A., "Boisil: An Irishman Hidden in the Works of Bede." *Peritia* 5 (1986): 400–403.
Ireland, Colin A. "Some Analogues of the Old English *Seafarer* from Hiberno-Latin Sources." *Neuphilologische Mitteilungen* 92 (1991): 1–14. Reissued in *The Otherworld Voyage in Early Irish Literature, An Anthology of Criticism*, edited by J. Wooding, 143–56. Dublin: Four Courts Press, 2000.
Ireland, Colin A. "Aldfrith of Northumbria and the Irish Genealogies." *Celtica* 22 (1991): 64–78.
Ireland, Colin A. "Aldfrith of Northumbria and the Learning of a *Sapiens*." In *A Celtic Florilegium: Studies in Memory of Brendan O Hehir*, edited by Kathryn A. Klar, Eve E. Sweetser, and Claire Thomas, 63–77. Lawrence, MA: Celtic Studies Publications, 1996.
Ireland, Colin A. "Penance and Prayer in Water: an Irish Practice in Northumbrian Hagiography." *Cambrian Medieval Celtic Studies* 34 (1997): 51–66.
Ireland, Colin A. "An Irish Precursor of Cædmon." *Notes and Queries* 44, no. 1 (March 1997): 2–4.
Ireland, Colin A. "Seventh-century Ireland as a Study Abroad Destination." *Frontiers: The Interdisciplinary Journal of Study Abroad* 5 (1999): 61–80.
Ireland, Colin A., ed. and trans. *Old Irish Wisdom Attributed to Aldfrith of Northumbria: An Edition of Bríathra Flainn Fhína maic Ossu*. Tempe: Arizona Center for Medieval and Renaissance Studies, 1999. https://archive.org/details/oldirishwisdomat00aldfuoft.
Ireland, Colin A. "The Poets Cædmon and Colmán mac Lénéni: The Anglo-Saxon Layman and the Irish Professional." In *Heroic Poets and Poetic Heroes in Celtic Traditions: A Festschrift for Patrick K. Ford*, edited by Joseph Falaky Nagy and Leslie Ellen Jones, 172–82. CSANA Yearbook 3–4. Dublin: Four Courts Press, 2005.
Ireland, Colin A. "From Protected to Protector: Some Legal Language in Cú Chulainn's Boyhood Deeds." In *Archaeology and Language: Indo-European Studies Presented to James P. Mallory*, edited Martin E. Huld, Karlene Jones-Bley, and Dean Miller, 15–22. Journal of Indo-European Studies Monograph 60. Washington DC: Institute for the Study of Man, 2012.
Ireland, Colin A. "Some Irish Characteristics of the Whitby *Life* of Gregory the Great." In *Early Medieval Ireland and Europe: Chronology, Contacts, Scholarship – Festschrift for Dáibhí Ó Cróinín*, edited by Pádraic Moran and Immo Warntjes, 139–78. Turnhout: Brepols, 2015.
Ireland, Colin A. "Where Was King Aldfrith of Northumbria Educated? An Exploration of Seventh-Century Insular Learning." *Traditio* 70 (2015): 29–73.
Ireland, Colin A. "Vernacular Poets in Bede and Muirchú: A Comparative Study of Early Insular Cultural Histories." *Traditio* 71 (2016): 33–61.
Ireland, Colin A. "What Constitutes the Learning of a *Sapiens*? The Case of Cenn Fáelad." *Peritia* 27 (2016): 63–78.
Ireland, Colin A. "Visionary Poets and the Aesthetics of Vision: Perspectives on Gaelic and Old English Poetic Practices." In *Fír Fesso: A Festschrift for Neil McLeod*, edited by Anders Ahlqvist and Pamela O'Neill, 125–31. Sydney Series in Celtic Studies 17. Sydney: University of Sydney, 2018.

Ireland, Colin A. "Lutting of Lindisfarne and the Earliest Recorded Use of Dionysiac *Anno Domini* Chronology in Northumbria." *Peritia* 31 (2020): 147–63.

Ireland, Colin A. "How King Oswiu Made the Northumbrian Church Orthodox: The Social and Political Background of the 'Synod' of Whitby (664)." In *Pre-Carolingian Computus and its Regional Contexts: texts, tables, and debates*, edited by Immo Warntjes, Tobit Loevenich, Dáibhí Ó Cróinín. Turnhout: Brepols, 2021. (forthcoming).

Jackson, Kenneth H. *Language and History in Early Britain: A Chronological Survey of the Brittonic Languages 1st to 12th c. A.D.* Edinburgh: Edinburgh University Press, 1953.

Jackson, Kenneth H. "On the Northern British Section in Nennius." In *Celt and Saxon: Studies in the Early British Border*, edited by Kenneth H. Jackson, Peter Hunter Blair, Bertram Colgrave, Bruce Dickins, Joan and Harold Taylor, Christopher Brooke, and Nora K. Chadwick, 20–62. Cambridge: Cambridge University Press, 1963.

Jackson, Kenneth H. "Angles and Britons in Northumbria and Cumbria." In *Angles and Britons*, 60–84. O'Donnell Lectures. Cardiff: University of Wales Press, 1963.

Jackson, Kenneth H. "Varia: I. Bede's *Urbs Giudi*: Stirling or Cramond?" *Cambridge Medieval Celtic Studies* 2 (Winter 1981): 1–7.

Jaski, Bart. "Marriage Laws in Ireland and on the Continent in the Early Middle Ages." In *'The Fragility of her Sex'? Medieval Irishwomen in Their European Context*, edited by Christine Meek and Katharine Simms, 16–42. Blackrock: Four Courts Press, 1996.

Jaski, Bart. *Early Irish Kingship and Succession*. Dublin: Four Courts Press, 2000.

Johnson, Máire. "The *Vita I S Brigitae* and *De Duodecim Abusiuis Saeculi*." *Studia Celtica Fennica* 9 (2012): 22–35.

Johnston, Elva. "Senchán Torpéist." In *Oxford Dictionary of National Biography vol. 49*, edited by H. C. G. Matthew and Brian Harrison, 753–54. Oxford: Oxford University Press, 2004.

Johnston, Elva. *Literacy and Identity in Early Medieval Ireland*. Woodbridge: Boydell Press, 2013.

Johnston, Elva. "Exiles from the Edge? The Irish Contexts of *Peregrinatio*." In *The Irish in Early Medieval Europe: Identity, Culture and Religion*, edited by Roy Flechner and Sven Meeder, 38–52. London: Palgrave, 2016.

Johnston, Elva. *When Worlds Collide? Pagans and Christians in Late Antique Ireland*. Kathleen Hughes Memorial Lectures 16. Cambridge: Department of Anglo-Saxon, Norse and Celtic, 2018.

Jones, Charles W., ed. *Bedae opera de temporibus*. Cambridge, MA: The Medieval Academy of America, 1943.

Jones, Charles W. *Saints' Lives and Chronicles in Early England*. Ithaca, NY: Cornell University, 1947.

Jones, G. R. J. "Some Donations to Bishop Wilfrid in Northern England." *Northern History* 31 (1995): 22–38.

Jones, Gwyn and Thomas Jones, trans. *The Mabinogion*. Everyman's Library. London and Melbourne: Dent, 1949.

Jones, Nerys Ann. "Hengerdd in the Age of the Poets of the Princes." In *Beyond the Gododdin: Dark Age Scotland in Medieval Wales, Proceedings of a Day Conference held on 19 February 2005*, edited by Alex Woolf, 41–80. St. John's House Papers, 13. St. Andrews: The Committee for Dark Age Studies, 2013.

Joynt, Maud, ed. *Tromdámh Guaire*. Mediaeval and Modern Irish Series 2. Dublin: Dublin Institute for Advanced Studies, 1931.

Kavanagh, Séamus. *A Lexicon of the Old Irish Glosses in the Würzburg Manuscript of the Epistles of St. Paul*, edited by Dagmar S. Wodtko. Wien: Verlag der Österreichischen Akademie der Wissenschaften, 2001.

Keating, Geoffrey. *The History of Ireland*. Translated by Patrick S. Dinneen. 2 vols. London: Irish Texts Society, 1908–1914.

Kelleher, John V., "The *Táin* and the Annals." *Ériu* 22 (1971): 107–27. Reprinted in *Selected Writings of John V. Kelleher on Ireland and Irish America*, edited by Charles Fanning, 205–28. Carbondale and Edwardsville: Southern Illinois University Press, 2002.

Kelly, Fergus. "A Poem in Praise of Columb Cille." *Ériu* 24 (1973): 1–34.

Kelly, Fergus. "Tiughraind Bhécáin." *Ériu* 26 (1975): 66–98.

Kelly, Fergus, ed. *Audacht Morainn*. Dublin: Dublin Institute for Advanced Studies, 1976.

Kelly, Fergus. *A Guide to Early Irish Law*. Early Irish Law Series 3. Dublin: Dublin Institute for Advanced Studies, 1988.

Kelly, Fergus, ed. *Marriage Disputes: A Fragmentary Old Irish Law-Text*. Early Irish Law Series 6. Dublin: Dublin Institute for Advanced Studies, 2014.

Kelly, Patricia. "Dialekte im Altirischen?" In *Sprachwissenschaft in Innsbruck*, edited by Wolfgang Meid, H. Ölberg, and H. Schmeja, 85–89. Innsbruck: Innsbrucker Beiträge zur Sprachwissenschaft, 1982.

Kendall, Calvin B. and Faith Wallis, trans. *Bede: On the Nature of Things and On Time*. Translated Texts for Historians 56. Liverpool: Liverpool University Press, 2010.

Kendall, Calvin B. and Faith Wallis, trans. *Isidore of Seville: On the Nature of Things*. Translated Texts for Historians 66. Liverpool: Liverpool University Press, 2016.

Kenney, James F. *The Sources for the Early History of Ireland: Ecclesiastical, An Introduction and Guide*. New York: Columbia University Press, 1929. Reprint, Dublin: Pádraic Ó Táilliúir, 1979.

Keynes, Simon and Michael Lapidge, trans. *Alfred the Great: Asser's Life of King Alfred and Other Contemporary Sources*. Hammondsworth and New York: Penguin Books, 1983.

Kimpton, Bettina, ed. *The Death of Cú Chulainn: A Critical Edition of the Earliest Version of Brislech Mór Maige Muirthemni with Introduction, Translation, Notes, Bibliography and Vocabulary*. Maynooth: School of Celtic Studies, National University of Ireland, Maynooth, 2009.

Kinsella, Thomas, trans. *The Tain: Translated from the Irish Epic Tain Bo Cuailnge*. London and New York: Oxford University Press, 1970.

Kirby, D. P. "Bede's Native Sources for the *Historia Ecclesiastica*." *Bulletin of the John Rylands Library* 48 (1965–1966): 341–71.

Kirby, D. P. "Bede, Eddius Stephanus and the 'Life of Wilfrid'." *English Historical Review* 98 (1983): 101–14.

Kirby, D. P. *The Earliest English Kings*. London: Unwin Hyman, 1991.

Kirby, D. P. "Cuthbert, Boisil of Melrose and the Northumbrian Priest Ecgberht: Some Historical and Hagiographical Connections." In *Ogma: Essays in Celtic Studies in Honour of Próinséas Ní Chatháin*, edited by Michael Richter and Jean-Michel Picard, 48–53. Dublin: Four Courts Press, 2002.

Knott, Eleanor. "Why Mongán was Deprived of Noble Issue." *Ériu* 8 (1916): 155–60.

Knott, Eleanor, ed. *Togail Bruidne Da Derga*. Mediaeval and Modern Irish Series 8. Dublin: Dublin Institute for Advanced Studies, 1936.

Koch, John T., trans. *The Gododdin of Aneirin: Text and Context from Dark-Age North Britain*. Cardiff: University of Wales Press, 1997.

Koch, John T. "Why Was Welsh Literature First Written Down?" In *Medieval Celtic Literature and Society*, edited by Helen Fulton, 15–31. Four Courts Press: Dublin, 2005.

Koch, John T. "Waiting for Gododdin: Thoughts on Taliesin and Iudic-Hael, Catraeth and Unripe Times in Celtic Studies." In *Beyond the Gododdin: Dark Age Scotland in Medieval Wales, Proceedings of a Day Conference held on 19 February 2005*, edited by Alex Woolf, 177–204. St. John's House Papers, 13. St. Andrews: The Committee for Dark Age Studies, 2013.

Koch, John T., ed. and trans. *Cunedda, Cynan, Cadwallon, Cynddylan: Four Welsh Poems and Britain 383–655*. Aberystwyth: University of Wales Centre for Advanced Welsh and Celtic Studies, 2013.

Koch, John T. with John Carey, eds. *The Celtic Heroic Age: Literary Sources for Ancient Celtic Europe & Early Ireland & Wales*. 4th ed. Aberystwyth: Celtic Studies Publications, 2003.

Krajewski, Elizabeth M. G. "Kildare and the Kingdom of God: A New Reading of Cogitosus' *Vita Sanctae Brigitae*." *Peritia* 28 (2017): 91–112.

Krapp, George Philip, ed. *The Vercelli Book*. Anglo-Saxon Poetic Records 2. New York: Columbia University Press, 1932.

Krapp, George Philip and Elliott van Kirk Dobbie, eds. *The Exeter Book*. Anglo-Saxon Poetic Records 3. New York: Columbia University Press; London: Routledge and Kegan Paul, 1936.

Krusch, Bruno and Wilhelm Levison, ed. "Vita Willibrordi Archiepiscopi Traiectensis." In *Monumenta Germaniae Historica*, 113–44. Passiones Vitaeque Aevi Merovingici 5. Hanover and Leipzig: Hahn, 1920.

Lacey, Brian. "Columba, Founder of the Monastery of Derry? – 'Mihi manet incertus'." *The Journal of the Royal Society of Antiquaries of Ireland* 129 (1998): 35–47.

Lacey, Brian. *Cenél Conaill and the Donegal Kingdoms AD 500–800*. Dublin: Four Courts Press, 2006.

Lacey, Brian. "Derry, the Cenél Conaill and Cenél nEogain." In *The Modern Traveller to our Past: Festschrift in honour of Ann Hamlin*, edited by Marion Meek, 65–69. Dublin: DPK, 2006.

Lacey, Brian. *Lug's Forgotten Donegal Kingdom: The Archaeology, History and Folklore of the Síl Lugdach of Cloghaneely*. Dublin: Four Courts Press, 2012.

Lacey, Brian. *Adomnán, Adhamhnán, Eunan: Life and Afterlife of a Donegal Saint*. Dublin: Four Courts Press, 2021.

Lambkin, Brian. "Blathmac and the Céili Dé: a Reappraisal." *Celtica* 23 (1999): 132–54.

Lapidge, Michael. "Aldhelm's Latin Poetry and Old English Verse." *Comparative Literature* 31/3 (Summer 1979): 209–31.

Lapidge, Michael. "'Beowulf', Aldhelm, the 'Liber Monstrorum' and Wessex." *Studi Medievali* 23. 3rd series (1982): 151–92.

Lapidge, Michael. "Columbanus and the 'Antiphonary of Bangor'." *Peritia* 4 (1985): 104–16.

Lapidge, Michael. "A Seventh-Century Insular Debate Poem on Divorce." *Cambridge Medieval Celtic Studies* 10 (Winter 1985): 1–23.

Lapidge, Michael. "The School of Theodore and Hadrian." *Anglo-Saxon England* 15 (1986): 45–72.

Lapidge, Michael. "Bede's Metrical *Vita S. Cuthberti*." In *St Cuthbert, His Cult and His Community to AD 1200*, edited by Gerald Bonner, David Rollason and Clare Stancliffe, 77–93. Woodbridge: Boydell Press, 1989.

Lapidge, Michael. *Bede the Poet*. Jarrow Lecture. Jarrow, 1993.

Lapidge, Michael, ed. *Columbanus: Studies on the Latin Writings*. Studies in Celtic History 17. Woodbridge: The Boydell Press, 1997.

Lapidge, Michael. "*'Precamur patrem'*: An Easter Hymn by Columbanus?" In *Columbanus: Studies on the Latin Writings*, edited by Michael Lapidge, 255–63. Woodbridge: The Boydell Press, 1997.

Lapidge, Michael. *The Anglo-Saxon Library*. Oxford: Oxford University Press, 2006.

Lapidge, Michael. "The Career of Aldhelm." *Anglo-Saxon England* 36 (2007): 15–69.

Lapidge, Michael. "Aldhelm and the 'Epinal-Erfurt Glossary'." In *Aldhelm and Sherborne: Essays to Celebrate the Founding of the Bishopric*, edited by Katherine Barker with Nicholas Brooks, 129–63. Oxford and Oakville, CT: Oxbow Books, 2010.

Lapidge, Michael. "The Earliest Anglo-Latin Poet: Lutting of Lindisfarne." *Anglo-Saxon England* 42 (2013): 1–26.

Lapidge, Michael, ed. and trans. *Bede's Latin Poetry*. Oxford: Clarendon Press, 2019.

Lapidge, Michael and Michael Herren, trans. *Aldhelm: The Prose Works*. Ipswich: D. S. Brewer; Totowa, NJ: Rowman and Littlefield, 1979.

Lapidge, Michael and David Dumville, eds. *Gildas: New Approaches*. Woodbridge: Boydell Press, 1984.

Lapidge, Michael and James L. Rosier, trans. *Aldhelm, the Poetic Works*. Cambridge: D. S. Brewer, 1985.

Lapidge, Michael and Richard Sharpe. *A Bibliography of Celtic-Latin Literature 400–1200*. Dublin: Royal Irish Academy, 1985.

Larson, Heather Feldmeth. "The Veiled Poet: *Liadain and Cuirithir* and the Role of the Woman-Poet." In *Heroic Poets and Poetic Heroes in Celtic Traditions: A Festschrift for Patrick K. Ford*, edited by Joseph Falaky Nagy and Leslie Ellen Jones, 263–68. CSANA Yearbook 3–4. Dublin: Four Courts Press, 2005.

Law, Vivien. "Fragments from the Lost Portions of the *Epitomae* of Virgilius Maro Grammaticus." *Cambridge Medieval Celtic Studies* 21 (Summer 1991): 113–25.

Law, Vivien. *Wisdom, Authority and Grammar in the Seventh Century: Decoding Virgilius Maro Grammaticus*. Cambridge: Cambridge University Press, 1995.

Laynesmith, Mark. "Anti-Jewish Rhetoric in the *Life of Wilfrid*." In *Wilfrid: Abbot, Bishop, Saint*, edited by Nicholas Higham, 67–79. Donington: Shaun Tyas, 2013.

Lazzari, Loredana. "Kingship and Sainthood in Ælfric: Oswald (634–642) and Edmund (840–869)." In *Hagiography in Anglo-Saxon England: Adopting and Adapting Saints' Lives into Old English Prose (c.950–1150)*, edited by Loredana Lazzari, Patrizia Lendinara, and Claudia Di Sciacca, 29–65. Textes et Études du Moyen Âge 73. Barcelona & Madrid: Fédération Internationale des Instituts d´Études Médiévales, 2014.

Lees, Clare A. and Gillian R. Overing. "Birthing Bishops and Fathering Poets: Bede, Hild, and the Relations of Cultural Production." *Exemplaria* 6 (1994): 35–65.

Lehmann, Ruth P. M., ed. and trans. *Early Irish Verse*. Austin: University of Texas Press, 1982.

Lendinara, Patrizia. "The World of Anglo-Saxon Learning." In *The Cambridge Companion to Old English Literature*, edited by Malcolm Godden and Michael Lapidge, 264–81. Cambridge: Cambridge University Press, 1991.

Lendinara, Patrizia. "Forgotten Missionaries: St Augustine of Canterbury in Anglo-Saxon and Post-Conquest England." In *Hagiography in Anglo-Saxon England: Adopting and Adapting Saints' Lives into Old English Prose (c.950–1150)*, edited by Loredana Lazzari, Patrizia Lendinara, and Claudia Di Sciacca, 365–497. Textes et Études du Moyen Âge 73. Barcelona & Madrid: Fédération Internationale des Instituts d´Études Médiévales, 2014.

Levison, Wilhelm. *England and the Continent in the Eighth Century: The Ford Lectures Delivered in the University of Oxford in the Hilary Term, 1943*. Oxford: Clarendon Press, 1946.

Löfstedt, Bengt, ed. *Der hibernolateinische Grammatiker Malsachanus*. Uppsala: Acta Universitatis Upsaliensis, 1965.

Lord, Alfred B. *Singer of Tales*. Cambridge, MA and London: Harvard University Press, 1960.

Lot, Ferdinand, ed. *Nennius et l'Historia Brittonum*. Paris: H. Champion, 1934.

Love, Rosalind. "The Library of the Venerable Bede." In *The Cambridge History of the Book in Britain, vol. 1 c.400–1100*, edited by Richard Gameson, 606–32. Cambridge: Cambridge University Press, 2012.

Loveluck, Christopher P. "The Development of the Anglo-Saxon Landscape, Economy and Society 'On Driffield', East Yorkshire, 400–750 AD." *Anglo-Saxon Studies in Archaeology and History* 9 (1996): 25–48.

Loyn, H. R. "The Conversion of the English to Christianity: Some Comments on the Celtic Contribution." In *Welsh Society and Nationhood: Historical Essays Presented to Glanmor Williams*, edited by R. R. Davies, Lawrence Hockey, Ralph A. Griffiths, and Kenneth O. Morgan, 5–18. Cardiff: University of Wales Press, 1984.

Lucy, Sam. "From Pots to People: Two Hundred Years of Anglo-Saxon Archaeology." In *'Lastworda Betst': Essays in Memory of Christine Fell*, edited by Carole Hough, Kathryn A. Lowe, foreword by R. I. Page, 144–69. Donington: Shaun Tyas, 2002.

Mac Airt, Seán, ed. *The Annals of Inisfallen (Ms. Rawlinson B. 503)*. Dublin: Dublin Institute for Advanced Studies, 1944. Reprint, 1988.

Mac Airt, Seán. "Middle Irish Poems on World Kingship." *Études Celtiques* 6 (1952–1954): 255–80; 7 (1955–1956): 18–45; 8 (1958–1959): 98–119, 284–97.

Mac Airt, Seán. "*Filidecht* and *Coimgne*." *Ériu* 18 (1958): 139–52.

Mac Airt, Seán and Gearóid Mac Niocaill, eds. *The Annals of Ulster (to A.D. 1131)*. Dublin: Dublin Institute for Advanced Studies, 1983.

Macalister, R. A. Stewart, ed. and trans. *Lebor Gabála Érenn: The Book of the Taking of Ireland Part V*. Dublin: Irish Texts Society, 1956.

Mac Cana, Proinsias. "On the Use of the Term *Retoiric*." *Celtica* 7 (1966): 65–90.

Mac Cana, Proinsias. "Mongán mac Fiachna and *Immram Brain*." *Ériu* 23 (1972): 102–42.

Mac Cana, Proinsias. *The Learned Tales of Medieval Ireland*. Dublin: Dublin Institute for Advanced Studies, 1980.

Mac Cana, Proinsias. "Early Irish Ideology and the Concept of Unity." In *The Irish Mind: Exploring Intellectual Traditions*, edited by Richard Kearney, 56–78. Dublin: Wolfhound Press, 1985.

Mac Cana, Proinsias. "Praise Poetry in Ireland before the Normans." *Ériu* 54 (2004): 11–40.

Mac Cana, Proinsias. "The Literary Language of Medieval Ireland." In *The Cult of the Sacred Centre: Essays on Celtic Ideology*, 275–82. Dublin: Dublin Institute for Advanced Studies, 2011.

McCann, Sarah. "*Plures de Scottorum regione*: Bede, Ireland and the Irish." *Eolas* 8 (2015): 20–38.

McCann, Sarah. "Cuthbert and Boisil: Irish Influence in Northumbria." In *The Saints of North-East England, 600–1500*, edited by Margaret Coombe, Ann Mouron, and Chritiania Whitehead, 41–68. Turnhout: Brepols, 2017.

MacCarron, Máirín. "Bede, *Annus Domini* and the *Historia ecclesiastica gentis anglorum*." In *The Mystery of Christ in the Fathers of the Church*, edited by Janet E. Rutherford and David Woods, 116–34. Dublin: Four Courts Press, 2012.
MacCarron, Máirín. "Christology and the Future in Bede's *Annus Domini*." In *Bede and the Future*, edited by Peter Darby and Faith Wallis, 161–79. Farnham and Burlington, VT: Ashgate Publishing, 2014.
MacCarron, Máirín. "Bede, Irish *computistica* and *Annus Mundi*." *Early Medieval Europe* 23, no. 3 (2015): 290–307.
Mc Carthy, Daniel P. "The Origin of the *Latercus* Paschal Cycle of the Insular Celtic Churches." *Cambrian Medieval Celtic Studies* 28 (Winter 1994): 25–49.
Mc Carthy, Daniel P. "The Chronology of St Brigit of Kildare." *Peritia* 14 (2000): 255–81.
Mc Carthy, Daniel P. "On the Shape of the Insular Tonsure." *Celtica* 24 (2003): 140–67.
Mc Carthy, Daniel P. *The Irish Annals: Their Genesis, Evolution and History*. Dublin: Four Courts Press, 2008.
Mc Carthy, Daniel P. "Bede's Primary Source for the Vulgate Chronology in his Chronicles in *De temporibus* and *De temporum ratione*." In *Computus and its Cultural Context in the Latin West, AD 300–1200*, edited by Immo Warntjes and Dáibhí Ó Cróinín, 159–89. Turnhout: Brepols, 2010.
Mc Carthy, Daniel P. "Synchronisms." 2008. http://www.irish-annals.cs.tcd.ie
Mc Carthy, Daniel P. "On the Arrival of the *Latercus* in Ireland." In *The Easter Controversy of Late Antiquity and the Early Middle Ages: Its Manuscripts, Texts, and Tables*, edited by Immo Warntjes and Dáibhí Ó Cróinín, 48–75. Turnhout: Brepols, 2011.
Mc Carthy, Daniel P. "The Chronology of St Columba's Life." In *Early Medieval Ireland and Europe: Chronology, Contacts, Scholarship – Festschrift for Dáibhí Ó Cróinín*, edited by Pádraic Moran and Immo Warntjes, 3–32. Turnhout: Brepols, 2015.
Mc Carthy, Daniel P. "Analysing and Restoring the Chronology of the Irish Annals." In *Maths Meets Myths: Quantitative Approaches to Ancient Narratives*, edited by Ralph Kenna, Máirín MacCarron, and Pádraig MacCarron, 177–94. Switzerland: Springer International Publishing, 2017.
Mc Carthy, Daniel P. "The Paschal Cycle of St Patrick." In *Late Antique Calendrical Thought and its Reception in the Early Middle Ages*, edited by Immo Warntjes and Dáibhí Ó Cróinín, 94–137. Turnhout: Brepols, 2017.
Mc Carthy, Daniel P. "The Genesis and Evolution of the Irish Annals to AD 1000." *Frühmittelalterliche Studien* 52 (2018): 119–55.
Mc Carthy, Daniel P. "Recovering Years Lost from the Irish Annals." In *Lost and Found III: Rediscovering More of Ireland's Past*, edited by Joe Fenwick, 267–76. Dublin: Wordwell, 2018.
Mc Carthy, Daniel P. and Aidan Breen. "Astronomical Observations in the Irish Annals and their Motivation." *Peritia* 11 (1997): 1–43.
Mc Carthy, Daniel P. and Aidan Breen. *The Ante-Nicene Christian Pasch "De ratione paschali": The Paschal Tract of Anatolius, Bishop of Laodicea*. Dublin: Four Courts Press, 2003.
McCarthy, Mike and Daniel Curley. "Exploring the Nature of the *Fráoch Saga* – An Examination of Associations with the Legendary Warrior on Mag nAí." *Emania* 24 (2018): 55–62.
McClure, Judith. "Bede and the Life of Ceolfrid." *Peritia* 3 (1984): 71–84.
McCone, Kim. "Brigit in the Seventh Century: A Saint with Three Lives?" *Peritia* 1 (1982): 107–45.

McCone, Kim. "Werewolves, Cyclopes, *Díberga*, and *Fíanna*: Juvenile Delinquency in Early Ireland." *Cambridge Medieval Celtic Studies* 12 (1986): 1–22.

McCone, Kim. "Dubthach Maccu Lugair and a Matter of Life and Death in the Pseudo-Historical Prologue to the *Senchas Már*." *Peritia* 5 (1986): 1–35.

McCone, Kim. *Pagan Past and Christian Present in Early Irish Literature*. Maynooth: An Sagart, 1990.

McCone, Kim. "An tSean-Ghaeilge agus a Réamhstair." In *Stair na Gaeilge, in Ómos do Pádraig Ó Fiannachta*, edited by Kim McCone, Damian McManus, Cathal Ó Háinle, Nicholas Williams, Liam Breatnach, 61–219. Maigh Nuad [Maynooth]: Roinn na Sean-Ghaeilge, 1994.

McCone, Kim, ed. and trans. *Echtrae Chonnlai and the Beginnings of Vernacular Narrative Writing in Ireland: a Critical Edition with Introduction, Notes, Bibliography and Vocabulary*. Maynooth: Department of Old and Middle Irish, 2000.

McCormack, Frances. "Those Bloody Trees: The Affectivity of *Christ*." In *Anglo-Saxon Emotions: Reading the Heart in Old English Language, Literature and Culture*, edited by Alice Jorgensen, Frances McCormack, and Jonathan Wilcox, 143–62. Farnham and Burlington, VT: Ashgate, 2015.

MacCotter, Paul. *Colmán of Cloyne: A Study*. Dublin: Four Courts Press, 2004.

McCready, William D. *Miracles and the Venerable Bede*. Studies and Texts 118. Toronto: Pontifical Institute, 1994.

Mac Eoin, Gearóid. "The Lament for Cuimíne Fota." *Ériu* 28 (1977): 17–31.

Mac Eoin, Gearóid. "The Four Names of St Patrick." In *Ogma: Essays in Celtic Studies in Honour of Próinséas Ní Chatháin*, edited by Michael Richter and Jean-Michel Picard, 300–11. Dublin: Four Courts Press, 2002.

McKenna, Catherine. "Between Two Worlds: Saint Brigit and Pre-Christian Religion in the *Vita Prima*." In *Identifying the 'Celtic'*, edited by Joseph Falaky Nagy, 66–74. CSANA Yearbook 2. Dublin: Four Courts Press, 2002.

McLaughlin, Roisin. *Early Irish Satire*. Dublin: Dublin Institute for Advanced Studies, 2008.

McLeod, Neil, ed. and trans. *Early Irish Contract Law*. Sydney Series in Celtic Studies 1. Sydney: Centre for Celtic Studies, University of Sydney, 1992.

Mc Manus, Damian. "A Chronology of the Latin Loan-Words in Early Irish." *Ériu* 34 (1983): 21–71.

Mac Mathúna, Liam. "The Designation, Functions and Knowledge of the Irish Poet: a Preliminary Semantic Study." *Anzeiger der phil.-hist. Klasse der Österreichischen Akademie der Wissenschaften* 119 (1982): 225–38.

Mac Mathúna, Liam. "Irish Perceptions of the Cosmos." *Celtica* 23 (1999): 174–87.

Mac Mathúna, Séamus, ed. and trans. *Immram Brain: Bran's Journey to the Land of the Women*. Tübingen: Max Niemeyer, 1985.

McMullen, A. Joseph. "Rewriting the Ecclesiastical Landscape of Early Medieval Northumbria in the Lives of Cuthbert." *Anglo-Saxon England* 43 (2014): 57–78.

McNamara, Martin, MSC. *The Apocrypha in the Irish Church*. Dublin: Dublin Institute for Advanced Studies, 1975.

Mac Neill, Eoin. *Celtic Ireland*. Dublin: Martin Lester; London: Leonard Parsons, 1921.

Mac Neill, Eoin. "Ancient Irish Law: The Law of Status and Franchise." *Proceedings of the Royal Irish Academy* 36C (1921–1924): 265–316.

Mac Néill, Eoin. "A Pioneer of Nations." *Studies* 11 (1922): 13–28, 435–46.

Mac Shamhráin, Ailbhe and Paul Byrne. "Kings Named in *Baile Chuinn Chétchathaig* and the Airgíalla Charter Poem." In *The Kingship and Landscape of Tara*, edited by Edel Bhreathnach, 159–224. Dublin: Four Courts Press for The Discovery Programme, 2005.

Magoun, Francis P. "Bede's Story of Cædmon: The Case History of an Anglo-Saxon Oral Singer." *Speculum* 30 (1955): 49–63.

Major, Tristan. "Words, Wit, and Wordplay in the Latin Works of the Venerable Bede." *The Journal of Medieval Latin* 22 (2012): 185–219.

Malone, Kemp. "Cædmon and English Poetry." *Modern Language Notes* 76 (1961): 193–95.

Maring, Heather. "Bright Voice of Praise: An Old English Poet-Patron Convention." *Studies in Philology* 108, no. 3 (Summer 2011): 299–319.

Márkus, Gilbert. "*Adiutor laborantium* – a Poem by Adomnán?" In *Adomnán of Iona: Theologian, Lawmaker, Peacemaker*, edited by Jonathan M. Wooding, with Rodney Aist, Thomas Owen Clancy, and Thomas O'Loughlin, 145–61. Dublin: Four Courts Press, 2010.

Martin, Martin. *Description of the Western Isles of Scotland*. London: Printed for Andrew Bell, at the Cross-Keys and Bible in Cornhill, near Stocks-Market, 1703.

Mayr-Harting, Henry. *The Coming of Christianity to Anglo-Saxon England*. 3rd ed. University Park: Pennsylvania State University Press, 1991.

Meehan, Denis, ed. *Adamnan's De Locis Sanctis*. Scriptores Latini Hiberniae 3. Dublin: Dublin Institute for Advanced Studies, 1958.

Meid, Wolfgang, ed. *Táin Bó Fraích*. Mediaeval and Modern Irish Series 22. Dublin: Dublin Institute for Advanced Studies, 1967.

Meid, Wolfgang, ed. and trans. *The Romance of Froech and Findabair or the Driving of Froech's Cattle: Táin Bó Froích*. Innsbruck: Innsbrucker Beiträge zur Kulturwissenschaft, 2015.

Meroney, Howard. "Irish in the Old English Charms." *Speculum* 20 (1945): 172–82.

Meyer, Kuno, trans. *The Voyage of Bran Son of Febal to the Land of the Living: An Old Irish Saga Now First Edited, with Translation, Notes, and Glossary*. London: David Nutt in the Strand, 1895. Reprint, Felinfach: Llanerch Publishers, 1994.

Meyer, Kuno. "Colcu úa Duinechda's Scúap Chrábaid, or Besom of Devotion." *Otia Mersiana* 2 (1900–1901): 92–105.

Meyer, Kuno, ed. and trans. *Liadain and Curithir: An Irish Love-Story of the Ninth Century*. London: David Nutt, 1902.

Meyer, Kuno, ed. and trans. *Cáin Adamnáin: An Old-Irish Treatise on the Law of Adamnan*. Anecdota Oxoniensia. Oxford: Clarendon Press, 1905.

Meyer, Kuno, ed. and trans. *The Triads of Ireland*. Todd Lecture Series 13. Dublin: Hodges, Figgis, & Co.; London: Williams & Norgate, 1906.

Meyer, Kuno, ed. and trans. *The Death-tales of the Ulster Heroes*. Todd Lecture Series 14. Dublin: Royal Irish Academy, 1906. Reprint, Dublin Institute for Advanced Studies, 1993.

Meyer, Kuno, ed. and trans. *The Instructions of King Cormac mac Airt*. Todd Lecture Series 15. Dublin: Hodges, Figgis & Co.; London: Williams & Norgate, 1909.

Meyer, Kuno. *A Primer of Irish Metrics with a Glossary, and an Appendix Containing an Alphabetical List of the Poets of Ireland*. Dublin: Hodges, Figgis, & Co.; London: David Nutt, 1909.

Meyer, Kuno, ed. "*Sanas Cormaic*, an Old-Irish Glossary Compiled by Cormac úa Cuilennáin King-Bishop of Cashel in the Tenth Century." In *Anecdota from Irish Manuscripts Vol. 4*, edited by Osborn J. Bergin, Richard I. Best, Kuno Meyer, and J. G. O'Keeffe. Halle: Max Niemeyer; Dublin: Hodges, Figgis & Co., 1912.

Meyer, Kuno, ed. and trans. *Hail Brigit: An Old-Irish Poem on the Hill of Alenn*. Halle: Max Niemeyer; Dublin: Hodges, Figgis & Co., 1912.
Meyer, Kuno. "Über die Älteste irische Dichtung: I. Rhythmische alliterierende Reimstrophen." *Abhandlungen der königlich preussischen Akademie der Wissenschaften* 6 (1913): 1–40.
Meyer, Kuno. "Masu de chlaind Echdach aird." *Zeitschrift für celtische Philologie* 11 (1917): 107–13.
Meyer, Kuno. "Bruchstücke der älteren Lyrik Irlands." *Abhandlungen der königlich preussischen Akademie der Wissenschaften* 7 (1919): 3–72.
Meyvaert, Paul. *Bede and Gregory the Great*. Jarrow Lecture. Jarrow, 1964.
Miller, Molly. "Eanfrith's Pictish Son." *Northern History* 14 (1978): 47–66.
Miller, Molly. "The Dates of Deira." *Anglo-Saxon England* 8 (1979): 35–61.
Mitchell, Bruce and Fred C. Robinson. *A Guide to Old English*. 4th ed. Oxford: Basil Blackwell, 1986.
Moisl, Hermann. "The Bernician Royal Dynasty and the Irish in the Seventh Century." *Peritia* 2 (1983): 103–26.
Mommsen, Theodor, ed. "Prosperi Tironis Epitoma Chronicon." In *Monumenta Germaniae Historica*, 385–499. Auctores Antiquissimi 9. Chronica Minora 1. Berlin: Weidmann, 1892.
Monge Allen, Exequiel. "Metamorphosis of *Eoin Bruinne*: Constructing John the Apostle in Medieval Ireland." *Études Celtiques* 43 (2017): 207–24.
Moore, Samuel and Thomas A. Knott, rev. by James R. Hulbert. *The Elements of Old English: Elementary Grammar, Reference Grammar and Reading Selections*. 10th ed. Ann Arbor, MI: George Wahr Publishing, 1977.
Moran, Pádraic. "Hebrew in Early Irish Glossaries." *Cambrian Medieval Celtic Studies* 60 (Winter 2010): 1–21.
Moran, Pádraic. "'A Living Speech'? The Pronunciation of Greek in Early Medieval Ireland." *Ériu* 61 (2011): 29–57.
Moran, Pádraic. "Language Interaction in the St Gall Priscian Glosses." *Peritia* 26 (2015): 113–42.
Moran, Pádraic. "Irish Vernacular Origin Stories: Language, Literacy, Literature." In *Anfanggeschichten/Origin Stories: Der Beginn volkssprachiger Schriftlichkeit in Komparatistischer Perspektive/The Rise of Vernacular Literacy in a Comparative Perspective*, edited by Norbert Kössinger, Elke Krotz, Stephan Müller, and Pavlina Rychterová, 259–73. Mittelalter Studien 31. Munich: Fink, 2018.
Moran, Pádraic, ed. and trans. *De origine Scoticae linguae (O'Mulconry's Glossary): An Early Irish Linguistic Tract, with a Related Glossary, Irsan*. Corpvs Christianorvm, Continuatio Mediaeualis, Lexica Latina Medii Aevi 7. Turnhout: Brepols, 2019.
Morris, John, ed. and trans. *Nennius: British History and The Welsh Annals*. History from the Sources. London and Chichester: Phillimore; Totowa, NJ: Rowman & Littlefield, 1980.
Mulchrone, Kathleen, ed. *Bethu Phátraic, the Tripartite Life of Patrick I: Text and Sources*. Dublin: Hodges Figgis & Co.; London: Williams & Norgate, 1939.
Mulchrone, Kathleen. "Flannacán mac Cellaigh Rí Breg Hoc Carmen." *Journal of Celtic Studies* 1 (1949–1950): 80–93.
Mulligan, Amy C. "'The satire of the poet is a pregnancy': Pregnant Poets, Body Metaphors, and Cultural Production in Medieval Ireland." *The Journal of English and Germanic Philology* 108, no.4 (October 2009): 481–505.
Mullins, Juliet. "*Herimum in mari*: Anglo-Saxon Attitudes towards *Peregrinatio* and the Ideal of a Desert in the Sea." In *The Maritime World of the Anglo-Saxons*, edited by Stacy S. Klein,

William Schipper, and Shannon Lewis-Simpson, 59–73. Tempe: Arizona Center for Medieval and Renaissance Studies, 2014.
Murphy, Gerard. "Bards and Filidh." *Éigse* 2 (1940): 200–207.
Murphy, Gerard. "On the Dates of Two Sources Used in Thurneysen's *Heldensage*." *Ériu* 16 (1952): 145–56.
Murphy, Gerard. "Finn's Poem on May-Day." *Ériu* 17 (1955): 86–99.
Murphy, Gerard. *Early Irish Metrics*. Dublin: Royal Irish Academy, 1961.
Murray, Kevin. "The Finding of the *Táin*." *Cambrian Medieval Celtic Studies* 41 (Summer 2001): 17–23.
Murray, Kevin, ed. *Baile in Scáil 'The Phantom's Frenzy.'* Irish Texts Society 58. Dublin: Brunswick Press, 2004.
Murray, Kevin. "Dialect in Medieval Irish? Evidence of Placenames." *Studia Celtica Fennica* 2 (2005): 97–109.
Murray, Kevin. "The Manuscript Tradition of *Baile Chuinn Chétchathaig* and its Relationship with *Baile in Scáil*." In *The Kingship and Landscape of Tara*, edited by Edel Bhreathnach, 69–72. Dublin: Four Courts Press, 2005.
Nagy, Joseph Falaky. *A New Introduction to Buile Suibhne, The Frenzy of Suibhne Being the Adventures of Suibhne Geilt, a Middle-Irish Romance*. Irish Texts Society, Subsidiary Series 4. Dublin: Elo Press, 1996.
Nagy, Joseph Falaky. *Conversing with Angels and Ancients: Literary Myths of Medieval Ireland*. Dublin: Four Courts Press, 1997.
Nees, Lawrence. "Ultán the Scribe." *Anglo-Saxon England* 22 (1993): 127–46.
Neidorf, Leonard. "The Dating of *Widsið* and the Study of Germanic Antiquity." *Neophilologus* 97, no. 1 (2013): 165–83.
Neidorf, Leonard, ed. *The Dating of "Beowulf": A Reassessment*. Cambridge: D. S. Brewer, 2014.
Neville, Jennifer. *Representations of the Natural World in Old English Poetry*. Cambridge: Cambridge University Press, 1999.
Ní Bhrolcháin, Muireann. *An Introduction to Early Irish Literature*. Dublin: Four Courts Press, 2009.
Nic Dhonnchadha, Lil, ed. *Aided Muirchertaig meic Erca*. Mediaeval and Modern Irish Series 19. Dublin: Dublin Institute for Advanced Studies, 1964.
Ní Chatháin, Próinséas. "Bede's Ecclesiastical History in Irish." *Peritia* 3 (1984): 115–30.
Ní Dhonnchadha, Máirín. "The Guarantor List of *Cáin Adomnáin*, 697." *Peritia* 1 (1982): 178–215.
Ní Dhonnchadha, Máirín. "Birr and the Law of the Innocents." In *Adomnán at Birr, AD 697: Essays in Commemoration of the Law of the Innocents*, edited by Thomas O'Loughlin, 13–32. Dublin: Four Courts Press, 2001.
Ní Dhonnchadha, Máirín. "The Law of Adomnán: A Translation." In *Adomnán at Birr, AD 697: Essays in Commemoration of the Law of the Innocents*, edited by Thomas O'Loughlin, 53–68. Dublin: Four Courts Press, 2001.
Ní Dhonnchadha, Máirín. "The *Prull* Narrative in *Sanas Cormaic*." In *Cín Chille Cúile: Texts, Saints and Places, Essays in Honour of Pádraig Ó Riain*, edited by John Carey, Máire Herbert, and Kevin Murray, 163–77. Aberystwyth: Celtic Studies Publications, 2004.
Ní Dhonnchadha, Máirín. "The Beginnings of Irish Vernacular Literary Tradition." In *L'Irlanda e gli Irlandesi nell'Alto Medioevo*, 533–97. Settimane di Studio della Fondazione Centro Italiano di Studi sull'Alto Medioevo LVII. Spoleto: Presso la Sede della Fondazione, 2010.

Ní Dhonnchadha, Máirín. "On the Meaning of *Baile (Buile)*, and the Interpretation of the Poem Beginning *Rop tú mo baile*." *Éigse* 39 (2016): 231–42.
Niles, John D. "*Widsith* and the Anthropology of the Past." *Philological Quarterly* 78, no. 1, 2 (Winter 1999): 171–213.
Niles, John D. "The Myth of the Anglo-Saxon Oral Poet." *Western Folklore* 62, no. 1 and 2 (Winter & Spring 2003): 7–61. Reissued in *Old English Heroic Poems and the Social Life of Texts*, 141–87. Turnhout: Brepols, 2007.
Niles, John D. "Query: How Real Are the Geats? And Why Does this English Poem Never Mention the English?" In *Old English Heroic Poems and the Social Life of Texts*, 65–71. Turnhout: Brepols, 2007.
Ní Mhaonaigh, Máire. "Of Saxons, a Viking and Normans: Colmán, Gerald and the Monastery of Mayo." In *Anglo-Saxon/Irish Relations before the Vikings*, edited by James Graham-Campbell and Michael Ryan, 411–26. Proceedings of the British Academy 157. Oxford: Oxford University Press, 2009.
Ní Mhaonaigh, Máire. "Cormac mac Cuilennáin: King, Bishop and 'Wondrous Sage'." *Zeitschrift für celtische Philologie* 58 (2011): 109–28.
Ní Mhaonaigh, Máire. "Of Bede's 'five languages and four nations:' The Earliest Writing from Ireland, Scotland and Wales." In *The Cambridge History of Early Medieval English Literature*, edited by Clare E. Lees, 99–119. Cambridge: Cambridge University Press, 2012.
Ní Mhaonaigh, Máire. "Poetic Authority in Middle Irish Narrative: A Case Study." In *Authorities and Adaptations: The Reworking and Transmission of Textual Sources in Medieval Ireland*, edited by Elizabeth Boyle and Deborah Hayden, 263–89. Dublin: Dublin Institute for Advanced Studies, 2014.
Ní Mhaonaigh, Máire. "*Légend hÉrenn*: 'The Learning of Ireland' in the Early Medieval Period." In *"Books Most Needful to Know": Contexts for the Study of Anglo-Saxon England*, edited by Paul E. Szarmach, 85–149. Old English Newsletter Subsidia 36. Kalamazoo, MI: Medieval Institute Publications, 2016.
Ní Shéaghdha, Nessa. "The Poems of Blathmac: The 'Fragmentary Quatrains'." *Celtica* 23 (1999): 227–30.
North, Richard. *Heathen Gods in Old English Literature*. Cambridge: Cambridge University Press, 1997.
North, Richard. "OE *scop* and the Singing Welsh Bishop." In *Northern Voices: Essays on Old Germanic and Related Topics Offered to Professor Tette Hofstra*, edited by Kees Dekker, Alisdair MacDonald, and Hermann Niebaum, 99–122. Germania Latina VI, Mediaevalia Groningana n.s. 11. Leuven: Peeters, 2008.
North, Richard and Michael D. J. Bintley, eds. *Andreas: An Edition*. Liverpool: Liverpool University Press, 2015.
O'Brien, Conor. "Exegesis as Argument: The Use of Ephesians 2, 14 in Cummian's *De controversia Paschali*." *Cambrian Medieval Celtic Studies* 67 (Summer 2014): 73–81.
O'Brien, Michael A. "A Middle-Irish Poem on the Birth of Áedán mac Gabráin and Brandub mac Echach." *Ériu* 16 (1952): 157–70.
O'Brien, Michael A., ed. *Corpus genealogiarum Hiberniae I*. Dublin: Dublin Institute for Advanced Studies, 1962.
O'Brien O'Keeffe, Katherine. *Visible Song: Transitional Literacy in Old English Poetry*. Cambridge: Cambridge University Press, 1990.
Ó Carragáin, Éamonn and Alan Thacker. "Wilfrid in Rome." In *Wilfrid: Abbot, Bishop, Saint*, edited by Nicholas Higham, 212–30. Donington: Shaun Tyas, 2013.

Ó Cathasaigh, Tomás. "The Semantics of 'Síd'." *Éigse* 17 (1977–1979): 137–55.
Ó Cathasaigh, Tomás. *"Cath Maige Tuired* as Exemplary Myth." In *Folia Gadelica: Aistí ó Iardhaltaí leis a bronnadh ar R. A. Breatnach i nDeireadh a Théarma mar Ollamh le Teanga agus Litríocht na Gaeilge i gColáiste Ollscoile Chorcaí,* 1–19. Corcaí [Cork]: Cork University Press, 1983. Reissued in *Coire Sois, The Cauldron of Knowledge: A Companion to Early Irish Saga,* edited by Matthieu Boyd, 135–54. Notre Dame, IN: University of Notre Dame Press, 2014.
Ó Cathasaigh, Tomás. "On the *Cín Dromma Snechta* Version of *Togail Brludne Uí Derga*." *Ériu* 41 (1990): 103–14.
Ó Cathasaigh, Tomás. "The Oldest Story of the Laigin: Observations on *Orgain Denna Ríg*." *Éigse* 33 (2002): 1–18.
Ó Cathasaigh, Tomás. *Táin Bó Cúailnge and Early Irish Law.* Osborn Bergin Memorial Lecture 5. Dublin: University College Dublin Faculty of Celtic Studies, 2005.
Ó Cathasaigh, Tomás. "The Literature of Medieval Ireland to c.800: St Patrick to the Vikings." In *The Cambridge History of Irish Literature,* edited by Margaret Kelleher and Philip O'Leary, 9–31. Cambridge: Cambridge University Press, 2006.
Ó Cathasaigh, Tomás. "Aspects of Identity and Memory in Early Ireland." In *Narrative in Celtic Tradition: Essays in Honor of Edgar M. Slotkin,* edited by Joseph F. Eska, 201–16. CSANA Yearbook 8–9. Hamilton, NY: Colgate University Press, 2011.
Ó Cathasaigh, Tomás. "Early Irish *bairdne* 'eulogy, panegyric'." *Studia Celtica Fennica* 9 (2012): 54–61.
Ó Cathasaigh, Tomás. "The Making of a Prince: *Áed Oll fri Andud n-Áne*." In *Rhetoric and Reality in Medieval Celtic Literature: Studies in Honor of Daniel F. Melia,* edited by Georgia Henley and Paul Russel, 137–54. CSANA Yearbook 11–12. Hamilton, NY: Colgate University Press, 2014.
Ó Coileáin, Seán. "Structure of a Literary Cycle." *Ériu* 25 (1974): 88–125.
Ó Coileáin, Seán. "The Making of *Tromdám Guaire*." *Ériu* 27 (1978): 32–70.
Ó Coileáin, *Seán*. "Some Problems of Story and History." *Ériu* 32 (1981): 115–36.
Ó Coileáin, Seán. "Mag Fuithirbe Revisited." *Éigse* 23 (1989): 16–26.
Ó Concheanainn, Tomás. "A Connacht Medieval Literary Heritage: Texts Derived from Cín Dromma Snechtai through Leabhar na hUidhre." *Cambridge Medieval Celtic Studies* 16 (Winter 1988): 1–40.
O'Connor, Ralph. "Compilation as Creative Artistry: A Reassessment of 'Narrative Inconsistency' in *Togail Bruidne Da Derga*." *Cambrian Medieval Celtic Studies* 65 (Summer 2013): 1–48.
O'Connor, Ralph. *The Destruction of Da Derga's Hostel: Kingship and Narrative Artistry in a Mediaeval Irish Saga.* Oxford: Oxford University Press, 2013.
Ó Corráin, Donnchadh. "Irish Origin Legends and Genealogy: Recurrent Aetiologies." In *History and Heroic Tales: A Symposium,* edited by Tore Nyberg, Iørn Piø, and P. M. Sørenen, 51–96. Odense: Odense University Press, 1985.
Ó Corráin, Donnchadh. "Creating the Past: The Early Irish Genealogical Tradition [Carroll Lecture 1992]." *Peritia* 12 (1998): 177–208.
Ó Corráin, D. "The Church and Secular Society." In *L'Irlanda e gli Irlandesi nell'Alto Medioevo,* 261–321. Settimane di Studio della Fondazione Centro Italiano di Studi sull'Alto Medioevo LVII. Spoleto: Presso la Sede della Fondazione, 2010.

Ó Corráin, Donnchadh. "Máel Muire, the Scribe: Family and Background." In *Lebor na hUidre: Codices Hibernenses Eximii I*, edited by Ruairí Ó hUiginn, 1–28. Dublin: Royal Irish Academy, 2015.

Ó Corráin, Donnchadh, comp. *Clavis Litterarvm Hibernensivm: Medieval Irish Books & Texts (c.400 – c.1600)*. 3 vols. Corpus Christianorum Claves. Turnhout: Brepols, 2017.

Ó Corráin, Donnchadh, Liam Breatnach, and Aidan Breen. "The Laws of the Irish." *Peritia* 3 (1984): 382–438.

Ó Cróinín, Dáibhí. "The Oldest Irish Names for the Days of the Week." *Ériu* 32 (1981): 95–114. Reissued in *Early Irish History and Chronology*, 7–27. Dublin: Four Courts Press, 2003.

Ó Cróinín, Dáibhí. "A Seventh-century Irish Computus from the Circle of Cummianus." *Proceedings of the Royal Irish Academy* 82C (1982): 405–30.

Ó Cróinín, Dáibhí. "Mo-Sinnu moccu Min and the Computus of Bangor." *Peritia* 1 (1982): 281–95. Reissued in *Early Irish History and Chronology*, 35–47. Dublin: Four Courts Press, 2003.

Ó Cróinín, Dáibhí. "Pride and Prejudice." *Peritia* 1 (1982): 352–62.

Ó Cróinín, Dáibhí. "Early Irish Annals from Easter Tables: A Case Restated." *Peritia* 2 (1983): 74–86. Reissued in *Early Irish History and Chronology*, 76–86. Dublin: Four Courts Press, 2003.

Ó Cróinín, Dáibhí. "The Irish Provenance of Bede's Computus." *Peritia* 2 (1983): 229–47. Reissued in *Early Irish History and Chronology*, 173–90. Dublin: Four Courts Press, 2003.

Ó Cróinín, Dáibhí, ed. *The Irish Sex Aetates Mundi*. Dublin: Dublin Institute for Advanced Studies, 1983.

Ó Cróinín, Dáibhí. "Rath Melsigi, Willibrord and the Earliest Echternach Manuscripts." *Peritia* 3 (1984): 17–49.

Ó Cróinín, Dáibhí. "Cummianus Longus and the Iconography of Christ and the Apostles in Early Irish Literature." In *Sages, Saints and Storytellers: Celtic Studies in Honour of Professor James Carney*, edited by Donnchadh Ó Corráin, Liam Breatnach, and Kim McCone, 268–79. Maynooth Monographs 2. Maynooth: An Sagart, 1989.

Ó Cróinín, Dáibhí. "The Date, Provenance and Earliest Use of the Works of Virgilius Maro Grammaticus." In *Tradition und Wertung: Festschrift Franz Brunhölzl zum 65. Geburtstag*, edited by Günter Bernt, Fidel Rädle, and Gabriel Silagi, 13–22. Sigmaringen: Thorbecke, 1989. Reissued in *Early Irish History and Chronology*, 191–200. Dublin: Four Courts Press, 2003.

Ó Cróinín, Dáibhí. "A New Seventh-Century Irish Commentary on Genesis." *Sacris Erudiri* 40 (2001): 231–65.

Ó Cróinín, Dáibhí. "Bede's Irish Computus." In *Early Irish History and Chronology*, 201–12. Dublin: Four Courts Press, 2003.

Ó Cróinín, Dáibhí. "The First Century of Anglo-Irish Relations (AD 600–700)." 31st O'Donnell Lecture. Dublin: National University of Ireland, 2003.

Ó Cróinín, Dáibhí. "A Tale of Two Rules: Benedict and Columbanus." In *The Irish Benedictines: A History*, edited by Martin Browne, OSB, and Colmán Ó Clabaigh, OSB, 11–24. Dublin: Columba Press, 2005.

Ó Cróinín, Dáibhí. ed. *A New History of Ireland I: Prehistoric and Early Ireland*. Oxford: Oxford University Press, 2005.

Ó Cróinín, Dáibhí. "Chapter VII: Ireland, 400–800." In *A New History of Ireland I: Prehistoric and Early Ireland*, edited by Dáibhí Ó Cróinín, 182–234. Oxford: Oxford University Press, 2005.

Ó Cróinín, Dáibhí. "Willibrord und die frühe angelsächsische Missionierung Kontinentaleuropas." In *CREDO Christianisierung Europas im Mittelalter, Band I: Essays*, edited by Christoph Stiegemann, Martin Kroker, and Wolfgang Walter, 239–49. Petersberg: Michael Imhof Verlag, 2013.

Ó Cróinín, Dáibhí. *Early Medieval Ireland, 400–1200*. 2nd ed. London and New York: Routledge, 2017.

Ó Cróinín, Dáibhí. "The Political Background to Columbanus's Irish Career." In *Columbanus and the Peoples of Post-Roman Europe*, edited by Alexander O'Hara, 53–68. Oxford: Oxford University Press, 2018.

O Daly, Máirín. "A Chóicid Choín Chairpri Crúaid." *Éigse* 10, no. 2 (1962–1963): 177–97.

Ó Dónaill, Caoimhín, ed. and trans. *Talland Étair: A Critical Edition with Introduction, Translation, Textual Notes, Bibliography and Vocabulary*. Maynooth Medieval Irish Texts 4. Maynooth: Department of Old and Middle Irish, 2005.

O'Donnell, Daniel Paul. *Cædmon's Hymn: A Multimedia Study, Archive and Edition*. Cambridge: D. S. Brewer, 2005.

O'Donnell, Thomas. "The Old English *Durham*, the *Historia de Sancto Cuthberto*, and the Unreformed in Late Anglo-Saxon Literature." *Journal of English and Germanic Philology* 113, no. 2 (2014): 131–55.

O'Donovan, John, ed. and trans. *Annála Rioghachta Éireann: Annals of the Kingdom of Ireland by the Four Masters, from the Earliest Period to the Year 1616*. 7 vols. Dublin: Hodges & Smith, 1848–51.

Ó Fiaich, Rev. Thomas. "Cérbh é Ninine Éigeas?" *Seanchas Ardmhacha* (1961–1962): 95–100.

Ó hAodha, D. "Rechtgal úa Siadail, A Famous Poet of the Old Irish Period." In *Seanchas: Studies in Early and Medieval Irish Archaeology, History and Literature in Honour of Francis J. Byrne*, edited by Alfred P. Smyth, 192–98. Dublin: Four Courts Press, 2000.

O'Hara, Alexander. "Columbanus *ad Locum*: The Establishment of the Monastic Foundations." *Peritia* 26 (2015): 143–70.

O'Hara, Alexander and Ian Wood, ed. and trans. *Jonas of Bobbio: Life of Columbanus, Life of John of Réomé, and Life of Vedast*. Translated Texts for Historians 64. Liverpool: Liverpool University Press, 2017.

Ohashi, Masako. "The Easter Table of Victorius of Aquitaine in Early Medieval England." In *The Easter Controversy of Late Antiquity and the Early Middle Ages: Its Manuscripts, Texts, and Tables*, edited by Immo Warntjes and Dáibhí Ó Cróinín, 150–72. Turnhout: Brepols, 2011.

Ó hUiginn, Ruairí. "The Background and Development of *Táin Bó Cúailnge*." In *Aspects of the Táin*, edited by J. P. Mallory, 29–67. Belfast: December Publications, 1992.

Ó hUiginn, Ruairí, ed. *Lebor na hUidre: Codices Hibernenses Eximii I*. Dublin: Royal Irish Academy, 2015.

Okasha, Elisabeth. "The Inscribed Stones from Hartlepool." In *Northumbria's Golden Age*, edited by Jane Hawkes and Susan Mills, 113–25. Thrupp: Sutton Publishinng, 1999.

O'Keeffe, J. G., ed. and trans. *Buile Suibhne (The Frenzy of Suibhne) Being the Adventures of Suibhne Geilt, A Middle-Irish Romance*. Irish Texts Society 12. London: David Nutt, 1913.

O'Leary, Aideen. "The Identities of the Poet(s) Mac Coisi: A Reinvestigation." *Cambrian Medieval Celtic Studies* 38 (Winter 1999): 53–71.

O'Leary, Philip. "*Fír Fer*: An Internalized Ethical Concept in Early Irish Literature?" *Éigse* 22 (1987): 1–14.

Olmstead, Garrett. "The Earliest Narrative Version of the *Táin*: Seventh-century Poetic References to *Táin bó Cúailnge*." *Emania* 10 (1992): 5–17.

O'Loughlin, Thomas. "The Exegetical Purpose of Adomnán's *De locis sanctis*." *Cambridge Medieval Celtic Studies* 24 (Winter 1992): 37–53.

O'Loughlin, Thomas. *Celtic Theology: Humanity, World and God in Early Irish Writings*. London and New York: Continuum, 2000.

O'Loughlin, Thomas. "Monasteries and Manuscripts: The Transmission of Latin Learning in Early Medieval Ireland." In *Information, Media and Power through the Ages*, edited by Hiram Morgan, 46–64. Dublin: University College Dublin Press, 2001.

O'Loughlin, Thomas, ed. *Adomnán at Birr, AD 697: Essays in Commemoration of the Law of the Innocents*. Dublin: Four Courts Press, 2001.

O'Loughlin, Thomas. "'A Celtic Theology': Some Awkward Questions and Observations." In *Identifying the 'Celtic'*, edited by Joseph Falaky Nagy, 49–65. CSANA Yearbook 2. Dublin: Four Courts Press, 2002.

O'Loughlin, Thomas. *Discovering Saint Patrick*. London: Darton, Longman & Todd, 2005.

O'Loughlin, Thomas. *Adomnán and the Holy Places: The Perceptions of an Insular Monk on the Locations of the Biblical Drama*. London and New York: T & T Clark, 2007.

O'Loughlin, Thomas. "The *De locis sanctis* as a Liturgical Text." In *Adomnán of Iona: Theologian, Lawmaker, Peacemaker*, edited by Jonathan Wooding, with Rodney Aist, Thomas Owen Clancy, and Thomas O'Loughlin, 181–92. Dublin: Four Courts Press, 2010.

Ó Máille, Tomás. "The Authorship of the Culmen." *Ériu* 9 (1921–1923): 71–76.

Ó Néill, Pádraig. "The Background to the *Cambrai Homily*." *Ériu* 32 (1981): 137–48.

Ó Néill, Pádraig. "*Romani* Influences on Seventh-Century Hiberno-Latin Literature." In *Irland und Europa: Die Kirche im Frühmittlealter/Ireland and Europe: The Early Church*, edited by Próinséas Ní Chatháin and Michael Richter, 280–90. Stuttgart: Klett-Cotta, 1984.

Ó Néill, Pádraig. "The Latin Colophon to the 'Táin Bó Cúailnge' in the Book of Leinster: A Critical View of Old Irish Literature." *Celtica* 23 (1999): 269–75.

O'Neill [Ó Néill], Patrick [Pádraig], ed. *King Alfred's Old English Prose Translation of the First Fifty Psalms*. Cambridge, MA: Medieval Academy of America, 2001.

Ó Néill, Pádraig. *Biblical Study and Mediaeval Gaelic History*. Quiggin Pamphlets on the Sources of Mediaeval Gaelic History 6. Cambridge: Department of Anglo-Saxon, Norse, and Celtic, 2003.

O'Neill [Ó Néill], Patrick [Pádraig]. "The Irish Role in the Origins of the Old English Alphabet: A Re-assessment." In *Anglo-Saxon/Irish Relations before the Vikings*, edited by James Graham-Campbell and Michael Ryan, 3–22. Proceedings of the British Academy 157. Oxford: Oxford University Press, 2009.

O'Neill, Timothy. *The Irish Hand: Scribes and Their Manuscripts from the Earliest Times*. Rev. ed. Cork: Cork University Press, 2014.

Opland, Jeff. *Anglo-Saxon Oral Poetry: A Study of the Traditions*. New Haven, CT and London: Yale University Press, 1980.

O'Rahilly, Cecile, ed. and trans. *Táin Bó Cúalnge from the Book of Leinster*. Dublin: Dublin Institute for Advanced Studies, 1967.

O'Rahilly, Cecile, ed. and trans. *Táin Bó Cúailnge: Recension I*. Dublin: Dublin Institute for Advanced Studies, 1976.

O'Rahilly, Thomas F. *Early Irish History and Mythology*. Dublin: Dublin Institute for Advanced Studies, 1946.

O'Reilly, Edward. *Containing a Chronological Account of Nearly Four Hundred Irish Writers Commencing with Earliest Account of Irish History, and Carried Down to . . . 1750; with a Descriptive Catalogue of Such of Their Works as Are Still Extant in Verse or Prose,*

*Consisting of Upwards of One Thousand Separate Tracts*. Transactions of the Iberno-Celtic Society for 1820. Vol. I, Part I. Dublin: A. O'Neill at the Minerva Printing Office, 1820.
Ó Riain, Pádraig, ed. *Cath Almaine*. Mediaeval and Modern Irish Series 25. Dublin: Dublin Institute for Advanced Studies, 1978.
Ó Riain, Pádraig, ed. *Corpus Genealogiarum Sanctorum Hiberniae*. Dublin: Dublin Institute for Advanced Studies, 1985.
Ó Riain, Pádraig. "Sanctity and Politics in Connacht c. 1100: The Case of St Fursa." *Cambridge Medieval Celtic Studies* 17 (1989): 1–14.
Ó Riain, Pádraig. "The Tallaght Martyrologies, Redated." *Cambridge Medieval Celtic Studies* 20 (1990): 21–38.
Ó Riain, Pádraig. *Anglo-Saxon Ireland: The Evidence of the Martyrology of Tallaght*. H. M. Chadwick Memorial Lecture 3. Cambridge: Department of Anglo-Saxon, Norse, and Celtic, 1993.
Ó Riain, Pádraig. "The Martyrology of Óengus: The Transmission of the Text." *Studia Hibernica* 31 (2000–2001): 221–42.
Ó Riain, Pádraig. *Feastdays of the Saints: A History of Irish Martyrologies*. Subsidia hagiographica 86. Bruxelles: Société des Bollandistes, 2006.
Ó Riain, Pádraig. *A Dictionary of Irish Saints*. Dublin: Four Courts Press, 2011.
Orchard, Andy P. McD. "'Audite omnes amantes': A Hymn in Patrick's Praise." In *St Patrick*, edited by David N. Dumville, with Lesley Abrams, T. M. Charles-Edwards, Alicia Corrĕa, K. R. Dark, K. L. Maund, and A. P. McD. Orchard, 153–74. Woodbridge: Boydell Press, 1993.
Orchard, Andy P. McD. *The Poetic Art of Aldhelm*. Cambridge: Cambridge University Press, 1994.
Orchard, Andy P. McD. "The *Hisperica Famina* as Literature." *The Journal of Medieval Latin* 10 (2000): 1–45.
Orchard, Andy P. McD. *A Critical Companion to "Beowulf."* Cambridge: D. S. Brewer, 2003.
Orchard, Andy P. McD. "Aldhelm's Library." In *The Cambridge History of the Book in Britain, vol. 1 c.400–1100*, edited by Richard Gameson, 591–605. Cambridge: Cambridge University Press, 2012.
Oroz Reta, José and Manuel A. Marcos Casquero, ed. and trans. *San Isidoro de Sevilla: Etimologías, Edición Bilingüe*. 2 vols. Madrid: Biblioteca de Auctores Cristianos, 1983, 1993.
Orschel, Vera. "Mag nEó na Sacsan: An English Colony in Ireland in the Seventh and Eighth Centuries." *Peritia* 15 (2001): 81–107.
Orschel, Vera. "The Early History of Mayo of the Saxons." In *Mayo: History and Society*, edited by Gerald Nolan and Nollaig Ó Muraíle, 77–99. Dublin: Geography Publications, 2014.
Ortenberg, Veronica. "The Anglo-Saxon Church and the Papacy." In *The English Church and the Papacy in the Middle Ages*, edited by C. H. Lawrence, 29–62. New York: Fordham University Press, 1965. Revised, Stroud: Sutton Publishing, 1999.
Oskamp, Hans P. A., ed. *The Voyage of Máel Dúin: A Study in Early Irish Voyage Literature*. Gröningen: Wolters-Noordhoff, 1970.
O'Sullivan, Tomás. "Texts and Transmissions of *Scúap Chrábaid:* An Old-Irish Litany in its Manuscript Context." *Studia Celtica Fennica* 7 (2010): 26–47.
O'Sullivan, Tomás. "The Anti-Pelagian Motif of the 'Naturally Good' Pagan in Adomnán's *Vita Columbae*." In *Adomnán of Iona: Theologian, Lawmaker, Peacemaker*, edited by

Jonathan M. Wooding, with Rodney Aist, Thomas Owen Clancy, and Thomas O'Loughlin, 253–73. Dublin: Four Courts Press, 2010.

Padel, Oliver J. "Aneirin and Taliesin: Sceptical Speculations." In *Beyond the Gododdin: Dark Age Scotland in Medieval Wales, Proceedings of a Day Conference held on 19 February 2005*, edited by Alex Woolf, 115–52. St. John's House Papers, 13. St. Andrews: The Committee for Dark Age Studies, 2013.

Palmer, James T. "The Adoption of the Dionysian Easter in the Frankish Kingdom (c.670–c.800)." *Peritia* 28 (2017): 135–54.

Parkes, Malcolm B. *Scribes, Scripts and Readers: Studies in the Communication, Presentation, and Dissemination of Medieval Texts*. London: Hambledon Press, 1991.

Parkes, Malcolm B. *Pause and Effect: An Introduction to the History of Punctuation in the West*. Aldershot: Ashgate, 1992.

Pascual, Rafael J. "Material Monsters and Semantic Shifts." In *The Dating of "Beowulf": A Reassessment*, edited by Leonard Neidorf, 202–18. Woodbridge: D. S. Brewer, 2014.

Patterson, Nerys T. *Cattle Lords and Clansmen: The Social Structure of Early Ireland*. 2nd ed. Notre Dame, IN: University of Notre Dame Press, 1994.

Pelteret, David A. E. "The Issue of Apostolic Authority at the Synod of Whitby." In *The Easter Controversy of Late Antiquity and the Early Middle Ages: Its Manuscripts, Texts, and Tables*, edited by Immo Warntjes and Dáibhí Ó Cróinín, 150–72. Turnhout: Brepols, 2011.

Pelteret, David A. E. "Diplomatic Elements in Willibrord's Autobiography." *Peritia* 22–23 (2011–2012): 1–14.

Pelteret, David A. E. "The Northumbrian Attack on Brega in A.D. 684." In *The Land of the English Kin: Studies in Wessex and Anglo-Saxon England in Honour of Professor Barbara Yorke*, edited by Alexander James Langlands and Ryan Lavelle, 214–30. Brill's Series on the Early Middle Ages 26. Leiden: Brill, 2020.

Pheifer, J. D., ed. *Old English Glosses in the Épinal-Erfurt Glossary*. Oxford: Clarendon Press, 1974.

Picard, Jean-Michel. "The Purpose of Adomnán's *Vita Columbae*." *Peritia* 1 (1982): 160–77.

Picard, Jean-Michel. "Bede, Adomnán, and the Writing of History." *Peritia* 3 (1984): 50–70.

Picard, Jean-Michel. "Church and Politics in the Seventh Century: The Irish Exile of King Dagobert II." In *Ireland and Northern France A.D. 600–850*, edited by Jean-Michel Picard, 27–52. Dublin: Four Courts Press, 1991.

Picard, Jean-Michel. "Tailoring the Sources: The Irish Hagiographer at Work." In *Irland und Europa im früheren Mittelalter: Bildung und Literatur / Ireland and Europe in the Early Middle Ages: Learning and Literature*, edited by Próinséas Ní Chatháin and Michael Richter, 261–74. Stuttgart: Klett-Cotta, 1996.

Picard, Jean-Michel. "Adomnán's *Vita Columbae* and the Cult of Colum Cille in Continental Europe." *Proceedings of the Royal Irish Academy* 98C, no. 1 (1998): 1–23.

Picard, Jean-Michel. "Bede and Irish Scholarship: Scientific Treatises and Grammars." *Ériu* 54 (2004): 139–47.

Picard, Jean-Michel. "Bède et ses sources irlandaises." In *Bède le Vénérable, entre Tradition et Postérité*, edited by Stéphane Lebecq, Michel Perrin, and Olivier Szerwiniak, 43–62. Villeneuve d'Ascq: Institut de recherches historiques du Septentrion, 2005. http://hleno.revues.org/310.

Picard, Jean-Michel. "Schaffhausen, Stadtbibliothek, Generalia 1: The History of the Manuscript." In *The Schaffhausen Adomnán (Schaffhausen, Stadtbibliothek, MS Generalia*

*1) Part II Commentary*, edited by Damian Bracken and Eric Graff, 56–69. Irish Manuscripts in Facsimile I. Cork: Cork University Press, 2014.

Pitman, James Hall, trans. *The Riddles of Aldhelm*. Yale Studies in English 67. New Haven, CT: Yale University Press, 1925.

Plummer, Carolus [Charles], ed. *Venerabilis Baedae Opera Historica*. 2 vols. Oxford: Clarendon Press, 1896.

Plummer, Carolus [Charles], ed. *Vitae Sanctorum Hiberniae*. 2 vols. Oxford: Clarendon Press, 1910. Reprint, Dublin: Four Courts Press, 1997.

Plummer, Charles, ed. and trans. *Bethada Náem nÉrenn: Lives of Irish Saints*. 2 vols. Oxford: Clarendon Press, 1922.

Plummer, Charles, ed. and trans. *Irish Litanies: Text and Translation*. Henry Bradshaw Society 62. London: Henry Bradshaw Society, 1925.

Plummer, Charles and John Earle, eds. *Two of the Saxon Chronicles Parallel: Text, Appendices and Glossary*. Oxford: Clarendon Press, 1892.

Pope, John C., ed. *Seven Old English Poems*. New York and London: W. W. Norton, 1981.

Poppe, Erich. "A New Edition of *Cáin Éimíne Báin*." *Celtica* 18 (1986): 35–52.

Poppe, Erich. "The List of Sureties in *Cáin Éimíne*." *Celtica* 21 (1990): 588–92.

Poppe, Erich. "Cormac's Metrical Testament: *Mithig techt tar mo thimna*." *Celtica* 23 (1999): 300–311.

Poppe, Erich. "Reconstructing Medieval Irish Literary Theory: The Lesson of *Airec Menman Uraird maic Coise*." *Cambrian Medieval Celtic Studies* 37 (Summer 1999): 33–54.

Poppe, Erich. "The Latin Quotations in *Auraicept na nÉces*: Microtexts and Their Transmission." In *Ireland and Europe in the Early Middle Ages: Texts and Transmission / Irland und Europa im früheren Mittelalter: Texte und Überlieferung*, edited by Próinséas Ní Chatháin and Michael Richter, 296–312. Four Courts Press: Dublin, 2002.

Poppe, Erich. *Of Cycles and Other Critical Matters. Some Issues of Medieval Irish Literary History and Criticism*. E. C. Quiggin Memorial Lectures 9. Cambridge: Department of Anglo-Saxon, Norse and Celtic, 2008.

Prosopography of Anglo-Saxon England (PASE). http://www.pase.ac.uk/index.html.

Pryce, Huw. "Conversions to Christianity." In *A Companion to the Early Middle Ages: Britain and Ireland, c.500–c.1100*, edited by Pauline Stafford, 143–59. Chichester: Wiley-Blackwell, 2009.

Purcell, Emer, Paul MacCotter, Julianne Nyhan, and John Sheehan, eds. *Clerics, Kings and Vikings: Essays on Medieval Ireland in Honour of Donnchadh Ó Corráin*. Dublin: Four Courts Press, 2015.

Qiu, Fangzhe. "Narratives in Early Irish Law: A Typological Study." In *Medieval Irish Law: Text and Context*, edited by Anders Ahlqvist and Pamela O'Neill, 111–41. Sydney: Celtic Studies Foundation, 2013.

Qiu, Fangzhe. "The Ulster Cycle in the Law Tracts." In *Ulidia 4: Proceedings of the Fourth International Conference on the Ulster Cycle of Tales*, edited by Mícheál Ó Mainnín and Gregory Toner, 9–22. Dublin: Four Courts Press, 2017.

Raby, F. J. E. *A History of Christian-Latin Poetry from the Beginnings to the Close of the Middle Ages*. 2nd ed. Oxford: Clarendon Press, 1953.

Rackham, Oliver, trans. *Transitus Beati Fursei: A Translation of the 8th Century Manuscript Life of Saint Fursey*. Norwich: Fursey Pilgrims, 2007.

Radner, Joan N. ed. *Fragmentary Annals of Ireland*. Dublin: Dublin Institute for Advanced Studies, 1978.

Radner, Joan N. "'Men Will Die': Poets, Harpers, and Women in Early Irish Literature." In *Celtic Language, Celtic Culture: A Festschrift for Eric P. Hamp*, edited by Ann T. E. Matonis and Daniel F. Melia, 172–86. Van Nuys, CA: Ford & Bailie, 1990.

Rauer, Christine, ed. and trans. *The Old English Martyrology: Edition, Translation and Commentary*. Cambridge: D. S. Brewer, 2013.

Raw, Barbara. "Alfredian Piety: The Book of Nunnaminster." In *Alfred the Wise: Studies in Honour of Janet Bately on the Occasion of her Sixty-Fifth Birthday*, edited by Jane Roberts and Janet L. Nelson with Malcolm Godden, 145–53. Cambridge: D. S. Brewer, 1997.

Ray, Roger. "Who Did Bede Think He Was?" In *Innovation and Tradition in the Writings of The Venerable Bede*, edited by Scott DeGregorio, 37–63. Morgantown: West Virginia University Press, 2006.

Rees, Alwyn and Brinley Rees. *Celtic Heritage: Ancient Tradition in Ireland and Wales*. London: Thames and Hudson, 1961.

Richards, Melville, ed. *Breudwyt Ronabwy, allan o'r Llyfr Goch o Hergest*. Caerdydd [Cardiff]: Gwasg Pryfysgol Cymru, 1948.

Riché, Pierre. *Education and Culture in the Barbarian West from the Sixth through the Eighth Century*. Translated by John J. Contreni. Columbia, SC: University of South Carolina Press, 1976.

Richter, Michael. "The Personnel of Learning in Early Medieval Ireland." In *Irland und Europa im früheren Mittelalter, Bildung und Literatur / Ireland and Europe in the Early Middle Ages, Learning and Literature*, edited by Próinséas Ní Chatháin and Michael Richter, 275–308. Stuttgart: Klett-Cotta, 1996.

Richter, Michael. *Ireland and Her Neighbours in the Seventh Century*. Dublin: Four Courts Press, 1999.

Richter, Michael. *Bobbio in the Early Middle Ages, the Abiding Legacy of Columbanus*. Dublin: Four Courts Press, 2008.

Ritari, Katja. "'Whence Is the Origin of the Gaels': Remembering the Past in Irish Pseudohistorical Poems." *Peritia* 28 (2017): 155–76.

Robinson, Fred C. "*Beowulf*." In *The Cambridge Companion to Old English Literature*, edited by Malcolm Godden and Michael Lapidge, 142–59. Cambridge: Cambridge University Press, 1991.

Rollason, David and Lynda Rollason, eds. *The Durham "Liber Vitae:" London, British Library, MS Cotton Domitian A.VII*. 3 vols. London: The British Library, 2007.

Rowland, Jenny, ed. and trans. *Early Welsh Saga Poetry: A Study and Edition of the "Englynion."* Cambridge: D. S. Brewer, 1990.

Russell, Paul. "The Sounds of a Silence: The Growth of Cormac's Glossary." *Cambridge Medieval Celtic Studies* 15 (1988): 1–30.

Russell, Paul. "*Dúil Dromma Cetta* and Cormac's Glossary." *Études Celtiques* 32 (1996): 147–74.

Russell, Paul. "'What Was Best of Every Language': the Early History of the Irish Language." In *A New History of Ireland I: Prehistory and Early Ireland*, edited by Dáibhí Ó Cróinín, 405–50. Oxford: Oxford University Press, 2005.

Russell, Paul. *'Read it in a Glossary': Glossaries and Learned Discourse in Medieval Ireland*. Kathleen Hughes Memorial Lectures 6. Cambridge: Department of Anglo-Saxon, Norse and Celtic, 2008.

Ryan, John, SJ. *Clonmacnois: A Historical Summary*. Dublin: Stationary Office, 1973.

Ryan, Martin J. "Latin Learning and Christian Art." In *A Companion to the Early Middle Ages: Britain and Ireland, c.500–c.1100*, edited by Pauline Stafford, 177–92. Chichester: Blackwell, 2009.

Schaller, Dieter. "Die Siebensilberstrophen 'de mundi transitu' – eine Dichtung Columbans?" In *Die Iren und Europa im früheren Mittelalter I*, edited by Heinz Löwe, 468–83. Stuttgart: Klett-Cotta, 1982.

Schaller, Dieter. "'*De mundi transitu*': A Rhythmical Poem by Columbanus?" In *Columbanus: Studies on the Latin Writings*, edited by Michael Lapidge, 240–54. Woodbridge: Boydell Press, 1997.

Schrader, R. J. "Caedmon and the Monks: The *Beowulf*-Poet and Literary Continuity in the Early Middle Ages." *American Benedictine Review* 31 (1980): 39–69.

Schwab, Ute. *Caedmon*. Messina: Peloritana, 1972.

Schwab, Ute. "The Miracles of Cædmon – Revisited." *Atti dell'Accademia Peloritana* 59 (1983): 5–36.

Scowcroft, R. Mark. "*Leabhar Gabhála* Part I: The Growth of the Text." *Ériu* 38 (1987): 79–140.

Scowcroft, R. Mark. "*Leabhar Gabhála* Part II: The Growth of the Tradition." *Ériu* 39 (1988): 1–66.

Scowcroft, R. Mark. "Abstract Narrative in Ireland." *Ériu* 46 (1995): 121–58.

Scowcroft, R. Mark. "The Irish Analogues to *Beowulf*." *Speculum* 74 (1999): 21–64.

Scowcroft, R. Mark. "*Recht Fáide* and its Gloss in the Pseudo-Historical Prologue to the *Senchus Már*." *Ériu* 53 (2003): 143–50.

Sharpe, Richard. "Hiberno-Latin *laicus*, Irish *láech* and the Devil's Men." *Ériu* 30 (1979): 75–92.

Sharpe, Richard. "*Vitae S Brigidae*: The Oldest Texts." *Peritia* 1 (1982): 81–106.

Sharpe, Richard. "St Patrick and the See of Armagh." *Cambridge Medieval Celtic Studies* 4 (Winter 1982): 33–59.

Sharpe, Richard. "*Quatuor Sanctissimi Episcopi*: Irish Saints before St Patrick." In *Sages, Saints and Storytellers: Celtic Studies in Honour of Professor James Carney*, edited by Donnchadh Ó Corráin, Liam Breatnach, and Kim McCone, 376–99. Maynooth: An Sagart, 1989.

Sharpe, Richard. *Medieval Irish Saints' Lives: An Introduction to Vitae Sanctorum Hiberniae*. Oxford: Clarendon Press, 1991.

Sharpe, Richard. *Adomnán of Iona: Life of St Columba*. Harmondsworth: Penguin Books, 1995.

Sharpe, Richard. *A Handlist of the Latin Writers of Great Britain and Ireland before 1540*. Turnhout: Brepols, 1997. Reissued with Additions and Corrections, 2001.

Sharpe, Richard. "The Naming of Bishop Ithamar." *English Historical Review* 117, no. 473 (2002): 889–94.

Sharpe, Richard. "Books from Ireland, Fifth to Ninth Centuries." *Peritia* 21 (2010): 1–55.

Shippey, Tom A. "Names in *Beowulf* and Anglo-Saxon England." In *The Dating of "Beowulf:" A Reassessment*, edited by Leonard Neidorf, 58–78. Cambridge: D. S. Brewer, 2014.

Sims-Williams, Patrick. "Thought, Word and Deed: An Irish Triad." *Ériu* 29 (1978): 78–111.

Sims-Williams, Patrick. *Religion and Literature in Western England 600–800*. Cambridge Studies in Anglo-Saxon England 3. Cambridge: Cambridge University Press, 1990.

Sims-Williams, Patrick. *The Iron House in Ireland*. H. M. Chadwick Memorial Lectures 16. Cambridge: Department of Anglo-Saxon, Norse, and Celtic, 2006.

Sisam, Kenneth. *Studies in the History of Old English Literature*. Oxford: Clarendon Press, 1953.

Smith, A. H., ed. *Three Northumbrian Poems: Cædmon's Hymn, Bede's Death Song and The Leiden Riddle*. London: Methuen, 1933. Revised, Exeter: University of Exeter, 1978.

Smith, Julia M. H. "Cursing and Curing, or the Practice of Christianity in Eighth-Century Rome." In *Italy and Early Medieval Europe: Papers for Chris Wickham*, edited by Ross Balzaretti, Julia Barrow, and Patricia Skinner, 460–75. Oxford: Oxford University Press, 2018.

Smith, Peter J. "Aimirgein Glúngel Tuir Tend: A Middle-Irish Poem on the Authors and Laws of Ireland." *Peritia* 8 (1994): 120–50.

Smith, Peter J. "*Mide maigen clainne Cuind*: A Medieval Poem of the Kings of Mide." *Peritia* 15 (2001): 108–44.

Smith, Peter J., ed. and trans. *Three Historical Poems Ascribed to Gilla Cóemáin: A Critical Edition of the Work of an Eleventh-Century Irish Scholar*. Studien und Texte zur Keltologie 8. Münster: Nodus Publikationen, 2007.

Smith, Peter J., ed. and trans. *Politics and Land in Early Ireland: A Poem by Eochaid Úa Flainn*. Éitset áes ecna aíbind. Berlin: Curach Bhán Publications, 2013.

Smith, Peter. J. "An Edition of *Tigernmas mac Follaig aird*." In *Clerics, Kings and Vikings: Essays on Medieval Ireland in Honour of Donnchadh Ó Corráin*, edited by Emer Purcell, Paul MacCotter, Julianne Nyhan, and John Sheehan, 458–76. Dublin: Four Courts Press, 2015.

Smith, Roland M. "On the Briatharthecosc Conculaind." *Zeitschrift für celtische Philologie* 15 (1925): 187–92.

Smithers, G. V. "The Meaning of *The Seafarer* and *The Wanderer*." *Medium Ævum* 26 (1957): 137–53.

Smyth, Alfred P. *Celtic Leinster: Towards an Historical Geography of Early Irish Civilization A.D. 500–1600*. Blackrock: Irish Academic Press, 1982.

Smyth, Alfred P. *Warlords and Holy Men: Scotland AD 80–1000*. Edinburgh: Edinburgh University Press, 1984.

Smyth, Marina. "The Physical World in Seventh-Century Hiberno-Latin Texts." *Peritia* 5 (1986): 201–34.

Smyth, Marina. *Understanding the Universe in Seventh-Century Ireland*. Woodbridge: Boydell Press, 1996.

Smyth, Marina. "The Date and Origin of *Liber de ordine creaturarum*." *Peritia* 17–18 (2003–2004): 1–39.

Smyth, Marina. "The Seventh-Century Hiberno-Latin Treatise *Liber de ordine creaturarum*: A Translation." *Journal of Medieval Latin* 21 (2011): 137–222.

Smyth, Marina. "From Observation to Scientific Speculation in Seventh-Century Ireland." In *Music and the Stars: Mathematics in Medieval Ireland*, edited by Mary Kelly and Charles Doherty, 73–98. Dublin: Four Courts Press, 2013.

Smyth, Marina. "The Word of God and Early Medieval Irish Cosmology: Scripture and the Creating Word." In *Celtic Cosmology: Perspectives from Ireland and Scotland*, edited by Jacqueline Borsje, Ann Dooley, Séamus Mac Mathúna, and Gregory Toner, 112–43. Toronto: Pontifical Institute of Medieval Studies, 2014.

Souter, Alexander, comp. *A Glossary of Later Latin to 600 A.D.* Oxford: Clarendon Press, 1949.

Stancliffe, Clare. "Red, White and Blue Martyrdom." In *Ireland in Early Medieval Europe: Studies in Memory of Kathleen Hughes*, edited by Dorothy Whitelock, Rosamond McKitterick, and David Dumville, 21–46. Cambridge: Cambridge University Press, 1982.

Stancliffe, Clare. "Kings who Opted Out." In *Ideal and Reality in Frankish and Anglo-Saxon Society: Studies Presented to J. M. Wallace-Hadrill*, edited by Patrick Wormald with Donald Bullough and Roger Collins, 154–76. Oxford: Blackwell, 1983.

Stancliffe, Clare. "Cuthbert and the Polarity between Pastor and Solitary." In *St Cuthbert, His Cult and His Community to AD 1200*, edited by Gerald Bonner, David Rollason, and Clare Stancliffe, 21–44. Woodbridge: Boydell Press, 1989.

Stancliffe, Clare. "Venantius Fortunatus, Ireland, Jerome: The Evidence of *Precamur Patrem*." *Peritia* 10 (1996): 91–97.

Stancliffe, Clare. "The Thirteen Sermons Attributed to Columbanus and the Question of Their Authorship." In *Columbanus: Studies on the Latin Writings*, edited by Michael Lapidge, 93–202. Woodbridge: Boydell Press, 1997.

Stancliffe, Clare. "Creator and Creation: A Preliminary Investigation of Early Irish Views and their Relationship to Biblical and Patristic Tradition." *Cambrian Medieval Celtic Studies* 58 (Winter 2009): 9–27.

Stancliffe, Clare. "'Charity with Peace': Adomnán and the Easter Question." In *Adomnán of Iona: Theologian, Lawmaker, Peacemaker*, edited by Jonathan M. Wooding, with Rodney Aist, Thomas Owen Clancy, and Thomas O'Loughlin, 51–68. Dublin: Four Courts Press, 2010.

Stancliffe, Clare. "Disputed Episcopacy: Bede, Acca, and the Relationship between Stephen's *Life of St Wilfrid* and the Early Prose Lives of St Cuthbert." *Anglo-Saxon England* 41 (2012): 7–39.

Stancliffe, Clare. "Dating Wilfrid's Death and Stephen's *Life*." In *Wilfrid: Abbot, Bishop, Saint*, edited by Nicholas J. Higham, 17–26. Donington: Shaun Tyas, 2013.

Stancliffe, Clare. "The Irish Tradition in Northumbria after the Synod of Whitby." In *The Lindisfarne Gospels: New Perspectives*, edited by Richard Gameson, 19–42. Leiden: Brill, 2017.

Stancliffe, Clare and Eric Cambridge, eds. *Oswald: Northumbrian King to European Saint*. Stamford: Paul Watkins, 1995.

Stanley, E. G. "St Cædmon." *Notes and Queries* 45, no. 1 (March 1998): 4–5.

Stansbury, Mark. *Iona Scribes and the Rhetoric of Legibility*. E. C. Quiggin Memorial Lecture 16. Cambridge: Department of Anglo-Saxon, Norse and Celtic, 2014.

Stansbury, Mark. "The Schaffhausen Manuscript and the Composition of the Life of Columba." In *The Schaffhausen Adomnán (Schaffhausen, Stadtbibliothek, MS Generalia 1) Part II Commentary*, edited by Damian Bracken and Eric Graff, 70–89. Irish Manuscripts in Facsimile I. Cork: Cork University Press, 2014.

Stansbury, Mark. "Irish Biblical Exegesis." In *The Irish in Early Medieval Europe*, edited by Roy Flechner and Sven Meeder, 116–30. London and New York: Palgrave, 2016.

Stephenson, Rebecca. *The Politics of Language: Byrhtferth, Ælfric, and the Multilingual Identity of the Benedictine Reform*. Toronto: University of Toronto Press, 2015.

Stevenson, Jane. "Bangor and the *Hisperica Famina*." *Peritia* 6–7 (1987–1988): 202–16.

Stevenson, Jane. "The Beginnings of Literacy in Ireland." *Proceedings of the Royal Irish Academy* 89C (1989): 127–65.

Stevenson, Jane. *The 'Laterculus Malalianus' and the School of Archbishop Theodore*. Cambridge Studies in Anglo-Saxon England 14. Cambridge: Cambridge University Press, 1995.

Stevenson, Jane. "The Monastic Rules of Columbanus." In *Columbanus: Studies on the Latin Writings*, edited by Michael Lapidge, 203–16. Woodbridge: Boydell Press, 1997.

Stevenson, Jane. "Altus Prosator." *Celtica* 23 (1999): 326–68.
Stifter, David. "Ulster Connections of *Cín Dromma Snechtai*." In *Ulidia 4: Proceedings of the Fourth International Conference on the Ulster Cycle of Tales*, edited by Mícheál Ó Mainnín and Gregory Toner, 23–37. Dublin: Four Courts Press, 2017.
Stokes, Whitley. "The Irish Ordeals, Cormac's Adventures in the Land of Promise, and the Decision as to Cormac's Sword." In *Irische Text mit Wörterbuch 3, no. 1*, edited by Ernst Windisch and Whitley Stokes, 183–229. Leipzig: S. Hirzel, 1891.
Stokes, Whitley. "The Annals of Tigernach: Third Fragment." *Revue Celtique* 17 (1896): 119–263. Reprint, Felinfach: Llanerch Publishers, 1993.
Stokes, Whitley. "The Bodleian *Amra Choluimb Chille*." *Revue Celtique* 20 (1899): 30–55, 132–83, 248–87, 400–437.
Stokes, Whitley. "A List of Ancient Irish Authors." *Zeitschrift für celtische Philologie* 3 (1901): 15–16.
Stokes, Whitley. "The Colloquy of the Two Sages, *Immacallam in dá Thuarad*." *Revue Celtique* 26 (1905): 4–64.
Stokes, Whitley, ed. and trans. *Félire Óengusso Céli Dé: The Martyrology of Oengus the Culdee*. London: Henry Bradshaw Society, 1905. Reprint, Dublin: Dublin Institute for Advanced Studies, 1984.
Stokes, Whitley and John Strachan, eds. *Thesaurus Palaeohibernicus: A Collection of Old-Irish Glosses, Scholia, Prose and Verse*. 2 vols. Cambridge: Cambridge University Press, 1901–1903. Reprint, Dublin: Dublin Institute for Advanced Studies, 1975 (vol. 1), 1987 (vol. 2).
Story, Joanna. "The Frankish Annals of Lindisfarne and Kent." *Anglo-Saxon England* 34 (2005): 59–109.
Story, Joanna. "Bede, Willibrord and the Letters of Pope Honorius I on the Genesis of the Archbishopric of York." *The English Historical Review* 127, no. 527 (August 2012): 783–818.
Strauss, Jürgen W. "Compounding in Old English Poetry." *Folia Linguistica Historica* 1 (1980): 305–16.
Swanton, Michael, ed. *The Dream of the Rood*. Rev. ed. Exeter: University of Exeter, 1987.
Swanton, Michael, trans. and ed. *The Anglo-Saxon Chronicles*. New ed. London: Phoenix Press, 2000.
Swift, Catherine. "Tírechán's Motives in Compiling the *Collectanea*: An Alternative Interpretation." *Ériu* 45 (1994): 53–82.
Swift, Catherine. "Patrick's Conversion of Ireland to Christianity and the Establishment of Armagh." In *Two Thousand Years of Christianity and Ireland*, edited by John R. Bartlett and Stuart D. Kinsella, 25–35. Dublin: Columba Press, 2006.
Tangl, Michael, ed. *Die Briefe des heiligen Bonafatius und Lullus*. Epistolae Selectae 1. Berlin: Weidmann, 1916. Reprint, 1955.
Thacker, Alan. "Bede's Ideal of Reform." In *Ideal and Reality in Frankish and Anglo-Saxon Society: Studies Presented to J. M. Wallace-Hadrill*, edited by Patrick Wormald with Donald Bullough and Roger Collins, 130–53. Oxford: Blackwell, 1983.
Thacker, Alan. "Lindisfarne and the Origins of the Cult of St Cuthbert." In *St Cuthbert, His Cult and His Community to AD 1200*, edited by Gerald Bonner, David Rollason, and Clare Stancliffe, 103–122. Woodbridge: Boydell Press, 1989.

Thacker, Alan. "*Membra Disjecta:* The Division of the Body and the Diffusion of the Cult." In *Oswald: Northumbrian King and European Saint*, edited by Clare Stancliffe and Eric Cambridge, 97–127. Stamford: Paul Watkins, 1995.
Thacker, Alan. "Bede and the Irish." In *Beda Venerabilis: Historian, Monk and Northumbrian*, edited by L. A. J. R. Houwen and A. A. Macdonald, 31–59. Mediaevalia Groningana 19. Groningen: E. Forsten: 1996.
Thacker, Alan. "Memorializing Gregory the Great: The Origin and Transmission of a Papal Cult in the Seventh and Early Eighth Centuries." *Early Medieval Europe* 7, no. 1 (1998): 59–84.
Thacker, Alan. "Boisil." In *Oxford Dictionary of National Biography vol. 6*, edited by H. C. G. Matthew and Brian Harrison, 452. Oxford: Oxford University Press, 2004.
Thacker, Alan. "Bede and the Ordering of Understanding." In *Innovation and Tradition in the Writings of The Venerable Bede*, edited by Scott DeGregorio, 37–63. Morgantown: West Virginia University Press, 2006.
Thacker, A., "Why did Heresy Matter to Bede? Present and Future Contexts." In *Bede and the Future*, edited by Peter Darby and Faith Wallis, 47–66. London and New York: Routledge, 2014.
Thomas, Mark, Michael P. H. Stumpf, and Heinrich Härke. "Evidence for an Apartheid-like Social Structure in Early Anglo-Saxon England." *Proceedings of the Royal Society B* (Biological Sciences) 273 (2006): 2651–57.
Thornbury, Emily. "Aldhelm's Rejection of the Muses and the Mechanics of Poetic Inspiration in Early Anglo-Saxon England." *Anglo-Saxon England* 36 (2007): 71–92.
Thornbury, Emily. *Becoming a Poet in Anglo-Saxon England*. Cambridge: Cambridge University Press, 2014.
Thornton, David E. "Communities and Kinship." In *A Companion to the Early Middle Ages: Britain and Ireland, c.500–c.1100*, edited by Pauline Stafford, 91–106. Chichester: Blackwell Publishing, 2009.
Thurneysen, Rudolf. *Zu irische Handschriften und Literaturdenkmälern*. Abhandlungen der königlichen Gesellschaft der Wissenschaften zu Göttingen, Philologisch-Historische Klasse, Neue Folge 14, no. 2. Berlin: Weidmannsche Buchhandlung, 1912. Reprint in *Rudolf Thurneysen Gesammelte Schriften II*, edited by Patrizia de Bernardo Stempel and Rolf Ködderitzsch, 586–683. Tübingen: Niemeyer, 1991.
Thurneysen, Rudolf. *Die irische Helden- und Königsage bis zum siebzehnten Jahrhundert*. Halle: Max Niemeyer, 1921. Reprint, Hildesheim and New York: Georg Olms Verlag, 1980.
Thurneysen, Rudolf. "Colmān mac Lēnēni und Senchān Torpēist." *Zeitschrift für celtische Philologie* 19 (1933): 193–209.
Thurneysen, Rudolf. "*Imbas for·osndai*." *Zeitschrift für celtische Philologie* 19 (1933): 163–64.
Thurneysen, Rudolf. *A Grammar of Old Irish*. Rev. ed. Dublin: Dublin Institute for Advanced Studies, 1946.
Toner, Gregory. "Reconstructing the Earliest Irish Tale Lists." *Éigse* 32 (2000): 88–120.
Toner, Gregory. "The Ulster Cycle: Historiography or Fiction?" *Cambrian Medieval Celtic Studies* 40 (Winter 2000): 1–20.
Twomey, Michael W. "On Reading *Bede's Death Song*." *Neuphilologische Mitteilungen* (1983): 171–81.
Tyler, Damian J. "Early Mercia and the Britons." In *Britons in Anglo-Saxon England*, edited by Nicholas J. Higham, 91–101. Woodbridge: Boydell Press, 2007.
Tyler, Damian J. "Bishop Wilfrid and the Mercians." In *Wilfrid: Abbot, Bishop, Saint*, edited by Nicholas J. Higham, 275–83. Donington: Shaun Tyas, 2013.

Tyler, Elizabeth M. *Old English Poetics: The Aesthetics of the Familiar in Anglo-Saxon England.* York: York Medieval Press, 2006.
van Hamel, Anton G., ed. *Compert Con Culainn and Other Stories.* Mediaeval and Modern Irish Series 3. Dublin: Dublin Institute for Advanced Studies, 1933.
van Hamel, Anton G., ed. *Immrama.* Mediaeval and Modern Irish Series 10. Dublin: Dublin Institute for Advanced Studies, 1941. Supplementary ed., 2004.
Waddell, John. "The Cave of Crúachain and the Otherworld." In *Celtic Cosmology: Perspectives from Ireland and Scotland*, edited by Jacqueline Borsje, Ann Dooley, Séamus Mac Mathúna, and Gregory Toner, 77–92. Toronto: Pontifical Institute of Mediaeval Studies, 2014.
Wadden, Patrick. "The First English Invasion: Irish Responses to the Northumbrian Attack on Brega, 684." *Ríocht na Midhe* 21 (2010): 1–33.
Wadden, Patrick. "The Pseudo-Historical Origins of the *Senchas Már* and Royal Legislation in Early Ireland." *Peritia* 27 (2016): 141–58.
Wadden, Patrick. "Dál Riata c.1000: Genealogies and Irish Sea Politics." *The Scottish Historical Review* 95(2)no. 241 (October 2016): 164–81.
Walker, G. S .M., ed. *Sancti Columbani Opera.* Scriptores Latini Hiberniae 2. Dublin: Dublin Institute for Advanced Studies, 1957.
Wallace-Hadrill, J. M. *Bede's Ecclesiastical History of the English People: A Historical Commentary.* Oxford: Clarendon Press, 1988.
Wallis, Faith, trans. *Bede: The Reckoning of Time.* Translated Texts for Historians 29. Liverpool: Liverpool University Press, 2004.
Walsh, Maura and Dáibhí Ó Cróinín, eds. *Cummian's Letter "De Controversia Paschali" together with a Related Irish Computistical Tract "De Ratione Conputandi" Edited by Dáibhí Ó Cróinín.* Studies and Texts 86. Toronto: Pontifical Institute of Mediaeval Studies, 1988.
Ward, Benedicta, SLG. "Miracles and History, a Reconsideration of the Miracle Stories used by Bede." In *Famulus Christi, Essays in Commemoration of the Thirteenth Centenary of the Birth of the Venerable Bede*, edited by Gerald Bonner, 70–76. London: Society for Promoting Christian Knowledge, 1976.
Ward, Benedicta, SLG. "'To my dearest sister': Bede and the Educated Woman." In *Women, the Book and the Godly: Selected Proceedings of the St. Hilda's Conference, 1993, Vol. 1*, edited by Lesley Smith and Jane H. M. Taylor, 105–111. Cambridge: D. S. Brewer, 1995.
Warner, Rubie D-N., ed. *Early English Homilies from the Twelfth Century MS Vesp. D.xiv.* Early English Text Society O.S. 152. London: EETS, 1917.
Warntjes, Immo. "The Earliest Occurrence of Old English *gerīm* and its Anglo-Irish Computistical Context." *Anglia: Zeitschrift für Englische Philologie* 127, no. 1 (2009): 91–105.
Warntjes, Immo, ed. and trans. *The Munich Computus: Text and Translation, Irish Computistics between Isidore of Seville and the Venerable Bede and its Reception in Carolingian Times.* Stuttgart: Franz Steiner, 2010.
Warntjes, Immo. "The Role of the Church in Early Irish Regnal Succession – The Case of Iona." In *L'Irlanda e gli Irlandesi nell'Alto Medioevo*, 155–213. Settimane di Studio della Fondazione Centro Italiano di Studi sull'Alto Medioevo LVII. Spoleto: Presso la Sede della Fondazione, 2010.
Warntjes, Immo. "The *Computus Cottonianus* of AD 689: A Computistical Formulary Written for Willibrord's Frisian Mission." In *The Easter Controversy of Late Antiquity and the Early*

*Middle Ages*, edited by Immo Warntjes and Dáibhí Ó Cróinín, 173–212. Turnhout: Brepols, 2011.

Warntjes, Immo. "Victorius vs Dionysius: the Irish Easter controversy of AD 689." In *Early Medieval Ireland and Europe: Chronology, Contacts, Scholarship – Festschrift for Dáibhí Ó Cróinín*, edited by Pádraic Moran and Immo Warntjes, 33–97. Turnhout: Brepols, 2015.

Warren, F. E., ed. *The Antiphonary of Bangor: An Early Irish Manuscript in the Ambrosian Library at Milan*. 2 vols. London: Harrison and Sons, 1893–1895.

Watkins, Calvert. "The Etymology of Irish *Dúan*." *Celtica* 11 (1976): 270–77.

Webster, Leslie. "The Iconographic Programme of the Franks Casket." In *Northumbria's Golden Age*, edited by Jane Hawkes and Susan Mills, 227–46. Thrupp: Sutton Publishing, 1999.

Webster, Leslie and Janet Backhouse, eds. *The Making of England: Anglo-Saxon Art and Culture AD 600–900*. London: British Museum Press, 1991.

Welch, Robert, ed. *The Oxford Companion to Irish Literature*. Oxford: Clarendon Press, 1996.

West, Philip J. "Rumination in Bede's Account of Caedmon." *Monastic Studies* 12 (1976): 217–26.

White, Nora, ed. and trans. *Compert Mongáin and Three Other Early Mongán Tales: A Critical Edition with Introduction, Translation, Textual Notes, Bibliography and Vocabulary*. Maynooth Medieval Irish Texts V. Maynooth: Department of Old and Middle Irish, 2006.

White, Roger. "Managing Transition: Western Britain from the End of Empire to the Rise of Penda." *History Compass* 11, no. 8 (2013): 584–96.

Whitelock, Dorothy. "The Interpretation of *The Seafarer*." In *The Early Cultures of North-West Europe: H. M. Chadwick Memorial Studies*, edited by Cyril Fox and Bruce Dickins, 259–72. Cambridge: Cambridge University Press, 1950.

Whitelock, Dorothy. "The Pre-Viking Age Church in East Anglia." *Anglo-Saxon England* 1 (1972): 1–22.

Whitelock, Dorothy, ed. *English Historical Documents c.500–1042*. 2nd ed. London: Eyre Methuen, 1979; New York: Oxford University Press, 1979.

Whitfield, Niamh. "Lyres Decorated with Snakes, Birds and Hounds in *Táin Bó Fraích*." In *A Carnival of Learning: Essays to Honour George Cunningham*, edited by Peter Harbison and Valerie Hall, 218–31. Collegeville, MN: Cistercian Press, 2012.

Wickham, C., *Framing the Early Middle Ages: Europe and the Mediterranean 400–800*. Oxford: Oxford University Press, 2005.

Wieland, G. R. "Caedmon, the Clean Animal." *American Benedictine Review* 35 (1984): 194–203.

Williams, Ifor, ed. *Pedeir Keinc y Mabinogi allan o Lyfr Gwyn Rhydderch*. Caerdydd [Cardiff]: Gwasg Pryfysgol Cymru, 1930. Reprint, 1978.

Williams, Ifor, ed. *Canu Llywarch Hen*. Caerdydd [Cardiff]: Gwasg Pryfysgol Cymru, 1935. Reprint, 1978.

Williams, Ifor, ed. *Canu Aneirin*. Caerdydd [Cardiff]: Gwasg Pryfysgol Cymru, 1938. Reprint, 1978.

Williams, Ifor. "The Juvencus Poems." In *The Beginnings of Welsh Poetry, Studies by Sir Ifor Williams*, edited by Rachel Bromwich, 89–121. 2nd ed. Cardiff: University of Wales Press, 1980.

Willis, K. E. C. "Mythologizing Thought *sine ambiguitate* in the Irish Augustine's *De mirabilibus sacrae scripturae*." *Medium Ævum* 85, no. 2 (2016): 187–207.

Wilson, Henry A., ed. *The Calendar of St Willibrord from MS Paris. Lat. 10837*. London: Henry Bradshaw Society, 1918. Reprint, Woodbridge: Boydell Press, 1998.

Winterbottom, Michael. "Aldhelm's Prose Style and its Origins." *Anglo-Saxon England* 6 (1977): 39–76.
Winterbottom, Michael, ed. and trans. *Gildas: The Ruin of Britain and Other Works*. London and Chichester: Phillimore, 1978.
Winterbottom, Michael, ed. and trans. *William of Malmesbury "Gesta Pontificvm Anglorvm:" The History of the English Bishops*. 2 vols. Oxford: Clarendon, 2007.
Wood, Ian N. "Ripon, Francia and the Franks Casket in the Early Middle Ages." *Northern History* 26 (1990): 1–19.
Wood, Ian N. "The Continental Journeys of Wilfrid and Biscop." In *Wilfrid: Abbot, Bishop, Saint*, edited by Nicholas Higham, 200–211. Donington: Shaun Tyas, 2013.
Wood, Ian N. "The Irish in England and on the Continent in the 7th Century: Part I." *Peritia* 26 (2015): 171–98.
Wood, Ian N. "The Irish in England and on the Continent in the 7th Century: Part II." *Peritia* 27 (2016): 189–214.
Wood, Ian N. "The Roman Origins of the Northumbrian Kingdom." In *Italy and Early Medieval Europe: Papers for Chris Wickham*, edited by Ross Balzaretti, Julia Barrow, and Patricia Skinner, 39–49. Oxford: Oxford University Press, 2018.
Woods, David. "On the Circumstances of Adomnán's Composition of the *De locis sanctis*." In *Adomnán of Iona: Theologian, Lawmaker, Peacemaker*, edited by Jonathan Wooding with Rodney Aist, Thomas Owen Clancy, and Thomas O'Loughlin, 193–204. Dublin: Four Courts Press, 2010.
Woolf, Alex. "Caedwualla *Rex Brettonum* and the Passing of the Old North." *Northern History* 41, no.1 (March 2004): 5–24.
Woolf, Alex. "Dún Nechtain, Fortriu and the Geography of the Picts." *The Scottish Historical Review* 85(2), no. 220 (October 2006): 182–201.
Woolf, Alex. "Apartheid and Economics in Anglo-Saxon England." In *Britons in Anglo-Saxon England*, edited by Nick Higham, 115–29. Woodbridge: The Boydell Press, 2007.
Woolf, Alex. "The Court Poet in Early Ireland." In *Princes, Prelates and Poets in Medieval Ireland: Essays in Honour of Katharine Simms*, edited by Seán Duffy, 377–88. Dublin: Four Courts Press, 2013.
Woolf, Alex. "Sutton Hoo and Sweden Revisited." In *The Long Seventh Century: Continuity and Disconintuity in an Age of Transition*, edited by Alessandro Gnasso, Emanuele E. Intagliagta, Thomas J. MacMaster, and Bethan N. Norris, 5–17. Bern: Peter Lang, 2014.
Woolf, Alex. "Imagining English Origins." *Quaestio Insularis: Selected Proceedings of the Cambridge Colloquium in Anglo-Saxon, Norse and Celtic* 18 (2017): 1–20.
Woolf, Alex. "Columbanus's Ulster Education." In *Columbanus and the Peoples of Post-Roman Europe*, edited by Alexander O'Hara, 91–102. Oxford: Oxford University Press, 2018.
Wormald, Patrick. "Bede and Benedict Biscop." In *Famulus Christi: Essays in Commemoration of the Thirteenth Centenary of the Birth of the Venerable Bede*, edited by Gerald Bonner, 141–69. London: Society for Promoting Christian Knowledge, 1976. Reissued in *The Times of Bede: Studies in Early English Christian Society and its Historians*, edited by Stephen Baxter, 3–29. Malden, MA: Blackwell Publishing, 2006.
Wormald, Patrick. "Bede, the *Bretwaldas* and the *Gens Anglorum*." In *Ideal and Reality in Frankish and Anglo-Saxon Society: Studies Presented to J. M. Wallace-Hadrill*, edited by Patrick Wormald with Donald Bullough and Roger Collins, 99–129. Oxford: Blackwell, 1983. Reissued in *The Times of Bede: Studies in Early English Christian Society and its Historians*, edited by Stephen Baxter, 108–34. Malden, MA: Blackwell Publishing, 2006.

Wormald, Patrick. "Appendix: St. Hilda, Saint and Scholar (614–680)." In *The Times of Bede: Studies in Early English Christian Society and its Historian*, edited by Stephen Baxter, 267–76. Malden, MA: Blackwell Publishing, 2006.
Wrenn, Charles L. "The Poetry of Cædmon." *The Proceedings of the British Academy* 32 (1946): 277–95.
Wright, Charles D. "The Irish 'Enumerative Style' in Old English Homiletic Literature, Especially Vercelli Homily IX." *Cambridge Medieval Celtic Studies* 18 (Winter 1989): 27–74.
Wright, Charles D. *The Irish Tradition in Old English Literature*. Cambridge Studies in Anglo-Saxon England 6. Cambridge: Cambridge University Press, 1993.
Wright, Charles D. "From Monks' Jokes to Sages' Wisdom: The *Joca monachorum* Tradition and the Irish *Immacallam in dá Thuarad*." In *Spoken and Written Language: Relations between Latin and the Vernacular Languages in the Earlier Middle Ages*, edited by Mary Garrison, Arpád P. Órban, and Marco Mostert, 199–225. Utrecht Studies in Medieval Literacy 24. Turnhout: Brepols, 2013.
Wright, Neil. "Aldhelm's Prose Writings on Metrics." In *Aldhelm: The Poetic Works*, translated by Michael Lapidge and James L. Rosier, 181–219. Cambridge: D. S. Brewer, 1985.
Wright, Neil. "Columbanus's *Epistulae*." In *Columbanus: Studies on the Latin Writings*, edited by Michael Lapidge, 29–92. Woodbridge: Boydell Press, 1997.
Wycherley, Niamh. *The Cult of Relics in Early Medieval Ireland*. Turnhout: Brepols, 2015.
Yocum, Christopher. "Wisdom Literature in Early Ireland." *Studia Celtica* 46 (2012): 39–58.
Yorke, Barbara. *Kings and Kingdoms of Early Anglo-Saxon England*. London and New York: Routledge, 1990.
Yorke, Barbara. *Wessex in the Early Middle Ages*. Leicester: Leicester University Press, 1995.
Yorke, Barbara. "The Anglo-Saxon Kingdoms 600–900 and the Beginnings of the Old English State." In *Der frühmittelalterliche Staat – Europäische Perspektiven*, edited by Walter Pohl and Veronika Wieser, 73–86. Vienna: Austrian Academy of Sciences Press, 2008.
Yorke, Barbara. "The *Bretwaldas* and the Origins of Overlordship in Anglo-Saxon England." In *Early Medieval Studies in Memory of Patrick Wormald*, edited by Stephen Baxter, Catherine Karkov, Janet L. Nelson, and David Pelteret, 81–97. Farnham, Surrey and Burlington, VT: Ashgate, 2009.
Yorke, Barbara. "Britain and Ireland, c.500." In *A Companion to the Early Middle Ages: Britain and Ireland, c.500–c.1100*, edited by Pauline Stafford, 41–56. Chichester: Blackwell, 2009.
Yorke, Barbara. "Kings and Kingship." In *A Companion to the Early Middle Ages: Britain and Ireland, c.500–c.1100*, edited by Pauline Stafford, 76–90. Chichester: Blackwell, 2009.
Yorke, Barbara. *Rex Doctissimus: Bede and King Aldfrith of Northumbria*. Jarrow Lecture. Jarrow, 2009.
Yorke, Barbara. "Aldhelm's Irish and British Connections." In *Aldhelm and Sherborne: Essays to Celebrate the Founding of the Bishopric*, edited by Katherine Barker with Nicholas Brooks, 164–80. Oxford and Oakville: Oxbow Books, 2010.
Yorke, Barbara. "Adomnán at the Court of King Aldfrith." In *Adomnán of Iona: Theologian, Lawmaker, Peacemaker*, edited by Jonathan M. Wooding with Rodney Aist, Thomas Owen Clancy, and Thomas O'Loughlin, 36–50. Dublin: Four Courts Press, 2010.
Yorke, Barbara. "From Pagan to Christian in Anglo-Saxon England." In *The Introduction of Christianity into the Early Medieval Insular World: Converting the Isles I*, edited by Roy Flechner and Máire Ní Mhaonaigh with the assistance of Eric Cambridge, 237–57. Turnhout: Brepols, 2016.

Yorke, Barbara. "Competition for the Solent and 7th Century Politics." In *The Middle Ages Revisited: Studies in the Archaeology and History of Medieval Southern England Presented to Professor David A. Hutton*, edited by Ben Jervis, 35–43. Summertown: Archaeopress Publishing, 2018.

Ziolkowski, Jan M. "Classical Influences on Medieval Latin Views of Poetic Inspiration." In *Latin Poetry and the Classical Tradition: Essays in Medieval and Renaissance Literature*, edited by Peter Godman and Oswyn Murray, 15–38. Oxford: Clarendon Press, 1990.

# Index

Page numbers in *italics* refer to Figures. The following abbreviations are used for texts:

ODR =   *Orgain Denna Ríg*
TBC =   *Táin Bó Cúailnge*
TBDD = *Togail Bruidne Da Derga*
TBF =   *Táin Bó Fraích*

abecedarian 203, 278
– see also Altus Prosator
Acca, bishop of Hexham (709–731; d.737x740) 259, 261–62, 279, 346
Acha, queen, wife of Æthelfrith 250
*Acts of Sylvester* 210, 212
*Additamenta* 44, 349
Adnae, *ollam filed* 47
Adomnán, abbot of Iona (679–704) 50, 181, 212
– *A maccucáin, sruith in tíag* (poem) 76, 78–80, 352
– *Adiutor laborantium* 76, 168, 367
– Aldfrith *sapiens*, relationship with 75–76, 79, 168, 172, 198, 200, 211, 240, 258, 266, 287, *290*, 292–94, 296, 310–11, 350–51
– *Cáin Adomnáin* (*Lex innocentium*) 76, 80, 94, 124, 168, 197, 207, 230, 311, 344, 347, 349
– *Colum Cille co Día domm eráil* 76, 169
– *De locis sanctis* 75, 76, 91, 124, 168–69, 172, 198–200, 234–35, 238, 240, 258, 285, 287, *290*, 293, 296, 351
– as diplomat 282, 340
– as *homunculus* 343
– Iona, as abbot of 75
– and Paschal controversy 310–11
– as teacher 222
– and tonsure 310
– Vergil, familiarity with 224
– *Vita Columbae* 30, 57, 75, *77*, 140, 158, 167, 172, 204, 208–12, 214, 222, 231, 240–42, 250, 256–58, 261, 301, 316, 325, 360
Æbbe, abbess of Coldingham 277

Ælfflæd, abbess of Whitby (680–714) 4, 213, 256, *263*, 320, 324, 332, 353
– and Aldfrith 158, 283–84, 288–89, *290*, 295, 354–55
– and Cuthbert 158, 283–84
– and Gaelic ethos of Whitby 238
– Hild, raised by 264, 267, 319, 354
– and *Vita Gregorii* 213, 238, 256, 289, 320, 324, 332, *354*
– and Wilfrid 288
Ælfric, abbot of Eynsham (d.ca.1012) 102–3, 262, 372
– homilies 135, 193
Ælfwine (d.679) *263*, 264, 278
Ælle, king of Deira 251
Ælle, king of South Saxons 246
Æthelbald, king of Mercians (d.757) 297
Æthelberht, king of Kent (d.ca.616) 184, 246, 255, 301
Æthelburh, wife of Edwin 255
Æthelfrith, king (ca.592–ca.617) of Northumbria 117, 248, 256, 276–77, 301
– and Chester, battle of 249
– and Dál Ríata 142
– defeat and death of 251–52
– and Degsastan, battle of 118, 139, 141, 249–50
Æthelhun, companion of Ecgberht 339, 342
Æthelred, king of Mercia (675–704) 264
Æthelthryth, queen (d.679), wife of Ecgfrith 239, 277, 279, 314, 359
Æthelwine, bishop of Mercia 291, *336*, 341–42
Æthelwold, bishop of Lindisfarne 352
Æthelwulf, *De abbatibus* 165, 296, 372
Áed, bishop of Sleaty (d.700) 206–8, 337, 349
Áed mac Diarmata 40
Áed Sláine, king of Tara (ca.604) 39, 41–42, 53, 141, 368

Áedán mac Gabráin, king of Dál Riata (d.606) 99, 117–18, 139–40, 142, 158, 249–50
– see also Echtrae Áedáin maic Gabráin
áer (satire; slander) see satire
áes admolta (people of praising) 28, 37
áes dána (people of the arts) 9, 132–33
– see also professional status
Agilberht, bishop (fl.650s) 221, 273–74, 318
– education of 119, 179, 217, 220, 222, 260–61, 313, 317, 321–22, 332–33
– at "synod" of Whitby 119–20, 229, 261, 313, 325–26, 333, 354–55, 358
Agilulf, king of Lombards 169, 312
aí (poetic inspiration) 12, 63, 363
Aidan, bishop of Lindisfarne (634–651) 238, 304, 317, 331, 342, 351, 354, 373
– Cuthbert's vision of Aidan ascending to heaven 212, 242
– death of 320–21, 330
– and Felix, bishop of East Angles 176, 313–14, 319, 354
– and Hild 232, 313, 319, 323–24
– and Honorius, bishop of Kent 319
– Lindisfarne, foundation of 176, 229, 259–60, 313, 318, 330, 352
– missionary work 259–60, 317–21, 341, 352
– and Oswald 176, 258, 262, 317–18, 352
– and Oswiu 268, 270
– and Oswine 158, 229, 268, 320
Aided Chonchobuir (Violent Death of Conchobar) 126–27, 130
Aided Fraích (Violent Death of Fróech) in TBC 136
Ailbe of Emly (Imlech Ibair) 173
Ailerán sapiens (d.665) of Clonard (Cluain Iraird) 180, 182, 186–87, 201, 238, 294
– Carmen in Eusebii canones 186
– Interpretatio mystica 172, 186
– Vita prima Brigitae 186, 202–3
Ailill, king 115, 363
– in TBC 122, 136, 143, 154
– in TBF 30–31, 130, 135–36
Áiliu poems 28
Aimirgein Glúngel Tuir Tend, poem see Amairgein Glúngel; Gilla in Choimded Úa Cormaic

Airbertach mac Coisse Dobráin, poet (d.1016), Saltair na Rann 103
airchetal 44
Airec Menman Uraird maic Coise (Stratagem of Urard mac Coise)
– tale list B 127–30, 144
– Widsith, compared to 128
Airgíalla 87
Aithirne Áilgesach (the Importunate), poet 43, 86
– Talland Étair (Siege of Howth) 19
Albinus, abbot 166
Albu (Britain) 17, 62, 115
Alcuin of York (c.735–804) 90, 186, 193, 195, 289, 328, 355
– and Ecgberht 341
– Life of Willibrord 345, 372
– and Mayo of the Saxons 224–25, 230, 328–29
– on the two Hewalds 347
– on Wihtberht 343–44
Aldfrith sapiens, king of Northumbria (685–704) 42, 188, 231, 235, 247, 263, 266–67, 339
– accession of 120–21
– and Adomnán 75–76, 79, 168, 172, 198, 200, 211, 240, 258, 266, 287, 290, 292–94, 296, 310–11, 350–51
– and Ælfflæd 158, 283–84, 288–89, 290, 295, 354–55
– and Aldhelm 73–75, 108, 142, 193–94, 200, 221–22, 228, 261, 266, 286, 293, 296, 333, 363
– and Bangor 284, 287, 290, 291, 293–94
– Bríathra Flainn Fhína maic Ossu 75, 150, 194–96, 258
– burial at Whitby 289, 290, 295
– and codex cosmographiorum 198, 200, 290, 291, 367
– coinage, use of 292–93, 295–96
– and Cuthbert's prophecy 120, 158, 283–84
– death of 288–89, 295–96
– and Dryhthelm 198, 200, 233, 291, 330
– education of 119, 199, 221–22, 258, 271, 333
– Gaelic speaker 3, 142, 245–46, 258, 294
– illegitimate (nothus) birth of 266, 285

- on Iona 282–84, 350
- as *magister* 194, 197–98, 200, 293
- marriage *290*, 291
- network of connections 289–96
- rebuilding kingdom 284–87
- as *sapiens* 50, 53, 70, 73–75, 94, 108, 119, 141, 169, *180*, 193, 198, *258*, 283, 289, 291–93, 295–96
- and Wearmouth-Jarrow, foundation of 197, 216, 287
- and Wilfrid 214, 287–89

Aldhelm, abbot of Malmesbury (d.709), bishop of Sherborne (705–709) 1–3, 50, 219
- and Aldfrith *sapiens* 73–75, 108, 142, 193–94, 200, 221–22, 228, 261, 266, 286, 293, 295–96, 333, 363
- *Altus Prosator*, familiarity with 68, 73, 168, 191, 220, 223, 228, 261, 316, 333, 350
- background of 73, 261, 291
- *Carmen de virginitate* 73, 153, 218, 334
- *Carmen rhythmicum* 73, 200, 223, 333, 350
- and Classical figures 224–25
- *De metris* 142
- *De pedum regulis* 142
- education of 221–25, 261, 329, 333, 339
- *Enigmata* 73, 333
- *Epistola ad Acircium* 73, 75, 108, 142, 193–94, 200, 218, 221, 228, 235, 286, 291, 296, 362–63
- and Gaelic influence 220–28, 261, 333–34
- and Gregory I the Great 165
- and Heahfrith, his pupil 116, 179, 187, 191, 223, 225–28, 328, 333
- as *homunculus* 343
- and Máeldub, as teacher 221, 333
- and Mayo of the Saxons 328
- *Prosa de virginitate* 74, 224, 228
- as *scop* 74
- sermons 315
- on sexual transgression 224
- Wihtfrith, letter to 153, 179, 187, 223–24, 227, 334

ale of sovereignty 40
Alexandrian Easter tables *see* Dionysiac reckoning

Alfred the Great of Wessex, king/poet (d.899) 87, 231
- *Handboc* 74
- laws 100
- as *rígbaird* 33
- translation project 9, 33, 97, 99–102, 105, 372

Alhfrith *see* Ealhfrith
Allen (Cath Almaine), battle of (722) 89
*Altus Prosator*, poem 168, 182, 238
- Aldhelm, known to 68, 73, 168, 191, 220, 223, 228, 261, 316, 333, 350
- Creator theme 56, 200, 361, 367
- prose preface 361
- Virgilius Maro Grammaticus as possible author 191, 223

Amairgen Glúngel, poet of Milesians 16, 26, 149
Amairgen mac Amloingid (fl.680) 191
*Amrae Choluim Chille*, poem 41, 146, 208–9
- Columba, in praise of 20–21, 35
- Dallán Forgaill, attributed to 20, 35
- prose preface 53

*Amrae Senáin see* under Cormac mac Cuilennáin
*anamain* (poetic meter) 143
*Andreas*, poem 20
Aneirin (Neirin), poet 11, 26, 70, 248
- *Y Gododdin* 12–13, 38, 98, 368

*Anglo-Saxon Chronicles* 11, 100, 245, 289
Anna, king of East Anglia (d.654) 176, 275, 277, 314, 317–18
*Annales Cambriae* 254, 264, 302
Annals of Inisfallen 102
Annals of Tigernach 72, 89, 126, 141, 250, 281, 338
Annals of Ulster 58, 87, 90, 96, 124, 280–81, 328, 338, 347
*annus Domini* 131
- Dionysiac chronology 305–7, 311
- Lutting of Lindisfarne 211, 280, 287, 291
*Anonymus ad Cuimnanum* 190
*ánṡruth* (second grade of poet) 109–10, 150, 196
Antiphonary of Bangor (680 x 691) 169–70, 203, 295, 312
Apuleius, *Florida* 152–53

Ard Machae *see* Armagh
Arianism 172
Armagh (*Ard Machae*) 92–93, 102, 143, 182, 236
- as bishopric 174, 177, 206–7, 210
- and Brigit, saint 202
- burning of 328
- and Sleaty 337
- *see also* Book of Armagh; Emain Macha; Ségéne, bishop of Armagh
*Ars Ambrosiana* 190
Asser, *De Vita et Rebus Gestis Alfredi* 99
*Atbret Iudeu* (Restitution of Iudeu) 267
Athanasius (d.373), *Vita Antonii* 204, 210–11, 242
*athláech* (ex-layman) 51, 197
- Cædmon as 364–65, 369
- *see also láechdacht*
*Audacht Morainn* (Testament of Morann) 17, 120
- as *speculum principum* 17, 19, 72, 121, 193, 368
Augustine, archbishop of Canterbury, saint 165, 184, 249, 300
Augustine, bishop of Hippo, saint 200, 239, 365
- *Soliloquies* 99–100
*Auraicept na nÉces* (Scholars' Primer), vernacular grammar 15, 189–90
*awen* (poetic inspiration) 11–12, 63, 363

Baducing *see* Benedict Biscop
Baeda *magister* (d.681) 210–11, 280, 308, 311
*baile* (frenzy; vision) 82–83 *see also* dreams/visions
*Baile an Scáil* (Frenzy of the Phantom) *see Fís Chuinn*
*Baile Chuinn Chétchathaigh* (Frenzy of Conn . . .) 119–21, 156, 158, 193, 281, 340, 368
*bairdne* (poetry of a bard; encomium, panegyric) 44, 97 *see also rígbaird*
Bamburgh (Dún Guaire) 11, 140, 248, 253, 259, 318
Banbán *sapiens* (d.686) 347
- as *sapiens* 50, 72, *180*, 191, 295
- *Cáin Fhuithirbe* (ca.680) 72, 191–92, 205, 207

*banfáith see* Fedelm
*banfili see* poetess
Bangor (*Bennchor*) 3, 75, 94, 117–18, 194, 236
- and Agilberht 217, 261, 313, 317
- and Aldfrith *sapiens* 284, 287, *290*, 291, 293–94
- bilingualism 222, 294–95
- foundation of 169
- importance of Latin learning at 119, 121, 163, 169–73, 187, 198, 222, 333
- name of 136
- *see also* Antiphonary of Bangor; *Hisperica Famina*
*bard(d)* (poet) 9, 11–12, *see also rígbaird*
Basil of Caesarea 21, 232
Beadohild, character in *Deor* 26
Bécán mac Luigdech, poet (fl.670) 74, 181, 188, 258, 271, 360
- Columba, poems praising 20, 41, 50, 57–64, 70, 168, 204, 209, 241, 363, 368
- Do-Bécóc of Cluain Ard 58
- as professional poet 63–64
- seafaring images 61–63
- vocabulary 63–64
Beccán *solitarius*, hermit of Rùm 58, 173–74
*Bechbretha* (Bee Judgements) 192–93
Bede, scholar/priest (d.735) 1–5, 9, 50, 52, 87, 117–18, 121, 131, 139–40, 169, 172–73, 177, 194, 198, 219, 270, 372
- and Adomnán 91, 168–69, 199, 209, 212, 234–35, 238, 240–41, 285, 310
- on Æthelthryth 278, 359
- on Aidan 318–20, 330–31
- and Aldfrith *sapiens* 75, 79, 169, 193, 196–98, 222, 235, 240, 266, 283, 285–88, 291, 293, 310
- on Aldhelm 73, 222, 293
- and Alfred's translation project 99–100
- biblical exegesis of 238–39
- on Cædmon 54, 64–65, *66*, 144–45, 149, 152, 353–55, 357–69, 373
- chronologies, choice of 239–42
- *De locis sanctis* 75–76, 91, 234–35, 238, 285, 288, 351
- *De orthographia* 191, 237
- *De temporibus* 211, 239–40, 307
- *De temporum ratione* 191, 237–39, 307

– death of 51, 87, 237, 351
– "Death Song" 81–83
– on Degastan, battle of 141
– and Ecgberht 80, 232, 235, 238, 243, 287, 293, 338–43
– on Ecgfrith 281–85
– on Edwin 251–56
– *Epistola ad Ecgbertum* 80, 287, 297
– *Epistola ad Plegwinum* 239, 288
– on Felix, bishop of East Anglia 313
– folkloric material 243
– on Fursa and Dryhthelm 60, 134–35, 232–33, 315, 330
– Gaelic influence, theme of 83, 229–43, 350
– heresy, accused of 239, 288
– on Hild 355
– *Historia abbatum* 184, 205, 216–17, 272
– *Historia ecclesiastica* (general) 1, 7–8, 33–34, 39, 80, 83, 99–100, 229–43
– and Iona 167–68, 240–42
– on kingship/*imperatores* 245–59, 263–66, 285
– *Martyrology* 274
– on Mayo of the Saxons 225, *231*, 327–28
– on missions, Gaelic 220–21, 230, 338–47
– on missions, Gregorian 165–66, 176, 184, 229, 300–4, 317
– names, Gaelic forms of *231*, 240, 242
– on Osred 296–97
– on Oswald 256–62
– on Oswiu 262–70, 275–76
– on Paschal controversy 174, 179, 212, 222, 236–37, 243, 269–70, 273, 306, 308–10, 324–26, 331, 350
– personal background 229, 238, 279–80, 324–25, 332, 355
– on Rath Melsigi 138, 230–31, 335, 337–38
– as *sapiens* 83
– on schooling, free 119, 164, 179, 181, 187, 201, 270–71, 294, 329
– "thought, word, deed" 233–34
– vernacular translations by 80–81
– *Vita Cuthberti (metrica)* (Life of Cuthbert) (ca.705) 212–13, 285, 296, 330, 341, 352, 359

– *Vita Cuthberti (prosa)* (Life of Cuthbert) (ca.716) 212–13, 237, 242, 285, 309, 330, 341, 352, 365
– on Whitby 323–26, 331, 357
– on Wilfrid 298, 331
Belach Mugna, battle (908) 39, 101
Benedict Biscop (Baducing) (d.689) 184, 198, 205, 214, 304
– and Aldfrith 216, *290*, 291
– death of 217
– and Ecgfrith 277
– and Oswiu 271–73, 276, 279, 323
– pictures and painted panels for Wearmouth and Jarrow 184, 205
– and Wearmouth and Jarrow, foundation of 216
– and Wilfrid 214, 272, 279, 323
Benedictine Rule 171, 215, 328
*Bennchor see* Bangor
*Beowulf*, poem 7, 11, 26, 69–70
– Christian values 112–13, 127, 213–14, 295
– chronological setting 25
– dialects 24, 82, 131
– digressions 31–32, 35, 88, 105, 125–26, 371
– extempore composition 20, 35, 110, 143, 363
– Finn episode 60, 105
– *gomela Scilding* 150
– hero, prowess of 130–31, *see also* Beowulf, character
– manuscript history 23
– mission to Frisians 230
– poets/harpers at court 26–27, 29–31, 33–34
– poets vs reciters of lore 129
– seafaring images 62
– "Song of Creation" 27
– syncretism 112–13
– TBC, compared to 130
– textual dating 24, 131, 295, 319, 334, 346
– unique copy Cotton Vitellius A.xv 23
– Weland the smith in 105
Beowulf, character 45, 234
– single combats 20, 25, 34, 125, 130–31
Berach, saint, Life of 140

Berht, *dux*, raid on Brega (684) 19, 42, 121, 280–81, 286–87, 368
Berhtwald, archbishop of Canterbury (d.731) 196, 214
*Bethu Phátraic* (*Tripartite Life of Patrick*) 44
Bicgu *abb sruithe* 183
bilingualism 163–64, 245–46, 258, 331, 352
 – at Bangor 169–73, 222, 294–95
 – code-switching 316
 – at Whitby 357–58
 – *see also* Aldfrith *sapiens*; Cædmon; *Cambrai Homily*; Cenn Fáelad *sapiens*; Oswald; Oswiu
 – *see also* under *sapientes*
Birinus, bishop (634–ca.650) of West Saxons (Gewisse) 176, 178, 220, 260, 304, 317, 332
Birr (*Birra*), Co. Offaly 336
 – synod at (697) 76, 168, *336*
*Birra see* Birr
blacksmiths (*gobae*) as *dóernemed* 107 *see also* Weland the smith
Blathmac mac Con Brettan, poet (fl.760) 87–89, 91
Blwchfardd, poet 11–12
Bobbio 119, 136, 169, 171–73, 312
Boethius (d.ca.524)
 – *De consolatione Philosophiae* 99–100
 – and personified *Philosophia* 116
 – Weland the smith in 105
Boisil, prior of Melrose (d.ca.664) 213, 232, *336*, 373
 – and Cuthbert 237, 309, 318, 330, 340, 351–52
 – death of 232, 237, 309, 341, 365
 – and prophecy 340, 342, 351, 365
Boniface IV, pope (608–615) 117, 172, 297, 305
Book of Armagh 44
Book of Cerne 233
Book of Leinster 32, 122, 125, 130
 – tale list 128–29
Bosa, bishop of York 324
"brain of forgetting" (*inchinn dermait*) 177, 188
Bran mac Febail *see Immram Brain*
Brandub mac Echach, king of Leinster (d.ca.605) 140

Brega (*Mag Breg*), attack by Berht 19, 41–42, 121, 134, 280–82, 286–87, 339–40, 350, 368
Brénann of Birr 173
*Bretha Crólige* (Judgements on Blood-lyings) 182, 266
*Bretha Déin Chécht* (Judgements of Dían Cécht) 182
*Bretha Étgid* (Judgements concerning Irresponsible Acts) 189
*Bretha Nemed* (Judgements of Privileged Persons) 19, 107–8, 110, 188–89
 – *Dédenach* 28, 39–40, 89, 97
bretwalda (ruler of Britain)/*imperator* 245–46, 257, 263 *see also* Bede, on kingship/*imperatores*; Edwin, as *imperator*; Oswald, as emperor/*imperator*; Oswiu, as emperor/*imperator*
*Breudwyt Ronabwy* 158
Brian Boru, Munster king 103
*Bríathra Flainn Fhína maic Ossu see* under Aldfrith *sapiens*
Brigit, saint (d.ca.526) 94–95, 187, 193
 – cult center (Kildare) of 207, 212, 349
 – *Vita prima* 202–3, 206, 212
 – *see also* Cogitosus, *Vita Brigitae*
*Brislech Mór Maige Muirthemni* (Great Rout of Muirthemne Plain) 98, 131
*brithemnacht ḟénechais* (jurisprudence of Gaelic law) 109, 111
Bruide mac Bili 281–82
*brytenwalda* (wide ruler) *see bretwalda*
*Buched Dewi Sant* 303–4
Burgh Castle *see* Cnobheresburg
Byrhtferth, author (d.ca.1020), *Enchiridion* 103

Cadfan, king of Anglesey 252–54, 303, 356
Cadwallon, king of Anglesey (d.634) 252, 254–56, 261, 263, 265, 301, 356
 – *Moliant Cadwallon* (Praise of Cadwallon) 368
Cædmon, poet (fl.670) 2, 33, 50, 52, 81, 144–45, 157, 168, 319–20, 324, 355
 – Aldhelm, compared to 74
 – analogues for 67–68

- as *athláech* 364–65, 369
- as bilingual Briton 4, 356–58, 369
- Colmán mac Lénéni, compared to 54–56
- Creator/creation theme 56, 68, 360, 365–67
- and dialects 81, 83, 357
- and divine grace 5, 151–52, 360, 363–64
- eulogy/encomium 13, 69–70, 367–69
- and Gaelic practices 4, 331, 354, 360–63, 373
- illiteracy/as untrained poet 64–65, 74, 149, 357–63, 369
- manuscript tradition 65–67, *66*
- and prophecy 158–59, 342, 365
- unwillingness to perform 34, 357–58
Caesarius of Arles 200
*Cáin Adomnáin see* Adomnán, *Cáin Adomnáin*
*Cáin Éimíne Báin* 349
*Cáin Fhuithirbe* 72, 368
Cairpre Cattchenn 19
"Caldron of Poesy", vernacular poetics
- and divine grace 151–53, 158
- and poetic inspiration 16, 34, 149–51, 363
*Cambrai Homily*, bilingual (macaronic) text 116, 172
*cano* (poetic grade) 109
Canterbury 213, 218, 274–75, 294, 367
- and Paschal controversy 270, 273, 320
- school of (est.669) 164–67, 200, 223–24, 226–27, 258, 276, 291, 320, 329, 350
- *see also* Gregorian missions, Canterbury
*Carmen in Eusebii canones* (text) *see* Aileán sapiens
*Carmen rhythmicum see* under Aldhelm
Cassian 21
catalogue poem *see Airec Menman*; *Widsith*
*Cath Maige Tuired* ([Second] Battle of Mag Tuired) 28–30, 98, 103, 129, 132–33, 135
Cathach, Gallican version of Psalms 168
Cathbad, druid 45
Catraeth *see* Catterick
Catterick (poss. Brittonic Catraeth) 12, 38, 257, 302
Ceawlin, king of West Saxons 246
Cedd, bishop of East Saxons (d.664) 158, 323, 341, 343
- Lastingham, foundation of 318, 330

- at "synod" of Whitby as interpreter 268, 318, 326, 330, 354–55, 358
*Céili Dé*, monastic movement 88–90, 92
*Celebra Iuda see* under Cuimmíne Fota sapiens
Cellán of Péronne (d.706) 228, 233, 261, 314, 333, 343
Cenél Conaill, northern Uí Néill sept 75, 97–98, 176–77, 286
- at Iona 178, 209, 270–71, 316
- and Oswiu 271–72
Cenél nÉogain, northern Uí Néill sept 53, 70, 74, 96, 141, 177, 188, 250, 258, 286, *290*, 322, 325
- and Oswiu 266–67, 271–72, 283
Cenn Fáelad *sapiens* (d.679) 74, 258, 271
- and *Auraicept na nÉces* 189–90
- bilingualism of 188–90, 295
- *Brislech Mór Maige Muirthemni* 71
- in law-tracts 188–89
- poems 71, 130, 188–89
- as *sapiens* 50, 70, 113, 141, 177, *180*, 188, 206, 258, 295
Cenred, king of Mercia 233
Cenwealh, king of West Saxons (642–672) 260, 317–18, 326, 333
Ceolfrith, abbot of Wearmouth-Jarrow (d.716) 209, 216–17, 270, 272, 280, 287, 310, 321
- *see also Vita Ceolfridi*
Ceollach, Middle Angles and Mercians 221, 269
Ceolred, king of Mercia 297
Cerball mac Muirecáin, king of Leinster 39
Ceredig, king of Elmet (d.616) 254, 356
Chad, bishop of Mercia and Lindsey (669–672) 269, 274, 291, *336*, 343, 354, 365
- death of 319
- education of 238, 318, 330, 341–42
Chaucer, Geoffrey 57
Chester, battle of 249
*Christ III* 89
*Chronicum Scotorum* 89, 96, 338
Christ 20, 54–55
- as charioteer 117

- crucifixion/passion of 88, 126, 130, 174, 306
- in *Dream of the Rood* 60
- as *logos* 238
- predictions of advent of 116–17
Cian, poet, *Gwenith Gwawd* (Wheat of Song") 11–12
Ciarán of Clonmacnoise 173
*Cín Dromma Snechtai* (Book of Druimm Snechtai [Drumsnat]) 2, 17, 105, 113, 182–83, 202, 295
- date of 114
- and Manannán mac Lir 117–18, 139
- "Midland Group" 119–21
- in tale lists 127
- texts in 114–21, 129, 133–34, 139–40, 156–57, 250 *see also Auducht Morainn*; *Baile Chuinn Chétchathaig*; *Compert Chonchobuir*; *Compert Con Culainn*; *Compert Mongáin*; *Echtrae Chonnlai*; *Immram Brain*; *Tochmarc Étaíne*; *Togail Bruidne uí Derga*; *Verba Scáthaige*
Cináed úa hArtacáin, poet (d.975) 102
Cissa 218
Clonfertmulloe (*Cluain Ferta Mo-Lua*) 114, 181–82, 201
Clonmacnoise (*Cluain maccu Nois*) 90, 92, 372
Cloyne monastery, Co. Cork (*Cluain Uama*) 39, 41, 51, 53
Cluain Aird Mo-Bécóc monastery, Co. Tipperary 58
Cnobheresburg (Burgh Castle) 135, 232, 314
*Cnoc Ailinne see* Knockaulinn
Cobthach Cóel, king in *Orgain Denna Ríg* 28, 37–38, 94–95, 137–38
Codex Ambrosianus C.301 40
*Codex cosmographiorum see* under Aldfrith *sapiens*
Codex Durmachensis (Book of Durrow) 231
*Codex sancti Pauli* 40
Cogitosus (fl.680) 184
- *Vita Brigitae* 191, 204–5, 207, 210–12, 348
Coifi, pagan priest 302
*coimgne* (joint knowledge, all-embracing knowledge; synthesis) 32, 109, 111, 113, 129

coinage *290*, 293
- dragon images on 334
- *see also* under Aldfrith *sapiens*
Colcu úa Duinechda, poet (d.796) 86, 90
- *Scúap Chrábaid* (Broom of Devotion) 89
Coldingham, Berwickshire 277–78
*Collectanea Patricii see* Tírechán
*Collectio canonum Hibernensis* 108, 166, 310
Colmán, bishop of Lindisfarne (661–664) (d.676) 4, 181, 229, 270–71, 322, 331, 342
- death of 327
- and Ireland, foundations in 187, 204, 225, 228, 230, 326–27, 350, 354 *see also* Inishboffin; Mayo of the Saxons
- "synod" of Whitby (664) 204, 230, 237, 258, 324–26
Colmán Elo, Hymn on St. Patrick 203
Colmán mac Lénéni, poet (d.606) 8, 41–42, 50, 64
- as *athláech* 364
- chronology 53
- Cloyne, established 51
- glosses to 55–56
- praise poems 39, 52–54, 60, 368
- as professional poet 51
- religious poems 54–56, 113, 163
- sleep/dreams, composes in 54–56, 161–62, 362, 364
Colmán of Hanbury 220–21, 333
Colmán Rímid, king (d.604) 42, 141, 321
Colmán úa Clúasaig 183
Colum Cille *see* Columba
Columba (Colum Cille; Crimthann), saint (d.593) 51, 161, 212, 304
- and angelic apparitions 250
- and Bangor 222, 292
- death of 167, 209, 241, 365
- Gregory I the Great, poem to honor 361
- Iona, founding of 53–54, 61–63, 75, 167, 209, 241–42, 292, 300, 316
- Life of 201 *see also* Adomnán, *Vita Columbae*
- missionary work 167–68, 300, 316
- *Mórdál Dromma Ceta*, support of 20
- name *231*, 240, 316
- and Paschal controversy 209, 326

– and prophecy 30, 158, 301, 342, 351, 365
– see also Adomnán, Colum Cille co Día domm eráil; Amrae Coluim Chille; Bécán mac Luigdech, Columba, poems praising; Cuimméne Find, De virtutibus sancti Columbae
Columbanus, missionary (d.615) 51, 163, 200, 261, 295, 372
– and Bangor 169–70, 312–13
– at Bobbio 119, 136, 169, 171–73, 312
– Boniface IV, letter to 117, 172, 305
– in Burgundy 312–14
– De mundi transitu 82, 170
– death of 172, 312
– education 3, 312
– Gregory I the Great, letter to 171–72, 227
– and Paschal controversy 175, 227, 305–6
– Precamur patrem 170
– Regula coenobialis 170
– Regula monachorum 170
– sermons 56, 171
– De fide 68
– see also Jonas of Bobbio, Life of Columbanus
Comgall, founding abbot of Bangor (d.602) 114, 169–70, 194, 222, 292, 304, 335
Compert Chonchobuir (Conception of Conchobar) 114
Compert Con Chulainn (Conception of Cú Chulainn) 114–15, 129
Compert Mongáin (Conception of Mongán) 117, 139, 250
competition among poets 46–48
– see also under Deor; Ferchertne fili, in Immacallam; Gilla in Choimded Úa Cormaic; Heorrenda; Immacallam in dá Thuarad; Néide mac Adnai; Senchán Torpéist
computus 103, 173–75, 205, 210–11, 216, 235–37, 305
– Computus Cottonianus 345
– Iona Chronicle 240
– Munich computus 179
– see also Cummian, De controversia Paschali; Dionysius Exiguus; latercus; Paschal controversy; Victorius of Aquitaine

Conailla Medb míchuru 15
Conaire Mór (mythic king), in TBDD 134, 159–60, 361–62
Conall Cernach (character) 44, 98, 136
Conall Cremthainne, king (d.480) 206
Conall Gulbain, ancestor of Cenél Conaill 63, 98
Conchobar mac Nessa (mythic king) 16, 45, 47, 98, 111, 114, 126–27, 130–31, 147, 160
– see also Aided Chonchobuir; Compert Conchobuir
Congal, king (d.639) 192
Conn Cétchathach (Conn of the Hundred Battles) 115–16, 120–21, 134
Constantine, Roman emperor 91, 212
coppersmiths (umaige), as dóernemed 107
Cormac mac Airt, legendary king 189, 253
Cormac mac Cuilennáin, king/bishop of Cashel (d.908) 39, 87, 100, 102
– Amrae Senáin 99, 101
– as rígbaird 33
– Uga Cormaic meic Cuilennáin (Cormac's Choice) 99, 101
– see also Sanas Cormaic
Cormac mac Diarmata, king of Uí Bairrche 291, 335
Cormac mac Fáeláin 124
Cormac of the Uí Liatháin, seafarer, miles Christi 54
Córus Bésgnai (Regulation of Proper Behaviour), law-tract 22, 108
Craiphtine, harper in ODR 28–29, 37, 137
Creation theme 68, 103, 200, 333, 365–67
– see also under Beowulf, "Song of Creation"; Cædmon
Crimthann see Columba
Críth Gablach (Branched Purchase), law-tract 27–28, 108, 281
Crónán, poet, poeta scoticus 30, 208, 316
cruit see harpers
Crúachu, Co. Roscommon see Rathcroghan
Cú Chulainn, legendary character 17, 45, 115, 118, 125, 136, 155
– Beowulf, compared to 25
– death of 71, 98, 130–31, 189
– and Scáthah, his female martial arts instructor 115, 363

- single combats 25, 130–31
- wife, Emer 156
- see also Compert Con Chulainn

Cúán úa Locháin, poet (d.1024) 103
Cuilmen see Etymologiae of Isidore
Cuimmíne Find (Cummeneus Albus; 657–669), abbot of Iona, De virtutibus sancti Columbae 77, 158, 204, 241
Cuimmíne Fota sapiens (d.662) 148, *180*, 229
- Celebra Iuda 184–85
- "Commentary on the Gospel of Mark" 185
- De figuris apostolorum 184
- penitential of 183–84

Cuirithir, éices 96, 148
Cúl Dreimne, battle (561) 53
Cummeneus Albus see Cuimmíne Find
Cummian (fl.632), De controversia Paschali 114, 163, *172*–76, 178, 185, 213, 235, *305*, 309, 323, 372
Cummianus see Cummian
Cuthbert, deacon, Epistola de obitu Bedae 80–81, 237, 310
Cuthbert, saint 52, 211–15, 237, 242, 265, 277, 294–95, 339, 372
- and Aldfrith sapiens 158, *290*, 365
- and Boisil 237, 309, 318, 330, 340, 351–52
- cult and relics of 291, 352
- and Ecgfrith 280–82
- immersion in water 242, 277, 330
- and prophecy 120, 158, 283–84
- see also Bede, Vita Cuthberti (metrica) and Vita Cuthberti (prosa); Vita Cuthberti (anonyma)

Cuthburh, wife of Aldfrith sapiens *290*, 291
Cyneburh, wife of Ealhfrith 265, 269
Cyneburh, wife of Oswald 220, 260, 317
Cynefrith, abbot of Gilling 217, 270, 273, 280, 321–22, 332
Cynegisl, king of West Saxons (Gewisse) (611–?642) 176, 220, 260–61, 317, 332
Cynewulf, poet (8th–10th c.) 87
- Christ II 90–91
- Elene 90–92, 162
- Fates of the Apostles 90–91, 185
- and Guthlac poem on 218
- Juliana 90–92

Cyriacus, saint, acta of 91

Dagobert, king of Franks 255
Daire Chalgaig (Daire Cholum Chille; Derry/Londonderry) 325
Daire Lúráin see Derryloran
Dál Fiatach 169, *231*, 243
Dál nAraidi 15, 117–18, 169, 177, 192–93, *231*, 243
Dál Riata, kingdom on both sides of Irish Sea 140, 142, 176–77, *231*, 242–43, 249–50
Dallán Forgaill, poet 20, 35, 41, 143, 146
Dallán mac Móre, poet (fl.900) 39, 102
dán (art; occupation) see áes dána; Maith dán ecnae; professional status
Daniel úa Liathaiti, poet (d.863) 96
De duodecim abusivis 72, 103, 124, 193–94, 372
De fáilsigiud Tána Bó Cúailnge (Finding (recovery) of the Táin) 21
- Fergus mac Roíg 21, 122–24
- fore-tales 121, 125–26
- and Isidore's Etymologiae 122–23
- and Senchán Torpéist 21, 121–22, 124, 147–48
- and Triads 123

De figuris apostolorum see Cuimmíne Fota sapiens
De locis sanctis see Adomnán, De locis sanctis; Bede, De locis sanctis
De mirabilibus sacrae scripturae (655) 182, 199, 238, 366
De ordine creaturarum see Liber de ordine creaturarum
De origine Scoticae linguae (O'Mulconry's Glossary) 175
Degsastan, battle of (ca.603) 118, 139, 141, 249–50
Denisesburn, battle of 256
Deor, poem 11, 25–26, 295
- competition among poets 46, 128, 147
- Germanic lore 26
- patronage 1, 7, 26, 36
- and professional status 26, 45–47, 49, 83, 359
- unique copy Exeter Book 23
- Weland the smith in 105

Derryloran (Daire Lúráin) 71, *180*, 188, 206

*Deus a quo facta fuit*, poem 178, 295
Deusdedit, bishop of Canterbury
  (d.664) 275, 329
Diarmiat mac Cerbaill, king of Ireland
  (d.ca.565) 209
Dialects
– in Early Gaelic (lack of) 50, *84*, 85–86
– in Old English 7, 50, *66*, 67, 81, 83, *84*, 85, 90, 131
– and poetic *koinē* 83, 85
– *see also* under *Beowulf*; Cædmon
*díberg* (marauding, pillaging, brigandage) 134, 224
*díchetal di chennaib* (lit. chanting from heads) *see under* extempore composition
Dícuill, *peregrinus* at Bosham 331
Dicullus (Dícuill), *peregrinus*, companion of Fursa 313
digressions *see* under *Beowulf*
Dímma *see* Diuma
Din Guayroi *see* Bamburgh
Dind Ríg, site near Rath Melsigi 29, 38, 94, 95, 138, *348*, 348–49
– *see also Orgain Denna Ríg*
*dindšenchas* (place lore) *18*, 48, 71, 96, 102–3, 131, 136, 227, 371
Dionysiac (Easter) practice *see* Dionysius Exiguus
Dionysius Exiguus (fl.525) 174, 205, 210–11, 215, 236, 287, 291, 294, *305*–11, 325, 338
*Disputatio Chori et Praetextati* (ca.600) 223, 240
Diuma (*Dímma*), bishop of Middle Angles and Mercians (ca.656–ca.658) 221, 269
divination *see* prophecy/divination
divine grace and poetic inspiration 149–53, 363–64, *see also* under Cædmon; "Caldron of Poesy"
*dóernemed* (base *nemed*, dependent professional) 27, 106–7
Domnall mac Áedo, king of Tara (628–642) 176–78, 188
Domnall (Ilchelgach) mac Muirchertaigh, co-high king of Tara (c.565/6) 39, 52–53, 368

Domnall mac Muirchertaigh, king
  (d.980) 127–28
Donatus 164, 189–90
Donn Cúailnge, bull named in TBC 115
Donnchad Midi mac Domnaill, king of Ireland (770–797) 39, 89
Dorbbéne, scribe (d.713) *77*, 204
Dorchester (Dorcic) 176, 220, 260, 317, 332
Dracontius 365
*Dream of the Rood* 20, 60
dreams/visions
– and Colmán man Lénéni 54–56, 160–61, 362
– and religious poems 161–62, *see also* Cædmon
– stereotype in poetry 361–64
– in TBC 160, 362
– in TBDD 159–60, 361–62
– *see also* prophecy/divination
*drécht* (pl. *dréchta*) (composition) 109–10, 129
Driffield, Yorkshire 289, *290*, 291, 295
druid (Old Gaelic *druí*; Old English *drȳ*; Latin *magus*) 116, 140, 218
– and divination 157–58, 187, 218, 362
– and *Vita prima* of St. Brigit 202, 218
Druimm Snechtai *see* Drumsnat
Drumsnat, Co. Monaghan (*Druimm Snechtaí*) 114, 182, 202
– *see also Cín Dromma Snechtai*
*druí* (druid) *see* druid
*drȳ* (magician) *see* druid
Dryhthelm, visionary 60, 193, 198, 200, 233, 242, *290*, 291, 330
Dublittir úa Úathgaile, poet (fl.1090), *Sex Aetates Mundi* 104
Dubthach Dóel, diviner 98, 160, 362
Dubthach maccu Lugair, poet 21–23, 37, 44, 112–13, 192, 206, 208, 337, 349
– *see also Senchas Már*, "pseudo-historical prologue"
Dún Guaire *see* Bamburgh
*dúnad* (conclusion, closure) 40–41, *95*
*Durham*, poem 87, 352, 371–72
Durrow 222, *231*, 242 *see also* Codex Durmachensis

Eadberht, bishop of Lindisfarne (688–698) 352
Eadfrith, bishop of Lindisfarne (post-698) 213, 352
Eadwine *see* Edwin
Ealhflæd 263, 265, 269
Ealhfrith, sub-king of Deira (d.ca.664) 262, 263, 265–66, 269
– and 'synod' of Whitby, initiation of 265, 272–73, 325, 332
– and Wilfrid 271–72, 274, 278
Eanflæd, wife of Oswiu 255–56, 263–65, 273, 275–76
– and Gilling abbey 217, 268–70, 322, 332
– and Whitby abbey 319
– and Wilfrid 271, 273
Eanfrith, king (d.634) 141, 256, 326
Easter controversy *see* Paschal controversy
Eata, bishop of Hexham, Lindisfarne (d.686) 258–59, 262, 265, 318, 326, 330, 341, 351
Ecgberht, bishop of York 80, 287
Ecgberht I, king of Kent 275, 329
Ecgberht of Rath Melsigi (*Eicbericht antistes*) (d.729) 169, 258, 266, 275, 292–94, 342
– and Æthelhun 339, 342
– and Bede 80, 232, 235, 238, 243, 287, 293, 338–43
– and Boisil 213, 232, 330, 340–41, 351
– and Brega 280–82, 339
– continental mission 340–41
– death of 338–39
– at Iona 243, 292, 338–39, 341, 351
– at Rath Melsigi 138, 188, 213, 232, 238, 243, 269, 292–93, 318–19, 330, 336, 338–39, 341, 343, 345
Ecgburh, abbess 218–19
Ecgfrith, king (670–685) 42, 120, 214, 216, 263, 264, 267, 274, 298, 356
– and Benedict Biscop 277, 279
– and Brega, battle at 17, 19, 42, 121, 339–40, 368
– and Cuthbert 120, 280–82
– death and burial of 279, 281–86, 289, 350
– as hostage to Mercians 268
– marriages of 277–78, 314

– military affairs 17, 19, 121, 279–86, 298, 339–40, 350, 368
– Wearmouth-Jarrow, foundation of 3, 216
– and Wilfrid 214, 277–80, 298, 345
Echaid Buide mac Áedáin 158
Echternach 336, 345, 372
*Echtrae Áedáin maic Gabráin* 140
*Echtrae Chonnlai* (Faring Forth of Connlae) 115–17, 119–20, 295
*Echtrae Maíl Umai maic Báetáin* 141
*Echtrae Mongáin maic Fiachnai* 140
*Ecloga de moralibus in Iob see* Laidcenn sapiens
*ecnae* (wisdom; *sapientia*; ecclesiastical scholar) 62, 75, 108, 111, 150, 186, 195–96, 198, 200, 224
– *Maith dán ecnae* 195
Edinburgh 12
Edwin (Eadwine), king of Northumbria (617–633) 3, 141–42, 245, 247, 263, 320, 356
– burial at Whitby 256, 282, 289
– conversion of 4, 175–77, 213, 229, 251, 255–56, 289, 301–4, 331
– death of 255–56, 317
– exile among Britons 250, 251–56, 301, 356
– as *imperator* 251–56
*éices* (poet) 9, 27, 124
*éicse* (poetic art, native lore, divination) 9, 47, 56, 86, 109, 141, 146, 358
*éicsíne* (student poet; apprentice) 358
*Elene* (poem) *see* Cynewulf
Elmet (modern Elfed), Brittonic kingdom 254, 353, 356
Emain Macha, Co. Armagh (Navan Fort) 16, 47, 92–93, 146
Emer, character, wife of Cú Chulainn 92, 156
Émíne ua Niníne, student poet 122, 124
Én mac Ethamain (*fili* and *senchaid*) 129
encomium 13–15, 19, 28, 36, 39, 41, 44, 52–54, 57–58, 63–64, 69–70, 88, 109, 137, 246–47, 367–69
– *topoi* 50
– *encomium urbis* 87, 352
– *see also* Cædmon; *Durham* (poem); patronage

*Enigmata see* Aldhelm
entertainers *see* harpers; horn players; jesters; jugglers; pipers; professional status, *gleoman*
Eochaid úa Flain, poet (d.1004) 102
*Eochu rígéices*, royal poet 48, 227
*Eoin bruinne* (John, apostle) 79, 308
Eosterwine, abbot of Wearmouth-Jarrow (d.686) 52, 192, 216
*Epistola ad Acircium see* Aldhelm
*Epistola de obitu Bedae see* Cuthbert, deacon
*Érmae*, caldron of *see* "Caldron of Poesy"
etiologies 21, 50, 113, 163 *see also* Cenn Fáelad; *De ḟailsigiud Tána Bó Cúailnge*; *Senchas Már*, "pseudo-historical prologue"
Eugenius, bishop of Toledo (646–658) 365
eulogy 12–14, 41, 69, 137, 367–69, *see also* encomium
Eusebius, *Chronicle* 97
Evagrius of Antioch (d.ca.388), translator of Athanasius's *Vita Antonii* 211, 218
ex-layman *see athláech*
Exeter Book
– Cynewulf poems 90
– *see also Deor; Seafarer; Widsith*
exile 53, 60–63, 122, 150, 214, 217–18, 232, 243, 246, 250, 314, 322, 339, 346
– *see also* under Edwin; Oswald; Oswiu; Wilfrid, expulsion from York
extempore composition 363
– in *Beowulf* 20, 35, 110, 143, 363
– *díchetal di chennaib* 20, 35, 110, 143–46

*fabula* 125
Fáelán *see* Fullanus
Fahan (*Othain*), monastery 96
*Failsigiud Tána see De ḟailsigiud Tána Bó Cúailnge*
Faricius, *life* of Aldhelm 73–74
*Fates of the Apostles see* Cynewulf
Faustus of Riez 170
Fedelm *banḟili, banḟaith*, poetess and prophetess 26
– and *imbas for·osna* 17, 20, 64, 110, 143
– prophecy of 17, 64, 148, 154–55, 363

– travelling to study poetry 43, 47, 86, 154–55
*Félire Óengusso see* Óengus mac Óengobann
Felix, bishop of East Angles (631–ca.648) 135, 246, 304
– and Aidan 176, 313–14, 319, 354
Felix of Crowland, Life of Guthlac 217–18, 372
*fénechas* (native law) 113, 177
Fenian (Finn) cycle 127
Feradach Find Fechtnach, king 121
Ferchertne *fili*, poet in ODR 28, 37
– as eulogist at Tara 137
Ferchertne *fili*, poet in *Immacallam* 16–17
– competition with Néide mac Adnai 47, 146–47
Fergus *fili*, pseudo-historical prologue 22, 112
Fergus mac Roíg, character in *De Ḟailsigiud* 16, 21, 122–24
Fergus Tuile, king of Uí Liatháin 39, 53, 368
Fiacc Finn Sléibte, poet/bishop 44, 192, 335, 337
– and Dubthach maccu Lugair 37, 113, 208
– Sleaty, foundation of 206, 208, 349
Fiachnae (Lurgan) mac Báetáin, king (d.628) 48, 99, 118, 139–40, 253
*fili* (pl. *filid*) (poet) 2, 9, 21–23, 32–33, 39, 55, 96, 133
– freedom to travel 42–44, 85, 106
– legal rôle of 109, 111
– poetic grades 109
– as *senchaid* 129
– *sóernemed* status/special status 27, 106–8, 113, 129, 143–44, 153, 187, 202, 358
– specialized skills 110, 143–45, 363
 *see also teinm láeda*
– training 86, 105–6, 110 *see also* professional status
– *see also* bard; Én mac Ethamain; Ferchertne; Fergus *fili*; Forgoll; Máel Muru Othna; *imbas for·osna*; patronage
*filidecht* (poetic art, native lore, divination) 9, 43, 86, 113, 154–55, 177
Fínán, bishop of Lindisfarne (651–ca.661) 141, 181, 188, 221, 229, 325, 354
– and Oswiu 271–72, 321–22
– and Paschal controversy 258, 323–24
– Peada, baptism of 265, 269

– and Rónán, defender of orthodoxy 323
– Sigeberht, baptism of 268
"Finding (recovery) of the *Táin*" see *De Ḟailsigiud*
Finn (Germanic) 31–32, 60, 105
– Finnsburh Fragment 32
Finnabair, daughter of Ailill and Medb 30, 135–36
Finnbennach, bull named in TBC 115
Finnsburh Fragment (Fight at Finnsburg) 32
Fínṡnechta Fledach, king of Tara (675–695) 17, 19, 42, 121, 134, 281–82, 286, 340
Fintan mac Bóchra, compared to Widsith 25–26
Fionn mac Cumhaill 96, 363
– *teinm láeda* 144, 146, 154
*fír aicnid* (truth of nature) 189
*fís* (vision) (Lat. *visio*) 134 see also dreams/visions
*Fís Chuinn Chétchathaig .i. Baile in Scáil* (Vision of Conn of the Hundred Battles) 134
*Fís Fursa* (Vision of Fursa) 134–35, 233
Flann Fína (mac Ossu "son of Oswiu") see Aldfrith *sapiens*
Flann mac Lonáin, poet (d.896) 96–97, 138
Flann mac Maíl M'Áedóc, poet (d.979) 102
Flann Mainistrech, poet (d.1056) 103
Flannacán mac Cellaig, king/poet (d.896) 87, 97–98, 99
– as *rígbaird* 33
*fodána* (subordinate professions) 107
Fomoiri see *Cath Maige Tuired*
fore-tales (*remscéla*) 105, 134, 371
– in *De Ḟailsigiud* 121, 125–26
– tale lists 105
Forggus, co-high king of Tara 53
Forgoll, poet 36, 47–48, 110, 129
Fragmentary Annals 72, 183
Franks Casket 105, 113, 295
Fróech 30–31, 119, 130, 135–36
Fullanus (Fáelán), companion of Fursa 313–14
Fursa, *peregrinus* (d.649) 218, 247, 277, 349
– burial at Péronne 228, 233, 314
– cult of 314–15

– Life of 201, 277, 349
– mission to East Angles 4, 135, 176, 178, 260, 313–14, 317–19, 331, 354
– visions of 60, 134, 176, 198 see also *Fís Fursa*

Gawain-poet 57
Genereus "*saxo*", witness in *Vita Columbae* 250
*gens ambronum* (race of gluttons) 284, 302
*gentraí* (laughter-inducing music) 29, 31, 133, 135
*gerīm* (number (of days)) see *computus*
Gertrude, abbess of Nivelles 314
*gidd* (song; tale) 33–34, 36, 110 see also lore
Gildas 163
Gilla Cóemáin, poet (d.1072) 104
Gilla in Choimded Úa Cormaic, poet (fl.1100) 2, 9, 104
– Aimirgein Glúngel Tuir Tend 9, 14, 16–17, 19, 21–22, 56, 87, 104, 352
– competition among poets 47, 147
Gilling (est. 651) 221, 269, 280
– foundation of 217, 229, 258, 268, 270, 273, 321–23, 332
– and Iona 321
Glendalough 92–93
*glēoman* 9, 49, 359
– and dialects 83
– freedom to travel 42–44
glossaries 223–24
– Corpus 200
– Épinal-Erfurt 200, 222
– Erfurt II 200
– see also *De origine Scoticae linguae*; *Sanas Cormaic*
Gobbanus (Gobbán), companion of Fursa 313
*Gododdin, Y* see under Aneirin
Góedel Glas 15
Gofraidh Fionn Ó Dálaigh (14th c.) 56–57
Goiriath, caldron of see "Caldron of Poesy"
*goltraí* (sorrow-inducing music, lament) 29, 31, 133, 135
Gospel of John see John, apostle (and Gospel of)
"Great Tradition" see *Senchas Már*

Gregorian missions  261, 299, 330
- Canterbury  3, 8, 163, 165–67, 169, 209, 229, 241, 246, 248–49, 300–1, 304–5, 310–12, 320
- Northumbria  175–77, 213, 251, 263–64, 289, 301–4, 353
Gregory I the Great, pope (590–604)  163, 186–87, 200, 251, 361
- on Benedict, saint  210
- and Columbanus  171–72, 227
- cult of  165–66, *172*, 175, 183, 185, 275, 329, 332
- *Dialogues*  212, 218, 242
- *Homilia in Evangelia*  172
- "Homilies on Ezekiel"  171–72
- *Moralia on Iob*  172, 175, 182, 202
- *Regula Pastoralis*  99–100, 171–72
- relics of  329
- *see also* Gregorian missions; *Vita Gregorii*
Gregory II, pope  166
Grendel, monster in *Beowulf*  20, 27, 29, 32, 34, 130
Grendel's mother, in *Beowulf*  32, 130, 234
Guaire Aidni, king (d.ca.663)  21, 124, 183
Guthlac, saint (d.714)  90, 217, 300 *see also* Wigfrith,*Vita Guthlaci*
Gwallawg  248

Hadrian, abbot of Canterbury (d.710)  166–67, 200, 219, 226–27, 258, 275–76, 309, 329
Hæmgisl, Bede's source for Dryhthelm  233, 330
Hæthfelth *see* Hatfield
hagiography (general)  3, 49, 65, 127, 163, 182, 280
- continental *vitae* of Gaelic saints  201
- early Anglo-Saxon  210–19, 289, 330
- Gaelic hagiographers  201–10, 371
harpers (*cruit*)  133, 360–61
- in *Beowulf*  27–28, 33–34
- and Cædmon  33–34
- *dóernemed* status  27–29, 107
- in law-tracts (*dóernemed*)  28
- in *Táin Bó Cúailnge* with Galeóin  31
- in *Táin Bó Fraích*  30–31
- *see also* Craiphtine; Scilling; Uaithne

Hartlepool (*Heruteu*)  264, 319–20, 323–24, 354
Hatfield, battle of  255
Heahfrith, pupil of Aldhelm  116, 179, 187, 191, 223, 225, 328, 333–34
Healgamen, poet in *Beowulf*  29–32
Heavenfield (*Hefenfeld*; *Caelestis campus*), battle of  257, 259, 261, 351
*Hefenfeld see* Heavenfield
Heorot, mead hall in *Beowulf*  26, 32, 34, 69, 319
Heorrenda, poet in *Deor*  26, 46–47, 128, 147
Hereric, king (d.ca.616), father of Hild  254, 356
*Heruteu see* Hartlepool
Hewald, Black  228, *336*, 341, 346–47
Hewald, White  228, *336*, 341, 346–47
Hexham  318, 324
- and Oswald, cult of  258–59, 261–62, 351
- and Wilfrid  216, 259, 277, 279
*Hibernensis see Collectio canonum Hibernensis*
Hild, abbess of Whitby (657–680)  135, 214, 318, 342, 356
- and Ælfflæd, raising of  264, 267, 319, 354
- baptism by Paulinus  254–55, 331, 353–55
- death of  319, 332, 354–55
- and Edwin  254–55, 353
- and Fursa  232, 313–14, 354
- at Hartlepool (Heruteu)  323–24, 354
- and "synod" of Whitby  280, 318, 326, 331, 354–55
- Whitby, as abbess of  4, 64, 238, 254, 259, 264, 319–20, 323–24, 354
- and Wilfrid's expulsion from York  280, 331, 345
Hildeburh, queen in *Beowulf*  32
*Hisperica Famina*  68, 119, 124, 169, 179, 181 187, 222, 227, 295
- and Creation theme  367
- and physical world  199, 367
*Historia abbatum* (ca.716) *see* Bede
*Historia Brittonum* (History of the Britons)  25, 248, 267, 284, 301, 363
- early poets  10–14
*Historia ecclesiastica see* Bede
"Homilies on Ezekiel" *see* Gregory the Great
*homunculus*  343

Honorius, bishop of Kent (ca.630–653) 304, 319
Honorius I, pope 176, 220, 260, 317, 332
horn players (*cornaire*) 107, 135
Hrabanus Maurus 186
Hrothgar (Hrōðgār), Danish king 26, 28–29, 31–34, 69, 150, 234, 363
Hygebald of Lindsey 233, 291, 319, *336*, 341, 343
Hygelac (king of Geats) 32, 88

Ida, king of Northumbria (r.547–ca.560) 248
Idle, River, battle of (616) 252
*imbas* (encompassing knowledge; inspiration) 63, 150–51, 153, 363
*imbas for·osna* (great knowledge which illumines) 63–64, 110, 115, 143–46, 153–56, 159, 361, 363
– and Fedelm 17, 20, 64, 110, 143, 154–55
– and Scáthach 115, 156, 363
– see also *imbas*
*Immacallam in Dá Thuarad* (Colloquy of the Two Sages) 92, 128, 150
– competition among poets 47, 146–47
– poets as judges 16
*immram* (pl. *immrama*) (sea voyages) 128
– see also *Immram Brain*
*Immram Brain* (Voyage of Bran) 115–18, 139, 295
*imperator* see *bretwalda*
*Imtheacht na Tromdháimhe* 123
*inchinn dermait* see "brain of forgetting"
Ingcél (character) 132, 134, 159, 361
*Inis bó finne* see Inishboffin
*Inis Éogain* see Inishowen
*Inis Medcoit* see Lindisfarne
Inishboffin (*Inis bó finne*) 204, 225, 230, *231*, 326–27, 350
Inishowen Peninsula 96, 118, 266, *290*, 325
inspiration, poetic see *aí*; *awen*; divine grace and poetic inspiration
intermarriage 245–46, 250, 317, 356
– Oswiu 263–67
*Interpretatio mystica progenitorum Domini Iesu Christi* see Ailerán *sapiens*
intertextuality 114–15, 117, 120, 123, 126–27, 208

– and cross-referencing 50, 105, 136, 371
Iona, monastery 58, 142, 204, 218, 222, 265, 342
– and Aldfrith *sapiens* 194, 282–84, *290*, 292
– Ecgfrith, burial of 282
– foundation of 53–54, 61–63, 75, 167, 209, 241–2, 292, 300, 316
– and Iona Chronicle 240–41
– and *latercus* 54, 79, 178
– literary and intellectual influence of 213, 330, 350–52
– and Mayo of the Saxons 226, 292, 334, 350
– and Melrose 232, 341
– mission to Northumbria 4, 163, 166–69, 178, 209, 211, 220, 229, 259–60, 309–10, 316–26
– and Paschal controversy 210, 269, 274, 280, 293–94, 306, 308, 310–12, 330–31, 338–39, 351
– and Rath Melsigi *336*
– see also *Altus Prosator*
Irish Sea culture-province 138–42, 243
– see *Compert Mongáin*; *Echtrae Áedáin maic Gabráin*; *Echtrae Maíl Umai maic Báetáin*; *Echtrae Mongáin maic Fiachnai*; *Slúagad Fiachnai maic Báetáin co Dún Guaire i Saxanaib*; *Slúagad Néill maic Echach co Muir nIcht*; *Tochomlud Dáil Riata i nAlbain*
"iron house" motif 138, 348
Isidore of Seville (d.636) 163, 178, 190, 199, 239–40
– *De ecclesiasticis officiis* 212
– *De natura rerum* 80, 365–66
– *Etymologiae* (*cuilmen*) 2, 21, 85, 97, 105, 116, 123, 146, 152, 366
– as exchange for the *Táin* 105, 122–23
Iurminburg [Eormenburh], wife of Ecgfrith 278–80

James, deacon 255
Jarrow (est.681) see Wearmouth-Jarrow
Jerome, saint 200, 204
– etymological works 186
– Vulgate Bible 168, 239
jesters (*fuirsire*) 107

John, apostle (and Gospel of) 54, 79–80, 91, 185, 236–38, 307–10, 365
- see also Eoin bruinne
John IV, pope-elect 177–78, 236
John of Beverley, bishop 235, 238, 259, 324–25, 332, 355
Jonas of Bobbio, Life of Columbanus 201, 312–13
Joseph, abbot of Clonmacnoise (d.794) 90
jugglers (*clesamnach*) 107
Justus 165

*Kanon euangeliorum rhythmica* see Ailerán sapiens, Carmen in Eusebii canones
Keating, Geoffrey (Seathrún Céitinn; historian, d.1644), *Foras Feasa ar Éirinn* (ca.1634) 158
Kildare (*Cill Dara*) 72, 92–94, *180*, 184, 191, 202, *348*
- and Cogitosus 204–5, 207, 212
- see also Brigit, saint
Kilian, bishop of Würzburg (d.687) 315
King (historical) cycle 128
kingship 19
- rôle of 132–34, 192–93, 368
- see also Audacht Morainn; Baile Chuinn; Bede, on kingship/*imperatores*; Cáin Fhuithirbe; Tara, (symbolic) kingship of
Knockaulinn (*Cnoc Ailinne; Ailenn*) 92–95, *348*, 349

Labraid Loingsech, character in ODR 29, 137–38
*Lacnunga*, medical text 181
*Læcboc* (Leechbook), medical text 181
*láechdacht* (lay state; martial life) 75, 195–98, 200, 224
Lagny, monastery 314
Laidcenn mac Bairchedo, poet 15–16, 96
Laidcenn *sapiens* (d.661) 72, 229
- Clonfertmulloe, foundation of 114
- *Ecloga de moralibus in Iob* 172, 183
- hagiography of 182–83, 201–2
- Life of Mo-Lua 182, 201–2
- *lorica* 181
- as *sapiens* 59, 114, 124, *180*, 181–83, 294

*Laídsenchas Laigen* (Versified Traditional Lore of Leinster) 137–38
Laisrén (d.639), abbot 347
*Langbaird* see Lombards
Langland, William 57
Lastingham 318, *336*, 341–42
"Laterculus Malalianus" 177
*latercus*, computus composed by Sulpicius Severus 54, 79, 173–74, 178, 205, 226, 236, 241, 273, *305*, 306–9, 312, 325, 331, 347
- see also Paschal controversy
Laurentius 165
law-tracts 9–10, 105, 109–10, 192
- and physicians, professional 182
- poets, legal rôle of 37, 109, 111
- poets recorded in 27, 49–50, 371
- and social hierarchies 106–10
- triads derived from 143
- see also Adomnán, Cáin Adomnáin; Bechbretha; Bretha Étgid; Bretha Nemed; Cáin Fhuithirbe; Córus Bésgnai; Críth Gablach; Laws of Ine; Míadslechtae; Senchas Már; Uraicecht Becc; Uraicecht na Ríar
Laws of Ine 356–57
lawyers (*brithem, aigne*) 9, 107
- see also *dóernemed*
*Lebor Gabála Érenn* (Book of Invasions of Ireland) 15–16, 25, 97, 102–4
*Lebor na hUidre* (Book of the Dun Cow) 131, 159
*leccerd* (*lethcerd*; type of poet) 147
*légend* (Latinate, ecclesiastical learning) 113, 177
Leiden Riddle 74
*lex diei* (rule of the day) 119
*Lex innocentium* (Law of the Innocents) see Adomnán, Cáin Adomnáin
Liadain, *banéices* (poetess) 148
*Liber de ordine creaturarum* (pre-680) *172*, 200, 239, 310, 366
*Liber ex lege Moysi* 100
*Liber monstrorum* 334
*Liber Vitae* 264–65
Life of Mo-Lua see Laidcenn sapiens

Lindisfarne 87, 204–5, 215, 259, 271, *290*, 295, 329, 341–42
– and Baeda *magister* 210–11
– foundation (by Aidan) 1, 4, 9, 176, 229, 232, 240, 259–60, 291, 299, 318, 352
– and *latercus*/Pashal controversy 54, 211–12, 269, 273, 287, 308, 310–12, 318, 326, 330, 354
– missionary work 166, 310, 316, 326
– Urien Rheged, blockaded by 248
– *see also* Cuthbert; Lutting
Lindsey 233, 289, 291–93, 295, 318, 321, *336*, 341–43, 346, 356
Lóegaire mac Néill, king 22, 37, 113, 192, 206, 208, 335, 349
Lombards 119, 136, 169, 172–73, 312
lore (*gidd*)
– *scél* (tale) 2, 110, 127–29
– *senchas* 2, 110, 112, 142
– *see also Beowulf*, digressions; etiologies; fore-tales
*lorica* (pl. *loricae*) 57, 59, 63, 76, 78, 101, 171
– and *Adiutor laborantium* 168
– and Columba 208, 316
– and Hygebald 343
– and Laidcenn *sapiens* 181
– and the *Táin* epic 124
Luccreth maccu Chíara, poet 15–16
Lug, hero in *Cath Maige Tuired* 129, 132–33
Lugaid maccu Óchae (Mo-Lua of Clonfertmulloe) 114, 172–73
– Life of *see* Laidcenn *sapiens*
Luigne maccu Blaí, witness in *Vita Columbae* 209, 241
Lutting, poet of Lindisfarne 210–12, 215, 280, 287, 291, 308, 311

Mac dá Cherda, wise fool 183
Mac Liag, poet (d.1016) 103
Macrobius, *Saturnalia* 223, 240
Máel Ísu úa Brolcháin, poet (d.1086) 104
Máel Muire, scribe 131
Máel Muru Othna, poet (d.887) 87, 231
– *Áth Líac Find, cia dia tá* 96
– *Can a mbunadus na nGoídel* 96–97
– as *fili eolach* and *rígfili* 96

– *Flann for Érinn* 96
– *Tríath ós tríathaib Tuathal Techtmar* 96
Máel Ruain of Tallaght 92
Máel Umai (d.ca.610), *rígḟéinnid* (royal champion) 141, 250
Máeldub, founder of Malmesbury 221, 261, 333
– teacher (?) of Aldhelm 73, 221
*Mag Breg see* Brega
Mag Léne, synod 173, 305
*Mag nÉo na Saxan see* Mayo of the Saxons
*Mag Roth see* Moira, battle of
*magister* (teacher) *see* Aldfrith *sapiens*; Baeda *magister*
*magus* (pl. *magi*) *see* druids
*Maildubi urbs see* Malmesbury
*Mainister Éimíne see* Monasterevin
*Maith dán ecnae* 195
Malmesbury (*Maildubi urbs*) 73, 168, 218, 221, 261, *290*, 333
Malsachanus, grammarian 190
Manannán mac Lir, Celtic sea god 117–18, 139
Manchéne, abbot of Old Leighlin (d.726) 347
Manchéne, abbot of Min Droichit (d.652) 72
martyrdom/martyrology 91, 116, 161, 315, 371
– the two Hewalds 346–47
– *see also* Bede, *Martyrology*; Martyrology of Tallaght; Óengus mac Óengobann, *Félire Óengusso*; Old English *Martyrology*
Martyrology of Tallaght 325
Maserfelth 261
Mayo of the Saxons (*Mag nÉo na Saxan*) 179, 187, 228, 292, 321, 334, 339, 344, 372
– burning of 328
– foundation of 217, 225, 299, 327–29, 350
– growth of 225–26, 328–29, 350
– and Iona 225, 226, 292, 327, 334, 350
– name of 230–31, 327
Medb, queen in TBC and TBF 17, 30–31, 64, 115, 122, 130, 135–36, 143, 154–55, 363
Mellitus, missionary 165, 268, 301, 322, 341
Melrose 232, 237, 265, 311, 318, 326, 341
– and Dryhthelm 198, *290*, 291, 330
– and Rath Melsigi 213, 233, 242, *336*
*Míadṡlechtae* (Sections on Rank) 108, 188
Milesians, sons of Míl 19

missions/conversion *see* Aidan, missionary work; Bede, on missions, Gaelic; Bede, on missions, Gregorian; *Beowulf*, mission to Frisians; Columba, missionary work; Columbanus, missionary; Ecgberht of Rath Melsigi, continental mission; Fursa, mission to East Angles; Gregorian missions; Iona, mission to Northumbria; Mellitus, missionary; Oswald, as missionary king; Paulinus, conversion of Edwin; Rath Melsigi, continental missions from; Rath Melsigi, missionaries trained at
Mo-Chuaróc maccu Sémuine, *Nonae Aprilis* 170
Mo-Chutu, saint (d.637) 78
Mo-Ling, monk and poet (d.697) 347
Mo-Lua *see* Lugaid maccu Óchae
Mo-Sinu maccu Min (Sinilis, Sinlán/Sillán) 169–70
Moira (*Mag Roth*), battle of 639 113, 177–78
Monasterevin (*Mainister Éimíne*), Co. Kildare 348, 349
"The Monastery of Tallaght" 89, 315
Mongán mac Fiachnai (d.627), hero 36, 47–48, 98, 129
– in *Compert Mongáin* 36, 117–18, 139
– in *Echtrae Mongáin* 140
*Moralia in Iob see* Gregory the Great
Morann mac Moín *see Audacht Morainn*
Morcant 248
*Mórdál Dromma Ceta* (Convention of Druimm Cet) 20
Moriath, lover of Labraid Loingsech 29
Muir nIcht "English Channel" *see Slúagad Néill maic Echach co Muir nIcht*
Muirchú maccu Machtheni (fl.690), *Vita Patricii* 21–22, 37, 113, 192, 203, 206–9, 335, 337, 348, 349
Muirgen mac Sencháin, student poet 122, 124
Muirgius mac Tommaltaig, king of Connacht (792–815) 39, 89

*natio*, Gaelic sense of 86, 134, 177, 190, 192
Navan Fort *see* Emain Macha
Nechtán, king of Picts 209, 287, 310

Nechtansmere, defeat of King Ecgfrith (685) 350
Néide mac Adnai, poet 16–17, 86, 150
– competition with Ferchertne *fili* 47, 146–47, 150
*nemed* (privileged status) 19, 27, 129, 143–44
– freedom to travel 106
– non-*nemed* 106–7
– *see also dóernemed*; *sóernemed*
Nessan of Mungret 173
Níall Noígíallach (Níall of the Nine Hostages, eponymous ancestor of Uí Néill), king 141–42, 206
Ninian (Nynias), saint 167, 300, 316
Niníne Éices, poet 123–24
Nivelles 314
Nothhelm, priest 166

Óengus mac Bronbachaill 158
Óengus mac Óengobann, poet (fl.832) 87, 92, 95, 348
– *Félire Óengusso* 52, 91–94, 135, 194, 230, 262, 282, 315, 320, 344, 349
Œthelwald, sub-king of Deira (d.651x655) 262, 268
Oftfor, bishop of Hwicce (d.693) 320, 324
Old English *Martyrology* 100, 135, 199–200, 213, 217, 262, 274, 304, 315–16, 318–20, 341–43
Old Leighlin (*Lethglenn*), Co. Carlow 72, 177, 180, 191, 347, *348*
*ollam* (expert, master, chief) 109–11
*ollam filed* (chief poet) 44, 47, 87, 109, 129, 147, 150, 362
*ór fírindi* (incantation of truth) 157, 362
oral-formulaic composition 49, 83, 358–59
*Orgain Denna Ríg* (The Destruction of Dind Ríg) (ODR) 28, 37–38, 94, 137–38, 348, 368
– "iron house" motif 138, 348
– *súantraí* in 29
Orosius, *Historiae adversum paganos* 97, 99–100
Orthanach úa Cóellámae, poet, bishop (d. ca.839) 87, *93*, 138, *348*, 348–49
– *Cuirrigh* 94

– *Slán seiss, a Brigit* 94–96
Osred, king of Northumbria (d.716) 296–97
Osric, king of Deira (d.634) 256
Osthryth, wife of Æthelred *263*, 264
Oswald, king of Northumbria (634–642) 194, 250, 312, 320, 354
– and Aidan 176, *258*, 262, 317–18, 352
– burial of 282
– Cadwallon, defeat of 256–57, 260, 301, 317
– and Columba, vision of 256, 301, 351
– cult and relics of 92, 230, 257–59, 346, 351–52
– death of 259, 261, 267
– as emperor/*imperator* 209, 247, 257, 351
– exile in Dál Riata 3, 176, 251, *258*, 263, 317
– Gaelic speaking 3, 142, 245–46, *258*, 260, 317, 352
– as missionary king 4, 176–78, 220, 259–62, 294, 317–18, 332, 351
Oswine, king of Deira (d.651) 158, 229
– and Aidan 158, 229, 320
– murdered by order of Oswiu 268, 270, 320, 332
Oswiu, king of Bernicia and Northumbria (642–670) 166, 193–94, 214, 278–79, 285, 294, 323, 329
– and Aidan 268, 270
– conversion of 176, *258*, 275
– death and burial of 276, 282, 289
– East Saxons, reconversion of 268, 322
– educational policy 179, 271, 294
– as emperor/*imperator* 247, 264, 267, 272, 275
– exile in Dál Riata 142, 176, 251, *258*, 263
– Gaelic speaking 3, 142, 245–46, *258*, 263
– Gilling, foundation of 217, *258*, 268, 270, 273, 321–22
– marriages 256, 263–67, 356
– Mercia, conversion of 220–21, 268–69, 322
– military matters 267–68, 298, 319
– Oswine, murder of 268, 270, 320, 332
– and Paschal controversy 262–63, 265, 267, 269–70, 272–76, 312
– at "synod" of Whitby 211, *258*, 262–63, 265, 269, 272–76, 326, 341, 354

Owain, son of Urien Rheged 13, 38, 368
Owun, scribe (10th c.) 102

Palladius, bishop of Ireland 300, 306
panegyric 13, 19, 36, 39–41, 70, 225 see also patronage
particularism (in the Church) 174–75
Paschal controversy 54, 79, 114, 171–79, 185, 205, 212, 215, 222, 232, 235–37, 243, 293, 304–12, 318, 347
– cycles, overview of 305–7
– *see also* computus; Cummian, *De controversia Paschali*; Dionysius Exiguus, computational cycle; *latercus*; Victorius of Aquitaine, computational cycle; Whitby, "synod of Whitby"
– *see also* under Adomnán; Bede; Columba; Columbanus; Fínán; Oswiu; Stephen of Ripon; Theodore, archbishop of Canterbury; Wilfrid
Patrick, saint 14, 21–22, 44, 145, 177, 192, 205, 300, 201, 203
– and Brigit, saint 202
– and computistical cycles 174, 309
– cult of 143, 210, 327, 337
– and poetic orders 163
– Sechnall's *Hymn* on St. Patrick 203–4
– *see also Additamenta*; *Bethu Phátraic*; Muirchú maccu Machtheni, *Vita Patricii*; *Senchas Már*, "pseudo-historical prologue"; Tírechán, *Collectanea Patricii*
patronage 7, 19, 36–42, 105, 147, 216, 279
– "begging" poems 128
– and freedom to travel 42–44
– and professional status 45–48, 359
– *see also Deor*; encomium; eulogy; panegyric; *Widsith*
Paulinus, bishop of York (625–633) (d.644) 174–77, 263–64, 317
– at Canterbury 165, 301, 303, 320
– at Catterick 257, 302–3
– Edwin, conversion of 4, 175–77, 213, 229, 251, 255–56, 289, 301–4
– Hild, baptism of 254–55, 331, 353–55
– identity of 303–4
– at Rochester 303–4, 319

– at Yeavering 257, 302–3
– York, as bishop of 304, 309
– *see also* Rhun mab Urien
Paulinus of Nola 211
Peada, son of Penda *263*, 265, 268–69
Pehthelm of Whithorn 233
Penda, king of Mercia (d.655) 221, 265, 275, 327
– death of 268, 269, 319
– and Edwin 255
– and Oswald 261, 267
– and Oswiu 220, 262, 267–68, 319
*Peronna Scottorum see* Péronne
Péronne, Francia 228, 233, 261, 314–15
Peter, apostle 54, 117, 172, 204, 306–8, 326
Philippus, presbyter 182, 238
physician (*liaig*) 9, 133
– as *dóernemed* 107
Pilu "*saxo*", witness in *Vita Columbae* 167, 209, 241, 250
pipers (*cuislennach*) 107
place lore *see dindṡenchas*
Plegmund, archbishop of Canterbury 99
Plegwine, friend of Bede 239, 288
poetess (*banfili*) *see* Fedelm; Liadain; Scáthach; Uallach
poetics (among Gaels) 106, 142–53, *see also* "Caldron of Poesy"; *imbas for·osna*; *Sanas Cormaic*, *prull* episode
praise *see* encomium, eulogy, panegyric
Priscian 164, 189
professional status 45–48, 50, 83, 85–86, 153, 202, 371
– *fodána* 107
– *gleoman* 43, 45, 359
– hierarchies 106–7, 151, 153, 187, 196
– *scop* 46, 49
– *see also áes dána*; *Deor*, professional status; *dóernemed*; *éices*; *fili*; *nemed*; patronage, and professional status; *sóernemed*; *Widsith*, professional status
prophecy/divination 17, 187, 210, 342, 362, 363
– of advent of Christ 116–17
– of Boisil 340, 342, 351, 365
– of Cædmon 158–59, 342, 365
– Columba 30, 158, 301, 342, 351, 365

– of Cuthbert 120, 158, 283–84
– of Feldelm 17, 64, 148, 154–55, 363
– political 19, 105, 120, 134, 143, 154–55, 157–58, 193, 256, 283–84
– *see also Baile Chuinn*; *imbas*; *imbas for·· osna*; *tarbfeis*; *teinm láeda*
prophetess (*banfáith*) *see* Fedelm
prosimetric narratives *see Orgain Denna Ríg*; *Táin Bó Cúailnge*;*Togail Bruidne Da Derga*
Prosper of Aquitaine, *Chronicon* 300
*prull* episode *see Sanas Cormaic*
"pseudo-historical prologue" *see Senchas Már*

Quartodecimans 306–7, *see also* Paschal controversy; *latercus*

Rædwald, king of East Angles (d.ca.625) 246, 252, 301
Rægenmæld *see* Rhiainfellt
*Ráth Máelsige see* Rath Melsigi
Rath Melsigi 4, 72, 191, 227, 232–33, *258*, 261, 332, *348*, 351
– and Aldfrith *sapiens* 290, 291–92
– and Bangor 292–94
– continental missions from 93, 228, 230, 343–47
– and Dind Ríg 349
– Ecgberht at 138, 188, 213, 232, 238, 243, 269, 292–93, 318–19, 330, *336*, 338–39, 341, 345
– missionary school at 39, 93, 179, 187, 228, 230, 243, 335–43, *336*, 372
– name of *231*
– networks of 213, *336*
– *see also* Wihtberht; Willibrord
Rathcroghan (*Crúachu*) 18, 30, 92–93, 135
Rechtgal úa Siadail, poet (fl.790) 39, 89
*Regula pastoralis see* Gregory I the Great
*remscél see* fore-tale
*retoiric* (Lat. *rhetorice*) 126–27, 130–31
Rhiainfellt [*Rieinmelth*], wife of Oswiu *263*, 264–65, 267, 269, 356
Rhun mab Urien 256, 264, 302–4
Rhydderch Hen 248
*ríastrad* (distortions) 155

Rieinmelth *see* Rhiainfellt
rígbaird (kingly bards) 89, 97–98, *see also* Alfred the Great; Cormac mac Cuilennáin; Flannacán mac Cellaig
Rígnach, wife of king of Loch Léin 39
Ripon 205, 210–11, 215, 265
– dedication of 277–78
– and Wilfrid 211, 265, 271–72, 274, 277–78, 280, 321, 326, 356
– and Willibrord 336, 345
– *see also* Stephen of Ripon
Rónán, defender of orthodoxy 323
Ruman mac Colmáin, poet (d.747) 87

St. Mullins 347, *348*
*Sanas Cormaic* "Cormac's Glossary" (Cormac mac Cuilennáin) 51, 99, 101–2, 253
– *imbas for·osna* 144–46, 154, 156, 361, 363
– on poetic skills 144–46
– *prull* episode 48, 102, 147–48
– vocabulary 53, 101
*sapiens* (pl. *sapientes*) 3, 62, 163, 179–81, *180*, 258, 372
– and bilingual world 188–200, 222, 294
– and students, peripatetic 179–87
– *see also* Ailerán; Aldfrith; Banbán; Cenn Fáelad; Cuimmíne Fota; Laidcenn
*sapientia* (wisdom) 62, 75, 195–96, 200, 224
– and "Caldron of Poesy" 150, 153
– personification of 116
– *see also* ecnae
satire, *áer* (slander) 39, 43, 48, 133
Scáthach, Cú Chulainn's female martial arts teacher 115, 156, 363
*scél* (pl. *scéla*) 2, 110, 127–29
*Scéla Cano meic Gartnáin* 40
*Scélšenchas Laigen* (Narrative Traditional Lore of Leinster) 137
Scilling, poet?/harper?/harp? in *Widsith* 25, 36–37
*scop* (pl. *scopas*) 9, 20, 27, 29, 31–32
– in *Deor* 46, 49, 359
– and dialects 83
– freedom to travel 43
– and patronage 128, 359
– social rank 49
– *see also* Aldhelm

*scriptio continua* 164
*Seafarer*, poem 61–62, 228, 337–38
Sechnall, Hymn on St. Patrick 203–4
Sedulius (*Scottus*) 82
Ségéne, abbot of Iona (623–652) 58, 173–74, 176, 207, 305, 318
Ségéne, bishop of Armagh (661–688) 207, 337
*senchaid* (reciter of lore, storyteller) 128–29, 133
Senchán Torpéist, poet 43, 86, 183
– competition among poets 48
– *De faílsigiud* 21, 121–22, 124, 147–48
*senchas* (lore; history; tradition) *see* lore
*Senchas Már* (Great Tradition), law-tract collection 182
– "pseudo-historical prologue" 14, 16–17, 19, 22, 47, 107, 112–13, 145–46, 153, 192, 208, 337, 372
– and poetic skills 143, 145
– and social hierarchy 107, 153
– and syncretism 112, 192
Sergius, pope (687–701) 291
*Serglige Con Culainn* (Sickbed of Cú Chulainn) 156, 362
– *see also* tarbḟeis
Sicgfrith, abbot 197
*síd* (peace) and (faerie folk) 30, 115, 119, 120, 135–36
Sigeberht, king of East Anglia (d.ca.653) 158, 176, 268, 275, 314, 322
Sigemund, character in *Beowulf* 35, 125
Síl nÁedo Sláine 41–2, 121, 53, 282, 286–87, 351, 368
– *see also* Uí Néill
Sillán *see* Mo-Sinu
silversmiths (*cerd*), as *dóernemed* 107
single combats *see* Beowulf, character; Cú Chulainn
Sinilis, Sinlán *see* Mo-Sinu
Sleaty (*Sléibte*) 206–7, 335, 337, *348*, 349
*Sléibte see* Sleaty
*Slúagad Fiachnai maic Báetain co Dún nGuaire i Saxanaib* 140
*Slúagad Néill maic Echach co Muir nIcht* 141–42
social hierarchy *see dóernemed; nemed; sóernemed*

sóernemed (noble *nemed*; noble dignitary)
– ecclesiastics as 107–8
– kings as 107
– poets as 106–8, 129, 153, 358
– *see also* under *fili*
Sofis, caldron of *see* "Caldron of Poesy"
*speculum principum* 19, 105, 121, 156, 193–94, 368
– *see also* under *Audacht Morainn*
*spiritus poematis* (spirit of poetry) 48, 148
Stephen of Ripon (hagiographer) 1, 372
– on Chad 342
– Gaelic influence, theme of 215, 262, 350
– on Osred 297
– on Paschal controversy 174, 211, 237, 273–74, 308–9, 325 350
– *Vita Wilfridi* 174, 196–97, 211, 213–14, 222, 237, 240, 259, 262, 271–74, 278–80, 282, 284, 288–89, 331
– date of 214, 289, 297
– and Wilfrid's ecclesiastical empire 214–15, 271, 279, 297
– on Willibrord's mission 345
Strathclyde 12, 247
*súantraí* (sleep-inducing music, lullaby) 29, 31, 133, 135, 137
*suí filed* (sage of poets) 107, 143
Suibne mac Maíle Umai (d.891) of Clonmacnoise 100, 372
Sulpicius Severus (d.420) 204, 305–6
– *Vita s. Martini* 78, 210–11, 218
– *see also latercus*
synchronism 111
syncretism 71, 112–13, 122, 177, 189, 205
– in *Beowulf* 112–13
– in "pseudo-historical prologue" to *Senchas Már* 112, 192
– in *Vita Patricii* 113, 192, 208, 337
– *see also coimgne*
"synod" of Whitby (664) *see* under Whitby
Synoptic Gospels 54, 79 307 *see also* John, apostle (and Gospel of)

*Táin Bó Cúailnge* (The Cattle Raid of Cooley) (TBC) 2, 16–17, 23, 31, 105, 363
– *Beowulf*, compared to 130
– chronological setting 24, 126

– and *Cín Dromma Snechtai* 114–15
– Conchobar in 127, 131
– Cú Chulainn in 115, 126
– dreams and visions in 160, 362
– Fedelm in 43, 47, 154–55
– Fergus mac Róig in 122
– Fróech episode and TBF 119, 130, 135–36
– intertextuality 119, 127, 130, 135–36
– and law-tracts 110
– place names in *18*, 25
– and poets' freedom to travel 43–44
– and poets' professional status 45
– recensions of 130–31, 156, 160
– *see also* Ailill; *De faílsigiud Tána Bó Cúailnge*; Fedelm *banfili*; Medb; *Táin Bó Fraích*
*Táin Bó Fraích* (The Cattle Raid of Fróech) (TBF) 30, 295
– date of 135
– intertextuality with TBC 119, 130, 135–36
– Lombards and the Continent 172–73
– narrative of 119
tale lists 99, 105, 127–38, 144, 253
– in Book of Leinster 128–29
– Lists A and B 127–30, 134, 140–42
Talhaearn Tad Awen, poet (Talhaearn father of the poetic muse) 11–12, 363
Taliesin, poet 11–12, 26, 37, 70, 98, 248, 368
– *Llyfr Taliesin* 11, 13–14
*Talland Étair* 43
Tara (*Temair*) 22, 28, 37, 41, 92–93, 103, 121, 129, 206
– kingship, symbolic, of 17, 19, 120, 132–34, 192, 368
– *feis Temrach* (feast of Tara) 137
– and St. Patrick 206, 209
*tarbfeis* (bull feast; bull sleep) 363
– description of 157–59
– purpose to predict kingship 120, 134, 145, 156, 193, 361–62, 368
"teat of wisdom" 116, 225, 333 *see also ubera sapientiae*
Tech Conaill, monastery, Co. Wicklow 57
*teinm láeda* (chewing the pith) 143–46, 153–54, 363

Theobald, brother of King Æthelfrith 141, 250
Theodore, archbishop of Canterbury (668–690) 214, 219, 269, 274–75, 277
– and Paschal controversy 308–9
– school of 165–67, 200, 226–27, 258, 276, 320, 324, 329, 350
– and tonsure 275, 308–9, 311
– and Wilfrid's expulsion from York 280, 331, 342, 345
Theodoric, character in *Deor* 26
Theodoric, son of King Ida 248
"thought, word, deed"
– in Bede 233–34, 315
– in *Beowulf* 234
– in Cynewulf 91
– in Hygebald's prayer 233, 343
Tilmon 52, 346
Tírechán, *Collectanea Patricii* 203, 205–7, 209, 212, 327, 349
*Tochmarc Emire* (Wooing of Emer) 156
*Tochmarc Étaíne* (Wooing of Étaín) 120, 134
*Tochomlud Dáil Ríata i nAlbain* (The Advance of Dál Ríata into Britain) 142
*Togail Bruidne Da Derga* (Destruction of Da Derga's Hostel) (TBDD) 120, 132–34, 224
– dreams and visions 159–60, 361–62
– intertextuality 120
– *tarbfeis* 157
*Togail Bruidne uí Derga* (Destruction of Uí Derga's Hostel) 119–20, 133–34, 157
– *see also* also*Togail Bruidne Da Derga*
Tondberht of the South Gyrwe 277
tonsure 198, 209, 273, 296, 308–11, 339
– and *latercus*, followers of 306, 325
– Petrine/coronal 212, 215, 275, 306, 326
– Theodore of Canterbury 275, 308–9
*Trecheng Breth Féne see* Triads (Gaelic)
Triads (Gaelic) (*Trecheng Breth Féne*) 123–24, 142–44, 347
*Trioedd Ynys Prydain* (Triads, Brittonic) 253–54
*Tromdám Guaire* (Burdensome Troop of Guaire) 43, 123
Trumberht, teacher of Bede 238, 342

Trumhere, bishop of Middle Angles (ca.659–ca.662) 179, 217, 221, 229, *258*, 269–70, 273, 321–22, 332
Trumwine, bishop of Abercorn 284
Tuaim Drecain (Tomregan), Co. Cavan 113
Tuán mac Cairill, compared to Widsith 26
Tuatha Dé Danann, mythical race 29, 103, 132–33, 182 *see also Cath Maige Tuired*
Tuda, monk (d.ca.664) 274, 326

Uaithne, harper of the Dagda 29–30
Uallach ingen (daughter) Muinecháin, poetess (d.934) 102, 149
*ubera sapientiae* 116, *see also* "teat of wisdom"
Uí Bairrche, territory/people in Leinster 291, 335, 337, 349
Uí Néill (descendants of Níall Noígiallach) 57, 59, 70–71, 74–75, 96, 98, 103, 115, 120, 141, 181, 192, 347
– and political prophecy 134, 158
– propaganda of 120–21
– rise/expansion of 101, 137, 177–78, 202, 206
– and St. Brigit 202
– and Síl nÁedo Sláine 39, 41–42
– *see also* Cenél Conaill; Cenél nEogain
Uisliu, sons of 98
Uisnech, Co. Westmeath 120
Ulster cycle 92, 98, 111, 114, 118, 127, 136
Ultán, scribe 165, 372
Ultán maccu Chonchobair, bishop (d.657) 203, 205–7
Ultanus (Ultán), companion of Fursa 313–14
*undecumque doctissimus* (very learned in all things) 73, 193, 293
*Uraicecht Becc* (Small Primer), law-tract 108
*Uraicecht na Ríar* (Primer of the Stipulations), law-tract about poets 50, 86, 108–11, 129, 147, 358, 362
Uraird mac Coise, poet (d.990), *Airec menman Uraird maic Coise* 102, 127–28
Urien Rheged (Urien of Rheged) 4, 248, 264, 302, 368
– in *Llyfr Taliesen* 13–14, 37

Venantius Fortunatus 365
*Verba Scáthaige* (Words of Scáthach) 115, 130, 156
Vercelli Book 90, 138, 349
Vergil 199–200, 211, 218, 222
– *Aeneid* 224, 284
Victorian (Easter) practice *see* Victorius of Aquitaine
Victorius of Aquitaine (fl.457), computus 174, 205, 210–11, 215, 236, 305–8
Virgilius Maro Grammaticus 68, 73, 82, 124, 187, 191, 223, 228, 261
– *Epistolae* 190
– *Epitomae* 190, 237–38
visions (*aislinge*; *baile*; *fís*) *see* dreams/visions
*Vita Antonii* (Life of Anthony) *see* Athanasius
*Vita Brigitae* (ca.680) *see* Cogitosus
*Vita Ceolfridi* (ca.716), anonymous 184, 216–17, 321
*Vita Columbae* (688–704) *see* Adomnán
*Vita Columbani* (ca.640) *see* Jonas
*Vita Cuthberti (anonymo)* (698–705) 158, 211–12, 215, 289, 296, 341, 352, 354
– date of *290*
– Gaelic characteristics 212, 294, 330
*Vita Gregorii* (704–714), anonymous of Whitby 165–66, 171, 175–76, 183, 185, 201, 213, 251–52, 256, 289, 296, 301–4, 320
– Gaelic characteristics 238, 294, 324, 332, 354–55
*Vita Guthlaci* (740s) *see* Felix of Crowland; *see also* Wigfrith, *Vita Guthlaci*
*Vita Martini see* Sulpicius Severus
*Vita Patricii see* Muirchú maccu Machtheni (fl.690), *Vita Patricii*
*Vita prima Brigitae see* Ailerán *sapiens*
*Vita Wilfridi* (712–714) *see* Stephen of Ripon
Vitalian, pope (657–672) 166, 258, 275, 329

Wærferth, bishop of Worcester 99–100
Walahfrid Strabo 186
Wearmouth (est.673) *see* Wearmouth-Jarrow
Wearmouth-Jarrow 197, 209–11, 217, 279–80, 287–88, *290*

– foundation of 4, 216, 291
– library of 240
– and Paschal controversy 211, 310
– pictures and painted panels at 184, 205
Weland (smith of Germanic legend) 26, 105
Whitby (founded ["set in order"] 657) 4–5, 34, 64–65, 171, 201, 205, 213, 238, 284, 319–20
– Aldfrith, burial at 289, *290*, 295, 354–55
– and bilingualism 357–58
– bishops, training of 320, 324–25, 355
– Edwin, burial at 256, 282, 289, 354
– ethnic mix and Gaelic ethos 353–55
– foundation of 291
– Oswiu, burial at 354
– "synod" of Whitby (664) 119, 167, 179, 204, 211, 220, 222, 225, 229, 258, 260–61, 263–64, 268, 289, 299, 308, 318, 329, 347, 351, 354
– initiation of 4, 265, 272–73
– Oswiu at 211, 258, 262–63, 265, 269, 272–76, 326, 341, 354
– and Paschal controversy 54, 185, 215, 232, 237, 272–76, 308, 310–11, 324–25, 330, 350
– and tonsure 273
– Wilfrid at 211, 220, 232, 265, 272–73, 280, 289, 313, 324–26, 331–33, 358
– *see also* Ælfflæd; Cædmon; Hild
Whithorn 167, 300, 316
*Widsith*, poem 7, 11, 26, 295, 319
– *Airec menman*, compared to 128
– author as professional poet 26, 30, 49, 83, 106–7
– Exeter Book, unique copy 23
– Germanic lore 25
– patronage (begging poem) 36–37, 42–44, 128, 359
"The Wife's Lament" 148–49
Wigfrith *librarius*, *Vita Guthlaci* 151–52, 159, 218–19, 299, 363
Wigheard, candidate (d.ca.664) 275, 329
Wihtberht, mission to Frisia 93, 228, 230, 336, 341, 343–44, 346
Wihtfrith, pupil of Aldhelm 153, 179, 187, 223–24, 227, 334

Wilfrid, bishop (d.710)  196–97, 214, 217, 239, 320, 328, 346
- and Aldfrith  214, 287–89
- and Benedict Biscop  214, 272, 279, 323
- and Ealhfrith  265, 271–72, 274
- ecclesiastical empire of  214–15, 271, 279, 297–98
- and Ecgfrith  277–80, 297
- Gaels, attitude towards  240, 259
- Hexham abbey, foundation of  259, 277, 279
- and Osred as adoptive son  297
- and Paschal controversy  237, 261, 273, 307–8, 331
- and prophecy  342
- and Ripon  211, 265, 271–72, 274, 277–78, 280, 321, 326, 356
- *schola* of  196, 215–16, 308
- South Saxons, conversion of  331
- "synod" of Whitby  211, 220, 232, 265, 272–73, 280, 289, 313, 324–26, 331–33, 358
- York, expulsion from  280, 288, 331, 342, 345
- *see also* Stephen of Ripon, *Vita Wilfridi*

William of Malmesbury  73–74, 334
- *Gesta pontificum*  73

Willibrord  188, 228, 230, 257–59, 304, 351
- *Calendar* of  165, 261, 274, 332, 345
- Echternach and Frisia, mission to  230, 259, 304, *336*, 341, 345–46, 372
- Oswald, cult of  230, 257–59, 261, 346, 351
- Rath Melsigi, training at  188, 332, *336*, 341, 345, 372
- and Ripon  *336*, 345
- Rome, visit to  341
- *see also* Alcuin of York, Life of Willibrord

Winwæd, battle of (655)  268

Witmer, learned man  193, 197, 200, 217, *290*, 291

woodworkers (*sáer*), as *dóernemed*  107

"Wulf and Eadwacer"  147

Wulfhere, king of Mercia (ca.658–674)  220–21, 269, 279, 342

Wulfstan, archbishop (d.ca.1023)  372
- *Institutes of Polity*  103
- *Sermo Lupi ad Anglos*  103

Würzburg (Germania)  315–16

Yeavering  257, 302–3

York  90, 274, 280, 304, 309, 331, *336*, 342, 372
- burning by Cadwallon  255
- Constantine's baptism at  212
- *see also* Wilfrid, York expulsion from

www.ingramcontent.com/pod-product-compliance
Lightning Source LLC
Chambersburg PA
CBHW031748220426
43662CB00007B/326